INTERPERSONAL RELATIONSHIPS

Professional Communication Skills for Nurses

Second Edition

Elizabeth Arnold, Ph.D., R.N., C.S.-P

Associate Professor
University of Maryland
School of Nursing
Baltimore, Maryland

Kathleen Underman Boggs, Ph.D., R.N.

Associate Professor
College of Nursing
University of North Carolina at Charlotte
Charlotte, North Carolina

W. B. SAUNDERS COMPANY
A Division of Harcourt Brace & Company
Philadelphia / London / Toronto / Montreal / Sydney / Tokyo

W. B. SAUNDERS COMPANY

A Division of Harcourt Brace & Company

The Curtis Center
Independence Square West
Philadelphia, PA 19106

Library of Congress Cataloging-in-Publication Data

Arnold, Elizabeth.
    Interpersonal relationships : professional communication skills for nurses /
Elizabeth Arnold, Kathleen Boggs. — 2nd ed.
      p. cm.
    Includes bibliographical references and index.
    ISBN 0-7216-6684-1
    1. Nurse and patient. 2. Interpersonal communication   I. Boggs, Kathleen Underman.
II. Title.
RT86.3.A76 1995
610.73'06'99—dc20

                                                   93-48584

INTERPERSONAL RELATIONSHIPS: Professional Communication Skills for Nurses   ISBN 0-7216-6684-1

Printed in the United States of America.

Last digit is the print number: 9   8   7   6   5   4   3

A Special Dedication

To George B. Arnold and our children,
Mary Beth, Brian, Karen, Julie, and Christy,
for their support and understanding during this project.

E.N.A.

and

To Michael John Boggs and our children,
Saretha Rebecca and Adam Underman,
who understand my own unique communication style.

K.U.B.

In Memoriam

Marilyn Jean Varner Bayne, M.S.N.
July 31, 1952–May 30, 1988

Contributors

Verna Benner Carson, R.N ., Ph.D., C.S.
University of Maryland
School of Nursing
Baltimore, Maryland
Chapter 8

Marcia Cooley, R.N., Ph.D.
Instructor
University of Maryland
School of Nursing
Baltimore, Maryland
Chapter 13

Ann O'Mara, R.N., Ph.D.
Assistant Professor
University of Maryland
School of Nursing
Baltimore, Maryland
Chapter 22

Cathy Carter Romeo, R.N., Ph.D.
Perinatal Program Manager
Obstetrics, Home Health Care
Curaflex-Birthcare Services
Columbia, Maryland
Chapter 7

Judith Ryan, R.N., Ph.D.
Assistant Professor
University of Maryland
School of Nursing
Baltimore, Maryland
Chapter 19

Virginia Sullivan, R.N., M.S.N., C.S.
Lecturer
University of North Carolina at Charlotte
Charlotte, North Carolina
Chapter 5

Reviewers

Barbara K. Boyer, R.N., B.S.N.
Mental Health Institute of Independence
Independence, Iowa

Janet Burton, R.N., M.S.N.
College of Nursing
Bob Jones University
Greenville, South Carolina
Staff Nurse
St. Frances Hospital
Greenville, South Carolina

Diane B. Hamilton, R.N., Ph.D., M.A., B.S.N.
Graduate Program
College of Nursing
Medical University of South Carolina
Charleston, South Carolina

Gail M. Houck, R.N., Ph.D.
College of Nursing
Oregon Health Sciences University
Portland, Oregon

Joyce Krothe, D.N.S.
Department of Community Health Nursing
School of Nursing
Indiana University
Bloomington, Indiana

Sarah Miller-Field, R.N., M.Ed., B.S.N.
School of Nursing
University of Alberta Hospital
Edmonton, Alberta, Canada

Agnes Natale, M.S.N., M.A.
Department of Gerontology, Psychiatric and Community
    Health Nursing
College of Nursing–Lincoln Division
University of Nebraska Medical Center
Lincoln, Nebraska

Karen Ruth Olson, R.N., M.N.
College of Nursing
Purdue University
West Lafayette, Indiana

Kathryn G. Pearson, R.N., M.S.
Assistant Professor
Psychiatric Mental-Health Nursing
College of Nursing
University of South Carolina
Columbia, South Carolina

Sandra J. Peterson, R.N., M.S., B.S.
School of Nursing
Bethel College
St. Paul, Minnesota

Terri Potts, R.N., B.S.N.
Independence, Iowa

Joy Ann Riley, R.N., M.S.N., C.S.
College of Nursing
Indiana University
Indianapolis, Indiana

Sharon C. Wahl, R.N., Ed.D.
Associate Professor
College of Nursing
San Jose State University
San Jose, California

Joyce M. Wallskog, R.N., Ph.D., M.S.N., B.S.N.
College of Nursing
Marquette University
Milwaukee, Wisconsin

Susan J. Wold, R.N., Ph.D., M.P.H.
Associate Professor
Metropolitan State University
St. Paul, Minnesota

Acknowledgments

This book represents the ideas and efforts of many people in our lives—students, valued colleagues, clients, and the editorial staff at W. B. Saunders. The evolution of this book began with an interpersonal relationship seminar, originally conceptualized by the University of Maryland faculty teaching in an upper-division baccalaureate nursing curriculum, which used an experiential methodology to teach students therapeutic communication skills. Our ideas, emotional understandings, and professional perspectives about the role of interpersonal relationships in professional nursing practice have developed in great measure from sympathetic and critical dialogues with these colleagues and others who have interest in developing comprehensive approaches to the study of interpersonal relationships in professional nursing practice. We especially want to recognize the contributions of Marilyn Bayne, Barbara Boland, Naomi Brooks, Verna Carson, Julie Fortier, Patricia Grimm, Suzanne Jimerson, Margaret Neal, Norma Rawlings, and Jody Robyler of the University of Maryland and those of Margaret Arroyo, Bettie Gordon Gray, Linda Moore, Ann Newman, and Joyce Ruth of the University of North Carolina at Charlotte. Many of our nursing students also have proved to be exemplar teachers of caring, creativity, and competence in working with clients in therapeutic relationships. Their voices find consistent expression in each chapter.

The ideas about interpersonal relationships and communication principles presented in this text build on the professional reflections of many nurse leaders, beginning with Hildegarde Peplau's classic work on interpersonal relationships in professional nursing practice. These leaders recognized the importance of interpersonal relationships and communication principles as the basis for effective clinical practice and have spoken, written, and researched their application in a wide variety of practice settings. The concepts also reflect the work of professionals outside the realm of nursing. Finally, there is the treasure chest of client gifts, which are found throughout the text. As each relationship is unique, so are the contributions of each of these stakeholders to the development of this book. Each contributor provides a deeper understanding of the communication process from different perspectives, which we hope blend together as a unitary concept in nurse–client relationships. Born of the many conversations, suggestions, and writings of all of these people in our lives, writing this book has compelled the authors to take a measured, thoughtful look at what we do with our clients in clinical settings and why we approach the process of relationship as the crux of professional nursing practice. We hope that your reading of the book will stimulate further questions and searching for the meaning of relationship in nursing practice that this text begins to address.

The editorial staff at W. B. Saunders deserves special acknowledgment for their commitment to the preparation of this book and their persistent belief in the worthiness of the topic. First, there is a need to fully acknowledge the part played by nursing editor Dan Ruth in the process. His firm support, creative ideas, challenging honesty, and sound attention to details kept us on track with the development of the book. He made many valuable suggestions regarding the style and content of the manuscript, which we incorporated into the book. When our energy faltered, Dan would have a new idea about how we could regain our momentum and accomplish the goal of making a substantive contribution to the literature on interpersonal relationships and communication in nursing practice. Another person who should be mentioned is Dan's assistant, Susan Bielitsky, for her cheerful handling of detail throughout the book's production.

We also owe a special debt of gratitude to Rachel Bedard, our development editor, who helped us in so many ways. She opened up new ways of looking at language and clarifying our ideas. Rachel's patience, clarity of thinking, sensitive understanding of the material, help with the development of the glossary, and suggestions about the mode of presentation were remarkable, and are deeply appreciated. We could not have developed this book without her expert assistance in refining our text.

Lorraine Kilmer, our production editor, was invaluable in managing the many details involved in the production of our manuscript. Without her efficient monitoring of the details necessary to the completion of the project, the book would not have seen the light of day.

We are very grateful to Fran Bartlett of G & H SOHO, Inc. for her tireless work in transforming the manuscript into a book, which was not always an easy task. She contributed far more than expert assistance in the production of the book, and it was a pleasure to work with her.

We also want to acknowledge the many useful and supportive suggestions made by our reviewers.

Last, but clearly not least, we need to acknowledge the loving support of our families. We are particularly grateful to our spouses, George B. Arnold and Michael J. Boggs, who supported us in our work with their presence and their constant encouragement, the real measure of which can never be fully expressed in words.

Contents

Preface

Despite technological advances in diagnosis and treatments available to clients and their families, communication remains the single most important, and sometimes most under-rated, dimension of nursing practice. The second edition of *Interpersonal Relationships: Professional Communication Skills for Nurses* provides the student with concepts and principles related to clinical and professional communication in health care settings. Communication strategies are presented in a relational context and highlight the therapeutic connections between people that are so necessary for healing the mind, body, and spirit.

Users of the first edition will note that this edition has been expanded to provide better access to and focus on essential topics. The chapters on basic therapeutic communication, relationships, values, and professional issues have been updated and rewritten for greater clarity. Previous discussions concerning intercultural and family communication, stress and crisis, and health teaching have been expanded into one and sometimes two chapters in their own right.

The second edition also reflects new demands for better critical thinking skills related to communication. In 1990 the National League for Nursing identified communication and critical thinking skills as essential outcomes in baccalaureate nursing education. We therefore encourage the student to examine the background of specific situations and the sequence of events by which the situation developed. A wealth of exercises offers students the opportunity to practice, observe, and critically evaluate their own communication skills and those of others.

When a student connects inwardly with another human being, whether another student or a client, a different and more significant form of learning occurs. Case examples provide a basis for discussion by helping students to understand and appreciate clients' perspectives and needs. Therapeutic communication strategies based on valid theoretical principles assist the student to consider and try out alternative approaches to care in a safe learning environment.

Even though the chapter topics in this edition cover a wide range of psychobiological health care situations, each chapter utilizes a standard, self-contained format that grants instructors and students flexibility in developing study and learning plans. Each chapter presents first the basic concepts of the chapter topic, then clinical applications and exercises.

The book is organized into five parts. Part I addresses the conceptual foundations of the nurse–client relationship, providing a theoretical framework and professional guides to action. In Part II the components of this interaction are explored in depth, including the evolution and resolution of the nurse–client relationship. New chapters discuss role relationships and potential barriers and specific strategies in the communication process.

Part III examines therapeutic communication and reviews communication styles and guidelines for skills development. This section also includes new chapters on intercultural communication and family communication. Health teaching content has been expanded to two chapters, Chapter 15 on assessing client learning needs and Chapter 16 on teaching interventions.

Part IV, "Responding to Special Needs," addresses lifespan issues in communication as well as clients experiencing communication deficits and those in stressful and crisis situations. Finally, Part V discusses professional issues in communicating with other health care providers and patient care documentation.

The second edition of *Interpersonal Relationships: Professional Communication Skills for Nurses* has been designed to be used for individual classes or across the curriculum. As a foundational text on communication it offers the student a thorough exploration of theoretical and practical applications of communication. As a supplemental text it can be used to integrate the learning of communication skills in a variety of health care settings.

Practicing nurses and graduate students will find the text useful as a comprehensive reference to enhance their knowledge base. Staff development nurses may be particularly interested in the more advanced chapters on intercultural communication, documentation, groups, assertiveness, health-promotion and teaching, and interprofessional communication. The exercises are fun and present a nonthreatening way to help students and clinicians alike become more involved in learning how to communicate more effectively.

Prologue

Those of us who accept the responsibility of professional nursing as a life commitment are most fortunate, for we can be constantly learning and growing personally and professionally from our interpersonal encounters with the clients we serve. In the process of learning about self and others in health care settings, we begin to explore and choose different behavioral responses that calm, educate, and promote the healing process of our clients. Some of these interpersonal encounters with clients will be remembered with joy and satisfaction, others with pain. But with each interpersonal encounter the nurse has yet another chance to appreciate the richness of human experience and the many different opportunities for fulfilling human potential in relationships, which is the foundation and purpose of our professional practice.

THE EXPERIENTIAL TEACHING–LEARNING PROCESS

The 23 chapters in this text are designed to provide the nurse with a comprehensive understanding of the principles of communication and of relationships. These principles can be used to establish and maintain therapeutic relationships with clients and collegial relationships with members of the interdisciplinary health team. In presenting this content, the authors have integrated a generous number of learning exercises designed to provide opportunities for active learner involvement in the teaching–learning process. These skills, first practiced in the classroom, can be used daily throughout a nursing career.

The Prologue is included in the text as well as in the Instructor's Manual because the authors believe that it is important for the student to understand the purpose and process of experiential learning. Although the term "student" is used, this term can apply equally to nurses in clinical practice wishing to use an experiential format to learn more about relationships and communication principles in nursing.

PURPOSE

The goal of the experiential format is to enable a student to learn, grow, and develop new insights about concepts brought to life through one's own activities in class. An experiential learning format provides a more humanistic alternative to the traditional lecture-discussion format, promotes creativity, and encourages the development of critical thinking skills. By requiring active participation, the student gains an understanding of the "meaning" behind the content. The exercises are designed to foster the development of self-awareness in a relationship and to provide an opportunity for students to practice communication skills in a safe learning milieu. The constructive feedback the student receives and the sharing of experiences encourage analysis and synthesis of attitudes, knowledge, and performance related to therapeutic communication skills.

THE LEARNING PROCESS

Engaging in the exercises presented in this text provides the student with a data base of shared experiences, thoughts, and feelings that can be described, explored, and analyzed.

Each structured exercise has a specific purpose. Some are designed to increase self-knowledge, whereas others focus on practicing a particular communication skill. The same learning process, however, is followed in all exercises. Each exercise procedure is to be implemented by the students, followed by reflection and discussion.

Goodstein and Pfeiffer (1983) have identified five distinct steps in the process of experiential learning that can provide a guide for students in understanding how they can get the most out of the exercises presented in this text. The steps involved in experiential learning include:

1. Active involvement in an exercise.
2. Collegial sharing of experiences.
3. Analysis and synthesis.
4. Integration of experiences with theory.
5. Applications to clinical practice.

1. ACTIVE INVOLVEMENT IN AN EXERCISE

Active involvement includes informed participation in a structured, preplanned exercise relevant to the concepts being studied. The more freely and completely a student is able to engage in the exercises and to learn from them, the stronger the learning potential. This definition of active involvement requires respect for self and others and the willingness to share and explore the meaning of professional relationships in an informed, reasoned manner. While active involvement means sharing of self, it does not require the student to reveal any personal details of one's life that would create a personal concern or special vulnerability. Only those details that the student feels comfortable sharing *and those that relate to the purpose of the exercise* help maximize learning. A desired outcome of active involvement is greater self-awareness, professional growth, deeper understanding of theoretical communication principles, and authenticity in professional nurse–client relationships.

2. COLLEGIAL SHARING OF EXPERIENCES

In the second step of the experiential learning process, students identify their reactions (feeling as well as thinking) associated with their participation in step (1) of the activity. This is done by sharing observations, feelings, and ideas with peers as they relate to the exercise. Reflective sharing helps students critically examine the underlying dynamics and feelings stimulated by the exercise. By focusing on common themes and feelings, students gain the objectivity needed to hear and respond constructively to what they are learning.

Feedback

Feedback provides factual and reflective input from others in the environment with an emphasis on individual professional growth and expanding proficiency in applying therapeutic communication skills. Feedback from peers may reinforce the correctness of a given action or may serve as a stimulus for changing nonproductive behaviors. Accurate feedback, delivered in a compassionate manner, can be viewed as a professional responsibility, a commitment to assist others with collegial professional growth. Constructive feedback is nonevaluative; it describes behaviors focusing only on behaviors that are relevant to professional development and only on those that can be changed.

3. ANALYSIS AND SYNTHESIS

Participation in each exercise should be followed by an analysis and synthesis of the key elements. This reflective process encourages critical thinking and provides insight into factors affecting the communication process. The analysis of an exercise or case study should include a systematic examination of those aspects of the experience common to all group members, with the focus on how certain behaviors affected others and how the exercise affected the group process. In addition to studying the meaning of common themes and feelings, ideas that are *different* from the general thinking of the group are also analyzed and reflected upon as important sources of information. Differences in observations, thinking, and feeling add to the critical examination of a topic. They should never be discouraged as irrelevant pieces of the group discussion.

Synthesis refers to developing a composite picture of a reality. As an essential component of the critical thinking process, it occurs when students take information obtained in a data analysis and develop a coherent blending of theoretical and personalized understandings based on the data. Crucial to the process of synthesis is enough time for participants not only to process their own personal reactions to the exercise but also to reflect on how others have perceived the same situation and how one behavior affects other behaviors. This synthesized data will become the foundation for applying communication principles in clinical practice.

4. INTEGRATION OF CONTENT

Class and group discussions need deliberately to link theory with the experiential learning. The structured exercises are not very useful unless the student learning dialogue serves to reinforce associations between behaviors demonstrated in the exercises and other class content, assigned readings, and prior life experiences. These data form the basis for applying the most appropriate communication principles in the clinical situation.

5. APPLICATION OF KNOWLEDGE TO CLINICAL PRACTICE

The final step in the experiential process involves use of the knowledge and skills about interpersonal relationships in nursing practice, in the service of the client. A connecting link exists between the last step, "application of knowledge to clinical practice," and the initial step, "active involvement in an exercise." Through active involvement in experiential structured exercises, students are able to make generalizations from isolated classroom experiences to the larger world of professional nursing practice. Ideally, the student will have the opportunity, simultaneously with course content, to practice application of communication principles in actual interaction with clients and colleagues. Bringing actual examples from the student's clinical experience into the classroom for discussion broadens the learning experience. If there is not an immediate opportunity to practice communication skills, students can speculate how this new knowledge could be applied in specific future professional nursing situations and can refer to the text for cues to action throughout their nursing career.

REFERENCE

Goodstein LD, Pfeiffer J (1983). The 1983 Annual Report for Facilitators, Training and Consultation. San Diego, CA, University Associates Publishers, Inc.

PART I
CONCEPTUAL FOUNDATIONS OF NURSE–CLIENT RELATIONSHIPS

Chapter 1
Theory as a Guide to Practice
ELIZABETH ARNOLD · KATHLEEN BOGGS

OUTLINE

Basic Concepts

DEFINITION OF THEORY
THEORETICAL MODELS OF NURSING

Applications

NURSING THEORY IN THE NURSE–CLIENT RELATIONSHIP
    Hildegard Peplau
CONTRIBUTIONS FROM OTHER DISCIPLINES
    Sigmund Freud
    Carl Jung
    Harry Stack Sullivan
    Martin Buber
    Carl Rogers
    Erik Erikson
    Abraham Maslow
COMMUNICATION FRAMEWORKS
    Linear theory
    Circular transactional theoretical models
    Therapeutic communication
    Neurolinguistic programming

Summary

OBJECTIVES

At the end of the chapter, the student will be able to:

1. Identify the four critical elements of nursing theory models.

2. Describe Peplau's theory as the nursing theoretical framework used in this text.
3. Identify psychological models relevant to nurse–client relationships.

4. Specify the use of communication theory in nursing practice.

Nursing theory ought to guide research and practice, generate new ideas, and differentiate the focus of nursing from other professions.

Chinn and Jacobs, 1987

Life for each individual is a personal tale of comedy and tragedy, joys and sorrows, peak moments and despondency, accomplishment and defeat, happiness and pain—an original adventure story, difficult to encapsulate in words alone. In every person's life, physical and emotional disturbances, injuries, or defects can occur. Such complex life experiences are hard to understand, and people have limited personal defenses or coping strategies to use against them. People in such situations seek help from professionals to reduce the sense of discomfort, to find relevant answers to difficult problems, and to reaffirm the sense of self.

In health care, the nurse often is the professional a person turns to for help. The person becomes the client, seeking nurturance. The nurse becomes the helping person, providing the help and support the client needs (Paterson and Zderad, 1988). Nurses share peak moments, both good and bad, with their clients—in birth, death, and much of life in between. Nursing interventions range from health promotion to caring for clients in home care to caring for critically ill clients in the hospital to caring for the dying client in a hospice. Nurse–client relationships are the means by which nursing care is delivered (Forchuk, 1991; Peplau, 1992).

This text is about professional interpersonal relationships in nursing practice. Nurses form interpersonal commitments with their clients and other health professionals to accomplish the work of professional nursing. They use their relationship skills as a tool for health promotion and healing just as they use their knowledge of antibiotic therapy to help clients achieve higher levels of physical health and well-being. Through deliberate use of self- and therapeutic communication strategies, the nurse enters a helping relationship with a client. Engaging in this helping relationship requires a mastery of relationship concepts and communication skills, just as administering an injection requires mastery of physiological concepts and psychomotor skills.

In each chapter, the authors develop key concepts related to communication and interpersonal relationships in nursing practice; the concepts are based in theory and are followed by relevant clinical applications. Although intended to be comprehensive, the text is not meant to be all-inclusive. It would be an impossible task to develop fully the richness of the communication possibilities in the nurse–client relationship.

The nurse–client relationship builds on three foundational components. The *theoretical* component consists of all the scientific principles that form the basis for establishing and maintaining professional interpersonal relationships in nursing practice. These principles are drawn from the disciplines of nursing, psychology, and communication. The second component is the *technical* aspect, seen in the application of specific commu-

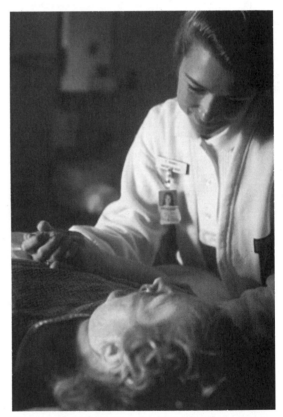

The nurse integrates three fundamental forms of nursing knowledge: theoretical, technical, and creative—in the nurse–client relationship. (Courtesy of the University of Maryland School of Nursing)

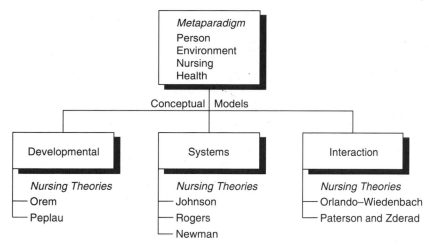

Figure 1–1 Nursing's Hierarchy of Knowledge

nication skills and strategies used to facilitate the purposes of the relationship. The *creative* element consists of the special and unique application of self for the express purpose of helping a fellow human being realize his or her fullest potential in a clinical setting. In this text the authors hope the reader will discover the nature and interplay of each of these variables in developing effective nurse–client relationships.

Chapter 1 identifies selected theoretical models relevant to the study of interpersonal relationships in nursing practice. Theory guides practice. Theoretical frameworks are useful in analyzing components and development of the relationship process, as well as in describing the behavioral changes occurring between nurse and client. An introduction to basic theoretical models—relevant to understanding communication, oneself, and relationships in nursing practice—provides a foundation for nurses learning to be effective communicators.

BASIC CONCEPTS

DEFINITION OF THEORY

Littlejohn (1989) defines *theory* as "any conceptual representation or explanation of a phenomenon" (p. 15). Phenomenon refers to an event or cluster of events about which one can draw hypotheses related to its meaning. Theoretical models represent an organized body of knowledge drawn from the scholarly thinking of experts who have studied a phenomenon at great length and developed conclusions about its nature. The theoretical model includes cause–effect and relational rules about what the experts have observed in addition to the description of the significant components of the phenomenon.

All theories are incomplete abstract constructions that can never fully capture the many variables contributing to the reality of a phenomenon. Different theories focus on different aspects of the same phenomenon, reflecting their authors' point of view. It is possible to take elements from several different theorists in developing a personally relevant theoretical guide to practice.

In examining theoretical frameworks or models, it is more important to explore their usefulness in explaining behaviors than to question their truthfulness. Theoretical models provide a framework for discussion, research, and the development of new thinking. They force the reader to challenge what is and to create fresh alternatives to the study of a phenomenon. All theoretical models are subject to change and adaptation as new information develops.

Theoretical models also make it easier to communicate with other professionals about complex behaviors and data. There is a common basis for discussing and organizing the information that everyone understands.

THEORETICAL MODELS OF NURSING

Paterson and Zderad (1988) assert that "the act of nursing involves a meeting of human persons. . . . It is a special or particular kind of meeting because it is purposeful" (p. 25). To consider the purpose of interpersonal relationships in nursing practice and how they fit into the delivery of professional nursing care, the reader needs to start with a general framework for understanding the nature of professional nursing. General theories of nursing lay out the domain of the profession, establish the boundaries of nursing practice, provide a basis for research, and serve as a guide for curriculum development. Theory as a guide to practice becomes more relevant as practice becomes more complex.

Theory development in nursing began with Florence Nightengale in her classic work *Notes on Nursing*. But it wasn't until the 1950s that professional nurse leaders began to insist on defining the domain of professional nursing practice. They saw a need to identify a logical theoretical structure of professional nursing practice with a clear linkage to what nurses actually do. Nursing theorists such as Virginia Henderson, Myra Levine, Martha Rogers, Imogene King, Sister Callista Roy, Madeline Leininger, Dorothea Orem, Jean Watson, Dorothy Johnson, Betty Neuman, and Rosemarie Rizzo Parse have devoted their professional lifetimes to developing theories about the body of knowledge that is unique to nursing. Adding to the value of these theories are the scholarly thinking of graduate nursing students in masters and doctoral programs throughout the nation. These graduate students have provided ideas, struggled to understand the language and meaning of concepts, critiqued ideas, and developed important research studies to support the validity of nursing theory. Thus the nursing theories that guide professional practice have a richness evolving from scholarly inquiry, and an integrity springing from the commitment to and continuous refinement of nursing theory by its primary and contributing authors.

Nursing knowledge proceeds from the general to the more specific in a structural hierarchy that includes a general metaparadigm, conceptual models, and theories. The first and broadest level of nursing knowledge is referred to as a metaparadigm. A **metaparadigm** contains the common ideas held across all paradigms. A conceptual model, or a *paradigm*, in nursing is defined as a worldview reflecting the knowledge developed about a phenomenon of interest within a scientific discipline (Parse, 1987). Examples of conceptual models of nursing include developmental models, systems models, and interaction models. Figure 1–1 provides a diagram of the structural hierarchy of knowledge beginning with the metaparadigm and dealing with these elements in specific nursing theory.

Nursing's metaparadigm reflects the central concepts of interest to all nursing theorists, namely concepts about (1) person, (2) environment, (3) nursing, and (4) health (Fawcett, 1994). Although nursing theorists make different assumptions about the relationships among each of these concepts, these four distinct elements are the focus for consideration in all theoretical models. Specific knowledge of pathophysiological processes, pharmacology and nursing interventions, communication, and the nursing process provides a tangible matrix through which each theorist threads specific theoretical concepts regarding the discipline of professional nursing (Fig. 1–2).

Person is viewed as a unitary concept that includes physiological, psychological, spiritual, and social elements. Circumstances arise that assault the well-being of a person, affecting body, mind, spirit, and role performance. At such times,

Figure 1–2 Critical Elements in Professional Nursing

the person may require the services of a professional nurse. The need for nursing care does not arise directly from the situation of illness or level of personal health but rather from the person's inability to cope with the changes resulting from the situation (Orlando, 1961). The centrality of self is key to effective nursing practice. The nurse views the client as a whole person, "not as an additive summation, but rather as a gestalt" (Paterson and Zderad, 1988, p. 25).

Just as the study of plant growth cannot be fully understood without an analysis of its environment, i.e., the soil, and the balance between sun and shade required for each plant's development, persons cannot be fully understood without an analysis of the environment that supports or retards their growth.

Environment refers to all of the cultural, developmental, physical, and psychosocial conditions external to an individual that influence the client's perception and involvement as a recipient of clinical nursing care. Some nursing theorists, such as King (1981), Levine (1978), and Paterson and Zderad (1988), broaden the concept of environment to include internal environmental states as well as external factors in terms of physiological, psychological, spiritual, and developmental variables. Each of these environmental elements influences how a person encounters and responds to life. The client's interpretation of health and perceptions of the nursing role have a direct relationship to societal beliefs. Current nursing theorists agree that environmental factors are critical inputs into the success or failure of nursing interventions.

"*Nursing* is the involved interaction with persons in a caring mode" (Marriner-Tomey, 1989, p. 197). It is practiced as a unique service designed to meet identified client health needs. Each theory defines nursing operations in a slightly different way, although the common themes of service to client cross all definitions. All nursing theorists agree that nursing activities are carried out through the nursing process, involving effective communication skills and a sound knowledge base. How client behavioral data are communicated depends on the nurse's theoretical orientation and the terminology associated with it.

The second level of nursing knowledge concerns the development of a conceptual model. **Conceptual models** are abstract images that explain the particular nursing theorist's assumptions, key concepts, and postulates about each of the four elements in nursing's metaparadigm. Concepts are broad and comprehensive ideas that serve as the building blocks of theory development. Assumptions are implicit and explicit principles that are essential foundations for understanding the conclusions drawn in the concept. Postulates are single-belief statements that help broaden the explanation of the concept. Conceptual models cannot be empirically validated because they represent abstractions and do not spell out the relationships between concepts. In nursing, conceptual models reflect developmental, systems, and interaction constructs.

Nursing theories develop from and are linked to conceptual models. They represent the third and most discrete level of nursing knowledge. Theories define the relationships among concepts, assumptions, and postulates implicit in each related nursing model. Nursing theories are capable of being tested empirically and give practical direction to clinical nursing practice. They also are used in nursing education to organize curricula.

Health is a broad concept used to describe an individual's state of well-being and level of functioning. More than the absence of disease, the personal meaning of health varies, affected by many factors, including the person's degree of wellness or illness (Kelly and Sime, 1990). Health has become a broad concept used to describe an individual's state of being, ranging from optimal well-being to death. The concept of health is developed in Chapter 15.

Key concepts as defined by various nursing theorists are presented in Box 1–1. For a more complete explanation of the concepts and theoretical models in nursing practice, the reader is referred to the original works of the theorists and nursing theory texts in the reference list of this chapter.

APPLICATIONS

NURSING THEORY IN THE NURSE–CLIENT RELATIONSHIP

Although principles of communication and relationship lend themselves to implementation of all nursing frameworks, those that specifically focus

---

BOX 1–1
Key Concepts as Defined by Various Nursing Theorists

Person	Environment	Nursing	Health	Terminology
Roy's Adaptation Model A person is viewed as a holistic "adaptive system."	"World within and around the person"; focal, contextual, or residual stimulus inputs.	Practical application of nursing science principles in nursing practice.	The process of becoming a fully functioning person in the face of environmental changes.	*Adaptive modes* Physiological Self-concept Role function Interdependent
Orem's Self-Care Model A person is viewed as a "unity that can be functioning biologically, symbolically, and socially."	Physical and psychosocial conditions external to the person that influence or motivate behavior.	Social, interpersonal, and psychomotor (regulatory) behaviors that foster responsible self-actions and assist clients in meeting self-care demands.	State of wholeness or integrity of human beings.	*Self-care requisites:* Universal Developmental Health deviation
Neuman's Systems Model A person is viewed as a whole: a dynamic physiological, sociocultural, spiritual, and developmental being.	Internal and external environment. Any interpersonal, intrapersonal, or extrapersonal stressor can disrupt normal lines of a person's defense.	Unique profession concerned with reducing environmental stressors and helping the client make needed adjustments for optimal wellness.	"Health is equated with optimal system stability" and a harmonious energy flow between client and environment.	Interpersonal, intrapersonal, extrapersonal lines of defense. Primary, secondary, tertiary prevention
Parse's Man-Living-Health Model A person is viewed as an open being, relating with the environment.	Inseparable in co-existing with a person.	A human science that emphasizes a person's subjective participation in health experiences.	A part of the process of becoming and reflects a person's relationship with the world.	Meaning, rythmicity, cotranscendence
King's Open Systems Model A person is viewed as a personalized social system capable of a wide variety of transactional behaviors.	Source of transactional stressors, with temporal, spatial, and developmental boundaries.	"Perceiving, thinking, relating, judging, and acting vis-à-vis the behavior of individuals who come to a nursing situation."	Constructive adaptation to internal and external stressors, and effective interpersonal functioning.	Personal, interpersonal, and social systems
Rogers' Life Process Model A person is viewed as an indivisible human energy field with identifiable characteristics.	An energy field, composed of a definable pattern, external to the individual.	A unique body of knowledge applied "in service to man" related to helping clients achieve maximum health, or "die with dignity."	Full expression of the life process, characterized by the dynamic interaction between human and environmental fields.	*Homeodynamics* Complementarity Heliacy Resonancy Integrality

---

on interpersonal relationships include Barnard and Mercer, (Marriner-Tomey, 1994), Erickson et al., Orlando, Peplau, Travelbee, Weidenbach, and Reihl-Sisca. The nursing theory framework chosen for the study of the nurse–client relationship in this text is that of Hildegard Peplau. Exercise 1–1 helps nurses apply theory to a clinical example.

Hildegard Peplau

Hildegard Peplau was the first nurse theorist to describe the nurse–client relationship as the foundation of nursing practice (Forchuk, 1991). In shifting the focus from what nurses do "to" clients to what nurses do "with" clients, Peplau engi-

EXERCISE 1–1
Application of Theory to a Clinical Example

Purpose: To help students apply nursing theory to a clinical example.

Time: 45 minutes plus preparation time

Procedure:

1. Break the large group into groups of four to five students. Select a nursing theorist and the nursing theorist's model for the case study. Suggestions for nursing theorists include Johnson, Levine, Neuman, Orem, Parse, and Roy. Describe how each theorist would assess the following situation:

    Mary Smith is a 63-year-old diabetic living alone in the community. The nurse is visiting her on a weekly basis for wound care related to her diabetes. Mary is noncompliant with her diet and is overweight. She does not like to test her blood because her eyesight isn't very good. Her daughter lives close by, but Mary likes her independence and does not want to rely on her for care.

2. After each group has developed the case according to the selected nursing theorist, reconvene and share the results.

neered a major paradigm shift from a model focused on medical treatments to an interpersonal relational model of nursing practice. She identified ways in which the nurse makes specialized use of a professional relationship to identify and intervene therapeutically in psychosocial nursing problems.

Peplau viewed nursing as a developmental educational instrument designed to help individuals and communities use their capacities to live more productively. Her theory is mainly concerned with the processes by which positive changes in health care status and well-being are achieved. Observation, interpretation, and intervention form the essence of a nurse-client relationship. Raw data must be interpreted and transformed into a meaningful explanation, acceptable in meaning to nurse and client.

The transformation process occurs as the nurse observes and listens to the client, developing impressions and general ideas about the meaning of the client's situation. These inferences are validated with the client for accuracy. Illness is viewed as an unique opportunity for experiential learning, personal growth, and improved coping strategies for living (Peplau, 1992).

The dynamic nursing approach is not that of a passive spectator observer. Peplau advocates being "participant observers" in therapeutic conversations, in which nurses observe not only the behavior of the client but their own behavior as well. Data are collected by interacting directly with the client. Nurses have a keen awareness of their own role and what is appropriate and also of the roles

the client may be projecting on them: friend, parent, protagonist, or sex object. None of these roles is useful in providing nursing care to clients. The social and personal needs of the nurse should not be a part of the nurse–client conversation.

In her classic work on the nurse–client relationship, *Interpersonal Theory of Nursing,* Peplau (1952) described four developmental phases of the relationship, which she characterizes as a dynamic learning experience out of which personal-social growth can occur. Two underlying principles of communication interwoven through each phase are clarification and continuity (Forchuk, 1991).

The nurse and client encounter each other for the first time during the *orientation phase* of the relationship. They enter the relationship as strangers to each other and must develop a working partnership before the work on health care problems takes place. Nurse and client begin to analyze a problem situation and related client needs. From this analysis, the nurse develops relevant *nursing diagnoses.*

Once the problem has been defined in the orientation phase, the nurse and client move into the *working phase.* The working phase is subdivided into two subphases: identification and exploitation. Correlated with the planning stages, the identification subphase is characterized by mutual clarification of ideas and expectations. It is important for the nurse to help clients express feelings they may not be aware of or fear societal disapproval of, such as helplessness, dependency, and despair. These data become the basis for developing an individualized *nursing care plan.* Nurse and client develop goals of the relationship related to resolution of identified client health needs. Types of assistance needed to achieve goals are confirmed. Planned nursing actions are evaluated from the perspective of effectiveness and efficiency of execution time.

The *exploitation* phase is used to assist the client in making full use of the services offered in resolving the issues for which the client initially sought treatment. Corresponding to the implementation phase of the nursing process, the nurse's role is to foster the self-direction of clients in promoting their health and well-being. The client's role is categorized as dependent, interdependent, or independent, based on the amount of responsibility the client is willing or able to assume for self.

The final phase of the relationship, corresponding to the evaluation phase of the nursing process, Peplau calls the *resolution* phase. The goals of this phase relate to the successful resolution of the issues that initially brought the client to seek health care assistance from the nurse. Modifications, including referrals, are made if goals have not been reached. Once health goals have been achieved, the nurse and client terminate the relationship. Peplau (1952, 1957) identifies six nursing roles relevant to the development of the nurse–client relationship (Box 1–2).

CONTRIBUTIONS FROM OTHER DISCIPLINES

Relationships take place between people, and the self is central to the development of any relationship. Exploring the meaning of feelings and behaviors is relevant to a full understanding of the client as a person. Nursing borrows theory principles from other disciplines in understanding what goes on in the successful nurse–client relationship. Representative psychoanalytic, interpersonal, and developmental theories are presented. For a complete description of these theories, the reader is advised to read the classic works identified in the reference list.

Sigmund Freud

Sigmund Freud is the original source of most theoretical formulations about the nature of person-

---

> **BOX 1–2**
> **Peplau's Six Relevant Nursing Roles**
>
> *Stranger role*—receives the client the same way one meets a stranger in other life situations.
> *Resource role*—answers questions, interprets clinical treatment data, gives information.
> *Teaching role*—gives instructions and provides training; involves analysis and synthesis of the learner experience.
> *Counseling role*—helps the client understand and integrate the meaning of current life circumstances.
> *Surrogate role*—helps the client clarify domains of dependence, interdependence, and independence.
> *Active leadership role*—helps the client assume maximum responsibility for meeting treatment goals in a mutually satisfying way.

---

ality. His model is of theoretical interest in the study of personality and behavior in nurse–client relationships for several reasons. First, Freud was the first to insist that talking about situations and the feelings accompanying them with a trained professional has a positive effect on reducing tension and resolving maladaptive behaviors. The therapeutic relationship, in which the focus is solely on the client, exists for the purpose of understanding and resolving client issues.

Second, Freud's ideas about *transference* (defined as behaviors in which the client projects irrational attitudes and feelings from the past onto people in the present) are useful in understanding difficult behaviors. For example, the client who says to the young nurse, "Get a real nurse—you're young enough to be my daughter and I don't want to talk with you about my personal life" has a transference reaction having little to do with the nurse's competence. This self-realization helps the nurse depersonalize the client's comment and allows for a more appropriate response. Peplau (1992) suggests that a constructive way of handling this situation would be: "(a) to get the patient to specify the similarity between the familiar other and the nurse, and (b) to specify some differences" (p. 15).

According to Freud, self-awareness of "counter-transference" feelings toward a client enables the helper to use one's personality consciously to help the client. *Counter-transference* feelings refer to the cluster of attitudes or feelings the nurse may develop toward a client. They can emerge in response to a difficult client's highly provocative transference behaviors. Or they can reflect the nurse's biases and past experiences with similar situations or people. For example, feeling anger or frustration, feeling strong attraction, acting on the basis of stereotypes, or feeling like a child with a powerful client can be critical counter-transference feelings that influence the nurse's behavior in the relationship.

Freud also was the first to identify biopsychosocial stages of development as a way of describing personality development. He maintained that every person passes through a series of age-related maturational stages of personality development, each with its own set of problems and conflicts (Freud, 1937, 1959). He strongly believed that most personality formation takes place during early childhood and can be altered only with intensive therapy. Because he believed that the personality is largely formed at an early age, Freud's stages of development do not address adult development. Although Freud's theoretical assumption that all personal growth takes place naturally during early childhood has been largely disputed, his ideas about the influence of past interpersonal experiences on present behavior continues to be relevant. The nurse needs to consider past experiences of clients as part of the environment. Neuman (1989), Paterson and Zderad (1988), and Roy (1976) are among the nursing theorists who emphasize the person's developmental internal environment as having an influence on present perceptions.

Freud proposed three structural components of personality: the id, the ego, and the superego. The *id* represents the pleasure principle, the *ego* the reality principle, and the *superego* family and societal norms for behavior. The ego is the central regulator of behavior, balancing the id's demands for instant gratification with the superego's insistence on adhering to society's values. When the ego malfunctions, behaviors reflect a loss of balanced control. Too much superego results in a constricted neurotic personality, and too much id without influence from the ego presents as irresponsibility. These terms remain relevant in behavior analysis.

Freud believed that people who are unable to resolve a specific maturational stage are destined to retain an immature behavioral response pattern for the rest of their lives. They remain "fixated" at that developmental stage. Many behaviors and emotional reactions that seem out of proportion to a situation may indicate a lack of psychosocial maturity in resolving earlier developmental stages. For example, a client who experienced little parental support in early childhood may develop a sense that it isn't possible to be treated fairly. These feelings become generalized unconsciously into "I can't trust anyone to communicate with me in a fair and honest way." The client demonstrates maladaptive behaviors that in turn affect the way people respond. The original erroneous conclusion about the relationship between self and other becomes a self-fulfilling prophecy.

Ego defense mechanisms protect the self from anxiety, but in the process severely compromise the flexibility of a person's behavioral responses (Freud, 1937). Mental illness develops when ego defense mechanisms replace adaptive coping strategies as a means of resolving difficult problems. Nurses use all of these concepts as they strive to understand their client's behaviors and focus on facilitating the individual's health and well-being.

Carl Jung

Another psychoanalytic model with implications for the nurse–client relationship was developed by Carl Jung. Jung's work has significant implications for nursing practice, first, because it views all people, regardless of race, socioeconomic status, religion, or culture, as sharing common human qualities. Jung believed culture and society play an important role in explaining behavior. As human beings, all people share some universal archetypes: gentleness, strength, love, and anger. A nurse's recognition of the common human bonds shared with all clients helps promote understanding and acceptance of self as well as others.

Jung's work is important in looking at the person as a gestalt, containing many and sometimes contradictory dimensions. According to Jung (1963, 1971), self represents an archetype or pattern of living within the larger society, characterized by an ongoing association and clash between the life instinct and self-extinction. Each dimension represents a partial truth about the nature of the self. Jung contends that we are all as capable of being destructive given certain life circumstances as we are of being loving. He encouraged every human being to find and acknowledge all parts of themselves, good and evil. For Jung, it is more important to be true to one's nature than to pattern one's life according to the whims of a conventionally adapted society (von Franz, 1975). The process by which this occurs Jung refers to as *"individuation."* Established hypotheses about "person" in nursing practice as unique but interconnected with others for survival are certainly compatible with Jung's ideas.

Other contributions to the study of behavior within and among people include Jung's persistence, despite criticism from his peers, in arguing that spiritual concerns are an important component of personality development. Jung also challenged the idea that men and women are automatically locked into roles and behaviors strictly because of gender. According to Jung, anatomy is not destiny, as Freud proclaimed. In men, there are strong needs for affiliation, just as in women there are equally strong needs for independence. Although all of these ideas were considered radical in Jung's day, today most people recognize the validity of his ideas. Jung introduced the idea of *"persona,"* describing the social masks that people show to the world. When the persona contradicts the nature of the self, the individual suffers.

Jung likened the role of a helping person in a therapeutic relationship to a "midwife, assisting in bringing into the light of day a natural process, the process of coming into one's self" (von Franz, 1975). The emphasis in a successful nurse–client relationship on a mutuality that supports the autonomy of the client is a very similar process.

Unlike Freud, who never considered adult development as a reality, Jung describes pivotal differences in self-development, occurring during the first and second halves of the life cycle. Before mid-life, the self-concept projects outward as a person establishes an identity, develops a career, and establishes intimate relationships. The external expectations of others are extremely important. It is not until the second half of life, for most people, that there is a turning inward. In midlife, a person begins to question the meaning of his or her life and to examine what is really important. Jung notes that "we cannot live the afternoon of life according to the values of life's morning" (1971). This concept is useful in understanding the inward turning of many older adults in their search for meaning.

Harry Stack Sullivan

Harry Stack Sullivan (1953), an American psychoanalyst, developed a theory of interpersonal relations that serves as the foundation of Peplau's work and of many of the concepts nurses use in therapeutic relationships. His work contains several interpersonal constructs of relevance to the nurse–client relationship. Sullivan defined three modes of experiencing. In the *prototaxic mode,* a person can focus only on the present and may not be able to recall past events or contemplate the future. In the *parataxic mode,* the person is able to describe the relationship between past and present. In the *syntaxic mode,* the person can connect past, present, and future. Individuals experiencing shock, panic, or brain damage function in the prototaxic mode. Understanding this behavioral construct allows the nurse to act empathetically with clients who simply cannot function at a higher level (Peplau, 1992). Parataxic distortions are similar to the transference reactions described by Freud.

Sullivan (1953) describes defensive behaviors as "security operations" designed to protect the self from experiencing anxiety. The self is viewed within an interpersonal context, a product of society.

Martin Buber

The I–Thou relationship described by Martin Buber (1958) captures the essence of the relationship desired in therapeutic conversations between nurse and client. Buber views an *I–Thou relationship* as one in which each individual responds to the other from his or her own uniqueness and is valued for that uniqueness in a direct, mutually respected reciprocal alliance. Neither person is an "object" of study. Instead there is a process of mutual discovery. Each person feels free to be authentic and to relate compassionately and responsibly with the other. The importance of responding to a client fully in a relationship has to do with confirming the essential dignity of the human being with unique capability and the potential for becoming more through the relationship. Paterson and Zderad (1988) suggest that "Buber's I–Thou relating emphasizes awareness of each being's uniqueness without a superimposing, or a deciding about the other without a knowing" (p. 44).

Buber's work also forms the theoretical foundation for confirming responses as a way of validating the self in a therapeutic relationship. He states that "Man wishes to be confirmed in his being by man and wishes to have a presence in the being of the other. Secretly and bashfully, he watches for a yes which allows him to be" (Buber, 1957, p. 104). Through the nurse–client relationship, nurses act as a primary resource in confirming the humanity of clients entrusted to their care.

Carl Rogers

Carl Rogers' theoretical model of a person-centered approach to therapeutic relationships is a useful framework for understanding the reciprocal roles of the professional nurse and client in nurse–client relationships. According to Rogers (1961), "If I can provide a certain type of relationship, the other person will discover within himself the capacity to use that relationship for growth and change, and personal development will occur." Rogers' work is important because of its focus on the client and because it identifies helper characteristics essential to the development of client-centered relationships: genuineness, unconditional positive regard, and empathy. These characteristics are found in successful nurse–client relationships.

Genuineness requires the nurse to be willing to enter a therapeutic relationship without presenting a false front. It means admitting that one has limitations, makes mistakes, and does not have all of the answers. Genuineness requires the nurse to take full responsibility for personal and professional choices.

Unconditional positive regard refers to a level of acceptance in which the nurse accepts all client feelings as legitimate even though boundaries may need to be set on the client's behavior. It means the nurse is willing to accept a client as a unique person of worth without any reservations. Empathy, the third characteristic of successful relationships, refers to the nurse's capacity to understand the client's world and to communicate that understanding to the client. These characteristics are part of the creative art of relationships in nursing practice and a fundamental component of all therapeutic communication strategies in the nurse–client relationship.

Erik Erikson

Erik Erikson's (1981, 1982) model of psychosocial development presents a useful framework for understanding the relationship between self and the interpersonal world the person inhabits. Erikson (1981, 1982) views a person as a potentially self-actualizing agent, capable of growing from birth to death. The word "development" means "unfolding." Brookfield (1986) notes that the "self-concept moves from dependency to independence as individuals grow in responsibilities, experience and confidence." Covey (1992) describes a third stage as interdependency, with many of the characteristics of generativity and wisdom described in the Erikson model. Within each person, developmental remnants of earlier experiences persist, to be constantly reworked and interwoven into the tapestry of life by each individual (Erikson and Erikson, 1981).

Erikson's (1981, 1982) stages of ego development refer to the process of expanding psychosocial development. His model upholds the interaction of the self with its surrounding social system as the fundamental core of maturation. Erikson describes identity as holistic. "Wholeness emphasizes a sound, organic, progressive mutuality between diversified functions and parts within an entirety, the boundaries of which are open and fluent" (1959, p. 92). The first three stages of psychosocial development prepare the person for the central life task of forming an identity, each by focusing on different elements essential for the development of a cohesive self-identity. Childhood forms of self-validation represent the core of self-identity. Yet the sense of identity defined in late adolescence or early adulthood is more than simply the total of self-images developed earlier. Integrated into identity are all previous developmental stages. The last three stages of ego development refine and elaborate on the core identity.

Erikson views self-definition as a lifelong process, occurring according to the epigenetic principle which states that "anything that grows has a ground plan . . . and out of this ground plan all parts arise, each part having its time of ascendency, until all parts have arisen to form a functioning whole" (1959). According to Erikson (1963), a person employs inner ego strengths to master each developmental life crisis. He refers to these inner strengths as "virtues." Although more than one strength may be used during the resolution of a particular developmental crisis, each assumes ascendancy or prominence during a particular segment of the life cycle.

The process by which psychosocial maturation occurs is through resolving psychosocial life tasks.

Developmental crises occur when previous patterns of adaptation are insufficient to handle the demands of life. To be successful, with each developmental task a person needs to move to higher levels of emotional mastery and interpersonal complexity. Society both presents and supports expanding development of identity through mandatory school attendance, confirmations, graduations, weddings, retirement, and other rituals marking self changes.

Unfortunately, all individuals do not have the same opportunity to develop a mature self-concept. Differences in parenting and life experiences can "fast forward" a child into assuming adult responsibilities without going through normal childhood phases. Other children exhibit retarded or arrested development occasioned by drug abuse or overprotection. Culture may influence the exact timetable and behavioral expression of different developmental stages.

Erikson views psychosocial development as a life cycle process following a linear biological timetable. But his theory also considers horizontal threads strongly interconnected with society and unexpected life circumstances that have an impact on the person's mastery of developmental life tasks. Horizontal threads are those life events that occur spontaneously. For example, illness, a promotion, marriage, and a job loss are horizontal threads. When they occur simultaneously with normal developmental crises, both situations are more intense. At any time sudden change can reactivate a psychosocial crisis (Dowd, 1990; Erikson, 1982). Exercise 1–2 analyzes normal psychosocial crises.

Although Erikson's theory of psychosocial development is no longer considered linear, as first believed (Logan, 1986 Oerter, 1986;), it offers nurses a concrete framework for examining the self-concept. Using a life-cycle approach offers nurses direction in looking at critical life issues the client may be facing concurrently with an illness. Accurate assessment of the client's mastery of psychosocial crises helps nurses differentiate between normal and abnormal psychosocial developmental patterns. It also provides a framework for understanding the significant identity issues that changes in circumstances create for people. Erikson's model helps the nurse select developmentally appropriate communication strategies. Box 1–3 contrasts some of these basic psychosocial constructs.

Abraham Maslow

Abraham Maslow's theory of self-development focuses on basic needs. According to Maslow, the self is the inner core of personality, holding some characteristics in common with others and possessing other characteristics not held by many others. Maslow describes ascending stages of personal growth needs, beginning with physiological survival needs and ending with self-transcendent needs. Self-actualization represents the growth potential within each of us to realize the fullest expression of our innate talents and personality assets, "the human being at his best." To become self-actualized, a person must achieve a sufficient level of need fulfillment at all the lower stages. If a

---

EXERCISE 1–2
Time Line

Purpose: To give students experience with normal psychosocial crises.

Time: 45 minutes

Procedure:
1. Draw a time line of your life to date. Include all significant events and the age at which they occurred. Identify horizontal threads.
2. Insert Erikson's stages as markers in your time line.

Discussion:
In a large group, discuss the following:
1. In what ways did Erickson's stages provide information about expected tasks in your life?
2. In what ways did they deviate or appear nonapplicable?
3. To what would you attribute the differences?
4. How could you use this exercise in your nursing care of clients?

BOX 1–3
Personality Development

Age (Years)	Erikson's Psychosocial Stages	Primary Person Orientation	Strengths	Qualities	Freud's Psychosexual Stages	Jung's Psychosocial Orientation
0–2	Trust vs. mistrust	Mother	Hope	To receive, to give	Oral	Largely unconscious
2–4	Autonomy vs. shame/doubt	Father	Will power	To control, to let go	Anal	
4–6	Initiative vs. guilt	Basic family	Purpose	To make, to play act	Oedipal	Beginning ego consciousness
6–12	Industry vs. inferiority	Neighborhood, school	Competence	To make things, to put things together	Latency	
13–19	Identity vs. identity diffusion	Peer groups	Fidelity	To be one's self	Puberty	Individual consciousness
Young adult	Intimacy vs. isolation	Partners in marriage, friendship	Love	To share one's self with another	Genitality	Social adaptation, achievement
Adult	Generativity vs. self-absorption	Children, community	Care	To take care of, to create		Inner reflection, individuation
Old age	Integrity vs. despair	Humankind	Wisdom	To accept being, to accept not being		Self-knowledge of the meaning of one's existence

Adapted from Erikson E (1982). The Life Cycle Completed. New York, Norton.

person is struggling to breathe or is starving, love and belonging needs are not as important.

Maslow's first stage is referred to as *physiological.* Meeting basic physiological needs has psychological as well as physical components. Satisfying hunger, thirst, and sexual and sensory stimulation needs has an emotional component requiring satisfaction as well. The second level of needs is labeled *safety and security.* Physical safety in the form of sufficient financial resources and personal protection leads to the desire for emotional security. Once safety and security needs are met, persons seek acceptance by the community of which they are part. Maslow refers to this need stage as *love and belonging.* In turn, the reciprocal commitment between self and others leads to self-esteem. Self-esteem requires only that one engage with life to the best of one's ability. A sense of dignity, respect, and approval by others for the self within is the hallmark of successfully caring for *self-esteem needs.*

Self-actualization is Maslow's name for the level of development in which a person balances interdependence with individual self-awareness. Self-actualized individuals are not superhuman— they are subject to the same feelings of insecurity and vulnerability all individuals experience. But they accept this part of their humanness and strive to share it with others. Self-actualized people take important personal stands on issues, saying no when it is appropriate and fully commiting themselves to personal goals that enrich their sense of self and contribute to the lives of others. Box 1–4 describes characteristics of self-actualized people.

Maslow's final level of development, *self-transcendence,* occurs when people fully realize their own unique place in a much larger cosmos. There is a detachment from petty annoyances in life and yet full involvement in making the world a better place in which to live.

Need deprivation in early childhood can lead to

BOX 1–4
Characteristics of Self-Actualization

A quality of genuineness
A passion for living
Ability to get along well with others
A strong sense of personal worth
A view of life situations as an opportunity, not a threat
Ability to experience each moment fully
Moments of intense emotional meaning, "peak experience"
Full acceptance of self and others
Identification with fellow human beings
High sense of responsibility with a strong desire to serve
   humanity
Integrity of purpose

an almost insatiable hope for need satisfaction in adulthood. Illness, trauma, environmental changes, and developmental stages during the lifespan are naturally occurring variables that affect need satisfaction in some immediate and strange ways. Deprivation can arise from unmet needs or from overindulgence. Adults who provide excessive need satisfaction—overfeeding and overprotection of children, as well as permissive child rearing—can cause children to expect similar treatment from others. When this behavior is not forthcoming, the individual feels insecure and sometimes bitterly deprived. Figure 1–3 presents needs of the client requiring nursing intervention as nursing diagnoses related to each stage of Maslow's theory.

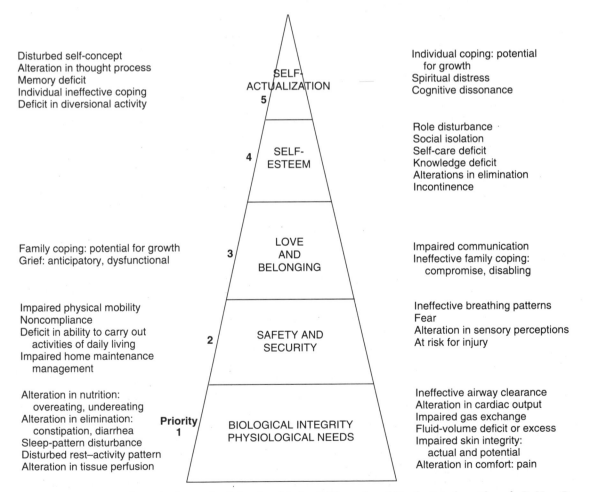

Figure 1–3 Nursing Diagnosis Categories Related to Maslow's Hierarchy of Needs. Based on Ebersole P, Hess P. Toward Healthy Aging: Human Needs and Nursing Response. St. Louis, Mosby, p. 150.

EXERCISE 1–3
Maslow's Hierarchy of Needs

Purpose: To help students apply theory to a clinical case example.

Time: 45 minutes

Procedure:
In groups of three or four students consider the following case study and apply Maslow's hierarchy of needs theory to Mr. Rodgers' case from the time of admission to the coronary care unit through his discharge and follow-up care. Include any considerations for changing priorities because of fluctuations in his condition.

Mr. Rodgers is admitted to the cardiac ICU with an acute myocardial infarction. He is an internationally known middle-aged businessman, a corporate vice president of a major company, and very well liked by his employees. His blood pressure for the past two years has never fallen below a diastolic reading of 95, and he is being treated with a mild diuretic. Before this hospitalization, he had never been admitted to a hospital. Mr. Rodgers is anxious and perspiring profusely. He has many of the predisposing factors for heart problems present in his history, family, and lifestyle.

Discussion:
1. In the large group, share your conclusions and recommendations for prioritizing Mr. Rodgers' care.
2. Discuss the rationales for the selections.

Maslow portrays his basic growth/need model as linear and progressive, but each stage of development is only partially independent of the others, and there is a feedback loop. Former stages are embodied in current developmental needs. People revisit earlier stages when circumstances force attention on satisfaction of basic needs.

The nurse can revise needs priorities whenever the situation dictates it. During a hospitalization, the nurse may need to update self-need priorities many times. Exercise 1–3 is designed to provide experience with applying Maslow's framework to a clinical situation.

The value of Maslow's model in nursing practice lies in establishing what is most important in the sequencing of nursing actions in the nurse–client relationship. For example, attempting to collect any but the most essential information when the client is in pain or suffering a heart attack is inappropriate. Basic needs come before growth needs. The nurse would meet the client's physiological need for pain relief before collecting general information for a nursing data base.

COMMUNICATION FRAMEWORKS

The limited discussion of communication theory in this section is based on several assumptions important to consider in professional relationships:

1. It is impossible not to communicate (Bateson, 1979).
2. Human beings are known and responded to by what they indicate about themselves in communication.
3. Faulty communication results in disordered thinking, feeling, and acting.
4. There is no way of judging a person's perception as truly accurate unless the person shares the experience with another.

Communication is a basic tool used in the helping relationship. It is recognized as an essential component of the theory and practice of nursing (Garvin and Kennedy, 1988). The quality of the communication process, to a large extent, determines the caliber of the relationship. Using a communication framework in nurse–client relationships helps facilitate communication with clients and colleagues (Schmieding, 1990). Nurses use communication skills to provide new information, correct misinformation, promote understanding of client responses to health problems, explore options for care, assist in decision making, and facilitate the well-being of clients. Knowledge of communication theory not only helps the nurse look at client interactions in a more systematic way but it also helps steer the direction of the relationship.

Ruesch (1961) asserted that "communication is a universal function of man that is not tied to any particular place, time, or context, and basically communication which produces a therapeutic effect in no way differs from what happens in ordinary exchanges" (pp. 30–31). Therapeutic communication is not a method but rather a specialized application of basic communication principles designed to promote the client's well-being and self-actualization.

Linear Theory

Historically, most communication models have been linear. *Communication* was viewed as an activity involving the transmission of messages by a source to a receiver for the purpose of influencing the receiver's behavior (Miller and Nicholson, 1976). Personal channels of communication are those sensory receptors through which information is transmitted. One or more of the five senses:—sight, hearing, taste, touch, and smell— are involved. From a linear perspective, there is a sender, a message, and a receiver—similar key elements—regardless of the message content, as diagrammed in Figure 1–4.

The *sender* is identified as the source or initiator of the message. By expressing an internal thought or feeling, the sender assumes responsibility for the accuracy of the content and the emotional tone of the message.

The *message* consists of a verbal or nonverbal expression of thoughts or feelings intended to convey information to the receiver and requiring interpretation by that person. To ensure that the message will be correctly received, a message needs

to be encoded by the sender, that is, put into verbal or nonverbal symbols that the receiver can understand. To encode a message appropriately requires a clear understanding of the receiver's mental frame of reference as well as knowledge of the desired objective of the communicated message. Clear communication is achieved when the sender thinks through what the message is supposed to achieve and organizes the content of the message to focus on key ideas.

The *receiver* is the recipient of the message. Once a message has been received, the receiver needs to decode it, that is, translate the message into word symbols that make sense. The receiver's open-minded attitude and suspension of judgment strengthens the possibility of decoding the sender's message accurately.

Circular Transactional Theoretical Models

Contemporary theorists favor viewing the communication process as circular rather than linear, as an integral part of a larger social system process. Originally developed by Bateson (1979), a circular transactional model proposes that communication is best understood within the context of a relationship: "Every communication has a content and a relationship aspect such that the latter classifies the former and is therefore metacommunication" (Waltzlawick et al., 1967, p. 54). *Communication* is viewed as a continuous, mutually interdependent activity involving communicators who reciprocally influence each other's behavior. Metacommunication results in confirmation, disconfirmation, or

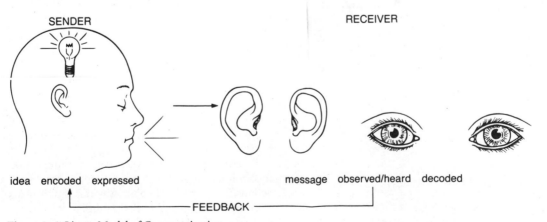

Figure 1–4 Linear Model of Communication

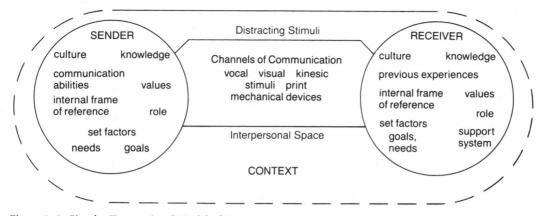

Figure 1–5 Circular Transactional Model of Communication

rejection. Confirmation acknowledges the existence of the other person as being of value. Disconfirmation fails to acknowledge either the existence or the value of the other person. Rejection is a negative appraisal of the sender's message.

People take either *symmetrical* or *complementary* roles in the relationship. The communicators are equal in a symmetrical relationship, with either assuming responsibility for the relationship. In complementary relationships, one participant assumes the leadership role and the other follows. The nurse–client relationship has elements of both types of roles.

With this transactional model, analysis of the meaning of a message reveals cues by which the receiver constructs a mental picture of the sender, including perceptions of the sender's attitude and background as well as the type of information the sender is conveying. The scope of the circular process in circular models expands linear constructs by adding systems theory concepts: feedback and validation.

Feedback is the response the receiver gives to the sender about the message. Feedback always occurs. Even by not responding, the receiver conveys feedback. The trouble is that feedback is easily misinterpreted when it does not provide usable information to the sender regarding the message sent. Feedback received by the sender affects all future communication (Dance, 1967).

Validation is a form of feedback involving verbal and nonverbal confirmation that both participants have the same basic understanding of the message and the feedback. Both concepts are discussed in detail in Chapter 10.

A circular model of communication allows the nurse to develop provisional data about differences in perceptions without passing judgment about the correctness of the information. The questions focus on the relationship between people, events, and behavior. Figure 1–5 is a diagram of the model.

Therapeutic Communication

Ruesch (1959) is generally recognized as the father of therapeutic communication. Together with Gregory Bateson, he merged concepts from communication theory with ideas from mental health dialogue to develop a theoretical model of therapeutic communication. Early nursing theorists used Ruesch's model to describe the communication needed in the nurse-client relationship (Abdellah et al., 1961).

Ruesch (1961) proposed that the process of therapeutic communication is "designed to enable the patient to experience fully, to accept what he has experienced and to share those experiences with others" (p. 37). Imogene King (1981), a contemporary nursing theorist, followed a similar theme. Communication is goal directed, designed to help a client achieve goals that are valued. Nurse and client are mutually present to each other: "Interactions can reveal how one person thinks or feels about another person, how each perceives the other and what the other does to him, what his expectation are of the other, and how each reacts to the actions of the other" (p. 85). Communication is both verbal and nonverbal. For King, all behavior serves as a form of communication (Fawcett, 1989).

Neurolinguistic Programming

Bandler and Grindler (1975) offer a different approach to the study of communication in their conceptual model, defined as *neurolinguistic programming* (NLP). This conceptual model focuses on the way a person takes in and internally processes verbal information. According to these theorists, people make sensory-based interpretations about the realities they observe. Individuals' model of the world reflects their preferred representational mode—visual, kinesic, or auditory. Although a person may use more than one representational mode, one is usually preferred. A person's language will reveal his or her primary representational system. Understanding a person's preferred representational system allows the nurse greater flexibility in communication. The nurse is able to decode the ways in which people represent their experiences to themselves and to frame their responses in ways that the client is most likely to hear. Examples of phrases for each representational system are given in Box 1–5.

Bandler and Grindler (1975) propose that people transform their original experience through one of three universal human modeling responses: generalization, deletion, and distortion. With generalization, a person splits off part of the original event and experiences only a portion of the event as the complete experience. Deletion refers to selective attention to some details and conscious or unconscious exclusion of others. Distortion reflects a shift in the meaning of the sensory data to represent greater compatibility with the self-concept. These concepts are important for nurses as they consider selective attention and information gaps in many assessment interviews.

SUMMARY

Chapter 1 introduces some of the theoretical concepts forming the foundation of the nurse–client relationship. Use of theoretical models in the implementation of the nurse–client relationship brings order to nursing practice, provides a cognitive structure for developing a body of knowledge identifiable with the profession, and contributes a basis for nursing research. Four elements critical to an understanding of nursing practice are person, health, nursing, and environment. These ele-

---

BOX 1–5
Common Phrases Used to Support Preferred Representational Mode

The key element to look for is the verb.

Visual	Auditory	Kinesic
I notice that . . .	What I hear you say . . .	I feel that . . .
I observe . . .	I would consider . . .	That really touches me . . .
Let's examine . . .	Please listen . . .	The way I would handle . . .
Upon inspection . . .	As I reflect on . . .	I fumbled that interview . . .
I would regard this as . . .	The way you express it, . . .	What are you groping for?
In my view . . .	By the tone of your voice . . .	I sense that . . .
Let's look at . . .	I would like to affirm . . .	The way I experience it . . .
It appears to me that . . .	Could I ask what you mean . . .	I have little control over . . .
This part resembles . . .	Might I inquire about . . .	I apply . . .
This looks like . . .	I would need to probe . . .	I operate on . . .
I would envision . . .	I would question . . .	If you could steer me . . .
I would foresee . . .	Please explain . . .	It's difficult to maneuver . . .
Looking back . . .	In answer to your question . . .	I need to make contact . . .
It's difficult for me to see . . .	My response is . . .	I can't put my finger on . . .
I have trouble picturing . . .	I would like to reply . . .	It's your move . . .
I have an image of . . .	What is your explanation?	I find it hard to connect . . .

ments form the metaparadigm for professional nursing and are common themes that recur in all current nursing theories.

Nursing borrows concepts and principles related to the development of interpersonal relationships from other disciplines. Sigmund Freud is the original source of most theoretical formulations about the nature of personality. His was the first model of personality development. Other Freudian contributions include the concept of transference/counter-transference and the influence of past experiences on present behavior. Carl Jung proposed several controversial ideas that today are recognized as valid regarding spirituality, the influence of culture and society on behavior, adult development, and gender roles. Erikson broadened the scope of earlier thinking on personality development to include man's interaction with the larger social environment. Maturational crises occur throughout life and require a different and more complex behavioral adaptation. Successful resolution enhances personal growth. Buber and Rogers offer basic concepts concerning the characteristics the nurse needs for developing effective interpersonal relationships with clients. Maslow's needs theory provides a basis for determining priorities in all phases of the nursing process.

Communication is viewed as the matrix of the nurse–client relationship. Three models of communication are presented: a linear model, circular transactional theoretical models, and neurolinguistic programming. Using the elements outlined in these models in creative applications of therapeutic conversations with clients will increase the depth and meaning of interpersonal interactions.

REFERENCES

Abdellah FG, Beland IL, Martin A, Matheny RV (1961). Patient-Centered Approaches to Nursing. New York, Macmillan.

Bandler R, Grindler J (1975). The Structure of Magic. Palo Alto, CA, Science and Behavior Books.

Bateson G (1979). Mind and Nature. New York, Dutton.

Brockopp, D (1983). What is NLP? American Journal of Nursing 83(7):1011–1014.

Brown KC (1991). Strategies for effective communication. AAOHN Journal 39(6):292–293.

Buber M (1957) Distance and Relation. Psychiatry 20:97–104.

Buber M (1958) I and Thou. (Smith R, trans.) (2nd ed.). New York, Scribner's.

Buber M (1970). I and Thou. New York, Scribner's.

Chinn P, Jacobs MK (1987). Theory and Nursing (2nd ed.). St. Louis, Mosby.

Chinn P, Kramer M (1991). Theory and Nursing: A Systematic Approach (3rd ed.). St. Louis, Mosby Year Book.

Covey S (1992). The Seven Habits of Highly Effective People. New York, Simon & Schuster (Fireside).

Creasia J, Parker J (1991). Conceptual Foundations of Professional Nursing Practice. St. Louis, Mosby.

Dance FEX (1967). Human Communication Theory. New York: Holt, Rinehart and Winston.

Dowd J (1990). Ever since Durkheim: The socialization of human development. Human Development 33:138–59.

Erikson E (1959). Youth and Identity. New York, Norton.

Erikson E (1963). Childhood and Society. New York, Norton.

Erikson E, Erikson J (1981). On generativity and identity: From a conversation with Erik and Joan Erikson. Harvard Educational Review 51:251.

Erikson E (1982a). Life Cycle Completed: A Review. New York, Norton.

Erikson E (1982b). The Life Cycle Completed. New York, Norton.

Fawcett J (1989). Analysis and Evaluation of Conceptual Models of Nursing. Philadelphia, Davis.

Forchuk C (1991). Peplau's theory: Concepts and their relations. Nursing Science Quarterly 4(2):54–60.

Forchuk C, Brown B (1989). Establishing a nurse–client relationship. Journal of Psychosocial Nursing 27(2):30–34.

Freud S (1937). The Basic Writings of Sigmund Freud (Brill AA, trans. and ed.). New York, Modern Library.

Freud S (1959). Collected Papers (Strachey J, ed.). New York, Basic Books.

Garvin BJ, Kennedy CW (1988). Confirming communication of nurses in interaction with physicians. Journal of Nursing Education 27(4):161–163.

Jung CG (1963). Memories, Dreams and Reflections. (Winston R, trans.). New York, Vintage, 1963.

Jung CG (1969). Psychology and religion: West and east. *In* Collected Works of CG Jung (1969). (Hull RFC, trans.). Princeton, Princeton University Press.

Jung CG (1971). The stages of life. *In* Jung CG, The Portable Jung (1971) (Campbell J, ed.). New York, Viking.

Kasch CR (1984). Communication in the delivery of nursing care. Advances in Nursing Science 6(1):71–88.

Kelly AW, Sime AM (1990). Language as research data: Application of computer content analysis in nursing research. Advances in Nursing Science 12(3):32–40.

King IM (1981). A Theory for Nursing: Systems, Concepts, Process. New York, Wiley.

Levine, M (1973). Introduction to Clinical Nursing (2nd ed.). Philadelphia, Davis.

Littlejohn S (1989). Theories of Human Communication (3rd ed.). Belmont CA, Wadsworth.

Loos F, Bell J (1990). Circular questions: A family interviewing strategy. Dimensions of Critical Care Nursing 9(1):46–53.

Marriner-Tomey A (1994). Nursing Theorists and Their Work (3rd ed.). St. Louis, Mosby.

Miller GR, Nicholson HE (1976). Communication Inquiry: A Perspective on Process. Reading, MA, Addison-Wesley.

Neuman B (1989). The Newman Systems Model (2nd ed.). Norwalk, CT, Appleton & Lange.

Parse RR (1987). Nursing Science—Major Paradigms, Theories and Critiques. Philadelphia, WB Saunders.

Parse RR (1993). *In* Randell B (1993). Nursing theory: The 21st century. Nursing Science Quarterly 5(4):176–184.

Paterson J, Zderad L (1988). Humanistic Nursing. New York, National League for Nursing.

Peplau H (1952). Interpersonal Relations in Nursing. New York, Putnam's.

Peplau H (1957). Therapeutic concepts. *In* Smoyak S, Rouslin S (eds.), A Collection of Classics in Pyschiatric Nursing Literature. Thorofare, NJ: Charles B. Slack. (Reprinted from National League for Nursing, League Exchange No. 26, Aspects of Psychiatric Nursing.)

Rogers C (1961). On Becoming a Person. Boston, Houghton Mifflin.

Roy C (1976). Introduction to Nursing: An Adaptation Model. Englewood Cliffs, NJ, Prentice Hall.

Ruesch J (1961). Therapeutic Communication. New York, Norton.

Schmieding NJ (1990). An integrative nursing theoretical framework. Journal of Advanced Nursing 15:463–467.

Sellick KJ (1991). Nurse's interpersonal behaviors and the development of helping skills. International Journal of Nursing Studies 28(1):3–11.

Sullivan HS (1953). The Interpersonal Theory of Psychiatry. New York, Norton.

Uys LR (1980). Towards the development of an operational definition of the concept "therapeutic use of self." International Journal of Nursing Studies 17:175–180.

Von Franz M (1975). CG Jung: His Myth in Our Time. Boston, Little Brown.

Waltzlawick P (1967). Pragmatics of Human Communication. New York, Norton.

Chapter 2

Professional Guides to Action in Interpersonal Relationships

ELIZABETH ARNOLD AND KATHLEEN BOGGS

OUTLINE

Basic Concepts

OBJECTIVES

At the end of the chapter, the student will be able to:

1. Discuss the implications of using theory-based interventions in the nurse–client relationship.
2. Identify the professional, legal, and ethical standards governing actions taken in the nurse–client relationship.

3. Describe the nursing process as it relates to the nurse–client relationship.

If a man's actions are not guided by thoughtful considerations, then they are guided by inconsiderate impulse, unbalance appetite, caprice or the circumstances of the moment.

John Dewey, 1933

Professional, legal, and ethical standards provide parameters for all professional nursing practice actions. This chapter, first, considers the numerous external factors affecting the nurse–client relationship, expanding the theoretical frameworks presented in Chapter 1 as important foundational concepts in professional interpersonal relationships. Second, the chapter provides a brief overview of the nursing process as a framework for the actions taken in the relationship. Both knowledge bases are necessary for implementing an effective nurse–client relationship.

Organizational and legal/ethical frameworks govern all professional practice disciplines. When a client goes to a physician, the client assumes the physician will use a defined body of knowledge and will provide care consistent with legal and ethical standards. The client expects the physician to use an organized, systematic method of data collection and to prescribe accurately the required treatment. Similar expectations are found in the legal system. Clients seek lawyers who have knowledge of specific legal codes and procedures. The lawyer is expected to know what information is important and how to use it in helping clients achieve their goals in legal matters.

Before a nurse initiates a professional relationship with a client, the nurse needs to have a knowledge of the professional context in which the relationship will occur, including legal and ethical constraints. In nursing practice, the object is "care of the whole person, not cure of disease or conditions" (Kinney and Erickson, 1990, p.94). Nurse practice acts define the scope of the practice of professional nursing in providing care and outline the nurse's rights, responsibilities, and licensing requirements. Developed independently by each state, the acts are based on standards of care developed by the American Nurses Association (ANA).

The nurse–client relationship is bound legally by the principles of tort law to provide a reasonable standard of care. This means that the nurse is obligated to provide a level of care that a reasonably prudent nurse would provide in a similar situation (Cournoyer, 1991). The American Nurses Association Professional Standards of Care are presented in this chapter. Professional standards for specialty areas may be found in most specialty nursing texts.

Nurses have a moral accountability to the clients they serve in addition to their legal responsibility to uphold professional standards of nursing practice (Fry, 1991). Guidelines for the nurse's moral imperatives in nurse–client relationships are found in the American Nurses Association codes of ethics.

Finally, an overview of the steps in the nursing process as the organizing framework for ordering and evaluating nursing care provides a consistent, comprehensive, and coordinated approach to the delivery of nursing care to clients. The nurse–client relationship is recognized as central to the implementation of the nursing process.

BASIC CONCEPTS

NURSE PRACTICE ACTS

The definition of nursing practice published by the ANA (1981) states that:

> The practice of professional nursing means the performance for compensation of professional services requiring substantial specialized knowledge of the biological, physical, behavioral, psychological and sociological sciences and of nursing theory as a basis for assessment, diagnosis, planning, intervention and evaluation in the promotion and maintenance of health; the case finding and management of illness, injury or infirmity; the restoration of optimum function; or the achievement of a dignified death. Nursing practice includes, but is not limited to, administration, counseling, supervision, delegation and evaluation of practice and execution of the medical regimen, including the administration of medications and treatments prescribed by any person authorized by the state to prescribe. Each registered nurse is directly accountable and responsible to the consumer for the quality of nursing care provided.

This is a broad and comprehensive statement of nursing practice. Most states use this generic ANA statement as the foundation for developing their own nurse practice guidelines. Each state identifies the nursing actions and functions defined as nursing practice, including, but not limited to, teaching, supervision, and delegation. The state legislature approves the state nursing practice act. State nursing boards, which meet monthly, interpret and enforce nurse practice acts through licensing requirements, close attention to legislation affecting nursing practice, and disciplinary actions if needed. Nurse practice acts are the single most important statutory law governing the provision of professional nursing care through the nurse–client relationship (Betts and Waddle, 1993). Since there are variations in state statutory definitions of nursing practice, nurses should become acquainted

with the nurse practice requirements in the state in which they are licensed to practice.

PROFESSIONAL STANDARDS OF CARE

Professional Standards of Care, developed by the American Nurses Association (ANA), provide guidelines for the provision and evaluation of professional nursing care. They are important criteria by which the nurse's actions will be evaluated should legal questions arise about adequate provision of care (Craven and Heinle, 1992). These standards of care are presented in Box 2–1.

LEGAL CONCEPTS

In addition to providing nursing care according to professional nursing standards and in accord with

---

BOX 2–1
Professional Standards Guiding the Nurse–Client Relationship

Standards of Care	*Standards of Professional Performance*
I. Assessment The nurse collects client health data.	I. Quality of Care The nurse systematically evaluates the quality and effectiveness of nursing practice.
II. Diagnosis The nurse analyzes the assessment data in determining diagnoses.	II. Performance Appraisal The nurse evaluates his/her own nursing practice in relation to professional practice standards and relevant statutes and regulations.
III. Outcome Identification The nurse identifies expected outcomes individualized to the client.	III. Education The nurse acquires and maintains current knowledge in nursing practice.
IV. Planning The nurse develops a plan of care that prescribes interventions to attain expected outcomes.	IV. Collegiality The nurse contributes to the professional development of peers, colleagues, and others.
V. Implementation The nurse implements the interventions identified in the plan of care.	V. Ethics The nurse's decisions and actions on behalf of clients are determined in an ethical manner.
VI. Evaluation The nurse evaluates the client's progress toward attainment of outcomes.	VI. Collaboration The nurse collaborates with the client, significant others, and health care providers in providing client care.
	VII. Research The nurse uses research findings in practice.
	VIII. Resource Utilization The nurse considers factors related to safety, effectiveness, and cost in planning and delivering client care.

Reprinted with permission from Standards of Clinical Nursing Practice, © 1991, American Nurses Association, Washington, DC.

nurse practice acts, other important legal tenets have particular relevance for the nurse–client relationship. The nurse is bound legally to respect the client's privacy except when the withheld information might be harmful to the client or innocent others. Other exceptions include the reporting of certain communicable diseases, gunshot wounds, and child abuse. Although in some states the courts require nurses to divulge confidential information, an increasing number of states have introduced legislation to protect privileged communication between nurse and patient statutorily. Confidentiality is discussed in Chapter 5 and 6.

In addition to protecting the client's privacy in terms of what is actually discussed in the relationship, the nurse has a legal responsibility to ensure against invasion of privacy related to the following:

- Releasing information about clients to unauthorized parties.
- Unwanted visitations in the hospital.
- Discussing client problems in public places or with people not directly involved in the client's care.
- Taking pictures of clients without their consent or using them without the client's permission.
- Performing procedures such as AIDS testing without the client's permission.
- Publishing data about a client in any way that makes the client identifiable without the client's permission (Cournoyer, 1991).

Informed consent is another aspect of legal considerations needed in the nurse–client relationship. Although it is the primary provider's responsibility to supply the information needed for informed consent, nurses play an important role in making sure the conditions for informed consent are met within the nurse–client relationship. Unless there is a life-threatening emergency, all clients have the right to give informed consent. For legal consent to be valid, it must contain three elements (Northrop and Kelly, 1987):

- Consent must be voluntary.
- The client must have full disclosure about the risks, benefits, cost, potential side effects or adverse reactions, and other alternatives to treatment.

- The client must have the capacity and competency to understand the information and to make an informed choice.

In 1991, Congress passed the Patient Self-Determination Act. This legislation gives clients the autonomy to choose whether or not to have life-prolonging treatment should they become mentally unable to make this decision. Individual preferences regarding treatment options can be put in writing and are recognized by state law. Advance directives provide a new dimension of care and respect for the autonomy of adult clients that formerly was not an explicit issue in nurse–client relationships.

There are several actions the nurse can take to legally safeguard the rights of clients in professional relationships and to protect the nurse's practice. Important protective strategies are knowledge of and adherence to professional nursing standards. Nurses also are responsible for careful documentation of nursing assessments, care given, and behavioral responses of the client. In the eyes of the law, failure to document in written form any of these elements means the actions were not taken (Betts and Waddle, 1993). Additionally, the nurse is accountable for informing other members of the health care team of changes in the client's condition, for appropriately supervising ancillary personnel, and for questioning unclear or controversial doctor's orders. Documentation is examined in Chapter 23.

ETHICAL CODES FOR NURSES

Ethical principles are guides to actions in the nurse–client relationship and should be a basic consideration in a nurse's choice of words and actions. The codes of ethics developed by the ANA and by the CNA, presented in Boxes 2–2 and 2–3 respectively, are not explicit definitions of right and wrong. Rather, they form a broad conceptual framework for identifying the moral dimensions of nursing practice and are important guides to choices of actions in nurse–client relationships. The authors hope that the reader will see applications of these codes threaded throughout the boxes, and exercises presented in this text (see Exercise 2–1). Of particular importance to the nurse–client relationship are directives related to

BOX 2–2
American Nurses Association Code for Nurses

1. The nurse provides services with respect for human dignity and the uniqueness of the client unrestricted by considerations of social or economic status, personal attributes, or the nature of health problems.
2. The nurse safeguards the client's right to privacy by judiciously protecting information of a confidential nature.
3. The nurse acts to safeguard the client and the public when health care and safety are affected by the incompetent, unethical, or illegal practice of any person.
4. The nurse assumes responsibility and accountability for individual nursing judgments and actions.
5. The nurse maintains competence in nursing.
6. The nurse exercises informed judgment and uses individual competence and qualifications as criteria in seeking consultation, accepting responsibilities, and delegating nursing activities to others.
7. The nurse participates in activities that contribute to the ongoing development of the profession's body of knowledge.
8. The nurse participates in the profession's efforts to implement and improve standards of nursing.
9. The nurse participates in the profession's effort to establish and maintain conditions of employment conducive to high quality nursing care.
10. The nurse participates in the profession's effort to protect the public from misinformation and misrepresentation and to maintain the integrity of nursing.
11. The nurse collaborates with members of the health professions and other citizens in promoting community and national efforts to meet the health needs of the public.

Source: Reprinted with permission from *Code for Nurses with Interpretive Statements,* © 1985, American Nurses Association, Washington, DC.

BOX 2–3
Relationship of the Nursing Proc ess to Patient Care Standards in the Nurse–Client Relationship

I. Assess
   Collects data — The nurse collects data throughout the nursing process related to client strengths, limitations, available resources, and changes in the client's condition.

   Analyzes data — The nurse organizes cluster behaviors, makes inferences based on subjective and objective client data, and personal and scientific nursing knowledge.

   The nurse verifies data and inferences with the client to ensure validity.

II. Diagnosis
   Formulates biopsychosocial statements — The nurse develops a comprehensive biopsychosocial statement that captures the essence of the client's health care needs/problems and validates the accuracy of the statement with the client; the statement becomes the basis for the nursing diagnoses.

   Establishes nursing diagnosis — The nurse develops relevant nursing diagnoses and prioritizes them based on the client's most immediate needs in the current health care situation.

III. Plan
   Identifies expected outcomes — The nurse and client mutually develop expected outcomes realistically, based on client needs, strengths, and resources.

   Specifies short-term goals — The nurse and client mutually develop realistic short-term goals and choose actions to support achievement of expected outcomes.

IV. Implement
   Takes agreed-upon action — The nurse encourages, supports, and validates the client in taking agreed-upon actions to achieve goals and expected outcomes through integrated, therapeutic nursing interventions and communication strategies.

V. Evaluation
   Evaluates goal achievement — The nurse and client mutually evaluate attainment of expected outcomes and survey each step of the nursing process for appropriateness, effectiveness, adequacy, and time efficiency, modifying the plan as indicated by evaluation.

EXERCISE 2–1
Applying the Nurses' Code of Ethics to Professional/Clinical Situations

Purpose: To help you identify applications of the nursing code of ethics.

Time: 30 minutes

Procedure:
1. In small groups of four to five students, think of three or four concrete professional or clinical situations in which you think the nursing code of ethics might apply.
2. Develop a rationale for why you think the code of ethics would be your guide for practice.

Discussion:
1. How difficult was it for you to develop applications?
2. Were there any common themes?
3. What implications does this exercise have for your future clinical practice?

the nurse's primary commitment to the client's welfare, respect for client autonomy, recognition of each individual as unique and worthy of respect, accountability, and collaboration with other health professionals.

APPLICATIONS

NURSING PROCESS

The nursing process represents a clinical management framework, recognized by all nursing theorists as an organizing structure for clinical nursing practice. Alfaro (1990) refers to it as an organized, systematic method of giving individualized care by identifying and treating responses to potential and actual alterations in health. It is used to organize test questions on the NCLEX, the state board examinations for professional licensing, and professional standards of nursing practice. The nursing process is used as the basic format for all of the activities carried out in the nurse–client relationship.

The nurse–client relationship serves as the matrix of the nursing process, allowing the nurse to analyze client information and to direct the nature of the relationship's activities. The nursing process is developed in five incremental phases: (1) assessment, (2) diagnosis, (3) planning, (4) implementation, and (5) evaluation. The progressive steps of the nursing process offer the nurse guidelines to identify the type of nursing a client requires, the scope of nursing activities needed to meet health goals, and the means to evaluate

whether the individual's nursing care needs were met. (Box 2–3)

Communication is integral to effective use of the nursing process, allowing the nurse to explain the purpose of the relationship. The goals of communication as they relate to the nursing process are directed toward:

- Helping clients to promote, maintain, or restore health or to achieve a peaceful death.
- Facilitating client management of difficult health care issues.
- Providing quality nursing care in an efficient manner.

Through use of therapeutic communication strategies, the nurse is able to help the client identify and clarify nursing problems in a systematic way. The nurse–client relationship acts as a continuous feedback system for the nursing process, as diagramed in Figure 2–1. This relationship affects every aspect of the nursing process.

Assessment

Assessment begins with the first contact between client and nurse. The nurse uses a structured format for collecting both subjective and objective data from a client and the client's family. *Subjective data* refers to the client's perception of data and what the client says about the data: "I have a severe pain in my chest. *Objective data* refers to data that are directly observable or verifiable through physical examination or tests, for exam-

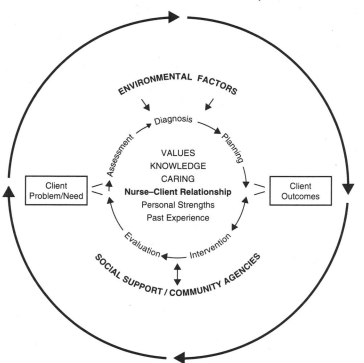

Figure 2–1 The Nursing Process and the Nurse–Client Relationship Feedback Loop

ple, an abnormal electrocardiogram. Combined, the data will present a complete picture of the client's health problem. One without the other is insufficient.

The data collected should include relevant past history, for example, previous hospitalizations, family history, past medical treatment, and medications. Christensen and Kenny (1990) advise that the data should reflect information from as many sources as needed. Sources of data would include interview, history, physical assessment, and review of records. Potential as well as actual problems are identified. These data will serve as the data base throughout the nursing process. As new information becomes available, nursing diagnoses and planned interventions are refined and updated.

It is important for the nurse to identify health deviations specific to the client and not to make global assumptions based on other clients' experiences. In each clinical situation, the client's behav-

ioral response might be assessed differently. For example, maintaining a sufficient intake of food would need to be assessed in terms of what is sufficient for this particular individual on the basis of age, activity, height to weight ratio, and present health status.

Assessments about the functional state of the client and previous experience provide a different type of specific information. For example, the mother of a newborn with Down's syndrome might know how to care for a normal infant but will need help adapting care strategies for her handicapped baby. Active listening skills will allow the nurse to obtain relevant data.

Observations of the client's nonverbal behaviors lead the nurse to make inferences. To be sure the inference is factual, the nurse validates the data with the client. For example, because a client withdraws and speaks in a flat tone, the nurse infers the client is depressed. To validate this inference,

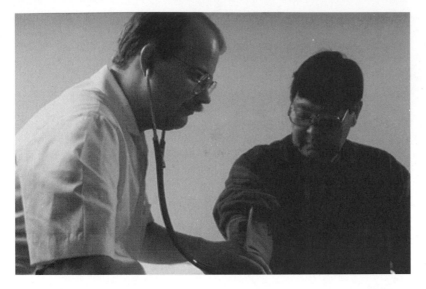

Client assessment begins with the first contact and may include physical measures. (Courtesy of the University of Maryland School of Nursing)

the nurse says, "You seem very quiet—as though you might be depressed. Tell me how you are feeling . . ." (Alfaro, 1990, p. 39).

Diagnosis

Once the data have been collected and the health deviation, problem, or need identified, the nurse analyzes the data and identifies gaps in the data collection. The client's data are compared with normal health standards, behavior patterns, and developmental norms to identify not only client problems but also client strengths. Those health care concerns judged amenable to nursing intervention form the basis for the selection of nursing diagnoses.

Nursing diagnoses provide a common language for discussing client problems (Creasia and Parker, 1991). Written as client-centered statements, an actual diagnosis consists of three parts (NANDA, 1992). The stem of the diagnosis labels the *problem* requiring nursing intervention. The second part of the statement identifies the *etiology* or risk factors associated with the health care problem. For example, "Impaired communication related to cerebral vascular accident" or "Alteration in body image related to partial mastectomy" are clear, simple connecting statements about client health care concerns requiring nursing intervention. The third part of the statement identifies the clinical evidence

that supports the diagnosis—for example, "Impaired communication related to a cerebral vascular accident, as evidenced by incomplete sentences and slurred words."

The nursing diagnosis should be written in clear, precise language so that any member of the health care team can look at the statement and be able to identify relevant issues for the client. Levine (1989) suggests that "the nursing diagnosis should be as informative and useful to the physician as the medical diagnosis is to the nurse" (p. 5). Exercise 2–2 gives practice in writing nursing diagnosis. Chapter 23 elaborates on the use of the nursing process with a focus on appropriate, accurate documentation.

Planning

Once the nursing diagnosis is established, the nurse develops nursing orders. These are defined as nursing actions needed to help the client achieve identified goals. Client goals are also referred to as outcome criteria. All short- and longer-term goals are stated as actions of the client. Nursing interventions are stated as actions the nurse will take to help the client meet identified goals. For example, the client's short-term goal might be written as: "The client will develop a support system within 1 month." The associated nursing intervention might be: "The nurse will

EXERCISE 2–2
Writing Nursing Diagnoses

Purpose: To help you develop skill in writing nursing diagnoses.

Time: 45 minutes

Procedure:
1. In small groups of two or three students, develop as many nursing diagnoses as possible for each of the following clinical situations based on the information you have. Indicate what other types of information you would need in order to make a complete assessment.
   a. Michael Sterns was in a skiing accident. He is suffering from multiple internal injuries, including head injury. His parents have been notified and are flying in to be with him.
   b. Lo Sun Chen is a young Chinese woman admitted for abdominal surgery. She has been in this country for only eight weeks and speaks very little English.
   c. Marisa LaFonte is a 17-year-old unmarried woman admitted for the delivery of her first child. She has had no prenatal care.
   d. Stella Watkings is an 85-year-old woman admitted to a nursing home following a broken hip.

Discussion:
1. What common diagnoses emerged in each group?
2. In what ways were the diagnoses different, and how would you account for the differences?
3. Were there any common themes in the types of information each group decided it needed in order to make a complete assessment?
4. How could you use what you learned from doing this exercise in your clinical practice?

encourage the client to attend a support group meeting on a weekly basis."

A care plan for nursing intervention takes into account the client's life situation, intellectual and emotional capabilities, and strengths and limitations, as well as the professional resources available. Care needs to be taken that the client's view of health is the primary referent for change and that the client participates to the fullest extent possible in arriving at nursing diagnoses and setting goals (Mitchell, 1991). Maslow's hierarchy of needs, described in Chapter 1, provides a rationale for prioritizing nursing actions, beginning with the most acute and basic needs. The care plan is continually updated as the client's condition changes.

Goal achievement forms the rationale for the nurse and client to engage in a therapeutic relationship. The nurse and client mutually develop goals related to the nursing diagnosis, which are stated as measurable objectives. Short-term goals are identified as the progressive steps needed to achieve a broader and more general long-term goal. For example, "The client will achieve dietary control of his diabetes" might be a long-term goal

for a diabetic client, and, "The client will identify a sample ADA diet plan for 1 week" might be a short-term goal. Time limits should be specified. They need to be realistic so that the client does not become discouraged with lack of goal achievement. It is important to establish priorities based on practical considerations and the wishes of the client.

Throughout this phase of the nursing process, the nurse and client select strategies to resolve the health care problem and analyze the practical advantages of using a variety of alternatives to achieve mutually established goals. As health-related issues emerge in the course of the therapeutic relationship, the nurse uses one or more listening responses to ensure accurate reception and understanding of client information. Accuracy of client data is validated with the client on an ongoing basis. Individualized nursing interventions and client actions designed to facilitate goal achievement are identified. Usually the plan is finalized in writing to ensure continuity of nursing care. In the planning phase, as in all other steps of the nursing process, mutual involvement and joint problem solving are emphasized.

Implementation

During the implementation phase, the client and nurse carry out the plan of care. Interventions appropriate to the purposes of the nurse–client relationship include giving physical, psychological, social, and spiritual support; health teaching; collaborating with other health professionals on behalf of the client; continuing to make ongoing assessments; documenting client responses; and updating/revising the care plan as needed.

Evaluation

The nurse uses the evaluation phase of the nursing process to compare projected behavioral responses and outcomes with what actually occurred. Nurse and client assess the client's progress or lack of progress toward identified goals. They mutually appraise the benefits and limitations of choices made for problem resolution. When there is a lack of progress, the nurse needs to ask the following questions.

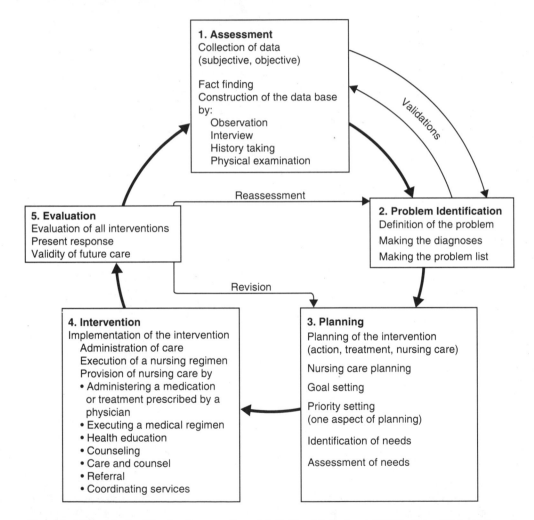

Figure 2–2 Steps in the Nursing Process. From McCaffery M, Beebe A (1989). Pain: Clinical Manual for Nursing Practice. St. Louis, Mosby, p. 35. Reprinted with the permission of C. V. Mosby Company and J. B. Lippincott Company

- Were the assessment data collected appropriate and complete?
- Was the nursing diagnosis appropriate?
- Were the goals realistic and achievable in the time frame alloted?
- Were the nursing interventions chosen appropriate to the needs of the situation and the capabilities of the client?

Each of these questions needs to be addressed. For example, the nursing diagnosis may be quite appropriate, but the intervention required may be more complex or not achievable in a limited time frame. The nurse needs to analyze the effectiveness, efficiency in terms of time, appropriateness, and adequacy of the nursing actions selected for implementation. Paying attention to the reality of the situation, the motivation of the client, and the setting in which the interventions need to be accomplished can prevent unnecessary frustration on the part of both nurse and client. The client gives input regarding actions perceived as helpful or not useful. Modifications are made in any area of the nursing process requiring alteration. Figure 2–2 diagrams the steps of the nursing process.

SUMMARY

Chapter 2 focuses on the nurse's need to have a basic knowledge of the externally imposed legal and ethical variables that influence the nurse's choice of actions in the nurse–client relationship. The chapter provides a brief overview of the nursing process as a framework for the actions taken in the relationship. Both knowledge bases are necessary for implementing an effective nurse–client relationship.

The nurse–client relationship is contained within the scope of nursing practice as defined by the nurse practice acts. Standards of professional practice provide a measurement standard that should form the foundation of professional nursing.

The nurse–client relationship is bound legally by the principles of tort law to provide a reasonable standard of care. This means that the nurse is obligated to provide a level of care that a reasonable prudent nurse would provide in a similar situation.

The American and Canadian Nurses Association codes of ethics provide a broad conceptual framework for identifying the moral dimensions of nursing practice and are important guides to choices of actions in nurse–client relationships.

Finally, the nursing process serves as a clinical management framework, recognized by all nursing theorists as an organizing structure for clinical nursing practice. It involves five phases: assessment, diagnosis, planning, implementation, and evaluation. The nursing diagnosis is established at the end of the assessment phase and forms the basis for the remaining phases of the nursing process.

REFERENCES

Alfaro R (1990). Applying Nursing Diagnoses and Nursing Process (2nd ed.). Philadelphia, Lippincott.

American Nurses Association (1981). Definition of the Practice of Professional Nursing. Kansas City, MO, American Nurses Association.

Betts V, Waddle F (1993). Legal aspects of nursing. *In* Chitty K (ed.) (1993), Professional Nursing: Concepts and Challenges. Philadelphia, W. B. Saunders.

Christensen P, Kenney J (1990). Nursing Process: Application of Conceptual Models (3rd ed.). St. Louis. Mosby Year Book.

Cournoyer, C (1991). Legal relationships in nursing practice. In Creasia J, Parker B (eds.) (1991), Conceptual Foundations of Professional Nursing Practice. St. Louis, Mosby Year Book.

Craven R, Heinle C (1992). Fundamentals of Nursing. Philadelphia, Lippincott.

Creasia J, Parker B (1991). Conceptual Foundations of Professional Nursing Practice. St. Louis, Mosby Year Book.

Fry S (1991). Ethics in health care delivery. In Creasia J, Parker B (1991), Conceptual Foundations of Professional Nursing Practice. St. Louis, Mosby Year Book.

Kinney C, Erickson H (1990). Modeling the client's world: A way to holistic care. Issues in Mental Health Nursing 11:93–108.

Levine M (1989). The ethics of nursing rehetoric. Image 21(1):4–6.

McCaffery M, Beebe A (1989). Pain: Clinical Manual for Nursing Practice. St. Louis, Mosby.

Mitchell GJ (1991). Nursing diagnosis: An ethical analysis. Image 23(2):99–103.

North American Nursing Diagnosis Association (NANDA) (1991). Classification of Nursing Diagnoses: Proceedings of the Ninth Conference. Philadelphia, Lippincott.

Northrop C, Kelly M (1987). Legal Issues in Nursing. St. Louis, Mosby.

Chapter 3
Self-Concept in the Nurse–Client Relationship

ELIZABETH ARNOLD

OUTLINE

Basic Concepts

DEFINITION
CHARACTERISTICS
    Dynamic process
    Holistic construct
    Unique construct
    Reflection of social and cultural norms
    Psychological centrality
FUNCTIONS OF SELF-CONCEPT
ERIKSON'S MODEL OF PSYCHOSOCIAL DEVELOPMENT
    Trust versus mistrust
    Autonomy versus shame and doubt
    Initiative versus guilt
    Industry versus inferiority
    Indentity versus identity diffusion
    Intimacy versus isolation
    Generativity versus stagnation and self-absorption
    Integrity versus despair

Applications

BODY IMAGE
    Functions of body image
    Types of alterations
    How body image develops
    Assessment strategies
    Planning and intervention
    Evaluation
PERSONAL IDENTITY
    Perception
    Cognition
    Emotions
    Spiritual aspects of personal identity
    Self-esteem
    Self-awareness

Summary

OBJECTIVES

At the end of the chapter, the student will be able to:

1. Define self-concept.
2. Describe the characteristics and functions of self-concept.

3. Identify the psychosocial stages of self-development.

4. Describe behaviors related to self-concept: body image, personal identity, self-esteem, and spiritual distress.
5. Identify nursing interventions relevant to nursing diagnoses of alteration of self-concept.

6. Describe the role of self-awareness in the nurse–client relationship.

The greatest gift I can conceive of having from anyone is to be seen by them, heard by them, to be understood and touched by them. The greatest gift I can give is to see, hear, understand and to touch another person. When this is done, I feel contact has been made.

Virginia Satir, 1976

Self is a concept central to understanding the person in the nurse–client relationship. No human being is ever defined by a diagnosis. This is as true for psychosocial nursing diagnosis as it is for any other medical or physical nursing diagnoses. The condition of a person, however catastrophic, does not provide an explanation of who that person is. It simply describes what the person has. Coombs, Avila, and Purkey (1980) have argued that self-concept is the most important single factor affecting behavior. Thus, knowledge of the human being behind the diagnosis, the meaning behind the behavior, is the key to effective nurse–client relationships.

Chapter 3 provides an overview of self-concept as a way of understanding the uniqueness of nurse and client, the basic units of a nurse–client relationship. The chapter defines self-concept, considers its complex nature, and provides applications of self-concepts in nurse–client relationships.

BASIC CONCEPTS

Illness and the circumstances that bring the client to the health care system to seek professional help are embedded in the personal story of the individual. Benner and Wrubel (1989) suggest that the personal story of how an illness affects a person's life, influencing body image, identity, spiritual worldview and role relationships, is as important as the description of a client's symptoms. Yet often physicians and nurses understand the pathophysiology of the disease process but have little comprehension of what the "lived experience" of illness is to the client.

"Lived experience" is a qualitative research term referring to the personal meaning of an experience as described by the person experiencing it. Phenomenological approaches to nursing care concerns specifically ask the client to describe the meaning of an experience. By entering the world of the client, the nurse learns firsthand how body, mind, and spirit interconnect to create the unique meaning of an illness.

The personalized meaning attached to the illness and the person's sense of its manageability have a direct effect on compliance. As a critical determinant of client response to illness and treatment, self-concept helps define the nursing interventions most likely to be successful in restoring a sense of well-being (Oliver, 1988)

DEFINITION

Self-concept is an abstract structural construct used to describe the different images making up the self in each person's mind (Westen, 1991). Although a person can't see or touch the self-concept, one can "know" it exists. Viewing the self-concept as a theoretical construct offers the nurse a point of reference for considering important relationships between self-concept and behavior.

Self-concept reflects a person's overall personality structure. At the heart of the self-concept lies a person's essential human nature, forming the foundation for all roles, motivations, behaviors, feelings, thoughts, and physical and psychological make-up (Whitbourne, 1985). The self-concept unfolds as a stable and adaptable construct, capable of being known and acted upon by the individual.

Expressed not as a recitation of elements but in the human language by which persons comprehend their lives and the fact of their mortality, self-concept is the underlying core construct that first introduces a person to the meaning of life. Throughout life, the self-concept continues to act as an interpreter of life's meaning. It represents "a self-knowledge of one's coherence and authenticity" (Hoare, 1991, p. 47).

Self-concept biases what a person focuses on in communication, what a person expects from others, and what a person remembers of a conversation. How open and honest a person is able to be in a relationship with another person is correlated with the self-concept. Self-concept accounts for differences in people's definition of personally meaningful behavior and those life events that affect them very little.

Self-concept affects treatment outcomes.

Unanticipated negative outcomes in an illness or during a crisis can reflect self-concept disturbances rather than a lack of motivation or knowledge (Koehler, 1989). People can unconsciously "will" themselves to die or fail to progress because to do otherwise doesn't fit with their self-concept.

A narrow self-concept tends to thwart adaptation. When dysfunctional thoughts challenge the self-concept, energy becomes bound by those thoughts and feelings. Defense of self-concept restricts thinking about alternatives, resulting in self-defeating behaviors.

Caring human connections often are as healing as medication and specific treatments in influencing human responses to an illness, because they touch and confirm self-concept. Even when the nurse is unable to promote healing through physical measures, the interpersonal process of understanding the meaning of the illness in the person's life provides a different type of healing. Through the nurse–client relationship the nurse helps clients lessen the impact of confusion, social alienation, and emptiness on the self-concept, which is activated by most illnesses.

CHARACTERISTICS

The self-concept is a dynamic, holistic, unique mental construct reflecting a person's interaction with the larger social community as well as intrapersonal characteristics. More than the sum of its parts, the self-concept acts as an inner snapshot of a person, helping people experience who they are and what they are capable of becoming physically, emotionally, intellectually, socially, and spiritually in community with others.

Dynamic Process

The self-concept is a *dynamic process,* increasing in both diversity and complexity (Markus and Wurf, 1987). Throughout life a person develops and defines self-concepts as generalizations about the self: "I am outgoing," "I have excellent analytical skills," "I am a loser." As the person develops from child to adult, the self-concept becomes increasingly complex, reflecting responses of the self to new challenges in the life cycle. Attitudes about the self are modified by life experience. (Cairns and Cairns, 1988).

Self-concepts allow roles to change and enlarge as a person matures. The self-concept of a child broadens through social interactions as the emerging person develops close associations with others to include that of adult, marriage partner, parent. James (1891) notes that a person "has as many different social selves as there are distinct groups of persons about whose opinion he cares." Appropriate psychosocial development requires the emerging adult to incorporate the self-identity of worker, contributor to the community, spouse, and parent in an evolving spectrum of self-identifying concepts.

Holistic Construct

Self-concept is a *holistic construct.* It represents the unified whole of a person with each functional aspect of self-concept fitting together and each single element affecting all other parts. Because self-concept functions as an organized whole, disorganization in any one dimension of self affects the functioning of the entire self. Alterations in body image influence personal identity, and vice versa. Depression and loss of meaning affect a person's attitudes toward the body and toward role relationships.

In health care the sensitive interconnections among mind, body, and spirit illustrate the close interdependence of self-concepts. Physical illness always creates some type of psychological tension. Current research demonstrates that it is possible to reduce the physical need for pain medication and to diminish the impact of physiological disorders by altering typical patterns of behavior and feelings (Heinrich and Schag, 1985). Irreversible physical ailments in the patient can create emotional exhaustion and moral dilemmas for the caregiver, including the professional nurse (Arnold, 1989). In 1986, NANDA developed a Unitary Person Framework for developing a nursing data base, further emphasizing the belief in the whole person as the fundamental concern of professional nursing care.

Unique Construct

The self-concept is *unique* to each person (Travelbee, 1971). Individual physiological features and inborn personality traits differ, as does ethnic and cultural heritage. Life experiences are both qualitatively and quantitatively different, even for two individuals living together within the same family environment. Position in the family has its effect. Neighborhood encounters, physical make-up, basic temperament preferences, and amount of social support are variables that account for contrasts in experience. The oldest child in a family experiences life differently than the youngest child, if for no other reason than that the parents are more experienced. One can think of the self-concept basically as being the response to the question, "Who am I?" For each person, the answer is a little different (see Exercise 3–1).

Reflection of Social and Cultural Norms

Self-concepts reflect *social and cultural norms.* Hormuth (1990) suggests that the self acts as a bond between the individual and society, in which the self-concept develops and grows (Damon and Hart, 1988; Mead, 1934). *Context* represents a person's environment, defined as all of the intrapersonal and interpersonal circumstances influencing

---

EXERCISE 3–1
Who Am I?

Purpose: To help you understand some of the self-concepts you hold about yourself.

Time: May be done as a homework exercise and discussed in class. The class should sit face to face in a circle.

Procedure:
Fill in the blanks to complete the following sentences. There are no right and wrong answers.

The thing I like best about myself is _____.

The thing I like least about myself is _____.

My favorite activity is _____.

When I am in a group, I _____.

It would surprise most people if they knew I _____.

The most important value to me is _____.

I like _____.

I most dislike _____.

I am happy when _____.

I feel sad when _____.

I feel most self-confident when I _____.

I am _____.

I feel committed to _____.

Five years from now I see myself as _____.

Discussion:
1. What were the hardest items to answer? the easiest?
2. Were you surprised by some of your answers? if so, in what ways?
3. Did anybody's answers surprise you? if so, in what ways?
4. Did anyone's answers particularly impress you? if so, in what ways?
5. What did you learn about yourself from doing this exercise?
6. How would you see yourself using this self-awareness in professional interpersonal relationships with clients?

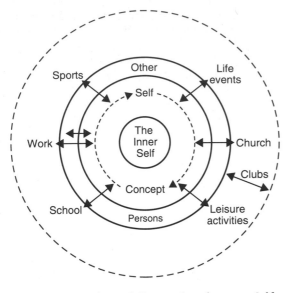

Figure 3–1 Reciprocal Connections between Self-Concepts and Social Influences

client behaviors. Self-concept is linked emotionally with context through culture and experience, but also serves to interpret the meaning of the context. Family, friends, and others in the community are part of a person's interpersonal context. (Fig. 3–1). They serve to confirm, support, or negate the self-concept. For example, an American woman might be respected for strong self-expression; the same behaviors would be frowned upon in a traditional Chinese woman.

The capacity of an individual to maintain a stable adaptive identity depends in part on the nature, timing, and number of the biological, environmental, or psychological assaults to the integrity of the self. For example, any job loss is difficult for a person to absorb emotionally. But a job loss for someone whose job has been a principal part of his or her identity can have the psychological impact of a significant death.

Threats to the self-concept occurring in rapid succession can have an additive effect, as can those occurring coincident with normal maturational crises. Consider the cumulative effects of losing both parents and undergoing emergency surgery in a three-month period. Cumulative tragedies result in significant assaults to self-concept.

Psychological Centrality

Clinically, certain aspects of the self-concept may be favored or valued more than others, thus achieving a "psychological centrality" (Adler et al., 1986). Psychological centrality refers to the level of emphasis a person places on different aspects of self-concept. For example, the health care team might emphasize body image or personal identity with a trauma victim having disfiguring injuries. Being attached to multiple equipment and restrained from movement will affect perception, with loss of orientation and confusion about self. Body image alterations are very obvious. But the same injury also may create significant spiritual distress and questions about the quality of life. Limited socialization and physical disability automatically redefine roles.

Circumstances usually determine which aspects of self-concept become psychologically central. Psychological centrality is temporary and changes as circumstances convert the focus from one element to another. When students study for a test, they usually focus on how well prepared they feel and on their cognitive ability. They mentally review past performance as an indicator of whether they will pass or fail the test. Even if they know the content, the positive or negative evaluation of their performance ability will affect their test achievement.

After the test, psychological centrality shifts from cognitive aspects of identity to other parts of the self. At the party after the test, social and physical aspects of self will be more primary. The self-concept remains the same, but psychological centrality shifts, much as designs do when seen through a kaleidoscope.

In health care, the impact of being in a hospital assumes psychological centrality for most clients. Differences in client experiences affect the level of shock. Previous experiences and the client's perception of their successful outcome are important, as are cultural values about hospitalization and helping professionals. The client who has never been hospitalized has more limited coping skills than one who has had the experience. Simple interventions such as providing anticipatory guidance about procedures, letting children manipulate equipment, and orienting the client and family to the unit help reduce the impact of being in a new and unfamiliar setting.

FUNCTIONS OF SELF-CONCEPT

Self-concepts

- Help explain behavior.
- Provide a conceptual framework for decision making.
- Shape expectations for the future.
- Provide bridges to meaning.

If self-images are consistent with reality, behavior is easily understood. When behaviors are incongruent with reality, others will experience the person's maladaptive behaviors as demanding and out of touch with reality. It becomes harder for people to respond effectively.

Self-concept acts as a decision-making framework within which the individual can evaluate current behaviors and weigh the legitimacy of feelings. Decisions congruent with self-concept affirm the sense of self-identity. Those that conflict with understandings of self diminish self-worth and affect the quality of a person's relationships with others.

Self-concepts serve to shape future expectations through the concept of "possible selves" (Cross and Markus, 1991). Possible selves unfold in the form of thoughts about goals, dreams, and fears about events still to come. Future thoughts provide either positive or negative input to the self-concept. For example, the nursing student might think, "I am a nursing student, but I can see myself, one day, as a nurse practitioner." Such thoughts help the novice nurse work harder to achieve professional goals. Possible selves have the capacity to prompt behaviors and aspirations, bringing about a self-fulfilling prophecy (Markus and Nurius, 1986).

Crises and illnesses provide the stage for considering possible selves that would not occur without these life interruptions. This concept is particularly important in health care because possible selves offer clients the hope that the current self-concept can be enlarged to include more positive possibilities. At the same time, negative possible selves (failure, incompetence, powerlessness) can work against the person, providing a negative context for evaluating the current self-concept. The nurse–client relationship provides support for positive possibilities of self and helps clients reframe the negative possible selves.

Self-concept provides interpersonal bridges to meaning. The journey to becoming completely one's own unique self is an intensely personal experience. At different points, the terrain appears dark, lonely, and unfamiliar. The nurse offers the client an interpersonal bridge between external events and internal perceptions, aiding clients in search of the deeper meaning of life. That interpersonal bridge can be simply one's presence and valuing of the client. For example, a nursing student wrote in her journal of a client encounter in which the client felt very depressed about her recent diagnosis of cancer. The student spent a long time with the client, answering her questions not only about her condition but also about why the student had chosen nursing. At the end of the encounter, the client thanked the student for listening and kissed her on the cheek, with tears in her eyes. For both participants, the interaction had meaning. The client felt hope and caring. For the student, it was a peak experience, reaffirming her self-concept as a professional nurse, as her statement reveals: "I *know* I made her feel much better and I comforted her a great deal; I was truly happy being there and this is what I think of when I picture myself as a future nurse" (Turnes, 1993). There was no one statement that made this meeting memorable; it was the genuine presence of the participants that gave this conversation its I–Thou qualities. Exercise 3–2 helps the nurse identify personality variations that contribute to self-concept.

ERIKSON'S MODEL OF PSYCHOSOCIAL DEVELOPMENT

Erik Erikson's (1963, 1982) seminal work on personality development is a primary developmental construct used by nurses in the nurse–client relationship. Concepts related to Erikson's model were described in Chapter 1. What follows is a description of each stage as the nurse might encounter it in the nurse–client relationship.

Trust versus Mistrust

Erikson labels the first stage of personality development trust versus mistrust. As an infant, a person is completely dependent on its caregiver for all of its needs. The infant needs to trust that the caregiver will respond appropriately. Trust is always a major

EXERCISE 3–2
Contribution of Life Experiences to Self-Concept

Purpose: To help you identify some of the many personality variations contributing to self-concept. There are no right and wrong responses.

Time: 45 minutes

Procedure:
1. Pair off with another student, preferably one with whom you are not well acquainted.
2. Student *A* spends five minutes questioning student *B* to collect a biography of facts, collecting such information as ethnic background, number of siblings, place of birth, job or volunteer experiences, unusual life experiences, types of responsibilities, favorite leisure activities. The process is then reversed, and student *B* interviews student *A*.
3. Each student introduces the other to the class, using the information gained from the interview.

Discussion:
1. What types of information were chosen for sharing and why?
2. Were you surprised by any of the information you found out?
3. How did your perception of other students change in light of the information shared?
4. In what ways were your perceptions different from your initial impression of your partner after the interview portion of the exercise?
5. To what would you attribute these differences?
6. What types of information were fairly similar and which ones were different among your classmates?
7. How did sharing information about self impact on the life of the group?
8. What did you learn about yourself from doing this exercise?
9. How do you think what you learned might apply to nursing practice?

issue for an infant. Simple interventions promote trust. Allowing the primary caregiver as much access as possible to the infant is particularly important. Assigning the same personnel to the infant is another nursing strategy likely to promote trust. If there is no primary caregiver available, the nurse can spend additional time with the infant, often talking to it and touching the infant.

As an adult, trust is a basic feeling that someone important to one's well-being will be there emotionally and physically when needed. Without trust, it is difficult to cooperate, to listen to instructions, or to share one's inner feelings. That is why it is such a basic and initial component in any meaningful relationship.

Whenever a person (because of age, illness, or temporary circumstances) becomes dependent on others for his or her existence, trust resurfaces as an issue. Any new experience will create this phenomenon, but an undesired experience in which one feels a lack of coping skills makes it even worse. There is a sense of insecurity and dependence; one feels a need to rely on others for direction and support. In the hospital, these feelings are quickly activated. The client feels like an outsider in an unfamiliar environment and looks to the nurse for assistance in reconstituting a meaningful self-identity. As a client develops confidence in the nurse's caring, the trust issue recedes into the background. Consistency and reliability foster trust.

Hope Is the Ego Strength Associated with Trust. A hopeful client expects a favorable outcome. Hope is expressed as an openness to explore the possibility of alternative options and other opportunities. Trusting others to support faltering identity provides some control over the aspects of the situation that can't be changed. Important sources of hope lie in the nurse's words and prompt responses to the client's needs, in reconnecting with a higher power, in finding a resource, or in simply getting in touch with personal strengths.

Autonomy versus Shame and Doubt

Once a baby becomes physically mobile, its interpersonal world looks quite different. Becoming mobile enlarges the baby's world. Erikson's second

The child in the initiative stage enjoys purposeful activities. (Courtesy of the University of Maryland School of Nursing)

developmental crisis involves developing motor autonomy. Coinciding with physical autonomy, the child learns the magic of the word "no" in choosing between alternatives. If denied an opportunity to practice independent behavior or family support to express legitimate feelings freely without fear of reprisal, the child may develop a sense of vulnerability and shame. Self-doubt replaces autonomy in situations calling for self-reliant action. An abnormal dependence or obstinacy can develop as the child learns that it is unsafe to choose any action autonomously.

On the other hand, failure to impose limits when they should be applied is equally destructive to self-concepts. The toddler is ill equipped physically and emotionally to be completely independent in making choices or decisions. Lacking judgment, many of the toddler's choices can lead to shame and self-doubt without parental direction. Providing direction and safeguards helps the child learn the limits of freedom in relationships. The child learns to express the self so that legitimate personal needs are met without significantly antagonizing others. Developing a sense of autonomy includes behaviors related to self-control, order, and reliability.

The Ego Strength Associated with Autonomy Is Will Power. Will power in the toddler is not the reasoned will of the adult but the beginning of a basic knowledge that it is possible to influence the reactions of others and that one's actions affect the outcome of an interpersonal situation.

Adults can experience loss of autonomy, and most health care situations promote dependency. Encouraging client participation in all aspects of health-related decision making is an essential nursing intervention. Respecting the dignity and rights of all clients, regardless of condition or age, supports autonomy.

Initiative versus Guilt

Initiative broadens the development of autonomy to include the skills involved in deliberately planning and undertaking activities. Independent actions become purposeful and goal directed. As the child discovers pleasure in manipulating tools and experimenting with different roles in play activities, thinking and behaviors become more complex.

The Ego Strength Associated with Initiative Is Purpose. The nurse can appreciate the change in complexity from autonomy to purpose in the increasing number of questions asked and in the eagerness with which the child seeks goal-directed activities. Playing games such as "house," doctor," and "store" allows the child to experience different life roles. Such experimentation prepares the child for the larger task of developing a career identity in late adolescence and early adulthood. In the process, the child learns beginning collaborative skills with other children and adults.

Purpose is important in adulthood. Without purpose, motivation disappears. Most people are unwilling to invest in a relationship that changes from intimate to casual acquaintance or in a work project about to be eliminated. With the increasing unemployment and serious social problems that are present in the 1990s, nurses are more likely to encounter clients who are experiencing conflicts in this area. Helping clients rediscover purpose and meaning in their lives is a first step in developing constructive coping strategies.

Industry versus Inferiority

Competency is important in this stage of psychosocial development. The child begins to experience the pleasures associated with task completion and pride in producing something. Children begin to see themselves as workers and to experience themselves in relation to others, both competitively and cooperatively, in mastering skills and tools.

Emotional mastery becomes more of a focus. Before adolescence, parental relationships were the child's primary guide to developing life strategies. In preadolescence, there is a shift in emotional energy from parents to peers. Group play becomes team play. Industry is a forerunner of the more integrated task of ego identity. The strategies learned in this developmental stage ideally lead to career and personal principled commitment.

Competence Is the Ego Strength Associated with Industry. Competence, defined as having the capability to perform required tasks, is relative. It is possible to be very competent in some areas and incompetent in others. For example, a brilliant scientist might be intellectually competent but socially inept. The car mechanic masters competency in fixing engines, a task physicians cannot usually perform with ease. Each person would find discomfort if held accountable for the other's competency. Adults lose their sense of competency in new and unfamiliar circumstances. It is easy to feel inferior. Inferiority refers to the sense of helplessness individuals feel when they sense their skills and abilities are insufficient to meet the current challenge. In the hospital, the nurse can provide activities and information leading to mastery in meeting new life demands. Helping the client use personal resources and helping only enough so that the client's self-help capacity takes over are other strategies to promote a sense of mastery. Social support groups offer validation to clients experiencing self-doubts about competency.

Identity versus Identity Diffusion

Erikson considers resolution of the psychosocial crisis of identity as the central life task. Establishing a clear, firm sense of identity promotes resilience in coping with the various assaults to the self-concept life invariably delivers in unfavorable life circumstances. Exercise 3–3 explores consistency and adaptability as they relate to self-concept.

Erikson characterizes identity as representing a continuity of self in which personal identity becomes clearer. Truths about self learned from others, self-motivations developed through competencies and values, and the expectations of significant persons in a person's life contribute to a person's self-identity.

Adolescence marks the transition from child to adult and a new sense of identity. The separation of self from parental figures, which began at birth, becomes more pronounced. A certain amount of identity diffusion or emotional upheaval in the process is considered healthy and normal. There is a loss associated with the necessary change in role to that of the adult. Much of the teenager's emotional turmoil and ambivalence relates to a search for identity—an identity separate from yet very much built upon what has gone before.

For many parents, watching teenagers experiment as they attempt to develop "an autonomous definition of self, apart from the nuclear family" (Hoare, 1991) is a painful time. But adolescents must establish an authentic sense of who they are, repudiating those elements they are not.

Since identity requires that each person become his or her own self-agent, Erikson spoke of commitment to ideals, career identity, and sex role identity as its benchmark. As a core construct of personality, people who choose a commitment corresponding with their talents, skills, and interests generally express self-satisfaction.

Culture and economic conditions play a role in

EXERCISE 3–3
Consistency and Adaptability of Self-Concepts

Purpose: To promote understanding of the consistency and adaptability of self-concepts.

Time: 45 minutes; written portions may be done as a homework exercise and the results shared in class.

Procedure:
1. Think back to when you were ten years old. Image yourself, and write as much as you can remember about yourself at that age, including what was most important to you, what activities you engaged in, who your friends were, and anything else that you can remember about yourself. Interview someone close to you who knew you at that age, and include this information on a separate piece of paper.
2. Now image yourself as you are today, and address the same topic areas.
3. Share your self-reports in groups of three, and common themes with the group as a whole.

Discussion:
1. In what ways were your self-concepts different today from what they were when you were ten years old?
2. To what do you attribute these differences?
3. In what ways are you still the same person today that you were when you were ten?
4. Did you notice any differences in your recollections of yourself as a ten-year-old and those of the person you interviewed?
5. If you found any differences, were you surprised by them? How do you explain the variance?
6. What did you learn about yourself from doing this exercise? about consistency and adaptability in your own self-concepts?
7. What common themes emerged in the groups regarding similarities and differences in self-concept across different age spans?

development and expression of identity. Western cultures foster an individualistic approach to identity, but group identity is the preference in many Asian cultures. For many people in today's society, building a solid career identity is threatened by economic uncertainty. Young adults are postponing major life commitments, including marriage, children, and home ownership, because of declining job opportunities and rising costs of housing and education. For economic reasons many adults in their twenties are still living at home with their parents. Midlife layoffs in previously stable work situations create serious assaults to self-identity. Some people emerge stronger, others are irreparably scarred. Marriage, parenting, and changes in responsibilities, lifestyle, or economic status are capable of re-creating a crisis of identity.

The Ego Strength Associated with Identity Is Fidelity. Fidelity represents a pledge of faith in an idea or person. Cults, causes, religious experiences, and many organizations provide important social agencies for the development of commitment. Whether the commitment that is chosen can provide the needed confirmation depends on the nature of the group. Colleges, career training, the armed services, and so on, provide institutional support for the development of identity. Political, conservation, and religious groups help people develop an identity around issues and values important to them. Support groups for different symptoms are important sources of identity building in health care. Not all groups support productive identity building. Identity diffusion is seen in groups that promote delinquency, irresponsibility, and fanatical behaviors.

Intimacy versus Isolation

Once a person has chosen a vocation, the next life task extends self-concept to a broader shared purpose with another human being. Intimacy is the ability to join with another human being, to connect emotionally as well as physically in mutually satisfying ways. It involves trust of another's good-will, a sense of personal identity, and confidence in one's ability to relate effectively with another human being. If a person does not have a clear sense of personal identity, intimacy is difficult to achieve. Other people can enrich, complement, and offer feedback about the self, but they should never be allowed to define it.

Love Is the Ego Strength Associated with Intimacy. Love is not romantic love. Love is a fundamental social tie consisting of a "natural sharing of one's real self" with another human being and a conscious commitment to that person evidenced in decisions and action (Bellah et al., 1985, p. 85).

Isolation is a feeling of emptiness, accompanied by the sense that nobody cares or wants to be there in times of trouble. People often compound the problem of isolation by withdrawing from important relationships and giving cues that they wish to be left alone when they feel bad about themselves.

Generativity versus Stagnation and Self-Absorption

Generativity, the developmental stage associated with midlife, encompasses "procreativity, productivity and creativity" (Erikson, 1982). This time, an individual reaffirms the sense of identity by investing the self in the interest of the larger society.

Caring Is the Ego Strength Associated with Generativity. Caring is expressed through commitment. Sharing one's talents with others becomes important. The benchmark associated with this stage of ego maturation does not relate to the number of family or community obligations a person has. It is possible to fill one's life with activity without being generative or to make many commitments without satisfying any of them. Instead, generativity reflects the quality of investment a person makes to his or her commitments. A person who commits to the betterment of humankind leaves a legacy of experience, knowledge, and caring that affects and inspires future generations. Work, community service, and creative projects, as well as child care, are avenues for generativity. A life in which one has no regrets generally is one that has been generative.

Self-absorption or stagnation evolves when an individual makes choices that compromise personal commitments to one's fellow human beings. In hospital settings, where one has little else to think about, it is easy to become self-absorbed. Taking time with a client to explore all aspects of the person, rather than focusing only on the part of the person that is ill, helps refocus clients caught up in self-absorption. The person's contribution to society or his or her sense of self may have to change, but life still can be fulfilling.

Integrity versus Despair

Erikson's final stage of ego development, integrity versus despair, focuses on the assessment of the meaning and worth of one's life. The crisis of ego integrity is not always age related. Young people facing death as well as old people need to assess their life during the last stage of ego development. They need to understand the meaning of their life as they prepare to exit it. All previous stages are incorporated into this stage of human development, so "a wise Indian, a true gentleman, and a mature peasant share and recognize in one another the final stage of integrity" (Erikson, 1968).

Life review is an important strategy in helping to resolve this stage. A sense of despair develops when an individual realizes that life is almost over and that the opportunity to act differently no longer exists. The nurse can help a client enhance the time left by making attitude changes that permit a different self-appraisal and accepting more fully the positive elements. Exercise 3–4 promotes an understanding of possible selves.

Wisdom Is the Ego Strength Associated with Integrity. Wisdom is defined as "your perspective on life, your sense of balance, your understanding of how the various parts and principles apply and relate to each other. It embraces judgment, discernment, comprehension. It is a gestalt or oneness, an integrated wholeness (Covey, 1989, p. 109). Wisdom comes from having lived life to the best of one's ability, from having few regrets about choices made, and from one's willingness to share this experience with others. Because wisdom stirs from within, there is a growing sense of detachment from the external world, with the realization that the true treasure lies within. Self-development is a lifelong process.

EXERCISE 3–4
A Life of Integrity through Imaging Possible Selves

Purpose: To promote understanding of the concept of possible selves.

Time: 45 minutes; written parts may be done as a homework exercise and the results shared in class.

Procedure:
Image yourself at a gathering to celebrate your life when you are 60 years old. Write down what you would like the main speaker to highlight about your life. Be as imaginative as possible, but include all of the things you would most like remembered about you if you had full control over how you would live your life.
    Share the speech you developed with your class group.

Discussion:
1. How did it feel to do this exercise? Were you surprised by any of the feelings you had or by the content of the speech? If so, in what ways?
2. In what ways do you feel the speech you developed reflects your values? life goals?
3. How did it feel to share your speech with your classmates?
4. What new information does the group have that could prove useful in understanding the power of possible selves in nursing practice?

Nurses use Erikson's model as an important part of client assessment. Exercise 3–5 can help apply Erikson's concepts to client situations. Analysis of behavior patterns, using Erikson's framework, can identify age-appropriate or arrested development of normal interpersonal skills (Table 3–1). A developmental framework helps the nurse know what types of interventions are most likely to be effective. For example, children in Erikson's initiative versus guilt stage of development respond best if they participate actively and ask many questions. Elderly clients respond to a life review strategy that focuses on the integrity of their life as a composite of experience.

EXERCISE 3–5
Erikson's Stages of Psychosocial Development

Purpose: To help you apply Erikson's stages of psychosocial development to client situations.

Time: 45 minutes; may be done as a homework exercise and the results shared in class.

Procedure:
To set your knowledge of Erikson's stages of psychosocial development, identify the psychosocial crisis(es) each of the following clients might be experiencing:
1. A 16-year-old unwed mother having her first child.
2. A 50-year-old executive "let go" from his job after 18 years of employment.
3. A stroke victim, paralyzed on the left side.
4. A middle-aged woman caring for her mother who has Alzheimer's.
5. A 49-year-old woman dying of pancreatic cancer.
6. A 63-year-old woman whose husband announces he has fallen in love with a younger woman and wants a divorce.
7. A 17-year-old high school athlete suddenly paralyzed from the neck down.

Discussion:
1. What criteria did you use to determine the most relevant psychosocial stage for each client situation?
2. In what ways were your answers similar or different from those of your peers?
3. What conclusions can you draw from doing this exercise that would influence how you would respond to each of these clients?

TABLE 3–1
Erikson's Stages of Psychosocial Development, Clinical Behavior Guidelines, and Stressors

Stage of Personality Development	Ego Strength or Virtue	Clinical Behavior Guidelines	Stressors
Trust versus mistrust	Hope	Appropriate attachment behaviors Ability to: • ask for assistance with an expectation of receiving it • give and receive information related to self and health • share opinions and experiences easily • differentiate between how much one can trust and how much one must distrust	Unfamiliar environment or routines Inconsistency in care Pain Lack of information Unmet needs, such as having to wait 20 minutes for a bedpan or pain injection Losses at critical times or accumulated losses Significant or sudden loss of physical function, such as a client with a broken hip being afraid to walk
Autonomy versus shame and doubt	Will power	Ability to: • express opinions freely and to disagree tactfully • delay gratification • accept reasonable treatment plans and hospital regulations • regulate one's behaviors (overcompliance, noncompliance, suggest disruption) • make age-appropriate decisions	Overemphasis on unfair or rigid regulations, for instance, putting clients in nursing homes to bed at 7 P.M. Cultural emphasis on guilt and shaming as a way of controlling behavior Limited opportunity to make choices in a hospital setting Limited allowance made for individuality
Initiative versus guilt	Purpose	Ability to: • develop realistic goals and to initiate actions to meet them • make mistakes without undue embarrassment • have curiosity about health care • work for goals • develop constructive fantasies and plans	Significant or sudden change in life pattern that interferes with role Loss of a mentor, particularly in adolescence or with a new job Lack of opportunity to participate in planning of care Overinvolved parenting that doesn't allow for experimentation Hypercritical authority figures No opportunity for play
Industry versus inferiority	Competence	Work is perceived as meaningful and satisfying Appropriate satisfaction with balance in lifestyle pattern, including leisure activities Ability to work with others, including staff Ability to complete tasks and self-care activities in line with capabilities Ability to express personal strengths and limitations realistically	Limited opportunity to learn and master tasks Illness, circumstance, or condition that compromises or obliterates one's usual activities Lack of cultural support or opportunity or training

TABLE 3–1 (*Continued*)
Erikson's Stages of Psychosocial Development, Clinical Behavior Guidelines, and Stressors

Stage of Personality Development	Ego Strength or Virtue	Clinical Behavior Guidelines	Stressors
Identity versus identity diffusion	Fidelity	Ability to establish friendships with peers Realistic assertion of independence and dependence needs Demonstration of overall satisfaction with self-image, including physical characteristics, personality, and role in life Ability to express and act on personal values Congruence of self-perception with nurse's observation and perception of significant others	Lack of opportunity Overprotective, neglectful, or inconsistent parenting Sudden or significant change in appearance, health, or status Lack of same-sex role models
Intimacy versus isolation	Love	Ability to: • enter into strong reciprocal interpersonal relationships • identify a readily available support system • feel the caring of others • act harmoniously with family and friends	Competition Communication that includes a hidden agenda Projection of images and expectations onto another person Lack of privacy Loss of significant others at critical points of development
Generativity versus stagnation and self-absorption	Caring	Demonstration of age-appropriate activities Development of a realistic assessment of personal contributions to society Development of ways to maximize productivity Appropriate care of whatever one has created Demonstration of a concern for others and a willingness to share ideas and knowledge Evidence of a healthy balance among work, family, and self demands	Aging parents, separate or concurrently with adolescent children Obsolescence or layoff in career "Me" generation attitude Inability or lack of opportunity to function in a previous manner Children leaving home Forced retirement
Integrity versus despair	Wisdom	Expression of satisfaction with personal lifestyle Acceptance of growing limitations while maintaining maximum productivity Expression of acceptance of certitude of death, as well as satisfaction with one's contributions to life	Rigid lifestyle Loss of significant other Loss of physical, intellectual, and emotional faculties Loss of previously satisfying work and family roles

Reprinted from The Life Cycle Completed by Erik H. Erikson with the permission of W. W. Norton & Company, Inc. Copyright © 1982 by Rikan Enterprises, Ltd.

APPLICATIONS

Figure 3–2 identifies the characteristics of a healthy self-concept. NANDA (1986) separates the nursing diagnosis "Alteration in self-concept" into four discrete elements: body image, personal identity, self-esteem, and role performance. The first three elements are described here. Role relationships are described in Chapter 6 because they have a dual function as an interpersonal bridge between the inner and the outer world of health care.

Although body image, personal identity, self-esteem, and role performance are described as separate processes, the separation is artificial. Sutherland (1993) notes that separation of different elements of self-concept "fails to do justice to the uniqueness of the self as a functioning whole" (p. 4). Throughout the chapter, the student must keep in mind that the simulated division of self-concepts into detached dimensions is for discussion purposes only.

BODY IMAGE

Body image represents the physical dimension of self-concept and a person's first awareness of self. *Perceptions* of the body and its associated elements, not its reality, make up body image. Physical structures associated with body image include not only the actual material body but all somatic sensations of pain, fatigue, pleasure, heat, and cold. The physical self-concepts include the senses, as well as the physical presentations of movement expressed through dancing, running, and gestures (Grassi, 1986).

Functions of Body Image

Schontz (1974) describes four functions of body image: *(1) a sensory image, (2) an instrument for action and source of drives, (3) a stimulus to self and others,* and *(4) an expressive instrument.* As a sensory register, the body recognizes important information through one or more of its sensory receptors. Touch, for example, provides information about temperature, pressure, and texture (Ackerman, 1990).

The physical self functions as a major instrument for action. Through a remarkable network of muscle, nerve, and cellular interactions, the human body can perform an infinite variety of independent actions. No other physical structure can autonomously decide to move on its own, be able to complete the action, reflect on the meaning of it, and discuss the meaning of it with another. Hormones and physiologic interactions stimulate sexual drives, removal of body wastes, and alarm reactions, all in a concerted way without a person even having to think about them.

As a stimulus to self, the mental picture of a person's body and associated feelings (e.g., body weight, shape, and size) affect the value we place on ourselves. Consider how you feel about yourself when you haven't showered, shaved, brushed your teeth, or combed your hair; then think how you feel when you know you look your best. Some mental disorders such as major depression, schizophrenia, and eating disorders reflect disturbed body images as part of their symptomatology.

Finally, body image serves as an *expressive*

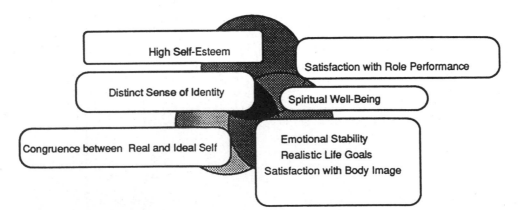

Figure 3–2 Characteristics of a Healthy Self-Concept

EXERCISE 3–6
Physical Cues to Behavior

Purpose: To increase your awareness of the interpersonal link between body image and interpersonal perceptions of behavior.

Time: 30–40 minutes for analysis and discussion.

Procedure:
1. Bring in magazine pictures of two or more people communicating with each other.
2. Put each picture on an easel, one at a time.
3. Without talking to one another, write down your impressions of what is going on in the picture interpersonally by looking at the people in the picture and observing their nonverbal cues.
4. Describe your impression of the relationship between the two people and why you are drawing the conclusions you are about what is going on between them.
5. Share your written observations and compare the results.

Discussion:
1. What physical characteristics were important to you in drawing interpersonal conclusions about the participants?
2. Were the conclusions drawn by your colleagues similar or different in nature?
3. What do you think might account for this similarity or difference?
4. What did you learn about the role of body image in drawing interpersonal conclusions from doing this exercise?

instrument giving interpersonal signals and information about the self to others. People who dress well and are well groomed generally command more respect than those who don't (Schlenker, 1985). Exercise 3–6 increases the nurse's awareness of the link between body image and perceptions of behavior.

Types of Alterations

Most people think of body image as describing visible changes in physical characteristics. But the concept includes more subtle variations related to loss of body function, loss of control, and deviations from the norm.

Loss of Body Function. Loss of body function is an aspect of body image that can be very obvious or well hidden by the client. Inability to move freely, infertility, impotence, and loss of bladder or bowel function are examples of functional loss. The loss is only part of the problem. Many people experience shame about their condition and avoid social situations because of their embarrassment. The mind and body interface so tightly that real or perceived inability to function biologically both affects and is affected by psychological factors.

Worrying about it can further compromise functioning. Talking about loss of function with a sympathetic listener makes it less unacceptable and more manageable to the client.

Loss of Control. Similar in impact to loss of function are alterations in control and loss of sensation. The client in pain and clients subject to seizures, alcoholism, cardiac arrhythmias, or periodic depressions may exhibit few obvious changes in body image. But the repeated loss of control over the body leaves the client with similar feelings of insecurity and uncertainty. Being able to talk about these realities that dominate some people's feelings about themselves can be enormously reassuring.

Deviations in Physical Characteristics. Body image is affected by subtle reactions to others. Those who are too thin or too fat or who look considerably older or younger than they are often are judged on the basis of their looks. Physical attractiveness and conformity to the norm unfortunately result in special treatment, and those who are different or unattractive are not treated so well (Burns et al., 1992). People who are different speak of feeling invisible, receiving subtle discrimination, and being misunderstood.

Significant deviations in physical, intellectual, or emotional characteristics have a profound effect on self-concept and self-esteem (Felker, 1974). For example, Johnnie is a two-year-old child with the physique of a six-year-old. He looks different from other children his age, and others expect him to act more mature than he is. With the limited cognitive skills of a two-year-old, the only conclusion Johnnie can draw is that he is not like other kids his age. There seems to be something intrinsically wrong with him; he is flawed. His perceptions are reinforced by significant others who also seem to finding him lacking. Ironically, being tall when he becomes an adolescent can be just as much of an advantage as it is a limitation now. Understanding differences and working with clients to develop effective coping strategies enhance self-esteem and self-efficacy.

Another response to people with longstanding physical deviations is to ignore them or to assume they have gotten used to being different. Lifelong experience with significant deviations in body image does not necessarily make the person unaware of it or any more comfortable with it. Sensitivity to the impact of physical differences is essential to effective communication. Otherwise nurses can overlook or minimize chronic alterations in body image that are of great importance in assessing the meaning of client behaviors.

Culture and Body Image. Culture plays a significant role in our perception of body image by emphasizing some physical characteristics as positive and others as negative. For example, in the United States a slim, trim figure is admired. The overweight individual is thought of as sloppy or unhealthy whether or not this is true. In other cultures, Africa and India, for example, obesity is viewed as a sign of prosperity (Ackerman, 1990).

How Body Image Develops

Self-knowledge about the body comes through the primary caregiver's human stimulation of the infant. When the infant nurses at the breast or is held, the physical and psychological stimulation enhances the infant's sense of well-being. Deprived of this pleasurable activity, the infant protests by crying and tightening its muscles. Children who never experience the physical and psychological satisfactions of being touched affectionately, kissed,

or held often have difficulty expressing and receiving affection in adult relationships. In life, Ackerman (1990) suggests, "touch seems to be as essential as sunlight" (p. 80).

Normal developmental stages affect body image. In adolescence, the rapid surge of physical growth and development, acne, the advent of secondary sex characteristics in puberty, and changes in the endocrine system make the adolescent more vulnerable to concerns about body image (Dempsey, 1972). For the adolescent cancer victim, the hair loss frequently accompanying chemotherapy may be a more difficult side effect to cope with than a more objectively disabling symptom of pervasive fatigue or nausea.

In later maturity, the body again undergoes major changes; looks fade, the skin becomes wrinkled, muscles sag, the eyes become dim, hearing diminishes, and physical movements slow. The perception of body image is no longer one of youth. To a lesser degree, pregnancy may have a temporary effect on body image.

Assessment Strategies

Alterations in body image always require some type of adaptation. The extent of adjustment is determined partially by the nature and magnitude of the alteration and the degree to which the alterations interfere with functioning or lifestyle. Highly visible changes usually require more of an adjustment. Likewise, sudden changes in body image may be more difficult to absorb than changes in appearance that occur over time. Important in the human response to alterations in body image are the feelings and attitudes of others, the potential capacity of the client to cope with change, and the availability of sources of support.

Beginning with the first encounter, the nurse seeks to understand the meaning behind the symptoms. The value placed on body image differs from person to person. Some individuals, like Helen Keller and Ray Charles, adapt an objectively negative physical feature of self in ways that benefit not only themselves but all whom they encounter. Others let a physical deviation so dominate self-image that it becomes their only defining characteristic.

The same medical treatment or surgical procedure stimulates different body images. For some women, the prospect of a hysterectomy is viewed with relief; for others, it has serious psychological implications related to attractiveness and physical enjoyment of sex. Understanding these variations in the meaning of physical changes enables the nurse to respond effectively. Instead of simply accepting a single behavioral response as a given, the nurse takes into consideration the personalized meaning of the change for each client in planning care.

Assessment data for a nursing diagnosis of self-concept disturbance in body image might include one or more of the following behaviors:

- Verbal expression of negative feelings about the body.
- No mention of changes in body structure and function or preoccupation with changed body image.
- Reluctance to look at or touch a changed body structure.
- Expression of worthlessness or hopelessness related to changes in body structure or appearance.
- Social isolation and loss of interest in friends.

The nurse would seek supporting data through open-ended questions or circular questioning related to the client's perception of altered body structure or function. For example, "What has it been like for you since you had your operation?" or, "Who do you think could be most helpful to you in making the transition back to work?" Often the concerns of clients relate not only to their perception of the changed appearance or function but also to perceptions of possible reactions of significant others. For example, a client with a speech impediment resulting from surgery or a stroke doesn't talk because she is anxious about the way her speech sounds to others. A cancer victim fears how she looks to others without her wig.

Other data should include the client's identified strengths and limitations, expressed needs and goals, the nature and accessibility of the client's support system, and the impact of body image change on lifestyle.

Planning and Intervention

Sensitivity to the client's need to absorb the implications of a change in body image is a critical component of support. Most clients need time to absorb physical changes. Interventions to modify alterations in body image might include:

- Providing information and support.
- Modeling acceptance.
- Introducing adaptive and compensatory functioning.
- Encouraging the client to share experiences with others.
- Enhancing social support.

Providing relevant information and creating opportunities for the client to ask questions makes it acceptable for the client to explore an anticipated or actual change in body image. In the case of a new diagnosis, it is important for the nurse to go over information more than once, even if it appears that the client understands it initially. Validation checks, asking if the client has any questions, and suggesting realistic responses can facilitate communication when the client seems very anxious.

Modeling acceptance starts with the nurse. Showing the client that a physical change does not frighten the nurse reduces the fear and panic that a significant change in appearance often presents. Nurses see clients with serious body image changes on a regular basis. For the client it is a unique and potentially horrifying experience. Finding that a significant physical change does not cause the nurse to recoil in disgust allows the client to reframe the situation and to see that the person within remains intact. For example, one client with extensive head and neck surgery would deliberately unwrap his wound to see how each new nurse would react. He needed to know that his nurse would not turn away from him because of his appearance.

As the client demonstrates beginning acceptance through inquiry or a willingness to talk about the physical change, the nurse can slowly introduce the idea of a resuming normal functions appropriate to the client's age and developmental level. A warm, supportive, yet tactfully objective interpersonal approach encourages expressions of feelings. For example, the nurse can help a client anticipate and respond with dignity to the reactions of others.

Sharing the experience with others with a similar ordeal recognizes the legitimacy of having feelings that otherwise might go unexpressed. For example, having a "Reach for Recovery" volunteer visit a mastectomy client to share feelings, hopes, alternative options, and practical suggestions for adapting to changes is a very simple intervention that helps increase the client's adjustment and acceptance of the change. With children, the nurse can act as an advocate in explaining alterations in body image to peers who otherwise might ridicule or avoid a child with a significant physical, cognitive, or emotional deficit.

Finally, the importance of *social support* from family and friends can not be overestimated. Social support does as much or more for a person than medication and technical skill in alterations in self-concept related to body image. Clients need to know that their altered appearance will not disturb their relationships. The nurse can suggest that the client call family or friends. Sometimes just a suggestion is enough to put the client in contact with others. At other times the nurse needs to provide encouragement and support to help the client take this step. Anticipatory guidance with visitors to prepare them for dramatic changes in their family member or friend's appearance helps promote acceptance.

Evaluation

Throughout the relationship, the nurse and client mutually evaluate the effectiveness of the rehabilitation process. Confirming statements about client effort and small steps taken, as well as goals attained, encourage the client to acknowledge short-term goals and point out areas of develop-

ment that require further modification of the nursing care plan. Appropriate adjustments, if needed, are mutually determined and implemented.

PERSONAL IDENTITY

Personal identity consists of all the psychological beliefs and attitudes people have about themselves—the *perceptual, cognitive, emotional,* and *spiritual* elements of self-concept. Personal identity is more difficult to characterize than the physical aspects of self-concept because the nurse can't actually see it, and it fluctuates with situations. Personal identity is seen in behavior (Rawlinson, 1990).

Perception

Perception is a personal identity construct by which a person transforms external sensory data into personalized images of reality. As an intrapersonal process, perceptions allow a person to choose among sensory images and to cluster sensory images into a meaningful design. Perception is the first gatekeeper of self-concept.

Perception is a function of the mind and not of the senses. Consider the two pictures in Figure 3–3. Depending on how one's eyes focus on the figures in each picture, it is possible to draw quite different

Figure 3–3 The Figure–Ground Phenomenon. Are the figures presented in white against a black background, or in black against a white background? Does it make a difference in your perception of the figures? From the Westinghouse Learning Corporation Self-Instructional Unit 12. Perception, 1970.

EXERCISE 3–7
Perceptual Differences

Purpose: To help you understand differences in perception.

Time: 45 minutes

Procedure:
The first part of this exercise is done outside the classroom. Pair up with another student and go to a fast food restaurant. Sit on opposite sides of a table. Pick out a person unknown to either of you and observe the individual's behavior for 20 minutes.
1. Write down your observations and inferences about this person without checking with each other.
2. After you leave the restaurant, compare your observations and the reasons for making your inferences.
3. Develop a composite picture of your observations.

Discussion:
1. In what ways were your observations similar or different from your partner's?
2. What was most surprising to you in doing this exercise?
3. What did you learn about yourself from doing this exercise?
4. How could you use this information in your nursing practice?

conclusions about the images. The same phenomenon is true in life. Reality lies in the eyes of the beholder. Perceptions differ because people develop mind sets that automatically alter sensory data in specific personal ways. Validation of perceptual data is needed because the nurse and the client may not be looking at the same phenomenon. Exercise 3–7 explores differences in perception.

Types of Perceptual Alterations in Self-Concept

DISTORTED REALITY

Perceptual processes contribute significantly to the self-concept in the way individuals think about themselves and others. When perceptions are colored by unresolved past conflicts, cultural values, or simple misunderstandings, they contribute to a false sense of self (Snyder, 1984). For example, a young boy with artistic abilities and little interest in sports might think of himself as odd or as not fitting in with his more aggressive, sports-minded schoolmates if there is no support from the environment for his more aesthetic inclinations. A sympathetic teacher or school art club, however, can dramatically reshape his self-concept in much the same manner as occurred in the story of the ugly duckling (Swann, 1982).

Perceptual distortions of reality are found in many mental and neurological disorders. People can create their own little world, which has little to do with reality. Usually if the perceptual distortions are significant, the client is unable to maintain independent living.

SELECTIVE ATTENTION

Selective attention is a less serious interpersonal perceptual process by which a person hears selected parts of a message and fails to absorb other parts because of defensive self needs. A person who has heard only part of the message is unlikely to respond appropriately. For example, people who are depressed hear only the one negative comment a person makes and fail to register the ten positive comments made in the same conversation (Segal, 1988). Some common perceptual filters associated with selective attention include culture, sex, age, physical condition, mood, past experience, similarity of problem, stereotyping, expectations, and interpersonal differences (Table 3–2).

Selective attention focuses on behavior extremes. People pay more attention to stimuli that are attention grabbing and remember them longer. Often it is difficult to erase the perceptual image created by a particularly intense or painful stimulus even if new information contradicts it, or the image was only a peripheral aspect of a larger situation. Interestingly, negative impressions are retained longer than favorable impressions (Adler and Rodman, 1988).

First impressions contribute to a subtle form of selective attention by blocking subsequent infor-

TABLE 3–2
Perceptual Filters Affecting Attention

Perceptual Filter	Implications
Culture	Is the object acceptable or alienating?
Sex	Is the object of specific gender interest?
Age	Does the object have relevance to the observer's age group?
Physical condition	Is a long period of attentiveness involved, requiring endurance for concentration?
Mood	What mood does the observer bring—receptive and focused or antagonistic and distracted?
Past experience	Is the observer distracted by early impressions or similar prior experiences?
Interpersonal differences	Is "chemistry," tolerance, or understanding lacking for focused attention?

mation that would contradict the initial assessment. For example, a co-worker tells you that Mrs. Jones in room 300 is difficult and cantankerous, and as you enter her room she glares at you. Mrs. Jones may be having a bad day, and her behavioral may not really reflect her normal behavioral responses. But the next time you work with her you may approach her as a "difficult" client. Reframing Mrs. Jones's angry symptoms as a cry for help could prevent this selective stereotype.

SELF-FULFILLING PROPHECY

When a person's perceptions of a certain outcome actually influence the person's present and future behaviors, the process is referred to as a self-fulfilling prophecy. For example, Martha receives an evaluation indicating a need for improved confidence. Martha interprets the instructor's comments as meaning she is awkward. Instead of seeing the instructor's comment as about a behavior simple to correct, Martha perceives it as a personal commentary on her self. This perception colors Martha's behavior, and from that point on she performs awkwardly and freezes when asked questions in the clinical area.

How Perception Develops

Perceptual development of a recognizable self-identity begins at birth when the infant first encounters his or her parents. The infant acquires perceptual attitudes about the self by observing the reactions of caregivers to his or her behavior. Over time, self-perceptions become more complex and flexible. Children who have multiple opportunities to experiment with different options and situations demonstrate greater perceptual flexibility, provided the experimentation is supported and guided.

Individuals who evidence healthy perceptual abilities characteristically are open minded. They develop realistic frames of reference for analyzing data and orienting self to time, place, and person. Problems and complex situations are viewed realistically, without significant distortions. When new information forces the conclusion that previous perceptions are no longer valid, the person can discard them with relative ease. Relationships with others reflect a healthy balance between dependent and independent behaviors.

Assessment Strategies

A nursing assessment of perceptual difficulty is based on knowledge of the expected developmental level of a particular client and observation of unsatisfactory behavioral responses to stress. Disturbances in perception can be inferred when the client seems to block out parts of his or her experience, projects the blame for personal frustration onto the environment, or is hypercritical of self or others. Hopelessness expressed as an inability to see alternative options also indicates limited perceptual functioning.

Health state, intelligence, life experience, and age are important considerations in assessing the client's perceptual capacity. For example, anxiety, brain trauma or dysfunction, disease, reaction to medication, certain abnormal blood values, sheltered living experiences, and the age-related evolution of thinking in childhood all have a significant impact on perceptual ability.

Assessment of perceptual patterns should take into account the environmental context in which the interaction takes place. People "edit" their behavior to meet their perceived expectations of the other person and the appropriateness of their communication to the current situation. They tend to be more guarded in unfamiliar and exposed settings. If the interview takes place in a less than ideal setting, this should be noted as an environmental variable.

Assessment data should incorporate the cultural diversity of the client if it is revelant. Major and minor language differences between client and nurse can affect the perception of the intent of the message sender or receiver. People are sometimes insulted by comments, gestures, and emblems they perceive as intrusive or degrading when this was not the intent of the message sender. Different cultures have culture-specific norms about the use of eye contact and deference to others. Without an understanding of cultural diversity, the nurse may unintentionally misinterpret a client's response or offend a client. Asking clients about their cultural world helps prevent insensitivity.

Perceptions of both nurse and client may be colored by interests, emotions, or needs that either party carries into the conversation. For example, if the nurse is worried about something happening that morning in her own family, it is likely that some of the client's data may go unnoticed or may be distorted because of the nurse's distraction.

Hospitalization by its very nature narrows perceptual ability. Adjusting to a major physical impairment and a radically different living situation simultaneously may prove overwhelming to a "normal" client and significantly affect that client's perceptual acuity (Swann, 1982).

CASE EXAMPLE

Mrs. Segal, a fiercely independent elderly woman, has suddenly been immobilized with a broken hip. After a short hospital stay, she is sent to a nursing home because she can no longer take care of herself. She is bewildered and acts slightly confused.

To reorient herself to the meaning of her new situation, Mrs. Segal might have some of the following concerns: In what ways is she like or unlike the other nursing home residents? Will she fit in, and is this a temporary or permanent arrangement? It's a whole new social milieu. Furthermore, physically helpless, elderly clients with all of their mental faculties are sometimes treated as though they are mentally incompetent because of stereotypes about aging. How will Mrs. Segal be able to communicate to the nursing staff that, just because she is 90, it

doesn't mean that she has significant memory problems? She has the same needs as they do—to be valued and treated with dignity. But how can she communicate her needs without being seen as demanding or out of line with her current condition? What happens when she has to go to the bathroom? Will they come the first time she rings, or will the overworked nursing staff think it's easier to clean her up if she soils herself? She is a large woman, and it is difficult to help her get to the bathroom. Each of these concerns represents and normal human response to a new situation.

The art of nursing involves protecting the integrity of her self-concept while giving Mrs. Segal the emotional support and compensatory assistance she needs. Providing information and cues for action are structural interventions the nurse can use. The nurse can also encourage the client to take advantage of activities with gentle verbal support.

Planning and Intervention

When perceptions are clouded, the nurse may intentionally provide a calm, unhurried interpersonal situation for therapeutic conversations. Timing and interpersonal space are critical in planning interventions. For example, the suspicious client needs shorter and more objective verbal interactions until trust is established. Sometimes the undemanding presence of a nurse allows the client to move closer without fear of reprisal. In the general hospital, taking time to make sure the newly admitted client or family is comfortable, offering a beverage, and introducing yourself are simple actions that reduce the anxiety most clients feel in unfamiliar settings. An uncomplicated game or small talk about a neutral topic can be a useful bridge in working with psychotic clients, for whom perceptions and the relationship are intertwined.

Tone of voice, choice of words, and nonverbal gestures create perceptual barriers if the person experiencing them feels devalued. The person receiving the message may not know the reason for being devalued, but the underlying communication is likely to affect every aspect of the nurse–client relationship and of goal accomplishment.

Perceptual Checks: A Useful Nursing Strategy

The interpersonal relationship offers an excellent means of reformulating false perceptions through perception checks. Adler and Rodman (1988) offer a three-step process for checking the validity of perceptual inferences.

The first step involves describing precisely the behavior of concern. All aspects of the problem, including the reasons the problem is of major concern at this time, as well as possible causes, are considered.

The second step involves offering two alternative explanations for the problem. Although in most situations the nurse asks only one question at a time to avoid confusing the client, clients with perceptual problems may need alternative suggestions. Adler and Rodman advocate using two possible cause-effect explanations rather than one interpretation as a way of broadening perspective. Most situations are multidetermined. Offering alternate explanations models the idea that most situations in life carry more than one possible explanation—and solution.

The third step involves requesting feedback. Feedback forces the client to interact with the helping person in checking reality. It reduces the chances of misinterpretations and false assumptions. This three-step process helps a person maintain an accurate picture of reality. In the process of developing shared meanings, people draw closer together. The knowledge that another individual cares enough to find out what is going on within the person affirms the value of the interpersonal relationship for both participants.

CASE EXAMPLE

Nurse: Mr. Jones, I notice that you didn't use the Ames glucose monitor this morning to test your blood for sugar. (*Focused description of behavior*)

Is that because you didn't understand fully what we went over yesterday, or is it difficult for you to consider using it for more personal reasons? (*Two alternative logical explanations of behavior*)

Client: The idea of pricking myself all the time isn't appealing.

Nurse: So it is the needle stick that disturbs you. Can you tell me more about your reluctance to test your blood? (*Asking for feedback*)

From the client's response, the nurse now knows that use of the glucose monitor, rather than a misunderstanding of instructions, is the major concern for the client. This perceptual check means that further instruction, support, and feedback will center on those parts of the problem of greatest import to the client. Equally important, the client feels heard.

Perceptual checks, combined with well-thought-out inferences about the meaning of client behaviors, enhance the quality of decision making in the nurse–client relationship. They allow the nurse to use perceptual data in a conscious, deliberate way to facilitate the relationship process. Because the client feels heard and communication focuses on matters of interest and concern to the client, mutuality occurs with greater frequency. Nursing interventions are more likely to fit the client's needs, resulting in deeper satisfaction and a more successful outcome.

The nurse–client relationship is not the only source of perceptual checks. Referent groups, defined as groups of persons having common interests and concerns, are a form of social support These informal support groups allow people who perceive they are alone with different physical, emotional, and spiritual situations to find themselves in others.

Evaluation

Behaviors indicating broader perceptual flexibility include the ability to develop different perspectives on the same subject. Willingness to enter a support group and to try different options also suggests perceptual adaptability.

Cognition

Thinking is a complex, creative cognitive process stimulated by conscious data, internal as well as external. Cognitive processes take perceptual images and categorize them into new informational sets through the process of reflective thinking. Through cognitive thinking processes, a person determines the accuracy of perceptual data and assesses the possible outcomes of alternate options. Without the ability to process the meaning of perceptual images cognitively, people would be unable to develop realistic goals, implement coherent patterns of behavior, and evaluate their efforts (Norem, 1988).

The cognitive aspects of self-concept are best characterized by the level, clarity, and logic of thinking. New cognitive images are stored in long- or short-term memory, capable of retrieval when needed. When illness, genetic factors, pain, accident, or injury affect cognition, they also have a profound effect on a person's overall sense of personal identity. Although images may enter the psyche, the normal cognitive processes directing behavior can no longer make sense out of them.

How Cognition Develops

Most of what we know about cognitive development of thinking processes emanates from the work of Jean Piaget, who described sensorimotor, preoperational, concrete operational, and formal operational stages of cognitive development. Stages of cognitive development are described in Chapter 18, "Communicating with Children."

Cognitive development proceeds from simple to complex. It is important to realize that a child thinks with images as well as with words. For example, the two-year-old child sees all four-legged animals as the same. As the child progresses in cognitive complexity, distinctions are made between horses and dogs. By the time the child grows up, subtle differences in breeds are also noted. Distinctions regarding the temperament, function, and so on, of different breeds are readily stored in and retrieved from memory. The adolescent is capable of making abstract inferences about the data and drawing conclusions about the relationships among them. Since imaging is so important with children, incorporating pictures and allowing children to handle equipment is a necessary part of their learning process.

Assessment Strategies

The information-processing characteristics of each client are different. Since people think differently about the same issues, it is logical to assume that individuals' cognitive approaches to problem solving differ. Time spent accurately assessing and responding appropriately to the individual learning characteristics of the client saves time for the nurse and minimizes frustration for the client.

Assessment data that might lead the nurse to suspect a disturbance in cognition start with the client's knowledge about his or her illness, treatment protocols, and expectations of therapy. Other information includes the client's knowledge of risk factors; previous illnesses; motivation; orientation to time, place, and person; and memory assessment.

Cognition can be compromised at any time by alterations in an individual's physiological and emotional state. For example, low blood sugar affects cognition in a very direct and immediate way. Pain, hunger, hormones, and chemical imbalances in the body influence cognitive functioning adversely. Strong emotions and intense psychological states can temporarily reduce the level of cognitive function and awareness. To lose one's cognitive functioning is one of the most horrifying circumstances affecting a human being, as Lear (1980) writes: "The most painful thing was what happened to my mind. Nothing in my life was ever worse than that, or ever will be" (p. 222). And his wife observed:

> It was not of course, no memory. It was damaged memory. Of all his disabilities, this was the most devastating. He had always taken memory so far for granted. Who does not when it works? He had no awareness how paralyzed one might be without it. Now he understood the obvious as philosophers do, profoundly. He understood that without memory, life was not human life but vegetation. Without memory, one could not tie a shoe. (Lear, 1980, p. 217)

It is not unusual to see an Alzheimer victim clutching his head as if to make sense out of a meaningless world. Taking into account the agony that loss of cognition creates in its victims enhances the development of appropriate nursing strategies.

It is important when assessing cognition to differentiate transient memory loss from more permanent loss in the elderly. Elderly clients can appear acutely confused when confronted with the unfamiliar context of a hospitalization, yet the disorientation completely disappears within approximately three weeks of their return home.

PLANNING AND INTERVENTION

Reflective thinking and the ability to express thoughts clearly contribute to effective functioning. Not all thinking processes are clear. Cognitive distortions occur as a result of thoughts about the meaning of a situation that have little to do with reality (see Box 3–1 for examples). Faulty perceptions lead to cognitive distortions, but it is the thinking about them that leads to disordered behavior. When this occurs, the nurse looks for the cause of the distortion and links the intervention to the nursing diagnosis.

Special modifications of the nurse–client relationship allow for individual differences in cognitive capacities. Clients with dementia have limited functioning because their ability to use knowledge constructively and to put facts together in a sys-

---

BOX 3–1
Examples of Cognitive Distortions

- All or nothing thinking (the situation is all good or all bad; a person is trustworthy or untrustworthy).
- Overgeneralizing (one incident is treated as if it happens all the time; picking out a single detail and dwelling on it).
- Mind reading and fortunetelling (deciding a person doesn't like you without checking it out; assuming a bad outcome with no evidence to support it).
- Personalizing (seeing yourself as flawed instead of separating the situation as something you played a role in but did not cause).
- Acting on "should" and "ought to" (deciding in your mind what is someone else's responsibility without perceptual checks; trying to meet another's expectations without regard for whether or not it makes sense to do so).
- "Awfulizing" (assuming the worst; every situation has a catastrophic interpretation and anticipated outcome).

---

tematic way is no longer available to them. Mentally ill clients often are unable to use cognitive problem-solving skills.

Keeping communication simple, breaking instructions down into smaller, sequential steps, presenting ideas one at a time, and using touch to emphasize directions or guide the client help compensate for cognitive deficits. Unless there is a pronounced cognitive deficit, knowledge of the client's educational level influences the type of language the nurse uses. Clients with flexible thinking styles may need less direct structural support from the nurse to assimilate new ideas than clients with more rigid thinking patterns. Older and chronically mentally ill individuals may need more time to process information. Sensory overload can compromise the assimilation of unfamiliar information in clients of all ages.

SELF-TALK

It is difficult to separate thoughts from feelings, and much of the reason that people feel badly about themselves has to do with negative self-talk. *Self-talk* is a cognitive process that produces a thought or thoughts which then lead to a feeling about a situation. Feelings attach a value to a person's thoughts, characterizing them as good or bad testimony about the self. When the thought carries a negative value connotation, it can affect the individual as if the thought represented the whole truth about the person. The thought "I stuttered in the interview" gets emotionally translated into "I had a terrible interview and I know I probably won't get the job." If the person thinks about it long enough, negative thoughts and associated feelings escalate to "I'm never going to get a job," "I don't ever interview well," "I'm no good." One part of one interview suddenly becomes a major defining statement of self. The pervading thoughts create a decrease in self-esteem. Changing the self-talk resets the thinking process. With positive self-talk as a therapeutic strategy, the person chooses the feeling he or she will have about a situation or person.

Through self-talk, a person can question the legitimacy of cognitive distortions, and often their irrationality becomes apparent. The nurse's comments can support the client's questioning. This can be done with direct challenge when appropriate—"Is that really true, you have *never* been successful at anything?" Or it can be done with humor, as in this case example.

CASE EXAMPLE

Grace Ann Hummer is a 65-year-old widow with arthritis, a weight problem, and failing eyesight. She looks older than she is. Admitted for a minor surgical procedure, Ms. Hummer tells the nurse she doesn't know why she came. Nothing can be done for her because she is too old and decrepit.

Nurse: As I understand it, you came in today for removal of your bunions. Can you tell me more about the problem as you see it? (*Asking for this information separates the current situation from an overall assessment of ill health.*)

Client: Well I've been having trouble walking, and I can't do some of the things I like to do that require extensive walking. I also have to buy "clunky" shoes that make me look like an old woman.

Nurse: So you are not willing to be an old woman yet? (*Taking the client's statement and challenging the cognitive distortion presented in her initial comments with humor allows the client to view her statement differently.*)

Client: (*Laughing.*) Right, there are a lot of things I want to do before I'm ready for a nursing home.

Nurse: What are some of the things you would like to do that will be possible after the surgery? (*Questions relating the shared experience of the surgery to shared possible outcomes of the surgery stimulates the client to think about possible options and subtly diminishes the validity of the client's overgeneralized negative thinking about life being over for her*).

EXERCISE 3–8
Correcting Cognitive Distortions

Purpose: To provide you with practice in recognizing and responding to cognitive distortions.

Time: 45 minutes; may be done in small groups of four to five students.

Procedure:
1. Using the definitions of cognitive distortions presented in the text, identify the type of cognitive distortion and the response you might make in each of the following situations:
   a. I shouldn't feel anxious about making this presentation in class.
   b. My wife never listens to me. If she really loved me, she would listen.
   c. I am boring and people don't like to talk to me.
   d. I shouldn't get upset when people don't approve of me.
   e. If I hadn't been raised in a dysfunctional family, I would be a different person.
   f. People should hire you because you can do the job, not because they like you or not.
   g. If I don't expect a situation to turn out well, it means that I won't be disappointed if it doesn't turn out the way I would like.
   h. If people really knew what I was like, they would never want to be my friend.
   i. Self-actualized people never make mistakes.
   j. If I don't get high grades, my family will think less of me.
   k. I can't experience true satisfaction unless I do things perfectly.

Discussion:
1. Which situations were hardest to develop answers for?
2. What were your thoughts and feelings in doing this exercise?
3. How do cognitive distortions affect behavior?
4. In what ways can you use this exercise to enhance your nursing practice and personal relationships?

Exercise 3–8 gives practice in recognizing and responding to cognitive distortions.

DEVELOPING A PREVENTION PLAN

A therapeutic intervention that combines self-talk strategies with social support forms the basis for a prevention plan designed to correct cognitive distortions. First, it is important to separate the person from the problem. This thinking process allows the client to step back and view the situation as an objective observer might, before beginning to resolve it. A certain amount of emotional distance is required to resolve difficult issues. When this condition is met, the client is able to develop and evaluate concrete strategies to cope with the issues. Even when the solutions chosen are appropriate and effective, however, the client may need to have ongoing support to implement them. Enlisting the help of others for support and advice gives rise to more effective problem solving.

CASE EXAMPLE

Johnnie's mother comes to the mental health clinic feeling depressed and feeling powerless. Johnnie brought home three interim reports indicating he is failing in school, skipping classes, and will most likely have to repeat tenth grade. As a single mother, it is all Johnnie's mother can do to make dinner and try to keep the household together on a very tight budget. She feels she is completely responsible for Johnnie's dilemma.

Some of the self-talk strategies the nurse might suggest to Johnnie's mother include:

1. Put boundaries on the situation.
   Cognitive distortion: "Johnnie is failing in school because I didn't help him with his homework." *Self-talk boundaries the mother can use:* "The homework is not the only reason Johnnie is failing." "Homework is Johnnie's responsibility, not mine." "I can help him get organized, but I can't do it for him."
   Once responsibilities are clarified, the homework issue remains a concern, but not the self-definition of the client as being responsible for Johnnie's failing performance.
2. Develop a plan to reinforce the idea that the problem is separate from the person. The plan should include:
   a. Assessing what the situation requires for resolution.
      Johnnie's mother schedules an appointment with Johnnie's teacher. She learns that Johnnie can't sit still long enough to grasp the material. He has particular difficulty with math, and he doesn't complete his homework. His mother now has a better idea of what exactly is needed.
   b. Identifying specific planned activities to resolve the problem.

Johnnie's mother shares the teacher's impression with Johnnie. She arranges for a professional evaluation to check for any organic components complicating Johnnie's educational progress. Together she and Johnnie specify a time when she can help him with his homework. Math tutoring may be necessary, so Johnnie's mother collects information about math tutors. A psychoeducational evaluation reveals an underlying attention deficit disorder.

c. Thinking of all the strategies a person can use to cope with stress.

Just because Johnnie's mother has made a plan doesn't mean that she can stop cognitively processing Johnnie's dilemma. *Self-talk* that encourages taking charge helps: "Worrying won't help anything." "Focus on what does help." "Taking one step at a time, I can handle this situation."

3. Get feedback and encouragement from other people.

a. Talking with friends, a pastor, or professionals helps to keep anxiety under control.

Feedback and social support are powerful antidotes to cognitive distortions about responsibility. Although a plan to correct cognitive distortions is easier to articulate than to implement, these guidelines have proved useful in helping people relinquish crooked thinking patterns and take constructive action.

Emotions

Emotions are an important part of personal identity. They clarify the nature of relationships as happy, sad, fearful, angry. For example, the person who is feeling angry and despondent because he has just lost a job and the person who is ecstatic because he has had a promotion are each expressing their self-consistent reactions to the relationship between self and the job. To the extent that a person, object, or situation has positive or negative value, there always is emotional involvement. Emotions color a person's perceptions and thinking processes through an additional filter of value-laden feelings.

Feeling awareness of self profoundly affects how we experience another person's humanity. Feelings allow people to experience compassion and sensitivity for another's experience even if they don't fully understand it. They also contribute to negative actions. Much of the brutality and inhumanity that occur in society relate to a suppression of feeling or strong negative feelings about the value of others.

Emotions are an inseparable part of all human experience. In nursing, emotions are an important part of the commitment to caring. Nursing actions performed with genuine feeling for a client are qualitatively different from those executed without feeling. A touch that communicates empathy for the client's situation differs from one that occurs without compassion. Conversations that value and respect the uniqueness of the client contrast markedly with halfhearted communications. The difference lies in the presence or absence of feeling for the client and/or one's work.

Almost without exception, feelings are significant pieces of information in the nurse–client relationship. Frequently it is the emotional sharing in the therapeutic relationship that stands out as most meaningful to both nurse and client. The emotional encounters are remembered with intensity, positively or negatively, long after the tangible nurse–client relationship has terminated.

Emotions as Social Responses

Expressions of feeling are influenced by culture as well as by the personal characteristics of the individual. They don't occur in a vacuum but in the form of a social response to a situation. To understand happiness, sadness, and anger one must also understand the situations and symbols that stimulate them (Kippax et al., 1988). How people handle emotions depends on the intensity of the experience stimulating the emotion, cultural norms, genetic temperament, and family constellation. Different cultures have express cognitive understandings about the meaning of sadness, shame, guilt, and the situations that should stimulate such feelings. In our culture, men until recently were socialized to repress feelings of emotional fragility. Exposing vulnerable feelings by crying or showing pain was not considered manly. Some cultures, such as Latin and Mediterranean cultures, permit free expression of emotions. Others, such as Oriental and British Isles cultures, restrict the use of spontaneous, openly expressed emotion.

Family rules in dysfunctional families often prevent members from understanding and accepting legitimate emotions. Unacceptable feelings are automatically replaced with absence of emotional expression or use of emotion in ways that protect the person from ridicule or punishment. They are very difficult to understand without knowledge of the family "script."

Interplay with Physical and Cognitive Processes

Although expression of emotion can occur verbally, it is more often and more truly communicated nonverbally through facial expression and behaviors such as smiling, laughing, frowning, striking out, and crying. Specific physiological changes in the body such as a quickening of the heartbeat, blushing, headache, muscle tension, or relaxation accompany the experience and expression of strong emotion. Thus, there is a close connection between physical and emotional expressions of personal identity.

Complexity of Emotions

Emotions can occur as simple expressions of a momentary feeling. They can also be so complicated that even the person experiencing the emotions is not fully aware of their existence or able to describe them. Persons may know *what* they feel but not why. A person may feel conflicting emotions simultaneously, about someone or something: outrage, fear, love, all at once. Nurses are an important resource in helping clients clarify their emotions and develop productive ways of expressing them.

Balanced Emotions

Healthy expression of feelings allows people to express who they are. People with a healthy emotional balance are able to let go of unhealthy feelings and search for ways to meet the new emotional demands of a situation.

In emotional maturity, emotions inform but do not dominate relationships. The person is able to feel the emotion, step back from it, and use it as a form of data without getting caught up in it. Likewise, a person may find it necessary to make a decision that causes painful emotions; the emotionally healthy person is able to make that decision and cope with the resulting emotions, for example, a decision to leave a destructive relationship. The emotionally healthy person does not deny the existence of emotions, even when they are irrational, but uses them as signals about life experiences in need of attention.

Properly harnessed, emotions provide energy to direct, motivate, and enrich life experiences. Careful expression of feelings can draw people closer as they strive to resolve difficult issues. Feelings energize relationships, inviting people to enter more deeply into a relationship or cautioning them to be wary of it. Emotionally healthy people generally have high self-esteem.

Unhealthy Emotional Expression

Feelings are dangerous only when they get out of control and serve to diminish the self or another person. Unresolved feelings tend to distance partners in a relationship because of emotional fears that needs will be misunderstood or remain unmet. Behavior usually suggests when something of an emotional nature is wrong, but if the reason for the behavior is not apparent, feelings have no chance of being met. "Unacceptable" feelings can be camouflaged by a calm, exterior demeanor or hidden behind a mask of superrationality. Strongly repressed feelings are expressed with an intensity that is significantly out of proportion to the situation.

CASE EXAMPLE

Joan is consistently late for shift report. She always has an excuse, and it always seems valid. Finally, after many weeks of starting report late because of Joan's tardiness, one of the nurses calls her on her behavior. Joan is astonished by the level of her colleague's anger and doesn't know how to respond. The nurse who brought the behavioral symptom to Joan's attention is surprised by the intensity of her own reaction, and although she meant everything she said, she is not pleased with how she confronted Joan. For both parties, it is an unpleasant experience that could have been avoided if the issues had been addressed when they first occurred.

When the receiver of a communication feels angry about a neutral message and there is no personal reason for having such a response, the receiver may be picking up strong hostile feelings the sender has little awareness of.

How Emotions Develop

People first learn about emotions from their families. They learn which emotions can be expressed in what interpersonal contexts and under what conditions. Emotional memories of subjectively significant events play an important role in self-esteem and in how people continue to express themselves emotionally as adults.

In dysfunctional families, children learn to internalize and mask legitimate feelings. Unacceptable feelings are unconsciously replaced with feelings of shame, unworthiness, or anger, which erupt unexpectedly whenever the person encounters a situation with similar elements. Unless the person is able to correct the emotionally distorted information about a situation and to accept, resolve, or discard that information as irrelevant, the feeling tones will continue to dominate human responses (Carr, 1984).

CASE EXAMPLE

A capable, intelligent young woman who developed and managed a successful small business had trouble seeing herself as competent. Her father had referred to her as "my dumb old girl" throughout childhood because she had trouble grasping math. She persisted in thinking she was not very bright with numbers well into adulthood, despite concrete evidence to the contrary in her successful business enterprise. The residue of unresolved feeling from her father's comment continued to color her self-image until she was able to regard the messages she received as a child as false.

Assessment Strategies

The emotions the nurse is most likely to encounter in health care settings include helplessness, frustration, hopelessness, powerlessness, anger, inadequacy, joy, anxiety, peacefulness, fearfulness, and apathy. In assessing the health of emotional self-concepts, the nurse considers several factors. Does the emotion fit the nature of the stimulus? Does it reflect a correct understanding of a situation or circumstances? When feelings do not match the

nature of the behavioral stimulus, e.g., too much, too little, contradictory, or unrelated, there may be an emotional block.

Does communication get blurred, or are tasks left unfinished for no known reason? For example, a client who refuses to take medication as instructed may be experiencing emotional barriers of anger or anxiety rather than a cognitive lack of understanding.

Do the emotions support the communicated message and match the body language of the participants? Emotions are important message carriers. Besides the actual verbal message, the sender and receiver steadily exchange emotionally laden nonverbal communication signals through facial expression, tone of voice, choice of words and gestures, emphasis, omissions, and timing of the communication.

The receiver of the message may hear only part of the message through an additional emotional filter that has little to do with the ongoing conversation. Feelings about the sender as well as about the content of the message influence how the message is received and interpreted. If the receiver feels threatened by the sender of the message or by the message itself, the receiver may read into the situation things that are not meant. The margin of distortion hides the true meaning of an experience to the client. Factors contributing to the margin of distortion in communication are presented in Figure 3–4. Exercise 3–9 helps develop skill in clarifying feelings.

CASE EXAMPLE

The nurse enters the client's room and says, "I need to draw some blood from you before we can start the chemotherapy." The client responds, "You only get one try at getting my blood." The client's comment may have little to do with the actual procedure. Most likely, the client is speaking from fear, or simply from a desire

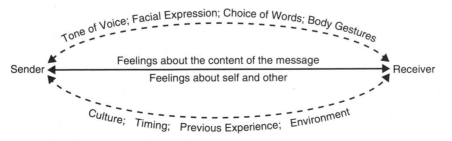

Figure 3–4 Affective Margin of Distortion in Communication

to have some control in a situation in which the client has very little control. If the nurse feels somewhat insecure about personal IV skills, the client's comment may trigger a defensive response. Even if the nurse is highly skilled, the client's remark will make it more difficult to draw the client's blood effectively. Instead of responding to the underlying concerns of the client, it is easy to turn the situation into a power struggle or inwardly to experience a loss of self-esteem. If the nurse can help the client identify the underlying fear, e.g., losing control or wondering if the staff really knows about chemotherapy or is competent to help the client, the interaction can be quite productive. Developing an appreciation for the emotional context and significance of a situation from the client's perspective is an important part of the nurse–client relationship.

PLANNING AND INTERVENTION

Feelings do not obey the rules of logic, so arguing the legitimacy of a feeling wastes time and energy. The presence of emotions needs no justification; feelings simply exist, in all people. However, acting on emotions is not always in the interest of the person experiencing the emotions. For example, it may be inappropriate to express anger to one's boss in the same way one might express anger to a friend.

Understanding that the language of emotion is telling you how the client is experiencing a life event or relationship is the key to giving a sensitive response. In highly charged emotional situations, for instance, the nurse frequently encounters angry,

---

EXERCISE 3–9
Clarifying Feelings

Purpose: To provide an opportunity to develop skill in recognizing underlying emotions and responding effectively to them.

Time: 45 minutes; break into small groups of three to five.

Procedure:
A class has been assigned a group project for which all participants will receive a common group grade. Each group consists of six students.
1. Identify two possible underlying feelings for each participant.
2. Develop a group understanding of the feelings and a response to each of the following situations. Consider the possible consequences of your intervention in each case.
   a. Don tells the group that he is working full time and will be unable to make any group meetings. There are so many class requirements that he also is not sure he can put much effort into the project, although he would like to help and the project interests him.
   b. Martha is very outspoken in group. She expresses her opinion about choice of the group project and is willing to make the necessary contacts. No one challenges her or suggests another project. At the next meeting, she informs the group that the project is all set up and she had made all the arrangements.
   c. Jackie is very quiet. She rarely says anything in group, and when she does it doesn't seem to get much response. Martha says, "Jackie, you are so quiet—don't you have anything to say?" to which Jackie replies, "Not at this time."
   d. Joan promises she will have her part of the project completed by a certain date. The date comes and Joan does not have her part completed.
   e. Mary agrees to edit the group project. She spends an entire weekend editing. When she presents her completed work to the group, they do not like how she has "altered their work." They don't feel it represents what they wanted to say.
   f. John feels like an outsider in the group. Every contribution he makes is challenged by Martha, or someone abruptly changes the subject. John is considered one of the weaker students in the class because English is his second language and he doesn't do well on objective written tests.

Discussion:
1. Identify common themes and difficulties in responding to emotional elements in a situation.
2. What would be the most appropriate response to each of these participants?
3. What are some actions the participants can take to move the group forward?
4. How can you use this exercise as a way of understanding and clarifying feelings in clinical work situations?

belligerent, out of control clients and families, and much of the emotion is projected onto the nurse or innocent family members. Armed with an understanding of the underlying feelings—intense fear, anguish about an anticipated loss, lack of power in an unfamiliar situation—the nurse provides the opening for the client to tell his or her story. The nurse might identify a legitimate feeling: "It must be frustrating to feel that your questions go unanswered," and then say, "How can I help you?" From a nonreactive position, the nurse can demonstrate caring about the client as a person by helping the client obtain the needed information and seeking validation of legitimate client concerns.

Clients caught up in the emotion of an event may need the nurse's permission to take a break. A simple comment from the nurse—"Why don't you go down to the cafeteria and get something to eat; we'll contact you immediately if your mother's condition changes"—gives the family needed respite from an overly intense emotional involvement. Recognizing escalating emotions before they get out of control and acknowledging their legitimacy helps relieve tension.

When setting limits on out of control behaviors, how the limit is presented is as important as the content of the message. In highly charged emotional situations, communication about limits can be expressed as clear, definite expectations (Lowe, 1992): "Mr. Smith, I can see that you are really upset about the doctor not being here. But your anger isn't helping your wife. Would you come with me, please, so that we can straighten this out." Expectations should be clear and not open to interpretation. In a qualitative research study, the categories that emerged as most important in defusing intense emotion included a calm, dispassionate approach, honesty, assessment of prodromal signs of escalating tension, the giving of opportunities for face-saving alternatives, positive reinforcement of appropriate emotional display, and use of touch (Gertz, 1980).

Spiritual Aspects of Personal Identity

Spiritual aspects of personal identity are sometimes spoken of as spiritual perspectives. Like other aspects of personal identity, they are intangible and are inferred from behaviors (Fig. 3–6). Hasse et al. (1992) define a spiritual perspective as "an integrating and creative energy based on belief

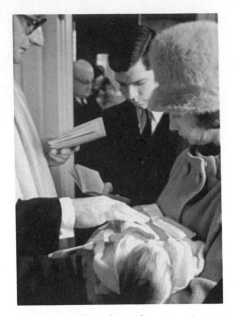

Figure 3–6 Spirituality plays a large part in personal identity

in, and a feeling of interconnectedness with, a power greater than self" (p. 143). This inner energy allows a person to consider possibilities one wouldn't ordinarily ponder. Even if one feels worthless, connections with a higher power can restore hope. Spirituality is also described as the "soul," or the core, of a person's humanness and basic self-integrity (Kinerk, 1985).

Fowler (1985) views spiritual perspectives as faith, "a patterned process or structure underlying and giving form to the contents of believing, valuing, knowing and committing" (p. 135). For other authors, spiritual self-concepts represent a worldview or self-transcendence (Hoschinko, 1993; Labun, 1988; Reed, 1991). Spiritual self-concepts help us answer vital questions about what is human, which human events have depth and value, and what are imaginative possibilities of being. Spiritual dimensions of self make significance possible and sustain a person's belief that he or she is worthy of respect as a human being. Although spiritual perspectives can occur within the framework of an organized religion, many deeply spiritual people do not embrace any organized religious group.

Having the courage and determination to do and say what one believes to be right rather than what is easy or currently fashionable are benchmarks for determining spiritual health. For the person with integrity, the goals or outcomes are important. The means by which the goals are achieved are equally significant. A person with integrity is motivated by a desire to create and to do things that matter to others as well as self. The language of the soul is found not only in words and actions but also in music, poetry, and art—mediums that stir our inner depths and create new and broader meanings in life.

Spirituality in Health Care

Tragedy and sorrow never leave us where they find us.
Perske, 1981

Suffering is a personal experience that summons a person to look more closely at unsettled questions of faith. The crisis of illness can be a time of spiritual renewal, when one discovers new inner resources, strengths, and capacities never before tested. Or it can be a time of spiritual desolation, leaving the individual feeling powerless to control or change important life circumstances.

Dugan (1987) describes spiritual pain as "a loss of one's sense of personal integrity, a fragmenting of one's sense of internal togetherness" (p. 27). The realization that there are some things beyond our control, some realities and circumstances that can leave us temporarily immobilized, perhaps never to be settled to our satisfaction, can be overwhelming. Since human spiritual nature touches on the innermost core of an individual, the depth of a spiritual need is not always readily observable either to the nurse or to the client. Unlike physical pain, spiritual pain can only be inferred from the client's behavior and what the client is willing to share verbally.

Spiritual well-being and being able to see the purpose and meaning of one's life are particularly important concepts when one is ready to leave this life. If the nurse can assist a client to find a connectedness with the meaning of his or her life in a larger cosmic process, the client can find healing and acceptance (Levine, 1987).

From the nurse's perspective, self-integrity through action embodies "the ultimate virtues of life in the form of hope, courage, faith, honor, love, acceptance, and meaningful encounter with death" (Arnold, 1989). Centering nursing practice on the development of these qualities strengthens the quality of care in the nurse–client relationship through commitment to personal integrity and high ethical standards.

How Faith Develops

Fowler's (1985) stages of faith development parallel those of Piaget, Erikson, and Kohlberg in that they emerge from a simple, global understanding to increasingly more complex self-understandings of faith. Described in progressive stages of development, people experience a growing self-awareness of faith beginning with the uncritical acceptance of the parent/family values (intuitive-projective faith). As the child develops a stronger sense of self, moral rules and attitudes are assigned to behaviors (mythic-literal faith). Rules are taken literally at first. But as the child's world and sense of self begins to expand, faith becomes increasingly more complex (synthetic-conventional faith). The next stage of faith development, the individuating-reflective stage, takes place in late adolescence. There is a qualitative shift in belief, with the individual realizing that he or she must take personal responsibility for choosing commitments to a certain lifestyle and set of beliefs. In the adult stages of spiritual development (paradoxical-consolidative faith), the person is able to recognize the integrity and truth of others as well as of self, although this may be a threatening prospect. Fowler's highest stage of faith development is reached by relatively few people. Fowler suggests that people who achieve this stage are able to "instinctively know how to relate to us affirmingly, never condescendingly, yet with pricks to our pretense and with genuine bread of life" (p. 141).

Like other aspects of personal development, people are an important source of learning: teachers, role models, and even momentary encounters with people who spark meanings for us. Life events also provide a stimulus to spiritual growth (Newman, 1989).

In coming to the conclusion that a person is a part of a larger scheme, disturbing questions of faith arise. Is there something or someone beyond ourselves that represents a deeper truth? Is it understandable? How then does one account for all of the evil that occurs or the misfortunes that beset innocent victims or the randomness with which catastrophe seems to strike some people and not others? There are no easy answers to these questions. Perhaps the mystery of life is that one can only live it successfully with faith. As people grow in faith, the presence of a higher power generally becomes a matter of knowledge and experience as well as of feeling.

Assessment Strategies

Spiritual distress can occur in the form of pain experienced through loss; separation from a faith community; or treatments that create spiritual anxiety, guilt, anger, or despair. Carson (1989) refers to four areas of spiritual concern as a framework for assessment:

- A person's personal concept of God.
- Personal sources of energy and hope.
- The relevance of specific religious practices to the individual.
- Areas of spiritual concern activated by the illness.

ASSESSING A PERSON'S PERSONAL CONCEPT OF GOD

The client's personal concept of God and spiritual needs may be quite obvious and initially responsive to clergy and pastoral counselors and to readings. The nurse notes the client's comments about God, a higher power, or "the man upstairs." Often, however, the spiritual needs of the client are ambivalent, cloaked in feelings of anger and disappointment toward a God who let this happen. For example, a lack of faith in the value of humanity may represent a need to find a spiritual meaning for life. Other clients may express the need in the form of anger. C. S. Lewis (1976), the noted author of traditionally spiritual books, calls his God "the cosmic sadist" as he experiences his personal grief following the death of his wife. Yet few would doubt the depth of his spirituality.

PERSONAL SOURCES OF HOPE

Spirituality evidences itself in the form of hope. Hope energizes a person to take steps that increase competency, peace, and self-transcendence (Hasse et al., 1992). Hope enables people to seek new alternatives for achieving positive future goals. Quite distinct from the optimism surrounding magical thinking, which may or may not be based

in truth, hope as a spiritual resource is grounded in reality (Progoff, 1985).

It is well known that hope is critical in maintaining the spirit of a person in health care settings (Miller, 1989). How else can one explain the will to live or the complete serenity of some individuals in the face of life's most adverse circumstances? Jourard (1964) suggests that "it is probably the spirit-response which is mobilized by any event that signifies hope or confidence in self or in the future; it is probably the spirit-response which, when weakened, permits illness to flourish." Societal sources of hope may be found in organized religions, in self-help books, in support groups, and in poetry and music. The nurse might ask the client, "What do you see as your primary sources of strength at the present time?" and, "In the past, what have been sources of strength for you in difficult times?" as ways of focusing attention on sources of hope and energy in the current situation.

CURRENT SPIRITUAL PRACTICES

When assessing the current spiritual preferences of the client, the nurse also needs to consider past religious affiliations. It is not unusual for the religion listed on the client's chart to be quite different from the religious practices the client actually follows. Cultural orientation and practices influence not only beliefs but the way they are expressed. Questions the nurse might ask during the nursing assessment interview are:

- Are there special spiritual practices that are particularly important to you now?
- Would it be helpful for me to arrange a visit from the hospital chaplain or your pastor? (There should be client data to warrant this question.)

AREAS OF SPIRITUAL CONCERN

The nurse also explores areas of special concern the client has expressed. Inquiring about religious rituals important to the client can be very helpful. Baptisms, last rites, and ethnic practices in preparing the body can occur within the hospital setting and can provide peace for a client experiencing spiritual and emotional pain.

CASE EXAMPLE

Nurse: Mr. Johns, I was wondering about something you told me earlier. You said you just started going to mass again. What brought about this change?

Client: To tell you the truth, fear pushed me back to the Church. When I first discovered I had this heart condition, I was so afraid I would die that I started to pray again.

Nurse: You started praying again? What made you stop?

Client: Several years ago, when my wife died, I found myself so angry at God that I didn't want to talk to Him. Now I find that I need Him again.

Nurse: So you returned to the Church out of fear? Has going to mass helped you?

Client: Yes indeed! I went back out of fear, but now I have a sense of peace. Even though the thought of the bypass surgery is frightening, I know that God is with me (Carson, 1989).*

Planning and Intervention

Carson (1989) suggests that the compassionate presence of the nurse in the nurse–client relationship is the most important tool the nurse uses in helping clients reinforce and confirm their spiritual self-concepts. From the moment the client enters the hospital, orientation to available religious services should be an essential component of the relationship. It is important, however, for the nurse to be aware of his or her own spiritual beliefs and not impose them on the client. This can be particularly tempting in times of crisis or when death seems imminent. Client autonomy requires that the client give the nurse permission for the pastoral counselor or clergy to visit.

Caring, information, prayers, and the thousand countless measures one human being takes for another simply to make the person more comfortable have a spiritual dimension in which healing can occur, even if it is only of the spirit. Praying with a client, even when the client is of a different faith, can be soothing. If the client professes no faith, the nurse can help the client identify actions that bring peace and meaning in times of stress. Exercise 3–10 helps in understanding spiritual responses to distress.

---

*From Carson, V (1989). Spiritual Dimensions in Nursing Practice. Philadelphia, W. B. Saunders, p. 156. Used with permission.

EXERCISE 3–10
Responding to Issues of Spiritual Distress

Purpose: To help you understand responses in times of spiritual distress.

Time: 45 minutes

Procedure:
Review the case situations below and develop an appropriate response to each.
1. Mary Trachter is unmarried and has just found out she is pregnant. She belongs to a fundamentalist church in which sex before marriage is not permitted. Mary feels guilty about her current status and sees it as "God is punishing me for fooling around."
2. Bert Smith, who is 18 years old, has been admitted to a psychiatric unit for conduct disorder. He tells you he is an atheist. His parents are strongly religious and believe he should be exorcised to get rid of the demons responsible for his delinquent behavior.
3. Linda Carter is married to an abusive, alcoholic husband. Linda reads the Bible daily and prays for her husband's redemption. She feels that God will turn the marriage around if she continues to pray for changes in her husband's attitude. "My trust is in the Lord," she says.
4. Bill Compton tells the nurse, "I feel that God has let me down. I was taught that if I was unfaithful to God, He would be there for me. Now the doctors tell me I'm going to die. That doesn't seem fair to me."

Discussion:
1. Share your answers with others in your group.
2. Give and get feedback on the usefulness of your responses.
3. Identify common themes.
4. In what ways can you use this new knowledge in your nursing care?

DEVELOPING THE NEXT STEP

Long-term goals are not always the primary focus in promoting, maintaining, or restoring spiritual health. Only the "next step" is important. Breaking down potentially overwhelming problems into manageable steps makes the problem seem workable and stimulates hope. The hopeful person also trusts in a transcendent source to show itself in the form of suggestion and direction about the next step. The answers may come from a personal encounter in the current or near-present environment, leading to other possibilities for personal growth and meaning.

SOCIAL SUPPORT

Social support can have a spiritual as well as an emotional and social effect on a client. Usually other people in the immediate situation play a critical role in the stimulation of hope through their encouragement and practical suggestions, and sometimes simply through their presence during a stressful time. Carson (1989) offers the following example of a caring intervention with a 16-year-old athlete with a bilateral amputation.

CASE EXAMPLE

One morning after shift report, Mrs. Johnson walked into Robert's room and found him crying. Her first response was to leave the room as she thought, "I can't handle this today." But she was able to stop herself and she went over to Robert and touched his shoulder. He continued to sob and said, "What am I going to do? I wish I were dead. My whole life is sports. I would have qualified for an athletic scholarship if this hadn't happened. I feel like my life is over at sixteen."

Mrs. Johnson recognized the feelings of despair that Robert was expressing and said to him, "It doesn't seem like life has any meaning at all. You are feeling that this is such an unfair thing to have happened to you. I agree with you, it is, but let's talk about it. We can't change what has happened, but maybe we can start to look at where to go from here. (Carson, 1989, p. 167)

To appreciate the influence of social support in reinforcing hope, consider encounters in your life that left you feeling refreshed, validated, or even transformed, and do Exercise 3–11. Most probably your encounters consisted of experiences with people who demonstrated their caring through their presence and willingness to be with you and listen to you when your self-value was low.

EVALUATION

Client outcomes suggestive of resolution of spiritual distress include reconnection with a higher

---

EXERCISE 3–11
Social Support

Purpose: To help you understand the role of social support in significant encounters.

Time: 45 minutes

Procedure:
1. Describe a "special" situation that had deep meaning for you.
2. Identify the person or people who helped make the situation meaningful for you.
3. Describe the actions taken by the people or person identified in (2) that made the situation memorable.

Discussion:
1. What common themes emerged from student descriptions of special situations?
2. What did you learn about yourself from doing this exercise?
3. What do you see as the role of social support in making memories?
4. How might you use this information in your practice?

---

power, decreased guilt, forgiveness of others, expressions of hope, and evidence that the client finds meaning in his or her current situation.

Self-Esteem

Self-esteem is not the same as self-concept, but it is intimately related to it (Hamachek, 1985). It refers to the value and significance people place on their self-concepts. It is an emotional process of self-judgment, an orientation to the self, ranging on a continuum from feelings of self-efficacy and respect to a feeling of being fatally flawed as a person (Branden, 1983).

Self-esteem is subjective. It develops from individuals' perceptions of their personal being and achievements, particularly in interpersonal relations. It is possible to have many objective achievements and to have low self-esteem. People with few achievements but with the knowledge that they have conducted themselves as well as possible can have high self-esteem. Although self-esteem can be reinforced by confirming relationships, the inner worth of a person can be experienced only by that person.

Self-esteem reflects a delicate balance between fitting into a larger social community and retaining the support and affirmation of others for being unique. Wanting the approval of others at the expense of personal integrity decreases self-respect, which in turn affects the admiration of others and leads to social alienation.

A relationship exists between self-esteem and level of psychological adaptation. People who value themselves become freer to know and to cherish the intrinsic value of others. Energy is not wasted on self-defensive behavior. People with high self-esteem have a strong emotional as well as intellectual conviction that they are worthy of respect and recognition, with something unique and useful to offer to society. When individuals do not feel as though there is much value to who they are as human beings or what they are able to contribute to others, they experience low self-esteem. Box 3–2 identifies characteristic behaviors related to self-esteem.

Self-esteem is not a fixed concept. It fluctuates whenever the self-concept is challenged by life transitions or crises, illnesses, or changes in status or role. Turning points of self-meaning related to developmental, situational, relational, and spiritual circumstances affect self-esteem. Sources of low self-esteem include loss of a job; loss of an important relationship; change in appearance, role, or status; and criticism by significant others. Suicide victims, convinced that their lives or presence on earth are of no value to anyone, represent perhaps the most graphic illustration of poor self-esteem.

Perceptions of the opinions and feelings of significant others have a profound effect on self-esteem. (Branden, 1983; Crouch and Staub, 1983; (Schlenker, 1985). Contrast, for example, a social situation in which you are considered an authority or a prized guest with one in which you clearly are on a different social level and have less life experience or fewer credentials than most of the other people present. Most probably there was a significant difference in the value you felt you had in each of these situations. If people feel valued by others, they begin to experience themselves as being worthy. Criticism, disconfirming comments, and devaluing by others through insensitive actions usually have the opposite effect.

Self-Esteem in Health Care

Epstein (1973) suggests that a sudden decrease in self-esteem is experienced as a greater loss than a more gradual decline. In most chronic or major illnesses, there is a lowering of self-esteem because the individual is no longer able to function as before in ways that inspired higher levels of self-esteem. In many cases, neither is there any real reason to believe there will be a return to normal activities or a positive change in functioning. Yet high levels of self esteem can accompany even the most debilitating illness if the client is given enough social support.

BOX 3–2
Self-Esteem Characteristics

People with High Self-Esteem	*People with Low Self-Esteem*
Expect people to value them.	Expect people to be critical of them.
Are active self-agents.	Are passive or obstructive self-agents.
Have positive perceptions of their skills, appearance, sexuality, and behaviors.	Have negative perceptions of their skills, appearance, sexuality, and behaviors.
Perform equally well when being observed as when not watched.	Perform less well when being observed.
Are nondefensive and assertive in response to criticism.	Are defensive and passive in response to criticism.
Can accept compliments easily.	Have difficulty accepting compliments.
Evaluate their performance realistically.	Have unrealistic expectations about their performance.
Are relatively comfortable relating to authority figures.	Are uncomfortable relating to authority figures.
Express general satisfaction with life.	Are dissatisfied with their lot in life.
Have a strong social support system.	Have a weak social support system.
Have a primary internal locus of control.	Rely on an external locus of control.

When illness occurs, at least two outcomes are possible. The client may become emotionally immobilized by the threat to self-identity that a symptom imposes, and loss of self-esteem results. Or the client may feel challenged by the illness to develop new coping skills, and there is an increase in self-esteem. The nurse in providing support and confirmation of the client's efforts plays an important role in a client's decisions and subsequent actions.

Assessment Strategies

Assessment of self-esteem tends to be observational. The nurse notes what clients say about themselves. Does the client devalue accomplishments, project blame for problems on others, minimize personal failures, or make self-deprecating remarks? "Oh, it was nothing really," or, "I don't want to be a burden to my children" are statements indicating low self-worth. Other data include: Does the client express shame or guilt? Does the client seem hesitant to try new things or situations or express concern about ability to cope with events? Lack of culturally appropriate eye contact, poor hygiene, self-destructive behaviors, hypersensitivity to criticism, need for constant reassurance, and an inability to accept compliments are behaviors associated with low self-esteem.

Planning and Intervention

When people have low self-esteem, they feel they have little worth and that no one really cares enough to bother with them. The nurse helps clients increase self-esteem by being psychologically present as a sounding board. Just the process of engaging with another human being who offers a different perspective can have a real effect in enhancing self-esteem. The implicit message the nurse conveys with personal presence and interest, information, and a guided exploration of the problem is twofold. First is confirmation of the client: "You are important and I will stay with you through this uncomfortable period." Second is the introduction of the possibility of hope: "There may be some alternatives you haven't thought of that can help you cope with this problem in a meaningful way." Once a person starts to take charge of his or her life, a higher level of well-being can result.

Self-esteem affects the ability to weather stress without major changes in self-perception. With a positive attitude about self, an individual is more likely to view life as a glass half full rather than half empty. There are several strategies the nurse can use to help a client experience deeper levels of self-esteem. Modeling is very effective. The nurse can convey a positive self-image, which is contagious.

The nurse's questions can be deliberately designed to assist clients in reflecting on their strengths and accomplishments. The nurse can ask, "Can you tell me the achievement you are most proud of?" or, "Can you tell me some things you like about yourself?" The nurse can give the client positive feedback: "The thing that impresses me about you is . . ." or, "What I notice is that although your body is so much weaker, it seems as if your spirit is stronger. Is that your experience as well?" Such questions help the client focus on positive strengths. Exercise 3–12 strengthens the nurse's skill in this area.

When the nurse helps the client to make independent judgments about health care, the process strengthens the client's self-esteem. The act of taking charge and choosing among alternatives indirectly suggests that the client can cope with difficult problems. Communication combined with compassionate health care information and actions confirms the value of a person as worthwhile. This strategy is appropriate even with clients who are dying. For example, the nurse can encourage clients to plan their funeral services or to get in touch with people important to them but currently not in their life.

Evaluation

Self-esteem behaviors are evaluated by comparing the number of positive self statements with those originally observed. Behaviors suggestive of enhanced self-esteem include:

- Taking an active role in planning and implementing self-care.
- Verbalizing personal psychosocial strengths.
- Expressing feelings of satisfaction with self and ways of handling life.

Self-Awareness

Self-awareness is the means by which a person gains knowledge and understanding of all aspects of self-

EXERCISE 3–12
Positive Affirmations: Contributions to Self-Esteem

Purpose: To help you experience the effects of interpersonal comments on self-esteem.

Directions:

1. This exercise may be done in a group or used as a homework assignment and later discussed in class.
2. List a positive affirming comment you received recently . . . something someone did or said that made you feel good about yourself.

_____

_____

_____

3. List a disconfirming comment you received recently . . . something someone did or said that made you feel bad about yourself.

_____

_____

_____

4. What have you done recently that you feel helped enhance someone else's self-esteem?

_____

_____

_____

5. In class, write phrases on a chalk board that capture the essence of the positive affirming comment.
6. Do the same for the negative disconfirming comment.

Discussion:

1. In general, what kinds of actions help enhance self-esteem?
2. What are some things people do or fail to do that diminish self-esteem?
3. What are some specific things you might be able to do in a clinical setting that might help a client develop a sense of self-worth?
4. What did you learn about yourself from doing this exercise?

concept. An interpersonal approach focusing on human responses in the client and nurse is quite different from one approaching self-understanding from a behavioristic or psychoanalytic perspective. In professional relationships with clients and colleagues, the nurse engages with other human beings from a position in which all that a person is capable of being becomes stretched to the utmost.

The nurse's self-concept in the nurse–client relationship is as important as the client's. Nurses who are comfortable with themselves can help clients use a similar process of self-reflection in understanding themselves. Creating an interpersonal environment that heals—one that permeates the human senses as well as meets daily needs—is possible only if self-awareness skills are built into the communication process (Rawlinson, 1990).

Self-awareness provides an inner frame of reference for connecting emotionally with the experience of another. Self-awareness occurs through the mechanism of *intrapersonal communication,* defined as communication taking place within the self, in contrast to *interpersonal communication,* which takes place between people. The two concepts are very much interwoven in most interpersonal relationships. Carl Rogers poses ten questions nurses should ask themselves as they enter into therapeutic relationships with their clients (Box 3–3). Through understanding themselves, nurses can better understand others.

BOX 3–3
Questions to Encourage Self-Awareness
in the Nurse–Client Relationship

1. Can I *be* in some way which will be perceived by the other person as trustworthy, dependable, or consistent in some deep sense?
2. Can I be expressive enough as a person that what I am will be communicated unambiguously?
3. Can I let myself experience positive attitudes toward this other person—attitudes of warmth, caring, liking, interest, respect?
4. Can I be strong enough as a person to be separate from the other?
5. Am I secure enough within myself to permit him his separateness?
6. Can I let myself enter fully into the world of his feelings and personal meanings and see these as he does?
7. Can I receive him as he is? Can I communicate this attitude?
8. Can I act with sufficient sensitivity in the relationship that my behavior will not be perceived as a threat?
9. Can I free him from the threat of external evaluation?
10. Can I meet this other individual as a person who is in the process of *becoming,* or will I be bound by his past and by my past?

From Rogers CR (1958). The characteristics of the helping relationship. Personnel and Guidance Journal 37(1).

Nurses can connect with the client's inner self more easily by understanding similar feelings within themselves. For example, a nurse looking at a client's photograph may experience certain images. Sharing these images with the client helps bridge the gap between their two perceptual worlds. The same is true of feelings. By identifying his or her own inner feelings of fear, sadness, anger, or joy, the nurse can appreciate their presence within the client even though the specific context for the behavioral stimulus is quite different. Through shared emotions, thoughts, and situations the nurse encounters and affirms the inner dignity of each human being in an interpersonal atmosphere marked with acceptance, authenticity, empathy, and a nonjudgmental attitude (Rogers, 1959).

Self-awareness provides an external structure for inquiring into and interpreting important behavioral inferences related to illness. Throughout the therapeutic relationship the questions, "How is this illness affecting the client?" "What is the meaning of the treatment process for this client?" frame the interpersonal experience. Describing the meaning of an illness and one's human responses to it is an interpersonal process that relies heavily on the client as a self-interpreting being. Within the jumbled chaotic events of life, the nurse and client begin to discover the threads of meaning that will restore the self-concept and the personalized meaning of the client's life.

Self-Reflection

Nurses learn about themselves through self-reflection and the feedback of others. *Self-reflection* is a mental process by which we are able consciously to examine the meaning of our motives and actions. It is a mental faculty available only to humans. Leary and Miller (1986) argue that "without the ability to think consciously about ourselves, we could not contemplate alternative courses of action, or consider the impact of our behaviors on other people. We would be unable to ponder the meaning of our actions and lives, systematically plan for the future, or purposefully attempt to better our lives." Taking time alone to explore and to discover what is happening or has happened in human relationships puts the pain and human suffering a nurse encounters on a daily basis into better perspective.

Self-reflection increases the nurse's capacity to be genuine. Knowing personal motivations, predjudices, strengths, and limitations helps nurses connect with clients in a straightforward manner. Self-awareness helps the nurse avoid using the therapeutic interpersonal relationship with clients to meet personal rather than client needs. Consider, for example, the nurse who strongly believes that breast-feeding is more beneficial than bottle-feeding. Without self-awareness, the nurse may unconsciously project her personal values about breast-feeding on a teenage mother who has no desire to breast-feed her infant.

Role Modeling

To be a role model for clients in a professional relationship, nurses need first to recognize their own needs and find ways to meet them in their personal lives. It is difficult for nurses to be considerate and sensitive to the needs of others if they are unable to be gentle and understanding of similar needs within themselves. If nurses cannot see themselves as worthy of being cared for, it is difficult to convince others of their worth. It is difficult to role model self-respect or to give to others from a barren stockpile.

Becoming Centered

The basic goal of any constructive relationship is to help the participants enlarge self-knowledge and enhance their potential by integrating disowned, neglected, unrecognized, or unrealized parts of the self into the personality. This process is referred to as being centered. Expected outcomes include:

- Enhanced self-respect.
- Increased resourcefulness and sense of what the person can do.
- Greater productivity.
- Increased personal satisfaction.

Attainment of these goals is impossible without a personal experiential knowledge of the self-concept and its effect on the development and maintenance of relationships.

SUMMARY

Self-concept is a major nursing diagnosis that involves four components: body image, personal identity, self-esteem, and role performance. Body image alterations encompass loss of function and control as well as physical changes. Included in personal identity are the psychospiritual, cognitive, emotional, and perceptual dimensions of self-concept. Erikson's model of psychosocial development is the framework used to assess client attainment of normal psychosocial tasks.

Self-concept influences communication through perceptual and cognitive processes such as selective attention and self-fulfilling prophecies. Emotional tagging of images affects how a person interacts with others in social situations. Spiritual self-concepts add meaning. Self-esteem, described as the emotional valuing of the self-concept, stems from perceptual images viewed by the person as good or bad assessments of self. A healthy self-concept results in behaviors reflective of satisfaction with body image, a realistic relationship between actual

and ideal self, high self-esteem, general satisfaction with role performance, and a distinct sense of identity and spiritual well-being. Strategies to enhance the development of a positive self-concept and psychospiritual well-being result in higher self-esteem.

REFERENCES

Ackerman D (1990). A Natural History of the Senses. New York, Random House.

Adler R, Rodman L (1988). Understanding Human Communication. (3rd ed.). New York, Holt, Rinehart and Winston.

Adler R, Rosenfal L, Towne N (1986). Interplay: The Process of Interpersonal Communication (3rd ed.). New York, Holt, Rinehart and Winston.

Arnold E (1989). Burnout as a spiritual issue. *In* Carson V (ed.) (1989), Spiritual Dimensions of Nursing Practice. Philadelphia, W. B. Saunders.

Bellah R, Madsen R, Sullivan W, Swidler A, Tipton M (1985). Habits of the Heart. New York, Harper & Row.

Benner P (1984). From Novice to Expert: Excellence and Power in Clinical Nursing Practice. Menlo Park, CA, Addison-Wesley.

Benner P, Wrubel J (1989). The Primacy of Caring: Stress and Coping in Health and Illness. Menlo Park, CA, Addison-Wesley.

Branden, N (1983). Honoring the Self. New York, Bantam Books.

Brookfield (1986). Understanding and Facilitating Adult Learning. San Francisco, Jossey Bass.

Cairns RB, Cairns BD (1988). The sociogenesis of self-concepts. *In* Bolger N, Caspi A, Downey G, Moorehouse M (eds.) (1988), Persons in Context: Developmental Processes. Cambridge, MA, Cambridge University Press.

Carr J (1984). Communicating and Relating. Dubuque, IA, William C. Brown.

Carson, V (1989). Spiritual Dimensions in Nursing Practice. Philadelphia, W. B. Saunders.

Coombs A (1962). Perceiving, Behaving, Becoming. Washington, DC, Association for Supervision and Curriculum Development.

Coombs A, Avila D, Purkey W (eds.) (1980). Helping Relationsips. Boston, Allyn & Bacon.

Covey S (1989). The 7 Habits of Highly Effective People. New York, Simon & Schuster.

Cross S, Markus H (1991). Possible selves across the life span. Human Development 34:230–255.

Crouch M, Staub M (1983). Enhancement of self-esteem in adults. Family and Community Health 2:65.

Damon W, Hart D (1988). Self Understanding in Childhood and Adolescence. Cambridge, MA, Cambridge University Press.

Dell P (1982). Beyond homeostasis: Toward a concept of coherence. Family Process 21:21–41.

Dempsey M (1972). Development of body image in the adolescent. Nursing Clinics of North America 7:609.

Dowd J (1990). Ever since Durkheim: The socialization of human development. Human Development 33:138–159.

Dugan D (1987). Death and dying: Emotional, spiritual and ethical support for patients and families. Journal of Psychosocial Nursing 25(7):21–29.

Epstein S (1973). The self-concept revisited: Or a theory of a theory. American Psychologist 5:414.

Erikson E (1959). Identity and the life cycle. Psychological Issues 1(1): New York, International Universities Press.

Erikson E (1963). Childhood and Society (2nd ed.). New York, Norton.

Erikson E (1964). Insight and Responsibility. New York, Norton.

Erikson E (1968). Identity: Youth and Crisis. New York, Norton.

Erikson E (1982). The Life Cycle Completed: A Review. New York, Norton.

Erikson E, Erikson J (1981). On generativity and identity: From a conversation with Erik and Joan Erikson. Harvard Educational Review 51:251.

Felker D (1974) Building Positive Self-Concepts. Minneapolis, Burgess.

Ferrucci P (1982). What We May Be: Techniques for Psychological and Spiritual Growth through Psychosynthesis. Los Angeles, JP Tarcher, p. 61.

Fowler J (1985). Stages of faith development. In Gorman M (ed.) (1985), Psychology and Religion. New York, Paulist Press; London, Farber & Farber, 1980.

Geary P, Hawkins J (1992). The ritual of healing. Health Care Trends and Transition 3(3):8–11.

Gertz B (1980). Training for prevention of assaultive behavior in a psychiatric setting. Hospital and Community Psychiatry 31:628–630.

Grassi J (1986). Changing the World Within. Mahwah, NJ, Paulist Press.

Hamachek D (1985). The self's development and ego growth: Conceptual analysis and implications for counselors. Journal of Counseling and Development 64:136–42.

Harre R (1987). The social construction of selves. In K. Yardley and T. Honess (eds.) (1987), Self and Identity: Psychosocial Perspectives. Chichester, U.K., Wiley.

Hasse J, Britt T, Coward D, Leidy NK, Penn P (1992). Simultaneous concept analysis of spiritual perspective, hope, acceptance and self-transcendence. Image 24(2):140–147.

Heinrich RL, Schag CC (1985). Stress and activity management: Group treatment for cancer patients and spouses. Journal of Consulting and Counseling Psychology 53:439–446.

Hoare C (1991). Psychosocial identity development and cultural others. Journal of Counseling and Development 70(1):45–53.

Holmes TH, Rahe RH (1967). The social readjustment rating scale. Journal of Psychosomatic Research 11:213–218.

Hormuth S (1991). An ecological perspective on the self-concept. In R Curtis (ed.) (1991), The Relational Self. New York, Guilford Press, pp. 94–108.

Hoshinko B (1993). Worldview as a model of spirituality. First Annual Conference on Spirituality. University of Maryland School of Nursing, Baltimore, May 7, 1993.

James W (1891). The Principles of Psychology. New York, Henry Holt.

Jourard S (1964). The Transparent Self. New York, Van Norstrand Reinhold.

Kinerk E (1985). Toward a method for the study of spirituality. In Gorman M (ed.) (1985), Psychology and Religion. New York, Paulist Press.

Kippax S, Crawford J, Benton P, Gault U, Noesjirwan J (1988). Contructing emotions: Weaving meaning from memories. British Journal of Social Psychology 27:19–33.

Koehler (1989). The relationship between self concept and successful rehabilitation. Rehabilitation Nursing 14(1):9–12.

Krueger D (1989). Body Self and Psychological Self: A Developmental and Clinical Integration of Disorders of the Self. New York, Brunner/Mazel.

Labun E (1988). Spiritual care: An element in nursing care planning. Journal of Advanced Nursing 13:314–320.

Lear M (1980). Heartsounds. New York: Simon & Schuster.

Leary M, Miller K (1986). Social Psychology and Dysfunctional Behavior. New York, Springer.

Levine S (1987). Healing into Life and Death. Garden City, NY, Anchor Press.

Lewis CS (1976). A Grief Observed. New York, Bantam Books.

Logan RD (1986). A reconceptualization of Erikson's theory. Human Development 29:125–136.

Lowe T (1992). Characteristics of effective nursing interventions in the management of challenging behavior. Journal of Advanced Nursing 17:1226–1232.

Markus H, Nurius P (1986). Possible selves. American Psychologist 954–969.

Markus H, Wurf E (1987). The dynamic self-concept: A social psychological perspective. Annual Review of Psychology 38:299–337.

Mead GH (1934). Mind, Self and Society. Chicago, University of Chicago Press.

Miller E (1986). Self Imagery: Creating Your Own Good Health. Berkeley, CA, Celestial Arts.

Miller J (1989). Hope-inspiring strategies of the critically ill. Applied Nursing Research 2:23–29.

Newman M (1989). The spirit of nursing. Holistic Nursing Practice 3:1–6.

North American Nursing Diagnosis Association (NANDA) (1986). Classification of Nursing Diagnoses: Proceedings of the Sixth Conference. St. Louis, Mosby.

Oerter R (1986). Development tasks through the life-span: A new approach to an old concept. In Featherman DL, Lerner RM (eds.) (1986), Life-span Development and Behavior, Vol. 7. San Diego, Academic Press.

Oliver J (1988). Client characteristics as determinants of intervention modality and therapy progress. American Journal of Orthopsychiatry 58:543–551.

Perske R (1981). Hope for Families: New Directions for Parents with Persons with Retardation and other Disabilities. Nashville, Abingdon Press.

Progoff I (1985). The Dynamics of Hope. New York, Dialogue House Library.

Radley A (1988). The social form of feeling. British Journal of Social Psychology 27:5–18.

Rawlinson J (1990). Self-awareness: Conceptual influences, contributions to nursing, and approaches to attainment. Nurse Education Today 10:111–117.

Reed P (1991). Spirituality and mental health in older adults: Extant knowledge in nursing. Family and Community Health 14(2):14–25.

Rogers C (1959). The essence of psychotherapy: A client centered view. Annals of Psychotherapy 1:51.

Rogoff B (1990). Apprenticeship in Thinking: Cognitive Development in Social Context. New York, Oxford.

Satir, V (1976). Conjoint Family Therapy. Palo Alto, CA, Science and Behavior.

Schlenker B (1985). Identity and self identification. In Schlenker B (ed.) (1985), The Self and Social Life. New York, McGraw-Hill.

Schontz F (1974). Body image and its disorders. International Journal of Psychiatric Medicine 5:464.

Segal Z (1988). Appraisal of self-schema construct in cognitive models of depression. Psychological Bulletin 103(2):147–162.

Snyder M (1984). When belief creates reality. In Berkowitz L (ed.) (1984), Advances in Experimental Social Psychology. San Diego, Academic Press.

Swann WB (1982). When our identities are mistaken: Reaffirming self-conceptions through social interaction. Journal of Social Psychology 43:59.

Sutherland J (1993). The autonomous self. Bulletin of the Menninger Clinic 57(1):4–23.

Travelbee J (1971). Interpersonal Aspects of Nursing. Philadelphia, Davis.

Turnes A (1993). Unpublished student journal, University of Maryland School of Nursing.

Westen D (1991). Cultural, emotional and unconscious aspects of self. In Curtis R (ed.) (1991), The Relational Self. New York, Guilford Press.

Whitbourne SK (1985). The psychological construction of the life span. In Birren JE, Scid KW (eds.) (1985), Handbook of the Psychiatry of Aging. New York, Van Nostrand Reinhold.

SUGGESTED READINGS

Antonucci TC, and Jackson JS (1983). Physical health and self-esteem. Family and Community Health 6(2):1–9.

Archibald J, Ulman M (1983). Is it really senility—or just depression? RN 46:49.

Averill JR (1980). A constructivist view of emotion. In Plutchik R, Kellerman H (eds.) (1980), Theories of Emotion. San Diego, Academic Press.

Branden N (1976). The Psychology of Self-Esteem. New York, Bantam Books.

Carper B (1978). Fundamental patterns of knowing in nursing. Advances in Nursing Science 1:13–23.

Damon W, Hart D (1982). The development of self understanding from infancy through adolescence. Child Development 53:841–864.

Festinger LA (1957). A Theory of Cognitive Dissonance. Palo Alto, CA, Stanford University Press.

Frankl V (1969). The Will to Meaning. New York, New American Library.

Freeman M (1984) History, narrative and life span developmental knowledge. Human Development 27:1–19.

Gillis L (1978). Human Behavior in Illness: Psychology and Interpersonal Relationships (3rd. ed.). London: Farber & Farber.

Hamachek D (1978). Encounters with the Self (2nd ed.) New York, Holt, Rinehart and Winston.

Jones E, Rodenwalt F, Berglas S, Skelton J (1981). The effects of strategic self presentation on subsequent self-esteem. Journal of Personality and Social Psychology 41:407.

Joseph L (1991). Character Structure and the Organization of the Self. New York, Columbia University Press.

Joseph P, Sturgeon D, Leff J (1992). The perception of

emotion by schizophrenic patients. British Journal of Psychiatry 161:603–609.

Lane (1987). Care of the human spirit. Journal of Professional Nursing 3:332–337.

Leary M, Miller K (1986). Social Psychology and Dysfunctional Behavior. New York, Springer.

Maslow AH (1954). Motivation and Personality. New York, Harper & Row.

Maslow AH (1956). Self-actualizing people: A study of psychological health. *In* Moustakas CE (ed.) (1956), The Self: Explorations in Personal Growth. New York, Harper & Row.

Peck S (1978). The Road Less Traveled. New York, Simon & Schuster.

Reed P (1987). Spirituality and well-being in terminally ill hospitalized adults. Research in Nursing and Health 10:335–344.

Schlenker B (1975). Self presentation: Managing the impression of consistency when it interferes with self-enhancement. Journal of Personality and Social Psychology 32:1030.

Smith MJ (1992). Enhancing esthetic knowledge: A teaching strategy. Advances in Nursing Science 14(3):52–59.

Uphold C (1991). Social support *In* Creasia J, Parker B (eds.) (1991), Conceptual Foundations of Nursing Practice. St. Louis, Mosby.

Zderad L (1969). Empathetic nursing: Realization of a human capacity. Nursing Clinics of North America 4.

Chapter 4
Structuring the Relationship
ELIZABETH ARNOLD

OUTLINE

Basic Concepts

OBJECTIVES

At the end of the chapter, the student will be able to:

1. Discuss key concepts in the nurse–client relationship.

2. Identify the four phases of the therapeutic relationship.

3. Contrast tasks in each of the four phases of the relationship.
4. Specify effective nursing interventions in each phase of the relationship.

Chapter 4 focuses on the structural aspects of developing a nurse–client relationship, offering specific guidelines to strengthen the process of shared humanness through caring communication. Unlike social relationships, a therapeutic relationship has definite boundaries, marked by purpose, person-centered communication, stages of development, and a health-related context. Although therapeutic relationships often seem just to happen, structuring a therapeutic relationship with a client requires a considerable amount of time, thought, sensitivity, and energy.

The therapeutic relationship in nursing practice is considered a basic building block underlying all biophysical, psychosocial, and cognitive treatments. Specific nursing responsibilities around which a therapeutic relationship develops range from providing total physical care to a client at one extreme of the illness–wellness continuum to providing health education and emotional support at the other. Most nurse–client relationships involve aspects of both types of interventions.

Certain guiding principles—purpose, mutuality, authenticity, empathy, active listening, confidentiality, and respect for the dignity of the client—strengthen the entire process and flow through the four identifiable phases of a relationship. Whereas some therapeutic relationships extend over weeks or months, others take place in the span of an eight-hour work shift.

Therapeutic relationships are essential to the healing process (Peplau, 1952). Healing involves more than medicine and treatment protocols. Since illness affects the whole person, it is as important to discover the particular personal meanings woven into the fabric of an illness as it is to address the physical and psychological origins of the disorder.

Interpersonal relationships directly affect the quality of a person's living and dying in health care situations. Client behavioral responses to illness differ. Two clients with similar symptoms may demonstrate different outcomes; one gets better, the other becomes worse. To achieve maximum well-being in any clinical setting, clients must be convinced that change is in their best interest. Only then will the necessary modification in attitude and active involvement in the treatment process occur. The treatment process can fail when a client does not understand a part of it or is indecisive, reluctant, anxious, doubtful, or opposed to engaging fully with it. In these situations, the nurse can represent a decisive intervening variable. The development of a therapeutic relationship between nurse and client often enables the client to perceive and react to illness in a more productive way. Besides the actual care and active listening delivered within the context of a human therapeutic relationship, new ways of coping and accepting difficult realities result from health teaching.

Personal meanings develop and change through talking with another about matters closest to one's heart and mind. They emerge from within the self, revealing themselves in human stories and behavior. Personal meanings are validated, transformed, or invalidated by others. Regardless of individual circumstances, every human being has a basic need for a cognitive-emotional-spiritual understanding of a world that is integrated, whole, purposeful, and coherent. The nurse offers a bridge to such understandings while respecting the client as a full and equal participant in the process of discovery (Paterson and Zedrad, 1988).

As clients share the human side of their illness, their fears, disappointments, and anger (natural by-products of their changed circumstances) become normalized. The client begins to make some sense out of what is happening. Hearing oneself say the unthinkable aloud and getting feedback allows for the development of different insights and alternative options. Several authors point to nurses helping clients achieve a sense of meaning from their illness and suffering as one of the most important and rewarding aspects of nursing practice (Frankl, 1955; Travelbee, 1971).

BASIC CONCEPTS

FOCUS OF THE RELATIONSHIP

Therapeutic relationships represent a "modified social relationship" and share many of the same characteristics (Ramos, 1992). All effective relationships involve personal contact and a discovery of the other person—his or her needs, feelings, and ideas. There is a give and take in discussion; an opening of self to other, the I–Thou dialogue described by Buber (1958). People engage in relationships because of a hope that the relationship will meet needs they are unable to meet on their own. Most people enter relationships seeking understanding and acceptance for their own uniqueness as a person.

Therapeutic relationships differ from social relationships in that the connections and bonding are purposeful and directed by the nurse. It is a specialized helper–helpee type of relationship. There is a specific reason for entering the relationship related to a helpee need. All behavior in the relationship is purposefully planned, carried out, and evaluated in terms of helping clients meet identified treatment goals. Unlike other relationships, the choice to enter the relationship or to like the helpee is not part of the helper's reason for participating in the relationship. The helping professional takes primary responsibility for maintaining the boundaries and guiding the relationship.

Giving of self is important in both types of relationships, but in therapeutic relationships "the sense of love for patients was differentiated from personal relationships in the intensity and depth that it was offered" (Clarke and Wheeler, 1992, p. 1286). Box 4–1 contrasts some of the fundamental differences between a social and a therapeutic relationship.

"Helping relationships" are not always therapeutic. When the nurse becomes overinvolved in the client's life, regardless of the rationale, the relationship loses its therapeutic value. Heinrich (1992) notes that nurses consistently walk a fine line between having compassion for a client and developing a relationship that is too close, resulting in a friendship with potential serious complications for the client as well as the nurse. Overinvolvement is most likely to occur when a client strikes an emotional cord within the nurse: The client reminds the nurse of a person or event that had meaning in the past. It is easy to become overinvolved with a strong therapeutic commitment that develops into something more because of shared positive feelings.

Another source of overinvolvement is the presence of unresolved guilt from previous relationships that is superimposed on the present one. The nurse may try to redo the original situation in a healthier way, but because the circumstances and people are different, the results will be question-

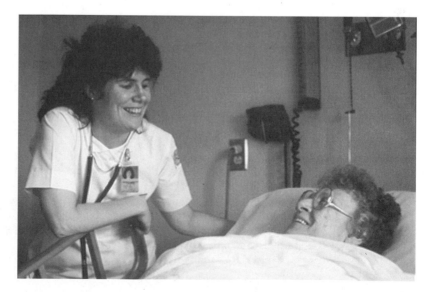

The underlying theme in all nursing interactions is respect for the client and a desire to understand the client as a unique person. (Courtesy of the University of Maryland School of Nursing)

BOX 4–1
Development of an Interpersonal Relationship

Comparison of a Helping Relationship with a Social Relationship
- Both involve at least two persons.
- There is a connection between the involved persons for an "established or discoverable reason."

Helping	*Social*
One person is taking the *responsibility* of helping while the other is seeking help.	Persons are not in a position of having responsibility for helping the other.
There is a specific *purpose* to the relationship.	Specific purpose is not necessary.
The relationship is *goal* directed.	The relationship is not necessarily goal directed.
The *focus* of the relationship is the needs of the helpee.	A person seeks to have own needs met as well as meet the needs of the other.
Behaviors are based on persons taking roles of professional and client respectively.	Certain social behavior is expected of persons in social roles.
The relationship is entered into through necessity.	The relationship is entered into by choice.
The *choice of whom* to enter the relationship with is usually not available to helper or helpee.	Persons can choose whom they care to become involved with.
Behavior on the part of the helper is purposefully planned, implemented, and evaluated.	Behavior on the part of participants is spontaneous.
It is not necessary that persons involved *like* each other.	Feelings of liking, fondness, or love for the other are usually involved.
The helping person seeks to be *nonjudgmental*.	Persons may be judgmental in attitude.
Sharing of personal or intimate *set factors* (self-disclosure) is usually a one-way process: helpee to helper.	There is mutual sharing of intimacies.
Empathetic feelings for the helpee are translated into helpful action.	Feelings for the other may enhance or prevent helpful action.
The helper is in control of the situation—meaning the helper is influencing behavior in a positive way.	Control is more evenly shared.
There is usually a definite and anticipated ending to the relationship—ideally, when the goals of the relationship have been accomplished.	The relationship may continue indefinitely, and the ending is usually not anticipated.
The helper possesses self-knowledge.	

able. Usually when past unresolved feelings create overinvolvement, the source is unconscious, and others recognize it is happening before the nurse involved does.

Whenever overinvolvement occurs, the nurse loses the necessary detachment and objectivity needed to support the client in meeting health goals. Lost is the needed balance between compassion and professionalism, a primary ingredient in successful nurse–client relationships. Ethical commitments made to the client to serve as protector and facilitator of the client's personal growth are placed in serious jeopardy. Boundaries meant to safeguard the purposes of the relationship become obscured.

The interpersonal boundaries of a professional relationship are what make it safe for the client (Fig. 4–1). The client must be able to trust that all kinds of feelings are possible without fear of misunderstanding or retaliation. Erasing or blurring relationship boundaries makes the relationship unsafe for the client. Although it is tempting to think of meeting the needs of an attractive or depleted client on a deeper level, to do so violates trust. Not only is the specific nurse–client relationship compromised but future relationships will be viewed as potentially risky. Interpersonal processes between nurse and client should always be restricted to meeting the health-related purposes of the relationship.

Overinvolvement has effects that extend beyond

choice must be respected, as long as it doesn't impinge on the rights of others. Unforeseen circumstances may require additional referral or modification of initial relationship goals.

A therapeutic interpersonal relationship in nursing practice can be a well-intentioned but ineffectual process if it lacks a planned direction or design to guide the participants. The relationship starts with the client and where he or she is at the time. No matter how worthy the nurse's goals may be for the client, they will not be effective unless they fit into the client's worldview. Dinkmeyer, Dinkmeyer, and Sperry (1987) note that "The proper therapeutic relationship, as we understand it, does not require transference but a relationship of mutual trust and respect. This is more than mere establishment of contact and rapport. Therapeutic cooperation requires an alignment of goals. When the goals and interests of the patient and therapist clash, no satisfactory relationship can be established" (p. 85). This axiom is true for all therapeutic relationships in which the client is capable of being a partner in the process, whether the relationship is of long or short duration.

It is the purposeful thinking behind the action taken in the relationship that best distinguishes the nurse's role from other types of relationships. Benner (1984) describes activities pertinent to the establishment and maintenance of healing relationships in nursing practices, as presented in Box 4–2. These actions are threaded through all stages of therapeutic relationships.

The underlying theme in all nursing actions is a respect for the human dignity of the client. A therapeutic relationship represents a conscious commitment on the part of the professional nurse to understand how an individual client and family perceive, feel, and respond to their world. From beginning to end, listening closely to verbal and nonverbal messages, focusing on the client's concerns, and attempting to understand the client as a unique person reinforces the client's value as a human being.

A therapeutic relationship is not one that a nurse can enter into passively. By accepting primary responsibility for the development of the relationship, the nurse consciously sets aside all personal prejudices, interests, and anxieties. The care of the client takes precedence, requiring the full attention and participation of the nurse. Curtin (1983) suggests that effective nursing practice depends as

---

BOX 4–2
Guidelines for the Healing Relationship

Creating a climate for and establishing a commitment to healing.

Providing comfort measures and preserving personhood in the face of pain and extreme breakdown.

Presencing: being with a patient.

Maximizing the patient's participation and control in his or her own recovery.

Interpreting kinds of pain and selecting appropriate strategies for pain management and control.

Providing comfort and communication through touch.

Providing emotional and informational support to patients' families.

Guiding a patient through emotional and developmental change: providing new options, closing off old ones.

Channeling, teaching, mediating—Acting as a psychological and cultural mediator

Using goals therapeutically

Working to build and maintain a therapeutic community.

Adapted from *From Novice to Expert* by Patricia Benner. Copyright © 1994 by Addison-Wesley Publishing Company. Reprinted by permission.

---

much on the humanity of the nurse as it does on the nurse's knowledge and technical skills.

CONTEXT

Professional relationships are controlled alliances in that they occur *within a particular context* and are *time limited*. Establishing and maintaining professional interpersonal relationships with clients places certain constraints, referred to as boundaries, on the professional nurse's activities. The nurse is ethically bound to observe all of the boundaries needed to make a relationship therapeutic. Clients seek health care in good faith from licensed professionals, from a vulnerable position as persons in need of help. They have every right to expect that the professionals who care for them will be active, responsive participants and guides in the client's progress toward optimal health and well-being. Typical boundaries in the nurse–client relationship include time, type of communication, role relationships, confidentiality, and purpose.

PERSON-CENTERED COMMUNICATION

The heart of the nurse–client relationship is *person-centered communication*. This is the medium

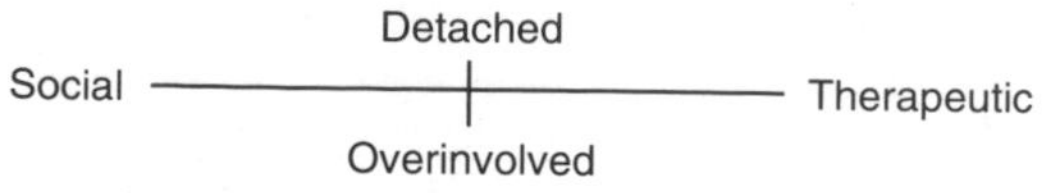

Figure 4–1 Types of Relationships

the individual client. It also can compromise the nurse's obligation to the institution, professional commitment to the treatment regimen, collegial relationships with other health team members, and professional responsibilities to other clients (Morse, 1991).

Warning signs that the nurse is becoming overinvolved include giving extra time and attention to certain clients, visiting the client in off hours, doing things for clients they could do for themselves, discounting the actions of other professionals, and feeling resentment about the ways other health team members are relating to the client.

When there is evidence that the nurse is becoming overinvolved, it is necessary to pull back from the situation and to regroup. Reviewing professional goals and seeking counsel from a mentor or peer not currently involved in the situation frequently helps the nurse gain perspective. It is important to recognize overinvolvement as the nurse's problem and not to withdraw from or become angry with the client because the nurse has overstepped the professional role, even if provoked to do so by the client.

At the other end of the spectrum are detached clinical relationships characterized by self focus rather than client focus. These relationships are not therapeutic; they do not enrich the client or permit genuine sharing. The nurse disengages from the client and fails to appreciate the reciprocal nature of a true therapeutic relationship. Communications are designed to keep the helper emotionally detached from the client's suffering.

Detached clinical relationships result when the nurse is unwilling or unable to meet the requirements of an engaged relationship with the client or the client's family. Causes differ: The nurse may lack experience and hesitate to become involved. Clients who fail to progress, who suffer, or who have significant changes in appearance or condition drain the nurse emotionally. Client behaviors that conflict with the nurse's values can affect the nurse's willingness to engage with the client. The nurse may limit involvement with certain clients because the constant exposure to their suffering is more than he or she can bear. Without self-awareness, the client is left to suffer alone. Morse et al. (1992) note that "sufferers watch for any signs of rejection, dismay or horror in their caregivers' faces. If the caregiver does reveal these feelings, and if the patient recognizes these feelings, he/she may become alarmed and lose hope" (p. 818).

Behaviors suggesting that the nurse lacks the emotional energy, inclination, or strength to engage in a therapeutic relationship include withdrawal, distancing through limited, perfunctory contact, minimizing the client's suffering, giving false reassurance, and defensive, judgmental, or rote communication. In cases of either overinvolvement or detached involvement, the nurse bears an ethical responsibility to work through his or her personal feelings with an objective peer or mentor.

PURPOSE

The goals of all therapeutic relationships are threefold: (1) to enhance client well-being, (2) to promote recovery, and (3) to support the self-care functioning of the client. A relationship between nurse and client is therapeutic when there is a goal-directed, helping focus related to an identifiable health care need: "In this type of relationship, two separately existing individuals come together for the sole purpose of helping one of them, the client, achieve maximum levels of self-care functioning and well-being" (Rogers, 1973). Health care needs can include health promotion and preventive care needs as well as distinct physiological and emotional needs requiring medical attention. The relationship terminates when the mutually determined treatment goals are met.

The nature of the goals and the time it takes to complete them determine the length and depth of the relationship. Client goals may be more limited than those of the nurse, or they may require a protracted length of time that extends beyond one nurse's time frame. The nurse engineers the interpersonal environment so that realistic goals are achievable within the context of the therapeutic relationship. But even with the best intentions and a realistic workable plan, the relationship doesn't always achieve its purposes. Sometimes the client simply doesn't want to move further in the relationship or in achieving treatment goals. This

through which the relationship takes place. Person-centered communication involves building an individualized relationship structure that allows clients to share their innermost personal experiences and the meanings they have for them (Kasch and Dine, 1988). The extent to which this occurs serves as a benchmark for evaluating the success of the therapeutic relationship. Through entering into the lived experiences of the client with empathy, the nurse makes a commitment to help the client resolve difficult problems related to health care. Standing outside the client's immediate stress related to health care, the nurse is in a unique position to provide the client with another perspective on a potentially overwhelming situation. Considering each person as a unique individual requiring a thorough understanding of the person as well as of the disease process helps earn the client's trust (Lamb, 1988).

Person-centered communication strategies are designed to meet the distinctive needs of each client. There is no one way to approach a client and no single interpersonal technique that works equally well with every client. Some clients clearly are more emotionally accessible and attractive than others. When a client seems unapproachable or uninterested in human contact, it can be quite disheartening for the nurse. It is not uncommon for the nurse to report the following kind of initial contact with a client: "I tried, but he just wasn't interested in talking to me. I asked him some questions, but he didn't really answer me. So I tried to ask him about his hobbies and interests. It didn't matter what I asked him. He just turned away. Finally, I gave up because it was obvious that he just didn't want to talk to me." From the nurse's perspective, this behavior may represent a lack of desire for a relationship. What isn't clear, however, is the reason for the rejection. In such cases, it is useful for the nurse to remember that this is usually not a personal rejection. The stress of hospitalization can heighten emotional responses, and coldness toward the nurse may be the only way a client can cope constructively with his or her predicament. All nurses have experienced some form of client rejection at one time or another. Usually a seeming rejection means that the client is bored, frightened, insecure, upset, or physically uncomfortable. Rarely does it have much to do with the personal approach used by the nurse in

the early stages of a relationship, unless the nurse is truly insensitive to the client's feelings or the needs of the situation.

On the other hand, it is useful for the nurse to explore whether the timing was right, whether the client was in pain, and what other circumstances might have contributed to the client's attitude. Occasionally a nurse is so eager to get the needed information for a client assessment or nursing care plan that the more subtle needs of the client in pain or emotional distress are overlooked. Behaviors that initially seem maladaptive may appear quite adaptive when the full circumstances of the client's situation are understood.

CASE EXAMPLE

A third-year student nurse, Joan Thoms, stops at the hospital to pick up her next day's assignment. Mrs. Groot, her client, is scheduled for a radical mastectomy. Joan enters Mrs. Groot's room to introduce herself, but finds her client in tears and unable to talk. Joan gives her a tissue and sits with her, holding her hand. After about five minutes, Joan asks, "Would you like to talk for a while? You seem really upset." Mrs. Groot replies, "I'd rather be alone." Joan states, "There are times when we all need to have some time alone. I'll pull your curtains around your bed to give you some privacy, and I will be back to see you later, before I leave the unit."

In this anecdote the nurse acknowledges the client's immediate need to be alone while at the same time setting the stage for further contact. Meeting the client's needs nonverbally when the client is reluctant to communicate verbally demonstrates respectful interest without pressure. You may have to use this technique several times before you see any results, but it is a highly effective therapeutic maneuver.

Seeking to understand the client and the circumstances surrounding the interaction is crucial. An initial rebuff may not represent a lack of desire for contact. It may be that the client had a restless night or is worried about the cardiac catheterization scheduled for later that afternoon. Such situations are another reason why it is important to interact with staff members before entering the client's room. They may have important data about the client that will influence your approach and response. Exercise 4–1 examines nonverbal cues in relationships.

EXERCISE 4–1
Nonverbal Cues in Relationships

Purpose: To increase awareness of nonverbal cues that support or negate the meaning of the verbal content.

Time: 20 minutes

Directions:
1. Compile a list of five body actions that might be observed during a conversation—lack of eye contact, for example.
2. Specify the possible meaning of each physical cue.
3. Compare data with those of other students.
4. Repeat this exercise in an actual clinical setting.

AUTONOMY

Autonomy is an important component of person-centered communication. Applying this concept means that the nurse leaves decision making to the client whenever possible and supports the client's decision unless there is a chance harm will be done to the client or others. With a clear understanding of the person's needs, the nurse recommends treatment options and gives the client sound reasons for the recommendations. It is up to the client to decide whether or not to follow the recommendations. Control and decision making are left in the client's hands in an interdependent nurse–client relationship (Roberts and Krouse, 1988).

INTERDEPENDENCE

The nurse–client relationship is an interdependent relationship. Each partner in the relationship has an impact upon the other. Each professional relationship represents a special opportunity for personal growth on the part of both participants (Yuen, 1986). The nurse enters each nurse–client relationship with a certain body of knowledge, a genuine desire to help others, and an openness to experiencing the client as a special and unique person who is worthy of personalized as well as professional attention and respect. For a shared moment in time, the nurse brings professional knowledge of physiology, pharmacology, human behaviors, birth, death, and suffering together with the client's rich reservoir of life experiences to achieve mutually established nursing care goals. Taylor (1992) notes, "Nurses and patients are different in terms of their knowledge and skills, but

they are also the same in terms of their essential humanness." Acknowledging their commonalities and exploring the nature of their differences is what makes each nurse–client relationship unique to its participants.

Having a professional interpersonal relationship with a client involves deliberately using the self as a tool, for the purpose of helping a client meet physical and psychological needs in a meaningful way. The nurse, in full command of the self, does not hide behind titles or roles for security but instead is free to interact with the client in a nondefensive, compassionate manner.

AUTHENTICITY

The most striking quality of an effective nurse–client relationship is the nurse's ability to be fully with another human being. This involves both empathy, discussed in Chapter 5, and the nurse's *authenticity* as a caring person. In successful relationships there is a physical, emotional, and even spiritual connectedness that is almost palpable. Fully being with another is not always comfortable or pleasant. It involves the capacity to know when to provide help and when to stand back, when to speak frankly and when to withhold comments because the client is not ready to hear them (Taylor, 1992b). Sometimes it is one of the hardest acts a nurse can perform for another human being. And yet the nurse–client relationship can be like none one has ever experienced before, filling the nurse with awe and respect for the humanness of suffering and the magnificence of humanity.

Relationships without authenticity are sterile applications of communication techniques. No matter what intellectual insights are shared, such relationships leave the client with questionable feelings about the meaning of the relationship to the helping person, and more important, with a sense of not being seen as a person.

Authenticity requires nurses to be clear about their personal values, feelings, and thoughts in responding to a client. For example, a homeless client tells the nurse, "I know you want to help me, but you can't understand my situation because you have money and a husband to support you. You don't know what it is like out on the streets." Instead of feeling defensive, a more appropriate response is to agree with the client that the nurse doesn't know what it is like to be homeless and to ask the client to tell her more about it. Following this discussion, the nurse might address the universality of the underlying themes. The loneliness, fear, and helplessness the client is experiencing are not foreign feelings for most people, including the nurse, from time to time.

Even mistakes can be a forum for genuine communication. For example, a nurse promises the client to return immediately with a pain medication and then forgets to do so because of other pressing demands. When the nurse brings the medication, the client accuses her of being uncaring and incompetent. It would be appropriate for the nurse to apologize for forgetting the medication and for any extra discomfort suffered by the client. To be truly effective, the nurse must have a keen sense of self-awareness that provides direction and acts as a barometer of the relationship process (Krikorian and Paulanka, 1982).

CONFIDENTIALITY

Confidentiality, developed as a fundamental concept in Chapter 5 is also an ethical issue in the development of the nurse–client relationship. As noted earlier, information shared by the client is considered privileged communication, except when withholding information would jeopardize the life or essential well-being of the client or others. Confidentiality is a judgment call. If the information is relevant to the care of the client, the nurse needs to reveal it only to those directly involved with the client's health care, and preferably with the client's permission. Paterson and Zderad (1988) suggest that nurses "in deciding what and how to convey of their knowledge must

decide freely, responsibly, personally and alone" (p. 55). To this statement must be added the need to use the counsel of more experienced nurses when appropriate.

SELF-DISCLOSURE

The nurse's self-disclosure represents limited emotional responses, particularly in the beginning stages of the relationship. It is the nurse, not the client, who is responsible for regulating the amount of disclosure needed to facilitate the relationship. What is appropriate in a personal relationship with a friend can be highly inappropriate in a therapeutic relationship. For example, letting a friend know the precise details of one's personal life and exactly how one feels about that person is a highly desirable goal in a personal relationship. There is little need to censor information shared with a friend.

By contrast, in a professional relationship, nurses do not share the more intimate details of their personal lives. It can be just as harmful to the goals of the professional relationship to divulge personal information as it is to withold such information in a personal relationship. Usually it is inappropriate for the nurse to share personal anxiety feelings with a client during the early stages of the relationship. Personal self-disclosure by the nurse should occur only when it helps the client focus on feelings and concerns (Anvil and Silver, 1984). Developing professional goals in a relationship and acting on them helps nurses become conscious of the range of behavioral responses that are most appropriate for the relationship.

If the client asks a nonoffensive question, the nurse may answer briefly with a minimum of information and return to a client focus. Client questions of a superficial social nature, such as, "Are you from around here?" "Where did you go to nursing school?" "Do you have any children?" may be simple client strategies to establish common ground for conversation (Morse, 1991). Answering them briefly with a return to focus on the client is appropriate.

Requests for intimate information about the nurse do not need to be answered. One way of defusing this type of request is to say that you are not sure that answering the question will really help the client cope with his or her health problem, or simply to indicate that you would prefer

EXERCISE 4–2
Recognizing Role Limitations in Self-Disclosure

Purpose: To help you differentiate between a therapeutic use of self-disclosure and spontaneous self-revelation.

Time: 30 minutes

Directions:
1. Make a list of phrases that describe your own personality, such as:
   I am shy.
   I get angry when criticized.
   I'm nice.
   I'm sexy.
   I find it hard to handle conflicts.
   I'm interested in helping people.
2. Mark each descriptive phase with one of the following:
   × = too embarrassing or intimate to discuss in a group.
   + = could discuss with a group of peers.
   RN = this behavior characteristic might affect my ability to function in a therapeutic manner if disclosed.
3. Share your responses with the group.

Questions for Discussion:
1. What criteria were used to determine the appropriateness of self-disclosure?
2. How much variation is there in what each student would share with others in a group or clinical setting?
3. Were there any behaviors commonly agreed upon that would never be shared with a client?
4. What interpersonal factors about the client would facilitate or impede self-disclosure by the nurse in the clinical setting?
5. What did you learn from doing this exercise that could be used in future encounters with clients?

not to answer the question and return to the client focus. Exercise 4–2 examines appropriate and inappropriate use of self-disclosure.

PHASES OF THE RELATIONSHIP

The four phases of a professional interpersonal relationship described in nursing literature are classified as preinteraction, orientation, working or active intervention, and termination (Peplau, 1952). Each phase is considered a separate stage of development for discussion purposes only. In actual practice, the phases are not mutually exclusive, and the nurse will need to consider their interconnections. For example, the needs of the termination phase are laid in the first encounter when the nurse indicates to the client the length of the relationship, if known: "I will be your primary nurse while you are in the hospital," or, "I will be caring for you on this shift." During the termination phase of the relationship, the nurse and client

review goals established in the orientation phase and evaluate the effectiveness of the actions that were chosen to meet them (Companiello, 1980).

The therapeutic relationship is more than the sum of its parts. The effects of each phase interact in ways that serve to broaden as well as deepen the scope of emotional connection. Different client needs are emphasized in each phase. The phases or stages of development are linear and overlapping, yet each retains a partial independence from the others through differences in characteristics and tasks. Though the nurse and the client are active partners in developing a therapeutic relationship, the nurse assumes different roles for ensuring the relationship's appropriate organization and progression through each phase, as diagrammed in Figure 4–2.

In any phase of the developing relationship, the process can break down. Remaining at the superficial, social level of the orientation phase hampers the active, problem-solving process needed for suc-

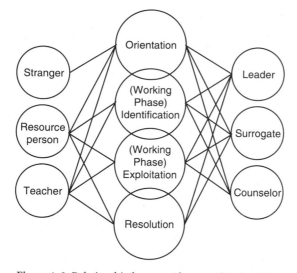

Figure 4–2 Relationship between Phases and Roles of the Nurse-Client Relationship, as Described by Peplau (1952)

cessful resolution of health care issues identified in the active intervention phase. Having developed a strong rapport with a client in the orientation and active intervention phases and then failing to terminate adequately with a client calls into question much of the effectiveness of the nurse's efforts during the earlier phases. The chances of the client trusting in the value of future relationships diminish when termination is treated casually. Threads of each phase are interwoven into a living fabric of meanings, unique to each relationship.

Flexibility in returning to more superficial levels may be necessary when the client is not ready to discuss sensitive issues. For example, a difficult diagnosis or beginning awareness of a terminal condition may cause the client to become silent. The client may need more time to absorb disturbing changes internally before using the therapeutic relationship to work through potentially overwhelming feelings about a situation. The client may have revealed a sexual indiscretion or fear that he is ashamed of or is not yet ready to handle. Client discomfort is evidenced by the fact that the client withdraws from the interaction, becomes fidgety, or changes the subject. Another indication is that the next session following significant self-disclosure seems sterile and nonproductive. The interpersonally sensitive nurse notices the client's

change in behavior and doesn't force the client to continue talking about the topic until there is more comfort with the topic and trust of the nurse.

APPLICATIONS

PREINTERACTION PHASE

The *preinteraction phase* is the only period in which the client is not actively involved. In this phase, the nurse explores his or her professional goals, creates a supportive environment, and plans with other staff the most appropriate ways to achieve relationship goals. Although it is impossible to anticipate every possible contingency, careful preparation usually makes the first encounter with a client go more smoothly. It also provides the nurse with a clearer idea of what realistically to expect from the relationship with a particular client (Box 4–3).

Identifying Professional Goals

Professional goals are like markings on a map, providing information about the best ways to arrive at a particular destination as well as about how far the nurse will have to go to arrive there. In a therapeutic relationship, professional goals relate to the role responsibilities the nurse assumes in helping clients achieve their goals in a time-limited, health-related alliance. Having a clear knowledge of the theoretical principles and role responsibilities associated with the relationship does not guarantee a successful outcome. It does, however,

---

BOX 4–3
Tasks of the Preinteraction Phase

Deciding on professional goals.
Assessing the environmental setting:
  evaluating personal characteristics, needs, values, and temperament that could have an impact on the relationship;
  evaluating the resources available for use in relationship;
  determining the kinds of conditions, facts, and circumstances likely to facilitate or hinder the development of a therapeutic relationship.
Establishing priorities.
Organizing time so relationship goals are realistic and achievable.

prevent the "lost" feeling that comes from not knowing what one is doing or what one hopes to accomplish through one's efforts. Developing professional goals helps the nurse select concrete, specific nursing actions that are purposeful and aligned with individualized client needs.

The role relations within the nurse–client relationship are unequal. The relationship is a one-way focus on the client's needs rather than a reciprocal focus on the needs of both partners (Peplau, 1952). The goals of a professional relationship dictate that the client is always the architect of the content, with the nurse supplying the coaching framework necessary for understanding the nature of the problem-solving process.

Professional goals provide a rationale for choosing the most appropriate communication strategies in each phase of the relationship. Two outcomes generally accompany these insights. First, a firm knowledge of appropriate professional goals allows the nurse to define concrete role responsibilities in the relationship. Second, having professional goals communicates to the client that the nurse is knowledgeable, in control of nursing role responsibilities, and ready to focus on the needs of the client. Professional goals rarely are communicated directly to the client, but they are implicit in all that the nurse does and says with a client.

Creating a Supportive Environment

In any relationship, participants may be responding to interpersonal stimuli or to factors having little or nothing to do with the current relationship. Effective therapeutic relationships require the nurse to consider all of the factors that potentially affect the emotional availability of both parties.

The psychological "mind set" of either the nurse or the client affects the person's emotional availability for developing the relationship. Preoccupation with other matters or biases about behaviors or classes of people can get in the way of therapeutic conversations. For example, if the nurse resents being on night duty or is preoccupied with personal matters, interpersonal availability will be affected. Stereotypes about the client's behavior, appearance, or illness make it easier or harder to relate empathetically. Prior to meeting the client, the nurse should reflect on the nature of these various factors and their implications for developing a therapeutic relationship.

Knowledge of differences in the client's mind set also is important. All of us have an invisible interpersonal shell that protects a basic human vulnerability. The thickness of this shell affects how receptive people can be in a relationship with another human being. Vulnerability ebbs and flows with the degree of emotional safety a person feels in the relationship.

Making the interpersonal environment a safe place in which to explore feelings and to work through painful issues is of critical importance in the beginning stages of the relationship. For example, the nurse on a maternity floor should have a different perspective in approaching a client whose infant is in the neonatal intensive care unit because of respiratory distress than in approaching a client who is rooming in with a healthy baby. The few minutes it takes to get a quick overview of client status prior to the initial meeting can make quite a difference in the choice of interpersonal approaches—and in the success of the initial encounter.

Obstacles are easier to handle when they have been anticipated. Thinking seriously about potential difficulties gives the nurse more leverage in responding appropriately in the relationship. For example, two clients might have a similar diagnosis of breast cancer. However, the client who has just received the diagnosis and the client who has known about her diagnosis for the past four months are likely to respond quite differently to the nurse. Two young women in the hospital to deliver a first child may have quite different needs in the relationship if one is happily married and the pregnancy was planned and the other is single and doesn't want the baby. Their personal demographic characteristics and antepartal history may be similar, but their interpersonal needs are likely to be different. Knowledge of the differences in their circumstances affords the nurse greater sensitivity in approaching the clients for the first time. This is what is meant by individualized nursing care. Treating critical yet sometimes subtle differences in individual circumstances as important information in the initial encounter respects the uniqueness of the person experiencing them.

Establishing a Comfortable Setting

The nurse carefully considers where the relationship should take place. Several factors should enter into this consideration, including the condition of the client, the emotional intensity of the client or family members, and the type of interaction.

Therapeutic relationships ideally take place in a quiet, undisturbed place. Trying to begin a relationship or expecting the client to reveal deep feelings in the presence of other people creates an unnecessary barrier. Similarly, it is best to avoid settings where the relationship is likely to be interrupted or where it is impossible to meet the immediate goals of the relationship. Both you and the client should be positioned comfortably, so that you are facing each other in an I–Thou position. Paying attention to these details communicates to the client the importance of the relationship and the commitment of the nurse to give the process the full attention it deserves. The room should be well lighted and not too hot or too cold. Validating that the space is available at the times needed prevents spending more time looking for a room than talking to the client.

Disturbing news and behavioral confrontations should always be delivered in private. Arrangements for significant others to be present when critical information is shared, especially with children, provides an additional support for the client in time of stress. In the hospital, relationships usually are carried out in the client's room or general living area. One-to-one relationships with psychiatric clients frequently take place in a designated, noiseless room, apart from the client's bedroom. In the client's home, the nurse is always the client's guest, and the client plays a stronger role in selecting the most appropriate place for the relationship.

Specific client needs also can dictate the most appropriate interpersonal setting. For example, the rape victim in a busy emergency room should be accorded privacy and an immediate interpersonal response from professionals. Although rape may not represent the most physically urgent triage situation, it is one of the most profound psychological emergency situations a woman can experience. The client needs privacy and someone to stay with her. Each time a nurse takes such factors into consideration in a nurse–client relationship, the nurse models consideration, respect, and empathy. Exercise 4–3 identifies environmental variables.

EXERCISE 4–3
Identifying Environmental Variables

Purpose: To identify the types of environmental factors that foster optimal nurse–client relationships.

Time: 30–40 minutes

Directions:
1. Using the format below, recall your first day of class.
2. Make a list of the factors that helped you get needed information.
3. List the factors that hindered getting needed information.
4. Share identified factors with fellow students.

Variation:
The same directions can be applied to an initial in-hospital nurse–client interaction.

	Facilitating Factors	*Hindering Factors*
In the physical (environmental) setting	*Example:* Temperature, 68° F 1. 2. 3. 4.	*Example:* Too hot, too cold 1. 2. 3. 4.
In the psychological (self-concept) setting	*Example:* Friend present 1. 2. 3. 4.	*Example:* High anxiety 1. 2. 3. 4.

Identifying Values and Feelings

Self-awareness is an important element of successful therapeutic conversations with clients. Some clients are highly provocative. They generate feelings in their caregivers similar to the countertransference feelings Freud described in psychoanalytic settings. Nurses need to explore their feelings and personal reactions to a client continually. Unrecognized feelings can become a significant barrier to the comfortable interpersonal atmosphere so necessary for successful professional relationships. It is not necessary for the nurse to compromise strongly held values, nor is it essential for the nurse to like all clients.

Professional nurses have an ethical responsibility to resolve potentially destructive feelings outside the therapeutic relationship. This applies to overly positive feelings toward the client or to exaggerated sympathy for the gravity of a client's condition as well as to negative feelings. Acting on any extreme feeling is not helpful to the client. Failure to resolve such feelings means the nurse is likely to act on them unconsciously, either by responding automatically to a preconceived impression of the client or by resenting and avoiding the client. Without self-awareness and a commitment to look consistently at personal feelings toward a client, the nurse is at a disadvantage by not being fully present and accountable to the client.

Self-awareness allows nurses to treat each person with respect as a person having value, even if the nurse cannot understand or approve of certain behaviors. It is always important to acknowledge one's behaviors of avoidance, anger, or frustration with a client and to work on developing a deeper understanding of the underlying interpersonal issues. When nurses are unsure of their initial reactions to a client, the counsel of a more experienced nurse should be sought. The ethical principle, "First, do no harm" should be foremost in the nurse's mind even before the relationship begins.

Example

Kelly, age 20, has been admitted with a tentative medical diagnosis, "Rule out AIDS." John is a 21-year-old student nurse assigned to care for Kelly. He expresses concern to his instructor about the client's sexual orientation. The instructor notes that John spends the majority of his time with his only other assigned client, who is in for treatment of a minor heart irregularity.

What conclusions might be drawn regarding the reason John spends so little time caring for Kelly? If you were John, what would be important to you in understanding and resolving your feeling?

Sharing Plans with Staff

Once the plan is formulated, the nurse should share care plans with the rest of the staff. This is critical to success. Though the nurse may have consulted the staff about different aspects of the plan, it is useful to summarize initial plans with other staff members. This simple strategy accomplishes two purposes: Staff will support the nurse's efforts, and often staff have additional input that can prove useful. Failure to involve staff in the initial planning stages can sabotage the most careful and creative plan.

ORIENTATION PHASE

The nurse–client relationship formally begins with the *orientation phase* (Box 4–4; Table 4–1). When nurse and client first meet in a therapeutic relationship, the client often comes with dual behavioral responses: the hope that the treatment process will be successful and the anguished doubt that anything can be changed or that life will ever be the same. The nurse enters the relationship in the stranger role.

All beginnings are important because they set the tone for the relationship. Psychological attitudes implicitly recognizing the dignity of the client form an important part of the interpersonal context. Human dignity and the client's personhood are acknowledged through simple nursing actions such as calling the client by the correct title (Mr., Mrs., Miss, or Ms.), providing the client with as much freedom and decision making as the client's condition and developmental status allow, and encourag-

---

BOX 4–4
Tasks of the Orientation Phase

Establishing contact.
Defining roles in the relationship.
Identifying client wants and needs.
Specifying mutually defined health goals.
Establishing the therapeutic contract.

TABLE 4–1
Phases of Nurse-Client Relationship*

Orientation Phase	*Working Phase*		*Resolution Phase*
	Identification	*Exploitation*	
Client	Participates in identifying problems.	Makes full use of services.	Abandons old needs.
Seeks assistance.	Begins to be aware of time.	Identifies new goals.	Aspires to new goals.
Conveys educative needs	Responds to help.	Attempts to attain new goals.	Becomes independent of helping person.
Asks questions.	Identifies with nurse.	Rapid shifts in behavior; dependent–independent.	Applies new problem-solving skills.
Tests parameters.	Recognizes nurse as a person.	Exploitative behavior.	Maintains changes in style of communication and inter-
Shares preconceptions and expectations of nurse due to past experience.	Explores feelings.	Realistic exploitation.	action.
	Fluctuates among dependence, independence, and interdependence in relationship with nurse.	Self-directing.	Positive changes in view of self.
	Increases focal attention.	Develops skills in interpersonal relationships and problem solving.	Integrates illness.
	Changes appearance (for better or worse).	Displays changes in manner of communication (more open, flexible).	Exhibits ability to stand alone.
	Understands purpose of meeting.		
	Maintains continuity between sessions (process and content).		
Nurse	Maintain separate identity.	Continue assessment.	Sustain relationship as long as patient feels necessary.
Respond to emergency.	Exhibits ability to edit speech or control focal attention.	Meet needs as they emerge.	Promote family interaction.
Give parameters of meetings.	Testing maneuvers decrease.	Understand reason for shifts in behavior.	Assist with goal setting.
Explain roles.	Unconditional acceptance.	Initiate rehabilitative plans.	Teach preventive measures.
Gather data.	Help express needs, feelings.	Reduce anxiety.	Utilize community agencies.
Help client identify problem.	Assess and adjust to needs.	Identify positive factors.	Teach self care.
Help client plan use of community resources and services.	Provide information.	Help plan for total needs.	Terminate nurse–client relationship.
Reduce anxiety and tension.	Provide experiences that diminish feelings of helplessness.	Facilitate forward movement of personality.	
Practice nondirective listening.	Do not allow anxiety to overwhelm client.	Deal with therapeutic impasse.	
Focus client's energies.	Help client to focus on cues.		
Clarify preconceptions and expectations of nurse.	Help client develop responses to cues.		
	Use word stimuli.		

Date Completed: _____   Signatures: _____

*Phases are overlapping.
From Forchik C, Brown B (1989). Establishing a nurse–client relationship. Journal of Psychosocial Nursing and Mental Health Services 27(2):32.

ing as much self-responsibility as possible given the client's level of self-care capacity.

From the very first encounter, the nurse conveys to the client the expectation that the relationship will be a partnership (Kasch, 1986). That understanding, in and of itself, sometimes stimulates an atmosphere of hope. The implicit assumption is that the client has something valuable to offer the relationship. Most important, the relationship should be based on "shared control and shared responsibility for health care decision making" (Roberts and Krouse, 1988, p. 51).

Introducing Purpose

The nurse needs to clarify the purpose of the relationship in the first session. Purposes differ, depending on client needs. A basic orientation given to a client by a nurse assigned for a day would be different from that given to a client when the nurse assumes the role of primary care nurse. If the interview is used to gather information, the focus can be on the type of information needed. When the relationship is to be of longer duration, the nurse should be prepared for a variety of secondary issues—length of sessions, frequency of meetings, role of the nurse in the process, basic orientation to what the client might expect from the relationship. It is important to ask the client what he or she would like to get out of the relationship.

The orientation phase of the relationship shares many of the characteristics of the assessment phase in the nursing process with a focus on gathering data, making inferences about client behaviors, and developing a beginning understanding of client needs, wants, and health goals. During the initial interview, the nurse observes behaviors, gestures, and body movements. Listening to the client's account of his or her current situation, the nurse begins to notice connections between different parts of the data. The sense of perceived self-validation the client experiences as a person in being able to tell his or her story to a person who cares to listen will enhance rapport.

Initial meetings should have two outcomes. First, the client should emerge from the encounter with a better idea of some of the beginning health issues and possible goals. Second, the client should feel that the nurse is interested in him or her as a person, not just a hospital number, because the nurse has taken the time to know more about the client's personal health care needs.

Establishing Contact

As noted earlier in the chapter, initiating a therapeutic relationship with some clients requires a great deal of effort, whereas other relationships seem to begin effortlessly. In both cases the beginnings are important. Even if the client is unwilling initially to engage, how the nurse presents the option will affect the client's willingness to participate later. Although nurses do not always see the fruits of their labor, the relationship that seems to require the most effort initially can turn out to be the most rewarding for both participants.

The most natural, time-tested way to begin talking to the client is to orient the client to the purpose of the relationship with a simple introductory statement. Your statement should include *who* you are, *what* your role will be, *what* you will be doing in the relationship, *when* and under *what* circumstances the relationship will take place, and *why*, and *what* the purpose of the relationship is. If the client's family or significant others are present, the nurse uses a similar introduction format. Role clarification and statement of purpose makes the relationship safe and provides direction for what follows.

Example

Good morning, Mr. Smith. I am Susan Stone, a nursing student, and I will be taking care of you until 3 P.M. today.

Or if the purpose of the interaction is to elicit information,

Hello, Mr. Smith, I am Susan Stone, a nursing student, and I will be asking you some questions about yourself and your family, so that we can know how best to take care of you.

These types of introductory statements should be made even to clients who are confused, aphasic, or unable to make an objective response because of mental illness or coma. All clients, regardless of condition, are entitled to be addressed by name and to be given this basic information. Since clients often have a number of nurses taking care of them, the introductory statement can take place on each of the first few days of care. Seyster (1987) suggests that the simple nursing intervention of greeting a client with interest and sincerity recognizes the inner humanity of the person and tempers the depersonalized experience of hospitalization. Exercise 4–4 is designed to give you practice in making introductory statements.

When you initially use this introductory strategy, the words may feel mechanical, and you might prefer to be more informal and spontaneous in your communication. Obviously, you

EXERCISE 4–4
Introductions in the Nurse–Client Relationship

The introductory statement forms the basis for the rest of the relationship. Effective contact with a client helps build an atmosphere of trust and connectedness with the nurse. The following statement is a good example of how one might engage the client in the first encounter.

> Hello, Mr. Smith. I am Sally Parks, a nursing student. I will be taking care of you on this shift. During the day I may be asking you some questions about yourself that will help me to understand how I can best help you.

Time: 30 minutes

Directions: After reading this introductory statement, identify the who, what, when, and why in the statement. The statement above is used as an illustration.

WHO: Sally Parks, student nurse

WHAT: Taking care of you and asking you some questions

WHEN: On this shift

WHY: To help me to understand how I can best help you

Think of a recent interaction you have had with a client. Write the statement and identify the who, what, when, and why in the statement.

_____

_____

_____

_____

WHO: _____

WHAT: _____

WHEN: _____

WHY: _____

Discussion Questions:
1. What was the client's response to the introductory statement?
2. If different students experienced a variation in client responses, what variables might have contributed to this finding?
3. What did you learn from doing this exercise?

Adapted from Carkhuff RR (1983). The Art of Helping V. Student Workbook. Amherst, MA., Human Resource Development Press. Copyright © 1983. Reprinted by permission of HRD Press, Inc., 22 Amherst Rd., Amherst, MA 01002.

can vary the words, but the verbal message needs to contain this combination of data. It may help to remember that clients do not know who you are or what your purpose is in interacting with them. It's frightening for many people to be asked questions without having any idea what is needed or why the person needs the information. By giving clients an opportunity to understand who you are, what you hope to accomplish by interacting with them, and what the boundaries of the relationship

are, you will be more likely to gain their cooperation. Having an idea of what you will say initially to a client also should decrease your anxiety.

Spontaneity can be expressed in the way you present yourself. Are you smiling and relaxed in manner? Do your posture and gestures support your genuine desire to get to know this client? Are you truly receptive to hearing what the client has to share with you? Your accompanying actions are no less important than the words you use. Both your actions and your words are data the client needs in order to begin trusting you.

Assessing Client Needs

Assessment, described in Chapter 2 as the initial component of the nursing process, is a key element of the orientation phase of the relationship. "At the core of every interpersonal relationship are two people with their own perceptions of reality" (Ersek, 1992). Since it is the client's perception of his or her circumstances that will form the basis for all that follows, it is important to understand how the client perceives the reasons for seeking treatment and what he or she expects of the helping professional. Initially the nurse focuses on the immediate crisis of the hospitalization or clinic visit and begins to identify factors with the client and the client's family that will facilitate or hinder the treatment process. Asking the client to tell you what brought him or her to the hospital (clinic) or to seek treatment elicits the client's perspective on the illness. Once the reason for seeking health care is established, a second question, "What kind of help can we provide for you?" yields information about client expectations. Asking the second question helps prevent client disappointment stemming from unrealistic expectations and provides the nurse with the opportunity to correct misinformation.

Direct, validated observation is an important source of information about a client. Mentally, nurses form impressions about the client's behavior, mental status, and anxiety level from the moment they enter the client's room. These impressions, when validated with the client, serve as guides for subsequent actions in the relationship.

The nursing history data collected in the orientation phase include a description of the client, the presenting problem, mental status, family background, relevant medical history, social and work background, and legal history if applicable. Also important are variables such as age, concurrent stressors, previous life experience, educational or socioeconomic background, and ethnic or religious orientation.

In assessing client needs, it is important to distinguish between behaviors and inferences about data. Perception involves a subjective interpretation of a situation and not necessarily objective reality. Behavior is a directly observable fact about a client. An inference represents the observer's translation of behavioral facts. Because it is an interpretation, it may or may not be accurate. To get the full picture, learning as much as possible about a client through data related to the illness experience is crucial.

Example

DYING CLIENT (*to the nurse*): It's not the dying that bothers me as much as not knowing what is going to happen to me in the process.

NURSE: It sounds as though you can accept the fact that you are going to die, but you are concerned about what you will have to experience. Tell me more about what worries you.

By asking for more information about the emotional context, before commenting on the content of the client's message, the nurse shows a desire to understand the situation from the client's perspective. Sometimes the full picture looks quite different from the initial presentation of the problem. Furthermore, the nurse is not relying on intuition or assuming the meaning of data without obtaining all applicable information from the client.

In less dramatic nursing situations, verbal strategies, such as a comment on the client's flowers or an observation about the client—"You look as though you would like to be alone" or "Are those pictures of your family?"—show the client that he or she is seen as a person having discernible individual characteristics.

Nurses need to be aware of the different physical cues clients give with their verbal messages. Noting the factors that seem to be preventing the establishment of the relationship—"You look exhausted" or "You look worried"—acknowledges the presence of these factors. Exercise 4–5 is designed to help you pick up another person's nonverbal cues.

An important aspect of client need assessment data relates to client strengths. When people enter the health care system, they do so because of problems or needs; they also enter with some healthy behavioral response patterns. Relevant historical data should include personal strengths and healthy coping responses as well as health-related deficits. Every client has healthy aspects of his or her personality and personal strengths that can be used to facilitate individual coping responses. Think about

EXERCISE 4–5
Inferences about Nonverbal Messages

Purpose: To provide practice in validation skills in a nonthreatening environment.

Time: 45 minutes

Directions:
1. Each student in turn tries to communicate the following feelings to other members of the group without words. They may be written on a piece of paper or the student may develop one directly from the list below.
2. The other students must guess what behaviors the student is trying to enact.

Pain	Anger
Sadness	Confidence
Anxiety	Disapproval
Relief	Uncertainty
Shock	Disbelief
Disgust	Acceptance
Disinterest	Rejection
Despair	"Uptightness"

Questions for Discussion:
1. Which emotions were harder to guess from their nonverbal cues? Which ones were easier?
2. Was there more than one interpretation of the emotion?
3. How would you use the information you developed today in your future care of clients?

a client you have had or a person you know who has a serious illness. What personal strengths does this person have that could have a healing impact on the illness? Using an assessment form as a guide ensures more complete data collection.

Relying exclusively on client information without soliciting the perceptions of significant others can distort and limit history taking. If there is any reason to suspect the reliability of the client as an historian, significant others can supply information. Nursing judgment is also needed when family and client disagree about diagnosis, treatment goals, or ways to provide care. Comparing client and family data for congruence and differences is an important source of client data. The differences can be just as important as the agreement in developing the most appropriate nursing interventions. For example, if the client has one perception about self-care abilities or other competencies and family members have a completely different perception, these differences become a nursing concern. Specific nursing diagnoses need to address the discrepancies in perceptions.

It is important to strike a balance between communicating with the client and with significant others accompanying the client. It happens that

health professionals ignore the interpersonal needs of a client who is elderly, an adolescent, or physically handicapped but not mentally incapacitated in assessment interviews. Talking only with the adult members of a family instead of including the client in the dialogue, or assuming the elderly or adolescent client has a limited understanding or interest, devalues the person. This subtle and usually unintentional devaluing of the individual increases a sense of dehumanization and loneliness—a frequent occurrence in health care settings.

The last part of the assessment process in the orientation phase relates to determining the kind of help needed, as well as who can best provide it. Assessment of the most appropriate source of help is an important but often overlooked part of the evaluation needed in the orientation phase.

Communication Strategies

Initial contacts should be exploratory and somewhat tentative. Both the conversation and behaviors in the orientation phase are usually of a superficial nature. Neutral topics rather than emotionally loaded subjects usually seem less invasive to the client in the beginning stages of the relationship. Initially a client feels vulnerable in examining sensitive subjects before a trusting bond is established. Discussion of deep feelings and core issues will come later.

Talking about the client's interests and non-controversial topics provides the nurse with important information about the client's choices, knowledge base, interests, and characteristic ways of thinking about life. At the same time, the nurse is accumulating information that can be used to assist the client in establishing workable, meaningful goals. Conversations about hobbies, the geographical area the client is from, and the type of work the client does are subjects most clients will respond to with ease. Sometimes an article in the client's room, such as a family picture or religious item, serves the same purpose.

Example

Mrs. Gayle T., age 24, has been admitted to the hospital in the early stages of labor. She is alone in the labor room, knitting a sweater, but she appears somewhat nervous. Karen K., a student nurse, is assigned to care for Mrs. T. Since Karen loves to knit, she begins a conversation with Mrs. T. by focusing the discussion on the art of knitting—of knitting layettes in particular.

Knowledge of the client's developmental stage and current health situation may suggest possible topics for conversation. For example, one of the best ways to engage an adolescent is to demonstrate an awareness of teenagers, their interests, and pastimes. If the client is on the maternity floor, asking about the labor and delivery is relevant, whereas most elderly clients are eager to share anecdotes about their earlier lives. Such topics usually feel familiar, yet they are perceived as nonintrusive to most clients.

During the initial encounters with the nurse, the client begins to assess the nurse's trustworthiness (Forchuk and Brown, 1989). Communication during the orientation phase is a two-way process. Kindness, competence, and a willingness to become involved are communicated through the nurse's words and actions. The client gains information about the nurse as a person from the approaches the nurse uses to gather information and make contact. Does the nurse seem to know what she is doing? Is the nurse tactful and respectful of cultural mores? Data regarding the level of the nurse's interest and knowledge base are fac-

tored into the client's decision to engage actively in a therapeutic relationship.

Honesty and committed purpose are foundational threads in all successful therapeutic relationships. The nurse can use several strategies. Consistency and adherence to ANA standards of practice ensures professionalism. If nurses define clear relationship expectations and make few promises but honor the promises that have been made to the best of their abilities, clients perceive them as trustworthy (Meize-Grochowski, 1984; Thorne and Robinson, 1988). When it is impossible to honor a commitment, the client receives a full explanation.

Example

A Mexican client on a psychiatric ward had an excellent working relationship with a young Spanish-speaking student nurse. Because most of the other staff members did not speak Spanish, they looked to the student nurse to serve as translator. One morning the client told the student nurse she had concealed a knife in her room to commit suicide the night before, but now had decided against it. The student nurse told the client she would have to tell the nursing staff. At this point the client became very angry. She reminded the student of pledged confidentiality and told her if she communicated with the staff, she, the client, would feel betrayed and would sever the relationship with the nurse because it would mean a loss of privileges.

Despite the client's threat, the student felt she needed to communicate the information about the knife to the appropriate nursing and medical staff. She explained her reasons for doing so and emphasized that the safety of the client was her most important concern. In a later dialogue between the client and the nurse, following the room search, the client was able to renew her sense of trust in the student nurse. Ironically, the relationship became mutually more trusting. Because the student acted in a manner consistent with her role and dealt with the human aspects of the relationship conflict in a firm but compassionate manner, the positive bond between nurse and client actually strengthened.

Trusting the nurse is particularly difficult for the seriously mentally ill, for whom the idea of having a nonexploitative relationship is incomprehensible. Having this awareness helps the nurse depersonalize the experience of momentarily feeling overwhelmed by intense human emotions that he or she does not always easily understand. Most mentally ill clients respond better to shorter, frequent contacts until trust is established. Schizophrenic clients often enter and leave the space occupied by the student, almost circling around a space that is within visual distance of the nurse. Yet when the nurse approaches the client for an interaction, the client indicates rejection. What the client usually is expressing nonverbally is a psychological ambivalence and fear of a relationship. With patience and tact the nurse engages the client slowly, respecting the client's apprehension. Brief meetings gradually held over time that involve an invitation and a statement as to when the nurse will return help reduce the client's anxiety (Morath, 1987). Reducing the client's anxiety might be accomplished with a dialogue such as the following:

CASE EXAMPLE

Nurse: (*said with eye contact with the client and enough interpersonal space for comfort*): Good morning, Mrs. O'Connell, my name is Karen Quakenbush. I will be your nurse today.

Patient: (*looks briefly at the nurse and looks away. Gets up and moves away.*)

Nurse: This may not be a good time to talk with you. Would you mind if I checked back later with you? (*The introduction coupled with an invitation for later communication respects the client's need for interpersonal space and allows the client to set the pace of the relationship.*)

Later, the nurse notices that Mrs. O'Connell is circling around the area the nurse is occupying but does not approach the nurse. The nurse can smile encouragingly and repeat short encounters with the client until the client is more willing to trust. Since clients with high anxiety sense the nurse's anxiety, creating an interpersonal environment that places little demand on either party initially allows the needed trust to develop in the relationship.

Defining Goals

Often a client needs assistance in developing relevant health goals, but the level of assistance always should coincide with the client's capacity for self-help. Treatment goals are client centered. Supplying the quick solution or giving timely advice may be easier, but usually the "quick fix" is ill-advised. "If you feed a man a fish, you feed him for a day; if you teach him *how* to fish, you feed him for life" is a valid maxim to follow. Unless clients are physically or emotionally unable to participate in their own care, they should be treated as active partners in developing meaningful personal goals.

Goals should have meaning to the client. Motivation increases when goals are significant to clients. Finding out the client's interests can influence the selection of environmental motivators and the development of specific nursing strategies. For example, modifying the diabetic adolescent exchange lists to include fast foods and substitutions that mimic normal adolescent eating habits may facilitate acceptance of unwelcome dietary restrictions imposed by the illness. Through a partnership in care, the nurse implicitly conveys confidence in the client's capacity to solve his or her own problems by expecting the client to provide data, to make constructive suggestions, and to follow through with the agreed-upon plan. Exercise 4–6 gives practice on establishing mutual goals with a client.

Developing a Therapeutic Contract

The final step in the orientation phase of the relationship is a concise verbal expression of what both the nurse and the client can expect from the relationship. Referred to as a therapeutic contract, the verbal agreement supports the aims of the relationship and spells out role expectations and goals. This nurse–client contract is a dynamic process statement that needs to be renegotiated as the original circumstances in the health care situation change. The contract formally commits the client to taking an active role in achieving the relationship goals. Each therapeutic contract is unique from a content perspective because it is tailored to meet individual client needs.

Included in the therapeutic contract are the parameters and terms of the relationship. The contract should contain information about the following:

- The frequency and nature of interpersonal contacts.
- The benefits and obligations.
- Mutually agreed-upon goals.
- Expected role behaviors of both participants.

Although the contract usually does not contain the specific details of the relationship, the broad outline of the relationship's structure allows each partner to know what to expect from the relationship and from each other. When the purpose,

EXERCISE 4–6
Establishing Mutual Goals

Purpose: To develop awareness of mutuality in treatment planning.

Time: 30 minutes

Directions:
1. Read the clinical situation below and subsequent nursing goals.
2. Identify each goal as nurse-centered, client-centered, or mutual, as follows:
   N = a nursing goal.
   C = a client goal.
   M = a mutual goal that takes into consideration both client and nursing concerns.
3. After completion, discuss correct answers. How could nurse or client goals be modified to become mutual treatment goals?

Nursing Situation:
Mr. S., age 48, a white, middle-class professional, is recovering from his second myocardial infarction. Following his initial heart attack, Mr. S. resumed his ten-hour work day, high-stress lifestyle, and usual high-calorie, high-cholesterol diet of favorite fast foods, alcohol, and coffee. He smokes two packs of cigarettes a day and exercises once a week by playing golf.

Mr. S. is to be discharged in two days. He expresses impatience to return to work but also indicates that he would like to "get his blood pressure down and maybe drop ten pounds." The student nurse caring for Mr. S. establishes the following treatment goals:
1. Following three dietary teaching sessions, Mr. S. will be able to identify five foods high in sodium content.
2. Following discharge, Mr. S. will nap for two hours each day.
3. During the dietary teaching session, Mr. S. will list five foods high in calories and five foods low in calories.
4. Mr. S. will exercise moderately for ten minutes a day and will limit his weekly golf game to three holes.
5. Mr. S.'s diastolic blood pressure will be below 90 at his one-month postdischarge examination.
6. Immediately following discharge, Mr. S. will resume his executive work schedule.
7. Mr. S. will remain symptom free until discharge.

terms, and nature of a therapeutic relationship are not clear, the relational experience may be unnecessarily difficult or painful.

The interpersonal contract puts closure on the orientation phase and sets the stage for the intervention phase of the relationship. With relationship goals firmly established, nurse and client develop strategies to resolve problem issues.

WORKING (ACTIVE INTERVENTION) PHASE

Peplau (1987) appropriately refers to the next phase of the nurse–client relationship as the *working phase.* Communication strategies and the nursing interventions that are needed for problem resolution and enhancement of self-concept are the focus of this stage (Box 4–5). By this stage an atmosphere of trust and candor has presumably

developed, making it easier for the client to discuss deeper, more difficult issues and to experiment with new roles and actions. By contrast with the orientation phase, in which roles are more individualistic, the working phase is characterized by interdependent role relationships, with the client assuming more of a partnership with the nurse in problem solving.

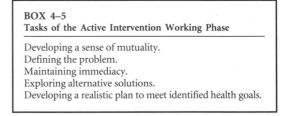

BOX 4–5
Tasks of the Active Intervention Working Phase

Developing a sense of mutuality.
Defining the problem.
Maintaining immediacy.
Exploring alternative solutions.
Developing a realistic plan to meet identified health goals.

The working phase requires mutuality that respects the client's autonomy. Integrating the client's perceptions of health needs and goals with those the nurse identifies as important to the client's well-being increases the probability of compliance with treatment protocols. The sorting-out process occurs more easily when the nurse is relaxed and willing to understand views different from his or her own. It is important to work with clients exactly as they are, without demanding that they be something different.

Mutuality in the working phase involves establishing a careful balance between the client's need for protection and his or her equally important need for self-determination. Unless a planned intervention has relevance for a client, it has little chance for success. Clients need to feel they have played a major role in developing a plan and implementing it in ways that make sense to them. The role of the nurse is to provide enough structure and guidelines for the client to explore problem issues and develop realistic solutions. Providing just enough support for the client to take control of the situation is important. The nurse may sometimes take more responsibility for an outcome than the client needs. Such an approach may be easier in the immediate situation, but important learning is lost. For example, a seemingly more efficient use of the nurse's time may be to give a bath to a stroke victim rather than to watch the client struggle through the bathing process with coaching when she falters. But what happens when the client goes home if she has not learned to bathe herself?

In developing mutuality in the working phase, the nurse respects the client's right to have opinions and feelings different from those of the nurse. The client's right to make important decisions, provided they do not violate self or others, is accepted by the nurse, even when it runs contrary to the nurse's thinking. This is not always easy when the nurse feels that the client is not acting in his or her own best interest. Consider what you would do as the community health nurse in the following situation.

Example

Mr. McEntee, 54 years old, is admitted for chest pain. His tests show increased occlusion of the cardiac vessels. All of the male members of his family died of coronary disease in their fifties. Three years ago he had coronary by-pass surgery. Since the surgery Mr. McEntee has conformed to a proper diet and exercised prudently. Although he was referred to the cardiac rehabilitation unit for after care, he has refused to go. A home visit shows that he is not adhering to his diet but that he goes to the gym daily to work out. The nurse questions his noncompliance and urges him to consider the implications.

Listening with heart as well as head, how would you try to understand Mr. McEntee's predicament? Why do you think he is acting in such a self-destructive way? What suggestions can you offer to home care nurse to increase compliance?

Defining the Problem

The working phase of the nurse–client relationship includes the planning and intervention phases of the nursing process. According to Peplau (1952), the success of the working phase lies in properly identifying the problems for which the client seeks treatment, followed by an evaluation of the client's interpersonal and problem-solving competencies. Including in the problem statement all elements that have the potential to interfere with goal achievement as well as defining the problem itself increases the probability of a satisfactory solution. The nurse acts as a sounding board, asking questions about parts of the communication that are not understood and helping the client describe the problem in specific and concrete terms.

The problem statement should be precise and concrete. "Mrs. K. started to cry when talking about her son's accident" is much more helpful than stating, "Mrs. K. is sad that her son was hurt in a motorcycle accident." The latter statement includes an inference about cause and effect that could be erroneous. In this case, the client's tears could relate to anger, disappointment, or hurt. Without validation from the client, the second statement about the cause of Mrs. K.'s tears could be incorrect, so that an intervention predicated on that information might be inappropriate.

Initially it might appear that developing the problem definition in more depth repeats the initial assessment data, but good problem definitions are evolving statements. Full participation by the client reinforces the client's feelings of being in control and free to communicate without being criticized. Clients vary in their ability to do this. For some clients there seems to be a genuine unawareness of a problem or of the connection between their behavior and the problem itself. Again, it is crucial for success to start where the client is in the process. If the client wishes to be active, use an action-oriented approach. But with a more passive client, forcing action-oriented solutions may prove counterproductive. Instead, gentle suggestions and a slower pace are indicated.

It is usually easier for the client to talk about factual data related to a problem rather than to express the feelings associated with the issue, or to talk about the feelings as if there were no factual data associated with the problem. Using open-ended questions and compound sentences to link situational facts and emotional effects allows for the most complete understanding. "It sounds as if you feel _____ because of _____" helps the nurse and client look at the strong interrelationship between the situational data and the emotional reactions to it. For many clients, events and feelings represent two separate and unconnected happenings. To experience the connections comes as a revelation.

Another way of helping clients recognize the significant details of critical issues is to describe the problem situation and the response in terms of who, what, where, when, and how—just as you did in your introduction and clarification of the nurse–client contract in the engagement phase. The difference is that now the communication focus is on a real or potential problem in need of nursing intervention instead of on the roles, purpose, and rules of the relationship. This strategy allows the client to perceive the problem in more complete form, and it gives the nurse an opportunity to observe the client's characteristic ways of handling difficult situations.

Whenever the nurse fails to understand a part of the client's problem or expectations, it is appropriate to ask for clarification or for more specific information. The nurse might ask for concrete data to bring the client's needs into sharper focus. For example, "Can you describe for me what happened next?" "Who else was there?" "Can you describe your feelings at the time?" "Can you tell me something about your reaction to (your problem)?" Time should be allowed between questions for the client to respond fully. Not infrequently,

the questions are asked, but not enough time is allowed for the client to respond.

In asking what, who, and why about problem situations, there must be careful observation of the impact of these questions on the client. "Why" questions are the hardest for clients to answer because motivational factors usually are the most difficult to understand and own. Most of the time behavior is multidetermined. Motivations are too complex and too sensitive to describe in answer to a simple "why" question. Often clients are not totally aware of what made them choose one behavioral response over another. The nurse needs to proceed slowly and carefully with such questions. It is important to challenge the client's thinking but not the client's integrity.

Pacing

Pacing refers to the deliberate exploration of client needs and solutions to health care problems, starting with where the client is in the process and respecting the client's need to be in as much control of the decision making as possible. The nurse needs to recognize the legitimacy of the client's need to proceed at a personally comfortable momentum. Throughout the active intervention phase, the nurse needs to be sensitive as to whether the client is still responding at a useful level. Looking at difficult problems and developing strategies to resolve those problems is not an easy process, especially when resolution will require significant behavioral changes. If the nurse is perceived as inquisitive rather than facilitative, communication breaks down.

Pacing the interview in ways that offer support as well as challenge is the responsibility of the nurse, not the client. The client's behavioral responses will serve as a guide for structuring deeper exploration and for understanding client needs. Changes in client behaviors often are the best indicators of data collection that is proceeding beyond the client's tolerance level. Examples of warning signs indicating increased anxiety include loss of eye contact, fidgeting, abrupt changes in subject, crying, inappropriate laughter, or asking to be left alone.

Although the nurse needs to be aware that heightened anxiety precludes discussion of difficult material, strong emotion should not necessarily be interpreted as reflecting a level of interaction stretching beyond the client's tolerance. Tears or an emotional outburst, even a more prolonged negative exchange, may reflect honestly felt emotion. A well-placed comment such as, "It seems to make you sad when we talk about your daughter" acknowledges the feeling and may also stimulate further discussion. The deciding factor as to whether to drop a subject or to support the client in exploring it is a clinical judgment about whether or not the feelings are appropriate in intensity to the behavioral stimulus, as well as about the capacity of the client to continue with the discussion. Forcing a client to continue with a painful discussion when it is clear that there is too much emotion fails to respect the client's need for self-determination in the relationship.

Sometimes just sitting with calm interest and an open posture is enough to help a client reduce the internal anxiety of expressing strong emotion. A simple statement, "It's all right to cry" or, "It's okay to feel angry; nobody would want this to happen to him" acknowledges the feeling component, gives the client permission to express it, and implicitly offers assistance in coping with difficult emotions.

Developing Realistic Goals

Once the client is able to describe a problem or need in comprehensive yet concise terms to the mutual satisfaction of the nurse and client, the problem in need of nursing care is reformulated as a nursing diagnosis. Initiated in the orientation phase, the working phase develops realistic short-term objectives to meet long-term treatment goals. This is easier said than done. Although the therapeutic alliance should be much stronger than it was in the orientation phase, it still is an interpersonal structure, easily threatened by anxiety and misunderstandings.

The nurse can provide a nonanxious presence in helping clients develop workable solutions based on goals that have meaning to the client and that are supportive of client well-being. Several possibilities explain client anxiety in health care situations and direct the most appropriate interventions in developing goals. In some instances, the client's anxiety relates to perceiving the problem as more complex than it actually is. By the time a client enters the health care system, the stress of the problem itself has been compounded by the tension created by the client's inability to cope successfully without help. Overestimating the likelihood of negative outcomes can create such an emotional strain that the impaired consequences can actually foster a self-fulfilling prophecy. Negative images about situations can drain the client's energy from thinking about more positive images and the actions needed to turn them into reality.

Breaking a seemingly insoluble problem down into simpler chunks makes it more manageable. Deciding on a course of action for even a small part of the problem helps the client to gain some control in the situation and usually reduces anxiety to a tolerable level. For example, a goal of eating three meals a day may seem overwhelming to a person suffering from nausea and loss of appetite associated with gastric cancer. A goal of having Jell-O or chicken soup and a glass of milk three times a day may sound more achievable. Packaging goals in terminology the client understands and accepts is more important than having a goal the client considers beyond his or her capabilities. To be effective, goals should be achievable, behavioral, and realistic.

Planning Alternative Solutions

All life situations have some element of choice. In even the most difficult nursing situations, there are some options, even if the choice is to die with dignity or to change one's attitude toward an illness or a family member. Once goals are determined, the nurse and client brainstorm all possible options and strategies to meet agreed-upon health objectives. In the process, they also discuss the implications of each possible choice and the anticipated reactions of others. Anticipating reactions of others is an important step in the process because even well thought out strategies can have unforeseen consequences for self and others. Thinking about whether this is tolerable and what the planned response might be strengthens the client's resolve and feeling of being in charge of his or her destiny.

The client should be encouraged to develop stronger problem-solving and interpersonal skills during the working phase. Although mistakes will happen, they will not destroy the work of this phase. The reality is that something can go wrong even with the most perfectly developed plan. Coping with unexpected responses can strengthen the client's problem-solving abilities by compelling the person to consider alternative options (plan B) when the original plan doesn't bring about the desired results.

Constructive coping mechanisms are as important to support as the actual plan. A useful comment might be, "It is important to keep in mind that you did a good job with this, and no one could have predicted the outcome." This statement removes the blame that so frequently accompanies failed efforts.

The client should be allowed to generate new ideas or possible solutions freely, without judgment, even if they initially do not seem to make much sense to the nurse. The more possibilities that are developed, the stronger the chances of settling on a strategy that has special meaning for the client.

During this phase of the relationship, nursing interventions should have a broader focus than simply correcting problem areas. For clients to experience lasting change, there also needs to be an emphasis on strengthening their healthy parts and on helping them to mobilize their resources.

Frequently clients are unaware that they possess assets they could be using in the resolution of difficult issues. Vocational skills, talents, community resources, and supportive family are advantages clients sometimes take for granted. They fail to appreciate the transferable skills that can be used in the current situation.

The next step in the process is to select the most promising alternative strategies in light of short- and long-term treatment goals. Anticipating possible consequences of using one strategy over another should be considered prior to implementation. For example, if a client wishes to go home rather than to a nursing home, how is this decision likely to affect other family members who will have to provide the necessary care? How does the client feel about his or her ability to provide self-care, and are these assumptions valid? Each of these questions will have a direct impact on the option chosen.

Strategies selected for implementation should be realistic and achievable in the light of the client's level of self-care capacity and potential environmental resources. The positive consequences of the course of action adopted should outweigh negative potential outcomes. Exercise 4–7 gives practice in developing alternative strategies.

EXERCISE 4–7
Selecting Alternative Strategies

Purpose: To help you develop a process for considering alternative options.

Time: 45 minutes

Procedure:
You have two exams within the next two weeks. Your car needs servicing badly. Because of all the work you have been doing, you haven't had time to call your mother, and she isn't happy. Your laundry is overflowing the hamper. Several of your friends are going to the beach for the weekend and have invited you to go along. How can you handle it all?
1. Give yourself five minutes to write down all the ideas that come to mind for handling these multiple responsibilities. Use single words or phrases to express your ideas. Don't eliminate any possibilities even if they seem far-fetched.
2. In groups of three or four students, choose a scribe, and share the ideas you have written down.
3. Select the three most promising ideas.
4. Develop several small, concrete, achievable actions to implement these ideas.
5. Share the small-group findings with the class group.

Discussion:
1. In what ways were the solutions you chose similar or dissimilar to those of your peers?
2. Were any of your ideas or ways of achieving alternative solutions surprising to you? to others in your group?
3. What did you learn from doing this exercise that could help you and the client to generate possible solutions to seemingly impossible situations?

Implementing the Plan

Both nurse and client monitor progress. As the client begins to implement certain actions for coping more successfully with anxiety-provoking situations, the nurse can offer anticipatory guidance and role rehearsal for the more difficult aspects of this process. Sometimes simply anticipating—"What is the worst that can possibly happen if I do _____?"—allows the client to see that the worst possibility is manageable.

Feedback for the client regarding possible modifications when the situation warrants it is an equally important element of the process.

Implementation does not always mean the course will be smooth and uneventful, even when the plan is appropriate. Most problems and health care needs have to be worked through slowly, with the client taking two steps forward and one step back. This slow progress sometimes is cause for discouragement, and yet, like small children taking their first steps, the process is usually not a straight linear progression.

Offering the client reassurance based on the fact that the two small steps were taken and that those steps cannot be erased, even if the client is unable to achieve a short-term goal to complete satisfaction, is a source of valuable support. Most people don't accomplish all of their goals on the first try. There is no reason to think the client has failed because a carefully though out plan has not worked. The more critical question is, What is it about either the goal, the strategies used to meet the goal, or the appraisal of the need or problem that needs reworking?

Handling Resistance in Implementation

Resistance to meeting treatment goals usually is related to parts of the process that are in conflict or are inconsistent with the client's underlying goals or important self-concepts. The client's perspective needs to be taken into account in planning and implementing strategies. Otherwise the new solution will be as unsuccessful as the initial one.

Careful observation of the client and attention to whether goals are being achieved provide indicators. When the behaviors or facial expression of the sender do not seem to match the words or the gravity of a situation emotionally, the message is classified as incongruent. If the words are positive but the tone of voice harsh and clipped, or if intense anger is expressed with a smile and a tightly controlled, neutral tone, the message is inconsistent. For example, a client may tell you he is not at all worried about his open-heart surgery in two days because he has read up on it and it doesn't seem dangerous to him, but then he spends most of the evening pacing the halls or yelling at his wife. This man is giving you a double message.

Any vague or uncomfortable feelings the nurse experiences about the progress of implementation are important. Assuming that the topic is not innately problematic to the nurse, attending to personal feelings of arousal or doubt in client conversations is one way of picking up feelings and attitudes that could sabotage implementation. In responding to a client's need, the nurse has to consider how verbal and nonverbal behaviors will be perceived by the client or family members. Therapeutic responses are clear and focused on the client's need. However, they also respect the nurse's integrity. The two responses to the client's need given below take the same amount of time. Which is potentially more satisfying?

CASE EXAMPLE

Jenny Johnson, RN, is on her way to the staff lounge to take a much needed break when Mr. Clemson stops her to discuss his concerns about the cardiac catheterization his son was scheduled for an hour ago. Jenny sighs, glances impatiently at her watch, and comments in a flat voice, "I'd be happy to talk with you about the procedure if you have any questions."

An alternative response, one that recognizes the legitimate needs of both client and nurse, might be as follows:

> NURSE (*in a warm voice and making direct eye contact*): It's natural to be concerned, but this procedure usually takes at least two hours. I'll phone the recovery room and find out if your son has arrived there yet. If he hasn't arrived, I'll leave a message for them to call me when he does arrive. I'll be off the unit for a short time now, but when I get back, I'd be happy to talk with you about the procedure if you have any questions.

In the second response, the nurse recognizes the legitimacy of the client's need as well as her own and responds accordingly. Because the message is clear and congruent with her expression and action, it is more likely to comfort the client.

Sometimes in the working phase it is necessary to challenge factors that may get in the way of goal achievement. Challenging resistant behaviors requires a special type of feedback because often the client is only partially aware of what is happening and of his or her role in the process (Garant, 1980). Because of a lack of awareness, these behaviors remain unavailable for direct exploration and negotiation. Before confronting a client, the nurse should determine carefully whether it is warranted and anticipate possible outcomes. It is not necessary to confront a client about a resistant behavior as soon as it occurs, nor is it always useful. Sometimes asking open-ended questions may elicit self-awareness, and the client may come to the same conclusion as the nurse about the existence of a problem in implementing certain actions.

If this strategy doesn't work and you must challenge the meaning of the client's message, it is important to proceed with interpersonal precision, sensitivity, and accuracy. The nurse needs to appreciate the impact of the confrontation on the client's self-esteem.

Calling a client's attention to a contradiction in behavioral response is usually threatening. It should be accomplished in a tactful manner that welcomes, but does not necessarily demand, an immediate resolution. Constructive feedback involves drawing the client's attention to the existence of unacceptable behaviors or contradictory messages while respecting the fragility of the therapeutic alliance and the client's need to protect the integrity of the self-concept. To be effective, constructive confrontations should be attempted only when the following criteria have been met:

- The nurse has established a firm, trusting bond with the client.
- The timing and environmental circumstances are appropriate.
- The confrontation is delivered in a nonjudgmental and empathetic manner.
- Only those resistances capable of being changed by the client are addressed.
- The nurse is willing to abide by the client's right to self-determination.

Timing is everything. Enough time and interpersonal space should be given to allow the client an opportunity to reflect on the feelings surrounding the behaviors as well as on the thoughts and feelings aroused by the nurse's comments. Discrepancies should never be challenged in a roomful of people unless there is no alternative and the client's behavior represents a danger to self or others. More specific guidelines regarding constructive feedback are presented in subsequent chapters.

CASE EXAMPLE

Mary Kiernan is 5 feet 2 inches tall and weighs 260 pounds. She has attended weekly sessions for weight management for the past six weeks. Although she lost eight pounds the first week and four pounds in weeks two and three, respectively, her weight loss seems to have plateaued. Jane Tompkins, her primary nurse, notices that she seems to be able to stick to the diet until she gets to dessert and then she can't resist temptation. Mary is very discouraged about her lack of further progress.

Consider the effect of each response on the client.

NURSE: You're supposed to be on a 1200-calorie a day diet, but instead, you're sneaking dessert. I think you need to face up to the fact that eating dessert while dieting is hypocritical.

Or:

NURSE: I can understand your discouragement, but you have done quite well in losing 16 pounds. It seems as though you can stick to the diet until you get to dessert. Do you think we need to talk a little more about what hooks you when you get to dessert? Maybe we need to find alternatives that would help you get over this hump.

The first statement is direct, valid, and concise, but it is likely to be disregarded or experienced as unfeeling by the client. In the second response, the nurse reframes a behavioral inconsistency as a temporary setback, a problem in need of a solution instead of a human failing. By bringing in the observed strength of the progress achieved so far, the nurse confirms her faith in the client's resourcefulness. Both responses would probably require similar amounts of time and energy on the part of the nurse. But the second response fits the goal of motivating the client to use inner resources. The external reinforcement of the nurse allows the client to continue progress toward her goal of losing 50 pounds over a six-month period.

Referral

There are times in the active intervention phase when it becomes obvious that the client needs a different interpersonal or more skilled approach to achieve treatment goals. Sometimes it is painful for the nurse to admit that the client's need surpasses the nurse's level of expertise, especially when genuine feelings and the nurse's ego are involved. Referral is an appropriate intervention whenever a client's needs exceed the level of care provided in the interpersonal relationship.

The nurse can play an important role in the referral process by thoroughly discussing with the client the reasons for the referral. Telling the client that you will pave the way or passing on some information about the person who has been referred is a good bridging technique that often alleviates unnecessary anxiety. The nurse should have the client's permission to transmit information to the referred resource. Often the nurse's summary of the relationship is helpful to the referral professional in planning future strategies. Summarizing goal achievement with the client and providing a copy of the summary information reinforces the client's sense of control and continuity of treatment.

TERMINATION PHASE

Termination should be mentioned well in advance of the actual ending of the relationship. The client needs to be allowed to express feelings related to termination and to discuss the effects of the anticipated loss. Encouraging the client to deal with reactivated feelings from former losses and the nurse's constructive sharing of relevant personal feelings about the relationship and the termination facilitate the process. Together the nurse and client examine the meaning and value of the relationship, including negative as well as positive elements. Finally, there is a mutual evaluation of goal achievement. Follow-up interventions are identified if needed.

The threads of termination are interwoven throughout the nursing process. Preparation for termination actually begins with the orientation phase, when the nurse explains to the client the times, duration, and focus of the relationship. Just as the orientation phase is linked with the assess-

---

BOX 4–6
Tasks of the Termination Phase

Summarizing goal achievement.
Making referrals if warranted.

---

ment phase, the termination phase of the nurse–client relationship shares characteristics with the evaluation phase (Box 4–6). The nurse and client mutually evaluate goal achievement and discuss needed modifications. Feelings surrounding the termination are discussed, and plans for follow-up are initiated, if indicated. With significant and long-term relationships, the nurse and client also evaluate the effectiveness of their communication in the relationship.

Endings are rarely comfortable, but the importance of the termination phase should not be underestimated. Sometimes there is a tendency to shortchange the termination phase because for both the nurse and the client it is more uncomfortable than some of the other stages. This is particularly true when the relationship has meaning—when the participants have invested a lot of themselves in the relational process, it is hard to give it up.

The process of termination will not be the same for every client. Different aspects of the relationship should be emphasized and, ideally, correlated with each client's individualized needs, temperament, and behavioral response. Not every relationship can tolerate a lengthy discussion of termination feelings. The nurse's behavioral response should match the level of other phases in depth and intensity. For very short-term relationships or for a superficial contact, a simple statement of the meaning of the relationship, factual reassurance based on client behaviors observed in the relational experience, and discussion of follow-up plans suffice.

The importance of the relationship, no matter how brief, should not be underestimated. The client may be one of several persons the nurse has taken care of that shift, but the relationship may represent the only interpersonal or professional contact available to a lonely and frightened person.

In personal relationships it is customary for the person who is leaving to acknowledge the fact to the people in the immediate surroundings. This custom should carry over into the clinical situation. Even if contact has been minimal, the nurse should endeavor to stop by the client's room to say good-bye. The dialogue in such cases can be simple and short: "Mr. Jones, I will be going off duty in a few minutes. I enjoyed working with (meeting) you. Miss Smith, the evening nurse, will be taking care of you this evening." Anticipatory guidance in the form of simple instructions or reiteration of important skills may be appropriate, depending on the circumstances.

Care should be taken to recognize the wide variety of behaviors accompanying termination, including regression and a temporary return of maladaptive ways of coping. Clients react in a variety of ways to separation. Some are grateful but very ready to move on with all they have gained in the relationship. Some get angry, others deny it is happening. Some clients appear to have lost all that was gained personally in the relationship. Behaviors the nurse may encounter with termination include avoidance; minimizing of the importance of the relationship; temporary return of symptoms precipitating the need for nursing care; anger; demands; or additional reliance on the nurse. Sometimes this phase is perplexing for both nurse and client. For the nurse there is a sense of pride in watching someone grow and develop as a person. It is difficult to give this up or to experience loss of gains during the termination phase. For the client there can be a fear of relapsing and losing ground with the new attitudes and competencies. All of these feelings are normal in the termination phase and are usually temporary. When the client is unable to express feelings about endings, the nurse may recognize them in the client's nonverbal behavior.

CASE EXAMPLE

A teenager who had spent many months on a bone-marrow transplant unit had developed a real attachment to her primary nurse, who had stood by her during the frightening physical assaults to her body and appearance occasioned by the treatment. The client was unable verbally to acknowledge the meaning of the relationship with the nurse directly, despite having been given many opportunities to do so by the nurse. The client said she couldn't wait to leave this awful hospital and that she was glad she didn't have to see the nurses anymore. Yet

this same client was found sobbing in her room the day she left, and she asked the nurse if she could write to her. The relationship obviously had meaning for the client, but she was unable to express it verbally.

In another clinical situation, a hospitalized formerly psychotic client, who had made remarkable progress in a one-to-one weekly relationship, failed to show up for the last appointment. Upon questioning the nursing staff, the primary care nurse found that the client had scheduled a clinic appointment off the ward at precisely the time of the nurse–client appointment. The nurse went to the clinic and found the client lying on a bench, waiting to be seen. The nurse told the client that she was disappointed when the client didn't come for the appointment and wondered if it had to do with termination. For the first time the client was able to cry and to address her feelings of abandonment, asking if she could go with the nurse and become her maid. Although her initial resolution of the termination phase was unrealistic, exploring the meaning behind the request with the nurse allowed this client to express the depth of her feelings about the impending separation.

The nurse was able to appreciate the significance of the relationship to the client and to help her work through some very strong feelings. The meaning and commitment the relationship held for the nurse were effectively demonstrated in her searching out the client, reinforcing the reality that the relationship had significance.

If the relationship has been rewarding, real work has been accomplished. Strong feelings were shared, and often there is a genuine sadness and sense of loss at parting. Nurses need to be sufficiently aware of their own feelings so that they may use them constructively without imposing them on the client. It is appropriate for nurses to share some of the meaning the relationship held for them, as long as such sharing fits the needs of the interpersonal situation and is not excessive or too emotionally intense.

Appropriate self-disclosure in the termination phase might include thanking the client for sharing his or her life with the nurse. Exploration of knowledge gained from the relationship and of attitudes and feelings of client and nurse during the relationship and as they relate to the specific health care concerns of the client add value to goal achievement. Shared meanings enhance the human outcomes of the therapeutic relationship (Marck, 1990).

In a successful relationship, the client demonstrates the following outcomes:

- Adaptive progression toward health or well-being.
- Adequacy of role performance according to developmental level and constraints of the illness.
- A self-reported or enacted value shift, indicating a deeper sense of personal integrity.

Evaluation of outcomes should take into consideration all phases of the nursing process. Was the problem definition adequate and appropriate for the client? Were the interventions chosen adequate and appropriate to resolve the client's problem? Could the interventions be implemented effectively and efficiently to both the client and nurse's satisfaction? Negative answers to any of these questions require adjustments in any or all phases of the nursing process.

There are occasions or circumstances when because of individual limitations, the policy of the agency, or the nature of the relationship dynamics, it is in the best interest of the client to terminate the relationship. If the relationship needs to be terminated for transfer, therapeutic, or policy reasons, the helping person should be honest, direct, and compassionate as he or she provides a full explanation of the circumstances surrounding the termination. Usually, if the nurse is tactful and considerate in explaining the unplanned end of the relationship, the client has a better chance of working through the termination than if the departure is precipitous and no attention is paid to its impact on the client. Follow-up planning should be initiated and resources identified for continued support. Termination as a loss process in nurse–client relationships is discussed in Chapter 8.

SUMMARY

The nurse–client relationship represents a purposeful use of self in all professional relations with clients and other people involved with the client. Respect for the dignity of the client and self,

mutuality, person-centered communication, and authenticity in conversation are process threads underlying all communication responses.

By contrast with social relationships, therapeutic relationships have specific boundaries, purposes, and behaviors. They are client focused and are mutually defined by client and nurse. Effective relationships enhance the well-being of the client and the professional growth of the nurse.

The professional relationship is a developmental process characterized by four overlapping yet distinct stages: preinteraction, engagement, active intervention, and termination. The preinteraction phase is the only phase of the relationship the client is not part of. During the preinteraction phase, the nurse develops the appropriate physical and interpersonal environment for an optimal relationship, in collaboration with other health professionals and significant others in the client's life.

The orientation phase of the relationship defines the purpose, roles, and rules of the process and provides a framework for assessing client needs. The nurse builds a sense of trust through consistency of actions. Data collection forms the basis for developing relevant nursing diagnoses. The orientation phase ends with a therapeutic contract mutually defined by nurse and client.

Once the nursing diagnosis is established, the working or active intervention phase begins. Essentially, this is the problem-solving phase of the relationship, paralleling the planning and implementation phases of the nursing process. As the client begins to explore difficult problems and feelings, the nurse uses a variety of interpersonal strategies to help the client develop new insights and methods of coping and problem solving.

The final phase of the nurse–client relationship occurs when the essential work of the active intervention phase is finished. Termination involves the deliberate separation of two or more persons from an intimate and meaningful relationship. Each relationship has its own character, strengths, and limitations, and what may be appropriate in one nursing situation may be totally inappropriate in another. Nevertheless, terminations are the final step in the nurse–client relationship, and the ending of it should be thoroughly and compassionately defined. Primary tasks associated with the termination phase of the relationship include summarization and evaluation of completed activities and when indicated the making of concrete plans for follow-up.

REFERENCES

Anvil CA, Silver BW (1984). Therapist self-disclosure: When is it appropriate? Perspectives in Psychiatric Care 22:57–61.

Benner P (1984). From Novice to Expert: Excellence and Power in Clinical Nursing Practice. Menlo Park, CA, Addison-Wesley.

Buber M (1958). I and Thou (2nd ed.). RG Smith (trans.). New York, Scribner's.

Buber M (1965). Between Man and Man. RG Smith (trans.). New York, Macmillan.

Carkhuff RR (1983). The Art of Helping V, Student Workbook. Amherst, MA, Human Resource Development Press.

Clarke J, Wheeler S (1992). A view of the phenomenon of caring in nursing practice. Journal of Advanced Nursing 17:1283–1290.

Companiello J (1980). The process of termination. Journal of Psychiatric Nursing 18(2):29.

Curtin L (1983). Trust: An idealistic or realistic goal? In Minckley B, Walters M (eds.) (1983), Building Trust Relationships in Nursing. Indianapolis, IN, Midwest Alliance in Nursing.

Dinkmeyer DC, Dinkmeyer DC, Jr, Sperry L (1987). Adlerian Counseling and Psychotherapy (2nd ed.). Columbus, OH: Merrill.

Ersek M (1992). Examining the process and dilemmas of reality negotiation. Image 24(1):19–25.

Forchuk C, Brown B (1989). Establishing a nurse–client relationship. Journal of Psychosocial Nursing 27(2):30–34.

Frankl V (1955). The Doctor and the Soul. New York, Knopf.

Garant C (1980). Stalls in the therapeutic process. American Journal of Nursing 80:2166–2169.

Heinrich K (1992). When a patient becomes too special. American Journal of Nursing 22(11):62–64.

Kasch C (1986). Establishing a collaborative nurse–patient relationship: A distinct focus of nursing action in primary care. Image 18(2):44–47.

Kasch C, Dine J (1988). Person-centered communication and social perspective taking. Western Journal of Nursing Research 10(3):317–326.

Krikorian DA, Paulanka BJ (1982). Self-awareness—the key to a successful nurse–patient relationship? Journal of Psychiatric Nursing and Mental Health Services 20(6):19–21.

Lamb HR (1988). One-to-one relationships with the long-term mentally ill: Issues in training professionals. Community Mental Health Journal 24(4):328–337.

Marck P (1990). Therapeutic reciprocity: A caring phenomenon. Advances in Nursing Science 13(1):49–59.

Meize-Grochowski R (1984). An analysis of the concept of trust. Journal of Advanced Nursing 9:563–572.

Morath J (1987). Theory-based intervention: A case study using Sullivan's interpersonal theory of psychiatry. Perspectives in Psychiatric Care 24(1):12–19.

Morse J (1991). Negotiating commitment and involvement in the nurse–patient relationship. Journal of Advanced Nursing 16:455–468.

Morse J, Bottorf J, Anderson G, O'Brien B, Solberg S (1992). Beyond empathy: Expanding expressions of caring. Journal of Advanced Nursing 17:809–821.

Paterson J, Zderad L (1988). Humanistic Nursing. New York, National League for Nursing.

Peplau HE (1952). Interpersonal Relations in Nursing. New York, Putnam's.

Ramos M (1992). The nurse–patient relationship: Theme and variations. Journal of Advanced Nursing 17:495–506.

Roberts S, Krouse J (1988). Enhancing self-care through active negotiation. Nurse Practitioner 13(8):44–52.

Rogers C (1973). My philosophy of interpersonal relationships and how it grew. Journal of Humanistic Psychology 13:3.

Seyster K (1987). A lesson in therapeutic relationship. Imprint 9:56–57.

Taylor B (1992a) From helper to human: A reconceptualization of the nurse as person. Journal of Advanced Nursing 17:1042–1049.

Taylor B (1992b) Relieving pain through ordinariness in nursing: A phenomonologic account of a comforting nurse–patient encounter. Advances in Nursing Science 15(1):33–43.

Taylor SG (1985). Rights and responsibilities: Nurse–patient relationships. Image 17(1):9–16.

Thorne SE, Robinson CA (1988). Reciprocal trust in health care relationships. Journal of Advanced Nursing 782–789.

Travelbee J (1971). Interpersonal Aspects of Nursing. Philadelphia, Davis.

Yuen FK (1986). The nurse–client relationship: A mutual learning experience. Journal of Advanced Nursing 11:529–533.

Chapter 5

Bridges and Barriers in the Therapeutic Relationship

VIRGINIA SULLIVAN

OUTLINE

Basic Concepts and Applications

BRIDGES TO THE RELATIONSHIP
    Caring
    Empowerment
    Trust
    Empathy
    Mutuality
    Confidentiality
BARRIERS TO THE RELATIONSHIP
    Anxiety
    Stereotyping and bias
    Violation of personal space

Summary

OBJECTIVES

At the end of this chapter, the student will be able to:

1. Identify concepts that enhance development of therapeutic relationships: caring, empowerment, trust, empathy, mutuality, and confidentiality.
2. Describe nursing actions designed to promote trust, empowerment, empathy, mutuality, and confidentiality.

3. Describe barriers to the development of therapeutic relationships: anxiety, stereotyping, and lack of personal space.
4. Identify nursing actions that can be used to reduce anxiety and respect personal space and confidentiality.

Life is a voyage in which we choose neither vessel nor weather, but much can be done in the management of the sails and the guidance of the helm.

Petty, 1962

Chapter 5 focuses on the conceptual components of the nurse–client relationship. The concepts and applications are integrated because they cannot logically be understood apart from one another. To establish a therapeutic relationship, the nurse must understand and apply the concepts of caring, empowerment, trust, empathy, and mutuality. Appreciation of other concepts, such as anxiety, stereotyping, personal space, and confidentiality, add to the quality of relationship strategies. Although these concepts are understood as abstract elements of the nurse–client relationship, implementing actions that convey feelings of caring, warmth, acceptance, and understanding to the client is an interpersonal skill that requires careful development. Caring for others in a meaningful way requires patience and practice. Novice students may experience interpersonal situations that leave them feeling helpless and inadequate (Chapman and Chapman, 1983). Feelings of sadness, anger, or embarrassment, although overwhelming, are common. Discussion of these feelings in peer groups, experiential learning, and theoretical applications help students to grow and learn from prior mistakes. The self-awareness strategies identified in Chapter 3 and the use of educational groups described in Chapter 12 provide useful guidelines for working through these feelings.

BASIC CONCEPTS AND APPLICATIONS

BRIDGES TO THE RELATIONSHIP

Caring

Caring is an intentional human action characterized by commitment and a sufficient level of knowledge and skill to allow the nurse to support the basic integrity of the person being cared for (Clarke and Wheeler, 1992). One person (the nurse) offers caring to another (the client) by means of the therapeutic relationship. The nurse's ability to care develops from a natural response to help those in need, the knowledge that caring is a part of nursing ethics, and respect for self and oth-

ers. The caring nurse involves clients in their struggle for health and well-being rather than simply doing for clients those actions they cannot perform for themselves.

Clayton (1991) describes four steps involved in caring. The first is *offering a presence,* during which the nurse introduces his or her purpose in developing a relationship with the client (meeting the client's health needs). The second is *attending,* in which the nurse provides evidence of an intent and ability to care. The third is *affiliating,* in which the client recognizes the value of the offered experience. The fourth is *empowering,* in which the nurse and client gain strength and confidence from the mutual experience while moving toward achievement of client outcomes.

The ability to become a caring person is influenced by previous thoughts, attitudes, and involvement with caring. The person who has received caring is more likely to be able to offer it to others. Caring should not be confused with caretaking. Although caretaking is a part of caring, it may involve giving care to others for the purpose of satisfying the nurse's unmet needs. Caretaking may lack the necessary intentional giving of self. Self-awareness about feelings, attitudes, values, and skills is essential for developing an effective caring relationship.

The focus of the caring relationship is the client and his or her needs. The nurse recognizes the client's need for help and basic vulnerability. Caring represents a selected and informed response to the client's need, the act of giving freely and willingly of oneself to another through warmth, compassion, and concern, and interest. Nurses care for others during times of physical discomfort, emotional stress, and need for health maintenance. Nursing leaders identify caring as an ethical responsibility (Fry, 1988; Harrison, 1990).

Caring has a positive influence on health status and healing. Caring individuals recognize others as separate and unique persons with varying needs. Clients are treated with kindness and consideration. Through caring, nurses identify client needs, implement appropriate nursing actions, make knowledgeable decisions, and bring about positive changes in their clients (Gault, 1983). In a caring relationship, the client can focus on accomplishing the goals of health care instead of worrying about whether care is forthcoming. The nurse gains from the caring relationship by experiencing the satisfaction of meeting the client's needs accurately and skillfully.

Some people criticize the use of caring as the essence of nursing practice and the foundational base of the nurse–client relationship on the grounds that it is not scientific, and perhaps, "feminine" in its origins. But if one considers competence as having a strong theoretical base from which one makes careful reflective judgments about every aspect of nursing care, then it becomes an important element of the science as well as the art of quality nursing practice. As you think about the concept of caring, it might be helpful, as a group, to consider all of the possible and different aspects of caring that might be applicable to nursing practice—and to ask yourself, "How is caring implemented in the nurse–client relationship?"

Empowerment

An important underlying thread in every nurse–client relationship is preparing and reinforcing clients to cope with difficult life situations created by alterations in their health and well-being. Hawks (1992) defines empowerment as "the interpersonal process of providing the proper tools, resources and environment to build, develop and increase the ability and effectiveness of others to set and reach goals for individual and social ends" (p. 609). Empowerment has to do with people power. It is a concept that explicitly encourages individuals and their families to take maximum control of their lives. Empowerment of another is pragmatic and action oriented. An empowerment model, such as presented in Figure 5–1, recognizes and builds on the strengths and talents of an actively involved person, group, or society to solve difficult problems. Empowerment is purposeful and related to client goals that are uniquely important to the person(s) involved. Because the client becomes the primary author of a new chapter in his or her life story, there is renewed energy and involvement in the issues. Personal responsibility, provision of appropriate resources, and ongoing support pro-

vide the catalyst and environmental support required for people to feel empowered. As you think about the concept of empowerment, you might want to reflect on the experiences you have had in which you felt empowered. What was it that made you feel empowered? Another relevant question is, "What groups in society are disempowered, and how might you as a nurse help these individuals feel more empowered?"

Trust

Trust is an element in our everyday structure. According to Erik Erikson (1963), trust is the reliance on the consistency, sameness, and continuity of experiences that are provided by an organized combination of familiar and predictable things and people. Trust is based on past experiences and begins in infancy through consistent and continual care by the same caregiver. It allows the infant to believe in self, in others, and in the external world. Through trust, one learns how to cope with the world and resolve frustrations and problems. There is consistency and predictability in behaviors and freedom from uncertainty and doubt (Meize-Grochowski, 1984). Once a sense of trust is established between two people, a sharing of feelings and emotions occurs.

Trust, however, can be broken. An alcoholic or abusive parent who is gentle one minute and explodes with anger the next leaves children and others unsure of how the parent will behave. The community health nurse who is inconsistent about keeping client appointments and the pediatric nurse who indicates falsely that an injection will not hurt are jeopardizing client trust. It is hard to maintain trust when one person cannot depend on another. Energy that should be directed toward coping with health problems gets rechanneled into assessing the nurse's commitment and trustworthiness. Having confidence in the nurse's skills, commitment, and caring allows the client to place full attention on the situation requiring resolution.

Among characteristics of a trusting relationship are respect, honesty, consistency, faith, caring, and hope, but a therapeutic relationship always begins with trust. Certain interpersonal strategies (Box 5–1) help promote a trusting relationship.

Clients can also jeopardize the trust a nurse has

NURTURING, CARING ENVIRONMENT

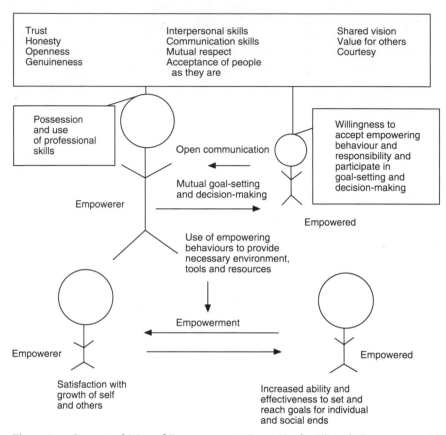

Figure 5–1 Conceptual Map of Empowerment. From Hawks J (1992). Empowerment in nursing education: Concept analysis and application to philosophy, learning and instruction. Journal of Advanced Nursing (17):613. Reprinted by permission of Blackwell Scientific Publications, Oxford, England.

in them. Sometimes clients "test" a nurse's trustworthiness by sending the nurse on unnecessary errands or talking endlessly on superficial topics. As long as nurses recognize testing behaviors and set clear limits on their roles and the client's role, it is possible to develop trust. Exercise 5–1 is designed to help students become more familiar with the concept of trust.

Empathy

Empathy is the ability of a person to perceive and understand another person's emotions accurately and to communicate the meanings of feelings to the other through verbal and nonverbal behaviors. The goal of empathy is to elicit and communicate hidden emotions and meanings of which the client is unaware. Objective and nonjudgmental nurses feel the emotions a client feels but at the same time maintain their own separate identities. The nurse should not overidentify with or internalize the feelings of the client. If internalization occurs, objectivity is lost, along with the ability to help the client move through the feelings. It is important to recognize that the client's feelings belong to the client, not the nurse.

Attaining high levels of empathy, although difficult, is rewarding to both nurse and client.

BOX 5–1
Techniques Designed to Promote Trust

Convey respect.
Consider the client's uniqueness.
Show warmth and caring.
Use the client's proper name.
Use active listening.
Give sufficient time to answer questions.
Maintain confidentiality.
Show congruence between verbal and nonverbal
    behaviors.
Use a warm, friendly voice.
Use appropriate eye contact.
Smile.
Be flexible.
Provide for allowed preferences.
Be honest and open.
Give complete information.
Provide consistency.
Plan schedules.
Follow through on commitments.
Set limits.
Control distractions.
Use an attending posture: arms, legs, and body relaxed;
    leaning slightly forward.

Carkhuff (1969) identifies five levels of empathy. From least to most empathetic, they are as follows, with clinical examples.

1. *Unawareness of the client's message of feelings* is the lowest level of empathy. Since there is no evidence of active listening or understanding of the client's feelings, the nurse's response communicates significantly less than the client's.

Example

CLIENT (*frantic*): Jamal (*10 months old*) has had a terrible cold for more than a week.
NURSE (*hurriedly, not looking at client*): Is he up to date on his immunizations?

In this example, the nurse ignores the feeling tone of the client and changes the subject to get the desired information. The nurse's insensitivity may arise from boredom, lack of interest, bias, or differing reasons for the interaction.

2. *Superficial acknowledgment of the client's message* minimizes the client's feelings. The nurse shows awareness of superficial feelings but responds in a way that noticeably ignores the client's emotions.

Example

CLIENT (*frantic*): Jamal (*10 months old*) has had a terrible cold for more than a week.
NURSE (*with a casual glance*): This is the time of year for colds. Everyone has one. He'll get over it.

In this example, the nurse responds to the content of the statement but not to the feeling tone of the client. The nurse minimizes the client's feelings.

3. *Recognition of the client's message and some of the client's feelings* is somewhat helpful. In level 3, the nurse responds to the meaning of the client's emotions. Verbal and nonverbal behaviors are congruent. The nurse's words reflect the client's concerns and feelings.

Example

CLIENT (*frantic*): Jamal (*10 months old*) has had a terrible cold for more than a week.
NURSE (*tone the same as the client's, making eye contact, leaning forward in chair*): You're upset that Jamal has had this cold for more than a week.
CLIENT (*crying*): Yeah. He's so little, and I want him to get better.
NURSE (*breaking eye contact*): He'll get better. The doctor will be in soon to examine him.

EXERCISE 5–1
Techniques That Promote Trust

Purpose: To identify techniques that promote the establishment of trust and to provide practice in using these skills.

Time: 50 minutes total: 15 minutes for exercise; 15 minutes for discussion; 20 minutes for role play.

Directions:

1. Read the list of interpersonal techniques designed to promote trust.
2. Describe the relationship with your most recent client. Was there a trusting relationship? How do you know? Which techniques did you use? Which ones could you have used?
3. In triads, one learner interviews a second to obtain a health history, while the third observes and records trusting behaviors. Rotate so that everyone is an interviewer. Interviews should last 5 minutes each. At the end of 15 minutes, each observer shares findings with the corresponding interviewer.

The nurse's first response shows a level 3 empathy. The nurse accurately interprets the superficial feeling tone of client. Because the nurse seems to understand, the client feels free to provide more information. The nurse then reverts to a level 2 response, however, and essentially ignores the client's tears. Level 3 responses are often a prelude to higher-level responses, which reflect the client's hidden emotions. Nurses who are unable to cope with deep feelings are unable to develop empathy beyond levels two and three.

4. *Acknowledgment of the message and obvious feelings* demonstrate the nurse's willingness to understand and care about the client's concerns. Although there are still deep, hidden meanings of which the nurse is unaware, there is a forum for discussion. The nurse probes for information to expand the client's awareness and the nurse's understanding of the situation.

Example

CLIENT (*frantic*): Jamal (*10 months old*) has had a terrible cold for more than a week.
NURSE (*same voice tone as client, making eye contact, with attending, open posture*): You are quite upset about this, aren't you?
CLIENT (*softly, spoken with tears*): Yes. He's so little, and he just has to get better.
NURSE: You're afraid it might develop into something worse? (*Level 4*)
CLIENT: Could he have pneumonia?
NURSE: I don't know. The doctor will examine him soon. How would you feel if he had pneumonia? (*Gathering data*)
CLIENT: Oh, I couldn't stand to have him in the hospital away from me.
NURSE: You feel anxious about the possibility of hospitalization, in which the two of you would be separated, and what it might do to your close relationship. (*Level 4*)
CLIENT: Yes, being separated would be awful.

In this example, the nurse begins responding on level 3 and then moves to level 4 responses. The nurse reflects slightly hidden feelings, but has not accurately perceived deeper feelings. Often level 4 responses build upon level 3 responses, as well as information-gathering questions, which increase the nurse's knowledge about the client and the probability of an accurate assessment of emotions.

5. *Full therapeutic acknowledgment of the client's hidden message and meaning* adds significantly to the meanings behind the feelings. Because the nurse has a clearer, more objective view than the client, the nurse is able to state deep, hidden feelings unknown to the client. Review the example from level 4 and begin with the client's response.

CLIENT: Oh, I couldn't stand to have him in the hospital away from me.
NURSE: What is it about the hospital separation from Jamal that makes you so anxious? (*Reflects hidden feelings, asks for more information*)
CLIENT: It's just his being in the hospital.
NURSE (*questions, still same feeling tone*): Have you or anyone close to you been in the hospital?
CLIENT: My brother, when he was young.
NURSE (*seeking more information*): And what was he there for?
CLIENT: Pneumonia. And he died there of complications!
NURSE: So now you're frightened that if Jamal has pneumonia and is hospitalized, he will die too, like your brother. (*Reflects deep feelings*)

Now that the nurse has full information, the interventions are more likely to address the client's individualized needs directly. The nurse then goes on to give information about pneumonia and provide reassurance that it is treatable. Armed with accurate data, the nurse can communicate the client's feelings to the physician so that the physician can discuss Jamal's diagnosis and treatment with the client to lessen the client's anxiety.

Levels of Nursing Actions

Nursing actions that facilitate empathy are classified by Gazda (1987) into three major skills: (1) recognition and classification of requests, (2) attending behaviors, and (3) empathetic responses. Two types of requests are for information and action. These requests do not involve interpersonal concerns and are easier to manage. Another form of request is for understanding involvement, which entails the client's need for empathetic understanding. This type of request requires greater interpersonal skills. It can be misinterpreted as a request for action or information. The nurse may have to clarify whether the client needs only what he or she

specifically asks for or whether further exploration of the meaning of the need is necessary.

Attending behaviors facilitate empathy and include an attentive, open posture, responding to verbal and nonverbal cues through appropriate gestures and facial expressions, using eye contact, and allowing client self-expression. They also include offering time and attention, showing interest in the client's issues, offering helpful information, and clarifying problem areas. These responses encourage clients to participate in their own healing.

The third major skill is empathetic response. The nurse helps the client identify emotions that are not readily observable and connect them with the current situation. Nursing actions recognize the client as a unique individual. The nurse calls the client by name, maintains an attentive, open posture, responds to verbal and nonverbal cues through appropriate gestures and facial expressions, uses intermittent eye contact, and allows self-expression by the client. Verbal prompts, such as "Humm," "Uh-huh," "I see," "Tell me more," and "Go on" facilitate expression of feelings. Repeating phrases and using silence are also useful responses. The nurse uses open-ended questions to validate perceptions and invite opinions. Informing behaviors enlarge the data base by providing new information. The nurse informs by providing honest and complete answers in language the client understands. The nurse also assesses the client's knowledge level and uses summarization to highlight important points. Examples of nursing actions associated with the five levels of empathy are presented in Box 5–2. Exercise 5–2 helps in identifying empathetic responses.

Mutuality

Mutuality basically means that the nurse and the client agree on the client's health problems and the means for resolving them and that both parties are committed to enhancing the client's well-being. The concept implies a dynamic partnership characterized by respect for the autonomy and value system of the other. In developing mutuality, the nurse maximizes the client's involvement in all phases of the nursing process. Mutuality includes shared communication and collaboration in problem solving. Reciprocal sharing grows as

---

BOX 5–2
Empathy: Levels of Nursing Actions

Level	Category	Nursing Behavior
1	Accepting	Uses client's correct name.
		Maintains eye contact.
		Adopts open posture.
		Responds to cues.
2	Listening	Nods head.
		Smiles.
		Encourages responses.
		Uses therapeutic silence.
3	a. Clarifying	Asks open-ended questions.
		Restates the problem.
		Validates perceptions.
		Acknowledges confusion.
	b. Informing	Provides honest, complete answers.
		Assesses client's knowledge level.
		Summarizes.
4–5	Analyzing	Identifies unknown emotions.
		Interprets underlying meanings.
		Confronts conflict.

---

the nurse–client relationship matures and is dependent upon caring, trust, and empathy. To foster mutuality within the relationship, nurses need to remain aware of their own feelings, attitudes, and beliefs. Negative, unresolved attitudes based upon typical stereotypes may quickly halt or impede mutuality and may actually jeopardize the relationship if the client suddenly views these attitudes as threatening.

Nurses who are truly sensitive to others' feelings and accept differences between their own lifestyles and those of others have the capacity to develop and attain mutuality in relationships. Such caring nurses involve clients in the decision-making process, and they do not belittle decisions made by clients. Effective use of values clarification assists clients in decision making. As clients clearly identify their own values, they are better able to solve problems effectively and arrive at decisions that have meaning to them, and thus a higher chance of being successful.

Mutuality does not end with decision making. The nurse and client must now implement the decisions, perhaps even difficult ones, a process that requires commitment, time, and patience for successful outcomes. As the client implements

EXERCISE 5–2
Identifying Empathetic Responses

Purpose: To correctly identify levels of empathy for clinical situations.

Time: 15 minutes for exercise; 10 minutes for group discussion.

Directions: Read the client statement, then identify the nurse's response as to the correct empathy level, 1, 2, 3, 4, or 5; place the number on the line to the left of the response.

1. CLIENT *(on the verge of tears)*: That doctor confused me so. He was in here for 10 minutes and I still don't know what's wrong with me.

   NURSE:
   _____ a. Doctors like that ought to give up medicine.
   _____ b. You feel the doctor was confusing and didn't explain your medical problem.
   _____ c. What time is it now?
   _____ d. You're angry that the doctor was unable to adequately explain your medical condition.
   _____ e. You feel exasperated about not knowing your current medical problem and helpless in knowing what you should do to take care of yourself.

2. CLIENT *(in a hostile voice)*: I'm sick of being poked at and stuck with needles. Go away and leave me alone.

   NURSE:
   _____ a. You're fed up with needles and wish to be left alone.
   _____ b. Getting needles is part of being in the hospital.
   _____ c. You're angry about having all these intrusive procedures and wish you didn't need them.
   _____ d. Just remember to fill out your menu for tomorrow.
   _____ e. With all these intrusive procedures, you feel vulnerable and defenseless, ready to go hide to get away from it all.

changes, regression to old behaviors and habits may occur temporarily. The nurse monitors the client for expected changes, supports the positive changes, and confronts the client about regressive behaviors.

Another aspect of mutuality is shared communication. Mutuality is an important part of an I–thou relation. The client never becomes an "it" in the nurse's eyes. Sharing feelings and emotions forms a stronger therapeutic relationship. When

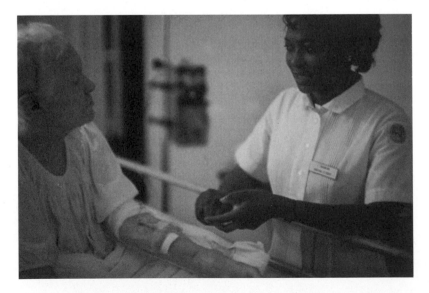

Mutuality is based on an I–Thou relationship between nurse and client. (Courtesy of the University of Maryland School of Nursing)

EXERCISE 5–3
Evaluating Mutuality

Purpose: To identify behaviors and feelings on the part of the nurse and the client that indicate mutuality.

Time: 15 minutes for exercise; 15 minutes for discussion

Directions: Complete the following questions by answering yes or no after terminating with a client; then bring it to class. Discuss the answers. How were you able to attain mutuality or why were you unable to attain it?
1. Was I satisfied with the relationship?
2. Did the client express satisfaction with the relationship?
3. Did I share feelings with the client?
4. Did the client share feelings with me?
5. Did I feel or communicate bias towards the client?
6. Did I make decisions for the client?
7. Did I persuade the client to act in a way the client did not want?
8. Did the client feel accepted or understood by me?
9. Did the client feel allowed to make his or her own decisions?
10. Did the client accomplish his or her goals?
11. Did I accomplish my goals?

appropriate, the nurse communicates aspects of having similar experiences with clients.

Mutuality encompasses all phases of the nursing process and enriches nurse–client relationships. Evidence of mutuality is seen in the development of individualized client goals and nursing actions that meet a client's unique health needs. A mutual relationship is terminated with both parties having a sense of shared accomplishment and satisfaction. Exercise 5–3 gives practice in evaluating mutuality.

Confidentiality

Confidentiality protects the client's right to decide who can have access to information about any aspect of health care or lifestyle. It refers to the idea that one person feels reassured that the other person will not divulge private information. Within the context of the nurse–client relationship, the client entrusts the nurse with intimate information and expects it to be held in confidence. The nurse has an ethical responsibility to protect the client's right to privacy.

Information obtained through professional interviewing and history taking is used by the nurse and other health team members to arrive at an individualized client care plan. This information is considered pertinent to an improvement in the client's health status, and it becomes a part of

the client's permanent health record. Emphasis is placed on *pertinent* information. Recorded client data should be neither too sketchy nor too detailed. Information that does not contribute to the direction of the client's care is not included. Data about the client or client's condition are not shared with the client's family or health professionals who are not directly involved in the client's care without the client's consent.

The following is an example of psychosocial data revealed to the nurse that could lead to the development of a relevant psychosocial diagnosis:

> Ben Langdon, age 32, is hospitalized for injuries related to a motorcycle accident. He discusses his feelings about a recent date with a woman he liked very much. The evening ended poorly because he was so nervous that he didn't know what to say or how to carry on a conversation. He usually stays at home by himself at night and rarely attends social functions.

This example shows how clients may reveal intimate real life stories that suggest underlying problems not directly associated with the reason they are in the hospital. In this client's case, the nurse may decide to help the client deal with his social isolation and inability to communicate in stressful situations because dealing with these problems will have an effect on his self-esteem and, indirectly perhaps, on his motivation to become rehabilitated. An appropriate nursing goal might be: The client will develop a relaxation technique to reduce anxiety in the presence of a significant other, and the intervention will be supportive-educative.

Although it would be important to use this information in planning total health care, the significant details of the event the client related to the nurse need not be divulged. Sometimes information is titillating and there is an urge to share it. The nurse who talks too much is easy to identify. Bringing up extraneous facts to show that you have the client's confidence or to share startling information is not only damaging to the development of a therapeutic nurse–client relationship, it is also unethical.

As professionals, nurses must be aware of their own tendencies and characteristics. Although some nurses enjoy discussing privileged information, others are quiet and rarely talk about their clients. A reluctance to share relevant information that could potentially help a client is an abuse of confidentiality. Nursing care conferences are designed to provide an outlet for the discussion of privileged communication. An explicit norm of such conferences is that the information and feelings shared about a client are not discussed outside the conference except in the direct application of nursing care (Greve, 1990).

Some nurses who are quiet by nature may need to be encouraged to attend conferences to discuss confidential client issues and their related feelings. They should feel comfortable discussing pertinent client information in a controlled and private environment. Nurses who miss or conceal pertinent information interfere with the complete formulation of the health care plan. Pieces of knowledge that are overlooked could contribute to a higher quality of nursing care and a more meaningful therapeutic relationship.

There are limits to confidentiality in the clinical setting. The nurse needs to inform the client what information will be shared with other health team members. The client should be fully informed regarding the limits of confidentiality, the purposes for which the information is being obtained, and how the information may be used (Kagle, 1984). Also, the nurse explains that the client's record is kept where only members of the health team have access to it, thus ensuring the client's privacy.

Sometimes clients want the nurse to promise not to tell before they reveal what is troubling

them, or they will try to swear the nurse to secrecy once information has been given. It is important for the nurse to be clear about the limits of confidentiality. An appropriate response might be, "I cannot make promises. You need to know that I may find it necessary to discuss this with the appropriate health professionals, especially if I think it affects your health or well-being." Beginning nurses may find it difficult to know when to keep secrets and when it is essential to the welfare of the client to share a privileged communication. A good example of sharing confidential information appropriately is presented in Chapter 4.

Another more easily learned aspect of confidentiality concerns the setting in which confidential information is disclosed. This setting should be separate from any public area. Discussions of client information should preferably take place in a conference room with the door closed so as to maintain privacy. This information includes change-of-shift reports, multidisciplinary conferences, one-to-one conversations with other health professionals about specific client care issues, and consultations with clients and their families.

Confidentiality is breached if conversations are heard by other clients, visitors, or anyone else not involved in the direct care of the client. When conference rooms are unavailable for the sharing of sensitive information among client, nurse, and family, the nurse may pull the curtains around the client's bed, close the door to the client's room, or perhaps ask an ambulatory roommate to leave the room if there is another place on the unit where clients are allowed to congregate. Exercise 5–4 gives practice in identifying situations that breach confidentiality and in learning to correct them.

The advent of computerized client information constitutes a new problem in the confidentiality issue. Once the information is entered into the computer, the nurse may not know under what circumstances it will be accessed. Therefore, much judgment is needed, and the most effective way to decide is to include only information that is necessary for good nursing care (Hard, 1990).

There are a few instances in which confidentiality is waived and clients are not allowed to restrict information to persons they approve or to those who have direct contact with their care. These are cases of suspicion of abuse of minors or elders, commission of a crime, or threat of harm to one-

EXERCISE 5–4
Confidentiality and Setting

Purpose: The purpose of this exercise is to identify situations that are a breach of confidentiality and then to correct them.

Time: 15 minutes for the exercise; 15 minutes for discussion.

Directions:
Regarding the following situations, all of which depict a breach of confidentiality.
1. State how confidentiality has been broken.
2. Given the situation, what might be an appropriate response?
3. Change the situation or setting so that confidentiality is maintained.

Situations:
1. You are eating lunch in the cafeteria with two fellow pediatric nurses who are discussing the behaviors of an abusive parent.
2. A nurse yells down the hall to you, "Your patient in 504 is ready to get off the bedpan."
3. On the postpartum unit, a nurse allows a husband to see his wife's chart.
4. You are riding in the elevator when two OR nurses step on and comment, "It took four of us to tie him down for that IV."
5. You are on rounds. One physician, learning over client *X*, suddenly remembers an order on another client, "Don't forget Mrs. Smith's enema. Give her a Fleet's enema this morning."
6. You are at your best friend's house for a dinner party. She is a nurse in the emergency room and begins to discuss a "terrible accident victim."

self or another person. Courts may also subpoena client records without the client's permission. Apart from these situations, the courts consider all communication between nurse and client as privileged communication.

BARRIERS TO THE RELATIONSHIP

There are barriers within the nurse, the client, and the health care system that can affect the development of the nurse–client relationship. They include, within the nurse, conflicting values, conflicting professional commitments, lack of a strong sense of self, and lack of value placed on caring. Within the health care system, barriers include lack of consistent assignment of nurse to client, lack of time, communication conflicts with other health professionals, conflicting values, poor physical arrangements, and lack of value placed on caring. Anxiety, stereotyping, and lack of personal space create barriers for the client.

Anxiety

Anxiety is a vague, persistent feeling of impending doom. It is a universal feeling; no one fully escapes

it. The impact on the self is always uncomfortable. It occurs when a threat (real or imagined) to one's self-concept is perceived. Anxiety is usually observed through the physical and behavioral manifestations of the attempt to relieve the anxious feelings. Although individuals experiencing anxiety may not know they are anxious, specific behaviors provide clues that anxiety is present. Similarly, although individuals may not be consciously aware of the factors that contribute to the anxiety-producing situation, others may be able to help them identify those factors, thus alleviating the anxiety. Four levels of anxiety are identified by Kreigh and Perko (1983). Exercise 5–5 identifies behaviors associated with anxiety. Expanding on this information, Box 5–3 shows how an individual's sensory perceptions, cognitive abilities, coping skills, and behaviors relate to the intensity and level of anxiety experienced.

A mild level of anxiety heightens one's awareness of the surrounding environment and fosters learning and decision making. Therefore, it may be desirable to allow a mild degree of anxiety when health teaching is needed or when problem solving is necessary. It is not prudent, however, to prolong even a mild state of anxiety. Behaviors

EXERCISE 5–5
Identifying Verbal and Nonverbal Behaviors Associated with Anxiety

Purpose: To broaden the learner's awareness of behavioral responses that indicate anxiety.

Time: 1 hour

Directions: List as many anxious behaviors as you can think of. Each column has a few examples to start. Discuss the lists in a group, and add new behaviors to your list.

Verbal	*Nonverbal*
Quavering voice	Nail biting
Rapid speech	Foot tapping
Mumbling	Sweating
Defensive words	Pacing

_____ _____

_____ _____

_____ _____

BOX 5–3
Levels of Anxiety with Degree of Sensory Perceptions, Cognitive and Coping Abilities, and Manifest Behaviors

Level of Anxiety	Sensory Perceptions	Cognitive/Coping Ability	Behaviors
Mild	Heightened state of alertness; increased acuity of hearing, vision, smell, touch.	Enhanced learning, problem solving; increased ability to respond and adapt to changing stimuli. Enhanced functioning.*	Walking, singing, eating, drinking, mild restlessness, active listening, attending, questioning.
Moderate	Decreased sensory perceptions; with guidance, able to expand sensory fields.	Loss of concentration; decreased cognitive ability. Cannot identify factors contributing to the anxiety-producing situation. With directions can cope, reduce anxiety, and solve problems. Inhibited functioning.	Increased muscle tone, pulse, respirations. Changes in voice tone and pitch, rapid speech, incomplete verbal responses. Engrossed with detail.
Severe	Greatly diminished perceptions; decreased sensitivity to pain.	Limited thought processes; unable to solve problems even with guidance. Cannot cope with stress without help. Confused mental state. Limited functioning.	Purposeless, aimless behaviors. Rapid pulse, respirations; high blood pressure; hyperventilation. Inappropriate or incongruent verbal responses.
Panic	No response to sensory perceptions.	No cognitive or coping abilities. Without intervention death is imminent.	Immobilization.

*Functioning refers to the ability to perform activities of daily living for survival purposes.

that show interest and concentration include listening, asking relevant questions, initiating problem solving, and formulating decisions. These behaviors promote individual functioning. Helping clients experiencing mild anxiety to focus on the objective to be attained, encouraging clients to use the heightened awareness as a catalyst to goal achievement, and validating the mild anxiety as a normal psychological response promotes learning and productive problem solving.

Anxiety, other than mild levels, decreases perceptual ability. The anxious state is accompanied by verbal and nonverbal behaviors that inhibit effective individual functioning. Once the presence of anxiety has been identified, the nurse needs to take appropriate action. Nurses can use a mild degree of anxiety to expand learning and problem solving, thus enhancing the nurse–client relationship.

Moderate to severe anxiety on the part of either nurse or client hinders the development of the therapeutic relationship. To accomplish goals and attain mutuality, higher levels of anxiety must be reduced. Although nurses may accurately identify their client's level of anxiety, they should also identify and reduce their own anxiety in order to help the client fully. Since anxiety can cloud one's perceptions, it can also interfere with relationships.

A moderate level of anxiety can be reduced sufficiently to allow problem solving and effective coping through the nurse's intervention in the therapeutic relationship. Some of the common strategies used to help clients reduce anxiety to a workable level include showing a calm, unhurried manner; setting limits; providing a definite structure; initiating a physical exercise program for the client; and adopting an active listening attitude that shows acceptance. Strategies to reduce client anxiety at mild and moderate levels are summarized in Box 5–4.

Severe anxiety requires medical and psychiatric intervention to alleviate the crisis-producing stress. A prolonged panic state is incompatible with life. It is such an extreme level of anxiety that without immediate medical and psychiatric assistance, suicide or homicide may ensue. Some of these interpersonal strategies used to reduce moderate anxiety also are used during severe anxiety and panic attacks as part of a team approach to client care.

Choosing from various strategies to reduce client anxiety can be difficult because not all meth-

---

BOX 5–4
Nursing Strategies to Reduce Client Anxiety

- Active listening to show acceptance.
- Honesty; answering all questions at the client's level of understanding.
- Clearly explaining procedures, surgery, and policies, and giving appropriate reassurance based on data.
- Acting in a calm, unhurried manner.
- Speaking clearly, firmly (but not loudly).
- Giving information regarding lab tests, medications, treatments, rationale for restrictions on activity.
- Setting reasonable limits and providing structure.
- Encouraging clients to explore reasons for the anxiety.
- Encouraging self-affirmation through positive statements, such as "I will," "I can."
- Using play therapy with dolls, puppets, games, drawing, for young clients.
- Using therapeutic touch, giving warm baths, back rub.
- Initiating recreational activities, such as physical exercise, music, card games, board games, crafts, reading.
- Teaching breathing and relaxation exercises.
- Using guided imagery.
- Practicing covert rehearsal.

From Gerrard B, Boniface W, Love B (1980). Interpersonal Skills for Health Professionals. Reston, VA: Reston Publishing Co.

---

ods are appropriate or work equally well with all clients. Application to clinical situations is discussed in Exercise 5–6.

Sterotyping and Bias

Stereotyping is the process of attributing characteristics or behavior, generalized opinions, attitudes, and beliefs to a group of people as if all persons in the identified group possessed them. People may be grouped by ethnic origin, culture, religion, social class, occupation, age, or other characteristics. Even health issues can be the stimulus for stereotyping individuals. For example, alcoholism, sexually transmitted diseases, and AIDS are fertile grounds for the development of stereotypes.

Stereotypes are learned during childhood and reinforced by life experiences. They may carry positive or negative connotations: If you are Jewish, you will be successful in business; Hispanics are basically dishonest—or honest. Nurses may have personal stereotypes or biases they act on unknowingly. Stereotypes negate empathy and erode the nurse–client relationship. Because direct nursing care may be affected by personal biases, nurses must assess their own beliefs about groups

EXERCISE 5–6
Anxiety: Application to a Clinical Situation

Purpose: To increase self-awareness of anxiety.

Time: 10–15 minutes

Directions:
1. Describe the circumstances surrounding an anxiety-producing situation for a client of yours and answer the following:
   a. What was the client's level of anxiety?
   b. How did the client attempt to cope with it?
   c. What strategies did you use to help the client reduce the anxiety?
   d. Which other ones could you have used?
2. Discuss in group session. Identify common factors.

of people. Exercise 5–7 gives practice in identifying stereotypes.

Biases are generalizations representing expectations and prejudgments about people or behaviors. Biases characterize all individuals having a similar characteristic—height, weight, race, religion, sex—as being the same. The characteristic is viewed as valid for each member of the group but is not shared by people outside the group. No allowance is made for individual differences within a subgroup. An implicit assumption is made that people who do not belong to the stereotype do not engage in the stereotypical behaviors, whereas the stereotyped individual does. Stereotypes are never completely accurate: There usually are more variations within a group than between groups.

The importance placed upon stereotypes and biases depends on several factors. Perceptions of people and interactions with them are affected by past feelings and opinions. Extreme differences in the lifestyles of members of different groups contribute to friction and conflict. The greater the difference, the stronger the conflict. Inadequate information and lack of exposure foster the development of stereotypes. All of us like to think that

our way is the correct way and that everyone else thinks about life experiences just as we do. The reality is that there are many roads in life, and one road is not necessarily any better than another.

Emotions play a role in the development of negative stereotypes. Stereotypes based upon strong emotions are called prejudices; they are extremely hard to break. The intensity and amount of interaction between people affect the strength of the stereotype. Less emotionally charged stereotypes are more amenable to change. Extreme stereotyping can result in discrimination. Discrimination is a term used to describe situations and actions in which a person is denied a legitimate opportunity offered to others because of bias or prejudice (Kavanaugh, 1991).

Stereotypes and biases are issues for nurses as well as clients. Nurses may bring their past biases with them to the clinical situation. Real and imagined attributes distort the nurse's perception and prevent client change and growth. To reduce bias in clinical situations, nurses need first to recognize clients as unique individuals, both different from and similar to themselves. Stereotypes are abandoned when the nurse is interested in learning about the client as a unique individual and as a member of

EXERCISE 5–7
Identifying Stereotypes

Purpose: To help you identify stereotypes in general and then to identify those you personally hold to be true.

Time: 15 minutes in small groups; 15 minutes for personal reflection (individual's time).

Directions:
1. Make up a list of stereotypes, both positive and negative, with which you are familiar.
2. In small groups, discuss how these stereotypes affect your ability to respond to individual clients.

a particular group. The nurse then becomes capable of accepting clients just as they are.

Acceptance of the other person needs to be total. Mr. Rogers, the children's TV star, ends his programs by telling his audience, "I like you just the way you are." How wonderful if we, as nurses, could convey this type of acceptance to our clients through our words and actions.

Conditional acceptance occurs when only certain attitudes and feelings are accepted. Approval, disapproval, agreement, and disagreement all convey a degree of judgment. Unconditional acceptance, described by Rogers (1961) as an essential element in the helping relationship, does not imply agreement or approval because acceptance occurs without judgment. The nurse who utilizes a nonjudgmental attitude with neutral responses conveys acceptance and develops meaningful client relationships. Exercise 5–8 examines ways of reducing clinical bias.

EXERCISE 5–8
Reducing Clinical Bias

Purpose: To identify examples of nursing biases that need to be reduced. Practice in identifying professional stereotypes and in how to reduce them is one component of maintaining high-quality nursing care.

Directions: Each of the following scenarios indicates a stereotype. Identify the stereotype and how it might affect nursing care. As a nurse, what would you do to reduce the bias in the situation? Are there any individuals or groups of people whom you would not want to care for?

Situation A

Mrs. Small, an ER nurse on night duty, reports to the day shift: "Oh, and a Mr. Johnson came in drunk last night around 3 A.M. He got into a fight and needs a few stitches in his forehead." The head nurse on days learns from Mr. Johnson that he has been sitting and sleeping in the waiting room for the past four hours and has not yet seen a doctor even though everyone else has been attended to.

Situation B

On break, Mrs. Smith complains about the three-year-old boy to whom she is assigned. "He sure knows when to pour on the tears. There's nothing wrong with him until he sees you, then the tears start, but they stop as soon as you leave or his mother comes. He's just spoiled because they have a nanny at home who waits on him hand and foot."

Situation C

Mrs. Daniels, an OB nurse who believes in birth control, comments about her client, "Mrs. Gonzales is pregnant *again.* You know, the one with six kids already! It makes me sick to see these people on welfare taking away from our tax dollars. I don't know how she can continue to do this."

Situation D

Mrs. Brown, an RN on a medical unit, is upset with her 52-year-old female client. "If she rings that buzzer one more time, I'm going to disconnect it. Can't she understand that I have other clients who need my attention more than she does? She just lies in bed all day long. And she's so fat; she's never going to lose any weight that way."

Situation E

Mrs. Waters, a staff nurse in a nursing home, listens to the daughter of a 93-year-old resident. "My mother, who is confused most of the time, receives very little attention from you nurses, while other clients who are lucid and clear-minded have more interaction with you. It's not fair! No wonder my mother is so far out in space. Nobody talks to her. Nobody ever comes in to say hello."

Situation F

During a nursing conference, the primary nurse for Sharon Penn, a 16-year-old girl with diabetes of three years' duration, comments, "I just don't understand why she refuses to take care of herself. She goes off her diet, makes her mother give her insulin shots, never tests her urine or blood glucose, and doesn't care. Doesn't she know she is killing herself? These teenagers today; they never want to take responsibility for themselves."

Violation of Personal Space

Personal space is an invisible boundary around an individual that changes under varying circumstances. The emotional personal space boundary provides a sense of comfort and protection to the person and is defined by past experiences and culture.

Proxemics is the study of an individual's use of space (Hall, 1996). Hall describes four distances surrounding an individual in interactive encounters. Many factors affect personal distance (Giger, 1980). Various cultures dictate the use of different distances in social conversations. In some cultures people approach each other closely, whereas in others more personal space is required. Men need more space than women in most cultures. People generally need less space in the morning. The elderly need more control over their space, whereas small children generally like to touch and be touched by others. Although the elderly appreciate human touch, they generally do not like it to be applied indiscriminately. Situational anxiety causes a need for more space. Persons with low self-esteem prefer more space as well as some control over who enters their space and in what manner. Usually people will tolerate a person standing close to them at their side more readily than directly in front of them. Direct eye contact causes a need for more space. Placing oneself at the same level, sitting while the client is sitting, for example, or standing at eye level when the client is standing, allows the nurse more access to the client's personal space because such a stance is perceived as less threatening. Exercise 5–9 helps identify individual needs for personal space.

Respect for Personal Space in Hospital Situations

Closely related to the interpersonal distance requirements in the nurse–client relationship is the client's need for territorial space. In a review of the literature Davis (1984) describes optimal territorial space needed by most individuals. A person needs 86 to 108 square feet of personal space. Other research has found that 60 square feet is the minimum needed for multiple-occupancy rooms and 80 square feet for private rooms in hospitals and institutions. Critical-care units offer even less square footage.

Obviously, there is a discrepancy between the minimum amount of space an individual needs and the amount of space hospitals are able to provide in multiple-occupancy rooms. Therefore, the nurse must recognize individual needs for privacy and implement actions to increase the sense of personal space. Respect for the client's personal space can be accomplished by:

- Providing privacy when disturbing matters are to be discussed.
- Explaining procedures before implementing them.
- Entering another person's personal space tentatively, slowly, and preferably with the person's permission.
- Providing an identified space for personal belongings.
- Encouraging the inclusion of personal and familiar objects on the client's nightstand.
- Decreasing direct eye contact during hands-on care.
- Minimizing bodily exposure during care.
- Using only the necessary number of people during any procedure.
- Appropriately using touch.

Hospitals are not home. Clients in the hospital are at times made to feel that they are trespassing on the territory of others (physicians, nurses, physical therapists, x-ray technicians). At the same time, many of the diagnostic and treatment procedures that must be instituted in providing nursing care represent a direct intrusion into the personal space of the client. Frequently procedures requiring tubes, such as nasal gastric intubation, administration of oxygen, catheterization, and IV initiation restrict the mobility of the client and the client's sense of control over personal territory. When more than one health professional is involved in implementing the procedures, the impact of the intrusion on the client may be even stronger. In many instances, personal space requirements are an integral part of a person's self-image. When a person loses control over his or her personal space, the client may experience a loss of individuality, self-identity, and self-esteem. Consider the issue of respect for personal space in the clinical examples presented in Box 5–5.

When hospitalized clients are able to incorpo-

EXERCISE 5–9
Personal-Space Differences

Purpose: The purpose of this exercise is to identify individual needs for personal space among different client populations.

Directions: Following is a list of factors affecting personal space. Each has a clinical example. Write another example (clinical or personal) for each factor.

1. *Culture*
   Mrs. Hopi, a native American who is in the ICU for a heart attack, is surrounded by her family and tribe members throughout her stay in the hospital.

   Your example: _____

   _____

2. *Sex*
   Mr. Smith, a retired steel worker, greets his community-health nurse with a smile and a gesture to enter his apartment. His ailing wife greets the nurse with outstretched arms.

   Your example: _____

   _____

3. *Degree of Acquaintance*
   The nurse meets Mrs. Parker at the prenatal clinic for the first time. They maintain a distance of 5 feet during the initial interview.

   Your example: _____

   _____

4. *Time of Day*
   Mr. Jones is an 86-year-old man in a nursing home. Every evening before retiring, he prefers to be in bed with the light out before the nurse comes to give him his medications and to say goodnight.

   Your example: _____

   _____

5. *Age*
   Katie Johnson, 17 months old, is always ready to hug her primary nurse when the nurse enters the room.

   Your example: _____

   _____

6. *Situational Anxiety*
   Mrs. Cook just returned from a brain scan, and she is quite anxious about the results. As the nurse attempts to comfort Mrs. Cook by placing her hand on Mrs. Cook's arm, Mrs. Cook snatches her hand away and retorts, "Just leave me alone."

   Your example: _____

   _____

Discussion:
Can you think of any other examples of factors relating to personal space?
What is your own preferred space distance? To what do you attribute this preference?
Under what circumstances do your needs for personal space change?

BOX 5–5
Clinical Examples of Personal Space Issues for Clients

1. The nurse places the client on the bedpan without drawing the curtain on a postpartum unit. When the client protests, the nurse states, "Well, we're all girls here."

2. The chief resident comes in with an entourage of interns and medical students. They draw the curtain and the chief resident, standing close to the client, informs the client that his cancer is terminal. The entourage moves on to the next client.

3. Miss Jones has just been brought to the emergency room as a rape victim. Because of the circumstances, she is unable to change her clothes until she has been examined. It is an unusually busy night in the ER, and the policy is to practice triage, and treat the most serious cases first. Since Miss Jones is not considered an emergency case, it will be some time before she is examined.

4. Dr. Michaels has had an auto accident for which he is receiving emergency treatment by a multidisciplinary team. He is conscious, but no one calls him by name or seems to notice his wife standing outside the door.

5. Barbara Burk has just been admitted to a psychiatric unit. The policy on the unit is to keep all valuables, razors, hand mirrors, and money locked up in the nurse's station. All clients must strip and shower under supervision soon after they arrive on the unit. It was not Barbara's choice to seek in-patient treatment, and she is very scared.

6. Mr. Novack is admitted to the coronary-care unit. He is hooked up to a cardioscope so his cardiac condition can be monitored continuously, and nasal oxygen is applied. The defibrillator is located close to his bed. His family is allowed to come in one at a time, for five minutes once very hour, as long as the visits don't interfere with nursing care of necessary treatment procedures.

---

rate parts of their rooms into their personal space, it increases their self-esteem and helps them to maintain a sense of identity. This feeling of security is evidenced when a client asks, "Close my door, please." Freedom from worry about personal space allows the client to trust the nurse and fosters a therapeutic relationship. When invasions of personal space are necessary—for example, when starting an IV on a two-year-old, performing emergency treatment, or collecting evidence in a rape case—the nurse can minimize their impact by establishing rapport with the client. Explaining why a procedure is needed or letting a child see the equipment is helpful.

To minimize the loss of a sense of personal space and associated behaviors, the nurse demonstrates a high regard for the client's dignity and privacy. Closed doors for private rest and periods of uninterrupted relaxation are respected. Personal belongings are arranged and treated with care, particularly with very old and very young clients for whom personal items may be highly significant as a link with a more familiar environment. Elderly clients can become profoundly disoriented in unfamiliar environments because their internal sensory skill in processing new information is often reduced. Encouraging persons in long-term facilities to bring pictures, clothing, and favorite mementos is an important nursing intervention with such clients.

Before rendering care, the nurse needs to assess the client's personal space needs. A comprehensive assessment includes cultural and developmental factors affecting the client's perceptions of space, how the client reacts to intrusions, how the client defends personal space, and nonverbal behaviors that may indicate loss of territory. All client populations require creative ways of handling personal space. In an attempt to increase the sense of personal space, nurses should decrease close direct eye contact and instead sit beside the client or position the chairs at angles for counseling or health teaching. Clients in ICU units, where there are many intrusive procedures, benefit from decreased eye contact during certain times, such as when being bathed or during suction, wound care, and changing of dressings. At the same time, it is important for the nurse to talk gently with the client during such procedures and to elicit the client's feedback, if appropriate. Conversation with clients at such times reinforces their feelings that they are human beings worthy of respect and not just objects being worked on.

Another important aspect of personal space is communicating client preferences to the members of the health team and including them in the client's care plan. If possible, personal space needs should be validated by the client to avoid misinterpretations by the nurse. However, the nurse may have to act as the client's agent to ensure this aspect of total nursing care if the client is unable to do so.

Similarly, nurses should be aware of their own space needs. Nurses who need more space themselves may feel uncomfortable or embarrassed at entering a client's intimate space. Taking into account variations in personal space for both parties in the relationship is important. The same nursing actions that promote privacy and respect for the client's personal space will increase the nurse's sense of space.

SUMMARY

Chapter 5 focuses on six essential concepts needed to establish and maintain a therapeutic relationship in nursing practice: caring, trust, empowerment, empathy, mutuality, and confidentiality. Respect for the client as a unique person is a basic component of each concept. Factors affecting the development of these behaviors, such as level of anxiety, clinical bias, and confidentiality, are described.

Caring is described as a commitment by the nurse that involves profound respect and concern for the unique humanity of every client and a willingness to confirm the client's personhood.

Trust represents an individual's emotional reliance on the consistency and continuity of experience, which are provided by an organized combination of familiar and predictable persons and things. In a trusting relationship with a client, the client perceives the nurse as trustworthy, as a safe person to be with and with whom to share difficult feelings about health-related needs.

Empathy is the ability to perceive accurately another person's feelings and to convey their meaning to the client. Nursing behaviors that facilitate the development of empathy are accepting, listening, clarifying and informing, and analyzing. Each of these behaviors implicitly recognizes the client as a unique individual worthy of being listened to and respected.

Mutuality includes as much shared communication and collaboration in problem solving as the client is capable of providing. To foster mutuality within the relationship, nurses need to remain aware of their own feelings, attitudes, and beliefs.

There are barriers as well as bridges in the establishment of a nurse–client relationship. Anxiety and stereotyping interfere with the development of a relationship. Anxiety is a vague, persistent, and uncomfortable feeling of impending doom. A mild level of anxiety heightens one's awareness of the surrounding environment, fostering both learning and decision making. Higher levels of anxiety decrease perceptual ability. The nurse needs to employ anxiety- and stress-reduction strategies when clients demonstrate moderate anxiety levels. Severe, sustained levels of anxiety and untreated panic are incompatible with life.

Stereotypes are generalizations representing an unsubstantiated belief that all individuals of a particular social group, race, or religion share the same characteristics. No allowance is made for individual differences within a subgroup. Developing a nonjudgmental, neutral attitude toward a client helps the nurse reduce clinical bias in nursing practice.

Personal space, defined as an invisible boundary around an individual, is another conceptual variable worthy of attention in the nurse–client relationship. The emotional boundary needed for interpersonal comfort changes with different conditions. It is defined by past experiences and culture. Proxemics is the term given to the study of the human being's use of space. To minimize a decreased sense of personal space, the nurse needs to demonstrate a high regard for the client's dignity and privacy.

A related concept is confidentiality: The nurse has an ethical responsibility to respect the client's right to decide who can have access to any information about any aspect of health care or lifestyle. There are limits to confidentiality in the clinical setting. Any information that, if withheld, might endanger the life or physical and emotional safety of the client or others needs to be communicated to the health team immediately. The nurse needs to inform the client what types of information will be shared with other team members.

REFERENCES

Buber M (1958). I and Thou (2nd ed.). RG Smith (trans.). New York, Scribner's.

Carkhuff RR (1969). Helping and Human Relations (Vol. 1). New York, Holt, Rinehart and Winston.

Chapman J, Chapman H (1983). The Psychology of Health Care: A Humanistic Perspective. Monterey, CA, Wadsworth.

Clarke J (1992). A view of the phenomenon of caring in nursing practice. Journal of Advanced Nursing 17:1283–1290.

Clay M (1984). Development of an empathetic interaction skills schedule in a nursing context. Journal of Advanced Nursing 9:343.

Clayton G (1991). Connecting: A catalyst for caring. *In* Chin P (ed.) (1991), Anthology of Caring. New York, NLN Press.

Davis J (1984). Don't fence me in. American Journal of Nursing 84:1141.

Erikson E (1963). Childhood and Society (2nd ed.). New York: Norton.

Fry S (1988). The ethic of caring: Can it survive in nursing? Nursing Outlook 36(1):48.

Gault D (1983). Development of a theoretically adequate description of caring. Western Journal of Nursing Research 5:313.

Gazda GM (1987). Foundations of Counseling and Human Services. New York, McGraw-Hill.

Greve P (1990). Keep quiet or speak up: Issues in patient confidentiality. RN 12:53.

Hall E (1966). The Hidden Dimension. Garden City, NY, Doubleday.

Hard R (1990). Computers help keep patient files confidential. Hospitals 64:49.

Harrison L (1990). Maintaining the ethic of caring in nursing. Journal of Advanced Nursing 15:125–127.

Hawks J (1992). Empowerment in nursing education: Concept analysis and application to philosophy, learning and instruction. Journal of Advanced Nursing 17(5):609–618.

Kagle J (1984). Privacy vs. accountability: A health care dilemma. Social Work in Health Care 9:25.

Kavanaugh K (1991). Values and beliefs. *In* Creasia J, Parker B (eds.) (1991), Conceptual Foundations of Professional Nursing Practice. St. Louis, Mosby, pp. 187–209.

Kreigh H, Perko J (1983). Psychiatric and Mental Health Nursing: A Commitment to Care and Concern (2nd ed.). Reston, VA, Reston Publishing Co.

Meize-Growchowski R (1984). An analysis of the concept of trust . . . in the nursing situation. Journal of Advanced Nursing 9:563.

Petty J (1962). Apples of Gold. New York: Walker & Co.

Rogers C (1961). On Becoming a Person. Boston, Houghton Mifflin.

Smith M, Walker M (1984). Empathy training for nursing students. Journal of the New York State Nursing Association 15:17.

SUGGESTED READINGS

Albarado R (1990). Computerized nursing documentation. Nursing Management 21:64.

Barron A (1990). Privacy: The right to personal space. Nursing Times 86:28.

Chinn P (ed.) (1991). Anthology of Caring. New York, NLN Press.

Colorado Society of Clinical Specialization in Psychiatric Nursing (1990). Ethical guidelines for confidentiality. Journal of Psychosocial Nursing and Mental Health 28:43.

Friedman FB, Hefferin E (1984). Are you out of touch with your patients? RN 47:51.

Gault D, Leininger M (1991). Caring: The Compassionate Healer. New York, NLN Press.

Gordon S (1991). Fear of caring: The feminist paradox. American Journal of Nursing 2:45.

Gould D (1990). Empathy: A review of the literature with suggestions for an alternative research strategy. Journal of Advanced Nursing 15:1167.

Grand Rounds (1989). A question of privacy: Should you protect a patient from himself? Nursing 19:66.

Hardiman M (1971). Interviewing or social chit-chat. American Journal of Nursing 71:1379.

Hoeman S (1989). Cultural assessment in rehabilitation nursing practice. Nursing Clinics of North America 24:277.

Killian W (1990). AIDS poses confidentiality risk. American Nursing 22:33.

Kirkpatrick N (1990). Frank needed more than surgery. . . . Nursing 20:44.

LaMonica E, et al. (1987). Empathy and Nursing Care Outcomes. Scholarly Inquiries in Nursing Practice 1:197.

Lane P (1989). Nurse–client perceptions: The double standard of touch. Issues in Mental Health Nursing 10:1.

Leininger M, Watson J (1990). Caring Imperative in Education. New York, NLN Press.

Maciorowski L (1991). The enduring concerns of privacy and confidentiality. Imprint 38:55.

Melroe N (1990). "Duty to warn" vs. "patient confidentiality": The ethical dilemmas in caring for HIV-infected clients. Nurse Practitioner 15:58.

Morse J (1991). Negotiating commitment and involvement in the nurse–patient relationship. Journal of Advanced Nursing 16:455.

Pike J (1990). On the nature and place of empathy in clinical nursing. Journal of Professional Nursing, 6:235.

Pultz B (1989). How to set boundaries without building walls. RN 52:21.

Reisman E (1988). Ethical issues confronting nurses. Nursing Clinics of North America 23:789.

Thorne S, et al. (1988). Reciprocal trust in health care relationships. Journal of Advanced Nursing 13:782.

Tingle J (1990). When to tell. Nursing Times 86:58.

Chapter 6

Role Relationship Patterns

ELIZABETH ARNOLD

OUTLINE

Basic Concepts

DEFINITIONS
FUNCTIONS OF ROLES
    Roles help define position
    Role relationships support identity
    Roles regulate communication
TYPES OF ROLES
    Ascribed roles
    Achieved roles
HOW ROLES DEVELOP
FACTORS AFFECTING ROLE PRESENTATION
    Social desirability
    External support
    Personal commitment
COMPONENTS OF THE PROFESSIONAL NURSE ROLE
    Steps toward the nurse role
    Sources of professional socialization
TYPES OF PROFESSIONAL NURSING ROLES
SOURCES OF ROLE STRESS
SELF-AWARENESS AND THE PROFESSIONAL ROLE
CHARACTERISTICS OF THE SICK ROLE

Applications

ASSESSMENT
INTERVENTION

Summary

OBJECTIVES

At the end of the chapter, the student will be able to:
1. Define role and role performance.
2. Describe the functions of roles.

3. Contrast the different types of roles.

4. Describe three ways roles are learned.
5. Identify factors influencing role presentation.

6. Describe the four components of professional role socialization.

7. Discuss the professional roles of the nurse.
8. Identify sources of role stress.

9. Discuss the characteristics of the sick role.

10. Apply the nursing process with clients having disturbances in role relationships.

HELMER: *Remember—before all else you are a wife and mother.*
NORA: *I don't believe that anymore. I believe that before all else I am a human being, just as you are.*

Henrik Ibsen
A Doll's House, 1879

This chapter explores the nature and functions of role relationships in the nurse–client relationship. Understanding role relationships is important for several reasons. How nurses perceive their professional role and their ability to fulfill it has a profound effect on the success of interpersonal communication in the nurse–client relationship. Clients invite nurses into the innermost spheres of their lives, almost without question, in the context of the nurse–client relationship. Within this professional relationship, the nurse functions as trusted friend, confidante, educational resource, and sounding board. In times of stress, with its predictable jolt to the self-concept, the nurse does for others what they cannot do for themselves in the health care system. Clients confide their private thoughts and feelings to the professional nurse because they are scared and their sense of self is faltering. They trust that nurses in their professional role will understand and help them regain self-control. Clients connect the nurse's presence with responsible caring when they are unable to perform this self-care function for themselves (Deers and Evans, 1980).

Role relationships are a significant part of self-definition. Hoare (1991) notes that "people are defined through their attachments, relationships and common purpose with others in community." Role performance is a common benchmark of health. Society considers clients who are able to function in their expected roles as healthier than those with a similar level of disability who are unable to perform in their functional roles. Role performance matters to people as a significant dimension of self-concept; this is seen in emerging symptoms of depression, feelings of emptiness, and even suicidal thoughts when a role ceases to exist. Causes of commonly lost role relationships include job loss, divorce, the "empty nest" syndrome when the last child leaves home, retirement, death of a significant person, and debilitating illness. Helping clients to grieve the loss of roles and to find new and meaningful roles is an important consideration in promoting, maintaining, and restoring client health and well-being.

BASIC CONCEPTS

DEFINITIONS

A *role* is defined as a set of expected standards of behavior established by the society or community to which the person belongs (Creasia, 1991). Roles represent the social aspects of self-concept. Relationships usually are influenced by role differences and similarities. The relationship patterns of roles help define a person's position and status in the community or group, providing commonly understood information as to how individuals perceive themselves in relation to others.

Role relationships do more than simply identify the behaviors people expect of each other. They evolve from the social self-concept, which describes all of the external ways one is known to others, including one's reputation and one's family, professional, and societal roles (Baumeister, 1986). Through the filter of the social self-concept, people consider their social status, noting its uniqueness and comparing it and merging it with that of others in the same social network. Role relationships of special significance in health care settings are the professional nursing role and the sick role.

Position incorporates the role, but it is not the same as a role. It represents an external context that formalizes a role and makes it understandable to others in the community or group. Social position relates to the status and identity the person holds in the community (Creasia, 1991). The social position a client or a client's family holds in the community can have a strong impact on the communication process in the nurse–client relationship. Helping professionals frequently treat clients in high positions with a deference that is not accorded people with low social status. Whereas it is important for the nurse to recognize differences in position, it is more important to view all clients as VIPs, treating them all with the same respect and giving them all quality care.

Position, or job, descriptions provide important information about roles. For example, the director of nurses would not be involved with bedside care except in an emergency; a staff nurse would not assume the responsibility for drafting the hospital budget. Although each person can implement a position in a personalized way, position descriptions dictate certain ways of behaving and implicitly prohibit others.

Positions carry strong and often unverbalized moral, competency, and social expectations that persons must live up to or suffer personal consequences. Consider politicians and community leaders who have engaged in questionable financial, sexual or organizational practices that are incompatible with the moral standards expected of them; the nurse who chooses not to complete assignments; or the spouse who chooses to have an affair. In each instance, the person violates the ethical standards implied in his or her position. Similarly, the nurse who is chemically impaired and the nurse who administers medication without knowing about the side effects of the drug compromise the role behaviors that are expected of the professional nurse The consequences of dishonoring any of these role expectations through improper behavior can ruin a career, an educational experience, or a relationship.

FUNCTIONS OF ROLES

Roles Help Define Position

Roles help define the position a person holds in society (Creasia and Parker, 1991). A person can have social, occupational, personal, and spiritual roles all in the same lifetime. For example, an individual might all at the same time be the president of a community organization, a nurse by profession, a spouse, a parent, a daughter, and a lay minister of a church. Role behaviors are recognized through membership, work responsibilities, cooperative activities, education, and social affiliations and through support of certain beliefs and norms. Authority, social customs, justice, and performance standards safeguard the role relationships between the individual and society (Damon, 1983).

Each role requires a different set of interpersonal communication skills. The familiarity inherent in the husband–wife relationship is not appropriate in the work setting. A woman would talk differently to her child than she would to her boss. Clients make distinctions in their communication styles with family members and health professionals based on their perceptions of differences in role relationships.

Role Relationships Support Identity

As an integral part of life experience, healthy role relationships create personalized meanings that affect one's identity and self-esteem. People's descriptions of themselves and of their feeling of self-esteem (or lack of self-esteem) reflect role performance more than any other aspect of self-concept. For example, adults evaluate their worth in terms of their work, marriage, parenting, and social roles. For children, their social, athletic, and school competencies are primary descriptors of themselves. As an older adult reflects back on his or her life, role performances, both positive and negative, account for most of the memories. Without a meaningful role, a person feels empty and worthless.

Roles develop from an individual's natural inclinations and resources. Most people choose, either consciously or unconsciously, how to present themselves to others. They want to feel that they are contributing to society in ways that other people consider useful. To be productive is equated with being of value. Consequently, people try to make their role activities match the expectations of others. The feedback from others introduces, strengthens, or invalidates a person's role perceptions. When people are able to meet expectations set by society, they demonstrate *role mastery.* Exercise 6–1 discusses role relations and self-concept.

Roles Regulate Communication

Role relationships help define both the content and process of communication because people always perceive themselves in relation to others. Every conversation touches on social norms, ways of thinking about and relating to others, feelings, values, and ideas that are unique, rich, and complex. Consider, for example, the function of role when one delivers the same message to a peer, to an instructor, to a staff nurse, to a doctor, to a client, and to a nursing aide. Of course, the role

> **EXERCISE 6–1**
> **Role Relations and Self-Concept**
>
> **Purpose:** To demonstrate the influence of the role of significant others in the formation of competence and personal identity.
>
> **Time:** 45 minutes; the essay may be written as a homework assignment.
>
> **Procedure:**
> 1. Think of a person or relationship that was particularly important as you developed an evaluation of your competence—a relative, friend, teacher, neighbor, or child, for example.
> 2. Describe how that person's evaluation of you contributed to your opinion of your self-competence.
> 3. In the group share with your classmates the way you feel about yourself.
>
> **Discussion:**
> 1. What were some of the common factors that led to an appraisal of competence?
> 2. What did people say or do that helped you feel more competent?
> 3. What helped you to hear their evaluation in a positive way?
> 4. In what ways do you think this exercise might help you be more effective in the nurse–client relationship?

relationship you have with each of these individuals affects the words you select, the spontaneity of your conversation, and the parts of the message you choose to emphasize. Professional roles help direct therapeutic conversations. They make the relationship safe for the client through role behaviors regarding confidentiality, level of involvement, and competency.

TYPES OF ROLES

Ascribed Roles

Ascribed roles are involuntary roles over which a person has no control, such as family position or gender. Usually an accident of birth determines whether an individual will be born a prince or a pauper. People have no control over whether they are born male or female, oldest or youngest. Each of these ascribed roles helps define people's behavior as well as the ways in which others will relate to them. For example, the role the oldest child assumes generally is quite different from that of the youngest child, simply because of family position. The oldest child is likely to be more serious and responsible, whereas the youngest child is likely to be more fun loving and less diligent. Despite significant advances toward gender equality, male children are socialized differently than female children.

Achieved Roles

The other major categorization of roles is defined as *achieved* roles. Achieved roles are earned or bestowed on a person. Although they may correspond to a person's background, they are not necessarily dependent on it. Achieved roles usually are consciously chosen and are voluntary—the occupations we choose or the decision to become a parent. Early signs of role preference and differentiation can be seen in the role playing of preschool children. For example, some children have a natural fascination for building things or for playing fireman or nurse. The adolescent often experiments with a wide variety of social roles before committing to adult roles; despite the turmoil this creates for their parents, this is a necessary component of the journey to an adult identity. Adults develop most social and professional roles through choice.

The assumption of other roles, however, is dictated by circumstances; they are neither consciously sought nor ascribed (Cox et al., 1989). Critical life events such as birth, death, serious illness, having children, leaving home, retirement, and marriage create new role responsibilities. The death of a parent or a personal illness can stimulate a significant role change, taken by or bestowed on an individual. For example, the 15-year-old daughter who loses her mother may acquire the role of a surrogate mother to her orphaned younger siblings. The spouse or adult child of an Alzheimer's victim must often accept some role reversals.

HOW ROLES DEVELOP

The concept of role has a social origin. Roles develop from two sources. They are the product of the values and expectations of others. Roles represent socially learned behaviors, communicated to the uninitiated through socializing agents, that is, by people considered expert in the individual's social network (Biddle, 1977). Each person subsequently adapts the social meaning of the role to fit inner self needs and values.

Role performance behaviors are learned through one of three processes: acculturation, assimilation, and socialization. *Acculturation* is the simplest way of learning cultural roles and behaviors. It occurs naturally without much conscious awareness as small children learn the language and the expected role behaviors of the larger society. Little children don't question the validity of their culture; they model themselves after their parents, as demonstrated by their clothing, language, and manners.

Assimilation is a more conscious learning process in which a person deliberately chooses to learn a language and expected role behaviors as a way of gaining acceptance into a dominant society. Most people who immigrate to this country choose to become U.S. citizens through the process of assimilation.

Socialization is a third mode of learning about expected role behaviors, values, and expectations. Socialization is a more specific learning of role behaviors, rather than the more global assimilation process needed for acceptance into a larger community. It is of particular importance in learning the professional culture of nursing. Socialization is the process through which nursing students learn expected role behaviors.

FACTORS AFFECTING ROLE PRESENTATION

The roles people assume represent an effort to influence the judgments of others about their self-concept. As a result, they emphasize certain parts of the self-concept and suppress those aspects they consider less desirable. Jung (1965) calls this public expression of self the "persona." The *persona* represents all the surface masks a person wears to bridge the gap between the inner self and society's expectations of the self. The persona ideally reflects socialized aspects of the inner self-concept. When the outer surface mask represents the inner self, behavior is congruent and understood by others. When it is different, it creates misunderstanding. The situation, the people involved, and a person's

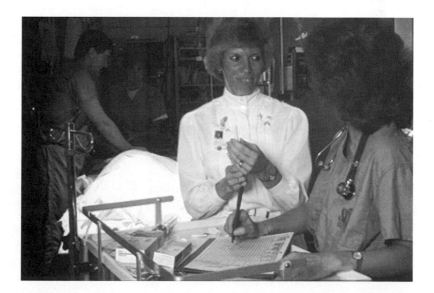

Nurses learn behavioral standards from instructors, nursing staff, and other students. (Courtesy of the University of North Carolina at Charlotte College of Nursing)

mood at the time influence how people present themselves to others, as does what a person anticipates and hopes to achieve in a given interaction.

Social Desirability

Most people try to present only the side of themselves that is likely to win the approval of others in a given interpersonal interaction (Schlenker, 1985). If a person wants to impress someone with the quality of personal accomplishments, the conversation is likely to include aspects of role performance related to personal skill and expressions of self-confidence. For example, a person might speak of his or her sales ability or most recent research project. The person who emphasizes the competency aspects of self-concept in this example might act quite differently at a party, stressing parts of the self-concept that suggest having a good time rather than achievement.

External Support

Society's support of a role largely determines its validity. For example, a century ago, women authors found it difficult to get published, so several famous novels were published under male pseudonyms. With today's increased gender equality, women now receive recognition as the authors of their own published works. Culture, described in more detail in Chapter 11, has an important influence on role behaviors. For example, male Iranian clients may have difficulty disclosing personal information to a female interviewer, and vice versa for Iranian women, because of cultural role expectations (Jalali, 1982).

Personal Commitment

Role development showcases a person's commitment. Skills required to learn role behaviors include language, motivation, role and personal flexibility, self-development, and risk-taking behaviors (Hardy and Conway, 1988). During a lifetime, an individual may participate in a wide variety of vocational, family, social, spiritual orientation, and community roles, some more satisfying than others. In each of these roles, the self may remain relatively consistent. Most people tend to value certain roles over others. This affects their commitment and performance One-sided role development—workaholism, for instance—means that other roles are suppressed or ignored. Neglect of leisure activities leaves an individual with notable life skill deficiencies. When illness, retirement, or adverse circumstances force a person who never developed leisure skills to take a different role in life, the transition can be difficult. Leisure skills, like work skills, are developed over time.

COMPONENTS OF THE PROFESSIONAL NURSE ROLE

Webster's dictionary defines *profession* as a "calling requiring specialized knowledge and often long and intensive academic preparation" and a *professional* as one "characterized by or conforming to the technical or ethical standards of a profession." In 1986, the American Association of Colleges of Nursing published examples of the essential values, attitudes, personal qualities, and professional behaviors associated with the profession of nursing. These examples are presented in Table 6–1.

Important components of professional behavior are technical and interpersonal competence. In the clinical setting, the professional nurse acts in a prescribed way. It is not enough to be pleasant and caring (Morse et al., 1991). The role demands a thorough knowledge of nursing and health care concepts and practices, delivered in relationships characterized by care and respect. Professional competence includes an acceptance and validation of certain behavioral standards, expressed through the nurse's words and behaviors in relationship with other health care providers and clients. Professional competence to process multiple, often indistinct behavioral data and the ability to think through problems without getting lost in detail are desired behavioral outcomes. Finally, professional competency includes oral and written proficiency. The nurse must be able to communicate in a clear, comprehensive, and timely manner and to confront difficult interpersonal issues with professional associates in an assertive but considerate manner.

Professionalism speaks to expectations held by consumers and others within the profession. In nursing practice, professional expectations are molded by and responsive to changes in societal

TABLE 6–1
Values, Qualities, and Behaviors Associated with Professionalism in Nursing Practice

Essential Values*	Examples of Attitudes and Personal Qualities	Examples of Professional Behaviors
1. Altruism Concern for the welfare of others.	Caring Commitment Compassion Generosity Perseverance	Gives full attention to the patient/client when giving care. Assists other personnel in providing care when they are unable to do so. Expresses concern about social trends and issues that have implications for health care.
2. Equality Having the same rights, privileges, or status.	Acceptance Assertiveness Fairness Self-esteem Tolerance	Provides nursing care based on the individual's needs irrespective of personal characteristics.† Interacts with other providers in a non-discriminatory manner. Expresses ideas about the improvement of access to nursing and health care.
3. Esthetics Qualities of objects, events, and persons that provide satisfaction.	Appreciation Creativity Imagination Sensitivity	Adapts the environment so it is pleasing to the patient/client. Creates a pleasant work environment for self and others. Presents self in a manner that promotes a positive image of nursing.
4. Freedom Capacity to exercise choice.	Confidence Hope Independence Openness Self-direction Self-discipline	Honors individual's right to refuse treatment. Supports the rights or other providers to suggest alternatives to the plan of care. Encourages open discussion of controversial issues in the profession.
5. Human Dignity Inherent worth and uniqueness of an individual.	Consideration Empathy Humaneness Kindness Respectfulness Trust	Safeguards the individual's right to privacy. Addresses individuals as they prefer to be addressed. Maintains confidentiality of patients/clients and staff. Treats others with respect regardless of background.
6. Justice Upholding moral and legal principles.	Courage Integrity Morality Objectivity	Acts as a health care advocate. Allocates resources fairly. Reports incompetent, unethical, and illegal practice objectively and factually.†
7. Truth Faithfulness to fact or reality.	Accountability Authenticity Honesty Inquisitiveness Rationality Reflectiveness	Documents nursing care accurately and honestly. Obtains sufficient data to make sound judgments before reporting infractions of organizational policies. Participates in professional efforts to protect the public from misinformation about nursing.

*The values are listed in alphabetic rather than priority order.
†From Code for Nurses (1976). American Nurses Association.
From American Association of College and University Education for Professional Nursing (1986). Final Report. Washington, DC, American Association of Colleges of Nursing.

norms, advances in education, technology, and the health care system. They range from expectations of clinical competence to dress codes. For example, only a few decades ago, it was considered unprofessional to wear a uniform of any color but white. A nurse caught without a cap was not in full uniform. Questioning a doctor's order and expressing doubt about the appropriateness of medical management were considered unacceptable professional behavior.

Today, because of the consciousness raising occasioned by the women's movement and evolving changes in the health care system, the professional nurse and the health care consumer expect that professional nurses will be held accountable for their actions. Questioning improper or inadequate doctor's orders is not only appropriate, it is a defined charge reflecting professional nursing competence. The modern nurse wears clothes appropriate to the clinical setting—cheerful, colorful clothes in pediatric and psychiatric settings, for example. The nursing cap, symbolically reminiscent of the "dust cap" and servitude associated with the popular image of nurses in a bygone era, is no longer considered an essential part of the nursing uniform.

The role of the nurse has moved far beyond its traditional, custodial, and charitable role definitions. Modern technology revolutionized the duties of the professional nurse and established nursing as the core element in the care of clients (Taylor, 1986). Intervening economic realities and the scarcity of prepared nurses in many health care settings stimulated the current revolution in the nursing education curriculum. Legislative support for third-party reimbursement of nurses recog-

nizes the changes in the expanded nursing role. Exercise 6–2 focuses on your development as a professional nurse.

Steps toward the Nurse Role

Role socialization is the means of learning behaviors associated with role performance. (Joos, Nelson, and Lyness, 1985). Nursing students learn the professional roles associated with nursing practice through the process of professional socialization. Cohen (1981) identifies four goals of professional socialization. The first is that the student must **"learn the technology of the profession—the facts, skills and theory."** The novice nursing student is expected to adjust to two different learning environments at the same time: clinical and academic. Entering a nursing-education program is a little like entering a strange country. The language and customs seem foreign and are not easily understood. During the initial stages of the socialization process, professional behaviors are limited and strictly defined. The novice student feels like an outsider. Sometimes it is helpful to realize that it is impossible to feel otherwise.

The second of Cohen's professional socialization goals is to **"internalize the professional cul-**

EXERCISE 6–2
Personal and Professional Assessment

Purpose: To help you focus on your self-development as a professional nurse.

Time: 45 minutes; the essay may be written as a homework assignment.

Procedure:
Answer the following questions in a one- or two-page essay. Let your thoughts and feelings emerge as you might share them with a good friend, without censoring them. There are no right or wrong answers; this is your story.
1. What are my reasons for choosing nursing as a profession?
2. What people, circumstances, or situations were instrumental in my making this choice?
3. What hopes do I have for myself in this profession?
4. What fears do I have about my ability to develop as a professional nurse?
5. How difficult will it be for me to integrate my professional role with other life roles?

Discussion:
Students who feel comfortable can share their stories.
1. In what ways is your story similar to or different from your classmates' stories?
2. As you wrote your story, were you surprised by any of the data or feelings?
3. What question was the hardest to answer? the easiest?
4. What did you learn about yourself from doing this exercise?
5. In what ways do you think doing this exercise can be helpful in your socialization process?

ture." Cohen suggests that nursing students need to merge all previously learned personal identity roles with professional role requirements and individual personality characteristics. The process of internalizing the culture varies from person to person, just as the normal learning curve for walking and talking varies among small children.

Usually behavioral standards related to professional integrity and client safety are inflexible because they form such an important part of the nurse's practice. But many other behaviors are negotiable. As with the beginnings of any relationship, establishing trust is the first priority. Once trust is confirmed, the student feels freer to experiment with new behaviors, though still using the instructor or preceptor as a guide.

Through self-initiated actions, the student develops skill and confidence in professional performance, adding flexibility and autonomy to the growing list of behaviors. Over time, students build a sense of identity that enhances self-esteem as they continue to grow and develop into professional nurses. Satisfactory resolution of a professional identity is evidenced in the nurse's reasoned clinical judgments, in compassionate administering of nursing care, and in competent performance of required psychomotor skills. Many of the skills and strategies discussed in earlier chapters are applicable to faculty–student and staff–student nurse relationships.

The third of Cohen's goals is that the student should **"find a personally and professionally acceptable version of the role."** The overall purpose of professional nursing is to act in the best interest of the client. To provide high-quality nursing care, nurses need to know themselves well, both personally and professionally, so they can be clear on where and how the professional use of self influences their delivery of client care. They must develop an authentic professional self-concept—one that moves away from defensiveness, facades, "ought to" behavior, and behavior aimed at pleasing others and toward development of the full self with the accompanying sense of self-direction and acceptance of self and others in clinical settings. Once the search for personal self-awareness has begun, the nurse can look at how to integrate personal self-images with a tangible, professional self-concept. Stability and flexibility are characteristics of a healthy professional concept of self, just as they are of the personal self-concept.

The fourth goal Cohen proposes, is that the student should **"integrate this professional role into all the other life roles."** Integrating a professional nursing role that is unique, arduous, and at times emotionally draining is not easy. Nursing students often experience a conflict between personally held values and the nursing role as defined by the clinical setting. When the student graduates, the role transition into the work world recreates a temporary sense of identity confusion. Instead of feeling confident, the new nurse feels bewildered and less sure of professional identity in the hospital setting. The psychosocial care one could give two or three clients during the eight-hour work shift is a far cry from the demand to meet the emotional needs of 10 or 20 clients during this same time period. Marlene Kramer (1974) describes the inner conflicts created by differing sets of expectations, philosophies, and behaviors as "reality shock." There is a natural period of discomforting confusion whenever one makes a change in job setting or role. Networking and maintaining collegial relationships diminish the unhealthy effects of this transition period. Securing appropriate mentorship and keeping abreast of current trends through continuing education decreases anxiety.

Sources of Professional Socialization

In nursing, the student learns expected standards of behavior from nursing instructors, preceptors, nursing staff on the unit, and other nursing students. Throughout the nursing program, the nursing faculty serve as important socializing agents, helping students learn the values, traditions, norms, and competencies of the nursing profession (Saarmann et al., 1992).

Recent developments in clinical supervision of students are the preceptor model and the clinical teaching associate model. Preceptors and clinical teaching associates are specially trained professional nursing staff who work with nursing students on a one-to-one basis on the unit. The student is assigned to the preceptor and follows the preceptor's schedule. On many clinical units, assigned staff nurses act as invaluable informal resources and role models for the nursing students. Fellow students also provide informal support and help other students who are experiencing temporary difficulty in the clinical area. This spontaneous support is often a critical, unexpected variable in the student's development as a professional nurse.

Interpersonal competencies with professional coworkers are often acquired informally through hands-on practice. Working with others as a collaborative effort to provide holistic nursing care to clients requires a strong capacity to listen carefully and empathize with others.

TYPES OF PROFESSIONAL NURSING ROLES

The professional roles associated with effective nursing practice in this decade include that of caregiver, teacher, client advocate, quality of care evaluator, manager, consultant, case manager, and researcher (Creasia, 1991). Selected role responsibilities are presented in Box 6–1.

Creative new professional roles include "entrepreneur, recruiter, editor, publisher, ethicist, labor relations expert, nurse anesthetist, lobbyist, culture broker" (Roberson, 1992). Hospitals no longer are the primary settings for nursing practice. Nurses practice in the community, in prisons, in schools, in homes, and with migrant workers in the field. They have an important role in health care of the military, during disasters, and when working with the homeless. Regardless of the setting and specific application of professional nursing skills, different role functions build on and

---

BOX 6–1
Professional Nursing Roles

Role	Role Responsibilities
Caregiver	Uses the nursing process to: a. Provide complete or partial compensatory care for clients who cannot provide these self-care functions for themselves. b. Implement supportive/educative actions to promote optimum health. c. Reinforce the natural, developmental, and healing processes within a person to enhance well-being, comfort, function, and personal growth.
Teacher	Provides health teaching to individual clients and their families. Develops and implements patient education programs to promote/maintain healthful practices and compliance with treatment recommendations. Guides individuals in their human journey toward wholeness and well-being through psychoeducation.
Client Advocate	Protects client's right to self-determination. Motivates individuals and families to become informed active participants in their health care. Mediates between client and others in the health care environment. Acts as client's agent in coordinating effective health care services.
Manager	Coordinates staff and productivity. Delegates differentiated tasks to appropriate personnel. Facilitates communication within and among departments. Serves on committees to improve and maintain quality of care. Makes decisions and directs relevant changes to ensure quality care.
Evaluator	Sets quality assurance/care standards. Reviews records and monitors compliance with standards. Makes recommendations for improvement.
Researcher	Develops and implements research/grant proposals to broaden understanding of important issues in clinical practice and validate nursing theories as a basis for effective nursing practice.
Consultant	Provides specialized knowledge/advice to others on health care issues. Evaluates programs, curricula, and complex clinical data. Serves as expert witness in legal cases.
Case Manager	Administers care for a caseload of clients. Coordinates cost-effective care options. Monitors client progress toward expected behavioral outcomes. Collaborates with other professionals to ensure quality care across health care settings.

reflect competence, critical thinking skills, and self-awareness. Respect is the thread that links all of these skills. Box 6–2 identifies professional nursing functions using a nursing process model. Exercise 6–3 develops the concept of the wide variety of nursing roles.

SOURCES OF ROLE STRESS

Professional roles are subject to stress originating as a response to environmental and internal stressors. The role demands a commitment that sometimes exceeds the physical, emotional, and psychospiritual resources of an individual nurse. When this occurs, there is a sensed loss of personal integrity and of role stress. For example, such stress may be experienced by the head nurse who assumes too much responsibility for staffing decisions or the nurse who feels torn between family demands and career needs. *Role stress* is a subjective experience that is associated with lack of role clarity, role overload, role conflict, or temporary role pressures. It affects the communication process because the nurse expends energy on the conflict rather than on the underlying issues. Important parts of the self-concept are suppressed,

---

BOX 6–2
Nursing Functions Using a Nursing Process Model

1. Interviewing to obtain accurate health assessment data.
2. Using all of the senses to assess and validate the health status of clients.
3. Developing relevant nursing diagnoses and care plan; referring clients to specialists and religious and community social service agencies if indicated.
4. Caring for clients with health care needs to include:
   a. Giving partial or wholly compensatory care for clients unable to perform normal self-care functions unassisted.
   b. Reinforcing the natural, developmental, and healing processes within a person to facilitate well-being, comfort, function, and personal growth.
   c. Teaching and guiding individuals in their human journey toward wholeness and well-being.
   d. Motivating individual clients and their families to become informed, active participants in their health care.
5. Collaborating with other health care professionals to ensure quality care of clients across clinical settings.
6. Evaluating adequacy, appropriateness, effectiveness, and efficiency of treatment programs and quality of nursing care with health care consumers, other health care professionals, and policy makers.

Adapted from Kelly L (1992). The Nursing Experience: Trends, Challenges and Transitions. New York, McGraw-Hill, pp. 144–145.

EXERCISE 6–3
Professional Nursing Roles

Purpose: To help the student develop an appreciation for the wide variation in professional nursing roles.

Time: Interview, 45 minutes; 45 minutes for discussion.

Procedure:
1. Do an occupational interview of a professional nurse in your community.

Questions You Might Ask
   What made you decide to go into nursing?
   What do you like best about your job?
   What would you do on an average work day?
   What is the most difficult aspect of your job?
   What kinds of preparation/credentials do you need to have for your job?
   What is of greatest value in what you do as a professional nurse?

2. Transcribe your notes from this interview to written form for class discussion.

Discussion:
1. Were you surprised by any of your interviewee's answers? If so, in what ways?
2. What similarities and differences do you see in the results of your interview compared with those of your classmates?
3. In what ways can you use what you learned from doing this exercise in your future professional life?

and the shared meaning respecting the needs of all participants in the relationship is built on false pretenses. Sooner or later the discrepancy leads to misperceptions by others, personal role conflict, and dysfunctional communication in relationships. Over time, role stress leads to the development of physical, emotional, or spiritual symptoms and burnout.

To function as an effective professional, the nurse must be self-directed, be able to live with ambiguity, create and work with alternative choices and diverse systems, and see the creative potential in all human beings. When role expectations are unclear, the work load is unreasonable, or several role demands occur simultaneously, professional as well as personal relationships suffer. There are times, both as a nursing student and in practice, when external role demands exceed the internal resources of the person. *Role pressures* are external or internal circumstances, capable of change, that interfere with role performance. Professional role pressures may be a result of perfectionism or of a confusion and uncertainty about the nature or validity of one's professional role. Role pressure can follow from role overload in clinical situations in which the nature of the role demands are appropriate but the nurse cannot meet the demands because there are too many of them occurring simultaneously. They also occur as a result of two competing responsibilities occupying the same space, for example, family and professional responsibilities. It is not always easy to make good decisions about putting your six-year-old on the schoolbus and being on time for work.

Role strains originate from within. The individual nurse may experience simultaneous pressure from clients, the client's relatives, nursing supervisors, and physicians. The nurse feels overwhelmed when each member of the interdisciplinary team, as well as the client's family and the client, has different expectations of the nurse's role. The extent to which the nurse is able to balance job expectations affects the level of role strain. It intensifies when the nurse tries to meet everyone's expectations without examining their relevance.

The key to avoiding role strain is to achieve balance in one's life. This can occur only if nurses are willing to define what is important to them and to focus on developing actions that enhance their self-definition. To achieve the goal of self-defini-

tion one must inwardly prioritize what needs to be done. This involves deciding which activities truly need intervention and which can be delegated or discarded as unimportant in the greater scheme of things. Learning to say no to requests that can't be handled immediately, or that need not be handled at all, is an interpersonal communication skill worth developing. Less damage is done when the nurse is able to set realistic expectations and meet them rather than trying to meet everyone's expectations and meeting none of them.

The changing role expectations of the registered nurse contribute to the role complexity, role conflict, and role stress experienced by modern nurses (Taylor, 1986). *Role conflict* is defined as an incompatibility between one or more role expectations. Sometimes role conflict becomes an overriding consideration for the professional nurse as well as for the client. For example, a physician asks a student nurse to perform a procedure with which the student has little or no experience. Rather than admit a lack of experience, the student nurse attempts to perform the procedure. If the student fails to perform the procedure correctly, the student feels compromised and angry at self and at the doctor for being put in this position. Exercise 6–4 explores multiple role relationships.

Role ambiguity occurs when roles are not defined clearly. As the person strives to meet role expectations that are not clear, frustration and immobilization result because the efforts never quite meet the mark. The staff nurse who finds that most of her time is spent on paperwork and little on the direct nursing care specified in her job description may experience professional disappointment, even though the work itself is easy.

SELF-AWARENESS AND THE PROFESSIONAL ROLE

Unless the therapeutic relationship supports the goals of the nursing interventions and is integrated with nursing tasks, it remains simply an interaction that occurs within a nursing situation. Professional role relations in the nurse–client relationship require self-awareness, caring, and an understanding of the nature of professional boundaries.

Self-awareness is a necessary precursor to professionalism. A strong sense of self is almost essen-

EXERCISE 6–4
Multiple Role Relationships

Purpose: To develop an awareness of the multiplicity of competing life roles.

Time: 30 minutes class time, homework assignment.

Procedure:
(1) and (2) may be done as a homework assignment
1. Identify all of the life roles you participate in and the activities associated with them.
2. Rank order them as to their importance in your life.
3. Put roles students have identified on a flip chart or chalkboard.

Discussion:
1. What were your thoughts and feelings as you made your individual choices?
2. Were you surprised at any of the rank orderings you gave your choices?
3. What roles do you hold in common with other participants in this exercise?
4. What does the learning from this exercise seem to suggest about possible role overload or conflict?
5. Identify one action you could take to reduce the strain of competing life roles.
6. What implications does this exercise have for nursing intervention?

tial for emotional survival in nursing practice. It is difficult, for example, to remain calm in adverse, unstable clinical situations without a strong sense of self. Yet as an integral part of the most basic struggles, joys, and ambiguities in health care situations, the nurse's role is critical. Nurses who are caring yet appear composed give the client confidence that they are emotionally able to provide competent care.

Professional self-awareness should reveal a fundamental respect for self and others. From professional self-awareness flows the ability to recognize what one needs to do with continuing education, the acceptance of accountability for one's own actions, the capacity to be assertive with professional colleagues, and the capability to serve as a client advocate when the situation warrants it.

In relationships, professional self-awareness reflects a balance between personal and professional use of self. The client expects the nurse to act in ways that show the nurse to be a person of feeling without getting caught up in those feelings. At the same time, professional expectations require the nurse to become actively involved with clients without becoming so overidentified with their concerns that it limits objectivity. Finally, the nurse should be spontaneous and genuine in communicating with clients, but not impulsive. Professional self-awareness allows the nurse to set the tone and to orient the client to expected role behaviors in the health care situation and to those essential to promoting, maintaining, and restoring health. To understand the nature of the client role in health care settings, the nurse begins by learning about the sick role and the changes the self-concept undergoes in physical and emotional illness.

CHARACTERISTICS OF THE SICK ROLE

Parsons' (1951) original framework for describing the sick role remains useful in describing this role in modern health environments. He states that as a role,

> the state of illness is partially and conditionally legitimized. That is, if a person is defined as sick, his failure to perform his normal functions is "not his fault" and he is accorded the right to exemption and to care. At one and the same time, however, the sick person is enjoined to accept the definition of his status as undersirable and the obligation to get well as expeditiously as possible. (Parsons and Fox, 1952, p. 52)

The client, in assuming the role of health care consumer, has to relinquish certain social, professional, and community roles, which are important dimensions of self-concept. Most people do not take on the sick role voluntarily. Illness or trauma can change an individual's social role from one of independent self-sufficiency to one of vulnerability and varying degrees of dependency on others. Preparing for work and engaging in the typical activities that constitute a person's life confirm a person's sense of self-worth. Without the capacity to engage in activities of normal daily living, a person can feel lost.

Adjustment to the presence of a health problem or self-care deficit requires a whole new set of coping skills without necessarily having the same social supports. Visitors come, but the routine daily conversations that so many of us take for granted in nourishing the sense of self are limited by visiting hours and lack of availability. Clients clearly need the support of the nurse to incorporate the rapidly changing meaning of the environmental and personal changes encountered in illness into an otherwise basically healthy self-concept.

When clients enter a health care situation, they encounter an interpersonal environment that encourages the development of feelings of anonymity and helplessness. At the hospital door, the client forsakes recognized social status in the family, work situation, and community. The sick person puts on the social persona of client, in need of help from health professionals. Regardless of how competent the person may be in other roles, when illness strikes, the sick role requires a new set of behaviors. Clients must learn behaviors that are unfamiliar and unsettling to previously held self-concepts.

The sick role has certain definable characteristics as well as a unique set of role expectations. To classify as "sick" and in need of professional care, the client must demonstrate a genuine self-care deficit over which the client has lost the capacity to assume sole responsibility for a successful resolution. The client meets this criterion if there is a distinguishable physical, cognitive, or emotional symptom, or if the doctor sanctions the existence of symptoms that are not visible to significant others. A person can meet the criterion without actually being sick in certain circumstances. For example, if there is enough psychological reason, as in the recent death of a spouse, society also may free the individual temporarily from the normal discharge of role responsibilities.

In meeting this criterion, the client is excused from performing expected role functions. The length of time and the level of excused absence from the exercise of normal role responsibilities depend on the severity of the self-care deficit. Until pronounced well, the individual has a legitimate excuse to avoid social commitments and work-related roles. During an illness, people tolerate client behaviors such as being demanding, helplessness, anger, and illogical decisions that they would not tolerate if the client were well. The sick individual can manipulate the environment in ways that are not possible without the label sick.

There are distinct disadvantages, however, to assuming the sick role. Having an illness, particularly a mental illness, carries a stigma. People may think of the ill person as being less competent or as having maladaptive behavior patterns that are attributed to the illness but that in reality have little or nothing to do with the illness (Wynne, Shields, and Sirkin, 1992). Stigmatization of the ill person occurs more frequently when the illness is protracted, recurrent, or seriously role disruptive. Chronic illness tends to lower self-esteem.

There also are major variations in the cultural contexts in which illness arises and in the role relationships surrounding it. Differences in perspectives play a major part in determining which illnesses and disorders are recognized as legitimate, the roles clients assume in their health care, and who becomes the culturally assigned expert in promoting, maintaining, and restoring health. For example, clients are expected to act as participating, cooperative agents in their recovery process. But an Asian client may appear as a passive recipient of health care, strikingly dependent on family and health caregiver for all guidance and care. Without a clear understanding of this culturally acceptable expression of the sick role, the nurse may respond inappropriately.

Natural in the acceptance of the sick role are unspoken rules to seek competent professional help for the restoration of health or the resolution of the self-care deficit. Society expects the sick person to cooperate fully with the health professionals with the goals of preventing further disability and promoting a higher level of wellness. Current thinking, however, in the form of advance directives and ethical/legal protections of the client's autonomy in declining treatment represents a modification of Parsons' original beliefs about the sick person's cooperation in the treatment process. Similar refinements are needed in the nurse's expectations of family involvement. Society anticipates that the client's immediate family or significant others will work with the client to identify the level of professional help needed and will participate in the treatment process. Sometimes there are reasons a family does not wish to be involved, and the family's right to decline participation in treatment needs to be respected.

APPLICATIONS

ASSESSMENT

Kleinman (1988) suggests that "inquiry into the meaning of an illness is a journey into relationships" (p. 186). Client assessment data need to consider not only the client's physical and emotional symptoms but also the social context in which the symptoms occur and the social networks that the symptoms affect. Role relationships are an inseparable part of the client's personal experience of an illness; role performance is considered such an important element of a person's self-concept that it warrants its own nursing diagnosis. Role performance falls under the NANDA human response patterns as "Relating, a human response involving establishing bonds" (NANDA, 1990). Included in the human response patterns are relationships with significant others and the ability to engage effectively with support systems. How a person functions in social roles, in sexual relations with a partner, in family roles, and in management of financial well-being are examples of assessment data associated with the nursing diagnosis.

Alterations in role performance indicate that the bond between self and established roles defining the person within a given community or group are compromised. In clinical settings, nurses assign the diagnosis of altered role performance related to:

- Change in physical, mental, or cognitive capacity affecting function.
- Addition, refinement, or deletion of work and/or family roles.
- Multiple life stressors.

For example, the client with a stroke may have significant role changes related to physical or cognitive impairment. Loss of a job, family member, or a club activity can all represent dramatic changes in role performance that affect self-image. Any disruption in the way a person views his or her role performance can provide evidence for a nursing diagnosis of Role performance, altered. In its most extreme forms, this nursing diagnosis can reflect a client's lack of hope about ever having a positive social identity or receiving acceptance from others as a functional member of society.

The nurse analyzes data related to role performance by looking at the client's functional performance and satisfaction associated with role responsibilities and relationships. How a client feels about roles and role responsibilities is just as important as the objective data. In an assessment interview, the nurse asks open-ended and focused questions about the client's family relationships, work, and social roles (see Box 6–3). Inquiry into how the client spends leisure time and the client's support systems and volunteer activities yields data about role performance. The nurse factors into the behavioral assessment understandings that role performance is jointly constructed by the client's developmental stage, socioeconomic environment, available social network, and intellectual and emotional potential. Role performance also is linked to gender (Bandura, 1986). Diagnoses associated with

---

BOX 6–3
Questions the Nurse Might Ask the Client in an Assessment Interview Centered on Role Relationships

Family
"Can you tell me something about your family?"
"How would you describe your family unit, e.g., age, sex, health status of members?"
"Who assumes responsibility for decision making?"
"What changes do you anticipate as a result of your illness (condition) in the way you function in your family?"
"Who do you see in your family as being most affected by your illness (condition)?"
"Who do you see in your family as being supportive of you?"

Work
"Can you tell me something about the work you do?"
"In general, how would you describe your satisfaction with your work?"
"Can you tell me something about how you get along with others on your job?"
"What are some of the concerns you have about your job at this time?"

Social
"How do you like other people to treat you?"
"To whom do you turn for support?"
"If _____ is not available to you, who else might provide social support for you?"

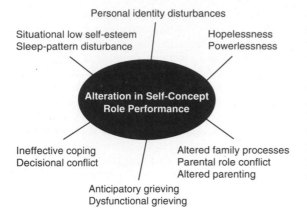

Personal identity disturbances

Situational low self-esteem
Sleep-pattern disturbance

Hopelessness
Powerlessness

**Alteration in Self-Concept
Role Performance**

Ineffective coping
Decisional conflict

Altered family processes
Parental role conflict
Altered parenting

Anticipatory grieving
Dysfunctional grieving

Figure 6–1 Alternate Nursing Diagnoses Associated with Alteration in Self-Concept: Role Performance

a primary diagnosis of Alteration in self-concept: role performance are presented in Figure 6–1.

INTERVENTION

Having a profound sense of loss about changes in role and social identity is normal and is part of the healing process involved with alteration in self-concept related to role performance. It is important to help the client grieve for the loss of important aspects of self-competency and its related status.

Validating the legitimacy of feeling hopeless, depressed, or angry helps the client acknowledge difficult feelings as part of the recovery process. Ventilation of disturbing feelings allows a person to put them in perspective. This step in the implementation process often is skipped because superficially it seems more logical to get on with the task of rebuilding a role identity.

The next step, helping the client to *identify personal strengths and "transferable skills,"* is an important strategy the nurse can use to help clients change perceptions about self and role performance. Transferable skills are talents and skills a person has that can be used in other ways. For example, the ability to analyze, to communicate easily with others, and to solve problems creatively are skills that can be employed in a variety of occupations and roles. Yet when people have lost a role, they often feel as if all the talents and skills associated with that role are also lost. Exercise 6–5 gives the nurse practice in identifying transferable skills.

Focusing on alternative options logically follows.

EXERCISE 6–5
Identifying Transferable Skills

Purpose: To help you identify the unique skills that can be transferred to other situations.

Time: 45 minutes; the essay may be done as a homework assignment.

Procedure:
1. Think of the one achievement you are most proud of.
2. List the strengths or personal actions that went into this accomplishment. "I was a good swim instructor," for example, can be recast into personal strengths such as, "I was a good swim instructor because I was dependable, organized, patient, and persistent." "I am able to relate easily to children," and "I was compassionate with slow learners and I was able to inspire others."
3. Identify the physical, psychological, and psychosocial characteristics that contributed to the accomplishment—for example, athletic ability, one of five children, ethnic origin.
4. Share your achievement with your classmates.

Discussion:
1. How difficult was it for you to write down the strengths that contributed to your finest achievement?
2. How many different aspects of yourself were you able to identify as being a part of your accomplishment?
3. What physical, psychological, and psychosocial characteristics contributed to your achievement?
4. As you listened to the other students' reports, did you think of any other factors present in your situation?
5. Do you see any of these talents or strengths as "transferable skills" you might use in other situations?
6. What did you learn about yourself in doing this exercise?
7. How might you apply what you learned in this exercise to working therapeutically with clients?

Assisting clients to think clearly about the options available instead of the options lost refocuses the client. The nurse can help the client develop a clearer understanding of realistic goals related to role performance and the steps needed to achieve them. Support groups assist with practical suggestions and emotional support. Clients identify "just knowing you are not alone" as a major strength of support groups.

Providing opportunities for the client to accomplish an activity successfully is a way of indirectly reinforcing the healthy, productive aspects of self. Similarly, *supporting clients by giving meaningful reassurance and positive feedback about achievements* is a simple way to help a client increase self-efficacy and self-esteem. Relevant client outcomes might include:

- Client verbalizes acceptance of changed role.
- Client expresses understanding of role expectations and responsibilities.
- Client develops realistic plans for adapting to changed circumstances.

SUMMARY

Chapter 6 develops the concept of role relationships as a major influence in nurse–client relationships. A role is defined as a set of behavioral standards and norms established by a society or community group to which a person belongs. Roles usually are ascribed—i.e., present at birth—or achieved—i.e., earned or bestowed on an individual—but sometimes they may be thrust upon a person. Roles also represent socially learned behaviors developed through one of three processes: acculturation, assimilation, and socialization. Position is the external context that defines role behaviors in a prescribed manner.

Factors influencing role behavioral presentations include social desirability, external support, personal commitment, and culture. Professionalism is the backbone of the professional nursing role. It consists of values of altruism, esthetics, autonomy, human dignity, the upholding of moral and legal principles, and faithfulness to truth. Competence, caring, and critical thinking are behavioral outcomes of professionalism.

Professional nursing roles include caregiver, teacher, client advocate, quality of care evaluator, manager, consultant, case manager, and researcher.

Professional role behaviors develop through comprehension of the profession's technology, internalization of the professional nursing culture, the finding of an acceptable personal and professional version of the role, and ability to integrate the role into other life roles.

Chapter 6 describes components of the sick role and role performance as a significant nursing diagnosis. Assessment and intervention strategies include validating the legitimacy of difficult feelings, identifying personal strengths and transferable skills, focusing on alternative options, and supporting risk-taking behaviors.

REFERENCES

American Association of Colleges of Nursing (1986). Values, Qualities, and Behaviors Associated with Professionalism in Nursing Practice. Washington, DC, the Association.

Bandura A (1986). Social Foundations of Thought and Action: A Social Cognitive Theory. Englewood Cliffs, NJ, Prentice Hall.

Baumeister R (1986). Identity: Cultural Change and the Struggle for Self. New York, Oxford.

Biddle BJ (1977). Role Theory: Expectations, Identities and Behaviors. New York, Academic Press.

Carroll-Johnson RM (ed.) (1992). Classification of Nursing Diagnoses: Proceedings of the Ninth Conference. Philadelphia, Lippincott.

Cohen H (1981). The Nurse's Quest for a Professional Identity. Menlo Park CA, Addison-Wesley.

Cox H, Hinz M, Lubno MA, Newfield S, Ridenour N, Sridaromont K (1989). Clinical Applications of Nursing Diagnosis. Baltimore, MD, Williams & Wilkins.

Creasia J (1991). Professional nursing roles. In Creasia J, Parker B (eds.) (1991), Conceptual Foundations of Professional Nursing Practice. St. Louis, Mosby Yearbook.

Creasia J, Parker B (1991). Conceptual Foundations of Professional Nursing Practice. St. Louis, Mosby Yearbook.

Damon W (1983). Social and Personality Development. New York, Norton.

Deers D, Evans D (1980). Excellence in nursing. Image 12:2.

Guzzetta C (1989). Developing a nursing data base prototype from the unitary person framework. *In* Guzzetta C, Bunton S, Prinkey L, Sherer A, Seifert P (eds.) (1989), Clinical Assessment Tools for Use with Nursing Diagnosis.

Hamilton J, Kiefer M (1986). Survival Skills for the New Nurse. Philadelphia, Lippincott.

Hardy ME, Conway ME (1988). Role Theory: Perspectives for Health Professionals (2nd ed). Norwalk, CT, Appleton and Lange.

Hoare C (1991). Psychosocial identity and cultural others. Journal of Counseling and Development 70(1): 45–47.

Jalali B (1982). Iranian families. In McGoldrick M, Pearce J, Giordano J (eds.) (1982), Ethnicity and Family Therapy. New York, Guilford Press.

Joos I, Nelson R, Lyness A (1985). Man, Health and Nursing: Basic Concepts and Theories. Reston, VA, Prentice Hall.

Jung CG (1965). Memories, Dreams, Reflections. (Recorded and edited by Aniela Jaffe. Richard and Clara Winston, trans.) New York, Vintage Books.

Kleinman A (1988). The Illness Narratives: Suffering, Healing and the Human Condition. New York, Basic Books.

Kramer M (1974). Reality Shock, St. Louis, Mosby.

Morse J, Bottorff J, Neander W, Solberg S (1991). Comparative analysis of conceptualizations and theories of Caring. Image 23(2):119–126.

North American Nursing Diagnosis Association (NANDA) (1991). Classification of Nursing Diagnoses: Proceedings of the Ninth Conference. Philadelphia, Lippincott.

Parsons T (1951). Illness and the role of the physician. A sociological perspective. American Journal of Orthopsychiatry. 21:452–460.

Parsons T, Fox RC (1952). Illness, therapy and the modern American family. Journal of Social Issues 13:31–44.

Roberson M (1992). Our diversity gives us strength: Comment and Opinion. American Nurse, May, p. 4.

Saarmann L, Freitas L, Rapps J, Riegel B (1992). The relationship of education to critical thinking ability and values among nurses: Socialization into professional nursing. Journal of Professional Nursing. 8(1):26–34.

Schlenker B (1985). Identity and self-identification. In Schlenker B (ed.) (1985), The Self and Social Life. New York, McGraw-Hill.

Steele S, Maravigilia F (1981). Creativity in Nursing. Thorofare, NJ, Charles B. Slack.

Taylor S (1986). Health Psychology. New York, Random House.

Wynne L, Shields C, Sirkin M (1992). Illness, family theory and family therapy: Conceptual issues. Family Process 31:4–17.

SUGGESTED READINGS

Burke GD, Scalzi CC (1988). Role stress in hospital executives and nursing executives. Health Care Management Review 13(3):67–72.

Campaniello JA (1988). When professional nurses return to school: A study of role conflict and well-being in multiple role women. Journal of Professional Nursing 4(2):136–140.

Corcoran S (1988). Toward operationalizing an advocacy role. Journal of Professional Nursing 4(4):242–248.

Crocker LM, Brodie BJ (1974). Development of a scale to assess student nurses' views of the professional role. Journal of Applied Psychology 59:233–235.

Hinshaw AS (1977). Socialization and resocialization of nurses for professional nursing practice. In Sams L (ed.) (1977), Socialization and Resocialization of Nurses (Publication No. 15–1659, pp. 1–15). New York, NLN Press.

Honan S, Krsnak G, Peterson D, Torkelson R (1988). The nurse as patient educator: Perceived responsibilities and factors enhancing role development. Journal of Continuing Education in Nursing 19(1):33–37.

McQueen P (1984). Resocializing the degree-seeking RN: A curriculum thread. Journal of Nursing Education 23(8):351.

Scearse P (1989). Quality of care: Another look. Journal of Professional Nursing 5(5):293–294.

Chapter 7

Clarifying Values in the Nurse–Client Relationship

CATHY ROMEO

OUTLINE

Basic Concepts

APPLICATIONS

Summary

OBJECTIVES

At the end of the chapter, the student will be able to:

1. Define terms related to values clarification.

2. Describe the seven steps (criteria) necessary for acquisition of a value.

3. Discuss the application of values clarification in professional relationships.

4. Analyze the role of personal values in ethical decision making.

All men are alike—true in that the difference between those who received many talents and those who received few is presently erased without mercy. But untrue when it is a question of how they employed them; then, there still stands the frontier between life and death, as it has been drawn for all eternity. . . . We are, all of us, at all times, confronted with the possibility of taking the step across that frontier—in either direction.

Dag Hammarskjöld, 1981

Chapter 7 examines the role of personal values and the importance of values clarification in the nurse–client relationship. A nurse's values often have a profound effect on the quality of care given to a client and the type of interaction that occurs. Value-laden issues such as abortion, "do not resuscitate" ("no" code) orders, clients' and nurses' rights, sexuality, alcoholism, quality of life, culture, and religion stir feelings in nurses that can be destructive in a therapeutic relationship if unrecognized. Differences in values can result in communication misunderstandings between client and nurse. Values clarification is a technique that can be used to help identify these feelings.

Most people don't pay much conscious attention to their values until called upon to do so by actions that conflict with their values. For example, what would you do if you witnessed a fellow student cheating on an examination? Some people would immediately call attention to the situation by summoning the exam proctor. Others might tell the proctor after the examination was over. Still others might wait several days and tell the proctor that "some student" was cheating the other day during the examination. Still others might choose not to do anything, believing that cheating will hurt the student in the long run. The ultimate decision on which action is taken often directly relates to the person's value system.

Nursing students are often surprised at how strong a value orientation they really possess on certain issues. Prior to entering a clinical setting, many students have never had to deal with value-laden controversial issues except perhaps in a very superficial manner. In our society, students may have had little opportunity to examine differences in cultural values and to draw the conclusion that differences represent variations in what is normal rather than a bizarre, alien lifestyle. They may be startled and confused when they experience the existence of two conflicting values at the same time, either in themselves or in a client.

This chapter introduces the nursing student to the process of values clarification. You will have the opportunity to explore your own values. In order to respond therapeutically to a client's needs, you need to have an understanding and acceptance of the client's value system. But you must understand your own value system first. Values clarification will help you to gain this understanding. The process of values clarification also will be a useful tool in helping you to understand and cope better with certain opposing values that your client might possess.

BASIC CONCEPTS

DEFINITIONS

Values

Values are a set of personal beliefs and attitudes about truth, beauty, and the worth of any thought, object, or behavior. They are action oriented and give direction and meaning to one's life (Uustal, 1978). As a noun, a "value" is something that is prized or cherished, like freedom, love, or life. As a verb, "value" implies action (Uustal, 1980)—for example, to fight for something you believe in. A value represents a way of life and is derived from life experiences. It affects a disposition one has toward a person, object, or idea. Values are almost never isolated but rather are interwoven with each other and with specific life events. They influence each other and are almost always changing. Values continually evolve as an individual matures in the ability to think critically, logically, and morally.

Values may be classified in several ways. One way is to classify them as either intrinsic or extrinsic. *Intrinsic values* are those related to the maintenance of life. For example, food has intrinsic value because it is essential for survival. Types of foods one values, however, differ significantly and are not intrinsic in and of themselves. *Extrinsic values* refer to values that are not essential to the maintenance of life. A client's selection of enjoyable music falls into this category (Steele and Harmon, 1983).

A second way to classify values is either as operative or conceived values. *Conceived values* are conceptions of the ideal (McNally, 1980). These are values that have been taught by one's culture, the ones most talked about in discussions concerning ethics or morality. Examples are such issues as right to life or freedom of speech. These values, though deeply held, have little practical application on a day-to-day basis. *Operative values,* by contrast, are values an individual uses on a daily basis to make choices about actions. For example, an individual who values honesty would probably give back the extra change that a cashier gave by mistake. When analyzing values, it is important to examine them not only in terms of what a person says but also in terms of what the person does in situations that involve an element of choice (McNally, 1980).

The *intensity* of one's values, how strongly one feels toward maintaining a value, or the amount of commitment an individual gives to his or her values can be measured in several ways. One way an intensity can be measured is by the amount of time and energy a person is willing to expend to preserve or act on a value. A nursing student might value high grades and be willing to give up weekend recreational time with friends and family in order to spend more time in the library, whereas another student might not.

A second way to identify value intensity is to measure the amount of satisfaction or guilt that is derived from holding onto a particular value. Many times, nursing students hold values that are belittled by their peers. Friends try to make them feel guilty or foolish for acting on their beliefs. The amount of satisfaction the student gets from staying faithful to his or her value system may determine the level of commitment to it. Strongly held values become a part of the integrity of a person's self-concept. Exercise 7–1 will assist you in exploring the intensity of your values. When doing this exercise, think about the commitment, the amount of time and energy you are willing to expend, the amount of satisfaction you are willing to give up, and the amount of satisfaction or guilt you obtain from holding onto a value.

Values System

A *values system* is a classification or hierarchy of individual values organized according to a continuum of relative importance. This system provides a meaningful and practical guide to everyday life. According to McNally (1980, p. 52), "The values

---

EXERCISE 7–1
Defining Values

Purpose: To help you clarify professional values.

Time: 15 minutes

Directions:
Fill in the blanks:
1. In giving care to an 18-year-old dying client, the most difficult aspect of care for me would be _____.
2. If a client with a diagnosis of cancer asked me to be truthful and tell him his diagnosis, I would _____.
3. If an attractive medical resident asked me out while I was assisting in performing a painful procedure on my client, I would _____.
4. If I was asked to administer a narcotic medication for pain relief to a client who clearly was not having any pain, I would _____.
5. If I was assigned to care for a client with a contagious disease and my employer did not provide protective equipment, I would _____.
6. When a long-term client is discharged, he gives me an expensive piece of jewelry. I would _____.
7. If I observed a colleague's unsafe practice, I would _____.
8. If an attractive client asked me out on a date, I would _____.

system helps to determine which beliefs, attitudes, values or actions are worth challenging, protecting, agreeing with or worth trying to change or influence." If this system is ideal or too far from reality, frustration, guilt, or conflict will result. In addition, individuals with few values tend to become conforming, apathetic, and inconsistent (McNally, 1980). A realistic values system allows flexibility and provides a general plan for conflict resolution and decision making.

Each day people make decisions regarding everyday life. Some are minor ("What should I have for dinner?" "Should I watch television or read?"). Major decisions include anything from "What car should I buy?" to "Is it time to place my grandfather in a nursing home?" Exercise 7–2 will give you an opportunity to practice choosing from alternatives and explaining or defending your choices. The exercise demonstrates that many issues require much more thoughtful consideration than most people tend to give them.

Values Indicators

Values indicators are attitudes, beliefs, feelings, worries, or convictions. They are not values because they have not been clearly established. The difference between values and values indica-

tors is that the latter do not fully meet the seven steps of the valuing process that describes and defines a values. For example, they may not meet the criteria of choice, prizing, and action.

HOW VALUES ARE FORMED

How do people learn or acquire values? Children initially learn their values from their parents. As the child's world expands, other people such as teachers, political heroes, and friends help a person shape and refine values that are personally meaningful. Simon, Howe, and Kirschenbaum (1972) identify four ways in which adults try to teach their children values. The first approach is moralizing. Traditionally, parents have tried to teach their children, starting a very young age, values that they believe will help their offspring to grow up and lead productive lives. Basically *moralizing* involves the transference of the parents' values directly onto the child. This approach has become increasingly less effective, especially as children are influenced by exposure to many different groups. Young people brought up by moralizing adults are not prepared to make their own decisions and form their own sets of values.

When children have not been taught how to form their values but rather just to believe what

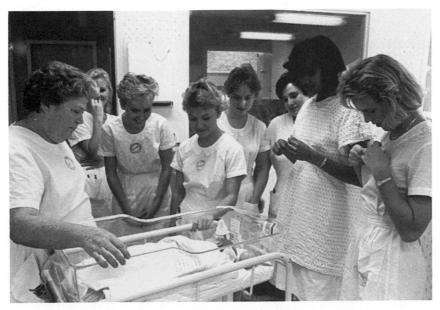

The values people hold often are observed in their interest, involvement, and commitment to people, places, and things. (Courtesy of the University of North Carolina at Charlotte College of Nursing)

EXERCISE 7–2
Examining Value Preferences

Purpose: To help you explore the meaning of your personal value preferences.

Time: 1 hour

Directions: Read each question and rank order it according to your own value-laden preferences. After the exercise has been completed, small-group discussion should be initiated in order to examine reasons for choices.

1. Whom would you prefer to marry? A person with
   _____ intelligence
   _____ personality
   _____ sex appeal
2. Which do you think more money should be spent on?
   _____ moon shots.
   _____ slum clearance.
   _____ cure for cancer.
3. Which would you be most likely to do about a person who has bad breath?
   _____ directly tell the person.
   _____ send the person an anonymous note.
   _____ nothing.
4. Which would you rather have happen to you if you had bad breath?
   _____ be told directly.
   _____ receive an anonymous note.
   _____ not be told.
5. You are married and have your own family. Your mother has died and your father is old. What would you do?
   _____ invite him to live in your home.
   _____ place him in a home for the aged.
   _____ get him an apartment for himself.
6. Which of the following measures should be taken to alleviate the overpopulation problems in other countries?
   _____ legalize abortion.
   _____ limit each family to two children and sterilize the parents afterwards.
   _____ distribute birth-control information everywhere.
   _____ trust people's common sense to limit the size of their families.
7. If you were with your family in a boat that capsized far from shore and there were only one life preserver would you
   _____ save your spouse?
   _____ save one of your children?
   _____ save yourself?
8. Which of these would be the most difficult for you to accept?
   _____ the death of a parent.
   _____ the death of a spouse.
   _____ your own death.
9. Which best describes the way you handle money?
   _____ spend freely.
   _____ always look for bargains.
   _____ budget carefully.
10. How would you rather spend a Saturday evening?
    _____ at a nightclub.
    _____ at home alone.
    _____ at a party at a friend's home.

From Simon, Howe, and Kirschenbaum, 1972.

they are told to believe, they may make important life decisions based on peer pressure. Or they may claim certain values merely to gain the approval of those influencing them, and then turn around and behave in an inconsistent manner.

Other adults adopt a *laissez-faire* attitude toward transmitting values. Their rationale is that no value system is right for everyone. They allow their children to do as they please without intervening, believing that eventually everything will turn out all right. Rather than form values, the children in such situations often experience confusion and conflict. Individuals who demonstrate arrested development of an ethical code can come from families at either extreme of the values-transmission continuum.

A third method of transmitting values is through **modeling.** The rationale for this approach is that if people present themselves in an attractive manner and live by certain sets of values, others will be impressed and will adopt and imitate those attitudes and behavior. However, young people are exposed to many different individuals who hold very different beliefs and attitudes and who act in very different ways. Even with good models, they can become confused. When it is time to make decisions, such as those involving choosing a career or a spouse or whether to have sex with someone, whom do they emulate? Should they stick to the old morals or try new ones? How do they develop their own sense of identity?

Values clarification, a fourth method of teaching values, was developed by Louis Roth and his associates (1966). This approach allows people to build their own values. It is not concerned with the *content* of people's values but rather with the *process of valuing.* The focus is on how individuals come to hold certain beliefs and values and how they establish certain behavior patterns based on these beliefs. Values clarification does not aim to instill any particular set of values but rather to help people use the process in their own lives for their own beliefs and behavior patterns (Simon, Howe, and Kirschenbaum, 1972). Two other concepts important in understanding values clarification are values acquisition and cognitive dissonance.

VALUES ACQUISITION

Values acquisition is a term used to indicate that a new value has been assumed consciously. As nurs-

ing students advance through their clinical experiences they take on some of the values of the nursing profession. Maintaining client confidentiality is an example of a professional value that a nursing student acquires. Before continuing with the chapter, reflect again on the questions in Exercise 7–2. Once you have thought about professional values in nursing from your own perspective, do Exercise 7–3.

COGNITIVE DISSONANCE

Cognitive dissonance refers to the holding of two or more conflicting values at the same time. If the nurse values a woman's right to choose yet believes that abortion is wrong, then the nurse's values are in conflict. The nurse is experiencing cognitive dissonance.

The world is a much more complicated place to live in today than ever before. Life is challenging and exciting, yet confusing as well. How does one think, feel, or act when facing today's many ethical dilemmas and situations? Ideally, choices should be made on the basis of the values that people hold, but frequently people cannot identify or are unclear about their own values and thus make their choices based on peer pressure, textbook theory, or family concerns. Typical areas of confusion and conflict include the following:

Policies or rules	War
Religion	Race
Work	Love, sex
Leisure time	Friends
Death	Personal taste
Abortion	Child rearing

VALUES CLARIFICATION

Values clarification is a process individuals use to help them sort through, analyze, and prioritize values. Once there is clarification, an individual is better able to act in a manner consistent with his or her chosen values. In other words, values clarification is a cognitive process that involves sorting through issues in an attempt to close the gap between what an individual says and what an individual actually does. The goal of values clarification is to facilitate self-understanding. The process is dynamic and ongoing, with emphasis on ques-

EXERCISE 7–3
Personal and Professional Value Descriptors

Purpose: To help you identify professional values. To focus on role functions of nursing curriculums.

Time: 15 minutes

Directions:
Mark each of the adjectives in the following word list:

S—if you feel it describes yourself
N—if you feel it is an ideal characteristic for a professional nurse
X—if it is undesirable

Any word may receive more than one mark.

Warm	Competent
Caring	Solitary
Concerned	Efficient
Opinionated	Aggressive
Reliable	Shy
Ambitious	Affectionate
Assertive	Thoughtful
Intellectual	Skillful

Discussion:
Compare the group of characteristics you feel reflected yourself (S) and those you marked only (N) nurse.
1. Which attributes labeled (S) might be useful to you in your career?
2. Which attributes marked (N) can be learned?
3. In class, identify the six attributes most frequently identified by class members as reflecting the ideal nurse.
4. With the instructor's assistance, identify curriculum content in your nursing program that may help a student develop these ideal characteristics. Do these curriculum areas include clinical learning experiences?

tioning, arguing, and challenging old ideas. The end result of a values clarification process should be increased awareness, empathy, and insight. According to Steele and Harmon (1983), values of paramount importance to an individual should be acted upon consistently and predictably. If a value is not acted upon with reasonable ease, it may be a value indicator rather than an established value. Acting on a value offers the strongest evidence of the values clarification process.

An important first step in values clarification is to understand yourself as a person and to know your own personally held values. For example, think about how you would respond if someone of significance to you asked you to steal a watch from an open case in a jewelry store. Would you do it? How about taking a monogramed towel from a hotel you were staying at, or claiming charitable donations on your tax return that, in fact,

you never made. In order to begin to examine yourself as an individual and as a future professional nurse, do Exercise 7–4.

In everyday life, people are faced with situations that require very little thought and only rote actions and others that require a great deal of thought and decision making, as well as carefully planned action. Whether minor or critical, all thoughts, opinions, and ultimate actions are based on consciously held beliefs, attitudes, and values. Exercise 7–5 provides practice in looking at the values present in everyday communication.

Values clarification holds a key position in the decision-making process. Values are a strong determinant in the selections made between competing alternatives. Values clarification is not a set of rules but rather an aid in making choices.

During a conflict that involves a values dilemma, people often form opinions prematurely based on

EXERCISE 7–4
Acquiring Professional Values

Purpose: To help students explore their professional values.

Time: 30 minutes

Directions:
Consider your answers to these questions.
1. What are some other professional values of nursing that I might expect to acquire when assuming the role of the professional nurse?
2. How might I go about acquiring these values?

their emotional reactions. Their initial reactions usually do not reflect their true beliefs. The ability to make decisions based on values becomes blurred. Often the values underlying decisions are unconscious or difficult to identify, and, as a result, behaviors and attitudes are inconsistent. As a person becomes more involved in a situation, these feelings often change. An individual with a clear sense of values is better able to choose and to initiate responses consistent with his or her value system. Values clarification is a process that is useful in completing this task.

APPLICATIONS

STEPS IN THE VALUES CLARIFICATION PROCESS

As a nursing student, it is important for you to examine each of the seven steps of the values clarification process to obtain a more comprehensive understanding of how a value is acquired. Once you see how the process works, you can apply it to your own life to identify and understand your own values. This will allow you to apply the values clar-

EXERCISE 7–5
Examining All Sides

Purpose: This exercise demonstrates that there are many facets to every issue. Howe do you determine your position? What factors influence your thoughts and feelings? How will your choice be reflected in your behavior?

Time: 45 minutes

Directions:
Discuss these questions with your peers in small groups. Then bring some of these issues to your clinical experiences and discuss options with staff nurses.

Indicate your responses to the following statements in this manner: SA—strongly agree, A—Agree, U—undecided, D—disagree, SD—strongly disagree

_____ 1. Clients have the right to participate in all decisions related to their health care.

_____ 2. Continuing education should be mandatory for nurses.

_____ 3. Clients should always be told the truth.

_____ 4. Standards of nursing practice should be enforced by state examining boards.

_____ 5. Nurses should be required to take relicensure examinations every five years.

_____ 6. Clients have the right to obtain their health records upon request.

_____ 7. Abortion should be legal.

_____ 8. Badly deformed newborns should be allowed to die.

_____ 9. There should be a law guaranteeing medical care for each person in this country.

ification process when trying to understand the value system of your clients. The seven criteria for acquisition of a value are as follows:

The value must be:

1. Freely chosen.
2. From alternatives.
3. After careful consideration of each alternative.

There must be:

4. Pride and happiness with the choice.
5. Willingness to make the value(s) known to others.

It must be acted upon:

6. In response to the choice.
7. In a pattern of behavior consistent with the choice (value is incorporated into the individual's lifestyle).

The criteria used for acquisition of a value may be divided into three major elements. The first three steps of the process relate to the idea that, in order for a value indicator to become a value, *it must be freely chosen* by an individual. The first step contends that individuals must identify value indicators that are suitable for guiding their lives. People must be in control and able to choose freely. The second step involves having alternatives. Selection of an alternative, *after careful consideration of* the consequences of each alternative, is the third step. Many people do not sort through options before committing themselves to an idea. In addition, many individuals approach value issues emotionally rather than logically and critically. Individuals are often surprised to find out how committed they are to an idea without having critically sorted through the alternatives. Exercise 7–6 gives practice in seeing the wide range of options that are possible in considering various issues.

The fourth and fifth steps of the process are based on the premise that, in order for a value indicator to be considered a value, *it must be prized* by the individual. In the fourth step, an individual believes that he or she deserves the prized value. This is a continuous process that represents a deepening awareness of one's feelings. The fifth step, which is very important, indicates the willingness to affirm and share the choice with the public. An individual might make the choices known through discussions with friends or colleagues, public speeches, and published letters and articles or possibly even through political activities. Often people find themselves acting one way and later wishing they had acted another way. Other people publicly affirm their beliefs but feel unable to act on them because of actual or perceived barriers to action. The clearer you are about your values, the more congruent your actions will

---

EXERCISE 7–6
The Range of Opinion

Purpose: When dealing with controversial topics, people tend to see things as either/or with nothing in between. The following exercise will help you see that there are often a wide range of possible positions on any given issue. This exercise will emphasize the importance of exploring all options before choosing freely.

Time: 30 minutes

Directions:
Divide the class into groups of 5. Each group is assigned a controversial issue. Sample issues include:

    Legalization of abortion
    Premarital sex
    Legalization of marijuana
    Legalization of euthanasia.

The group then divides the issue into 5 positions. These include an ultraconservative stand, a moderate stand, a liberal stand, a radical stand, and a revolutionary stand. Each student selects a stand. A mock debate with a narrator is then initiated. Discuss the result of the debate with spectators from the rest of the class and participants.

be with your beliefs. Exercise 7–7 gives practice in breaking through obstacles to action.

The sixth and seventh steps state that to be a true value, *the value must be acted upon in a consistent manner*. These last two steps of the values-clarification process demonstrate the willingness of an individual to act on his decision. A shift from insight to behavioral change exemplifies the sixth step. The seventh step occurs when the choice made is consistently acted upon. This is the most difficult step because it involves the integration of the choice into an individual's lifestyle (Uustal, 1980). Exercise 7–8 gives practice in exploring values.

Understanding Your Own Values

Professional values ultimately are an expansion and reflection of an individual's personal values. Many of the things you as a student value may have had an impact on why you decided to become a nurse in the first place. At this time, take a few minutes to contemplate your reasons for wanting to become a nurse. Next, think about aspects of your life that you value a great deal. Examples might include health, friends, and socialization. Examine the two lists and see if they have any commonalities.

Values clarification is a valuable tool for the nurse because it serves as a base for helping clients search successfully for and find the values they identify as important. The way your clients respond to the health care system, to their individual diagnoses, or to your therapeutic interventions are influenced by their personal value systems. Unless you are able to identify your client's values and can appreciate the validity of those values, you run the risk of imposing your own values on others rather than modifying, teaching, and working with your client's value system. It is not necessary for your values and your client's values to coincide—this is an unrealistic expectation. However, whenever possible and appropriate the client's values should be taken into consideration during every aspect of the nursing process.

APPLICATION OF VALUES CLARIFICATION TO THE NURSING PROCESS

The nursing process offers many opportunities to incorporate values clarification into care of the client. During the assessment phase, the nurse can obtain an assessment of the client's values with regard to the health system. For example, the nurse might interview a client for the first time and learn that he has obstructive pulmonary disease (COPD) and is having difficulty breathing. The client insists on smoking. As the nurse caring for the client, is it appropriate to intervene? if so, to what extent? This is an example of having knowledge that smoking is detrimental to a person's health, and as a nurse, finding the value of health in conflict with the client's value of smoking. In this case, it is important to examine your own values and to try to identify and understand your client's values. Although your values differ, whenever possible you must attempt to

---

EXERCISE 7–7
Removing Barriers to Action

Purpose: This exercise will be helpful in assisting students to practice identifying and removing barriers to action.

Time: 1 hour

Directions:
Write at the top of a piece of paper some action that you would like to take or decision that you would like to make. It should be an action that you are having some difficulty taking or that you fear to take. Next, draw a line lengthwise down the middle of the paper. On the right-hand side of the paper, list all of the perceived or real barriers that seem to be keeping you from acting. On the left-hand side of the paper, list steps that could be taken to help move or reduce each of the barriers. On the back of the paper, develop a plan of action for actually removing the barriers.

This exercise can be completed individually or in small groups. The group can help the individual in listing barriers and developing a course of action for removing barriers.

EXERCISE 7–8
Values Grid

Purpose: When learning a new process, it is always helpful to practice before applying it to actual clinical practice. This exercise will help you to integrate all 7 steps of the values clarification process into practical nursing applications.

Time: 1 hour

Directions:
On the grid below, write a statement that reflects a belief you have related to a specific nursing application. This statement should reflect an area of conflict or confusion in nursing that you wish to examine. An example might be, "A nurse should never lie to a patient about anything." To the right of this statement you should then go through the values-clarification process step by step, checking as you go along each of the seven steps that reflect your beliefs. In other words, you might choose freely never to be dishonest to a patient, but in certain real situations you might not be able to act on this belief and therefore cannot check that box.

Listed below are some examples of conflicts or confusions in nursing that you may wish to focus on.

Peer review	Professional organizations	Confidentiality
Accountability	Patient's rights	Euthanasia
Continuing education	Informed consent	Abortion
Licensing	Refusal of care	Nurses' rights

	Freely chooses	From alternatives	Examine consequences	Proud	Able to disclose	Action	Acts repeatedly
Statement	1	2	3	4	5	6	7

Is your belief a value according to the theory? What step(s) must you consider more carefully and completely?

---

care for this client within his realm of value. A client has the right to make decisions that are not always congruent with those of the health care system. These decisions may cause the nurse to feel uneasy unless there is a commitment to respect the rights of the client (Steele and Harmon, 1983). Exercise 7–9 gives practice in understanding values and rights.

When identifying specific nursing diagnoses, it is important for the nurse to continue to reflect on his or her own values and on those of the client so that the diagnoses reflect a specific problem and

are not biased by the nurse's values. When caring for a client from another culture, diagnoses may involve potential or actual problems. Examples of conflicts indicating differences in values orientation might be spiritual distress related to a conflict between spiritual beliefs and prescribed health treatments or ineffective family coping related to restricted visiting hours for a family in which full family participation is a cultural value.

In the planning phase, it is important to identify and understand the client's value system as the foundation for developing the most appropriate

EXERCISE 7–9
"Rights"

Purpose: To help you understand the relation between values and rights.

Time: 30 minutes per questionnaire

Directions:
Choose any or all of the following questionnaires. Answer the questions. Use the questionnaires as catalysts to generate discussion. If time allows, use role play to further explore some of the issues discussed in the questionnaires.

Questionnaire 1
Children's Rights

Please indicate how much you agree with the following statements by placing the number that most closely indicates your value next to each statement.

Strongly Disagree 1	Disagree 2	Ambivalent 3	Agree 4	Strongly Agree 5

_____ 1. Children's rights should be the same as adults' rights.
_____ 2. The "age of reason" is accurately set at 18 years of age.
_____ 3. Voting in political elections should be extended to children who want to vote.
_____ 4. Children should be allowed to read records that have information about them.
_____ 5. Children under 18 are incompetent and cannot make decisions that affect their lives.
_____ 6. Children should be consulted about treatment for their illness.
_____ 7. Children should be consulted before they are removed from abusive homes.
_____ 8. Child agents should be available to assist children with limited capacities.
_____ 9. Parents should have the "final say" in situations involving their children.
_____ 10. Society needs to be protected from incompetent children, and parents are the best persons to perform this role.

From Steele SM, Harmon VM (1983). Values Clarification in Nursing (2nd ed.), Norwalk, CT, Appleton-Century-Crofts.

Consider the rights and values involved in helping Maria and her parents:

Case Study

Maria, age four, has been recently diagnosed with a second exacerbation of acute lymphocytic leukemia. She is receiving prednisone and an experimental drug intravenously. Nurses must check the rate of infusion every hour as well as administer other medication and monitor urinary output. To monitor therapeutic progress she is scheduled for bone-marrow aspirations every three days, which she finds extremely painful. Maria complains of abdominal pain almost constantly in addition to the severe vomiting and diarrhea caused by the medication.

Maria is so fearful that she screams every time a nurse enters her room. Initially her parents were told she had a 95 percent chance for recovery. With her second relapse, however, standard treatment protocols have failed to produce remission of her disease. One estimate of 10 percent or less possibility of recovery was given to her parents. Since they heard this news they have reduced their visits to 10 minutes once every other day. Maria frequently cries for her mother.

Questions for Discussion:
1. What values should be communicated to parents about painful treatment procedures undertaken in the care of ill children?
2. What verbal and nonverbal means of communication could be used by staff to reassure Maria about care that will be less painful?
3. How does the change in prognosis affect your feelings about performing invasive, painful procedures?

EXERCISE 7–9 *(Continued)*

4. You are asked to restrain Maria for her next bone-marrow aspiration. Discuss possible ways to prepare Maria for this procedure to reduce her anxiety.
5. A co-worker expresses anger to you about Maria's parents' absence. Identify some therapeutic communication responses you might use in your conversation with this coworker. What interventions might you use with the parents?

The following questionnaires can help you get in touch with some of the personal and professional issues inherent in values clarification.

Questionnaire 2
Professional Values

Please indicate your belief in the values presented below by placing the number that most closely represents your feelings next to the statement.

Strongly Disagree	Disagree	Ambivalent	Agree	Strongly Agree
1	2	3	4	5

_____ 1. I should be able to help every client.
_____ 2. The client's needs are more important than mine.
_____ 3. If I make a medication error, I probably should look into a profession other than nursing.
_____ 4. I consider it my responsibility to challenge my client's value system if it does not seem to be in the client's best interest.
_____ 5. I would find it difficult to work with an AIDS client.
_____ 6. If a client's condition is terminal, I believe the choice to use extraordinary measures is not mine to make; it belongs to the family.
_____ 7. I can be most effective with clients who have a similar value system.
_____ 8. It is not possible to express caring without having time to sit down and talk with a client.
_____ 9. I would find it difficult to work with a client who has strict fundamentalist religious beliefs.
_____ 10. I would find it difficult to be empathetic with a child abuser.
_____ 11. Relating to an atheist would be very difficult for me.
_____ 12. Terminally ill and severely handicapped individuals should be allowed to end their own lives.
_____ 13. Severely ill clients should be encouraged to make a living will that allows the medical and nursing staff to withhold lifesaving treatment.
_____ 14. Nurse have an ethical responsibility to tell clients of the limits of confidentiality.
_____ 15. A mentally retarded girl should be given the option to decide whether or not she should be sterilized.
_____ 16. It's okay to talk about client problems in a general way as long as the client's name or any identifying information is not included in the discussion.
_____ 17. Consulting with family or outside agencies without the client's permission is appropriate in certain situations.

Questionnaire 3

Read the statements below. Think about each situation carefully. How would you want to respond if you were the primary nurse in the situation?

1. A 40-year-old man tells you of his ongoing extramarital affair. He is very physically and verbally affectionate with his wife when she comes to visit.
2. A gay client tests HIV-positive, but he doesn't want to tell his partner because it might jeopardize the relationship.
3. An eight-year-old girl is admitted to the emergency room, immaculately dressed, with many bruises and welts on her arms and legs. Her mother states she was hurt on the playground.

(Continued)

EXERCISE 7–9 *(Continued)*

4. You note that your student partner has alcohol on her breath when she picks up her assignments. This has happened on more than one occasion.
5. A client has been told his bone scan shows metastatic lesions. He tells you not to tell his wife because she will just worry.
6. An adolescent client tells you that her friend brought some marijuana to the hospital to help her calm her nerves.
7. A client admitted to the psychiatric unit refuses to take his medication and wants to sign out of the hospital against medical advice.

Discussion:
1. How did your answers compare with those of your peers?
2. If you implemented them, what would be the consequences for you? For the client?
3. In what ways did your values enter into your choices?
4. What did you learn about yourself and your preferred value choices from doing this exercise that might help you in your nursing practice?

interventions. Care plans that support rather than discount the client's health care beliefs are more likely to be received favorably.

The intervention used identifies values as guidelines for care. The nurse can also use the values-clarification process as a therapeutic technique. The process may be used to help clients sort out feelings, identify conflict areas, examine and choose from alternatives, set goals, and act in a manner consistent with their value systems and according to their physical and emotional health. During the evaluation phase, the results of therapeutic intervention can be examined in terms of how well the nursing and client goals were met while keeping within the guidelines of the client's value system.

SOLVING ETHICAL DILEMMAS IN NURSING

Nurses are having to deal more and more frequently with ethical dilemmas in and out of clinical settings. Ethical issues may include anything from euthanasia to who should receive an organ transplant to caring for a client with AIDS. With the expanded technological advances in health care there is an ever-increasing need for ethical decisions to accompany these advances. As a result, nurses may feel a growing pressure to be proficient in ethical decision making.

There are three general categories related to ethical issues that nurses are commonly faced with today. These include moral uncertainty, moral or

ethical dilemmas, and moral stress. *Moral uncertainty* occurs when the nurse is uncertain as to which moral rules (i.e., values, beliefs, ethical principles) apply to a given situation. For example, should a terminally ill client who is in and out of a coma and chooses not to eat or drink anything be required to have intravenenous therapy for hydration purposes? Does giving IV therapy constitute giving the client extraordinary measures to prolong life? Is it more or less comfortable for the dying patient to maintain a high hydration level? When there is no clear definition of the problem, moral uncertainty develops because the nurse is unable to identify the situation as a moral problem or to define specific moral rules that apply. Strategies that might be useful in dealing with moral uncertainty include using the values-clarification process to clarify values, developing a specific philosophy of nursing, and acquiring knowledge about ethical principles.

Ethical or moral dilemmas arise when two or more moral issues are in conflict. An ethical dilemma is a problem in which there are two or more conflicting but equally right answers. Organ harvesting of a severely brain-damaged infant is an example of an ethical dilemma. Removal of organs from one infant may save the lives of several other infants. However, even though the brain-damaged child is definitely going to die, is it right to remove organs prior to the child's death? It is important for the nurse to understand that in many ethical dilemmas there is often no single automatically right solution. Some decisions may be "more right" than others, but often what one nurse decides is best differs significantly from what another nurse decides.

The third most common kind of ethical problem seen in nursing today is *moral distress.* Moral distress results when the nurse knows what is "right" but is bound to do otherwise because of legal or institutional constraints. When such a situation arises (e.g., a terminally ill client who does not have a "do not resuscitate" medical order and for whom, therefore, resuscitation attempts must be made) the nurse may experience inner turmoil.

Values clarification plays a very important role in solving ethical dilemmas in nursing. Since values underlie all ethical decision making, nurses must understand their own values thoroughly before making an ethical decision. Instead of responding in an emotional manner on the spur of the moment (as people often do when faced with an ethical dilemma), the nurse who uses the values-clarification process as a tool can respond rationally. It is not an easy task to have sufficient knowledge of oneself, of the situation, and of legal and moral constraints to be able to implement ethical decision making quickly and under less than ideal circumstances. Many nurses who have been practicing for years still struggle over ethical dilemmas. Values clarification does not eliminate the problem, but it can be useful in minimizing the struggle.

Examination of real-life situations can be helpful to the student when attempting to use values clarification to address ethical dilemmas in nursing. Take some time now to read the case studies in Exercise 7–10. Try to put yourself in the place of the nurse in each study and determine how you would respond to a similar situation.

SUMMARY

A nurse's values often have a profound effect on the quality of care given to a client and on the type of interaction that occurs. This chapter introduces the process of values clarification. Individuals acquire values through interactions with others. Moralizing, adopting a laissez-faire attitude, modeling behaviors associated with certain values, and practicing values clarification are strategies that foster the development of certain values. Basically, values clarification is concerned with the process of valuing. The focus is on how individuals come to hold certain beliefs and values and establish behavior patterns based on these beliefs. An important first step in values clarification is developing an understanding of oneself as a person and identifying one's own personally held values.

Values represent a personalized set of beliefs and attitudes about truth and the intrinsic worth of persons, objects, and behaviors. The intensity of a value is measured by the amount of commitment and of satisfaction one is willing to give up on its behalf, as well as by the amount of satisfaction derived from holding on to a particular value.

Values are classified as either operative or conceived. The conceived worth of an object is taught by one's culture. Usually conceived values have less applicability to everyday situations than operative values, which individuals use daily to make choices about their actions.

A values system is a classification or hierarchy of individual values. A realistic value system allows flexibility and provides a general plan for conflict resolution and decision making. Values acquisition describes the process of procuring a new value.

The outcome of a values-clarification process should be more awareness, empathy, and insight. Seven steps are involved in the values-clarification process. To acquire a value, the person chooses freely from more than one alternative after careful consideration of each option. The person prizes the value chosen and shows pride in the choice by making the value known to others. Additionally, the person acts on the basis of the chosen value; behavior is congruent with the choice and is incorporated into the person's lifestyle.

Professional values are ultimately an expansion and reflection of an individual's personal values. To understand and work with a client's value system, one must first understand the nature of one's own value system. Value-laden issues that are unrecognized can be destructive to the goals of the nurse–client relationship.

Values clarification is used throughout the nursing process to direct the type of care that is most compatible with the client's recognized cultural belief and value system. Although ethical issues often require a deeper understanding of val-

EXERCISE 7–10
Difficult Case Examples

Purpose: To help you develop a practical approach to ethical decision making by understanding your value responses.

Time: 1 hour

Directions:
The following case studies can be used as discussion catalysts or for role-play situations in order to examine values and to explore possible responses in terms of values only. After reading each study, try to respond to the following questions.
1. What would your reaction be to this situation?
2. What would you do if you were the nurse?
3. What conflicts in values does the situation pose for you?
4. How can you as the nurse respect the integrity of your client's decision when it conflicts with your own value system?
   A. *Prolongation of life*—Kim is a 25-week gestational-age newborn who is surviving in the neonatal intensive-care unit with major life-support systems. Kim's parents are showing increasingly less interest in Kim's progress. One day when you are caring for Kim, the father yells "stop poking and prodding at her! What are you trying to prove by keeping her alive? Turn off those machines." Discuss how you might react in this situation.
   B. *Abortion*—Mrs. Smith requested to have amniocentesis in order to determine whether her fetus would have Tay-Sachs disease. She finds out that the fetus is a girl. Even though it does not have Tay-Sachs, she decides to terminate the pregnancy because of her desire to have a boy. Her husband agrees with her decision. Discuss your reactions to this request.
   C. *Euthanasia*—An elderly male client of yours is suffering from terminal cancer. He is continuously in a great deal of pain. He says that he has had a good life and does not want his family to suffer. He tells you that he is going to commit suicide. What would be your reaction? Next consider how you would react if the elderly client was your grandfather.
   D. *Refusal to accept blood*—You are an obstetrical nurse. You have a client, Mrs. Jones, who refuses to receive blood because it is against her religious beliefs. After a difficult cesarean section she delivers a healthy baby girl. She has lost a great deal of blood and is continuing to hemorrhage. Without a blood transfusion it is very likely that she will die. She refuses to receive blood. What would be your response to this situation?
   E. *Sexual advances*—As the nurse, it is your responsibility to care for a very attractive, seductive male or female client who has had foot surgery. He or she continues to make subtle sexual advances to you. How would you respond?
   F. *Refusal to care for a client*—You are the head nurse on a medical–surgical unit. You have assigned Nurse Brown to care for Mr. Adams, a 28-year-old homosexual, who has recently been diagnosed as having AIDS. Nurse Brown refuses to care for this patient because she does not want to get AIDS and says she does not like "that kind of person." As the head nurse, how would you deal with this situation? How might Nurse Brown use values clarification to deal with this ethical dilemma?

ues clarification, the nurse can use the values-clarification process as a basic tool for responding to such a dilemma.

REFERENCES

Cunningham N, Hutchinson S (1990). Myths in health care ethics. Image 22(4):235.

Davis AJ (1990a). Ethical issues in nursing research: Ethical similarities internationally. Western Journal of Nursing Research 12:685.

Davis AJ (1990b). Ethical issues in nursing research. Western Journal of Nursing Research 12:413.

Ericksen JR (1990). Making choices: The crux of ethical problems in nursing. ARON Journal 52(1):394.

Fowler MD (1989). Ethical decision making in clinical practice. Nursing Clinics of North America 24(4):955.

Hammarskjöld D (1981). Markings, New York, Knopf, p. 44. (Translated from the Swedish by Sjöberg L, Auden W).

McNally JM (1980). Values: Part II. Supervisor Nurse 11:52.

Pederson C, Duckett L, Maruyama G (1990). Using structured controversy to promote ethical decision making. Journal of Nursing Education 29(4):151.

Roth L, Harmen M, Simon S (1966). Values and Teaching. Columbus, OH, Charles E. Merrill.

Simon SB, Howe LW, Kirschenbaum H (1972). Values Clarification: A Handbook of Practical Strategies for Teachers and Students. New York, Hart Publishing.

Steele SM, Harmon VM (1983). Values Clarification in Nursing (2nd ed.). Norwalk, CT, Appleton-Century-Crofts.

Uustal DB (1978). Values clarification in nursing: Application to practice. American Journal of Nursing 78:2058.

Uustal DB (1980). Exploring values in nursing. ARON Journal 31:183.

SUGGESTED READINGS

Avery GB (1985). Ethical considerations in the intensive care nursery. *In* Gottffried AW, Gaiter JL (eds.) (1985), Infant Stress under Intensive Care, Environmental Neonatology. Baltimore, University Park Press.

Eddy JM, St. Pierre RW, Alles WF (1985). A re-examination of values clarification for the health educator. Health Education 16:36.

Edwards BJ, Haddad AM (1988). Establishing a nursing bioethics committee. Journal of Nursing Administration 18:30.

Hazinski, MF (1988). Pediatric organ donation: Responsibilities of the critical care nurse. Pediatric Nursing 13:354.

Pence T, Cantrall, J (1990). Ethics in Nursing: An Anthology. New York, National League for Nursing.

Steele SM (1986). AIDS: Clarifying values to close in on ethical questions. Nursing and Health Care 7:247.

Thompson, JE (1988). Living with ethical decisions with which you disagree. MCN: American Journal of Maternal Child Nursing 13:245.

Wilson-Barnett J (1986). Ethical dilemmas in nursing. Journal of Medical Ethics 12:123.

Wright J (1991). Counseling at the cultural interface: Is getting back to roots enough? Journal of Advanced Nursing 16:92.

Chapter 8

Losses and Endings in the Nurse–Client Relationship

VERNA BENNER CARSON

OBJECTIVES

At the end of the chapter, the student will be able to:

1. Define termination and identify common behaviors associated with endings in the nurse–client relationship.

2. Discuss the termination of death.

3. Describe the nurse's role as facilitator of termination.

4. Discuss the role of the nurse with clients who are dying.

Because I could not stop for Death,
He kindly stopped for me;
The carriage held but just ourselves
and Immortality.

Emily Dickinson, 1878

Chapter 8 describes termination as a universal and profound life experience. As such, the termination process tends to defy neat, concise explanations. Attempts can certainly be made to understand and to help others as they experience loss, but there will always be other ways to explain loss and the feelings generated by it. Good-byes themselves often leave people with the longing to have said more, to have given more, and to be able to feel less pain. Terminations are a part of every relationship. How the client works through saying good-bye and coping with the loss of relationships determines whether the process serves as an opportunity for personal growth or diminishes the self. It is both a blessing and a challenge to the nurse to be able to share and participate in a client's deepest and most meaningful life experiences—including the experience of loss.

BASIC CONCEPTS

What do a quote from Shakespeare, ("Parting is such sweet sorrow") and a line from a John Denver song ("Why do we always fight when I have to go?") have in common? They both have a theme that conveys the difficulty of saying good-bye, a theme that is repeated in music, literature, and fine arts.

Endings of relationships are an inevitable part of life, a sorrow that is woven into the fabric of life. No one is exempt. The sadness of good-byes is repeated many times as we make our way into adulthood. We are always confronted with saying good-bye to something familiar and cared for and saying hello to something unfamiliar and unknown (Bozarth-Campbell, 1982). Consider the following normal life events:

- A two-year-old leaves his mother for the first time to spend the day at a babysitter's home while his mother works.
- A five-year-old goes to kindergarten for the first time.
- A teenager transfers to a different school.
- A grandmother dies.
- A couple is granted a divorce.

- A student graduates from nursing school.
- A young woman receives the news that she has tested positive for HIV.

All of these events are linked by an element of leaving, of saying good-bye to what was and beginning anew, of building on the past but not returning to it. Sometimes termination involves ending a relationship through death or separation. In other cases, the termination involves a major change in the relationship that requires the participants to give up former expectations and move on to new ways of relating. In still other cases, the termination involves giving up an old role for a new one. In any event, all leavings have in common feelings of sadness, loss, a longing for the past, and ambivalence about the future. The feelings differ only in the intensity that they are experienced.

Nurses experience termination in their personal relationships, as well as in the professional relationships they develop with clients. The ending of a professional relationship carries with it the same feelings of sadness, loss, and anger that accompany other good-byes. Whether the nurse is able to facilitate the termination process so that it is a growth-producing experience for both participants is greatly influenced by how the nurse has handled past termination experiences. Nurses who have openly acknowledged and shared their feelings of past losses will be better prepared to assist their clients. If, on the other hand, they have tended to avoid saying good-bye in their personal lives, their difficulty will be reflected in their professional relationships. The more pain is denied, the deeper it tends to go inside our bodies and souls. Burying pain only makes it harder to identify, deal with, and ultimately grow beyond (Bozarth-Campbell, 1982). Yet there are good ways to say good-bye. Exercise 8–1 will help you examine certain aspects of termination.

DEFINITION

Termination involves the deliberate separation of two or more persons from an intimate and meaningful relationship. Companiello (1980) suggests

EXERCISE 8–1
Saying Good-bye

Purpose: To consider what saying good-bye means.

Time: 10 minutes

Directions:
Reflect on the words of the song "Hey, There's No Way to Say Good-bye" and ask yourself:
1. What makes a "good" good-bye?
2. What place do tears have in saying good-bye?
3. How do you usually say good-bye?
4. How do you feel when you say good-bye?
5. How do you interpret the meaning of the words in the song that suggest: "Our steps will always rhyme"? How does this apply to all relationships?
6. How do you let someone know how his or her relationship with you has touched your heart?

that the terminations of nurse–client relationships provide a stage for the reenactment of childhood conflicts of separation and individuation. The concept of termination has been examined more fully in psychological literature than in nursing literature. It is clear in the writings that deal with termination that unresolved issues in the early separation from one's mother surface and influence an adult's terminations. Agoraphobia, adolescent alcoholism, borderline personality disorder, bulimia, and depression have been linked to these very first separations (Dubrul, 1988; Mijuskovic, 1988; Stuart et al., 1990; Zitrin and Ross, 1988). Exercise 8–2 explores the feelings associated with our first good-byes.

How an individual is able to handle the feelings aroused by termination provides a good measure of the individual's maturity and psychological well-being. For this reason, termination is a significant aspect of the nurse–client relationship. It is both a here-and-now experience and a process that is affected by earlier experiences with loss and

separation. Consequently, how termination is handled can lead either to growth or to pain for both the client and the nurse.

The process of termination is a feeling-laden experience, one that can be as difficult for the nurse as it is for the client. Therefore, it is essential that nurses deal directly with all aspects of their own struggles with termination if they are to be effective in helping clients understand their feelings and behaviors. Before continuing with the chapter, you may find it helpful to take 15 minutes of quiet time to reflect on the questions in Exercise 8–3.

THE PROCESS OF TERMINATION

In order to understand termination it helps to look at the process. Termination moves through three stages—denial, grief, and integration. These phases are similar to what occurs as an individual faces grief-work. It is important to remember, though, that termination is a journey and as such may

EXERCISE 8–2
Early Leave-Takings

Purpose: To remember early leave-takings.

Time: 10 minutes

Directions:
Consider the answers to these questions.
1. What is your earliest recollection of leaving your primary caregiver?
2. What did it feel like?
3. How did you deal with it?

EXERCISE 8–3
The Meaning of Loss

Purpose: To consider what losses mean.

Time: 20 minutes

Directions:
Consider your answers to the following questions.
1. What losses have I experienced in my life?
2. How did I feel when I lost something or someone important to me?
3. How was my behavior affected by my loss?
4. What was the most helpful thing to me in terms of resolving my feelings of loss?
5. How has my experience with loss prepared me to deal with further losses?
6. How has my experience with loss prepared me to help others deal with loss?

meander onto paths that do not fit neatly into an analysis by stages.

Denial

The first phase consists of denial; the individual does not acknowledge either the reality of the loss or the feelings associated with the loss. *Denial* is evident when a client repeatedly changes the subject when the nurse tries to discuss termination, or when a nursing student expresses nothing but relief that a long-term relationship is coming to an end. In both instances, denial is being used to ward off painful feelings. The client, by refusing to discuss termination, can avoid focusing on the impending loss. The nursing student, by acknowledging only his or her relief, may be denying feelings of frustration and depression at not being able to be more effective with the client.

Grief

When the denial begins to break down and is no longer effective in blocking feelings, the person begins the second phase, characterized by considerable grief, sadness, and anger. A client may feel very sad about not being able to see the nurse again and feel the loss of their relationship profoundly, but may simultaneously experience extreme anger toward the nurse for abandoning him or her. Feelings of abandonment and the anger that accompanies them occur in response to the loss of a relationship, a job, a capability, an ideal, or some highly prized material possession

(Cerney and Buskirk, 1991). According to Cerney and Buskirk (1991), the fear of abandonment can stimulate an unrelenting rage in persons (e.g., clients) placed in a vulnerable position. The nurse may share this dichotomy of feelings—sadness over the loss but anger at the same time. It is not uncommon for nursing students to feel anger toward an instructor whom they see as responsible for placing them in this painful situation. The reader can find a more complete description of the grieving process in Chapter 20.

The feelings generated by this second phase are so intense that frequently the client as well as the nurse may want to withdraw from the relationship. The withdrawal can occur either by canceling planned meetings, so that there is an actual physical removal from the relationship, or by relating on a superficial level so that the withdrawal occurs on an emotional level. The process of withdrawal is a defense against the pain of the loss. The client is saying, in effect, "I will abandon you before you have the chance to abandon me." The following example illustrates this:

CASE EXAMPLE OF DENIAL

At the fifth meeting that nursing student Brown had with Mr. James, she reminded him that they had only three more meetings to go before they would have to say good-bye. When the student asked how Mr. James felt about this, he replied, "Well, that will give me some extra time to do the things I need to do!" (use of denial). The student told Mr. James that she felt sad about the impending termination and that perhaps they could talk about it the next time they met.

When the time arrived for their sixth meeting, Mr. James was not to be found (withdrawal from the relationship). On inquiring as to his whereabouts, the student was told that Mr. James had canceled his clinic appointment for that day. The student decided to call Mr. James to let him know that she had missed him and to remind him of their next meeting. Mr. James arrived for the seventh meeting, but he would discuss only the weather and other superficial topics.

In addition to withdrawal from the relationship, other behaviors accompany the sadness of the second phase. Clients may experience a temporary return of disabling symptoms, or they may display indifference. Both responses represent the client's unconscious attempt to hold on to the relationship. This can be understood in the following way: If the nurse enters the relationship to assist the client to deal with a particular problem and then the problem intensifies, perhaps the nurse will change her mind about terminating the relationship and stay to help the client. The fact is that if the client shows signs of illness or increased dependency, the nurse may feel guilty and find termination extremely difficult. The following example illustrates this point.

CASE EXAMPLE OF DEPENDENT RESPONSE

Mrs. Lynch was leaving her position as a diabetic specialist at the community hospital to return to graduate school. She had informed all of her clients of her intended job change months before it was to occur so that she could adequately prepare them for her leaving. As the time drew closer, she noticed that several of her clients were experiencing increasing difficulty controlling their diabetes (return of disabling symptoms). Two of the clients had been admitted to the hospital for hypoglycemic episodes. When Mrs. Lynch went to see these clients, they both told her that they didn't know how they could manage their diabetes without her support (increased dependency), despite the fact that they had done well for two years. Mrs. Lynch was torn between her desire to further her education and her feelings of responsibility to her clients. She sought the advice of another colleague, who helped her to recognize that the clients were expressing their difficulties with termination and suggested ways for Mrs. Lynch to help the clients to cope with their feelings in a constructive way.

Integration

The third phase of termination occurs as the client works through the reality of the loss and the feelings of sadness and anger associated with it and is able to integrate the relationship into other life experiences. This phase may continue even after the nurse and client are no longer seeing each other. As essential as integration is for both participants, it is possible that it may never be completely achieved. To the extent that it is achieved, integration frees both participants from emotional ties and allows them to invest themselves in other relationships and activities. This relationship has ended, but both the nurse and the client have been enriched by what has transpired between them and are ready for new life experiences.

GIFT GIVING

Even in this working-through phase the feelings of sadness that arise can lead to some problematic issues for the nurse to confront. Gift giving and requests to continue the relationship through the exchange of phone numbers, Christmas or birthday cards, or even future visits are the client's last attempt to hold on to the relationship. It is not uncommon at the end of a meaningful relationship for the participants to wish to exchange gifts as a lasting remembrance of the experience. In a nonprofessional relationship it would be totally appropriate to exchange gifts. However, in a professional relationship the issue of gift giving requires closer examination.

Morse (1989) believes that clients sometimes desire to give nurses gifts because nurses have given care to them: The client perceives that the giving has been one way and is unable to recognize his or her own contributions to the relationship. After all, nurses are the listeners; they assist clients with intimate personal tasks; nurses are the doers. The uneven nature of the nurse–client relationship violates a basic characteristic of all human interactions—that relationships are characterized by the obligation to give, the obligation to receive, and the obligation to reciprocate (Mauss, 1967). A gift from the client to the nurse may be an attempt to restore balance and achieve greater reciprocity between client and nurse. Or a gift may have other meanings. Examined in this light, gift giving during the termination phase is an especially delicate matter that does not lend itself to absolute caveats but instead invites reflection. There is a difference between a gift given to convey a sincere thank-you and a gift given to make the receiver feel guilty about leaving the relationship or even a gift that blocks a critical evaluation of the relationship. These are issues the nurse needs to assess. Exercise 8–4 may help in examining the issue of gift giving.

Sometimes the nurse feels a need to give a gift to a client. The need can arise out of feelings of deep caring or out of guilt for not having been able to accomplish all that was needed. This situation can be confusing to a client and, in general, it should be avoided.

CASE EXAMPLE

Ms. Johnson, a nursing student, had approached the idea of a nurse–client relationship with great anxiety, and the thought of termination totally unnerved her. She had been unable to establish mutual goals with her client and had never moved beyond a superficial level of relating. As the final meeting drew near, Ms. Johnson had not prepared her client for termination. As a parting gift Ms. Johnson took her client out to lunch for their final meeting. The setting of the restaurant was not conducive to talking about termination, so that Ms. Johnson's gift served to block a meaningful termination experience.

Some nurses are strongly opposed to ever accepting a gift from a client. Sometimes the agency or institution where the nurse is employed has a policy prohibiting the acceptance of gifts. In any event, regardless of the nurse's personal feelings or the policies of the employer, the nurse needs to identify his or her feelings about gift giving before the final interaction with the client. The nurse needs to be prepared to deal with this issue in a gentle and tactful way so that gift giving does not become a stumbling block to a positive termination. One strategy is to reflect on all the intangible gifts that the client has given the nurse. The relationship itself, where the client shares deep feelings and revelations of self, is indeed a beautiful and lasting gift. In turning down a material gift nurses need to acknowledge the value of all they have received from a client, thus reinforcing the worth of the client and of the relationship they shared.

A last word about gift giving responds to the question, "What do I do?" There is no one answer about whether gifts should or should not be exchanged. In fact, if the nurse handled every situation in the same fashion, the nurse would be denying the uniqueness of each nurse–client relationship. Each relationship has its own character and its own strengths and limitations, so that what might be appropriate in one situation would be totally inappropriate in another. Although the answer is not simple, it involves being true to what you know and feel about the client, assessing the meaning of the gesture, and using your best professional judgment in every situation. Most important, give freely of yourself.

In addition to giving gifts, some clients attempt to extend the relationship by requesting the nurse's phone number or address so that they can "keep in touch." Clients may ask the nurse either to call or to visit them. There are two possible explanations for this behavior. The client may not want to conclude a meaningful relationship with the nurse, or the client may be testing the reliability of the nurse who has said that today is our last meeting.

EXERCISE 8–4
The Issue of Gift Giving

Purpose: To consider the problem of clients giving gifts.

Time: 10 minutes

Directions:
Consider your answers to the following questions.
1. Would you react differently if a client gave you a gift of $200 or a hand-crocheted scarf? If so, why?
2. What factors would influence your reaction to accepting a gift from a client?
3. Are there gifts the clients give a nurse that are intangible? How should these gifts be acknowledged?

Termination, as the word implies, should be final. To provide the client with a hint that the relationship will continue is unfair because it keeps the client emotionally involved in a relationship that has no future. Nurses need to be clear that good-bye means just that. This is a very difficult issue for nursing students, who either see no harm in telling the client they will keep in contact or who feel that they have used the client for their own learning needs and to leave is grossly unfair. However, this perception underestimates the positive things the client received from the relationship and denies the fact that good-byes, painful as they may be, are a part of life and certainly not new for the client or the nursing student. Exercise 8–5 develops this theme.

THE TERMINATION OF DEATH

In a chapter that examines termination it is fitting to include the process of dying and the termination of death, for it is the final leave-taking. Death is the ending of all that life holds—successes, failures, relationships, careers, laughter, and pain. Death seeks the young as well as the old, the rich as well as the poor—it knows no favorites. Yet in light of the certainty of death for everyone, we struggle against it, we deny the reality of it, we pretend that it will not touch us.

Death is feared, even by those who believe in a spiritual afterlife. There is the fear of the unknown, the fear of losing everyone and everything, the fear of pain. Nurses are not immune to that fear. Nurses cling to life and struggle against death with the same intensity as the clients they compassionately care for, yet nurses are called upon to rise above their feelings and fears so that they can provide solace and support to dying persons and their loved ones. In so doing, nurses must achieve a balance between maintaining their own professional objectivity and psychological well-being and providing the empathy and support their clients need.

Death is an event and a process. Once death occurs, it is final. It may come suddenly without warning, or it can stalk us over a long period of time. If it comes slowly, the individual, his or her family, significant others, and health care providers are confronted with the dying process. As Chenitz (1992), a nurse diagnosed with AIDS, so eloquently stated: "Like many people with AIDS, I am not

EXERCISE 8–5
Gift-Giving Role Play

Purpose: To help students develop therapeutic responses to clients who wish to give them gifts.

Time: 45 minutes

Situation

Mrs. Terrell, a hospice nurse, has taken care of Mr. Aitken during the last three months of his life. She has been very supportive of the family. Because of her intervention, Mr. Aitken and his son were able to resolve a longstanding and very bitter conflict before he died. The whole family is grateful to Mrs. Terrell, particularly his wife, for her special attention to Mr. Aitken.

Role Play Directions to Mrs. Aitken
You are very grateful to Mrs. Terrell for all of her help over the past few months. Without her help, you don't know what you would have done. To show your appreciation, you would like her to have a $300 gift certificate at your favorite boutique. it is very important to you that Mrs. Terrell fully understand how meaningful her caring has been to you during this very difficult time.

Role Play Directions to Mrs. Terrell
You have given the Aitken family high-quality care and you feel very good about it, particularly the role you played in helping Mr. Aitken and his son reconcile before Mr. Aitken's death. Respond as you think you might in this clinical situation, given the above data.

Discussion:
1. Discuss the responses made in the role-playing situation.
2. Discuss other possible responses and evaluate the possible consequences.

afraid of death. I am afraid of dying. The dying process and how that will be handled is of great concern to me. Everyone is going to die. Death is part of life. However, AIDS brings with it a terrible, painful, often humiliating dying process and that terrifies me" (p. 454). Chenitz's concerns are our concerns. How will we continue to provide compassion, assurance, and competence when we are faced with the dying person's pain, overwhelming losses, and feelings of sadness and anger? The feelings that precede and follow death and other losses are called grief.

Grief

"Grief is a journey toward healing and recovering from the pain of a significant loss" (Gyulay, 1989, p. 1). It is a multifaceted process that affects every aspect of one's person, including the physical, emotional, social, spiritual, cognitive, and behavioral dimensions. Grief is often referred to as grief work. It is probably the most difficult work one does in life. Gyulay (1989, p. 2) suggests that grief is often a "blurred and muddy journey that is not easily understood in a step-by-step sequence." Many grievers do not come to acceptance, but it is a certainty that the *only* way to arrive at peace, serenity, recovery, healing, and acceptance is to *work through grief.* There is no way around it. One must experience the pain of the loss before healing is possible.

Initially, the griever experiences shock, denial, depression, and bargaining in sequence. Beyond these initial reactions, the griever is most likely to experience recurring, wavelike, roller-coaster responses. These responses are not one-time experiences that lead easily and predictably to a new stage; instead they move the griever along on a rocky, tumultuous course of progress.

Nurses are confronted with their own grief as well as the grief of clients, their families, and significant others. Nurses confront their own grief through quiet introspection and in dialogue with supervisors and peers. Nurses deal with the grief in others through presence, compassion, and quiet assurance. It is difficult for anyone to remain in a relationship with someone whose pain will not go away. This is the challenge for nurses—to remain in relationships with their clients and loved ones even though they feel inadequate to the task.

Sometimes all that is needed on the part of the nurse to encourage the grieving process is listening and assisting those who are grieving to understand their own feelings and behaviors through the use of open-ended statements. ("And then . . ., Tell me more . . ., You felt . . ., How did you do that? Who was with you? How did you feel?") Nurses must be aware that grieving is not a yes or no process, nor is it cut and dried. An appropriate opening response by the nurse might be, "It is true that your loved one has died of AIDS. He will never come back." But beyond these simple realities, the grief process is complex.

Reflecting on Personal Experiences with Grief and Death

Just as it is important to examine their past experiences and feelings about termination, it is equally important for nurses to examine their experiences with and feelings about grief and death. How have we handled our grief experiences? Were we able to arrive at acceptance? Did we work our way through grief and not try to sidestep the pain of the loss? How would we cope if we were faced with what our client faces? This examination is ongoing, stimulated by losses in the nurse's personal and professional life. Exercise 8–6 is designed to assist in this process.

Elisabeth Kübler-Ross (1971) has said that it is always easier to consider someone else's death than one's own. Yet to consider one's own mortality is essential in order to be effective with the dying client. Nurses need to face their feelings about death, to examine them, and to analyze the effect these feelings have on their lives. Exercise 8–7 is designed to assist in this process.

THEORETICAL MODEL OF THE DYING PROCESS

Kübler-Ross (1971) provids a framework for understanding the process of dying. She identifies various stages that a dying person experiences, including denial, anger, bargaining, depression, and acceptance. The framework of these stages is only a rough guide to understanding a client's feelings and behaviors; not every client will exhibit the behaviors of every stage. Some clients may seem to accept the reality of their death from the

EXERCISE 8–6
Personal Grieving Style Inventory

Grief is a natural response to a loss, a way of repairing emotional damage. Each person grieves differently from everyone else, and each time a person's grief is different than before. But a pattern forms that becomes a person's grieving style.

This worksheet is intended to help you, in a somewhat systematic way, reflect upon and better understand your own grieving style. To accomplish this goal it is important that you be honest with yourself, even if some of the memories are difficult and painful to recall.

Take your time. This worksheet is not to be used as a classroom exercise and shared, but rather as an opportunity for your own personal reflection. If you are not able to complete it at the first sitting, return to it later.

I. Responses to Past Losses

Please complete the following sentences. In case you have not yet had a traumatic loss from death in your life, think of another major loss from divorce or separation, a broken romance, a relocation, and so on.

A. The First Remembered Significant Loss
1. The first death (major loss) I experienced was that of my _____. I was _____ years old.
2. When I heard of the death (loss) I was (e.g., at work, studying, awakened from a sleep) _____.
3. I responded by (e.g., continuing what I had been doing, crying, swearing) _____.
4. My predominant emotional tone for the next few days was _____.
5. The other major change in my life that occurred just before or soon after my first experience of death (loss) was _____.

B. The Most Recent Loss
1. The most recent death (loss) I experienced was _____.
2. When I heard of the death (loss) I was _____.
3. I responded by _____.
4. My predominant emotional tone for the next few days was _____.
5. The other major change in my life that occurred just before or soon after this death (loss) was _____.
6. My reactions to this death (loss) compared to the first were similar in that _____.
7. My reactions were different in that _____.

C. How I Respond to Losses
Sit back for a moment, close your eyes, and try to recapture other losses in your life. You may think of an incident from childhood when a favorite toy was taken from you, or when you moved from one house to another. Memories of teenage romance or the loss of a job may come to mind. Try to remember as many losses as you can and as many details as possible. Focus especially on the feelings that were evoked. Can you discern any patterns to your reactions?

When you are ready, complete these unfinished sentences.
1. Usually when I first hear of a death (loss) or impending death (loss) I react by _____.
2. After a while my initial reaction is replaced by feelings of _____.
3. My predominant emotional reaction for the first few days is _____.
4. Upon reflection, I would describe the way I grieve as _____.

From Dershimer RA (1990). Counseling the Bereaved. New York, Pergamon Press, p. 129. Copyright © 1990 by Allyn and Bacon. Reprinted by permission.

beginning. Others struggle until the end before finally accepting that death will come. And still others never find acceptance but rather come to a sort of resignation characterized by a negative state of mind. Furthermore, the stages are not neat and orderly. Clients may experience more than one stage simultaneously, or they may be fixated at a particular stage. However the client deals with the knowledge of his or her dying, it is helpful for nurses to have a knowledge and understanding of these stages so that they can be a support and not a hindrance to the client.

EXERCISE 8–7
A Questionnaire About Death

Purpose: To explore your feelings about death.

Time: 20 minutes

Directions:

Answer the following questions

1. Who died in your first personal involvement with death?
   a. Grandparent or great-grandparent
   b. Parent
   c. Brother or sister
   d. Other family member
   e. Friend or acquaintance
   f. Stranger
   g. Public figure
   h. Animal
2. To the best of your memory, at what age were you first aware of death?
   a. Under three years old
   b. Three to five years old
   c. Five to ten years old
   d. 10 or older
3. When you were a child, how was death talked about in your family?
   a. Openly
   b. With some sense of discomfort
   c. Only when necessary and then with an attempt to exclude the children
   d. As though it were a taboo subject
   e. Never recall any discussion
4. Which of the following most influence your present attitudes toward death?
   a. Death of someone close
   b. Specific reading
   c. Religious upbringing
   d. Introspection and meditation
   e. Ritual (e.g., funerals)
   f. TV, radio, or motion pictures
   g. Longevity of my family
   h. My health or physical condition
   i. Other
5. How often do you think about your own death?
   a. Very frequently (at least once a day)
   b. Frequently
   c. Occasionally
   d. Rarely (no more than once a year)
   e. Very rarely or never
6. If you could choose, when would you die?
   a. In youth
   b. In the middle prime of life
   c. Just after the prime of life
   d. In old age

7. When do you believe that, in fact, you will die?
   a. In youth
   b. In the middle prime of life
   c. Just after the prime of life
   d. In old age
8. Has there been a time in your life when you wanted to die?
   a. Yes, mainly because of great physical pain
   b. Yes, mainly because of great emotional upset
   c. Yes, mainly to escape an intolerable social or interpersonal situation
   d. Yes, mainly because of great embarrassment
   e. Yes, for a reason other than those above
   f. No
9. What does death mean to you?
   a. The end: the final process of life
   b. The beginning of a life after death; a transition; a new beginning
   c. A joining of the spirit with a universal cosmic consciousness
   d. A kind of endless sleep; rest and peace
   e. Termination of this life but with survival of the spirit
   f. Don't know
10. What aspect of your own death is the most distasteful to you?
    a. I could no longer have any experiences
    b. I am afraid of what might happen to my body after death
    c. I am uncertain as to what might happen to me if there is a life after death
    d. I could no longer provide for my dependents
    e. It would cause grief to my relatives and friends
    f. All my plans and projects would come to an end
    g. The process of dying might be painful
    h. Other
11. To what extent do you believe that psychological factors can influence (or even cause) death?
    a. I firmly believe that they can
    b. I tend to believe that they can
    c. I am undecided or don't know
    d. I doubt that they can

(Continued)

EXERCISE 8–7 *(Continued)*

12. What is your present orientation to your own death?
    a. Death-seeker
    b. Death-hastener
    c. Death-accepter
    d. Death-welcomer
    e. Death-postponer
    f. Death-fearer
13. If you had a choice, what kind of death would you prefer?
    a. Tragic, violent death
    b. Sudden but not violent death
    c. Quiet, dignified death
    d. Death in line of duty
    e. Death after a great achievement
    f. Suicide
    g. Homicide victim
    h. There is no "appropriate" kind of death
14. If it were possible would you want to know the exact date on which you are going to die?
    a. Yes
    b. No
15. If your physician knew that you had a terminal disease and a limited time to live, would you want him or her to tell you?
    a. Yes
    b. No
    c. It would depend on the circumstances.

16. What efforts do you believe ought to be made to keep a seriously ill person alive?
    a. All possible effort: transplantations, kidney dialysis, and so forth
    b. Efforts that are reasonable for that person's age, physical condition, mental condition, and pain
    c. After reasonable care has been given, a person ought to be permitted to die a natural death
    d. A senile person should not be kept alive by elaborate artificial methods
17. If or when you are married would you prefer to outlive your spouse?
    a. Yes; I would prefer to die second and outlive my spouse
    b. No; I would rather die first and have my spouse outlive me
    c. Undecided or don't know
18. What effect has this questionnaire had on you?
    a. It has made me somewhat anxious or upset
    b. It has made me think about my own death
    c. It has reminded me how fragile and precious life is
    d. Other effects

Stages of Death and Dying

Denial

Frequently when a client learns that his or her condition is terminal, the initial reaction is shock and disbelief. The very thought of one's own death is so overwhelming that a person cannot deal with the feelings generated by such a thought. These feelings can be allowed into conscious awareness only gradually. Consequently, in order to defend against such terrifying and devastating feelings, the client uses denial. The client may say things like, "This can't be," or, "They must have made a mistake." Kübler-Ross (1971) characterizes this stage as the "No, not me" stage.

Anger

As the client allows the reality of his or her death gradually to come into awareness, denial no longer works and is replaced with anger—some-times rage as the client reels against the unfairness of the situation. The client is angry at no one in particular but angry at everyone. A client in this stage is angry for what those around him have and what they symbolize. They have life and everything the client is losing. Who can argue against the unfairness of it, the cruelty of it? Surely no one. So the client lashes out at family, friends, and staff members. The client is angry that people are oversolicitous and angry that people don't do enough. The client is angry at life and angry at God.

The client feels powerless and alone, and essentially such perceptions are correct. The client is alone with death—no one can die for him. And no matter how much he wills it, he cannot control his own death. The enormity of the situation is inescapable. There is no alternative to dying but to die, and the client fights back with all the anger he can muster. Kübler-Ross characterizes the anger as the "Why me?" stage.

Bargaining

After dying clients have vented their anger they often enter a stage of bargaining. Usually the bargaining is done with God. Most of the time the client makes a promise to be a better person in exchange for more time. "If you just let me stay alive until my son's graduation, I'll go to church every Sunday." This stage is reminiscent of childhood when children pleaded with their parents. It's almost as if the client is saying, "If God didn't respond to my anger, maybe He'll hear me if I ask very nicely for just a little more time." Kübler-Ross (1971) says the client characteristically says, "Yes, me, but . . ." when in the bargaining stage.

Depression

After the bargaining is complete, the client comes to the "Yes, me" stage. Clients recognize that not only will they die but also that they will be saying good-bye to all that they love. During this stage clients are sad as they grieve for what they are losing. They cry. They silently mourn. They become quiet and introspective. They are working through their losses, and in this process they begin to separate from all that has been their life until, finally, they no longer need family and friends but only one loved one to sit quietly and wait with them until death comes.

Acceptance

Clients are at peace in the acceptance stage. They are not happy, but not terribly sad either. They know they cannot change the inevitable. They have brought to a closure all of their unfinished business; they have said all the words that need to be said. There is nothing left to do but to be with the people they love and just wait.

APPLICATIONS

NURSE'S ROLE AS FACILITATOR OF TERMINATION

Long-Term Relationships

Up to this point the focus has been on the phases of termination and the feelings and behaviors a client may exhibit in each phase. With this knowledge and understanding the nurse can facilitate a client's movement through these phases so that the ending is a positive, growth-enhancing experience. In examining the nurse's role it is appropriate to apply the steps of the nursing process.

Assessment

The nurse needs to assess the client's response to the issue of termination and to be aware of both behavioral and affectional cues that the client communicates when the topic of termination is discussed. If possible, the nurse should determine the client's prior experiences with losses and learn how the client has coped with them. This information will help the nurse to plan an individualized approach to termination for this client.

In addition to assessing the client's feelings, behaviors, and past experiences in regard to termination, nurses must apply the same assessment process to themselves. They need to ask themselves, "In general, how do I feel about saying good-bye?" "Specifically, how do I feel about saying good-bye to this client?" Nurses need to examine their own reactions to past losses and how those experiences still affect their present behavior. They also need to examine the relationship in terms of goal achievement and strengths and limitations. Only after examining these issues can nurses effectively guide the termination process.

The assessment of behaviors and feelings relative to termination provides the nurse with the basis for arriving at a nursing diagnosis. A number of diagnoses are appropriate to the termination process. These include:

1. Anxiety related to the impending termination of the nurse–client relationship.
2. Ineffective client coping (return of disabling symptoms) with the impending termination of the nurse–client relationship.
3. Powerlessness related to the impending termination of the nurse–client relationship.
4. Depression and sadness related to the impending termination of the nurse–client relationship.
5. Grieving related to the impending termination of the nurse–client relationship.
6. Alteration in self-concept related to the impending termination of the nurse–client relationship.

Plan

From the nursing diagnosis the nurse derives a plan related to termination and develops objectives. Some of the objectives are mutually decided between the nurse and the client, whereas the nurse develops other objectives independently. The nurse's independent responsibilities include planning the best time to inform the client of the termination date. If the relationship is a time-bounded one, in which the nurse knows ahead of time that he or she will have only a certain number of meetings with the client, then termination should be included in the original contract. In subsequent meetings, the nurse needs to plan times to remind the client of the impending termination date.

If the termination of the relationship is open-ended, to be determined by the client's achievement of certain goals, then the nurse needs to plan an ongoing evaluation of goals, thus keeping the client up to date on his or her progress. In addition to goal evaluation, the nurse needs to plan and inform the client about how much longer they will probably meet. If at all possible terminations should never be a surprise.

The nurse must also plan how to deal with his or her own feelings about termination. Sometimes it is enough for the nurse simply to plan time to think about the issue of termination. At other times and in other relationships, the nurse needs to talk with a supervisor or peer about the feelings associated with the termination so that these feelings do not interfere with the nurse's effectiveness with the client.

In planning with a client it is helpful for the nurse to ask the client how he or she would like to handle the termination. The client may have specific ideas and feelings related to the process, and these ideas and feelings should be included in the plan.

The planning phase also includes the establishment of specific behavioral goals. These goals, derived from the behaviors the nurse has collected, are directly related to the nursing diagnoses. Box 8–1 lists the nursing diagnoses related to specific client goals.

Interventions

Although the nurse intervenes with actions that are specific to client needs, there are eight general interventions that are appropriate in any planned termination. The first one is to *prepare clients* by informing them of the termination date (if possible, the contract date) and reminding them of this date throughout the relationship. Keeping the date in mind allows clients to become aware of their own feelings and lets the nurse and client prepare for termination.

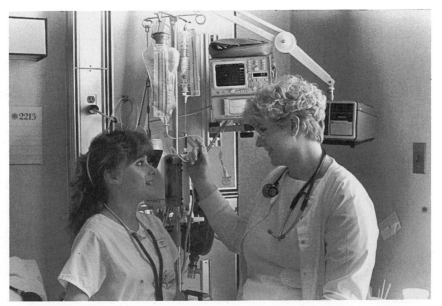

Exploring the meaning of a significant relationship helps both participants terminate, feeling valued and enriched by the experience. (Courtesy of the University of North Carolina at Charlotte College of Nursing)

BOX 8–1
Nursing Diagnoses and Behavioral Goals in the Nurse–Client Relationship

Nursing Diagnosis	*Client Goal*
Depression and sadness related to the impending termination of the nurse–client relationship.	1. The client will express feelings of sadness and relate them to termination. 2. The client will examine other experiences that have produced similar feelings. 3. The client will explore ways of coping with sadness and depression.
Grieving related to the termination of the nurse–client relationship.	1. The client will express feelings of loss related to termination. 2. The client will explore the positive and negative aspects of the relationship. 3. The client will examine how he or she coped with past experiences of loss. 4. The client will examine the availability of support to help cope with the loss.
Alteration in self-concept related to impending termination of the nurse–client relationship.	1. The client will examine how the relationship affected self-perception. 2. The client will examine how the termination affects self-concept.
Anxiety related to the impending termination of the nurse–client relationship.	1. The client will report a decrease in anxious feelings related to the discussion of termination. 2. The client will display a decrease in behaviors indicative of anxiety (nail biting, foot tapping) when termination is discussed.
Ineffective client coping (return of disabling symptoms) related to fear associated with the impending termination of the nurse–client relationship.	1. The client will express feelings of fear related to the impending termination. 2. The client will explore the relationship between symptom return and fear. 3. The client will identify alternative ways of coping with fear.
Feelings of powerlessness related to the impending termination of the nurse–client relationship.	1. The client will express feelings of powerlessness related to impending termination. 2. The client will examine related experiences that produce similar feelings. 3. The client will explore ways to cope with feelings of powerlessness.

The second intervention is to *allow clients to express their feelings* about termination. The nurse must be aware of the client's readiness to discuss such feelings. If the client is in the denial phase, the nurse should not force the client to discuss those feelings until he or she is ready. However, the nurse may use interventions that gently confront the denial. A response such as, "It is difficult to talk about saying good-bye and certainly easier to talk about the weather, isn't it?" acknowledges the client's denial without a confrontation that may result in the erection of an insurmountable barrier of denial.

The third intervention is to *encourage the client to experience and to discuss the effects of the anticipated loss.*

The fourth intervention is to *encourage the client to deal with reactivated feelings* from former losses. Questions such as, "As you think about saying good-bye to me, are you reminded of other situations when you had to say good-bye? What

experiences are you reminded of when you were confronted with loss?"

The fifth intervention involves *the nurse's constructive sharing of his or her own feelings* about the relationship and the termination.

The sixth intervention involves *examining the value of the relationship* to both the client and the nurse, including both the positive and negative components.

The seventh intervention includes *mutually evaluating the goals of the relationship.* Have the goals been achieved? If not, has progress been made? What work remains to be done?

The eighth and final intervention involves *helping clients to identify supportive people in their families, communities, or work situations* who can assist them with feelings of loss.

Koehne-Kaplan and Levy (1978) propose a technique to assist the nurse and client to focus effectively on termination. Their approach involves assigning both the nurse and the client

homework. The task includes the steps described in Box 8–2. Exercise 8–8, although geared to assisting nursing students, is valuable for any nurse who must deal with the termination of a relationship. Tilden and Gustafsen (1979) suggest that the exercise be utilized one week before the final nurse–client meeting.

A final suggestion for handling the last interaction is for both nurse and client to graph or map out their experience, depicting the high and low points of their time together. This technique is helpful in summarizing the accomplishments and the feelings associated with the relationship.

Although the last step of the nursing process is generally presented as the evaluation phase, evaluation is actually an ongoing process. The nurse continually makes evaluations and assessments to determine whether he or she has been accurate in analyzing the client's behaviors and feelings related to termination. If not, then the nurse collects more behaviors and perhaps analyzes the data differently. Likewise, the goals are also continually evaluated, not only for goal attainment but for the appropriateness of the goals to the client's needs. Interventions are also evaluated in terms of their effectiveness. Did the interventions assist the client in talking about feelings of sadness and loss? If not, what modification is necessary? Box 8–3 illustrates the complete nursing process applied to one nursing diagnosis.

Thus far, the discussion has focused primarily on a planned termination of a long-term relationship. Terminations of short-term relationships or unplanned terminations also need to be examined.

Short-Term Relationships

A short-term relationship could be of varying duration—from 15 minutes to a few days. Obviously, the termination of a relationship of short duration is probably not going to generate the same intense feelings as the termination of a long-term relationship. The amount of personal investment in a relationship and the personal meaning ascribed to the relationship is partially determined by the length of time spent in the relationship. However, there are still certain interventions that the nurse should use in terminating relationships of short duration. These include identifying feelings related to the relationship and summarizing

---

BOX 8–2
Sample Dialogue for Terminating a Long-Term Relationship

The nurse says to the client:

1. "Before we meet again I want each of us to take some time to be alone, as much time as we choose but no less than a half hour. We must plan for this time well so that we ensure that we are undisturbed and undistracted.

2. "Give careful thought to the place and the time of day you choose for this time alone. Plan well so that nothing deprives you of this time and that this time alone is exactly the way you want it to be. Most important, spend this time alone. I will do this, too.

3. "While alone let yourself reminisce about our relationship. Recall the first session we had together and review historically any moments that come clear to you. Give yourself the luxury of staying with these moments as long as you want to. Ask yourself: 'What has this experience been for me? What has touched me?' Most important, think about you in this relationship and feel whatever feelings come up inside you. I will do this, too.

4. "Next, while you are alone, let yourself imagine and/or fantasize how you want the last session to be. Include as many details as possible. At first this may be very difficult to do. Stay with the task, nevertheless, allowing yourself to think and feel whatever comes to you. I will do this, too.

5. "Having done this imagining, practice this scene. So many of us have never had a satisfactory good-bye. Allow thoughts and feelings of previous partings to come to you. How were they? How do you want this one to be? You and I must say good-bye. Practice your chosen scene for our parting over and over, changing or modifying it until your image of the last session is perfect for you. I will do this, too."

From Koehne-Kaplan NS, Levy KE (1978). An approach for facilitating the passage through termination. Journal of Psychiatric Nursing 16:11. Reprinted with permission.

---

the goal achievements. The following example illustrates this process.

CASE EXAMPLE

Nurse Brown assisted Ms. Johnson, a new mother, with breast-feeding at the end of the day, Nurse Brown went to Ms. Johnson and said: "As I mentioned to you this morning, I end my shift at 3:30, and it's about that time. I just wanted to tell you that I enjoyed working with you today. You did very well with breast-feeding the baby. I'm sorry we weren't able to go over baby bathing, but I will tell the evening nurse to be sure to review that with you. Do you have any questions or concerns that I should know about before I leave?"

EXERCISE 8–8
Termination

Purpose: To examine the feelings involved in termination.

Time:

Directions:
The instructor gives the following directions to the students: "Make yourselves as comfortable as possible in your chairs; relax your arms and legs, close your eyes and inhale and exhale deeply in order to 'sigh out' all the tension. Gently focus your awareness just on my voice and put as many distracting thoughts out of your mind as possible. Follow my directions in your mind only. There are no right or wrong answers; no speaking out loud."

1. Think of your patient.
   Imagine him.
   Develop a mental picture of him.
   How does he appear to you?
   What is he doing?
   How has he changed since you've known him?
   How have you changed since you've known him?
2. Now, imagine that you are meeting with your patient for the last time.
   How are you sitting?
   How do you appear?
   How does he appear?
   Just stay with that image for a minute.
3. Now, take a moment to plan what you'd like to say to him in this last meeting. Think it through until you have it just the way you want it.
   Now, imagine yourself saying it.
4. Is there anything in particular that you'd like to say to him that you probably won't?
   Let yourself be in touch with that. Be free in your mental image to go with whatever comes to mind.
5. What feelings do you experience now as you look at your patient?
   Let yourself experience these feelings as fully as possible.
6. What is it you'd like your patient to say to you?
   Imagine him saying it.
   Indulge yourself.
   • Is he thanking you?
   • Is he telling you how much you've meant to him?
   Now be aware that this is your need, not his.
7. Now it's time to say good-bye.
   Imagine that happening.
   How will it go?
   What will it be like?
   Set it up for yourself, how you want it to be.
   What words will you use? Will you shake hands?
   The journey that you've made together is ending.
   Each of you has been touched in some way by the other.
   Let yourself be aware of that, and stay with whatever feeling it evokes.

Bit by bit, at your own pace and readiness, let go of your mental pictures and return your awareness to the room, to the chair you're sitting in, to the people on either side of you. Inhale and exhale deeply, and when you are ready, open your eyes. (Note: The instructor will read the entire exercise slowly, allowing sufficient pauses throughout for the students to develop each fantasy called for. At the conclusion of the exercise, you should discuss your experience of the exercise. Some of you might wish to share, and others might elect not to. You are free to share only what you choose.)

BOX 8–3
The Nursing Process: One Diagnosis

Nursing Diagnosis	Goal	Intervention	Evaluation	Modification
Depression and sadness over the loss of the nurse–client relationship.	The client will verbally express feelings of sadness related to the loss.	Using therapeutic communication skills the nurse will: a. Show warmth. b. Display empathy. c. Reflect on the client's affect of sadness and ask for client validation.	Client acknowledges feelings of sadness but does not want to discuss them at this time.	1. Look for cues of client readiness to discuss feelings of sadness. 2. Reflect on sadness without pressuring client to discuss until ready. 3. Communicate understanding that feelings are sometimes difficult to discuss.

The nurse's statement brings closure to the relationship. It focuses the client's attention on what has been accomplished and what remains to be done.

Unexpected Terminations

Unexpected terminations can come about for a variety of reasons. The client may be unexpectedly discharged without the nurse's receiving adequate warning, or the client may abruptly decide to end the relationship. The nurse might also have to end the relationship without having adequate time to say good-bye. Whatever the reason, unexpected termination leaves both the client and the nurse at loose ends in regard to their feelings. This unfinished business can be emotionally unsettling and tends to tie up energy that needs to be available for other relationships.

In such cases, a number of possible interventions are available to the nurse. The nurse may decide to write a letter or to telephone the client. If neither of these interventions is possible, the nurse may need to discuss his or her feelings with a colleague or a supervisor in order to resolve them and bring the relationship to a close. It is important for nurses to find ways to deal with their own feelings so they are emotionally free to involve themselves with other clients.

ROLES OF THE NURSE IN WORKING WITH DYING CLIENTS

Working with dying clients and their families is an extremely demanding task, but it can be also an emotionally enriching experience for the nurse. Not every nurse can be intimately involved with every dying client and his or her family, but it is to be hoped that at least one nurse will be available to become involved in the client's pain, to withstand the client's anger, and to help the client in whatever way is needed in this experience of death. It is this nurse who accepts the client's denial as long as the client needs to use this defense. It is this nurse who can say to the client, "I can see how angry you are, and I wish that I could make you better." It is this nurse who can assist the client to see that berating his or her family may not be the best method for dealing with the sense of powerlessness. It is this nurse who communicates a care plan to the rest of the staff so that everyone has an understanding of the client's changing needs. And, finally, it is this nurse who helps the family deal with their own grief as they prepare to say good-bye. In planning care for the dying client, the nurse applies the steps of the nursing process.

Assessment

There are a number of important areas for the nurse to assess when working with the dying client. These areas include the feelings that the client has toward death and the client's cultural response to and spiritual beliefs regarding death, life experiences with death, developmental level, role within the family, and support system. All of these factors interact to shape the client's response to his or her own death.

The assessment of feelings was addressed in the

discussion of the stages of death and dying. What was not covered was the manner in which the client expresses his or her feelings. Most likely clients will not discuss death in an open and direct way, at least not until they have ascertained that they have a listener who can handle this difficult topic. Generally, clients give hints about their underlying feelings and concerns. Thus, the nurse must be attuned not only to nonverbal clues that the client communicates but also to the client's use of symbolic language.

Clients may refer to their deaths as "a great struggle," "a last train ride," "the biggest fight of my life." The use of symbolic language serves a dual purpose. The first purpose is to avoid the pain associated with the word "death" itself, and the second is to test the waters. The client is throwing out bait to a sensitive listener, hoping to be allowed to talk about issues of loss, of saying good-bye, and of taking care of unfinished business. The nurse assesses the client's readiness to discuss death openly, and it is to be hoped responds in a way that says, "You can talk to me. I can't change your situation, but perhaps I can make it less lonely." Sometimes the nurse is the most convenient or the only person to allow the client this freedom.

In assessing the family's feelings about their loved one's death, the nurse must be aware that the family's reaction may not be synchronous with the client's. For instance, the client may be ready to grieve openly, whereas the family is still denying the reality of death. The nurse must also help family members deal with their feelings so that they can provide empathetic and loving support to the client.

Culture and the Dying Client

Culture plays an important role in how a dying person and his or her family cope with death, and it behooves the nurse to consider this area (Sankar, 1991). For instance, expression of grief reflects a person's culture (Bozarth-Campbell, 1982). In general, American culture does not encourage or value "falling apart." Instead, what is valued are a stoicism and general denying of grief. It is important for nurses to examine their own cultural biases so that they are not judgmental about cultural beliefs and practices that are important to clients and their families.

Ross (1981) identifies a number of areas that are affected by cultural beliefs about death:

1. *Affecting assessment of comfort needs of the dying and the kind of care provided.* Sometimes families feel the need to provide the client with special food or other comforting measures that are unique to a specific ethnic group.

2. *Influencing the selection, perception, and evaluation of health care providers and their skills.* Some cultures rely on nonprofessional healers—American Indians have medicine men and herbalists. Professional health care providers may be viewed with fear and distrust.

3. *Influencing beliefs about the causes of illness and death.* Some cultures attribute illness and death to the activities of evil spirits, whereas others believe that illness and resulting death are caused by an imbalance in the system between hot and cold (yin and yang in Chinese culture) or a disequilibrium between God and man.

4. *Determining funeral or burial rites.* Religious practices and rituals are important to clients and may enhance their spirituality. The nurse needs to assess the importance of such rites and facilitate their performance. For instance, a Roman Catholic client may desire to see a priest to receive the sacraments of Reconciliation, Holy Communion, and the Anointing of the Sick. The nurse should provide a private environment for the priest and the client and should inquire if there is anything the priest requires, such as a covered table for the placement of religious articles. The nurse's attitude toward the client's need for specific religious practices should be one of reverence and respect. Although the nurse may not understand the exact meaning of the ritual for the client, the nurse can be sure that the practice touches the client's inner core and helps him or her move toward a peaceful death. Different cultures have important religious rituals that have special meanings to families. American Indians perform specific deathbed rituals and choose to bury their dead on an Indian reservation. The Islamic family washes the body of the loved one and then turns the body toward Mecca. Orthodox and some Conservative Jews oppose autopsy and cremation. The dead are cleansed by a ritual burial society, and burial is carried out as expeditiously as possible.

5. *Patterning acceptable sick role behavior and grief responses.* Among Arabs, Jews, and Italians it is acceptable to be very emotional in expressions of grief and pain. Conversely, clients of Chinese, Japanese, Filipino, and American Indian cultures

generally do not express their feelings openly to persons outside the family.

Spiritual Needs

Spiritual beliefs and religious practices regarding death are yet another crucial area for the nurse to assess. In doing so, the nurse must differentiate between spirituality and religiosity. Spirituality is a broad concept that refers either to a unifying life force or to a relationship with a supreme being. Religiosity refers to membership in and adherence to the practices of a particular denomination or sect. An individual can be very spiritual but not be religious. On the other hand, an individual can adhere closely to his or her religious rules and rituals but not have a well-defined relationship either with God or with any unifying life force.

In assessing spiritual needs the nurse needs to be attuned to clients' verbal and nonverbal behaviors indicative of their feelings and thoughts toward God. Clients may refer to God in a guarded, indirect way or they may joke about God or they may openly plead with God. Their expressions may indicate anger toward God, feelings of abandonment, a belief that death is a way of making retribution to God for wrongdoing, or just that they are seeking a benevolent God to comfort them in their pain. The psalms of the Old Testament are replete with all of these themes as David the Psalmist approaches God. All expressions related to spirituality require direct and sensitive intervention from either the nurse or a member of the clergy. Clients are indicating their need to talk about and to God, and addressing this need is as essential for the nurse as administering pain medication. The dying process, grief, and death itself herald a spiritual crisis for most individuals. This is a crisis of faith, hope, and meaning, the resolution of which is integral to emerging from grief healed and whole and confronting death with peace and acceptance. Exercise 8–9, "The Unfolding Tapestry of My Life," helps nurses examine the patterns and meaning in their own lives and may be a useful strategy for assisting clients to do the same.

Life Experiences

How satisfied people are with the way in which they have led their lives affects their attitude toward death. In general, if persons have few regrets and feel they have engaged life to the best of their abilities, death is easier. Conflicts about life and ambivalence in relationships contribute to the unrest many people have in facing the unknowns in the dying process.

Previous life experiences with death may also affect a client's attitude toward his or her own dying. For instance, if clients experienced the death of a loved one or a friend who was able to face death with equanimity, they may not view death as something to be feared. On the other hand, if they watched someone die through a prolonged and painful struggle, then they may expect the worst.

The client's developmental level is an influencing factor in his or her attitude toward death. The young child views death entirely differently from the elderly client, and this difference certainly impinges on nursing care. A child under three years old has no clear concept of what death means. A three-year-old may even play at death, as if it is a game, without any conception of the finality associated with the reality. Very young children react to the anguish and the grief of those around them but are confused as to why everyone is sad. Preschoolers understand that death involves leaving, but they believe that it is gradual and temporary. This belief is reinforced by cartoons on television, which frequently depict characters dying and coming back to life.

Children between six and nine years tend to personify death and to view it as a person who causes people to die. The 10- to 12-year-old school-aged child understands that death is the cessation of bodily life. The adolescent may vacillate between a very mature and a very childlike attitude toward death.

Adults between 18 and 45 years of age are fully aware of the finality of death, but they tend to believe that only old people die. They are so involved with the tasks of generativity, family, and career that death is not a common thought. Between the ages of 45 and 65 years of age adults accept their own mortality. They have probably already experienced the death of their parents and some of their peers. Adults over 65 years may view death with several different attitudes. They may see death as a reunion with deceased family members, or they may fear that their deaths will be prolonged and painful and will cause hardship to their children.

EXERCISE 8–9
Blueprint for My Life Story

This is a two-part exercise. First, make a single life line across a blank sheet of paper, beginning with your birth. Identify the significant events in your life, and insert on your worksheet the age that you were when the event/moment occurred. When you have completed Part I, answer the questions below.

Childhood
1. What was your happiest time as a child?
2. What were your saddest times?
3. What were your chores or responsibilities as a child?
4. What did you hope to become when you grew up?
5. Who were your companions as a child?
6. How did you view your mother? your father? your grandparents?
7. How did you feel about your home? your neighborhood?
8. As a child, who was your most important relationship with?
9. Were boys and girls treated alike in school? in the family?
10. Where was your favorite space?
11. Where did you live as a child?

Adolescence
1. What subjects did you like best in school?
2. How and when did you get your first job?
3. Who were your companions as an adolescent, and what did you do with them?
4. Who was your first girlfriend (boyfriend)?
5. Who had the most significant influence on you as an adolescent? in what ways?
6. What was most important to you as an adolescent?
7. Where did you live as an adolescent?

Adult
1. What was the best job you ever had? the worst?
2. If you could choose your career again, what would you choose?
3. How did you meet your partner (husband, wife, significant other)?
4. If you have children, when were they born, and what are they like?
5. If you could relive any part of your life, what would it be?
6. What parts of your life are you particularly proud of?
7. Look back over your life; when were you happiest? saddest?
8. What have you learned about life from the process of living?
9. What was the most exciting part of your life?
10. Who has influenced your life most, as an adult?
11. If you could make three wishes, what would they be?

Record your answers in whatever way seems most appropriate to you. Spend some time thinking about the events you have identified on your life line and the answers you have provided in the narrative. Reflect on your life as a whole, with *you* as the primary actor, producer, and director. Think about ways in which you could write the remaining chapters of your life so they have special meaning to you.

Family role is still another area that the nurse needs to assess in relation to the dying client. An unmarried woman with a terminal illness will have different concerns than a dying mother; an older widower will have different concerns than a newly married young man. Different roles within the family carry with them differing amounts of responsibility. A young mother's death may engender anger and guilt because she feels she is deserting her family. A single person who is dying may also feel anger, but it will probably relate more to a loss of independence.

Last, the client's support system needs to be examined by the nurse. The presence or absence of a loving and supportive family is a determining factor in the client's ability to cope with death. The nurse needs to be aware that the family is subject to all of the same feelings and influences regarding death the client is subject to. For this reason, family members may need as much support as the client to assist them to be a help to the client (Piemme and Bolle, 1990). For instance, if clients express anger and are particularly abusive to their spouses, the spouses may be confused and frightened. Such a situation requires mediation on the part of the nurse, not only to help the client to deal with the anger more appropriately but also to provide the spouse with an understanding of the client's behavior.

Analysis

The nurse, having made a careful assessment of the areas of concern, analyzes the data he or she has collected and determines the nursing diagnosis for the problems that have been identified. Any or all of the following nursing diagnoses are appropriate when working with the dying client and his or her family:

- Ineffective coping related to impending death.
- Coping, potential for growth related to impending death.
- Anticipatory grieving related to expected death.
- Dysfunctional grieving related to expectant death.
- Fear related to known and unknown factors of expected death.
- Alteration in self-concept related to death.
- Spiritual distress related to impending death.

Planning

Working with dying clients and their families requires open and consistent communication among all members of the health team. Usually the nurse coordinates the planning and evaluation of care.

Ideally, one nurse is responsible for the primary care of the client and keeps the rest of the health team members informed of new issues, seeking their input to plan and to evaluate care. This approach prevents fragmentary and inconsistent care and allows the client to be cared for totally.

Although the goals for care are individualized for clients and their families, the following general goals provide a framework for developing more specificity:

1. The client will verbalize feelings of anger.
2. The client will vent anger in appropriate ways.
3. The client will express feelings of grief and loss.
4. The client will explore and evaluate his or her life experiences.
5. The client will identify areas of concern over unfinished business.
6. The client will express feelings about God in relation to dying.
7. The client will utilize religious practices appropriate to his or her beliefs.
8. The client will verbalize a sense of personal order and meaning associated with the dying process.
9. The client will spend private, uninterrupted time with his or her family.

Intervention

In meeting these goals, most of the nurse's interventions focus on communication. Lindemann (1972), who studied dying persons and their families for 30 years, summarizes three key components in providing care for them: open, empathic communication; honesty; and tolerance of emotional expression. The following quote from Lindemann succinctly and poignantly identifies these components: "Rely on open communication. Don't lie. The family or the patient always will know if you do, just as children always know. That's number one, and for me it is the basis of helping" (p. 110).

The second important skill is to be able to take the client's position. Even if what is said seems silly to you, take time to listen to the client because there may be a very good reason for the client's attitude. So don't brush the client aside. The third skill is to understand that being sad and crying for awhile are not bad for the client. Don't assume that you have to keep a smooth surface and that the client must smile—he or she may smile just to keep you happy.

Talking about death is not easy for the nurse. Few schools of nursing actually teach nurses how to converse with the dying client. In addition, nurses are subject to the same societal influences the client is. These influences paint death as a topic to be avoided at all costs. Nurses frequently feel ill prepared to deal with the emotional turmoil generated by the task. Yet the dying person often has a very strong need to express these feelings, and nurses can be facilitators of this process if they allow themselves to be. Guidelines for communicating with terminally ill clients and their families are presented in Box 8–4.

In addition to communication, the nurse's other interventions include helping the client take care of unfinished business, which might involve finalizing a will or taking care of some financial matters. Providing spiritual care through the use of clergy and through the nurse's own interventions of presence, touch, prayer, and scripture reading are all important in meeting the client's identified spiritual needs. A last intervention is to provide the client and family the privacy necessary to talk and comfort one another, to share thoughts and physical closeness not possible when there are frequent interruptions by the nursing staff.

Evaluation

The evaluation of care of dying clients and their families is an ongoing and continuous process. In some cases nurses may consider their interventions successful if the client dies in peace surrounded by loved ones. For some clients, though, this kind of death is not possible, and yet this does not mean that the nursing interventions were ineffective. If a client persists in a state of denial until the end, this is the client's right. Although nurses might feel this is not the ideal way to depart from life, it is the client's needs that are paramount in directing care. In general, nursing care of the dying client is successful when the nurse is sensitive to the needs of the client and family and meets those needs in a loving and gentle way. For one client such care will involve the nurse's quiet presence while the client cries and mourns; for another client it will involve the nurse's faithfulness in light of the client's angry behavior; and for still another

---

BOX 8–4
Guidelines for Communicating with Terminally Ill Clients and Their Families

1. Remember that what people want most is a peaceful death, a sense of completion, and through their legacy, a continuity with the future.
2. Actively listen for what the client is communicating nonverbally as well as through words. Use client-initiated themes as the basis for conversation.
3. Talk with the client as a unique individual with emotional, physical, and spiritual needs. Do not assume that you know what these needs are or what they should be.
4. Talk with clients about their feelings; do not talk to them out of having their feelings.
5. Provide comfort measures frequently, such as mouth care, positioning, and arrangement of covers. Inquire about and provide appropriate cultural and religious supports.
6. Encourage the client to make as many active choices as possible within the limits of his or her condition. Let the client take the lead in conversations.
7. Do not attempt to change the dying client's life-long patterns of coping with stress. Recognize the client's need to withdraw or to deny the impending reality of death as normal protective mechanisms in the dying process.
8. Offer frequent opportunities for dialogue, but respect the client's need for privacy.
9. Encourage clients to connect with significant people in their lives and to say the things they feel to the person, either verbally or through letters.
10. Let the client know when you are leaving and who will be caring for him or her after you go. This decreases the client's sense of abandonment by caregivers.
11. Be honest, direct, and tactful. If you don't know the answer, it is appropriate to say so.
12. Maintain a calm presence during all interactions. Your calming presence can emotionally ground the interaction. It is OK, even beneficial, to display sadness, but the feelings of the nurse should not overshadow the situation or overwhelm the client.

---

client it will be the nurse's willingness to pray with him or her for a peaceful death. Death is experienced differently by everyone, and it is the uniqueness of the experience that the nurse attempts to tap into and to facilitate.

SUMMARY

This chapter examines the concept of termination—how it feels to terminate, how people behave when faced with termination, the phases of termination, and how the nurse can be effective in dealing with termination. The chapter concludes with an examination of grief as a process, the final termination that occurs with death, and the nurse's role in assisting dying clients and their families to say good-bye.

All leave-takings have in common feelings of sadness, loss, a longing for the past, and ambivalence about the future. The feelings differ only in the intensity with which they are experienced. Terminations are characterized by three developmental phases: denial, grief, and the working through of the reality of the loss.

The nurse follows the nursing process in selecting appropriate termination strategies. Different types of terminations require different strategies. The strategy chosen should correspond to the depth of the relationship. Deep, meaningful relationships require a longer termination, whereas the ending of a short-term relationship is best acknowledged by mutual identification of feelings related to the relationship and a summary of the goals achieved.

Grief is the response to a significant loss, whether it is the loss of a loved one, an ideal, a material possession, or even a long-held aspiration. Grief is a process that begins with the anticipation of the loss and extends until the griever has learned to live with the loss. Nurses are subject to feelings of grief, but at the same time are expected to respond in a helpful manner to grieving in clients, their families, and their significant others.

Death represents finality in a relationship. Kübler-Ross (1971) identifies a framework for understanding the process of dying: denial, anger, bargaining, depression, and acceptance. In planning care for the dying client, the nurse applies the steps of the nursing process to individualize nursing care.

REFERENCES

Bozarth-Campbell (1982). Life Is Goodbye Life Is Hello. Minneapolis, CompCare Publications.

Cerney MS, Buskirk JR (1991). Anger: The hidden part of grief. Bulletin of the Menninger Foundation 55:228–237.

Chenitz WC (1992). Living with AIDS. In Flaskerud JH, Ungvarski (eds.) (1992), HIV/AIDS: A Guide to Nursing Care. Philadelphia, W. B. Saunders.

Companiello J (1980). The process of termination. Journal of Psychiatric Nursing and Mental Health Services 1:29.

Dickinson E (1978). "Because I could not stop for death." Quoted in Dunlop R (1987), Helping the Bereaved. Bowie, MD, Charles Press.

Dubrul T (1988). Separation-individuation roller coaster in the therapy of a borderline patient. Perspectives in Psychiatric Care 25(3–4):10–14.

Epstein C (1975). Nursing the Dying Patient. Reston, VA, Reston Publishing Co.

Gyulay JE (1989). Grief responses. Issues in Comprehensive Pediatric Nursing 12:1–31.

Kellar MH (1983). What is it like to be dying? Nursing '83 13:65.

Koehne-Kaplan NS, Levy KE (1978). An approach for facilitating the passage through termination. Journal of Psychiatric Nursing 16:11.

Kübler-Ross E (1971). What is it like to be dying? American Journal of Nursing 71:54.

Lindemann E (1972). Symptomatology and management of acute grief. American Journal of Psychiatry 8:101.

Mauss M (1967). The Gift. New York, Norton.

Mijuskovic B (1988). Loneliness and adolescent alcoholism. Adolescence 23(91):503–516.

Morse JM (1989). Reciprocity for care: Gift giving in the patient–nurse relationship. Canadian Journal of Nursing Research 21:33–46.

Piemme JA, Bolle JL (1990). Coping with grief in response to caring for persons with AIDS. American Journal of Occupational Therapy. 44:266–269.

Ross HM (1981). Societal/cultural views regarding death and dying. Top Clinical Nurse 10:1.

Sankar A (1991). Ritual and dying: A cultural analysis of social support for caregivers. Gerontologist 31:43–50.

Stuart GW, Laraia MT, Ballenger JC, Lydiard RB (1990). Early family experiences of women with bulimia and depression. Archives of Psychiatric Nursing 4(1):43–52.

Tilden VP, Gustafsen L (1979). Termination in the student–patient relationship: Use of a teaching tool. Journal of Nursing Education 18:9.

Zitrin CM, Ross DD (1988). Early separation anxiety and adult agoraphobia. Journal of Nervous and Mental Disease 175(10):621–625.

SUGGESTED READINGS

Bass DM, Bowman K, Noelker LS (1991). The influence of caregiving and bereavement support on adjusting to an older relative's death. Gerontologist 31:32.

Kelly B (1991). Emily: A study of grief and bereavement. Health Care for Women International 12:137.

Kübler-Ross E (1968). On Death and Dying. New York, Macmillan.

Peloquin SM (1990). AIDS: Toward a compassionate response. American Journal of Occupational Therapy 44:271.

Ross HM (1981). Societal/cultural views regarding death and dying. Top Clinical Nurse 10:1.

Ross-Algolmolki K (1985). Supportive care for families of dying children. Nursing Clinics of North America 20:457.

Sowell RL, Bramlett MH, Gueldner SH, Gritzmacher D, Martin G (1991). The lived experience of survival and bereavement following the death of a lover from AIDS. Image 23:89.

Travelbee J (1970). Intervention in Psychiatric Nursing. Philadelphia, Davis.

Worden JW (1990). Grief Counseling and Grief Therapy. New York, Springer.

PART III

THERAPEUTIC COMMUNICATION

Chapter 9

Communication Styles

KATHLEEN BOGGS

OUTLINE

Basic Concepts

COMPONENT SYSTEMS
    Spoken language
    Vocalization
    Nonverbal communication
    Metacommunication

Applications

BODY CUES AND FACIAL EXPRESSION

    Cultural implications
    Gender differences
    Clothing as a nonverbal message
INTERPERSONAL COMPETENCE
STYLE FACTORS INFLUENCING RELATIONSHIPS
    Responsiveness of participants
    Roles of participants
    Validation of individual worth
    Context of the message
    Involvement in the relationship

Summary

OBJECTIVES

At the end of the chapter, the student will be able to:

1. Describe the component systems of communication.

2. Cite examples of body cues that convey nonverbal messages.
3. Identify cultural implications of communication.
4. Describe the effects of gender on the communication process.
5. Define interpersonal competence.
6. Identify five communication style factors that influence the nurse–client relationship.

. . . the term dialogue implies communication, but in a much more general sense. It is not restricted to the notion of sending and receiving messages verbally and nonverbally. Rather, dialogue is viewed as communication in terms of call and response.

Paterson and Zderad, 1988, p. 23

Chapter 9 explores the component systems of communication as a basis for applying communication skills and strategies in the nurse–client relationship. The clues a client provides through gestures, vocal tones, body movements, and facial expressions help make sense out of the client's words. Sharpening observational skills to gather data needed for nursing assessments, diagnosis, and intervention is of special value to the nurse in planning care for clients. Knowledge of communication styles allows a more client-centered, goal-directed approach to resolving difficult health care issues.

BASIC CONCEPTS

COMPONENT SYSTEMS

Communication is a complex composite of verbal and nonverbal behaviors integrated for the purpose of sharing information. Within the nurse–client relationship, any exchange of information between the two individuals also carries messages about how to interpret the communication. Rothman and Sward (1958) describe three interrelated component systems of communication: *spoken language, vocalization,* and *nonverbal/body language.*

Spoken Language

Language is the tool people use to think about ideas, to share experiences with others, and to validate the meaning of perceptions about the world and one's place in it. Without the use of language symbols, people would be severely limited in their ability to classify and order information in ways that can be understood by self and others.

The meaning of words, however, extends beyond the symbols. The interpretation of the meaning of words may vary according to the individual's background and experiences. It is dangerous to assume that words have the same meaning for all persons that hear them. Language is useful only to the extent that it accurately reflects the experience it is designed to portray. Consider, for example, the difficulty an American has communicating with a person who speaks only Vietnamese, the dilemma of the young child with a limited vocabulary trying to tell you where it hurts, or the anguish of the victim of Alzheimer's disease who is desperately attempting to communicate, using words that no longer have an understandable meaning.

There are two levels of meaning in language: denotation and connotation. Both are affected by culture (Samovar and Porter, 1985). *Denotation* refers to the generalized meaning assigned to a word, whereas *connotation* points to a more personalized meaning of the word or phrase (Berko, Wolvin, and Wolvin, 1981). For example, most people would agree that a dog is a four-legged creature, frequently domesticated, with a characteristic vocalization referred to as a bark. This would be the denotative or explicit meaning of the word.

When the word is used in a more personalized way, it reveals the connotative level of meaning. "What a dog" and "His bark is worse than his bite" are phrases some people use to describe personal characteristics of a human being rather than a four-legged creature. Translating such phrases for individuals not familiar with their connotation requires explanation of their more personalized meaning. The nurse should be aware that many communications convey only a part of the intended meaning. One should never assume that the meaning of a message is the same for the sender and the receiver until mutual understanding is verified. For example, a three-year-old child remarked to her mother, who was pregnant at the time, that the mother was getting fat. The mother, assuming the child was referring to changes associated with the pregnancy, launched into an elaborate, theoretically correct explanation of why she was fat. "But, that's not what I meant, Mommy!" her daughter said. "I meant your legs are getting fat." Mother and child were talking to each other, but they were not communicating about the same issue.

Cultural Implications

According to Giger and Davidhizar (1990b), many nurses lack an understanding of communication principles and the techniques necessary to communicate effectively with clients from backgrounds other than their own. Developing an awareness of potential communication differences is the first step toward effective cross-cultural communication.

Language is culturally specific not only to ethnic, geographic, and religious groups but to a lesser degree to specific occupational and age groups. For example, entering a nursing program entails learning new language sets and new word connotations. The students' initial feelings of being overwhelmed are quite similar to those of any person entering a new and poorly understood culture.

English as a Second Language

Many adults think in their native language, translating words into a more familiar dialect before processing it in or out, even though they speak a second language fluently. Extra time needs to be allowed for information processing, especially when clients are experiencing emotional tension and are more likely to rely on their native language to assist them in sending and receiving information. Verification of message content is even more essential with clients from different cultural backgrounds to make sure that nuances of language do not get lost.

Black English

The nurse who works with black Americans may identify some barriers to communication resulting from incorrect assumptions about the message being sent. Giger and Davidhizar (1990a) caution nurses not to regard black English as substandard, noting that at least some of the time 89 percent of blacks use this form. Like those with dialects, speakers of black English use unique pronunciations, nonstandard grammar, and slang. For example, the final "th" in a word may be pronounced as "f," such as "baf" instead of "bath," or the unconjugated form of the verb "to be" may be used, such as "he be walking" instead of "he is walking."

Slang/Jargon

Different age groups in the same culture may attribute different meanings to the same word. For example, an adult who says, "That's cool" might be referring to the temperature, whereas an adolescent might be expressing satisfaction. A black teenager might convey his satisfaction by using the term "chilly." The "food pyramid" is understood by most health professionals to represent the basic nutritional food groups needed for health. But the term has limited meaning for individuals not in the health professions or for those with little knowledge of the body's nutritional requirements.

For successful communication, the words used should have a similar meaning to both individuals in the interaction. An important part of the communication process is the search with the client for a common vocabulary so that the message sent is the same as the one received.

Gender Differences

Many studies have found differences between men and women in both the content and the process of communication. In health care communication there is evidence to suggest that more effective communication occurs when the provider of the care and the client are of the same gender (Weisman and Teitelbaum, 1989). In general, men have been shown to use less verbal communication than women in interpersonal relationships (Juang and Tucker, 1991). Among the many gender differences noted in relation to verbal communication is that women tend to disclose more personal information than men and to use more supportive words. Men, on the other hand, are more likely to interrupt, to use hostile verbs, and to talk more about issues (Cotton-Huston, 1989).

Vocalization

The second system involved in communication is vocalization. The oral delivery of a verbal message, expressed through tone of voice and inflection, sighing, or crying, is referred to as *paralanguage.* This system of communication is important to understand because it affects how the verbal message is likely to be interpreted. For example, the nurse might say, "I would like to hear more about what you are feeling" in a voice that sounds rushed, high-pitched, or harsh. The same statement might be made in a soft, unhurried voice that expresses genuine interest. In the first instance the message is likely to be misinterpreted by the client, despite the good intentions of the nurse; the caring intent of the nurse's message is more apparent to the client in the second instance. Voice inflection suggests mood and either supports or contradicts the content of the verbal message. When the tone of voice doesn't fit the words, the message is less easily understood and is likely to be discounted. For example, expressing anger in a flat tone of voice as if the matter is of no consequence contradicts the meaning of the message and the intensity of the emotion the individual is feeling. Thus it is very difficult for the person receiving the message to respond appropriately. A message conveyed in a firm, steady tone is more reassuring than one conveyed in a loud, abrasive, or uncertain manner.

Cultural Implications

Culturally specific modes of emotional expression can sometimes confuse as well as clarify the meaning of a verbal message. The vocal emphasis given to certain sounds and tone modulations is in part culturally determined. In some cultures sounds are punctuated, whereas in others sounds have a lyrical or singsong quality. Contrast, for example, the vocalization of an Oriental client with that of a German or Spanish client. The vocal inflections are quite different. Nurses need to orient themselves to the characteristic voice tones associated with different cultures to avoid being distracted by them in the process of communication. The tone of voice used to express anger and other emotions varies according to culture and family. For example, it is sometimes difficult for an American nurse to tell when someone from an Indian or Oriental culture is angry because vocalization of strong emotion is more controlled than in most Western cultures. By contrast, a Latin American's vocalization may seem more angry than it is intended to be because of the characteristic Latin emotional intensity of verbal expression. Through repeated interaction with clients, the nurse learns to understand the message the client is trying to communicate.

Gender Differences

Studies indicate that women have a greater range of pitch and also tend to use different informal patterns of vocalization than do men. Females use more tones signifying surprise, cheerfulness, unexpectedness, and politeness (Cotton-Huston, 1989).

Nonverbal Communication

The third system of communication, which includes facial expression, eye movements, body movements, posture, gestures, and proxemics (the use of space), is commonly referred to as *body language* or nonverbal communication. Whereas words direct the content of a message, emotions accentuate and clarify the meaning of the words. Often the emotional component of a message is communicated indirectly through body language, particularly facial expression. The vast majority of person-to-person communication is picked up by monitoring subtle nonverbal communication (Cooper, 1990). Although there is potential for misreading nonverbal cues, researchers have demonstrated that nonverbal behavior can be correctly used to make accurate inferences about a person (Gifford, 1991).

Generally, nonverbal manifestations of communication are considered useful for expressive and social communication (Harrison, 1989) and may be more reliable than their verbal counterparts. To be effective, nonverbal behavior should be congruent with and reinforce the verbal message. For example, if Mark Beam, RN, smiles as he tells his manager that his assignment is more than he can handle, he negates the seriousness of the message (Raudsepp, 1991).

Nonverbal behaviors may be seen as a one-time or occasional occurrence or as part of a generalized pattern of behavior in communication. Knowing the client's usual nonverbal pattern of communication is important in assessing the nature and meaning of changes in behavior.

Metacommunication

Metacommunication is a broad term used to describe all of the factors that influence how the message is received. People communicate not only information, they also communicate a message about how that information is to be interpreted.

This ancillary information is known as metacommunication. Metacommunicated messages may be hidden within verbalizations.

CASE EXAMPLE

Crowther (1991) describes a case example of a crack-addicted client who has been in and out of treatment a number of times. In a therapy session the client discusses a peer who doesn't attend the therapy sessions at the rehabilitation center, saying "They don't kick her out because she could always turn around . . . maybe next week. . . ." Crowther interprets this as a message from his client expressing his own ambivalence about remaining in therapy.

In another example the nurse conveys a message of caring to her client during their conversation verbally by making appropriate, encouraging responses and nonverbally by maintaining direct eye contact, presenting a smooth face without frowning, and using a relaxed, fluid body posture without fidgeting.

In a professional relationship verbal and nonverbal components of communication are intimately related. When the verbal message is incongruent with the visual image, it is important to help the client understand and assimilate the discrepancy so that content can be dealt with directly. The nurse nonverbally communicates acceptance, interest, and respect for the client through eye contact, body posture, head nodding at pivotal points in the conversation, and frequent smiling. Studies of nurses' touching of clients has been reported to be perceived both positively as an expression of caring and negatively as a method of control (Mulaik et al., 1991). When nonverbal cues are incongruent with the verbal information, messages are likely to be misinterpreted.

APPLICATIONS

The nurse's assessment of nonverbal behaviors and their meanings must be verified with the client because body language, though suggestive, is imprecise. When communication is limited by the client's health state, the nurse should pay even closer attention to nonverbal cues. Pain, for example, can be assessed through facial expression, even when the client is only partially conscious (Enlow and Swisher, 1986).

BODY CUES AND FACIAL EXPRESSION

Posture, rhythm of movement, and gestures accompanying a verbal message are other nonverbal behaviors associated with the overall process of communication. Body stance may convey a message about the speaker. For example, speaking while directly facing a person conveys more confi-

Emotional meanings are communicated through body language, particularly facial expression.

dence than turning one's body at an angle (Duryea, 1991). A slumped, head-down posture and slow movements give an impression of lassitude or low self-esteem, whereas an erect posture and decisive movements suggest confidence and self-control. Rapid, diffuse, agitated body movements may indicate anxiety. Vigorous, directed actions may suggest confidence and purpose. More force with less focused direction in body movements may symbolize anger.

Eye contact and facial expressions appear to be particularly important in signaling our feelings (Cooper, 1990; Harrison, 1989). Throughout life, individuals respond to the expressive qualities of another's face, often without even being aware of it. Research suggests that individuals who make direct eye contact while talking or listening create a sense of confidence and credibility, whereas downward glances or averted eyes signal submission, weakness, or shame (Duryea, 1991). We speak of a person as having an open expression or a kind face. Almost instinctively, individuals use facial expression as a barometer of another person's feelings, motivations, approachability, or mood.

Facial expression is important in getting a message across. It connects the words presented in the message and the internal dialogue of the speaker. Facial expression either reinforces or modifies the message the listener hears. When the verbal message is inconsistent with the nonverbal expression of the message, the nonverbal expressions assume prominence and generally are perceived as more trustworthy than the verbal content. Mehrabian (1971), in a simulated study of the impact of words, vocalization, and facial expression on the receiver, notes that the power of the facial expression supporting the verbal content far outweighs the power of the actual words.

Six photos of common facial expressions are presented in Figure 9–1. The examples represent global, generalized interpretations of facial expressions. Although facial expression is often a strong indicator of emotional response to a situation, there are exceptions. Some clients control their facial expressions by masking the underlying emotion completely or by expressing it in a different way. A smile may be used to express joy or pleasure, or it may cover other emotions that cannot be expressed. A stoic facial expression and limited affect may hide the intense vulnerability a client is actually feeling when facing a potentially overwhelming situation. In an assessment of facial expression, the nurse notes a *lack* of appropriate facial expression as well as evidence of strong emotion in the facial expression. Since the eyes and corners of the mouth are least susceptible to control, they may provide the most informative data to support or contradict the overall communication picture the client presents.

CASE EXAMPLE

A client smiles but narrows his eyes and glares at the nurse. An appropriate comment for the nurse to make might be: "I notice you are smiling when you say you would like to kill me for mentioning your fever to the doctor. It would seem that you might be angry with me."

Cultural Implications

Most nonverbal behaviors are culturally specific and contextually bound. They are learned unconsciously through observation of the behaviors of significant people. Sometimes a cultural taboo tends to inhibit nonverbal behaviors. For example, different cultures have distinct rules about eye contact. Black clients culturally tend to avoid eye contact when listening and to use it when speaking. The nurse who thinks the black client is inattentive to her explanations because there is little eye contact during her discourse may actually be experiencing a normal, culturally specific nonverbal behavior (Atkinson, Morton, and Sue, 1985). There are cultural differences in the meaning attached to the use of touch. For example, some Native Americans use touch in healing, so that casual touching may be taboo (Giger and Davidhizar, 1990b).

Gender Differences

Gender differences in communication have been shown to be greatest in terms of use and interpretation of nonverbal cues (Hyde, 1990). In contrast to males, women tend to demonstrate more effective use of nonverbal communication (Cotton-Huston, 1989). Females are more likely to be better decoders of nonverbal expression (Keeley-Dyreson, Burgoon, and Bailey, 1991). Empirical studies have documented gender differences. For example, women smile more than men, whereas men prefer

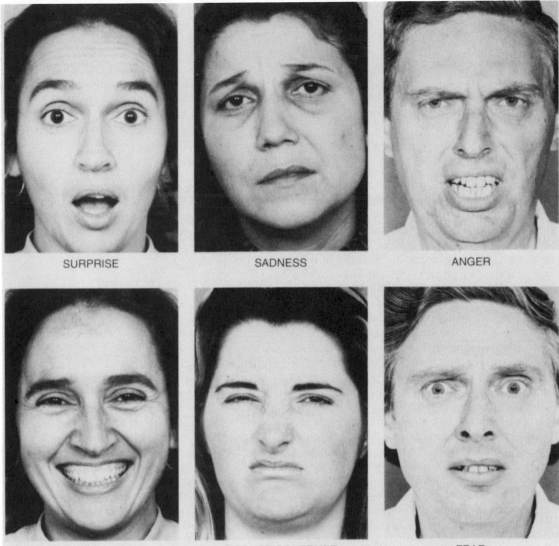

SURPRISE   SADNESS   ANGER

HAPPINESS, JOY   DISGUST, CONTEMPT   FEAR

Figure 9–1 Facial Expressions. From Ekman P, Friesen W (1975). Unmasking the Face. Englewood Cliffs, NJ, Prentice-Hall.

a greater interpersonal distance between themselves and others. Women are taught at a young age to keep arms, hands, and legs close to their bodies.

Clothing as a Nonverbal Message

Everyone is familiar with sayings like "Dress for success." The business world has long noted the role clothing plays in conveying an image of a seri-

ous professional. Mangum and associates (1991) surveyed clients, nurses, and administrators to determine whether different styles of nursing uniforms are associated with variations in the professional image of nursing. Findings supported client preference for traditional white uniforms (with nurse caps). Lab coats conveyed a less professional image, as did colored uniforms, scrub clothes, and so on. Most modern nurses have discarded the "dust cap" of previous dress codes. As more men enter the profession of nursing and traditional nursing is replaced by a wider variation in acceptable professional attire, nurses are being defined more by what they do than by what they wear. Exercise 9–1 is designed to help you reflect on nonverbal perceptions of professionalism in the nurse–client relationship.

INTERPERSONAL COMPETENCE

Communication is a process through which the nurse can establish a human-to-human relationship and fulfill the purpose of nursing. Through effective communication, the nurse can assist individuals and families to prevent and cope with the experience of illness and suffering and, if necessary, can assist them in finding meaning in these experiences.

Kasch (1984) proposes that nurse–client communication processes are based on the nurse's interpersonal competence. Interpersonal competence develops as the nurse comes to understand the complex cognitive, behavioral, and cultural factors that influence communication. This understanding together with the use of a broad range of communication skills helps the nurse in her interactions with the client and with the demands placed on him or her by the social environment.

In dealing with the client in the sociocultural context of the health care system, two kinds of abilities are required. *Social cognitive competency* is the ability to interpret message content within interactions from the point of view of each of the participants. By embracing the client's perspective, the nurse begins to understand how the client organizes information and formulates goals. *Message competency* refers to the ability to use language and nonverbal behaviors strategically in the intervention phase of the nursing process to achieve the goals of the interaction (Harrison, 1989; Kasch, 1984). Communication skills are then used as a tool to influence the client to maximize his or her adaptation.

STYLE FACTORS INFLUENCING RELATIONSHIPS

Having a knowledge of communication styles is not enough to guarantee successful application. The nurse needs to understand the interconnected relationships among intangible aspects of the communicators in the relationship.

Responsiveness of Participants

How responsive the participants are affects the depth and breadth of communication. Some clients are naturally more verbal than others. It is easier to have a therapeutic conversation with extroverted clients who want to communicate. The nurse will want to increase the responsiveness of less verbal clients, and there are many ways to enhance communication responsiveness. Verbal and nonverbal approval encourages clients to express themselves. Therapeutic skills and strategies that promote responsiveness include active listening, demonstration of empathy, and acknowledgment of the content and feelings of messages. Sometimes acknowledging the difficulty a client is having expressing certain feelings and praising the efforts the client is making helps. Using more than

---

EXERCISE 9–1
Nurses' Clothing as Nonverbal Communication
Clothing communicates a nonverbal message about competence and professionalism to a client, which can influence the nurse–client relationship. Mangum et al. (1991), in describing the conclusions of their study, wrote, "The nurse is judged primarily by what is worn and presented as professional at the bedside" (p. 130).

Directions:
In group discussion answer the following questions:
1. What are the external symbols of nursing?
2. if you were taking a picture for public relations purposes, how would you dress the nurse?
3. What would different items of clothing suggest about you as a nurse?

one sensory channel and filling in awkward silences can also promote ease in conversation.

Roles of Participants

Paying attention to the role relations surrounding the content is just as important as deciphering the meaning of the message (Northouse and Northouse, 1992). The relationships between the roles of the sender and of the receiver influence how the communication is likely to be received and interpreted. The same constructive criticism made by a good friend and by one's immediate supervisor is likely to be interpreted differently, even though the content of both messages may be quite similar and both are delivered in a similar manner. The quality of the relationship will be harmed if the nurse fails to follow through on verbal commitments, fails to pay attention to details, is uncertain or lacks experience, or attempts to reassure without documentation.

Validation of Individual Worth

Confirming responses validate the intrinsic worth of the person. These are responses that affirm the right of the individual to be treated with respect. They also affirm the participant's right ultimately to make his or her own decisions. For example, in a nurse–client relationship the nurse acts deliberately to accept and confirm the humanity of the client.

Disconfirming responses, on the other hand, disregard the validity of feelings by either ignoring them or imposing a value judgment. Such responses take the form of changing the topic, offering reassurance without supporting evidence, or presuming to know what a client means without verifying the message with the client. In a study of communication interactions between nurses and physicians, Garvin and Kennedy (1988) found that more experienced nurses used more confirming communication than did younger, less experienced nurses. These findings suggest that communication skills are learned, developing over time.

Context of the Message

Communication is always influenced by the environment in which it takes place. It doesn't occur in a vacuum but is shaped by the situation in which the interaction occurs. Taking time to evaluate the physical setting and the time and space in which the contact takes place, as well as the psychological, social, and cultural characteristics of each individual involved, gives the nurse flexibility in choosing the most appropriate context (Weaver, 1984).

Involvement in the Relationship

Relationships generally need to develop over time because communication changes with different phases of the relationship. In building a caring, therapeutic nurse–client relationship, more is involved than what is actually said or acted out. Early in the development of a therapeutic relationship, the client may test the nurse's involvement—for example, using the call bell for a minor request to see whether the nurse will answer it. Such preliminary testing is necessary if clients are to develop feelings of trust and confidence that the nurse will care for them until they are able to do so themselves. If the client is unable to develop trust in the nurse or to accept the illness situation, the client may become withdrawn or manifest "difficult" behavior (Morse, 1991). Box 9–1 displays communication behaviors that tend to increase or decrease involvement in the nurse–client relationship.

SUMMARY

Communication between nurse and client or nurse and another professional involves more than the verbalized information exchanged. Professional communication, like personal communication, is subtly altered by changes in pitch of voice and use of accompanying facial expressions or gestures. This chapter describes three component systems intrinsic to communication: spoken language, vocalization, and nonverbal communication. Cultural and gender differences associated with each of these three areas of communication are discussed. For professional communicators, maintaining congruence is important. Style factors affecting the communication process include the responsiveness and role relationships of the participants, the types of responses and context of the relationships, and the level of involvement in the relationship. Confirming responses acknowledge the value of a person's communication, whereas disconfirming

BOX 9–1
Behavioral Communication Styles in Nurse–Client Relationships

To Increase Involvement	*To Decrease Involvement*
	Nurse	

To Increase Involvement	*To Decrease Involvement*
Demonstrates commitment.	*Depersonalizes the client.*
• Responds to client as an individual.	• Refers to client by bed number of diagnosis.
• Uses close physical distance.	• Uses formal terms of address.
• Gives time to the client.	• Does not make eye contact.
• Establishes common ground.	• Has no time to talk.
• Anticipates needs.	
	Maintains superefficient attitude.
Shows perseverance.	• Gives impression of business.
• Gets to know client's family.	• Interactions focus on physical care.
• Follows through on promises and goals.	• Ignores emotional behavior and cues that client wants to discuss difficult questions.
	• Does not provide meaningful information to client about his condition.
Acts as an advocate.	
• Becomes involved.	*Does not trust client.*
• Connects the client with the system.	• Suspects ulterior motives.
• Acts as a buffer or go-between.	• Keeps client "in the dark."
• Adapts/bends rules to meet client needs.	

To Increase Involvement	*To Decrease Involvement*
	Client	

To Increase Involvement	*To Decrease Involvement*
Testing behavior.	*Avoids therapeutic relationship.*
Is nurse a "good person"?	• Does not self-disclose.
• Tests for dependability.	• Is late or absent from scheduled meetings/activities.
• Evaluates "likability."	• Focuses conversation on symptoms rather than feelings.
• Requests personal disclosures.	
Is nurse a "good nurse"?	*Does not trust the nurse.*
• Obtains information from other clients.	• Is manipulative.
• Looks for indicators of empathy.	• Becomes overly demanding.
• Evaluates competency.	
• Tests for ability to keep a confidence.	*Expresses discomfort nonverbally.*
	• Avoids direct eye contact.
Makes overtures.	• Fidgets when conversation "gets personal."
• Acts like "a good patient."	• Refuses to talk.
• Is friendly, jokes.	• Turns head/body away from nurse.
• Seeks time with nurse.	
Makes decision to trust.	
• Conversation content less social, more meaningful.	
Relinquishes vigilance.	

Adapted from Morse J (1991). Negotiating commitment and involvement in the nurse–patient relationship. Journal of Advanced Nursing 16. Reprinted by permission of Blackwell Scientific Publications, Oxford, England.

---

responses discount the validity of a person's feelings. Nonverbal strategies to facilitate nurse–client communication are discussed in later chapters.

REFERENCES

Atkinson D, Morten G, Sue D (1985). Minority group counseling. *In* Samovar L, Porter R (eds.) (1985), Intercultural Communication: A Reader (4th ed.). Belmont, CA, Wadsworth.

Baumeister R (ed.) (1986). Public Self and Private Self. New York, Springer.

Berko R, Wolvin A, Wolvin D (1981). Communicating: A Social and Career Focus (2nd ed.). Boston, Houghton Mifflin; 4th ed., 1988.

Brown KC (1991). Strategies for effective communication. AAOHN Journal 39(6):292–293.

Cooper MG (1990). I saw what you said: Nonverbal communications and the EAP. Employee Assistance Quarterly 5(4):1–12.

Cotton-Huston A (1989). Gender communication. *In* King S (ed.) (1989), Human Communication as a

Field of Study. Albany, State University of New York Press.

Cowan KM, Wilcox JR, Nykodym N (1990). A comparative analysis of female–male communication style as a function of organizational level. Communications 15:291.

Crowther D (1991). Metacommunications: A missed opportunity? Journal of Psychosocial Nursing 29(4):13–16.

Duryea EJ (1991). Principles of nonverbal communication in efforts to reduce peer and social pressure. Journal of School Health Nursing 61(1):5–10.

Ekman P, Friesen W (1975). Unmasking the Face. Englewood Cliffs, NJ, Prentice-Hall.

Enlow A, Swisher S (1986). Interviewing and Patient Care (3rd ed.). New York, Oxford.

Garvin BJ, Kennedy CW (1988). Confirming communication of nurses in interaction with physicians. Journal of Nursing Education 27.

Gifford R (1991). Mapping nonverbal behavior on the interpersonal circle. Journal of Personality and Social Psychology 61(2):279–288.

Giger JN, Davidhizar R (1990a). Developing communication skills for use with Black patients. ABNF Journal 1(2):33–35.

Giger JN, Davidhizar R (1990b). Transcultural nursing assessment. International Nursing Review 37(1):199–202.

Harrison RP (1989). Nonverbal communication. *In* King S (ed.) (1989), Human Communication as a Field of Study. Albany, State University of New York Press.

Holtgraves T (1991). Interpreting questions and replies. Social Quarterly 54(1):15–24.

Hyde JS (1990). Meta-analysis and the psychology of gender differences. Signs 16(1):55–73.

Juang S, Tucker CM (1991). Factors in marital adjustment and their interrelationships. Journal of Multicultural Counseling and Development 19(1):22–31.

Kasch CC (1984). Communication in the delivery of nursing care. Advances in Nursing Science 6:71–88.

Keeley-Dyreson M, Burgoon J, Bailey W (1991). Human Communication Research 17(4):584–585.

Lynch T, Anchor K (1991). Use of humor in medical psychotherapy. *In* Lynch T(ed.) (1991), Handbook of Medical Psychotherapy: Cost Effective Strategies in Mental Health. Toronto, Hogrefe & Huber, pp. 153–165.

Mangum S, Garrison C, Lind A, Thackery R, Wyatt M (1991). Perceptions of nurses' uniforms. Image 23:127.

Mehrabian A (1971). Silent Messages. Belmont, CA, Wadsworth, p. 44.

Morse J (1991). Negotiating commitment and involvement in the nurse–patient relationship. Journal of Advanced Nursing 16:455–468.

Mulaik JS, Megenity J, Cannon R, Chance KS, Cannella K, Garland LM, Gilead MP (1991). Patients' Perceptions of Nurses' Use of Touch. Western Journal of Nursing Research 13(3):306–323.

Northouse P, Northouse L (1992). Health Communication: A Handbook for Health Professionals (2nd ed.). Englewood Cliffs, NJ, Prentice Hall.

Patterson J, Zderad LT (1988). Humanistic Nursing (3rd ed.). New York, Wiley.

Raudsepp E (1991). Six steps to becoming more assertive. Nursing 91 21(3):112–116.

Rothman T, Sward K (1958). *In* Hoch P, Zubin J (eds.) (1958), Psychopathology of Communication. New York, Grune & Stratton.

Samovar L, Porter R (eds.) (1985). Intercultural Communication: A Reader (4th ed.). Belmont, CA, Wadsworth, p. 201; 6th ed., 1991.

Sellick, KJ (1991). Nurse's interpersonal behaviors and the development of helping skills. International Journal of Nursing Studies 28(1):3–11.

Weaver RL (1984). Understanding Interpersonal Communication. Glenview, IL, Scott, Foresman.

Weisman CS, Teitelbaum MA (1989). Women and health care communications. Patient Education and Counseling 13(2):183–199.

Wilkinson S (1991). Factors which influence how nurses communicate with cancer patients. Journal of Advanced Nursing, 16(6):677–688.

SUGGESTED READINGS

Egan G (1990). The Skilled Helper (4th ed.). Monterey, CA, Brooks/Cole.

Greenwald S (1991). Cancer nursing: What to know before you can offer emotional support. Nursing 91 21(6):32N.

Kelly AW, Sime AM (1990). Language as research data: Application of computer content analysis in nursing research. Advances in Nursing Science 12(3):32–40.

Kennedy CW, Camden CT, Timmerman G (1990). Relationships among perceived supervision communication, nurse moral and sociocultural variables. Nursing Administration Quarterly 14(4):38–46.

Meeuwesen L, Schaap C, Vander Staak C (1991). Verbal analysis of doctor–patient communication. Social Science and Medicine 32(10):1143–1150.

Raines RS, Hechtman SB, Rosenthal R (1990). Nonverbal behavior and gender as determinants of physical attractiveness. Journal of Nonverbal Behavior 14(4):253–267.

Thorne S (1988). Helpful and unhelpful communications in cancer care: The patient perspective. Oncological Nursing Forum 15(2):167–172.

Chapter 10

Developing Therapeutic Communication Skills in the Nurse–Client Relationship

ELIZABETH ARNOLD

OBJECTIVES

At the end of the chapter, the student will be able to:

1. Define therapeutic communication.
2. Identify the purposes of therapeutic communication.
3. Describe the characteristics of therapeutic communication.

4. Apply active listening and therapeutic communication strategies and skills.

5. Describe selected verbal strategies to facilitate therapeutic communication.

The fundamental fact of human existence is person with person. . . . That special event begins by one human turning to another, seeing him or her as this particular other being, and offering to communicate with the other in a mutual way, building from the individual world each person experiences to a world they share together.

Stewart, 1986

Relationships need the human touch of communication to bring them alive. The purpose of this chapter is to promote the development of therapeutic communication skills in professional interpersonal relationships. These skills are necessary to understand and to make emotional connections with clients so clients can achieve health-related goals and personal well-being. The quality of relationships is directly linked with the quality of the communication process (Stewart, 1986).

Included in the chapter are basic concepts of therapeutic communication as the main point of contact between two or more people in a relationship. Strategies specifically adapted to different client populations are discussed in other chapters, but all modifications in the therapeutic communication process build on the fundamental principles presented here.

BASIC CONCEPTS

DEFINITION

Therapeutic communication is a goal-directed, focused dialogue between nurse and client, specially fitted to the needs of the client (Severtsen, 1990). The process involves the exchange of ideas, feelings, and attitudes related to the desired health care outcomes. Here "client" refers to individuals, family, and groups who seek nursing care. The physical environment in which therapeutic communication takes place may be a hospital, a client's home, a community health care center, a school, or a nursing home. Therapeutic communication takes place within an interpersonal environment that, in addition to the client and nurse, may include the health care team, the family, and anyone else involved in the health care of the client.

Therapeutic communication develops in a conversational format. It is a complementary process in which all parties must be actively engaged. Effective therapeutic conversation is a lot like playing ball. To play successfully, the participants must be active players and pay careful attention to the ball in the air. Throwing and receiving the ball are not random occurrences. The ball must be thrown in such a way that it can be caught easily by the receiver. It is thrown with as much precision as the sender can muster. The receiver deliberately stands in the proper position to catch it. Once caught, the ball is returned to the sender with a similar degree of accuracy and care. When fast balls, curves, and slow balls are thrown, they catch the receiver off guard and frequently miss their mark.

Therapeutic communication works in a similar manner. The nurse takes the role of sender and receiver in an interaction. In the role of sender, giving a verbal message requires careful precision if the receiver is to "catch" it. If the message is thrown too high (e.g., vocabulary beyond the receiver's comprehension level), too fast (e.g., manipulative or sarcastic communication), too slow or too low (vague or tangential statements), or as a curve ball (message with a hidden agenda), it is difficult for the receiver to "catch" the message and to respond appropriately.

The nurse as receiver must be prepared to catch the client's communication accurately and to respond with precision. This means that the nurse must be in an open, waiting position to receive the message. Careful attention to the sender's body cues and to how the message is being delivered enhances the chances of catching the message. Once the message is received, the nurse deliberately chooses the most appropriate response (feedback) and returns the message to the sender.

Tannen (1991) notes that "life is a series of conversations." Many communication strategies discussed in this chapter are ones used spontaneously in social conversations. The primary differences between social and therapeutic communication have to do with purpose and focus. In health care, therapeutic conversations between nurse and client have a serious purpose. Through therapeutic conversations, clients learn about their illness and how to cope with it. Therapeutic conversations comfort dying persons and assure living persons that someone is there to be with them and ease their suffering. They make illness bearable by reinforcing self-esteem and supporting the natural healing powers of a person.

PURPOSE

Ruesch (1961), the originator of the term "therapeutic communication," notes that "the aim of therapeutic communication is to improve the patient's ability to function alone, with one other person, and in groups." Specific objectives of therapeutic communication between client and nurse can emerge as one or more of the following:

- A critical factor in helping clients to reassess priorities.
- An opportunity for clients and their families to explore new information about themselves.
- An interpersonal experience of discovering meaning in current life circumstances.
- An avenue for the discovery of new possibilities to achieve well-being.

Therapeutic communication is a mutual process, with both participants seeking to understand each other's position and support the goals of the relationship. But it is not a completely reciprocal process in the sense that both parties can expect their needs to be met through their conversation. In social interactions between two people, there is a give and take in exploring the personal dimensions of each person. This is not true of therapeutic conversations. Whereas the nurse's humaneness, feelings, attitudes, values, and behavior all show through in therapeutic communication, they are indirect contributors to the success of the relationship and not the focus of discussion. Intimate details of the nurse's life experience, except as they might facilitate the relationship, are deliberately excluded from discussion (Barron and Morrison, 1990).

CHARACTERISTICS

Goal Directed

The process of therapeutic communication is much more than simply the transfer of information and ideas from one person to another (Williams, 1991). Emphasis is placed on reaching realistic solutions to health care problems and client needs. Discussions occur within the context of clear definitions of values, purposes, and goals related to the specific nursing diagnoses and the relationship needs of the client. Always the nurse considers "What is the purpose or objective of sharing this information or asking this question?" "What are the main points to be shared, and in what order?" Adhering to relationship goals is an art requiring conscious effort and considerable practice. The client's health care needs dictate a sense of timing and sensitivity, a coordination of interpersonal skills to meet the demands of each situation.

Descriptive and Nonjudgmental

Therapeutic communication is a specific form of dialogue that is descriptive, problem focused, and supportive of the client's strengths. Such communications consider the client's perspective, readiness, ways of relating to others, physical and emotional condition, and sociocultural norms as relevant factors in planning and implementation of nursing interventions. Principles of therapeutic communication in the nurse–client relationship involve the whole person (Barnlund, 1986). Communication strategies are effective only when they are viewed as a process, or as a point of reference, not simply as a technical competency. Each therapeutic skill is a part of the larger I–Thou relationship (Buber, 1970; Duldt, 1991).

Defined Rules and Boundaries

Therapeutic communications have defined rules guiding their implementation and prescribed interpersonal boundaries. Comments are descriptive rather than judgmental. The communications take place within health care settings, and interactions usually are time limited. Each person's role, abilities, and boundaries are clearly recognizable by all participants. When the purposes of the relationship no longer require continued interaction, the nurse and client terminate the process. This is important to remember because some clients and nurses would like to allow a satisfying relationship to extend beyond goal achievement. To do so can compromise the therapeutic relationship, no matter how tempting it is to continue a rewarding experience.

Focused on the Client

Therapeutic communication requires that the focus of any conversation be on the client's needs. Although the conversation is a two-way, shared process, understanding and responding appropriately to client needs form the rationale for having the conversation. Free and open exchange of ideas helps the nurse and client develop a shared system of symbols and meanings that become the basis for therapeutic movement.

It is important for the nurse to see potential or actual health problems and needs from the client's perspective. To do so the nurse needs to listen reflectively until he or she understands the client's viewpoint and frame of reference (Wachtel, 1993). The nurse's response should proceed from the specific data the client presents. The nurse communicates an understanding of the central themes and feelings the client conveys.

The nurse and client mutually define health care problems and the client's needs. Words and accompanying actions serve the objectives of the relationship. For example, the nurse might deliberately choose conversation topics that interest the client and that are suitable for the client's level of functioning. Mutuality and reciprocity in the nurse–client relationship account for the greatest depth in therapeutic communication (Ramos, 1992).

Individualized Strategies

With practice the nurse learns to adapt broad communication principles, keeping the individualized communication needs of each client, family, or specific health care situation as a central focus. Adapting a communication strategy to meet client needs in different circumstances resembles the modifications a skilled cyclist needs to make to accommodate to different terrains in different locales. For example, the skills needed to ride a bicycle up a steep hill are different from those needed to coast down a road or maneuver a sharp curve. Each circumstance requires different judgment and skills. Similarly, nurses can adapt communication strategies to meet the requirements of different conditions and circumstances because they understand a variety of basic communicating principles.

Choosing the right communication strategy to meet the unique needs of each situation is the art of nursing. For example, the conversation that takes place during an acute emergency, when a client is in pain, will be different from one that occurs when the client is comfortable or has visitors. The resistant client needs a different approach from the one

Whether you are sitting or standing, your posture should be relaxed and, if possible, the upper part of your body should be inclined toward the client. (Courtesy of the University of Maryland School of Nursing)

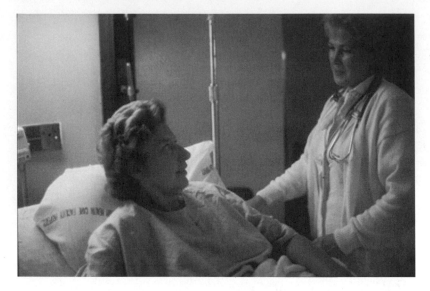

Confirming responses respect and support the uniqueness of a client's experience. (Courtesy of the University of Maryland School of Nursing)

used with a client who is eager to learn about his or her treatment. In the recovery room, after surgery, the nurse takes into account the client's diminished level of consciousness and lack of physical orientation in choosing appropriate ways to communicate (Severtsen, 1990). Children require different communication strategies than adults. In each of these situations, knowledge of the principles of therapeutic communication allows the nurse to pick and choose the most appropriate strategy. Strategies that are responsive to the individual, that have a sound theoretical base yet clearly reflect the nurse's natural communication style and personality, are most effective (Corey, 1982).

ACTIVE LISTENING

Active listening is an interpersonal skill essential to therapeutic communication (Duldt, 1991; Edwards, 1991). It is a dynamic process, whereby a person hears a message, decodes its meaning, and conveys an understanding about the meaning to the sender. In the communication process, active listening is as important as talking. Although other means, such as lab values, chart information, and end of shift reports, provide valuable information in client assessment, they are not a substitute for active listening in face-to-face contact with the client.

Listening differs from hearing. It is possible to hear a message without really listening to it. Hearing is a sensory process by which words and

sounds are transmitted to the brain. Listening involves taking the original sounds and words and constructing meaning from them (Adler and Rodman, 1991). The meaning derived from the listening process may be different from what the sender intended because the listener's values, expectations, and experiences impose a perceptual filter on the communicated message. Two people may hear the same conversation and derive entirely different meanings from it. For this reason validation and self-awareness are important components of the communication process.

To develop shared meanings, active listening requires thinking critically and choosing responses that will aid in gaining a clear understanding of the client's perspective. Active listening includes recall and the integration of many factors. Nonverbal cues, such as body posture, gestures, and tears, are part of the communicated message. The listener notes tone of voice, pauses in the conversation, and his or her own intuitive feelings in receiving the message. Previous conversations with the client and observations of the present client and other similar or different clients provide the historical context. For example, the mild-mannered client who suddenly expresses angry dissatisfaction with his care engages the listening skills of the nurse differently than the client who habitually complains about his care. One way to develop active listening skills is to begin to listen to yourself. How do you transmit messages (hearing)?

How do you decode a client's message (understanding) and give feedback related to the decoded message (remembering)? Exercise 10–1 utilizes principles of active listening in familiar situations.

Active listening responses have other benefits in the development of the nurse–client relationship. They provide evidence of the nurse's recognition and validation of the humanness of the client. When someone listens to another person and tries to understand and respond to that person's fears, feelings, and ideas, the person feels validated. Feeling confirmed as a person of worth can be as important as understanding the nursing diagnosis in promoting, maintaining, and restoring the health of an individual.

Presence

To be a good listener a person must focus on the other person and temporarily suspend any personal thoughts or ideas on the subject at hand. Only then can one person truly hear another per-

> **BOX 10–1**
> **Attending Behaviors in the Nurse–Client Relationship**
>
> - Erect posture with the upper torso slightly inclined toward the client.
> - Direct eye contact.
> - Use of open, expansive gestures.
> - Minimal encouraging cues.
> - Nonverbal cues such as nodding and smiling.

son's perspective. This concept is sometimes referred to as presence or attending (Charkhuff, 1983; Egan, 1982). Presence refers to the ability of the nurse to remain physically, spiritually, and emotionally attuned to a client's communication and being. Gardner (1992) identifies presence as a therapeutic gift of self and "the embodiment of caring in nursing" (p. 193). Attending behaviors (Box 10–1) invite the client to communicate with the nurse and demonstrate the nurse's interest in a person-to-person relationship. They convey interest and a sincere desire to understand.

EXERCISE 10–1
Active Listening

Purpose: To allow you to practice principles of active listening using a familiar situation.

Time: 25 minutes

Directions:
1. Choose a partner.
2. In five minutes, Person *A* describes events and feelings on an important life occasion such as a birthday or anniversary; a religious occasion like first communion or a bar or bas mitvah; a championship competition; or the first day in nursing school or on a clinical unit
3. Person *B* assumes the role of the active listener and practices skills relevant to active listening. Person *B*
   - Sits 2 feet away, facing *A*.
   - Makes frequent eye contact.
   - Uses alert body language such as leaning forward, nodding head, tilting head while listening.
   - Pays attention to what is being said (the words) and how it is being expressed (the feelings *A* is expressing, for example, noting variations in tone of voice).
   - Observes all nonverbal cues.
4. After *A* finishes, *B* demonstrates that he or she did indeed actively listen by (a) stating in his or her own words what *A* said and (b) summarizing his or her perception of *A*'s affective message—the feelings *A* was expressing.
5. Since active listening requires *B* to be able to understand completely everything *A* is saying and to communicate to *A* that both *A*'s content and feelings are understood and accepted, *B* now asks *A* whether step 4 was an accurate summary of *A*'s ideas and feelings. If *A* agrees, then *B* can be sure he or she correctly utilized active listening skills.

Discussion:
Follow several of these experiences with a general discussion about difficulties inherent in developing active listening skills.

Context

Physical Setting

Factors that occur dynamically between the individual and his or her environment, social supports, family and developmental history, culture, and the emotional relationship between helper and helpee have a profound effect on the communication process (Mahoney, 1993). The environmental context in which the communication takes place has an important influence on active listening. Contrast trying to speak with a close friend in a crowded restaurant versus in a small, intimate restaurant seated at a table apart from other customers. In which setting would you be more likely to express your deep-seated feelings? In the general hospital setting, the client's room or a room in which the nurse and client will not be disturbed is the best setting for serious therapeutic conversations. Drawing the curtain around the bed is a possible alternative when no other space is available. There should be enough room to have eye-to-eye contact and for both parties to be comfortable physically.

Home settings require a more complex assessment, including whether other family members should be included or excluded. In the home setting, the nurse is a guest who looks to the host or hostess to determine where the conversation will take place. The same protocol as in the hospital is required of the nurse in the client's home. Where the communication takes place is the client's call.

Timing

Timing of communication is important. The nurse needs to take cues from the client's behavior to determine emotional readiness and available energy. Sensitivity of the nurse to the presence of pain, variations in energy levels, and differences in relationship needs under different circumstances enhances communication. Planning for communication during periods when the client is more receptive to the idea is time efficient and respectful of the client's needs.

Interpersonal Space

The amount of personal space a client requires regulates the nature of the physical space and the positions of nurse and client (Hall, 1959). For example, sitting very close to a client who needs more space to feel comfortable can prove highly distracting to the client. The client won't hear the nurse's words because the inner tensions created by an invasion of personal space preoccupy the client. Persons from North American, Indian, Afro-American, Pakistani, and Asian cultures require greater interpersonal space for successful interaction than Hispanics, Arabs, and southern Europeans (Richmond, McCroskey, and Payne, 1987).

Circumstances can dictate the amount of physical space clients need. Most therapeutic conversations take place within a social distance. But clients experiencing high anxiety levels and difficulty with trust need more physical space between themselves and the helping person for successful conversation. More space is needed by a client on the first day of admission and by a paranoid client. On the other hand, clients experiencing a sudden physical injury or undergoing a painful procedure appreciate having the nurse talk them through the process, close by their head and possibly holding their hand. With experience, the nurse learns to gauge the amount of space the client needs. Nonverbal cues such as shifting position, rapid eye movements, or actually moving away slightly offer important cues about the client's space needs.

Role Relationships

Dramatic lifestyle differences between the nurse and the client related to socioeconomic status, previous life experience, education level, and occupational status influence the language, attitudes, and format of therapeutic communication. For example, the interpersonally sensitive nurse expresses the same concepts in different words to a construction worker, an adolescent, and a physician. The words chosen reflect client differences in education, styles of establishing familiarity and recognition, and developmental level.

Knowing the client's background gives the nurse greater flexibility in listening and responding appropriately. Faced with a client with a higher educational or social status, the average nursing student feels intimidated. Establishing a therapeutic relationship with a nurse or physician who is hospitalized with a serious illness can be poten-

Most conversations take place within a social distance.

tially overwhelming. "What will my client think of me?" is of concern when the nurse perceives the client as having a higher status than the nurse. Remember, the nurse has skills and knowledge in this particular situation that the client lacks. The client, regardless of status, feels strange and ill at ease. Introducing oneself and asking clients to describe their problems helps set the stage for mutual work in areas in which nurse and client will assume a team approach for resolution.

Unusual lifestyles make it more difficult for the participants in the nurse–client relationship to empathize with each other. Understanding the needs of a homeless client or the behaviors of a drug-addicted teenage mother may be difficult for a nurse who has never experienced the stresses associated with these lifestyles (Berne and Lerner, 1992). Although homosexuality is much more acceptable than it used to be, some nurses may find it more difficult to relate to clients with this lifestyle because of personal values and biases. Although the nurse may not understand different life experiences of the client, it is important to recognize that they represent the practices of the culture to which the client belongs. To question a client's lifestyle or

health practices is like denouncing an entire culture and its belief system to the client. The nurse has the responsibility to learn enough about cultural and lifestyle differences to be able to care for sick and well people, regardless of their background. Giving the best care involves providing patterns of care congruent with the client's values, beliefs, and practices (Leininger, 1991). By knowing and understanding another's lifestyle, the nurse can better serve the needs of the client and thereby provide more relevant health care.

Client Autonomy

When the client makes choices the nurse finds hard to accept, it can have a strong impact on communication. The alcoholic who persists in drinking and the HIV positive mother who continues to get pregnant discourage the nurse's investment in communicating with these clients. Watching a client make choices that indicate the client has given up also makes therapeutic conversations difficult. For example, an 80-year-old woman with multiple health problems requiring nursing home care may be hard to motivate. Why should she live?

Likewise, the teenager suddenly rendered a paraplegic in an auto accident may not want to engage in rehabilitation. So much has been lost that, from the client's perspective, there is little reason to try. Working with clients who have given up is a communication challenge for the nurse. At such times, it is important to remember the ethical principle of autonomy governing all aspects of the relationship. It is essential interpersonally to meet and respect clients where they are rather than trying to change them.

Intrapersonal Factors

Accurately *hearing* a message is not always easy. There are many reasons why a message fails to reach its target. The nurse can become so involved with giving physical care that listening to the client becomes secondary. And the client may be preoccupied with illness, pain, or worry. It is possible to become so intent on arriving at a destination (goal) that one forgets to pay attention to or enjoy the journey (process). Sometimes nurses listen only to the parts of the communication that interest them or to those that they assume are relevant. Included in each participant's communicated message are important instructions (metacommunication) about the interpretation of the message. The nurse or client may hear the content of a message but fail to register the nonverbal contradictions or qualifiers. To hear the communicated message fully, it is necessary to decipher the instructions as well as the actual verbal message (Crowther, 1991).

In tense situations, or because a situation taps into the nurse's vulnerability and professional insecurity, a nurse's anxiety level can get high enough to obstruct receptive listening. Because of a particular topic or a personal reaction to a given client, the nurse becomes immobilized, overidentifies with the client, or takes too much responsibility for coping with the problem. The client may not be ready to cope with a situation, and this affects listening. For example, to ask a newly diagnosed cancer client what her goals are reflects a lack of sensitivity to the client's need. The nurse's purpose in asking the question may be legitimate, but the inappropriate timing reflects the nurse's anxiety.

The client's speech patterns, anxiety, or behavioral mannerisms can make it difficult to attend fully or to understand a client's message. For example, many clients become increasingly vague when attempting to communicate about emotionally charged material, so that understanding what the core issues are is difficult. Some clients consistently communicate in a dull and uninteresting manner, making it hard for the nurse to maintain concentration. A strong foreign accent or an abrasive vocal tone grates on the ears, making it difficult to follow what the client is saying. Similarly, clients who consistently use poor grammar constructions or who use socially unacceptable language divert attention from the content of their message. Awareness of the effects of these factors on conversation provides the nurse with opportunities to work through them with clients in ways that are mutually satisfying.

VERBAL EXPRESSION

Weingarten (1992) notes, "Every conversation creates an opportunity for connection and disconnection; reflection and haste; dialogue and monologue; understanding and misunderstanding; collaboration and instruction; no change and change" (p. 45). Verbal messages are decisive factors in the nurse–client relationship. The nurse can make or break interpersonal bonds with the words used with clients. Verbal messages are central to all forms of nursing care. The nurse uses language to help clients connect different parts of their stories and to let the stories of their lives as they relate to the current health care situation flow freely. Verbal messages are used as a means of problem solving; they also comfort, challenge, and provide information to clients in distress.

Conversation is considered the art of nursing practice. Each nurse adapts communication strategies to reflect his or her personality, knowledge, experience and talents. But all therapeutic verbal strategies take into account the principles listed in Box 10–2.

Effective verbal messages are encoded in a clear, concise manner, and they address core issues. The nurse delivers the message in a spirit of caring and is aware of the client's reactions. Relevant background information is included so that

BOX 10–2
Guidelines to Effective Verbal Expressions in the Nurse–Client Relationship

1. Keep messages clear, concrete, honest, and to the point.
2. Match content and delivery with each client's developmental and educational level, experiential frame of reference, and learning readiness.
3. Define unfamiliar terms and concepts.
4. Put ideas in a logical sequence of related material.
5. Relate new ideas to familiar ones when presenting new information.
6. Repeat key ideas.
7. Keep language as simple as possible; use vocabulary familiar to the client.
8. Focus only on essential elements; present one idea at a time.
9. Reinforce key ideas with vocal emphasis and pauses.
10. Use as many sensory communication channels as possible for key ideas.
11. Make sure that nonverbal behaviors support verbal messages.
12. Seek feedback to validate accurate reception of information.

the client can move from the familiar to the unknown with greater ease.

The nurse considers the developmental and educational level of the client in framing responses. Expectations concerning the client's participation reflect the client's condition and age. Every attempt is made to deliver messages that carry mental images of cultural significance to the client. The nurse uses conventional, everyday language, which is spoken in a general spirit of inquiry and concern for the client.

Concentrating on issues of greatest importance and delivering clear verbal messages as precisely as possible is most likely to engage the client's attention. Messages that camouflage core ideas in a scrambled jumble of irrelevant side issues are difficult to follow. Introducing new ideas one at a time in chunks of simple information allows the receiver to process data without having to adjust to several different ideas at the same time. Illness is viewed as a stressor that can significantly alter the client's comprehension of important material. Repeating key ideas and reinforcing information with concrete examples of concepts facilitates understanding. It also provides another opportunity for the client to ask important questions that affect treatment compliance.

APPLICATIONS

ASSESSMENT STRATEGIES

Physical Cuing and Observation

Physical cues first inform the client of the nurse's interest and involvement. Eye contact constitutes an invitation or readiness to interact (Richmond, McCroskey, and Payne, 1987). Similarly, breaking eye contact is sometimes used to indicate nonverbally that the interaction is about to cease.

Communication is most effective when both participants are positioned so that their eyes are at the same level. It is easier to engage a client lying in bed if you sit in a chair at eye level than if you are standing and the client must look up at you. The next time you are in a client's room, try communicating from a standing position with your eyes looking down at the client; then sit in a chair facing the client with your eyes at the same level. Notice the differences in the flow of communication. Moving a chair close to the client in a wheelchair enhances communication (Miller, 1991). Whether you are sitting or standing, your posture should be relaxed, and if possible, the upper part of your body should be inclined toward the client. Physical behavioral cues characteristically include the behaviors summarized in Box 10–3.

When using attending strategies, it is necessary to bear in mind cultural differences among clients. For example, some cultures, such as the Puerto Rican, Japanese, Appalachian, and Native American, favor a more limited use of eye contact in communicating with others than do Western and some Latin American cultures. Withdrawal of eye contact in Western cultures may indicate discomfort, whereas in the cultures mentioned above, it might represent deference or respect.

Observing behavior as the client talks is an essential component of active listening strategies used in assessment. People tend to understand the meaning of a communicative message as a unified perceptual experience having nonverbal as well as verbal components. Nonverbal messages reinforce, expand, clarify, or contradict the meaning of verbal messages. When the verbal and nonverbal components of a message are incongruent, the impact of the nonverbal part becomes stronger and is more likely to be believed.

BOX 10–3
Physical Behavioral Cues

Emblems: Gestures or body motions having a generalized verbal interpretation, e.g., handshaking, baby waving bye-bye, sign language.

Illustrators: Actions that accompany and exemplify the meaning of the verbal message. Illustrators are used to emphasize certain parts of the communication, e.g., smiling, a stern facial expression, pounding the fist on a table. Illustrators usually are not premeditated.

Affect Displays: Facial presentation of emotional affect. Similar to the illustrators used above, the sender has more control over their display, e.g., a reproving look, an alert expression, a smile or a grin, a sneer. Affect displays seem to be more pervasive nonverbal expressions of the client's emotional state. They have a larger range of meaning and act to support or contradict the meaning of the verbal message. Sometimes the generalized affect is not related to a specific verbal message; e.g., a depressed client may have a retarded emotional affect throughout the relationship that has little to do with the communicated message.

Regulators: Nonverbal activities that adjust the course of the communication as the receiver gives important information to the sender about the impact of the message on the sender. Regulators include nodding, facial expressions, some hand movements, looking at a watch.

Adaptors: Characteristic, repetitive, nonverbal actions that are client specific and of long duration. They give the nurse information about the client's usual response to difficult emotional issues. Sample behaviors include a psychogenic tic, nervous foot tapping, blushing, twirling the hair.

Physical Characteristics: Nonverbal information about the client that can be gleaned from the outward appearance of the person, e.g., skin tone, descriptions of height and weight and their relation to body shape, body odor, physical appearance (dirty hair, unshaven, teeth missing or decayed teeth, etc.).

Adapted from Blondis M, Jackson B (1982). Nonverbal Communication with Patients: Back to the Human Touch (2nd ed.). New York, Wiley, pp. 9–10.

Besides listening for auditory cues and patterns, the nurse looks for visual indicators of meaning. The nurse takes special notice of the client's facial expression, body movements, posture, breathing rate, and so on, as cues indicating either support or nonsupport of the spoken message. For example, the client who verbally declares that he is ready for surgery and seems completely calm may be sending a very different message through the tense muscles the nurse accidentally touches. Poor hygiene suggests low self-esteem (Kramer and Akhtar, 1992). Dress and hair style can superficially classify a person as a liberal or conservative. Even behaviors that are seemingly external to the client, for example, the half-eaten lunch and noncompliance with treatment, can provide nonverbal clues that a client is in distress. Ekman and Friesen (1975) describe guidelines for interpreting facial expressions (Box 10–4) that may be useful in deciphering the nonverbal meaning of behaviors observed in nursing practice.

Facial expression is a major source of information when it is interpreted accurately. In stressful situations, however, it can be highly deceptive. Birdwhistell (1970), for example, found significant variation in the meaning of a smile. A smile can indicate pleasure, sarcasm, doubt, and acceptance, or it can cover the intent of a very angry statement. In the clinical setting, the nurse should always verify the meaning of nonverbal communication. Exercise 10–2 gives practice in identifying nonverbal behavior.

Questions

If someone asked you for directions to a particular place, you would need to start with where the person is at the time. Otherwise the person would have little idea of how to move from where he or she is to the new destination. The same is true of therapeutic relationships. The nurse can find out where the client is by asking questions. When using questions as an active listening response, it is important to respect the client's needs. The number of questions is determined by the client's condition and the information needed. It is important to ask enough questions so the client feels the nurse is listening, but not so many that the client feels he or she is being interrogated (Renwick, 1992). Questions to elicit information for a psychosocial assessment address human concerns such as those listed in Box 10–5.

The nurses questions fall into three categories: open-ended, closed, and circular. The differences between the first two are similar to the differences between essay and multiple-choice tests. In general, open-ended questions, like essay questions, go beyond the facts to elicit the person's subjective view of a topic. They represent a richer and more informative way of eliciting information than the other types of questions.

BOX 10–4
Facial Expressions Associated with Different Emotions

Anguish/distress	Eyebrows down and together, forming "worry triangle"; cheeks stretched and flattened down; corners of lips turned down, eyes without life in them; client may have difficulty looking at nurse.
Anger/rage	Mouth and jaw firmly set; eyes narrow and alert; facial muscles taut; speech fast; lips curled under and tense; client usually looks directly at nurse with cold, hard stare.
Guilt/shame	Head down; shoulders slumped; eyes down, avoiding direct eye contact; some twitching of facial muscles; face flushed; client may lick lips.
Happiness/joy	Face smiling, laughing, life in the eyes; muscles relaxed, stretched upward and outward, nostrils flared; client looks directly at nurse.
Contempt	Lips pursed, tense with corners turned up; jaw tense; eyes narrowed and focused.
Interest	Forehead drawn upward; eyes wide open; smiling, mouth open; facial muscles relaxed.
Fear	Muscles tense; head lowered; eye contact limited, mouth closed.
Caring	Eyes soft; muscles relaxed, smiling.

Based on Ekman P, Friesen W (1975). Unmasking the Face: A Guide to Recognizing Emotions from Facial Clues. Englewood Cliffs, NJ, Prentice-Hall.

Open-Ended Questions

An *open-ended* question is open to interpretation: It cannot be answered by yes, no, or a one-word response. Such questions are designed to permit the client to express the problem or health need in his or her own words. Open-ended questions are used to:

- Assess the client's ability to articulate ideas.
- Elicit the client's thoughts without presenting the direction of an acceptable response.

Open-ended questions usually begin with "how," "what," "where," "when," "in what way," or "can you tell me about?" The following are examples:

"How do you feel about having chemotherapy?"
"What happened after you . . . ?"
"When would you say this problem started?"
"In what ways do you think this treatment might be helping you?"
"Can you tell me about the accident?"

Open-ended questions are desirable in most clinical situations. Exceptions include emergencies or other circumstances when information is needed quickly or in a structured format. For example, open-ended questions may not be appropriate to use with a woman in active labor.

A variation of the open-ended question is the

EXERCISE 10–2
Observing Nonverbal Behavior

Purpose: To help you accurately identify nonverbal behaviors.

Time: 1 hour

Directions:
1. The group leader makes up 3 × 5 cards prior to class. On each card is the name of a feeling, e.g., sad, happy, lonely, scared, afraid, confident, shy, proud, lovable, dejected, hopeless, helpless, hostile, annoyed, attractive, pleased.
2. Students draw a card and, in turn, act out the emotion nonverbally.
3. The other students guess the emotion expressed nonverbally.

Discussion:
1. How difficult was it to express an emotion without words?
2. Did some of the nonverbal expressions of the emotion have multiple meanings? If so, why do you think this occurred?
3. Were some of the emotions expressed more or less universal in nature?
4. What were some of the nonverbal cues that made it easier to guess certain nonverbal communications of feelings?

BOX 10–5
Phenomena of Concern in a Psychosocial Assessment

Comfort/pain	Spirituality
Growth and development	Psychosexuality
Perception	Self-concept
Psychological state (mood, level of anxiety)	Self-esteem
Stress	Family/social relations
Security/trust	Sociocultural attachments
Communication	Suicide assessment
Mental status (orientation, cognition)	Teaching/learning needs

focused question, which limits the response to a certain informational area but requires more than a yes or no answer. This format is used when specific information is needed or when a generalized description of an issue or situation is too vague or too universal to describe fully the client's personal experience. The following are examples:

"Can you tell me any more about the pain in your arm?"
"You mentioned that you had the problem with your back before. How did this problem develop before?"

"Can you give me a specific example of what you mean by . . . ?"
Exercise 10–3 identifies open-ended questions.

Closed Questions

Closed questions can be answered with a yes, no, or one-word answer. Although they limit full expression and can control the other person's response, closed questions are essential in emergency situations when the goal is to obtain information quickly and the client's emotional reactions are of secondary importance. They also are used to check facts:

"When was your last tetanus shot?"
"Does the pain radiate down your left shoulder and arm?"
"Have you had these symptoms before?"

Sometimes clients with limited social skills respond better to closed questions until they are relaxed enough to answer more completely. Again, the sensitivity of the nurse in noticing this interpersonal need is central to the success of the relationship.

A variation of closed questions are questions that

EXERCISE 10–3
Identifying Open-Ended Questions

Purpose: To help you identify open-ended questions.

Time: 5 minutes for test; 10 minutes for discussion.

Directions:
Examine the following questions: Mark those that are open-ended with an asterisk (*). Mark a focused question with a plus sign (+). Mark a closed question with a minus sign (–).
 1. Ms. Gai, did you have a productive therapy session?
 2. How do you feel about it now that you've learned that you will be staying at your daughter's house?
 3. What did the doctor say about your lower-back pain?
 4. Your tray will be here soon. Are you hungry?
 5. And when you heard that, you felt . . .?
 6. When the doctor walked away, you felt rejected?
 7. No one likes to be in pain; can I get you something for it?
 8. In the past when your leg ached, what kinds of things helped it?
 9. What do you think about being transferred to a nursing home?
10. Tell me, what brought you to see the doctor today?
11. Are you having that problem with arthritis in your hand again?
12. What would you like to discuss today while we take a walk?
13. How are you?
14. What happened to you after you fell down?
15. And then what did you think?
16. Do you feel like taking your medicine now or later?

BOX 10–6
Examples of Circular Questions

Definition	*Example*
Difference type: Explores differences between people, between relationships, and between times.	"Who is most upset about your father's illness?" "The last time your father was hospitalized, what was most helpful?"
Behavioral effect type: Explores connections between the effect of one person's behavior on another.	"How do you make sense out of the fact that your brother won't visit your father?" "How is your mother handling this?"
Hypothetical type: Explores possible alternative actions and meanings.	"If your father doesn't make it, who will assume responsibility for the care of your mother?" "If you could identify what would be most helpful at this time, what would it be?"
Triadic type: Explores the person's perception of the relationship between two other people.	"If your brother wanted to be supportive to you and your mom, what would he do?" "How does your father respond to his son's lack of interest?"

Adapted from Loos F, Bell J (1990). Circular questions: A family interviewing strategy. Dimensions of Critical Care Nursing 9(1):47. Copyright 1990 Hall Johnson Communications, Inc. Reproduced with permission. For further use contact the publisher at 9737 West Ohio Avenue, Lakewood, CO 80226.

begin with "why." Why questions limit responses to a discussion of motivation, and they implicitly demand a justification of behavior. They should be used with discretion because the client may be only vaguely aware of why he or she chooses a certain behavior, and it is rare that only one type of motivation is present. The answer is therefore likely to be incomplete. Moreover, such questions usually put the client on the defensive (Muldary, 1983).

Circular Questions

By contrast with linear questions, which explore the descriptive characteristics of a situation, *circular questions* focus on the interpersonal context in which an illness occurs. They are designed to identify family relationships and differences in the impact of an illness on different family members. Circular questions are particularly useful when the family needs to be involved in the client's care (Loos and Bell, 1990). Such questions are categorized as difference, behavioral effect, hypothetical, and triadic types, as presented in Box 10–6.

What the Nurse Listens For (Box 10–7)

Themes

It is essential to explore another's reality before one can be of any help. Attending to themes means listening for the important thoughts and feelings underlying the client's words and nonverbal behaviors. Each client experiences a situation differently. For example, the client says to the nurse, "I'm worried about my surgery tomorrow." This is one way of framing the problem. The client might also say, "I'm not sure I will make it through the surgery tomorrow," which changes the focus of the communication from a generalized worry to a more personal one about survival. Or the client might say, "I don't know whether my husband should stay tomorrow for the surgery. It is going to be a long procedure, and he gets so worried." The

BOX 10–7
What the Nurse Listens For

- Content themes.
- Communication patterns.
- Discrepancies in content, body language, and vocalization.
- Feelings, revealed in a person's voice, body movements, and facial expressions.
- What is not being said as well as what is being said.
- The client's preferred representational system.
- The nurse's own inner responses.
- The effect communication produces in others involved with the client.

focus of her concern now includes her relationship with her husband. In each of these communications, concern about the upcoming surgery is expressed. The focus in each instance is a little different, however. For maximum impact, the nurse needs to assess accurately the difference in focus and should structure the response according to the client's emphasis.

Listening for themes includes understanding what the client is not saying as well as what the person actually reveals to you. For example, a client may tell you that he is not afraid of his surgery the next day. It's a simple in-and-out procedure, he says, and he plans to be back at work on Monday. At the same time, he is distressed that his girl friend won't be able to go out with him the night before the operation "to get his mind off the surgery." The discrepancy in the mixed messages is important assessment data.

It is important to respond to underlying themes as they are presented objectively to the nurse. "Objectivity here refers to seeing what an experience is for another person, not how it fits or relates to other experiences, not what causes it, why it exists, or what purposes it serves. It is an attempt to see attitudes and concepts, beliefs and values of an individual as they are to him at the moment he expresses them—not what they were or will become" (Moustakas, 1974). Understanding the nature of central and recurring themes helps ensure that the nurse's response is appropriate to the client's needs and the interpersonal requirements of the situation. Exercise 10–4 provides practice in listening for themes.

Communication Patterns

In addition to content themes, the nurse who listens looks at the client's way of relating to others. How does the client's conversational style affect the reception of communicated messages (Fig. 10–1)? Some clients exaggerate information, whereas others characteristically leave out highly relevant detail. Some talk a lot; others say very little. Verbal manipulation, aggressiveness, helplessness, martyrdom, obsequiousness, complaining, and humor used to disguise fear, anger, and hurt represent

---

EXERCISE 10–4
Listening for Themes

Purpose: To help you identify underlying themes in messages.

Time: Approximately 45 minutes

Directions:
1. Divide yourselves into groups of five students.
2. Take turns selling a short story about yourselves—about growing up, important people or events in your life, significant accomplishments, getting your first job, for example.
3. As each student presents a story, the other students in the group take mental notes of the important themes. Write them down so you won't be tempted to change them as you hear the other students. Notice nonverbal behaviors accompanying the verbal message. Are they consistent with the verbal message of the speaker?
4. When the story is completed, each of the other people in the group shares his or her observations with the speaker.
5. After all students have shared their observations, validate their accuracy with the speaker.

Discussion:
1. Were the underlying themes recorded by the group consistent with the speaker's understanding of his or her communication?
2. As other observers related their interpretations of significant words or phrases, did any of you change your mind about the nature of the underlying theme?
3. Were the interpretations of pertinent information relatively similar or significantly different? If they were different, what implications do you think such differences have for nurse–client relationships in nursing practice?
4. What did you learn from doing this exercise?

Figure 10–1 Wiley, © 1993, The Washington Post Writers Group. Reprinted with permission.

coping strategies that over time become recurrent interactional patterns for some clients. Some of these patterns are simply products of habit, but most of them are used by clients to gain control over their circumstances. Knowledge of their existence allows the nurse to respond empathetically to the underlying issues of powerlessness the client is experiencing. The nurse can also use this information to coach the client on communication strategies that are likely to be more effective in meeting the client's goals. Coordination of communication patterns with content themes provides the nurse with a more complete understanding of the communicated message.

A good assessment of communication patterns is comprehensive and objective. Evaluation of the client's present overall pattern of interaction with others includes strengths and limitations, family communication dynamics, and developmental and educational levels. The impact of external environmental influences such as culture, roles, sources of interpersonal support, and ways of handling conflict and of dealing with emotions on communication patterns forms a critical dimension of interpersonal communication.

Preferred Systems of Giving and Receiving Data

Neurolinguistic programming (NLP) is a useful listening format for decoding the client's preferred representational system for giving and receiving data (Knowles, 1983). Knowing whether a person organizes data about personal experience predominantly from a visual, auditory, or kinesthetic mode permits the nurse a wider access to the client's communication pattern and may suggest the images or examples the nurse might use in dialogue with the client. To determine which representational mode is preferred, pay attention to the verbs the client uses in conversation because they are the least vulnerable to distortion (Mercier et al., 1984). If the client uses phrases such as "I feel" or "I think," the preferred mode is likely to be kinesthetic, whereas the client who says, "I just can't see myself," "It is hard for me to envision . . .", or "When I look at . . ." is using a visual representational system. Auditory representational systems are exemplified in statements such as, "The doctor told me" or, "All I hear is that the chemotherapy is necessary, but nobody will tell me what my options are." The verbs the client chooses to describe his or her experience give the nurse clues about how the client internally processes information.

As a nurse working with the client using a kinesthetic mode, one might phrase informational feedback focused on the types of feelings the client is likely to experience. The nurse might tell the client going for a cardiac catherization, "When they first inject the dye, you may feel a funny sensation, but the feeling will subside very quickly." If the client uses a visual representational system, the nurse might say, "Now the room will be dark, but that is because it is easier to see what the doctor will be looking for with this procedure." For the client who prefers an auditory mode, the nurse might focus on the verbal directions the client is likely to receive: "When the doctor is ready to inject the dye, he will probably tell you that you may feel a momentary pressure that will pass quickly." When the information is phrased in the client's preferred pattern of informational processing, it is accepted more readily. An interesting way to understand the nature of your preferred representational mode is to ask yourself how you learned your name and what you remember about getting from your house to the elementary school. If the mental answer that first comes to your mind is auditory, e.g., "That's what my mother called me," and your description of getting to school lacks visual impressions, chances are you favor an auditory representational system. Conversely, seeing your name in written form as your first mental answer suggests a visual mode, and describing your walk to elementary school as "I felt cold in the winter" and "It seemed as though I would never get there" suggests a kinesthetic mode. Most people use more than one mode in general conversation, but generally there is a preferred system of communication. Talking the same language increases with the use of similar representational mode phrasing in dyadic communication.

Personal Intuitions

Assessment can occur as a personal response from within the nurse. The nurse may feel intuitively that something is amiss, but observed data fail to reveal the nature of functional discrepancies. This inner sense can be stimulated by the content of the message, by the client's behavior or expressions, or even by internal feelings about self-behaviors that capture the nurse's attention.

Personal feelings of anxiety, anger, or depression that the nurse occasionally experiences in a relationship are worth noting. If the nurse has no particular personal reason for reacting to the client with these feelings, the inner response may reflect the unexpressed feeling in the client's tone of voice. Behavioral reactions that the nurse feels are out of proportion to the situation—e.g., complete calm before surgery, excessive anger, noncompliance or passive compliance with no questions asked, guarded verbalizations, incongruent facial expressions or body language, and social withdrawal—are danger signals.

Superficial observations that fail to go beyond a client's abrasiveness or guarded verbal expressions to the loneliness and hurt inside touch only surface issues. When the nurse feels there are missing pieces of data upon which to base a diagnosis, it is useful to ask oneself, "How would most clients I have cared for face a similar situation?" Reflecting the nurse's inner response back to the client helps the client clarify or validate the nurse's observation. Before acting on any intuition, nurses need to validate their assumptions with the client. Only those intuitions that the client is ready to hear and that would facilitate the relationship are shared with the client.

Therapeutic Listening Responses

Feedback in the form of a listening response shows the client that the nurse is interested in processing the information and in remembering important facts about the client in an accurate data assessment. The nurse uses words and touch as listening responses to encourage further disclosure, to convey understanding, and to provide immediate feedback to the client related to his or her needs and health problems. Minimal verbal cues, clarification, restatement, paraphrasing, reflection, summarization, silence, and touch are examples of skilled communication strategies the nurse can use to elicit a complete data base. Examples of these strategies are presented in Box 10–8, followed by their descriptors and guidelines for use.

Minimal Cues and Leads

Simple, encouraging leads communicate an interest in the message the client is imparting. Minimal cues through body actions, e.g., smiling, nodding, and leaning forward, are designed to stimulate further communication and encourage clients to go on with their story. By not detracting from the client's message and by giving permission to tell the story as the client sees it, minimal cues are uniquely suited to a client-centered dialogue, as shown in Exercise 10–5.

BOX 10–8
Listening Responses

Listening Response	*Example*
Minimal cues and leads	Body actions: smiling, nodding, leaning forward. Words: "mm" or "uh huh," "Oh really," "go on."
Clarification	"Could you describe what happened in sequence?" "I'm not sure I understand what you mean; can you give me an example?"
Restatement	"Are you saying that . . . (repeat client's words)?" "You mean . . . (repeat client's words)?"
Paraphrasing	CLIENT: I can't take this anymore. The chemo is worse than the cancer. I just want to die. NURSE: It sounds as though you are saying you have had enough.
Reflection	"It sounds as though you feel guilty because you weren't home at the time of the accident." "You sound really frustrated because the treatment is taking longer than you thought it would."
Summarization	"Before moving on, I would like to go over with you what I think we accomplished thus far."
Silence	Briefly disconnecting, but continuing to use attending behaviors following an important idea, thought, or feeling.
Touch	Gently rubbing a person's arm during a painful procedure.

Clarification

Clarification seeks to understand the message of the sender by asking the client for more information or to elaborate on a point. The strategy is most useful when parts of a client's communication are ambiguous or not easily understood. Failure to ask for clarification when part of the communication is poorly understood means that the nurse will act on incomplete or inaccurate information.

Clarification responses are expressed as a question or statement followed by a restatement or paraphrasing of part of the communicated message. "You stated earlier that you were concerned about your blood pressure. Can you tell me more about what concerns you?" The tone of voice used with a clarification response should be neutral, not accusatory or demanding. Practice this response in Exercise 10–6.

Restatement

Restatement is a communication strategy used to broaden a client's perspective or when the nurse

---

EXERCISE 10–5
Minimal Cues and Leads

Purpose: To practice and evaluate the efficacy of minimal cues and leads.

Time: 30 minutes

Directions:
1. Think of a recent interpersonal problem you have encountered. Break up the group into groups of three: *A,* the protagonist, *B,* the helping person, and *C,* the observer. *A* should relate the problem and indicate how he or she dealt with it and what the outcome was. *B* should use encouragers, minimal cues, and leads as outlined in the text. *C* observes the interaction and provides feedback.
2. Reverse roles, and this time the helping person should not use verbal cues and minimal leads as a listening response strategy. If time permits, each student can have an opportunity to practice each role.

Discussion:
1. What were the differences when encouragers were not used? Was the communication as lively?
2. How did it feel to you when telling your story when this strategy was used by the helping person?

EXERCISE 10–6
Using Clarification

Purpose:

1. To make clear the actual meaning of the client's message.
2. To check the accuracy of your perception of the client's message.
3. To demonstrate to the client that you actually heard what the client was saying.

Time: 45 minutes

Directions:
For each of the following statements, respond by acknowledging receiving the message, expressing your uncertainty about what was said, and asking for clarification.

1. "Things are a mess in our apartment, I'll clean later."
   Example response: "I understand that you're planning on cleaning up, but I'm not sure what you mean by later or whether you feel I should help."
   Other Possible Responses:

   _____

   _____

2. "Please pick up your client assignment before going on duty."
   Response: to seek clarification about when, where.

   _____

   _____

3. "Soak your hand in salt water every day."
   Response: to clarify how much salt in what amount of water, how often, and for how long.

   _____

   _____

4. Client: "The doctor was just in here and said they found something. I feel so bad. I just wish I didn't have to go through all this."
   Response:

   _____

   _____

5. Client: "Ever since I had this stroke, I can't do any of the things I used to do. I'm no good to anyone."
   Response:

   _____

   _____

needs to provide a sharper focus on a specific part of the communication. Restatement is like bracketing a phrase in a paragraph. It can be viewed as a brief interruption designed to highlight a defined element of a message. Restatement is particularly effective when the client overgeneralizes or seems stuck in a repetitive line of thinking. To challenge the validity of the client's statement directly could be counterproductive, but repeating parts of the message in the form of a query serves a similar purpose. Restating a self-critical or irrational part of the message momentarily focuses the client's attention on the possibility of an inaccurate or global assertion. It also is used to strengthen an ego-enhancing self statement. Restatement should be used sparingly and only as a point of emphasis.

Otherwise it can sound stilted and adds little to the client's frame of reference in exploring issues.

Paraphrasing

Paraphrasing is a response strategy designed to help the client elaborate more on the cognitive part (content) of a verbal message. The nurse takes the original message and transforms it into his or her own words without losing the meaning. The paraphrase is a little more specific than the client's initial statement and is shortened so that the focus is on the core elements. Presented as a tentative statement, the paraphrase listening response invites but does not force a specific answer. Paraphrasing is particularly useful in the early stages of a relationship or when the client is raising a troublesome topic for the first time. It is also valuable in checking whether the nurse's translation of the client's words is an accurate interpretation of the message. Exercises 10–7 and 10–8 use paraphrasing as a listening response.

Reflection

The *reflection* response focuses on the emotional overtones of a message. It is a listening response used to help clients look at the relation between the content and the emotional aspects of a message. By reflecting the client's words, the nurse helps the client connect seemingly unrelated pieces of information and blend feelings with associated data. Reflective listening responses help the client clarify important feelings and experience them with their appropriate intensity in relation to a particular situation or event. They give the client permission to have feelings. Often clients are tremendously relieved to find that having conflicting emotions is a normal emotional response in new and unfamiliar circumstances. It is important when using this strategy to put into words the feelings that underscore the client's comments without either adding or subtracting from them.

Timing is critical in the use of reflection. Reflective listening responses have more impact if they are used sparingly to accentuate only the important themes. Using a "you feel" statement after each client statement suggests a shallow approach rather than genuine listening. Most important, the nurse should be sensitive to the client's readiness to discuss feelings and attitudes. Otherwise the listening response will appear lacking in feeling or purpose, despite the "feelings-associated" words that are used.

Reflection is most useful when it is used in a

EXERCISE 10–7
Practice in Paraphrasing

Purpose: To practice using paraphrasing as a listening response.

Time: 20 minutes

Directions:
1. The class forms into groups of three students each.
2. Participants *A* and *B* will hold a discussion on why *A* chose to be a nurse or some other important decision or event in *A*'s life. Participant *B* may respond to *A* only with a paraphrasing response. Participant *C* will act as observer.
3. At the end of five minutes, *C* shares his or her observations.
4. Then for the next five minutes, *C* acts as the protagonist in describing his or her first day on the clinical unit or the first day in a nursing course. *A* responds to *C* with paraphrase while *B* acts as observer.
5. After five minutes, the process may be repeated with another scenario to give *C* the chance to practice the paraphrase response.

Discussion:
1. Discuss the difficulties in trying to paraphrase the statements of clients.
2. Did the paraphrased statement encourage you to continue? Did you feel more understood as a result of hearing the listener's response? What did you learn personally from this exercise about the paraphrase as a listening response?

EXERCISE 10–8
Practicing Paraphrasing

Purpose:
1. To validate with the client the accuracy of your perception of the objective content of the client's message.
2. To convey to the client that you are interested and actually heard what was said.

Time: 1 hour

Directions:
For each statement, write one appropriately rephrased sentence.
1. "I'm on a diet but I seem to be gaining a lot of weight even though I usually try to stick to it faithfully."
   Appropriately paraphrased example:
"You want to lose weight but your diet isn't working?"
   Inappropriate: "You can't stick to your diet?"
2. "I need an operation but can't take the time to have it until my business is doing better."
   Appropriate paraphrase:

   _____

   _____

3. "The doctor just told me I have cancer, but I'm not sure what he means."
   Appropriate paraphrase:

   _____

   _____

compound sentence that connects the feeling with the appropriate content (Charkhuff, 1983; Cormier, Cormier, and Weisser, 1984). The nurse links the probable feeling with the content of the message through the use of a compound sentence. "It sounds as though you feel _____ because _____."

Sometimes nursing students feel they are putting words into the client's mouth when they "pick" an emotion from their perception of the client's message. This would be true if they were picking an emotion out of thin air, but not when the nurse empathetically considers the client's situation. Reflective responses serve to validate the nurse's accuracy in perceiving the client's feelings about a situation. Exercise 10–9 gives practice in using reflecting responses.

Reflecting a feeling is not the same as interpreting it. Interpretation, which goes beyond the client's communication, represents a psychological decoding of the message rather than a linkage between the manifest content and the emotional response to a current situation. Interpreting the meaning of a feeling rather than reflecting it back to the client for validation is a misuse of the strategy.

Summarization

Summarization is a listening skill used to review the communication achieved at the end of an interaction or series of comments. Summarization pulls several ideas and feelings together. The ideas may relate to the same interaction or to different ones. The nurse reduces a lengthy interaction or discussion to a few succinct sentences. A summary statement is particularly useful before moving on to a different topic area. Exercises 10–10 and 10–11 give practice in summarization.

Silence

Silence, used deliberately and judiciously, is a powerful communication strategy. It allows the client to think, and it is often beneficial for the nurse to step back momentarily and process what he or she heard before responding. Too often a quick response addresses only a small part of the message and/or gives the client an insufficient opportunity to formulate fully a complete idea. A short silence to get in touch with one's personal anxiety aroused by a client's response is appropri-

EXERCISE 10–9
Practicing the Use of Reflecting Responses

Purpose: To practice the use of reflection as a listening response.

Time: 30 minutes

Directions:
1. May be done alone or in any size class group.
2. Read the following situation.

> Jamie, age seven, is dying of a chronic respiratory condition. His small stature and optimistic sense of humor have made him a favorite on the unit. Jamie's Mom breaks down crying one day, saying to you, "I try to do good, to help out on the unit these last four weeks. Why is God punishing me this way? I can't take much more of this staying here constantly, watching Jamie struggle for every breath. Only his IVs and oxygen keep him alive. Sometimes I think it would be better to stop them and let him die in peace."

3. Write appropriate nurse responses that reflect back to the mother several statements she made.
4. Then write other responses that reflect your perception of her feelings.
5. Combine the responses to attain an appropriate reflection of content and feeling. It may be easier to do this exercise for each sentence in the situation.

Discussion:
1. Was it more difficult to use reflection as a communication strategy? if so, why?
2. What did you personally learn from this exercise?

ate before responding. On the other hand, long silences become uncomfortable. The silent pause should be just that, a brief disconnection followed by a verbal comment.

Silence is used to accent an important point in a verbal communication. By pausing briefly after presenting a key idea and before proceeding to the next topic, the nurse encourages the client to notice the

EXERCISE 10–10
Practicing Summarization

Purpose: To provide practice in summarizing interactions.

Time: 15 minutes

Directions:
1. Choose a partner.
2. For five minutes the two of you discuss a medical ethics topic such as euthanasia, heroic life support for the terminally ill, or "Baby Doe" decisions to allow malformed babies to die if the parents so desire.
3. After five minutes, both must stop talking until *A* has summarized what *B* has just said to *B*'s satisfaction, and vice versa.

Discussion:
After both partners have completed their summarizations, discuss the process of summarization, answering the following questions:
1. Did knowing you had to summarize the other person's point of view encourage you to listen more closely?
2. Did the act of summarizing help clarify any discussion points? Were any points of agreement found? What points of disagreement were found?
3. Did the exercise help you to understand the other person's point of view?
4. What should an effective summary contain? Is it hard to summarize a long conversation?
5. How did you determine which points to focus on in your summarization?

EXERCISE 10–11
Summarizing Conflicts

Purpose: To provide experience with summarizing complex issues.

Time: To be done out of class.

Directions:
1. Watch a television talk show (such as Donahue or Sally Jessy Raphael or a political debate or a show such as Face the Nation) in which two individuals are expressing conflicting opinions.
2. At the end, write a one-paragraph summarization of each point of view.

Discussion:
1. Discuss difficulties inherent in summarizing complex issues.
2. Were you surprised at what you learned when you attempted to summarize two conflicting opinions?

most important elements of the communication. Brief silence following an important verbal message dramatizes the significance of the nurse's statement.

When a client falls silent it can mean that something has touched the client profoundly. Respecting the client's silence and sitting without breaking the mood can be important in sharing the meaning of the communication. Clients often marvel at the nurse's willingness to sit quietly and without awkwardness in their moments of silence. Practice in this skill is developed in Exercise 10–12.

Touch

Touch represents a person's first experience in communicating with another human being. As infants, touch was the primary means through which we knew how those important in our lives felt about us. Touch was also the predominant pathway through which we explored our world. Throughout life touch is a vital form of communication. It can be used as a powerful listening response when words would break a mood or verbalization would fail to convey the empathy or depth of feeling between nurse and client.

Touch is a reciprocal process; those who touch others experience being touched. Touch can reach the depths of spirit for many individuals in ways that words cannot match. A hand tenderly placed on a frightened mother's shoulder or a gentle squeeze of the hand can speak far more eloquently than words in times of deep emotion, whether sad or joyful. Clients in pain, those who feel repulsive to others because of altered appearance, lonely and

EXERCISE 10–12
Therapeutic Use of Silence

Purpose: To experience the effect of the use of silence as a listening response.

Time: 30 minutes

Directions:
1. Two people act as *A* and *B*.
2. Individual *A* plays the role of the nurse while individual *B* is a healthy, ambulatory 80-year-old client in an extended-care facility, having been placed there against her will by her family, who are moving to another state.
3. *B*'s role is to describe her feelings (shock) at being institutionalized and to discuss her slow adjustment to new surroundings and new companions, describing both the positive and the negative aspects.
4. *A*'s objective is to make at least three deliberate efforts to use silence during their conversation (as a therapeutic device to encourage *B*'s consideration of her life and problems).

Discussion:
After 15 minutes of role playing, have a general discussion to share feelings about the effective use of silence.

dying clients, and those experiencing sensory deprivation or feeling confused respond positively to the nurse who is unafraid to enter their world and touch them (Miller, 1990).

Touch can also deepen the meaning of language. When combined with words, e.g., in a back rub, touch tends to enhance the feeling of comfort. Holding a small child or placing your hand in another's during a painful procedure is as important a means of communication in the therapeutic relationship as knowing the right words to say.

There is variation in the amount of touch people are comfortable with. Some people are demonstrative and enjoy being touched, whereas others are more reserved. Distrustful clients will shrink from such closeness. There should be some visual indication that the client would not be disturbed by touch before this intervention is used as part of a listening response. When in doubt, the nurse should ask the client before proceeding.

INTERVENTION STRATEGIES

In the nurse–client relationship the client is not really looking for brilliant answers from the nurse but for feedback and support that suggests a compassionate understanding of his or her dilemma. Since, ultimately, the client is the one who should assume full responsibility for implementing solutions to health-related self-care deficits, the role of the nurse in giving leads, cues, and information is that of guide, not director, of the communication process. An essential step in using communication strategies as interventions is to structure creative responses and provide relevant feedback so that the client's inner strengths are mobilized and environmental supports are used.

This goal should underscore all of the nurse's interventions and feedback. No matter what level of communication exists in the relationship, the same questions arise: "Who am I?" "What is the meaning of my current experience?" "How can I cope with what is happening to me?" The same needs—"Hear me," "Touch me," "Respond to me," "Feel my pain and my joys with me"—are identifiable as basic underlying themes. Communication behaviors that encourage the development of nurse–client relationships are as follows:

- Allowing the client enough time to answer questions.

- Informing the client of what the nurse is going to do, and why.
- Asking the client what his or her feelings were about what was happening (Duldt, 1991).

In the planning and intervention phase of the nursing process, the nurse employs a number of strategies, including framing responses, metaphors, humor, confirming responses, reframing, providing relevant feedback, and validation. Each communication strategy is designed to foster mobilization of the client's inner strengths and natural healing powers. Sensitivity to the situation as well as to the client should frame all interventions.

Framing Responses

The nurse's basic responses to the client should match the client's message in level of depth, meaning, and language (Johnson, 1980). The client needs to lead the way to any exploration of deeper feeling. If the client makes a serious statement, the nurse should not respond with a flip remark. Likewise, a superficial statement does not warrant a profound discourse. Responses that correspond to the client's depth of feeling or that encourage a client to explore feelings about limitations or strengths at a slightly deeper level are likely to meet with more success.

To encourage a client to expose vulnerabilities and feelings before the client is ready to encounter them can be an irresponsible use of communication in a relationship. Newly diagnosed clients or clients who are struggling with realities that are strange, upsetting, and incompatible with their concept of self may need time to reflect before they are willing to share with another. Some clients, for example, choose to remain in a state of denial throughout a terminal illness. This is their choice, and it may be the right one for them.

When communicating with clients, the nurse's response should neither expand nor diminish the meaning of the client's remarks. Notice the differences in the nature of the following responses to a client:

CLIENT: I feel so discouraged. No matter how hard I try, I still can't walk without pain on the two parallel bars.

NURSE: You want to give up because you don't think you will be able to walk again?

The nurse's response adds meaning to the client's statement. At this point it is unclear that the client wants to give up. Although it is possible that this is what the client means, it is not the only possibility. The more important dilemma for the client may be whether or not her efforts have any purpose. The next response focuses only on the negative aspects of the client's communication.

> NURSE: So you think you won't be able to walk independently again.

In this statement, the meaning of the client's statement is diminished by the first part of the communication: The client's reference to her efforts with no results is ignored. Yet the relation of the client's efforts to her progress would appear to be a major theme in her message to the nurse.

In the third statement, both parts of the client's message are addressed in the nurse's comments, and the appropriate connection is made between them. By giving a complete response, the client is free to choose and develop the part of the communication that is more important to her.

> NURSE: It sounds to me as if you don't feel your efforts are helping you regain control over your walking.

The final match needed for successful communication relates to the client's ability to understand the nurse's language. Using jargon or a linguistic style that is beyond the client's educational level and experiential frame of reference generally means that little information will be retained. Unless the client is able to associate new ideas with familiar words and ideas, the nurse might as well be talking in a different language. Often clients will not inform the nurse that the vocabulary or presentation style is at too high a level for fear of offending her or of acknowledging their own sense of discomfort. By the same token, talking down to a client or giving information that fails to take into account the client's previous experiences also tends to fall on deaf ears.

Once the data base is established, the nurse can move easily between listening and responding modes of communication to accomplish the goals of the relationship. Underlying all feedback and information the nurse gives to the client is the need to take into account the client's unique personal set of circumstances as they exist in the here and now. Here is where the nurse uses creativity in choosing the most appropriate communication strategies for building and maintaining rapport. Some clients need a straightforward, concrete format. Others respond favorably to more imaginative formats.

Metaphors

Metaphors are teaching anecdotes in which one idea or object is substituted for another in a way that implies their similarity (Billings, 1991). They are abstractions that reframe a problem and allow a person to think and feel differently about it. People use metaphors all the time to describe personal characteristics: "happy as a lark," "pain in the neck," "sharp as a tack," "pillar of strength." Many children's stories build metaphors in developing their central theme, for example, *The Emperor with No Clothes* and *The Ugly Duckling.* In *The Tale of the Velveteen Rabbit,* the reader understands the process of becoming real through the metaphor of a young boy and his toy rabbit.

Metaphors are useful in health care settings to reduce tension and stimulate insight. The metaphor enables the client to view a difficult problem as outside the self. The mirroring capacity of the metaphor offers less threat than actual confrontation with difficult issues. The metaphor introduces a new perspective and provides the client with a foundation for learning new ways of functioning. To be maximally effective, the metaphor should mirror the client's concerns and suggest alternative solutions to the client's problems.

Reframing Situations

Reframing communication strategies are used to help clients modify their perspective and change their outlook, feelings, or emotional state. Reframing a situation expands the way a person thinks about it and changes the focus of the intervention (Pesut, 1991). The example of looking at life or a situation as a half-empty glass or a half-full glass captures the essence of reframing strategies. Reframing strategies originally developed from NLP and the human modeling processes proposed by Bandler and Grinder (1975): generalization, deletion, and distortion (see Chapter 1). An individual's use of these processes leaves out important pieces of data. Helping the client to make constructive shifts in the experiencing of this sensory data "reframes" the attitudes, values, and experiencing of a situation.

Steps in the reframing process call for the nurse to discover a positive or useful element in the client's situation. For example, the nurse might ask a seriously ill client if the illness has brought him closer to a family member or caused him to contact a faraway friend. Looking at a crisis as an opportunity for personal growth that might not have occurred otherwise is another example.

Another focus of reframing is to look for the aspect(s) of the situation that might be used to provide a different meaning. People assume that an action develops from motivations that they understand. This is not always true. The nurse might help the client to separate intention from behavior and to consider alternative explanations for motivation. For example, the reason a person fails to take medication or continues to drink alcohol may have little to do with the individual's significant others. Helping the family to see these behaviors as part of the client's symptoms and not as a commentary on the significant others helps reframe the situation and allows for needed detachment. It refocuses the internal dialogue.

Self-blame for illness or misfortune is a waste of time. Nothing can be done to change the past. Reframing strategies can modify the present. The client with a family history of serious heart problems risks the development of cardiac pathology no matter how well he takes care of himself. Helping the cardiac client acknowledge the relevance of his cardiac family history and what is and isn't within his power to change helps the client reduce taking undue responsibility for the current symptoms. At the same time, the nurse might point out that without the careful attention the client pays to his health, he might be dead instead of in the hospital. Reframing strategies emphasize client strengths and promote client control. The new meanings, co-created through interaction with another person, are thoughtfully designed to redefine unhealthy interpretations, conclusions, and attributions in ways that suggest positive actions. Alternative actions, based on the new information, are an essential component of reframing as a therapeutic intervention.

Humor

Feedback can be either serious or humorous, depending on the needs of the situation. Humor is a powerful communication technique when used with deliberate intent for a specific therapeutic purpose. It is not a clever assemblage of words to demonstrate the wit of the sender, nor should it be used as sarcasm. Sarcasm is humor with a twist that diminishes the humanity of a person. It is a dysfunctional use of humor in the nurse–client relationship. McGhee's (1985) definition of humor is, "The mental experience of discovering and appreciating ludicrous or absurdly incongruous ideas, events, or situations" (p. 6). A sense of humor, which most people have, is a form of social connection that enhances most relationships.

Often the surprise element in humor can cut through an overly intense situation. Humor has the capacity to encourage a sense of intimacy, acceptance, and warmth, which can reduce emotional distance in the nurse–client relationship (Lynch and Anchor, 1991). Laughter helps create natural highs by increasing the presence of B endorphin, a neurotransmitter agent known to stimulate positive chemical changes in the body that encourage healing (Cousins, 1976). Humor reframes an impossible situation by putting it into perspective. Once a person can appreciate the many absurdities and incongruities of life, the spirit lifts. For all of these reasons, humor plays an important role in therapeutic communication.

A good joke creates a distraction, but it needs the proper context. Humor is most effective when rapport is well established and a level of trust exists between the nurse and client. A shared joke becomes a bond and in some cases almost a password in well-established relationships. When humor is used, it should focus on the idea, event, situation, or something other than the client's humanity. Humor that ridicules is not funny. Occasional use of humor is more effective than constant use. Consistent use of humor can lead the client to minimize personal recognition of serious issues. It is up to the nurse to maintain the appropriate level of intensity and heightened interpersonal awareness in the relationship to help clients meet health goals. The following factors contribute to the successful use of humor:

- Knowledge of the client's response pattern.
- An overly intense situation.
- Timing.
- The client's developmental level.

It is essential that the nurse collect enough data on the client to have a working knowledge of how a humorous remark or joke might be received. Some clients respond well to humor; others are insulted or perplexed by it. They may not see it as appropriate or culturally acceptable in a helper–helpee relationship. Small children cannot relate to humor as well as adults because of their concrete thinking. Adolescents respond enthusiastically to some types of humor and can be emotionally devastated by other humorous remarks, particularly if the comments directly relate to them as persons.

Professional judgment is a critical factor in using humor a a strategy. Humor is less effective when the client is tired or emotionally vulnerable. But it is an effective tool to introduce therapeutic change when the client is emotionally immobilized. Humor can reduce aggression or tension in ways that a serious comment cannot. However, if the client is very frustrated or on the verge of losing control, humor may be inappropriate intervention. Instead, the client may need structure and calming support.

Confirming Responses

Confirming responses are designed to validate the client and enhance self-esteem. They respect and support the uniqueness of a client's experience. For example, the nurse might say to a mother reluctant to leave her small child, "It's hard for you to speak at a time like this" or, "I can see that it is hard for you to say goodnight to your little boy, knowing that he does not understand why you have to leave. Is there anything I can do to make it easier for you?" To the client who tells the nurse, "I know it is silly to worry about general anesthesia with one-day surgery. I don't know why I am so uptight about it," the nurse might say, "No, it is not silly; many people approach anesthesia with apprehension. Can you tell me more

about what worries you?" With each confirming response the nurse acknowledges the legitimacy of the client's feelings and invites the client to explore further the meaning of the message.

Communication that contradicts, minimizes, or denies the client's feelings lowers self-esteem and limits full disclosure (Heineken, 1982). Examples of disconfirming responses include giving a client reassurance without supporting data, discounting the client's perceptions or feelings, changing the topic of conversation abruptly, focusing on topics of little relevance to the client, and stating opinions as established facts.

CASE EXAMPLES

Nurse: Don't worry about leaving your little boy with us. We're quite capable of taking care of him.

Nurse: They hardly give you any anesthesia with one-day surgery, so I wouldn't worry about it.

Both responses disconfirm the validity of the client's feelings. In the first statement, the nurse assumes an understanding of the client's communicated feelings without validating them with her. The second response minimizes the impact of a new and potentially frightening surgical experience by suggesting that the client's feelings are foolish in light of the objective reality. The client is treated as an object and not as a person. For the client with a psychiatric disorder, confirming responses are particularly important. Such clients enter therapeutic relationships with a history of ineffective communication characterized by disconfirmation of the client as unique and worthy of respect (Heineken, 1982). Examples of disconfirming responses are given in Box 10–9.

Feedback

Feedback is a special form of giving information to another person about behaviors, actions, attitudes, and ideas. If offered in a supportive interpersonal environment, it can have a profound impact on the recipient's behavior. Helpful feedback is *descriptive* in nature. By simply describing one's reaction to a behavior and avoiding any evaluation of it, the receiver is free to use or discard the feedback. For example, the nurse might say to a noncompliant diabetic client,

---

BOX 10–9
Disconfirming Responses That Block Communication

Category of Response	Explanation of Category	Examples
False reassurance	Using pseudocomforting phrases in an attempt to offer reassurance.	"It will be okay." "Everything will work out."
Giving advice	Making a decision for a client. Offering personal opinions. Telling a client what to do; using phrases such as "ought to," "should do."	"I feel you should . . ." "If I were you I would . . ."
False inferences	Making an unsubstantiated assumption about what a client means. Interpreting the client's behavior without asking for validation. Jumping to conclusions.	"What you really mean is you don't like your doctor." "Subconsciously you are blaming your husband for the accident."
Moralizing	Expressing your own values about what is right and wrong, especially on a topic that concerns the client.	"Abortion is wrong." "It is wrong to refuse to have that operation."
Value judgments	Conveying your approval or disapproval about the client's behavior or about what client has said. using words such as "good," "bad," or "nice."	"I'm glad you decided to." "That really wasn't a nice way to behave." "She's a good patient."
Social responses	Polite superficial comments that do not focus on what the client is feeling or trying to say. Use of clichés.	"Isn't that nice?" "Hospital rules, you know." "Just do what the doctor says." "It's a beautiful day."

NURSE: I was disappointed when you didn't ask any questions about rotating sites for your insulin injection.

instead of,

NURSE: You should have asked questions about rotating sites if you didn't understand it.

With the first response the nurse expresses the nature of the relationship and a personal reaction to the client's noncompliance. The second response places all of the responsibility for noncompliance on the client, which may be appropriate in essence, but it is unlikely to activate behavioral change. Nor is it necessarily a valid assumption.

Effective feedback is *specific* rather than general. Telling a client he or she is shy or easily intimidated is less helpful than saying, "I noticed when the anesthesiologist was in here that you didn't ask her any of the questions you had about your anesthesia tomorrow." Precise information about an observed behavior can suggest a solution; a generalization about a wide range of behaviors cannot.

Timing of feedback is crucial for effectiveness. Generally, feedback given as soon as possible after a behavior is observed is most effectual. To be constructive, however, other variables, such as the person's readiness to hear feedback, the appropriateness of the environment for giving responses, and the availability of support from others, need to receive consideration.

Feedback should be *appropriate* to the needs of the situation and the client. A behavioral response that takes into account the needs of both the receiver and the giver of feedback is most fitting. For example, a very obese mother in the hospital was feeding her newborn infant 4 ounces of formula every four hours. She was very concerned because the infant vomited a considerable amount of the undigested formula following each feeding. Initially the nursing student gave the mother instructions about feeding the infant no more than 2 ounces at each feeding in the first few days of life, but the mother's behavior persisted, and so did that of her infant. The nursing student then began to assess the mother's relevant life experiences and discovered that the mother's mother had fed her 4 ounces right from birth with no problem. By considering the mother's past experience, the nurse was able to help the client correct misperceptions and take the necessary actions to feel comfortable and confident in feeding her infant.

Even though the feedback may be appropriate objectively in that it gives the receiver information, the interpersonal context or the information itself may not be appropriate. Information should not be imparted to the client if the client is too vulnerable to receive it, if unusual circumstances exist, or if the sender would have to reveal intimate material that would destroy the purposes of the relationship.

Feedback in the form of global comments is likely to be inaccurate. The client's behavior probably contains some but not all of the relevant behavioral actions subsumed under a category. The benchmark for deciding whether or not feedback is appropriate is to ask, "Does the feedback advance the goals of the relationship?" and, "Does it consider the individualized needs of both participants?" If the answers are no, the feedback may be accurate but inappropriate in the therapeutic relationship.

Usable feedback is perceived as interest and concern. Behavioral responses that address behaviors a person can do nothing about are likely to increase frustration. For example, telling a cardiac client in the hospital with his second heart attack, "You should have known better than to go back to work so soon" is informational feedback the client already knows and cannot use in his present situation. Similarly, it is not useful to tell a 350-pound client, "You should lose some weight." Surely the client is aware of her weight problem. Providing feedback about behaviors over which the client has little control only increases the client's feelings of low self-esteem.

As with other forms of proactive communication, feedback needs to be *clear and honest*. Feedback that expresses opinions as if they were facts and that uses "authorities" as evidence can impede communication. It is very difficult to refute "They say" or to argue with someone's opinion when it is expressed as a proven reality. Feedback is more acceptable when it is presented as accurately as possible in a supportive, responsible way, commensurate with the experience and education of the provider.

Feedback *presented by a nonthreatening knowledgeable resource* or trusted colleague will be believed, whereas the same feedback from a person without the credibility of interest, experience, and/or credentials is not accepted. For example, the same feedback given to the client by the client's wife and by his doctor may be accepted quite differently. Depending on the faith the client has in either party, one's feedback may be heard and acted upon whereas the other's may be discounted or ignored.

Reassurance supported by documentation is believable, whereas reassurance without documentation is perceived by many clients as unfeeling or lacking in credibility. To illustrate from your nursing school experience: If you were told that you would have no trouble passing any of the exams in nursing school, you would wonder if the statement was true. But if your instructor said, "Based on past performance and the fact that your score on the entrance exams was high, I think you should have little problem with our tests as long as you study," you would have more confidence in the statement.

Assumptions stated as facts are difficult for the client to respond to. When the nurse tells the client, "I know what you mean" without asking the client if the communication or situation has the same meaning for both, the nurse is making a global statement about something that may be quite specific. Use of the words "always" and "never" are misleading. Since most events in life fall somewhere between these two extremes, adopting a less certain attitude in communicative statements allows the client more flexibility in response.

Switching the topic or focus of the conversation tends to bring communication to a dead halt or to leave it at a superficial level. It also undermines the feelings of trust that develop when the nurse really wants to explore issues in depth with the client. Feedback is relevant only when it addresses the topics under discussion.

CASE EXAMPLE

A nursing student had a client with pancreatic cancer who was in considerable pain, so that even shaving required effort almost beyond his endurance. It was one of the first days of spring, and the weather was bright and sunny. The client said to the nurse, "I wish I were dead; there is nothing to live for." The nurse's response, "It's such a beautiful day, at least that should have some meaning" acted to disconfirm the meaning of the client's feeling and represented a complete switch in topic to one that had no connection with the ongoing subject. By responding to the client as she did, the nurse was ignoring the client's emotional needs and focusing on her own. The client became quite angry, and communication was paralyzed. In such a situation, the nurse who recognizes her own discomfort as the basis for making such a switch might apologize to the client, acknowledge her own discomfort, and refocus the conversation back onto the client's needs.

Validation

Validation is a special form of asking for feedback from a client. It is a way of checking out the accuracy of the message received by the nurse and of confirming that a given message sent by the nurse was received by the client in the manner intended (Fig. 10–2).

Usually any new information creates a certain amount of anxiety. The nurse should ask the client to validate each chunk of information directly after delivery. This rule of thumb is especially important for explanations of complex diagnostic and medical protocols. Asking the client, "How do you feel about what I just said?" or, "I'm curious what your thoughts are about what I just told you," or, "I wonder how you heard what I just said?" conveys to the client an expectation that new information has both a cognitive and affective impact on the client, which the nurse respects and

"I meant on *that* wall."

Figure 10–2 Validation Is a Way of Confirming the Message Sent Is the Same as the One Received! ("Laugh Parade,"® by Bunny Hoest and John Reiner. *Washington Post*, October 11, 1992)

is willing to help the client process. Even if the client initially indicates that the information has no effect, raising the issue as a normal response and as a legitimate part of learning new information leaves the door open for further discussion.

The nurse might follow the preliminary communication with the statement, "Many people do find they have reactions or questions about [the issue] after they have had a chance to think about it, and I would be glad to discuss them with you if you find you have some later on." Helping clients to assign meaning to new information and to acknowledge their feelings about it affirms the feeling of being emotionally understood and fosters the clients' sense of being a full participant in their care. It involves asking the client if the message the client communicated either verbally or behaviorally is the same as the one the nurse received. Also, validation is a communication technique that is used to allow clients an opportunity to express further feelings. It is not the same as asking the client a question that requires only a yes or no answer. Effective validation of an inference requires that nurses:

1. *Describe* the observed client *behavior(s)* (verbal and nonverbal).
2. *Verbalize* the client's *own perceptions* of the behavior's intended meaning, especially if the inference is made about hidden feelings.
3. Remain *nonjudgmental.*

Simply asking a client if he or she understands what was said is not an adequate method of validating message content. Nurses need to rephrase or verbally reflect back to the client their perceptions of what they hear and observe.

CASE EXAMPLE

Mr. Brown (to nurse taking his blood pressure): I can't stand that medicine. It doesn't set well. (*Grimaces and holds his stomach.*)

Nurse: Are you saying that your medication for lowering your blood pressure upsets your stomach?

Mr. Brown: No, I just don't like the taste of it.

Sometimes the validation is seen in the client's behavior. For example, after learning information about cancer risk factors, Mr. Goden stops smoking and increases his use of high-fiber cereals and breads.

An additional indirect method for validating accuracy of inference involves evaluating the types of questions the client asks. If the questions are relevant to the client education provided by the nurse, they can serve as an initial indicator of understanding.

CASE EXAMPLE

Following a diabetic diet instruction class, Mr. Oxam questions the nurse as to whether the potato served him at lunch was an equivalent exchange for the toast he ate at breakfast. The nurse has behavioral evidence that the client has a basic understanding of the concepts related to food exchanges in diabetic diets. However, Mr. Oxam may need further information and practice to make concrete applications in his life.

Using validation as an integral part of the communication process is essential to the success of the therapeutic relationship. It allows the client to confirm that the nurse's perception of what the client meant is correct. Different parts of the rela-

tionship will emphasize certain communication skills, as presented in Box 10–10.

Indirect Communication

Ideally, all communication should involve face-to-face contact. Interpretations lend themselves to distortion when facial expression is not available to help clarify the meaning of the message. When visualizing the speaker is not possible, nurses should consider how their words might be interpreted. Telephone conversations and messages delivered over the intercom can be misinterpreted by clients.

Direct communication with clients or family members is not always possible. The need to communicate in forms other than face-to-face interactions is more likely to occur at the beginning or near the end of the relationship. There may be times, for instance, when a nurse must end with a client, because of a sudden transfer, without being able to say good-bye. Or a child dies on an off shift and the nurse would like to share thoughts with

---

BOX 10–10
Interviewing and Relationship Skills

Phase	Stage	Purpose	Skills
1. Orientation phase	Rapport and structuring.	To build a working alliance with the client.	Basic listening and attending; information giving.
2. Assessment, engagement, and beginning active intervention phase	Gathering information, defining the problem, identifying strengths.	To determine how the client views the problem and what client strengths might be used in their resolution.	Basic listening and attending; open-ended questions, verbal cues, and leads.
3. Planning, active intervention phase	Determining outcomes. What needs to happen to reduce the self-care demand? Where does the client want to go?	To find out how the client would like to be. How would things be if the problems were solved?	Attending and basic listening; influencing; feedback.
4. Implementation, active intervention phase	Explaining alternatives and options.	To work toward resolution of the client's self-care demand.	Influencing; feedback balanced by attending and listening.
5. Evaluation, termination phase	Generalization and transfer of learning.	To enable changes in thoughts, feelings, and behaviors. To evaluate the effectiveness of the changes in modifying the self-care demand.	Influencing; feedback; validation. Validation; feedback.

Adapted from Ivey A (1983). Ivey's five stage model of interviewing. In Ivey A (1983), Intentional Interviewing and Counseling. Monterey, CA, Brooks/Cole. Richmond V, McCroskey J, Payne S (1987). Nonverbal Behavior in Interpersonal Relations. Englewood Cliffs, NJ, Prentice Hall.

the family. Telephoning the client or writing a note at least acknowledges the meaning of the relationship. When notes are necessary or messages must be given over the phone, the nurse should carefully consider possible interpretations of the message.

Indirect communication cues, such as the formality of the message, typed versus handwritten notes, or the nature of the closing remarks, may have an impact on the way the person at the other end interprets the message. The number of behavioral cues decreases as communication becomes removed from direct interpersonal contact. Phone calls represent a more distant way of communicating, whereas written communication is the most detached form of interpersonal contact. Even so, a written message is better than nothing when the interests of the relationship warrant it.

Frequently it is the nurse who calls the family when a client is near death or has died. Before making such a call the nurse should consider what the impact of the person's loss will be on the family member. Overestimating the meaning is preferable to underestimating it. When placing a call, the nurse first clarifies that the person on the other end of the line is the right significant other. Addressing the client's significant other by name centers the person. It is important to explain who you are and the reason for your call at the outset. Details are not given at this time. The nurse keeps communication simple while providing clear directives as to the next step. In calling a client's responsible significant other, the nurse might use the following format: "Hello, is this Mr. Peters? My name is Judy Cooper and I am a nurse at Bayley Hospital. Your son has been in an accident and was admitted to our emergency room. I know this must be a terrible shock to you, and I think it is important for you to come to the hospital as soon as possible. Are you familiar with the route to the hospital?"

If the family asks if the client has died, the nurse needs to answer truthfully. Other details are better discussed once the family has arrived on the unit. Nurses should make every effort to deliver bad news in person. Learning the details of a serious injury or the death of a relative with the direct support of hospital staff who were there is comforting. Nursing personnel can interpret baffling medical data and provide practical advice regarding the next steps in caring for the client and the family. If the client has died, the nurse represents an anchor and calming presence in the face of an overwhelming crisis (Jacob, 1991). Having an opportunity to see the client in death and being able to say good-bye in person is important to families. It allows natural closure on an important relationship.

Periodic informational phone calls are useful communication strategies to enhance family involvement in the long-term care of clients. Over time some families lose interest or find it too painful to continue active commitment. Interest and support from the nurse reminds families that they are not simply nonessential, interchangeable parts in their loved one's lives. Their input is important. Strategically placed phone calls designed to inform, not blame, reinforce and sustain the family–client connection. The call also serves as a reminder that the nurse is a resource to the family member as well as the client during difficult times.

SUMMARY

This chapter discusses communication strategies designed to enhance the interactional process between nurse and client and outlines the basic principles of successful communication. Application of communication strategies should fit the purposes of the relationship and the communication style of the nurse. Clarification is used to obtain more information when data are incomplete. Restatement is appropriate when a particular part of the content is needed. Paraphrasing addresses the content or cognitive component of the communication. Reflection is a technique used more specifically to get at the underlying feelings, or the affective part of the message.

Silence gives the client additional opportunity to clarify thoughts and to process information. Touch is a nonverbal strategy that underscores verbal understanding or is used in place of verbal expression when words would fail as a response to the deep of feeling expressed by the client.

Summarization integrates the content and feeling parts of the message by rephrasing two or more parts of the message. All of these techniques are intertwined and overlapping. Nurses who actively listen are able to paraphrase what the client has stated while at the same time tuning into the nonverbal aspects of the client's message, e.g., body language, eye contact, and other behaviors that support or contradict the verbal message.

Open-ended questions give the nurse the most information because they allow clients to express ideas and feelings as they are experiencing them. By contrast, focused and closed questions narrow the range of possible answers. They are most appropriate in emergency clinical situations when precise information is needed quickly.

The nurse as the source of communication uses another set of interpersonal skills. Basic responses should fit the client in terms of level, meaning, and language. Other strategies include use of metaphors, reframing, humor, confirming responses, feedback, and validation. Feedback provides a client with needed information. Validation is used as a perceptual check to ensure that the message given is the same as the one received.

Dialogue that validates the client as a person facilitates relationships between people. Giving reassurance without supportive data, changing the topic, or confining the discussion to superficial topics are considered blocks in the interactive process and prevent full disclosure.

REFERENCES

Adler R, Rodman G (1991). Understanding Human Communication (4th ed.). Fort Worth, TX, Holt, Rinehart and Winston.

Bandler R, Grindler J (1975). The Structure of Magic. Palo Alto, CA, Science and Behavior Books.

Barnlund D (1986). Toward a meaning centered philosophy of communication. In Stewart J (ed.) (1986), Bridges Not Walls (4th ed.). New York: Random House.

Barker L (1971). Listening Behavior. Englewood Cliffs, NJ, Prentice-Hall.

Barron J, Morrison E (1990). Answers professionally speaking. . . . When a relationship with a patient ceases to be therapeutic. Journal of Psychosocial Mental Health Nursing Services 28(10):42–43.

Berne M, Lerner HM (1992). Communicating with addicted women in labor. American Journal of Maternal Child Nursing 17(1):22–26.

Billings C (1991). Therapeutic use of metaphors. Issues in Mental Health Nursing. 12:1–8.

Birdwhistell R (1970). Kinesics and Context. Philadelphia, University of Pennsylvania.

Blondis M, Jackson B (1982). Nonverbal Communication with Patients: Back to the Human Touch (2nd ed.). New York, Wiley.

Brunau T (1973). Communicative silences: Forms and functions. Journal of Communication (23):17–46.

Brockopp D (1983). What is NLP? American Journal of Nursing (7):1012–1014.

Buber M (1970) I and Thou. New York, Scribner's.

Buckman R (1992). How to Break Bad News: A Guide for Health Care Professionals. Baltimore, Johns Hopkins University Press.

Burgoon J, Buller D, Hale J, and Deturk M (1984). Relational messages associated with nonverbal behaviors. Human Communications Research (10):351–378.

Burnside I (1973). Touching is talking. American Journal of Nursing 73(12):2060–2063.

Carr J (1984). Communicating and Relating. Dubuque, IA, William C. Brown, pp. 322–323.

Charkhuff R (1983). The Art of Helping (5th ed.). Amherst, MA, Human Resources Development Press.

Cohen MR (1991). Why good communication is so important. Nursing 21(6).

Corey G (1982). Theory and Practice of Counseling and Psychotherapy (2nd ed.). Monterey, CA, Brooks/Cole, p. 240.

Cormier L, Cormier W, Weisser R (1984). Interviewing and Helping Skills for Health Professionals. Monterey, CA, Wadsworth.

Cousins N (1976). Anatomy of an illness. New England Journal of Medicine 295(26):1458–1463.

Cox M (1988). Structuring the Therapeutic Process. London, Kingsley Press.

Crowther DJ (1991). Metacommunications: A missed opportunity? Journal of Psychosocial Nursing and Mental Health Services 29(4):13–16.

Duldt B (1991). I–Thou in nursing: Research supporting Duldt's theory. Perspectives in Psychiatric Care 27(3):5–12.

Edwards K (1991). The importance of good nurse/client communication. Nursing Standard 5(37):13.

Egan G (1982). The Skilled Helper. Monterey, CA, Brooks/Cole.

Ekman P (1972). Universals and cultural differences in facial expressions of emotion. In Cole J (ed.) (1972), Nebraska Symposium on Motivation, pp. 207–283.

Ekman P (1976). Movements with precise meanings. Journal of Communication (22):14–26.

Ekman P, Friesen W (1971). Constants across cultures in the face and emotion. Journal of Personality and Social Psychology (17):124–129.

Ekman P, Friesen W (1975). Unmasking the Face: A Guide to Recognizing Emotions from Facial Clues. Englewood Cliffs, NJ, Prentice-Hall.

Farrell G, Salmon P (1989). Communication: Caring expressions. Nursing Standard 3(41).

Furman B, Tapani A (1992). Solution Talk: Hosting Therapeutic Communications. New York, Norton.

Gale J (1991). Conversation Analysis of Therapeutic Discourse: The Pursuit of a Therapeutic Agenda. Norwood, NJ, Ablex Publishing Co.

Gardener J (1992). Presence. *In* Bulechek G, McCloskey J (eds.) (1992), Nursing Interventions: Essential Nursing Treatments. Philadelphia, W. B. Saunders.

Granger B (1992). Talking to Theresa. Nursing 22(3):120.

Hall E (1959). The Silent Language. New York, Doubleday.

Heineken J (1982). Disconfirmation in dysfunctional communication. Nursing Research 31(4):211–213.

Heineken J (1983). Treating the disconfirmed psychiatric client. Journal of Psychosocial Nursing 21(1)21–25.

Hodson P (1991). Communication: A listening ear. Nursing Times 87(6):30–1.

Hiakawa SI (1941). Language in Action. New York, Harcourt, Brace.

Jacob S (1991). Support for family caregivers in the community. Family and Community Health 14(1):16–21.

Johnson M (1980). Self disclosure: A variable in the nurse–client relationship. Journal of Psychiatric Nursing 18(1):17–20.

Kannah A (1991). The need to communicate. Nursing Standard 5(5):19–21.

Kasch C (1984). Interpersonal competence and communication in the delivery of nursing care. Advances in Nursing Science 71–88.

Knapp M, Hall J (1992). Nonverbal Communication in Human Interaction. Fort Worth, TX, Holt, Rinehart and Winston.

Knowles RD (1983). Building rapport through neuro-linguistic programming. American Journal of Nursing 83(7):1010–1014.

Kramer S, Akhtar S (eds.) (1992). When the Body Speaks: Psychological Meanings in Kinetic Clues. Northvale, NJ, Arons.

Krieger M (1975). Therapeutic touch: The imprimatur of nursing. American Journal of Nursing. 75(5):784.

Leathers D (1986). Successful Nonverbal Communication: Principles and Applications. New York, Macmillan.

Leebov W (1991). Handling phone calls effectively. Nursing 21(9):98, 100–101.

Leininger M (1991). Culture Care Diversity and Universality: A Theory of Nursing. New York, National League for Nursing Press.

Littlejohn S (1989). Theories of Human Communication (3rd ed.). Belmont, CA, Wadsworth.

Livingston S (1991). Watch your language. Nursing Standard 5(20):11.

Loos F, Bell J (1990). Circular questions: A family interviewing strategy. Dimensions of Critical Care Nursing 9(1):47.

Lynch T, Anchor K (1991). Use of humor in medical psychotherapy. *In* K. Anchor (ed.), Handbook of Medical Psychotherapy. Lewiston, NY, Hogrefe & Huber.

Mahoney M (1993). Theoretical developments in the cognitive psychotherapies. Journal of Consulting and Clinical Psychology 61(2):187–193.

McGhee M (1985). Humor. *In* Snyder M (1985), Independent Nursing Functions. New York, Wiley.

McKaru L (1991). Therapeutic use of self: Emphasis. Nursing 1(1):73–77.

McCroskey J, Richmond V, Stewart R (1986). One to One: The Foundations of Interpersonal Communication. Englewood Cliffs, NJ, Prentice Hall.

McKinney S (1992). The nurse who listened. Nursing 22(5):71.

Miller C (1990). Understanding the psychosocial challenges of older adulthood. Imprint 37(4):67–69.

Moustakas C (1974). Finding Yourself: Finding Others. Englewood Cliffs, NJ, Prentice-Hall.

Peplau H (1960). Talking with patients. American Journal of Nursing 60(7):964–966.

Pesut D (1991). The art, science, and techniques of reframing in psychiatric mental health nursing. Issues in Mental Health 12(1):9–18.

Ramos MC (1992). The nurse–patient relationship: Theme and variation. Journal of Advanced Nursing 17(4):196–206.

Renwick P (1992). Teaching the use of interpersonal skills. Nursing Standard 7(9):31–34.

Richmond V, McCroskey J, Payne S (1987). Nonverbal Behavior in Interpersonal Relations. Englewood Cliffs, NJ, Prentice Hall.

Rogers C (1951). Client-Centered Therapy. Boston: Houghton Mifflin.

Ruesch J (1961). Therapeutic Communication. New York, Norton, p. 32.

Ruesch J, Bateson G (1951). Communication. New York, Norton.

Severtsen BM (1990). Therapeutic communication demystified. Journal of Nursing Education 29(1): 190–192.

Stewart J (ed.) (1986). Bridges Not Walls (4th ed.). New York, Random House.

Tamparo C, Wilburta L (1992). Therapeutic Communications for Allied Health Professions. Albany, NY, Delmar Publishers.

Tannen D (1991). You Just Don't Understand: Women and Men in Conversation. New York, Balantine, Preface.

Wachtel P (1993). Principles of Therapeutic Communication. New York, Guilford Press.

Weingarten K (1992). A consideration of intimate and non-intimate interactions in therapy. Family Process 31:45–59.

Williams J (1991). Meaningful dialogue. Guidelines for

effective communication with elderly patients. Nursing Times 87(4):52–53.

SUGGESTED READINGS

Adler R, Rosenfeld L, Towne N (1986). Interplay: The Process of Interpersonal Communication (3rd ed.). New York: Holt, Rinehart and Winston.

Baxter J (1970). Interpersonal spacing in natural settings. Sociometry (33):444–546.

Chisolm M (1991). Communication: Roots within nursing. Clinical Nurse Specialist 5(3):169.

Corey G (1982). Theory and Practice of Counseling and Psychotherapy (2nd ed.). Monterey, CA, Brooks/Cole, p. 240.

Cosper B (1977). How well do patients understand hospital jargon? American Journal of Nursing (12):1932–1934.

Cox M (1988). Coding the Therapeutic Process: Emblems of Encounter. London, Kingsley Publishers.

Druckman D, Rozelle R, Baxter J (1982). Nonverbal Communication: Survey, Theory and Research. Beverly Hills, CA, Sage Publications.

Duncan E (1991). Listening: A communication. Psychoanalytic Review 78(1):127–133.

Friedman H, DiMatteo M (1979). Health care as an interpersonal process. Journal of Social Issues 35(1):1–11.

Goldsborough J (1969). Involvement. American Journal of Nursing (69):66–68.

Hall E (1969). The Hidden Dimension. Garden City, NY, Anchor Books.

Hamid P (1968). Style of dress as a perceptual cue in impression formation. Perceptual and Motor Skills (26):904–906.

Heslin R, Alper T (eds.) (1983). Nonverbal Communication. Beverly Hills, CA, Sage Publications.

Knapp M (1984). Interpersonal Communication and Human Relationships. Boston, MA, Allyn and Bacon.

Lickee L, Perel, I, Wallace CJ, Davis J (1976). It's the staff that keeps the patients talking. Journal of Psychiatric and Mental Health Services (5):11–14.

Lynch T, Anchor K (1991). Use of humor in medical psychotherapy. Handbook of Medical Psychotherapy: Cost-Effective Strategies in Mental Health. Toronto: Hogrefe & Huber.

Kriekorian D, Paulanaka B (1982). Self awareness—the key to a successful nurse–patient relationship? Journal of Psychosocial Nursing 20(6):19–21.

Leininger M (1991). Culture Care Diversity and Universality: A Theory of Nursing. New York, National League for Nursing Press.

Lore A (1970). Nursing students help children express their feelings. Journal of Nursing Education (1):39–43.

Mallandro L, Barker L (1983). Nonverbal Communication. Reading, MA, Addison-Wesley.

Mehrabian A (1971). Silent Messages. Belmont, CA, Wadsworth.

Mehrabian A (1972). Nonverbal Communication. Chicago, Aldine-Atherton.

Meyerscough P (1992). Talking with Patients: A Basic Clinical Skill. New York, Oxford.

Miller FE, Rogers LA (1976). A relational approach to interpersonal communication. In Miller G (ed.) (1976), Explorations in Interpersonal Communication. Beverly Hills, CA, Sage Publications, pp. 87–103.

Montagu A (1978). Touching. New York, Harper & Row.

Moustakas C (1974). Finding Yourself: Finding Others. Englewood Cliffs, NJ, Prentice-Hall.

Pazola KJ, Gerberg AK (1990). Privileged communication—Talking with a dying adolescent. MCN: American Journal of Maternal Child Nursing 15(1):16–21.

Petrello J (1969). Your patients hear you, but do they understand? RN (2):37–42.

Ray B (ed.) (1992). Case Studies in Health Communication. Hillsdale NJ, Erlbaum.

Reik T (1972). Listening with the Third Ear. New York, Pyramid.

Rosenfeld L, Plax T (1977). Clothing as communication. Journal of Communication (27):24–31.

Ruggiero V (1975). Beyond Feelings: A Guide to Critical Thinking. New York, Alfred Publishing Co.

Seegar P (1977). Self-awareness and nursing. Journal of Psychiatric Nursing (8):24–26.

Shanken W, Shanken P (1976). How to be a helping person. Journal of Psychiatric Nursing and Mental Health Services (2):24–28.

Sheflen A (1964). The significance of posture in communication systems. Psychiatry (27):316–331.

Stewart J (1974). Clear interpersonal communication. In Cathcart R, Samovar L (eds.) (1974), Small Group Communication: A Reader. Dubuque, IA, William C. Brown.

Tilden P, Porter K (1978). Manifest and latent content in communication: Genesis of an instructional module in psychiatric nursing. Journal of Nursing Education (4):11–16.

Veninga R (1973). Communications: A patient's eye view. American Journal of Nursing (73):320–322.

Watzlawick P, Beavin J, Jackson D (1967). Pragmatics of Human Communication. New York, Norton.

Wieman J, Knapp M (1975). Turn-taking in conversations. Journal of Communication (25):75–92.

Zderad L (1969). Empathetic nursing. Nursing Clinics of North America (4):655–662.

Chapter 11

Intercultural Communication

ELIZABETH ARNOLD

OBJECTIVES

At the end of the chapter, the student will be able to:

1. Define culture and describe related terminology.

2. Identify a nursing framework for the study of culturally congruent nursing care.
3. Discuss the concept of intercultural communication.
4. Apply the nursing process to the care of the culturally diverse client.
5. Discuss characteristics of selected cultures as they relate to the nurse–client relationship.

If we are to achieve a richer culture, rich in contrasting values, we must recognize the whole gamut of human potentialities, and so weave a less arbitrary social fabric, one in which each diverse human gift will find a fitting place.

Mead, 1935

The focus of this chapter is the interpersonal context that surrounds the nurse and client who come from different cultures. Culture is primarily a social concept. Nurses interact with large numbers of clients with different individual characteristics and from a variety of cultural backgrounds. This chapter offers guidelines for interacting with the culturally diverse client. The chapter develops basic characteristics of the African-American, Hispanic, Asian, and Native-American cultures and those associated with the culture of poverty. The nurse's ability to understand the fundamental customs and practices of different cultures determines the effectiveness of his or her care.

The U.S. population is changing, and health care consumers increasingly are people of color. Recent estimates indicate that by the year 2000, more than 25 percent of the American population will consist of people of color and will include approximately six million more immigrants (DHHS, 1991). The health care system will have to redirect its focus from the white middle class to serve clients from many different backgrounds who speak many different languages. It will also have to respond to recent, unprecedented social changes in the dominant culture. The emergence of new roles for men and women; far-ranging economic uncertainty; and increases in the number of single-parent families, in the elderly population, and in poverty-stricken populations add to the diversity of the health care consumer.

To be an effective communicator with culturally diverse clients, the nurse must assume a more proactive role. Basic to intervention is an understanding of the different social structures and norms that shape the clients' values and behaviors. Such knowledge helps the nurse examine unfamiliar behavior patterns without dismissing or devaluing them. Communication competence with culturally diverse clients requires appropriate ways of speaking to the clients and a knowledge of culturally congruent ways to manage intercultural health care events.

BASIC CONCEPTS

DEFINITION

Leininger (1977) defines *culture* as "a common collectivity of beliefs, values and shared understandings and patterns of behavior of a designated group of people." Culture provides the community with its strength and vitality. It needs to be viewed as a human structure with many variations in meaning (Westbrook and Sedlacek, 1991). Each cultural community develops fundamental standards of behavior that differentiate those who "belong" and those who are outsiders. Personal patterns of emotional expression, language, child-rearing practices, values, rules, and even physical objects such as dress and equipment trace their origin to cultural experience. They contribute to the development of a cultural worldview that includes the individual's perceptions of his or her relationship with the larger community (Sue, 1978). Differences in cultural expectations, ways of being in the world, and meanings can partially account for the individual behavior patterns found in clinical events. As Shweder (1991) notes, "When people live in the world differently, it may be that they live in different worlds" (Exercise 11–1).

CHARACTERISTICS OF CULTURE

Culture is a *learned social experience*. Primary cultural behavior patterns are handed down from generation to generation. People interpret reality and present themselves through a continuous connectedness with others in their community that grounds their life experience. Over time, norms become established that direct behavior in culturally defined ways. These norms provide safety and security for the community. A person within the culture is respected and treated as an equal, whereas one who is not a part of the culture is treated with misgivings and suspicion.

EXERCISE 11–1
The Meaning of Culture

Purpose: To help students appreciate the many dimensions of culture.

Time: 45 minutes

Procedure:
Frequently the attitudes, feelings, and understandings people have about a culture are found in the words they associate with that culture.
1. Think about the word "culture" and write down all of the words and phrases you can think of in response to the word. There are no right or wrong answers.
2. Assign a negative (–) sign to the words you perceive might have a negative value. Assign a positive (+) sign to the words you perceive might have a positive value. Do not assign any value to words you perceive as being without a value.
3. Share your results with the other members of your class group.

Discussion:
1. Were you surprised at any of the words that popped into your mind?
2. What does your list tell you about your attitudes and feelings about culture?
3. In what ways were your words and phrases similar or different from those of your classmates?
4. In what ways did your answers reflect your own cultural background?
5. How could you use the information you gained from doing this exercise to provide culturally congruent care?

CASE EXAMPLE

Mohan is an Asian nursing student trying to cope in an American society characterized by autonomy, self-assertiveness and self-disclosing responsiveness. By contrast with American students, Mohan seems nonaggressive and doesn't always act in his own best interest. Sometimes he is late for class, and he is guarded, by American standards, in what he reveals about himself. Viewed from an Asian perspective, Mohan's behavior is not at all unusual. In India, the individual does not seek personal attention. Each person is part of the larger cosmos, and seeks to blend harmoniously with traditions and the community. Achievements count, but it is culturally incorrect to view them as part of a personal identity. (Kakar, 1991)

Multiculturalism

Multiculturalism describes a heterogeneous society in which diverse cultural worldviews can coexist with some general ("etic") characteristics shared by all cultural groups and some ("emic") perspectives that are unique to a particular group. Combining the two perspectives provides the multicultural perspective. The term "implies a wide range of multiple groups without grading, comparing, or ranking them as better or worse than one another and without denying the very distinct and complementary or even contradictory perspectives that each group brings with it" (Pederson, 1991b, p. 4). Since today's global social environment is characterized by rapidly changing demographics and an increasingly interdependent world economy, the term "multiculturalism" seems fitting (Exercise 11–2).

RELATED TERMINOLOGY

Acculturation

Culture represents an *adaptive process*. As the social environment and biological needs of a people change, so do the traditional forms of the culture. For example, the adult children of a second-generation Vietnamese living in America are likely to demonstrate a watered-down loyalty to traditional Vietnamese values. Likewise, changes from a rural lifestyle to an urban lifestyle require for survival a significant modification in cultural values. The process by which a person consciously learns and accepts the values of a new culture is referred to as *acculturation* (Exercise 11–3).

EXERCISE 11–2
An Appreciation of Cultural Behaviors within the Dominant Culture

Purpose: To help students appreciate the cultural components of everyday life.

Time: 45 minutes

Procedure:
1. Describe a formal social group to which you belong. Examples include religious, ethnic, work, professional, social, neighborhood, and school groups.
2. Identify specialized "norms" in the group culture related to dress, time, expression of role, language, values, and expected behaviors.
3. How does a person become a member of this culture?
4. What are some of the advantages and disadvantages of being a member of this group?
5. How would a person violate the group customs, and what would be the consequences?

Discussion:
1. Are there any special symbols, dress, or language that are shared with others in the cultural group?
2. As you discuss the advantages and disadvantages of being a member of this group with your class group, what common themes do you see?
3. What new information did you learn about the effects of culture on group behaviors?
4. What did you learn from this exercise that can help you communicate more effectively with culturally different clients?

Subculture

Subculture is defined as an ethnic, regional, or economic group of people joined by distinguishing characteristics that differentiate the group from the predominant culture or society (Samovar and Porter, 1988). Examples of subcultures in the United States include Amish, Appalachians, Jehovah's Witnesses, Hare Krishnas, the homeless, and migrant workers. Although the cultural differences of these groups might not seem pronounced, meaningful communication can be difficult because the communication of subcultures reflects the cultural meaning the groups attach to the content of a message. Communication that is not understood and is negatively distorted can be worse than that which never occurred.

Cultural Diversity

Cultural diversity describes the fact that there are differences among cultural groups. Diversity is becoming the norm in our society rather than the

EXERCISE 11–3
Cultural Experiences

Purpose: To help students appreciate how culture is learned.

Time: 45 minutes

Procedure:
1. Identify and describe one family custom or tradition. It can relate to special family foods, a holiday custom, a or child-rearing practice.
2. Describe the custom or tradition in detail.
3. Ask your parent or a grandparent where the custom came from.
4. If the custom or tradition has undergone change, ask why it has changed.

Discussion:
1. Share your family tradition with your classmates.
2. Discuss how knowledge of family customs can influence health care promotion.

exception. It can include such variables as nationality, ethnic origin, gender, educational background, geographic location, economic status, language, politics, and religion (Pederson, 1991a).

Diversity also occurs within the same community—for example, age or work cultures. Situations that are culturally significant to adolescents and young adults may not have the same meaning to their grandparents, and vice versa. Such gaps also occur within a work culture. For example, acknowledgment of diversity in health care settings can mean different levels of personnel (physician, social worker, ward clerk, nurse, and physical therapist), which can affect decision making and task allocation. These differences are aspects of cultural diversity that are not usually considered relevant, but to overlook their importance is a mistake.

The fact that people are different from one another in culturally specific ways is not important to the development and maintenance of a therapeutic relationship. What is very important is for nurses to understand, acknowledge, and respect these differences in the nurse–client relationship. Having this understanding can mean the difference between success and failure in providing effective nursing care (Tripp-Reimer, Brink, and Saunders, 1984).

Cultural Relativism

Cultural relativism refers to the belief that cultures are neither inferior nor superior to one another and that there is no single scale for measuring the value of a culture. Furthermore, cultural behaviors change as people within a culture come into contact with "outsiders" and blend their cultural beliefs with those outside the original culture.

Within a culture there are many variations in behaviors and in how individuals interpret their cultural heritage. In fact, there may be more individual differences among members of the same culture than there are among dissimilar cultures. Bromwich (1992) notes, "An artist, of any race or sex or ethnic identity, has more in common with other artists, however remote, than with other members of the same 'cultural' group." This point has implications for the nurse–client relationship in that the individualized needs of the client should determine the degree to which cultural

variations require modifications of the treatment plan. For some clients, the modifications mandated by culture will be extensive; for others, an understanding of sensitive issues is sufficient. Customs, beliefs, and practices must be understood in context and according to the needs of each client.

Ethnicity

The word "ethnic" derives from the Greek word *ethnos,* meaning "people." An *ethnic group* is a social grouping of people who share a common racial, geographic, religious, or historical culture. Ethnicity is different from culture in that it represents a personal awareness of certain symbolic elements that bind people together in a social context. In contrast to culture, which does not always involve a conscious awareness of norms and symbols, ethnicity is a chosen awareness and commitment to a cultural identity. In the United States, common ethnic groups include African-American, Native American, Hispanic, Asian, Indian, Jewish, Irish, Italian, and Amish. Ethnic identity is very meaningful to people, and it is important to them to have their ethnic differences recognized and valued by the dominant culture.

Ethnic norms and values play an important role in the personalized meaning of symptoms and in the client's responses to treatment. Behaviors considered healthy and acceptable in one culture may be viewed as dysfunctional in other cultures. For example, seeking professional treatment to achieve personal growth or to resolve problems of daily living is acceptable in the United States, but an Asian family would consider seeking treatment to improve mental health a disgrace.

Ethnocentrism

Ethnocentrism refers to a belief that one's own culture is superior to others (Leininger, 1977). It is fine to be proud of one's culture, but ethnocentrism narrows effective communication with people from other cultures. It can turn into prejudice without a person's being aware of it. Ethnocentrism is sometimes used to justify treating persons within one's own culture with favor and behaving in a derogatory manner toward others. The deadly extremes of ethnocentrism were apparent in the Nazi persecution of the Jews in the name of the

Aryan race during Hitler's regime. Similar perse-cutions for ethnic reasons are ongoing today in parts of Europe and the Middle East. But ethno-centrism occurs daily on a smaller scale with the physically or mentally disabled, the urban poor, the homeless, persons with AIDS, and certain minority groups. The culture of poverty and the social stigma of AIDS preclude access to health care for some people and result in a low level of health care for many others. Age and racial dis-crimination are subtle forms of ethnocentrism that add to the feelings of devaluation and inferi-ority experienced by minority members of a dom-inant culture. Although not described as a typi-cally cultural phenomenon, the following human perspective carries many of the values of ethno-centrism.

CASE EXAMPLE

I knew a man who had lost the use of both eyes. He was called a "blind man." He could also be called an expert typist, a conscientious worker, a good student, a careful listener, a man who wanted a job. But he couldn't get a job in the department store order room where employees sat and typed orders which came over the phone. The personnel man was impatient to get the interview over. "But you are a blind man," he kept saying and one could almost feel his silent assumption that somehow the inca-pability in one aspect made the man incapable in every other. So blinded by the label was the interviewer that he could not be persuaded to look beyond it. (Lee, quoted in Allport, 1982)

This case example shows how a small part of a complex human reality can replace individual characteristics with stereotyped impressions. When the stereotyped label corresponds to undesirable personal traits, whether the deviation from the norm has a cultural, physical, or psychological ori-gin, the person is at a distinct disadvantage because of the implied negative value judgments. To coun-teract this tendency, Allport (1982) suggests using ethnic labels as adjectives rather than nouns. Thus the nurse would speak of the "person of color" rather than "the African American." Recognizing implied value judgments and taking the time to be sensitive to the subtle interpretations of value-laden ethnic terms in conversation can prevent misunderstanding and hurt feelings. To provide quality care for clients from different cultures, the nurse must make a conscious effort to see each client as a unique individual with many complex characteristics, one of which happens to be differ-ent from those of the majority norm. Exercise 11–4 makes it easier to see the prevalence of stereotypes.

Ethnography

Ethnography is a qualitative research approach that seeks to study and understand culturally spe-cific human behavior by describing what people know and do. Instead of using quantitative statis-tical measures, the ethnographic researcher asks questions of people and elicits themes from the data that describe the meaning of behavior from the individual's perspective.

THEORETICAL FRAMEWORK

Leininger's (1991) Sunrise Model is used to por-tray a nursing theory of cultural care diversity and universality (see Fig. 11–1). The model incorpo-rates all of the cultural factors that influence health care expressions and practices related to a client's health and well-being. The interaction among these factors takes place in a wide variety of health care settings, ranging from informal folk medicine to professional systems of care. The nurse–client relationship frequently acts as an interpersonal bridge between health care systems, with the nurse providing nursing care that integrates valued cul-tural remedies with the modern sophistication of professional care systems. Nursing care decisions represent a mixture of preserving positive cultural home remedies and negotiating to accommodate client and family requests without compromising essential treatment. Examples of accommodation include attention to religious practices, cultural food preferences, and requests for additional fam-ily contacts.

INTERCULTURAL COMMUNICATION

Samovar and Porter (1988) define *intercultural communication* as a communication in which the sender of an intended message is a member of one culture and the receiver of the message is from a different culture. Different languages create and express different personal realities. Many experts note that language has four primary functions:

EXERCISE 11–4
Exploring Stereotypes

Purpose: To help students examine the prevalence and different types of ethnic, racial, and social issues present in our society.

Time: 45 minutes

We learn about people who are different from us by many methods. Stereotypes are negative or positive attitudes, which are transmitted by family members, friends, religious institutions, schools, the media, and popular culture. Usually we don't know where our attitudes come from because they come from so many different sources (Eliason and Macy, 1992).

Procedure:

The first part of this exercise should be written at home, anonymously, to encourage honest answers. The following list represents some of the groups in our society that carry familiar value-laden stereotypes.

American Indians	People on welfare
African Americans	Teenage mothers
Asians	AIDS victims
Hispanics	Migrant workers
Homosexual men	The elderly
Lesbians	People with sensory deficits
The homeless	Mentally ill persons

1. Write down the first three words or phrases that come into your mind regarding each of these groups.
2. Make a grid to show stereotypes. Use three columns, with each cultural group. On the vertical column at the left, list positive, neutral, and negative connotations at the top.
3. As a class group, take the collected words and phrases and decide whether they represent one or more culturally specific connotations. Place each word or phrase under the appropriate column for each group. Use an X to indicate repetitive words or phrases.

Discussion:

For each cultural group, consider the following:

1. Why do you think people believe that this cultural group possesses these characteristics?
2. What were the common themes of these groups? Did certain groups have more negative than positive responses? If so, how would you account for this?
3. In what ways did this exercise help you to think about your own cultural socialization process?
4. Did doing this exercise cause you to question any of your own assumptions about culturally different values?
5. From your view, what implications do these stereotypes hold for providing appropriate nursing care?
6. How can you use this exercise in your future care of culturally different populations?

Adapted from Eliason M, Macy N (1992). A classroom activity to introduce cultural diversity. Nurse Educator 17(3):32–35.

(1) to direct actions, (2) to interpret the meaning of events and situations, (3) to connect past experiences with the present through imagination, and (4) to establish and maintain relationships with people. These functions are woven into the fabric of every culture. Customary ways of thinking and categorizing situations affect how a person experiences and responds to situations. People name objects, situations, events, qualities, and feelings in their own language symbols. Socially acceptable and adaptive behaviors are reinforced through language. Human cooperation, achieved best through verbal communication, consists of understanding a person's motivations and responding to them in a relevant way. Through language, people begin to understand the intentions of others and are better able to make their intentions known to others (Littlejohn, 1989). Meanings develop from social interactions in the present, and their interpretation is influenced by significant interpersonal experiences from the past.

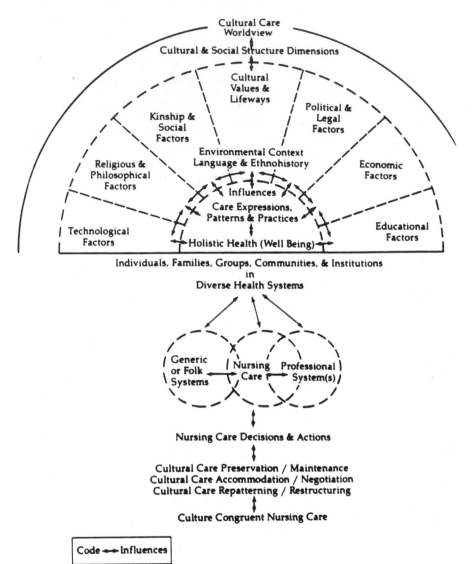

Figure 11–1 Leininger's Sunrise Model to Depict the Theory of Cultural Care Diversity and Universality. From Leininger M (ed.) (1991). Cultural Care Diversity and Universality: A Theory of Nursing. New York, National League for Nursing.

Thus, cultural differences in language affect every aspect of the behavior and relationships that occur between nurses and their clients and can function as a major barrier to mutual understanding (Geissler, 1991a). Breakdowns in communication can occur because one of the parties does not understand the cultural context and misinterprets the message, the relationship, or the emotions surrounding it (Primeaux, 1977). Subtle but important language differences can color the meaning of words and concurrently can change the understanding of related life experiences. It is essential to use clear, precise language and to avoid slang and clichés with clients who display limited English skills.

CASE EXAMPLE

A nursing student from the Philippines said she was thoroughly confused by her instructor's slang expression, "I want to touch base with you." The student did not know how to respond, because her literal translation of the sentence did not express its meaning to her. Had the instructor said, "I would like to talk with you," the student would have known how to respond.

Ease of understanding the language and knowledge of culturally relevant teaching strategies also play a significant role in the learning process. When teaching does not take into consideration the client's cultural strengths and language limitations, the client often does not comprehend the meaning of the nurse's communication, and part or all of the teaching is lost. Because the content is difficult to absorb, or is considered irrelevant, less attention is paid to it. Strategies the nurse can use include using pictures and developing "flash cards" with commonly used hospital terms such as "pain," "medicine," "bathroom," "can't sleep," "hungry," "hot," "cold," "doctor," and so on, with the words in the client's language written beside them (Thompson, Thompson, and House, 1990). Learning a few specific words related to the client's health care in the client's language and teaching the client some simple English words to express needs also helps. Exercise 11–5 can help you experience language differences.

Intercultural communication is more than simply an issue of language translation. Cultural interpretations of illness, behaviors, and symptom expressions are important considerations. So are issues related to traditions about treatments, family hierarchy, and decision making in each culture. Sometimes the cultural differences are striking, involving language, dress, diet, and behavioral styles that are completely foreign to the nurse. At

EXERCISE 11–5
Understanding Language Barriers

Purpose: To help students understand the role of language barriers in health care.

Time: 45 minutes

Procedure:

Situation 1

Lee Singh is a 24-year-old Korean patient who speaks no English. She was admitted to the maternity unit and has just delivered her first child, a 9-pound infant. It was a difficult labor because the baby was so big. Lee Singh speaks no English. The initial objectives of the health care providers are to help the client understand what is happening to her and to help her become comfortable with her baby.

Situation 2

Jose Perot is a 30-year-old Hispanic male who was admitted to the emergency department with multiple injuries following a car accident. His family has been notifed, but the nurse is not sure they understand what has happened. They have just arrived in the emergency room.

1. Break up into two groups of four or five students. Each group acts as a unit. The groups role play situation (1) and reverse roles for situation (2).
2. The *client group* should completely substitute bogus words that only they understand for the words they would normally use in the situation. The bogus words should have the same meaning to all members of the client group.
3. The *health provider group* must figure out creative ways to understand and communicate with the client group.

Discussion:
1. In what ways was it different being the client and being the health provider group?
2. What was the hardest part of this exercise?
3. In what ways did this exercise help you understand the frustrations of being unable to communicate?

other times, variations are more subtle, perhaps involving the meaning of a gesture, the interpretation of a remark, consciousness of space and time, or the role of self in the larger community. An educated nurse consciously incorporates knowledge of the client's culture into every interaction.

Even if a person has been in a country for a long time, original cultural values and norms continue to remain important in a client's life. It is not unusual for a client and family members for whom English is a second language to revert to their native language in times of stress (Thompson, Thompson, and House, 1990). Conversation slows because the person is trying to have two conversations, one with the interviewer and one within himself or herself about the meaning of the message. Although words and phrases are expressed in English, they are translated into, and processed in, the client's native language. Sometimes it is difficult for the nurse to appreciate this double cognitive processing because the responses are in English and the nurse is aware only that the client seems to be taking more time than usual. If the client experiences anxiety about what to say next, ease in communicating is further compromised. Asking the right questions, providing verbal cues, and allowing more time for clients with limited language skills to answer conveys interest and respect; this kind of communication also helps decrease unnecessary anxiety.

APPLICATIONS

ASSESSMENT

The assessment forms the basis for planning culturally sensitive interventions. It includes not only the collection of relevant data but also the analysis and synthesis of that data into a meaningful appraisal of the client's culturally specific health care needs. It is important to learn about clients' cultural realities from their particular frames of reference. The way a client presents symptoms will reveal which aspects of the client's complaints are culturally acceptable and how the client's culture permits their expression. For example, pain is expressed with great intensity in some cultures. Latin cultures express it with deep emotion, whereas Asian and Pacific Islands cultural norms mandate controlled emotional expression (Giger

and Davidhizar, 1991). Being able to recognize that a behavior may be characteristic of a culture rather than "abnormal behavior" places a nurse at an advantage in effectively and therapeutically relating with clients from differing cultures.

One method currently being utilized today by nurses to enhance the care of culturally diverse patients is the use of a cultural assessment. A *cultural assessment* is defined as a "systematic appraisal of beliefs, values, and practices conducted in order to determine the context of client needs and to tailor nursing interventions" (Tripp-Reimer and Afifi, 1989, p. 613). The data base should include the information presented in Box 11–1. The cultural assessment is comprised of three progressive interconnecting elements: (1) a general assessment, (2) a problem-specific assessment, and (3) the cultural details needed for successful implementation of the care plan. This structure represents a logical way of organizing relevant cultural data and is easy for the client to follow. Exercise 11–6 provides practice with cultural assessment.

The general assessment provides the nurse with a beginning appraisal of issues that could potentially affect health care delivery. Common areas of cultural variation include client responses to pain, the need for privacy and body exposure, eating

---

BOX 11–1
Data Base for the Culturally Diverse Client

Information should focus on:
1. Patterns or lifestyles of an individual or group.
2. Specific cultural values, norms, and experiences of a client or group regarding the health and caring behavior of their culture.
3. Cultural taboos or myths.
4. The worldview and ethnocentric tendencies of an individual (or group).
5. General features the client (or group) perceives as different from, or similar to, other cultures in or near their environment.
6. The health and life-care rituals and rites of passage to maintain health and avoid illness.
7. Folk and professional health–illness systems.
8. Detailed caring behavior and nursing care for self and others.
9. Indicators of cultural changes and acculturation processes influencing health care.

From Leininger M (1978). Transcultural Nursing. New York, Wiley, pp. 88–89. Reprinted with permission.

EXERCISE 11–6
Cultural Assessment

Purpose: To help students identify cultural assessment data.

Time: 45 minutes

Procedure:
1. Select a specific culture and review the characteristics of culture described in this chapter.
2. Using Leininger's model for data areas, interview someone from the same culture.
3. Compare your findings in the interview with the basic characteristics of culture identified in the chapter.

Discussion:
1. What important values did you uncover?
2. In what ways were your actual findings similar to or different from those presented in the chapter? If you found differences, how would you account for them?
3. How might you incorporate these cultural values in your care of clients?

preferences and style, consciousness of space and time, isolation and quiet, the number of people involved in decision making, hygiene practices, religious and healing rituals, eye contact, and touch. Most people find comfort in sharing their culture with others and appreciate the nurse who asks. Usually clients will not volunteer such information without being asked.

The second stage of the cultural assessment is problem specific. Here the nurse gathers data related to the condition or problem for which the client is seeking treatment. This strategy allows the nurse to place a particular client problem or need within its unique cultural context. Nurses need to be careful that their own ethnocentrism about the superiority of traditional health care measures over folk medicine does not get in the way of understanding. Sample questions are found in Box 11–2.

The final phase of the cultural assessment focuses on the specific cultural details needed for client acceptance of treatment plans. It is a way to engage the client as an active co-participant in the treatment process. For example, if diet is a major part of the treatment protocol, the nurse elicits information about diet preferences that are culturally related and works with the client to include relevant foods whenever possible in a therapeutically restricted diet.

NURSING DIAGNOSES

Current nursing diagnoses that are specifically designed to address the communication difficulties of the culturally diverse client include (1) impaired verbal communication related to cultural differences, (2) impaired social interaction related to sociocultural dissonance, and (3) noncompliance related to a patient's value system: beliefs about health and cultural influences (NANDA, 1989). Although these diagnoses are in current use, they often fail to inform the nurse fully of the complexity of the cultural issues that led to the diagnosis and should be used with caution. As Geissler (1991) notes, each of these diagnoses has features that imply a negative clinical judgment about the person. For example, in the first diagnosis, is communication impaired because a person cannot speak the language? Impairment implies a disability. Furthermore, cultural expression includes non-

---

BOX 11–2
Sample Assessment Questions

- Can you tell me something about the reasons you are seeking health care for . . .?
- Can you tell me something about how a person in your culture would be cared for if they had a similar condition?
- Have you been treated for a similar problem in the past? (If the client answers yes, more information about the precise nature of treatment is elicited.)
- Can you tell me what people do in your culture to remain healthy?
- Can you tell me something about the foods you like and how they are prepared?
- Are there any special cultural beliefs about your illness that might help me give you better care?

verbal expressions that are "critical to mutual understanding and may have nothing to do with knowledge of the dominant language" (p. 192). In what ways, then, does "impaired verbal communication" really describe the communication problem of the culturally diverse client?

The second diagnosis has similar problems. Is the social isolation experienced by the culturally diverse client truly an impairment, or should this diagnosis be described differently? The third diagnosis assumes that the client is being noncompliant. This is a negative value judgment that may have little to do with the client's motives or desire to cooperate in treatment. When the noncompliance gets linked to the client's value system, there is an implicit assumption that the client is doing something wrong when, in fact, the client may be acting in total accord with his or her own religious or cultural beliefs. To comply with Western medical protocols would place the client at odds with personal cultural values. Thus the nursing diagnosis, while descriptive of the client's difficulty, may not be completely usable as a valid descriptor of the culturally diverse client. If one accepts this premise, should the nurse still assume that the client is noncompliant and try to change the client's behavior? If you as a professional nurse wanted to make these diagnoses culturally congruent, how would you change the wording of them?

PLANNING

Developing Culturally Congruent Care Plans

Planning that incorporates knowledge and acceptance of the client's right to seek alternative health care practices dictated by the client's culture can make a major difference in compliance and successful outcome. Health care professionals sometimes mistakenly assume that illness is a single concept, but illness is a complex personal experience, strongly colored by cultural norms, values, social roles, and religious beliefs (Deetz and Stevenson, 1986). For example, some lower-income, rural African Americans, who are not integrated into the predominant culture, consider illness from a natural and unnatural perspective. Natural illness occurs because the individuals have not protected themselves sufficiently from the forces of nature. Unnatural illness happens when the person receives a "hex" from bad spirits, usually of a supernatural nature. Clients who believe in an unnatural origin

for their illness often require the services of a folk healer in addition to medical treatments as part of their treatment process (Campinha-Bacote, 1992). Some illnesses have stronger negative values than others for certain cultures. For example, in Chinese cultures it is more acceptable for an individual to have venereal disease than to have tuberculosis; physical explanations for behavioral symptoms are acceptable, but psychological explanations are denied outside the family circle (Kleinman, 1980). Vaccinations for smallpox cannot be given in some parts of India because smallpox is considered a god in rural areas (Brophy, 1983).

There are physical considerations as well. Drug responses vary across cultures. For example, it has been documented that Asians have a tendency to metabolize drugs more slowly and thus achieve a higher therapeutic effect with smaller doses of medication (Keltner and Folks, 1992; Lin, Porland, and Lesser, 1986). Sickle cell anemia is found almost exclusively among African Americans, and Tay Sachs disease is a genetic disorder unique to the Jewish community.

Clients from different cultures frequently identify language barriers as the most frustrating aspect of cultural diversity. They feel helpless, even desperate, when they cannot express their thoughts and feelings to someone who must be able to understand their meaning in order to help them. The nurse needs to assess the extent of language barriers and to explore what it means to the client. Acknowledging language difficulties and trying to find creative ways to share experiences are important for the client's acceptance of the nurse.

Role relationships also are important. Cultural customs may require role relationships to be more formal, with well-defined boundaries and clearly verbalized expectations. For example, Asian clients respond best to a formal relationship. They favor an indirect communication style characterized by polite phrases and marked deference (Tsui and Schultz, 1988). The nurse would not expect an Asian client to question the nurse actively or to ask for more information about treatment. Typically, the client waits for the information to be offered by the nurse as the authority figure. This behavior does not mean that the Asian client is timid, passive, or unwilling to participate in the treatment process. It simply is a cultural characteristic that needs to be acknowledged, respected, and accounted for in developing an individualized plan of care for a

Ethnocultural differences need not be barriers to acceptance in a relationship.

client exhibiting such culturally determined behavior. On the other hand, Hispanic clients need a more personal, informal interpersonal format to feel comfortable. They respond best to a health professional who is open, warm, and willing to respond to personal questions (Pagani-Tousignant, 1992).

Another area of concern in planning has to do with the level of family involvement. For example, the degree of family involvement among Asian, Hispanic, and African-American cultures is apt to be much greater than the norm in the United States. Within these cultures, the extended family is the basic social unit. Health problems affecting one family member have direct implications for all other members of the family. In most instances the number of potentially involved caregivers is correspondingly larger than in the main culture. Moreover, there also is a sex-linked hierarchy, with the oldest male being the final authority on family matters in Asian and Hispanic cultures. For this reason, the nurse might address the husband first, even if another adult family member is the actual client. Identifying and including all those who will be taking an active part in the care of the client from the outset recognizes the communal nature of family involvement in health care.

A common characteristic of most minority cultures is an unspoken tendency to view health professionals as authority figures, treating them with deference and respect but disregarding their advice. This value is so strong a client frequently will not question the nurse or in any way indicate mistrust of the authority figure's counsel. But such clients simply will not follow the nurse's recommendations or will withdraw from treatment. A participatory style that follows the flow of the ethnic client or family's concerns helps to prevent this situation.

INTERVENTION

General Guidelines

Culturally sensitive nursing interventions affect the teaching process. Those interventions that are integrated with culturally specific values empower the client to build on what she or he already knows and accepts as reality. New knowledge is accepted more readily because it seems familiar to the client.

Interventions that take into consideration the specialized needs of the culturally diverse client follow the guidelines for LEARN: "Listen, Explain, Acknowledge, Recommend and Negotiate" (Campinha-Bacote, 1992, p. 11). With this process, the nurse listens carefully to the client's perspective on his or her health problem, including the cause, expectations for treatment, and information about others who traditionally are involved in the client's care. It is important to find out the client's expectations of health care and to inquire about family lifestyle. Once the nurse has a clear understanding of the *client's* perception of the problem, the nurse can explain his or her understanding of it, using simple, concrete terminology. The nurse needs to address the same areas the client talked about. Following this discussion, the nurse can acknowledge the differences and similarities between their perceptions. The information serves as a basis for planning interventions, with the nurse making specific recommendations to the client and negotiating a mutually acceptable treatment approach (Campinha-Bacote, 1992). Throughout the negotiation process, the nurse is respectful of the client's right to hold different cultural views. Strategies to minimize conflict and disagreement enhance the effectiveness of the intervention. If family members traditionally are involved in decision making, they should be made an integral part of the relationship. Otherwise the treatment process is likely to fail, no matter how worthy the intervention.

Teaching strategies can be culturally based. For example, incorporating storytelling as a teaching strategy is likely to facilitate success with the Native-American client, who is used to learning in this manner (Moody and Laurent, 1984). Providing a maternity client with booklets about breastfeeding written in her native language is a small yet meaningful gesture. The offering is tangible evidence of the nurse's acknowledgment of cultural differences. Box 11–3 provides general teaching guidelines for use with culturally diverse clients.

Interpreters can be used if attempts to communicate with a client fail to meet the client's needs. In fact, federal law mandates the use of a trained interpreter in such situations, according to standards established by the Joint Commission on Accreditation of Hospitals and criteria published under Title VI of the Civil Rights Act. Having someone act as an intermediary, who can communicate with the client and who can understand the subtle nuances of the culture, often allows the client greater freedom in expression (Newhill, 1990). Interpreters should be chosen with care, keeping in mind differences in dialects as well as the sex and social status of the interpreter and the client if this is likely to be

---

BOX 11–3
General Communication Guidelines
for Interacting with Culturally Diverse Clients

- Use the same sequence and repeat phrases, expanding on the same basic questions.
- Speak slowly and clearly and use concrete language the client can understand. Make the sentence structure as simple as possible.
- Encourage the client by smiling and by listening. Provide cues such as pictures and gestures.
- Avoid the use of technical language, and choose words that incorporate cultural terms whenever possible.
- Allow enough time, and do not assume that simply because the client nods or smiles the communication is understood.
- Identify barriers to compliance such as social values, environment, and language.
- Help the client develop realistic, culturally relevant goals.
- Incorporate culturally specific teaching formats. For example, use an oral or storytelling format with clients who have oral teaching traditions.
- Close with cultural sensitivity: "I've really learned a lot today about . . . (restate highlights). Thanks for sharing with me."

---

an issue. In societies with strong cultural biases and social class distinctions, clients may not want to discuss intimate information with a person of the opposite sex or with someone they perceive as their social inferior (Santopietro, 1981).

Cultural Brokering

Cultural brokering is part of the advocacy role of the professional nurse. It is defined as "the act of bridging, linking or mediating between groups or persons of differing cultural backgrounds for the purpose of reducing conflict or producing change" (Jezewski, 1993). Ideally, the process is used to help clients understand the health care system and to help health care personnel better understand the culture gaps between the lay culture of the client entering the system and the medical culture of the health care system. A cultural brokering model (Fig. 11–2) diagrams the feedback system involved in the advocate-as-broker role. The intervening conditions presented at the top of the model provide a guide to appropriate assessment of the problem and recognition of the need for the nurse's intervention. Usually there is an imbalance in power that creates the need for cultural brokering. Interventions to resolve the

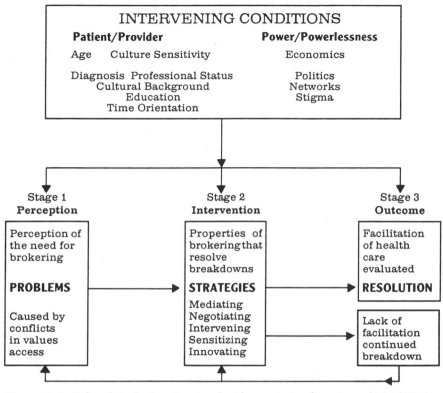

Figure 11–2 Cultural Brokering. Reprinted with permission from Jezewski M (1993). Culture brokering as a model for advocacy. Nursing and Health Care 14(2):81. Copyright 1993 National League for Nursing.

problem involve a number of interrelated strategies. Successful outcomes represent a resolution of the conflict between the client's set of values, beliefs, and behavior and changes in the desired direction of increased health and well-being.

APPLICATIONS TO SPECIAL POPULATIONS

Some basic concepts about the traditional characteristics of the larger minority groups living in the United States are included in this chapter. In no way are they intended to be all-inclusive or completely descriptive of the culture. It also seems essential to emphasize that not everyone associated with a particular culture demonstrates the same characteristics or has the same desire for an ethnic identity. The nurse needs to use the basic information about different cultures as a basis for

inquiry and must engage the client as the primary resource in learning the best ways to provide culturally congruent care for each individual.

African-American Clients

African Americans account for 12 percent of the U.S. population, making it the largest minority group in the nation (DHHS, 1991). They are referred to as blacks, Afro Americans, or African Americans. For many African Americans, their ethnic culture traces back to slavery and deprivation. The vestiges of this heritage are evidenced in a seriously disproportionate level of poverty, with its attendant social and health problems, and a visible need for further efforts to ensure equal opportunity for this group. A smaller group emigrated from other countries such as Haiti and Jamaica.

In addition to health care issues directly related

to lack of education, cost, and access, lower-income African-American clients statistically are less likely to use regular health services and are more likely to use the emergency room for routine medical care. They tend to rely on informal helping networks in the community until a problem becomes a crisis. Use of folk-healing measures is common. From a cultural perspective, this strategy is understandable for people with a worldview, developed from experience, in which racism, oppression, and devaluation of their lives were commonplace. Many African Americans have not had positive experiences with traditional health services (Williams, 1992). It is hard for them to trust in the goodwill and cultural sensitivity of health care providers when subtle and overt discrimination have been a part of their lives for as long as they can remember.

Establishing trust is a critical element for success with African-American clients, who are more willing to participate in treatment when efforts are made to involve them as co-participants in their care (Gunnings and Lipscomb, 1986). Allowing these clients to have as much control over their health care as possible helps reinforce personal strengths and enhances their self-concept. This is a useful strategy with any client who feels oppressed and stigmatized by the health care system. Understanding the reasons behind a client's hostility and mistrust of the health care provider allows the nurse to be more patient and proactive.

In the traditional African-American culture, disease is thought to occur because of a lack of harmony with nature. Voodoo is still practiced in some rural communities.

CASE EXAMPLE

Ms. Jones was a 56-year-old African-American female who was brought to the psychiatric emergency service of a large city hospital by her family. She claimed that she had been poisoned by her husband's lover. After a psychiatric examination, Ms. Jones was given the diagnosis of delusional disorder—jealous type. She was admitted to the inpatient psychiatric unit and started on a neuroleptic medication. However, the diagnostician failed to conduct a culturological assessment, which would have revealed that Ms. Jones felt she was experiencing voodoo illness. A more culturally relevant treatment would have included consultation with a folk healer. (Campinha-Bacote, 1992)

Health care concerns of African Americans cover a variety of social and physical diseases. The rate of AIDS, homicide, and drug abuse—social diseases associated more with poverty and substandard living conditions than ethnicity—are significantly higher for black than for white Americans. African Americans are subject to higher rates of hypertension, adolescent pregnancy, diabetes, and stroke. If you are a black male, you have a significantly greater chance of developing cancer and of dying from it (DHHS, 1991).

The family is the rallying point of the African American's social life. Loyalty to the extended family is a dominant value, and family members rely on each other for support. Many low-income African-American children grow up in extended families. If one or both parents cannot assume child care, the role is assumed by grandparents. As a result, generational boundaries are not always clear-cut. This is not true of the large black middle class. These individuals are more likely to have intact families and to enjoy high socioeconomic and professional status in their communities. Their health care behaviors more closely resemble those of the dominant culture.

Decision making is largely matriarchal in low-income families. Sex roles are more flexible, in part because women have often had to become the heads of their families because of racial discrimination (McGoldrick and Rohrbaugh, 1987). African-American families stick together in times of trouble, and it is not uncommon for a whole entourage of family visitors to camp out in the hospital waiting room during a serious illness.

The church plays a central role in black culture and even today is viewed as more than a religious institution. For many centuries it served as the primary social, economic, and community life center. It continues to provide a resource in times of stress and to serve as a source of identity affirmation and inspiration to the black community. In fact, families often turn to their minister when they have marital problems before going to a mental health clinic. Many African-American leaders, for example, Jesse Jackson, Ralph Abernathy, and the late Martin Luther King, Jr., have been recognized church leaders. Because of the central meaning of the church in African-American life, incorporating the appropriate clergy in treatment plans is a useful strategy. Likewise, readings from the

Bible and gospel hymns are sources of support during hospitalization. Most African Americans are Christian. The Black Muslim religion is a strict fundamentalist religion favored by some African Americans. It has a militant flavor and strongly endorses ethnic identity through dress and actions. The religion does not permit the eating of meat.

Hispanic-American Clients

Spanish-speaking Americans are the second largest minority group in the United States (DHHS, 1991). They usually identify themselves as Hispanic Americans or Latinos. Mexican Americans are referred to as Chicanos. Typically, Hispanic clients identify their country of origin, for example, Puerto Rico, Colombia, and San Salvador, in their self-description. The Hispanic client typically uses the formal health care system only as a short-term, problem-solving strategy. Many Hispanics rely on *curanderos* (local folk healers and herb doctors) for most of their medical advice. The *curandero* uses a combination of healing practices, medicines, and herbs to cure illness. Hispanics like to keep their problems within the family, so talking with a "stranger" is difficult. In a health care situation, the Hispanic client needs to develop *confianza* (trust) in the health care provider and frequently will ask personal questions to establish the bonding necessary for disclosure. This practice is not based on a desire to invade the nurse's privacy but rather is the normal way the Hispanic client establishes an acceptable context for conversation (Pederson, 1988). Consequently, if asked, the nurse might provide simple information about marital status, number of children, or other nonintrusive data.

Many Hispanics view illness as a punishment from God. They also believe that physical diseases and the treatments used to cure them are related to dietary practices. It is important to determine if the client ascribes to the hot and cold theory of treating illness. For example, many Hispanic clients view arthritis as a "cold" disease that should be treated with "hot" foods such as corn meal, garlic, alcohol, coffee, onions, and chili peppers. "Hot" diseases such as constipation, diarrhea, or ulcers would be treated with "cold" medication, such as bicarbonate of soda and milk of magnesia

(Cowell, 1988). In this framework, illness can also be caused by a great fright (*susto*).

Health care concerns of particular relevance to the Hispanic population are teenage drug abuse, adolescent pregnancy, lack of preventive and of prenatal health care, and a higher incidence of HIV infections in women and children than in the white population. Heart disease and cancer are the most frequent causes of death in the United States.

The family is the center of the Hispanic client's life and serves as a primary source of emotional support. Hispanic clients are "family members first, and individuals second" (Pagani-Tousignant, 1992, p. 10). Social interactions, often on a daily basis, take place among the nuclear and extended family and a few close friends. Close friends are considered a part of the family unit. In the Hispanic culture, cooperation is more important than competition, and competitive situations are avoided whenever possible.

Sex roles are relatively rigid, and it is very important that the male remain in control of his feelings (machismo). Hispanic men are trained from early childhood not to show their feelings, particularly to a strange woman. Hispanic women are socialized to serve their husbands and children without question (*la sufrida* = "the long-suffering woman") (Pagani-Tousignant, 1992). The nurse needs to be sensitive to the role of these cultural beliefs in treatment situations.

Hispanic clients are usually deeply religious, with the predominant religion Catholicism. They view illness and suffering with a fatalistic acceptance having religious overtones (*Si Dios quierre*, "if God wishes"). The relationship between God and the individual is a close, intimate one. In fact, the relationship is so close that it is acceptable for individuals to experience visions and dreams in which God or the saints speak directly to the individual. In many Western cultures, such behaviors might be labeled as hallucinatory, and psychiatric treatment might be recommended.

Asian-American Clients

The third most common minority group in the United States is the Asian. Pagani-Tousignant (1992) notes that there are over 32 ethnic groups comprising the cultural community of Asians and Pacific Islanders. Traditionally, the Asian client exercises significant emotional restraint in communication. It is hard to tell what Asian persons are really thinking or feeling because, typically, their facial expressions are not as flexible and their words are not as revealing as those people in the dominant culture. For this reason the nurse can underestimate or neglect the Asian client's suffering. Asking the client about pain and suggesting possible feelings are helpful interventions. The Asian client also appreciates a clinician who is willing to provide advice in a matter of fact, concise manner. Health care concerns specifically relevant to this population include a higher than normal incidence of tuberculosis, hepatitis B, and some forms of cancer (DHHS, 1990).

The Asian client traditionally perceives illness as an imbalance of yin and yang. In this ancient representation yin is the female force containing all the elements that represent darkness, cold, and weakness. Yang represents the male elements of strength, brightness, and warmth. Acupressure and herbal medicines are among the medical practices used by Asian clients to reestablish the balance between yin and yang. As long as these medical practices are not harmful, they should be encouraged (Giger and Davidhizar, 1991).

The family is crucial and all-encompassing. There is a lot of family pressure on members to do well academically, and family members assume a great deal of responsibility for each other, including financial assistance. Sons have a higher value than daughters, and sex roles are well defined, with the male viewed as the breadwinner and the female designated the caretaker. In contrast with many other societies, the elders in an Asian community are highly respected and well taken care of by younger members of the family (Pagani-Tousignant, 1992).

The Asian client views the nurse as an authority figure. In the Asian culture, a person must show complete respect for authority figures. It is almost impossible for the Asian client to argue or disagree with the nurse. Consequently, the nurse has to ask open-ended questions and clarify issues consistently in *every* interaction. If the nurse uses questions that require a yes or no answer, the answer may reflect the client's polite deference rather than an honest response. A participatory approach in which the nurse asks the client how things are done in his or her culture and then works with the client to develop a culturally congruent solution usually is most effective. Incorporating the Asian client's need to focus on problem-solving facts rather than on feelings as a manner of speaking is also an effective communication strategy.

It is extremely important to Asian clients that they not lose face. Criticizing an Asian person in front of others is never acceptable. The practice carries much more weight than it does for a non-Asian person, so that it is important for nurses or anyone in a superior position to realize the significance of shame in the Asian culture. If an individual loses face, the family and community share that shame.

CASE EXAMPLE

Jone was an Asian nursing student who missed part of a clinical conference because he was distracted by another experience. Although he apologized to his instructor and explained his distraction, he perceived that the instructor did not believe him. He did well in the course but he never forgot his shame. Six months later, this student shared the shame of not being believed with his faculty adviser. It had continued to haunt him despite his getting a good grade in the course. Other students might have viewed the incident differently, but for this Asian student it was a matter of losing face.

Males in Asian cultures may have a difficult time disclosing personal information to a female nurse without an explanation, because in serious matters women are not considered as knowledgeable as males. Asian clients may be reluctant to be examined by a person of the opposite sex, particularly if the examination or treatment involves the genital area. Many Asians consider the head the repository of the soul, so that touching the head is seen as damaging the equilibrium of the soul. For this reason, it is useful to explain the reason for touching the head before doing so (Santopietro, 1981).

The three major religious groups in Asian culture are Hinduism, Sikhism, and Islam. Religious beliefs are tightly interwoven into the social fabric of everyday life and affect every aspect of it. Hindus are required to pray regularly, and they are devoted to the ideals of pacifism, reincarnation, and a God who can be worshiped in many forms. There is a well-defined caste system that is important because what a person is and does in this life affects life after reincarnation (Abrahams, 1985).

Hindus are vegetarians because it is against their religion to kill living creatures. Sikhism is a reformed variation of Hinduism in which women have more rights in domestic and community life. Islam is the world's fastest-growing religion, and it is found predominantly in South and Southeast Asia. Stoddard (1988) notes that it is both a religion and a way of life centered around God, or Allah. The Muslim submits entirely to Allah and follows Allah's basic rules about everything from personal relationships to business matters, including personal matters such as dress and hygiene. In the end, Allah decides whether a person has been successful in following the rules and whether the person will be allowed to enter paradise. The five major tenets of the faith are (1) to bear witness to Allah and acknowledge Muhammad as his messenger, (2) to pray five times a day facing Mecca, (3) to fast during the daylight hours of the ninth lunar month, (4) to give alms, and (5) to make the pilgrimage to Mecca at least once during a lifetime. Islam has some strong tenets that affect health care, such as that God is the ultimate healer. There can be no physical contact between a woman and a man who is not her husband. Physical modesty is a high value. Only the body part to be examined can be exposed, and only in private. The following is a case example of an Asian client in an American hospital.

CASE EXAMPLE

Hollingsworth, Brown, and Brooten (1980) describe a case study in which a young Vietnamese woman, Mrs. N., gave birth to a healthy baby boy. During labor, the mother was smiling and said nothing. Seemingly, the labor process caused her no stress. The father remained at the hospital during the labor but assumed a passive role, entering the delivery room only to translate some instructions to his wife. On the postpartum unit, Mrs. N. refused to take her medications with the ice water offered to her. She seemed reluctant to get out of bed other than to use the bathroom, and she refused to eat. Despite a smiling, polite posture during most of her postpartum course, she became visibly upset when the nurse brought her baby to her and made pleasing remarks about the infant.

To the casual observer, Mrs. N.'s behavior was perplexing. But if the nurse viewed the same behaviors from a transcultural perspective, they made complete sense. Mrs. N.'s composure during her labor and her politeness during postpartum were cultural responses dictated by an aversion to strong emotional display. In Vietnam, the newborn is bathed and clothed before the father has contact with it. This custom explains Mr. N.'s behavior in exiting the delivery room quickly and not spending initial time with his newborn infant.

Mrs. N.'s postpartum behavior also has cultural origins. The Vietnamese view childbirth as disturbing the balance between yin and yang (hot and cold) in the body. Mrs. N.'s refusal of medications was related to a fear of disturbing the balance between yin and yang in her body. Likewise, her poor eating pattern can be explained by this humoral imbalance. Only certain foods, such as chicken, rice, and pork, are thought to be "warm" foods. Beef, seafood, and salads are not traditionally eaten by postpartum women. Vietnamese women traditionally avoid early ambulation because of a belief that too much movement will prevent their distended internal organs from resuming their prepregnancy state. Finally, the nurse's enthusiasm in recognizing her new infant was unacceptable to Mrs. N. because of a cultural belief that should a spirit overhear the comments and find the child desirable, the spirit might attempt to steal it away.

This case example demonstrates the importance of cultural knowledge in implementing and evaluating the effectiveness of nursing care. With a more culturally specific awareness of Mrs. N.'s needs, the nurse could respond in an individualized, caring manner. No more time need be expended, but planning would be practical and simple, with clear attention given to the cultural implications of each intervention. Although this case example may seem extreme, subtle misunderstandings and problems can occur in any nursing situation in which the nurse and client are not of the same ethnic background.

Native-American Clients

Although Native Americans represent the smallest of the major ethnic groups in the nation, there are almost four hundred tribes in the United States. Very few Native Americans still dwell on Indian reservations (Pagani-Tousignant, 1992). Native Americans, living in or around Alaska, refer to themselves as Alaska natives. Those living in other states prefer the label American Indian (DHHS, 1991). As an ethnic group, the Native Americans are less verbal and are much more comfortable with long periods of silence than other groups. Native Americans are private persons who respect the privacy of others. They are less likely to speak of their feelings and prefer to talk about the facts rather than the accompanying emotions. Native-American clients respond best to health professionals who stick to the point and do not engage in small talk. They are suspicious of interviewers who ask many questions, and they are hesitant to volunteer information about anyone other than themselves. For this reason, it is better to ask questions in short sessions rather than all at once and to ask each person directly for information. Native Americans live in the present and have little appreciation of time commitments. The nurse can experience frustration with Native Americans' reluctance to plan for the future and with their inability to honor appointments unless these cultural needs are acknowledged and understood. One way to alleviate this problem is to engage the client as the responsible party for health care.

HEALING CIRCLE

A healing circle is a Native-American intervention in which a person in trouble is able to talk without interruption. No feedback is offered, but familiar cultural symbols are used to facilitate the group interaction. This group format is very healing, whereas a more traditional group format in which confrontation and feedback are used would not be as effective for this population group (Scott, 1991).

If a person is in harmony with the supernatural forces in the universe, the person will not experience disease. Illness is viewed as an imbalance, a punishment from God for some real or imagined imbalance with nature; it is felt to be divine intervention to help the individual correct evil ways. In some cases, recovery is likely to occur only after the client is cleansed of the "evil spirits."

The religious beliefs of Native Americans are strongly linked with nature and the earth. Symbols and metaphors are used to explain and make sense of reality. Inanimate objects such as rocks and the elements of weather are imbued with spiritual

qualities. Since person and nature are one and the same, most healing practices are strongly embedded in religious beliefs. Native Americans may seek medical help from their tribal elders and *shamans* (highly respected spiritual medicine men and women). The shaman uses spiritual healing practices and herbs to cure the ill member of the tribe (Pagani-Tousignant, 1992). Native Americans view death as a natural process, but they fear the power of dead spirits and employ numerous tribal rituals to ward them off.

Health concerns of particular relevance to the Native-American population are unintentional injuries, of which 75 percent are alcohol related—suicide, cirrhosis, alcoholism, and obesity. Juvenile diabetes is a major problem, and the death rate from the disease is significantly higher than it is in the white population. It is estimated that 95 percent of American Indian families are affected directly or indirectly by alcohol abuse (DHHS, 1991).

The family is highly valued by the Native American. Sex roles are less rigid than in other cultures, and family boundaries are extended to include people who are not blood related. For example, it is not unusual for a child to have several mothers and siblings who are not related but are considered a part of the person's family. The nurse may need to include these people in care planning because they can be a very important social support to the Native-American client. Tribal identity is maintained through regular pow-wows and other ceremonial events. Both men and women feel an obligation to promote tribal values and traditions through their crafts and traditional ceremonies. Children are taught Indian crafts at an early age. In addition to the economic value of the products, the making of crafts reinforces the Native-American identity (McGoldrick, Pierce, and Giordano, 1982).

The Culture of Poverty

In addition to ethnic cultural variation, societal differences that have an impact on the communication process reflect a person's socioeconomic status and geographic location (rural vs. urban). There are enough differences in the cultural worldview of those who fall below the poverty line to warrant special consideration of their needs in the nurse–client relationship. The culture of poverty is characterized by acute deprivation. The poor generally are disadvantaged educationally and have a higher incidence of problems related to school performance, deviant social behaviors, and mental and physical challenges. Access to the health care system and preventive health care are limited, in many cases, by cost and availability. The poor who seek health care are also subject to long waits and sometimes very rude treatment by health professionals who don't seem to want to help. Consequently, health-seeking behaviors among the poor and homeless tend to be crisis oriented. Medical help is sought only when a person is acutely ill and is discontinued when obvious symptoms disappear. The nurse needs to treat and health teach aggressively during the time permitted.

Equally significant are intrapersonal issues that make it more difficult for poor people to take seriously a relationship with health care providers except in time of crisis. In our society, being poor means being powerless. Taking individual responsibility for preventive and prenatal care is not a prevalent norm among the poor even when that care is free and is proactively offered. It is important for nurses to understand why this is so and to appreciate the emotional impact of powerlessness on the full utilization of health care services by poor people. Many poor people experience virtually no control over meeting their basic needs— things that we take for granted such as food, housing, and clothing or the chance for a decent job and the opportunity for education. Often they have experienced violence rather than social justice as the means to provide their fundamental needs. Consequently, the idea that they can exercise choice in their lives and can make a difference in their health care is not part of their worldview. They look to and expect others to take responsibility and to make things better. Poor people often do not take the initiative simply because their life experiences tell them they cannot trust that their own efforts will produce any change. This is a very difficult but important cultural concept for nurses to incorporate into their relationships with people of poverty. Understanding the origin of low expectations and the depth of powerlessness helps nurses to withstand discouragement about rejection of services and to take the proactive, persistent, and patient stance required in interpersonal

relationships with this population. Communication strategies that acknowledge, support, and empower the poor to take small steps to independence are most effective. Talking about abstract feelings and expecting major changes or independence through information alone are less likely to be successful.

Having poverty and refugee status compounds the problem. Often refugees have come from situations in which sanitary conditions were poor and infection rampant. Strange as it may seem, many refugees from poorer areas have had no previous exposure to refrigeration or indoor plumbing (Santopietro and Lynch, 1980). Many refugees have lost contact with family members, so that their support system may not be in this country. Socially isolated from familial and cultural support systems, the stress of an illness may be superimposed on other stresses due to emigration, job, and financial problems. With little more than a rudimentary grasp of English and few educational skills with which to learn it, these clients present an essentially passive orientation toward the acquisition of knowledge about their illness and treatment protocols. Immigrants fleeing an intolerable life in their country of origin frequently feel out of place, scorned, and unable to compete effectively in a cultural community in which they stand out because of language, skin color, or dress.

In a society in which articulate communication is a sign of status and native treatments are suspect, the refugee client is at a distinct advantage. Furthermore, financial problems, lack of marketable skills, and language deficits may preclude planning an expensive health care intervention without the financial and social resources to support it (Atkinson, Morten, and Sue, 1989). Exercise 11–7 provides practice with a practical application of cultural differences.

EVALUATION

Evaluation of goals achieved and the effectiveness of nursing interventions should reflect the client's cultural values. Questions to guide the evaluation process might include: Were the learning activities culturally specific and sufficient to produce the desired outcome? Does the evaluation of treatment outcomes fit the objectives from a cultural perspective? What cultural modifications are

EXERCISE 11–7
Applications of Cultural Diversity Affecting Nursing Care

Purpose: To familiarize you with culture-specific elements of nursing care for several populations.

Time: 45 minutes of personal time; varied class time.

Directions:
1. Read the admission information on the following client.
2. Select one of the clients described in the list following.
3. Look up and apply the cultural information you discover in an assessment and nursing care plan.
4. Resulting information may be shared in class, placed in displays, or turned in.

A client presents with an acute infection, requiring hospitalization for 10 days, with IV antibiotics, rest with progressive ambulation, passive ROM exercises progressing to active ROM, teaching about nutrition and infection control, and supportive emotional care.

- An Amish farmer from Pennsylvania.
- A Navaho Native American from a reservation in Arizona.
- A Vietnamese immigrant living in a southern city.
- A Shiite Moslem from Lebanon (female).
- An African American living in an urban ghetto.
- A Haitian newly arrived in an American city.
- A Christian Scientist living in a small town.
- An older woman who has lived all her life in rural West Virginia (religiously fundamentalist).
- A member of the British peerage.
- A famous foreign film star (French).
- A member of an Eskimo tribe living in remote Alaska.
- A gay AIDS patient from an urban area.

needed to provide the client with the content and process the client needs to achieve the objectives? Ideally, the nurse also learns from the client and consequently might ask, "What learning skills did I learn from working with this client that I can transfer to use with other clients from a similar culture?" It is important for the nurse to assess any potential biases that may have been in the way of providing culturally congruent care. Self-awareness of cultural blind spots remind the nurse that people are different. They occur in one of two ways: (1) when nurses view everyone as the same, regardless of their cultural background, or (2) when nurses automatically categorize persons as having certain behaviors because they belong to a certain cultural or minority group. If nurses act on the former assumption, they may conclude that their ethnic clients share the same expectations for treatment and will be surprised to find that this is not so. If they assume that all ethnic minority clients follow the norms of their cultural group, the client is likely to know at a very basic level that

he or she is not important enough to warrant consideration as a unique individual. Both outcomes can be avoided if attention is paid to the development and implementation of culturally congruent care strategies in the nurse–client relationship.

SUMMARY

The focal point of this chapter is the interpersonal context that surrounds the nurse and client from different cultures. Culture is defined as a common collectivity of beliefs, values, shared understandings, and patterns of behavior of a designated group of people. It needs to viewed as a human structure with many variations in meaning.

Multiculturalism describes a heterogeneous society in which diverse cultural worldviews can coexist with some general (etic) characteristics shared by all cultural groups and some (emic) perspectives that are unique to a particular group. Combining the two perspectives provides the multicultural perspective. Related terms include cultural diversity, cultural relativism, subculture, ethnicity, ethnocentrism, and ethnography. Each of these concepts broadens the definition of culture. Intercultural communication is defined as a communication in which the sender of a message is a member of one culture and the receiver of the message is from a different culture. Different languages create and express different personal realities.

A cultural assessment is defined as a "systematic appraisal of beliefs, values, and practices conducted in order to determine the context of client needs and to tailor nursing interventions." It is comprised of three progressive, interconnecting elements: (1) a general assessment, (2) a problem-specific assessment, and (3) the cultural details needed for successful implementation.

Knowledge and acceptance of the client's right to seek and support alternative health care practices dictated by culture can make a major difference in compliance and successful outcome. Health care professionals sometimes mistakenly assume that illness is a single concept, but illness is a personal experience, strongly colored by cultural norms, values, social roles, and religious beliefs. Interventions that take into consideration the specialized needs of the culturally diverse client follow the guidelines for LEARN: "Listen, Explain, Acknowledge, Recommend, and Negotiate."

Some basic thoughts about the traditional characteristics of the larger minority groups (African American, Hispanic, Asian, Native American) living in the United States relating to communication preferences, perceptions about illness, family, health, and religious values are included in the chapter. The culture of poverty is discussed.

REFERENCES

Abrahams J (1985). Asian expectations. Nursing Times 81:44–46.

Allport G (1982). The language of prejudice. *In* Eschholz P, Rosa A, Clark V (eds.) (1982), Language Awareness (3rd ed.). New York: St. Martin's.

Atkinson DR, Morten G, Sue S (1989). Counseling American Minorities: A Cross-Cultural Perspective (3rd ed.). Dubuque, IA: William C. Brown.

Barrett R (1984). Culture and Conduct: An Excursion in Anthropology. Belmont, CA, Wadsworth.

Boyle JS, Andrews MM (1989). Transcultural Concepts in Nursing Care. Glenview, IL, Scott, Foresman.

Bromwich D (1992). Politics by Other Means: Higher Education and Group Thinking. New Haven, CT, Yale University Press.

Brophy K (1983). Personal communication.

Bullough V, Bullough B (1982). Health Care for the Other Americans. East Norwalk, CT, Appleton-Century-Crofts.

Campinha-Bacote J (1991). Community mental health services: A culturally specific mode. Archives of Psychiatric Nursing 5(4):229–235.

Campinha-Bacote J (1992). Voodoo illness. Perspectives in Psychiatric Care 28(1):11–16.

Carmichael C (1985). Cultural patterns of the elderly. *In* Samovar L, Porter K (eds.) (1985), Intercultural Communication: A Reader. Belmont, CA, Wadsworth.

Castaneda C (1974). The Teachings of Don Juan: A Yaqui Way of Knowledge. New York, Touchstone.

Cowell D (1988). Keynote address. Cultural Implications of Health Care: Proceedings. Washington, DC, National Institutes of Health.

Deetz S, Stevenson S (1986). Managing Interpersonal Communication. New York, Harper & Row.

Department of Health and Human Services (DHHS) (1991). Healthy People 2000: National Health Promotion and Disease Prevention Objectives. Washington, DC, DHHS Publication No. (PHS) 91–50212.

Geissler EM (1991a). Nursing diagnoses of culturally diverse patients. International Nursing Review 38(5):150–152.

Geissler EM (1991b). Transcultural nursing and nursing diagnoses. Nursing and Health Care 12(4):190, 192, 203.

Giger J, Davidhizar R (1991). Transcultural Nursing: Assessment and Intervention. St. Louis, Mosby Year Book.

Grasska MA, McFarlane T (1982). Overcoming the language barrier: Problems and solutions. American Journal of Nursing 89:1376.

Gunnings T, Lipscomb D (1986). Psychotherapy for black men: A systematic approach. Journal of Multicultural Counseling and Development 14:17–24.

Hollingsworth AO, Brown LP, Brooten DA (1981). The refugees and childbearing: What to expect. RN (43):45–48.

Jezewski MA (1993). Culture brokering as a model for advocacy. Nursing and Health Care 14(2):78–84.

Jones DC, Van Amelsvoort-Jones GM (1986). Communication patterns between nursing staff and the ethnic elderly in a long-term care facility. Journal of Advances in Nursing Science 11:265–272.

Kakar S (1991). Western science, eastern minds. Wilson Quarterly 15(1):109–116.

Keltner N, Folks D (1992). Culture as a variable in drug therapy. Perspectives in Psychiatric Care 28(1).

Kleinman A (1980). Patients and Healers in the Context of Culture. Berkeley, University of California Press.

Klineman A, Eisenberg L, Good B (1978). Culture, illness and care. Annals of Internal Medicine 88:251.

Lee I. Quoted in Allport G (1982). The language of predjudice. In Eschholz P, Rosa A, Clark V (eds.) (1982), Language Awareness (3rd ed.). New York, St. Martin's.

Leininger M (1977). Cultural diversities of health and nursing care. Nursing Clinics of North America. 12(1):5–18.

Leininger M (1978). Transcultural Nursing. New York, Wiley, pp. 88–89.

Leininger M (1991). Transcultural nursing: The study and practice field. Imprint April/May, pp. 55–65.

Lin K, Poland R, Lesser I (1986). Ethnicity and psychopharmacology. Culture, Medicine and Psychiatry 10:151–165.

Littlejohn S (1989). Theories of Human Communication. Belmont, CA, Wadsworth.

McGoldrick M, Pearce J, Giordano J (eds.) (1982). Ethnicity and Family Therapy. New York, Guilford Press.

McGoldrick M, Rohrbaugh M (1987). Researching ethnic family stereotypes. Family Process 26:89–99.

Mead M (1935). Sex and Temperament in Three Primitive Societies. New York.

Moody LE, Laurent M (1984). Promoting health through the use of storytelling. Health Education 15(1):8–10, 12.

NANDA (1989). Taxonomy I Revised—1989 with Official Diagnostic Categories. St. Louis, NANDA.

Newhill C (1990). The role of culture in the development of paranoid symptomatology. American Journal of Orthopsychiatry 60(2):176–185.

Pagani-Tousignant C (1992). Breaking the Rules: Counseling Ethnic Minorities. Minneapolic, MN, The Johnson Institute.

Pederson P (1988). A Handbook for Developing Multicultural Awareness. Alexandria, VA, American Association for Counseling and Development.

Pederson P (1991a). Multiculturalism as a generic approach to counseling. Journal of Counseling and Development 70:6–11.

Pederson P (1991b). Introduction to the special issue on multiculturalism as a fourth force in counseling. Journal of Counseling and Development 70:4.

Primeaux M (1977). American Indian health care practices: A cross-cultural perspective. Nursing Clinics of North America 12(1).

Rempusheski V (1989). The role of ethnicity in elder care. Nursing Clinics of North America 24(3): 717–724.

Rosenbaum J (1991). A cultural assessment guide: Learning cultural sensitivity. Canadian Nurse 87(4):32–33.

Samovar L, Porter R (1988). Approaching intercultural communication. In Samovar L, Porter R (eds.) (1988), Intercultural Communication: Reader (5th ed.). Belmont, CA, Wadsworth.

Santopietro M (1981). How to get through to a refugee patient. RN (44):43–48.

Santopietro M, Lynch B (1980). What's behind the "inscrutable" mask? RN 43:55–61.

Scott JK (1991). Alice Modig and the talking circles. Canadian Nurse 87(6):25–26.

Shubin S (1980). Nursing patients from different cultures. American Journal of Nursing 10:78.

Shweder RA (1991). Thinking through Cultures. Cambridge, MA, Harvard University Press, p. 23.

Stoddard P (1988). Culture, values and health beliefs in the middle east. Cultural Implications of Health Care: Proceedings. Washington, DC, National Institutes of Health.

Sue D (1978). World views and counseling. Personal and Guidance Journal 56:458–462.

Taylor CM, Mereness D (1990). Essentials of Psychiatric Nursing (13th ed.). St. Louis, Mosby.

Taylor S (1986). Health Psychology. New York, Random House.

Thiederman SB (1986). Ethnocentrism: A barrier to effective health care. Nurse Practitioner 11:52, 54, 59.

Thompson WL, Thompson TL, House RM (1990). Taking care of culturally different and non-English speaking patients. International Journal of Psychiatry in Medicine 20(3):235–245.

Tripp-Reimer T, Afifi L (1989). Cross-cultural perspective on patient teaching. Nursing Clinics of North America 24(3):613–619.

Tripp-Reimer T, Friedl MC (1977). Appalachians: A neglected minority. Nursing Clinics of North America 12(1):41–54.

Tsai P, Schultz G (1988). Ethnic factors in group process: Cultural dynamics in multiethnic therapy groups. American Journal of Orthopsychiatry 58(1):136–142.

Westbrook F, Sedlacek W (1991). Forty years of using labels to communicate about nontraditional students: Does it help or hurt? Journal of Counseling and Development 70:20–28.

Williams O (1992). Ethnically sensitive practice to enhance treatment participation of African American men who batter. Families in Society 588–593.

SUGGESTED READINGS

Abu-Saad H (1984). Cultural group indicators of pain in children. Maternal Child Nursing Journal 13:187–196.

Anderson JM (1986). Ethnicity and illness experience: Ideological structures and the health care delivery system. Social Science and Medicine 22:1277–1283.

Anthony-Tkach C (1981). Care of the Mexican-American Patient. Nursing and Health Care 8:424.

Bal P (1981). Communicating with non-English speaking patients. British Medical Journal 283:368.

Boyle JS (1991). Transcultural nursing care of Central American refugees. Imprint April/May, 73–77.

Campbell T, Chang B (1976). Health care of the Chinese in America. Nursing Outlook 21:245.

Carter J (1974). Recognizing psychiatric symptoms in black Americans. Geriatrics 29:95.

Chavez LR (1984). Doctors, *curanderos* and *brujas*: Health care delivery and Mexican immigrants in San Diego. Medical Anthropology 15:31–37.

Clinton J (1982). Ethnicity: The development of an empirical construct for cross-cultural health research. Western Journal of Nursing Research 4: 281–300.

DeGracia RT (1979). Cultural influences on Filipino patients. American Journal of Nursing 8:1412.

Dixon S, LeVine R, Richman A (1984). Mother–child interaction around a teaching task: An African-American comparison. Child Development 55:1252.

Duh SV (1987). Physician-patient communications: Sensitivity is what breaks culture barriers. Public Health Report 102:560–561.

Fitzpatrick JP, Gould RE (1970). Mental illness among Puerto Ricans in New York: Cultural or intercultural misunderstanding? American Journal of Orthopsychiatry 15:238–239.

Fleming J (1989). Meeting the challenge of culturally diverse populations. Pediatric Nursing 6:566, 634, 648.

Gaitz C, Scott J (1974). Mental health of Mexican-Americans: Do ethnic factors make a difference? Geriatrics 29:103.

Grosso C, Barden M, Vieau MG (1981). The Vietnamese American family . . . and Grandma makes three. American Journal of Nursing 6:177.

Hall LK (1988). Providing culturally relevant mental health services for Central American immigrants. Hospital and Community Psychiatry 39(11):1139–1140, 1144.

Hilker MA (1991). Generational viewpoints in culturally diverse literature. International Journal of Aging and Human Development 33(3):211–215.

Jein RF, Harris BL (1989). Cross-cultural conflict: The American nurse manager and a culturally mixed staff. Journal of the New York State Nurses Association 20(2):16–20.

Kline F, Acosta FX, Austin W (1980). The misunderstood Spanish-speaking patient. American Journal of Psychiatry 137:1530–1533.

Lawson LV (1990). Culturally sensitive support for grieving parents. MCN: American Journal of Maternal and Child Nursing 15(2):76–79.

Lin EH (1983). Intraethnic characteristics and the patient–physician interaction: "Cultural blind spot syndrome." Journal of Family Practice 16:91–98.

Malgrady RG, Rogler LH, Constantino G (1987). Ethnocultural and linguistic bias in the mental health evaluation of Hispanics. American Psychologist 42:228–230.

Malgrady RG, Rogler LH, Constantino G (1990). Culturally sensitive psychotherapy for Puerto Rican children and adolescents: A program of treatment outcome research. Journal of Consulting and Clinical Psychology 58(6):704–712.

Manson A (1988). Language concordance as a determinant of patient compliance in emergency room use in patients with asthma. Medical Care 26:1119.

Mead M (1956). Understanding cultural patterns. Nursing Outlook 5:260.

Moffic HS (1983). Sociocultural guidelines for clinicians in multicultural settings. Psychiatric Quarterly 55:47–54.

Morris TM (1990). Culturally sensitive family assessment: An evaluation of the family assessment device used with Hawaiian-American and Japanese-American families. Family Process 29(1):105–116.

Perez-Stable (1987). Issues in Latino health care. Western Journal of Medicine 146:213–218.

Powers BA (1982). The use of orthodox and black American folk medicine. Advance in Nursing Science 3:35.

Primeaux M (1977). Caring for the American Indian patient. American Journal of Nursing 77:91.

Putsch RS (1985). Cross-cultural communication: The special case of interpreters in health care. Journal of the American Medical Association 254:3344–3349.

Ridley CR (1984). Clinical treatment of the non-disclosing black client: A therapeutic paradox. American Psychologist 39:1234–1244.

Rosendal N (1987). Understanding Italian-American cultural norms. Journal of Psychosocial Nursing 25(2):29.

Sachdev PS (1990). Whakama: Culturally determined behavior in the New Zealand Maori. Psychological Medicine 20(2):433–444.

Samovar L, Porter R (1988). Approaching intercultural communication. *In* Samovar L, Porter R (eds.) (1988), Intercultural Communication: A Reader (5th ed.). Belmont, CA, Wadsworth.

Sarell M, Baider L (1984). The effects of cultural background on communication patterns of Israeli cancer patients. Psychopathology 17:17–23.

Schwartz D (1985). Carribbean folk beliefs and western psychiatry. Journal of Psychosocial Nursing 23(11):26.

Smith SC (1987). Barriers to cross-cultural counseling: The American Black perspective. Birth Defects 23:183–187.

Tripp-Reimer T (1983). Retention of a folk-healing practice (matiasma) among four generations of urban Greek immigrants. Nursing Research 32(2):97.

Tripp-Reimer T, Brink P, Saunders J (1984). Cultural assessment: Content and process. Nursing Outlook 32(2):78–82.

Tsai P, Schultz GL (1985). Failure of rapport: Why psychotherapeutic engagement fails in the treatment of Asian clients. American Journal of Orthopsychiatry 55:561–569.

Tyler L (1981). Individuality. San Francisco, Jossey-Bass.

Watson P (1986). Communication: Towers of Babel? Nursing Times 82:401–403.

White EH (1977). Giving health care to minority patients. Nursing Clinics of North America 12(1):27–40.

Wood PR, Zeltzer LK, Cox AD (1987). Communicating with adolescents from culturally varied backgrounds: A model based on Mexican-American adolescents in South Texas. Seminars in Adolescent Medicine 3:99–108.

Chapter 12

Communicating in Groups

ELIZABETH ARNOLD

OBJECTIVES

At the end of the chapter, the student will be able to:

1. Define group communication.
2. Identify the differences between primary and secondary groups.
3. Discuss factors that influence group dynamics.

4. Identify the stages of group development.

5. Compare and contrast group and individual communication.
6. Apply group concepts in clinical settings.

7. Contrast different types of groups in health care settings.

He knew intuitively how to be understanding and acceptant. . . . This kind of ability shows up so commonly in groups that it has led me to believe that an ability to be healing or therapeutic is far more common in human life than we might suppose. Often it needs only the permission granted by a freely flowing group experience to become evident.

Rogers, 1972

This chapter introduces concepts related to group communication in health care settings, identifies types of groups commonly found in these settings, and offers basic guidelines for implementation. The material may be used effectively as a resource by nurses who wish to take a fresh look at small-group communication, as well as by those who are exploring group communication principles for the first time.

At its most basic level, group communication in family, social, and work relationships supports a person's physical, emotional, and social development. Men and women are social animals; they employ groups to satisfy a wide range of personal and professional needs. Most people depend on the cooperation of others for survival. Groups are used as natural bases to gather support, obtain information, and take action (Abrahams, 1973). Much of what people know about themselves and others are learned in a group. Since most human beings seek relationships and community, groups are a natural resource. Lewin (1951) observes that "the *person* we are does not happen in isolation, but rather takes place as the result of exposure to the attitudes and habits of the social groups to which we belong." Social behaviors and self-concept are shaped by the approval, feedback, and modeling of group members in the social, religious, and work groups a person engages in during a lifetime.

From a professional perspective, group communication skills are essential for well-being, effective nursing interventions, and professional growth. Nurses, as the largest work group in health care, use group communication skills on a daily basis to accomplish nursing goals. In work settings, groups represent one of the most effective mechanisms for effecting change and establishing work policies. Groups are a communication forum for health care professionals with common interests and diverse backgrounds, allowing consistent and collaborative interactions for effective health care delivery (Cathcart and Samovar, 1988). Group communication skills are essential tools in communicating with peers, instructors, and other health care professionals. Student evaluations often specifically reflect the student's ability to express ideas in clinical conferences, group learning projects, and interdisciplinary team meetings.

From a therapeutic standpoint, nurses use group formats to provide information and emotional support for clients and their families in a wide variety of health care settings. Therapeutic groups help people cope with difficult life tasks and maximize their human potential. Support groups foster creative problem solving and expand the number of supportive relationships with people who have similar interests and are experiencing the same kinds of problems. Educational groups are important for health-promotion purposes and help clients and their families develop skills for coping with difficult health problems.

BASIC CONCEPTS

DEFINITION

A *group* is a gathering of two or more individuals who share a common purpose and meet over a period of time in face-to-face interaction to achieve an identifiable goal. Every group is a unique social community of individuals. Within the group, members develop characteristic perspectives and patterns of behavior as central guides to their actions. A *group culture* emerges, which is the unique interrelationships among a particular group's purpose, norms, roles, status distinctions, and ways of interacting. Each group's culture is different from that of other groups because group dynamics reflect the differences in group functions and the makeup of the membership. Groups may have similar memberships and purposes but be quite different in level of functioning and goal achievement. Communication is understood by group members but not necessarily by anyone outside the group. The relationships among members are interdependent, so that each member's behavior influences the behavior of other group members. Group cultures develop through shared images and the meanings of the communication that takes place in the group. Shared meanings become stories, myths, and metaphors about the group and how it functions. Group values are woven together into a meaningful whole, which becomes the group's unique history or story.

PRIMARY AND SECONDARY GROUPS

Groups are categorized as primary natural groups or secondary groups. *Primary* groups are spontaneous group formations characterized by an informal structure and social process. Membership can be natural and automatic—family, for example. Or membership is freely chosen because of common interests, such as bridge groups, scouts, team sports, and community, religious, and other organized groups. Primary and natural groups usually do not have a defined time limit. People stay or leave as they choose.

So important are primary-group identifications that many people make their group membership and their relationship with others a part of their self-identification, "I am a Catholic," "I am a student at the university," "I am Jamie's mother." Special initiation rites symbolize the solemnity and significance of entering group membership, for example, baptism, bar mitzvah, sorority or fraternity rush week. Other ceremonies, such as retirement parties or graduation, mark the exit of an individual from a formal work group or school. When people die, those who knew them best and cared about them as a member of one or more natural groups hold a funeral, joining together to bid a group member farewell. Throughout a person's life, primary groups serve as a fundamental context for communication and source of relationship.

Secondary groups are artificially made groups. Most groups found in health care settings are secondary groups. Secondary groups differ from primary groups in structure and purpose. They are formally established to achieve certain agreed-upon goals. In contrast with natural primary groups, they have a prescribed structure, a designated leader, and last for a specified length of time. When the group achieves its goals, the group disbands. Secondary groups include therapy groups, work groups, and educational groups (Fig. 12–1).

Principles of group relationships in secondary groups originate from and build on the human behavior that occurs in natural groups. People join secondary groups for one of three reasons: to meet personally established goals, to develop skills to make better adaptations to the environment, or to satisfy the expectation of a larger group system to which the individual belongs. A study of the number and types of groups a person belongs to provides valuable data about values and interests. Exercise 12–1 is designed to give you an idea of the role groups play in a person's life.

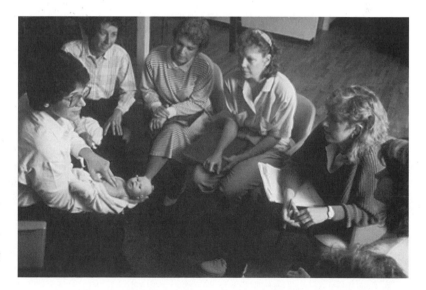

Figure 12–1 Secondary groups are formed for a specific purpose and disband when the purpose is achieved. (Courtesy of the University of Maryland School of Nursing)

EXERCISE 12–1
The Role of Group Communication

Purpose: To help students gain an appreciation of the role group communication plays in their lives.

Time: 25 minutes

Directions:
1. Write down all of the groups in which you have been a participant, e.g., family, scouts, swim team, and community, religious, work, and social groups.
2. Describe the influence membership in each of these groups had on the development of your self-concept.
3. Identify the ways in which membership in different groups was of value in your life.
4. Identify the primary reason you joined each group. If you have discontinued membership, specify the reason.

Discussion:
1. How similar or dissimilar were your answers from those of your classmates?
2. What factors account for differences in the quantity and quality of your group memberships?
3. How similar were the ways in which membership enhanced your self-esteem?
4. If your answers were dissimilar, what makes membership in groups such a complex experience?
5. Could different people get different things out of very similar group experiences?
6. What implications does this exercise have for your nursing practice?

All groups have a structure (group process) and an emotional life based on the communication and meaning of the group to individual members (group dynamics) that facilitate or impede the accomplishment of group goals.

GROUP DYNAMICS

Group dynamics includes all of the communication processes that take place within a group. It is influenced by individual communication and group variables that bind the individual to the group purpose and that cause group membership to become important. A model of the common determinants of group dynamics is presented in Figure 12–2. Groups in which members possess commitment and are reasonably similar in functional capabilities and cultural background and that operate with a democratic leadership style are most likely to function smoothly.

INDIVIDUAL VARIABLES

Commitment

Commitment denotes responsibility and involvement. Successful groups are constituted of members who are motivated to fulfill their responsibilities as group members. *Motivation* "refers to the

forces that activate behavior and direct it toward one goal instead of another" (Meichenbaum, 1989). It helps to have a goal that members can support, but a motivated group can develop appropriate and meaningful goals. Members committed to the goals of a group derive satisfaction from their efforts. They attend meetings through choice and feel a sense of responsibility for the well-being of other group members. Group members who are unwilling to participate actively in the accomplishment of group goals must find ways to bring their individual goals in line with established group goals. Otherwise they should consider leaving the group. For a member to remain without resolving his or her fundamental conflicts with the goals of the group can jeopardize goal achievement.

Functional Similarity

Numbers alone do not make a group. Regardless of the group's purpose, members should have enough in common to communicate with each other. This is called functional similarity (Yalom, 1985). For professional groups, commonalities might include credentials, level of experience, or cooperative interests. For social groups, common denominators might be educational or functional level. Similar expertise and interest in an issue are

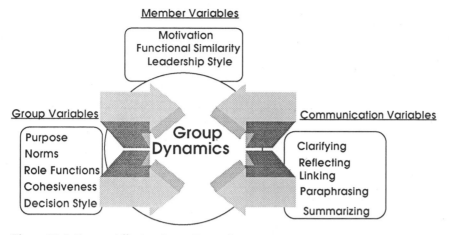

Figure 12–2 Factors Affecting Group Dynamics

other indicators. In therapy groups, the experiencing of the same kinds of problems, for example, co-dependency, loss, or abuse, provides grounds for a group relationship.

Some examples illustrate. Medication groups require a certain level of cognition because their goal is to provide education related to taking medication. The Alzheimer victim, lacking the cognitive ability to acquire new information, generally does not benefit from such groups. An adolescent girl placed in a group composed of adolescent boys or an older Ph.D. put into a group of very young adults with limited verbal and educational skills creates problems in communication because the new member who is different lacks functional similarity to the other members. In each of these actual circumstances, the "different" one became a group casualty. Member mismatches can be avoided if attention is paid to functional similarity.

Functional similarity should not be confused with sameness in communication style or personality profile. Whereas it is imperative that group members speak enough of a common language to understand one another, differences in interpersonal styles help clients learn a broader range of behavioral responses (Goldberg and Goldberg, 1973). Diversity of ideas and communication styles improves the adaptive survival characteristics of all members. Group members with complementary rather than similar views on task group issues potentially ensure a more lively discussion and a more productive outcome.

GROUP VARIABLES

Purpose

The purpose of the group represents the functional design of the group; it lays the foundation for the group's existence. Group purpose provides direction for membership decisions, development of group norms, and type of communication. Group purpose differs from a group goal in that it relates to the functional framework of the group rather than to the anticipated outcome. For example, the group goal might be improved health of the client. But the functional purpose of the group might differ depending on whether the "improved health" outcome relates to anticipated changes in interpersonal functioning, medication compliance, or greater self-awareness. If the purpose is medication compliance, the interventions would be educational, quite different from a therapy group focused on improved interpersonal functioning in which the intervention would be insight oriented. It is critical for the professional nurse to understand the purposes and communication focus of each type of group. Most client-focused groups in health care settings have either a therapeutic or an educational purpose and design. Common group purposes are presented in Box 12–1.

Norms

Every group needs to have a certain order and standard of operation. Group norms represent the

---

BOX 12–1
Identifying Group Purpose

Type of Group	Group Category Provides Opportunities for
Therapy groups	Reality testing.
	Encouraging personal growth.
	Inspiring hope.
	Strengthening personal resources.
	Developing interpersonal skills.
Support groups	Giving and receiving practical information and advice.
	Supporting coping skills.
	Promoting self-esteem.
	Enhancing problem-solving skills.
	Encouraging client autonomy.
	Strengthening hope and resiliency.
Activity groups	Getting people in touch with their bodies.
	Releasing energy.
	Enhancing self-esteem.
	Encouraging cooperation.
	Stimulating spontaneous interaction.
	Supporting creativity.
Education groups	Learning new knowledge.
	Promoting skill development.
	Providing support and feedback.
	Supporting development of competency.
	Promoting discussion of important health-related issues.

---

unwritten communication rules and standards of behavior expected of group members. Communication rules are particularly important in group interactions because different personalities are involved. Norms are developed by group members. Ideally, they support the purpose and goals of the group.

Behavioral standards enhance the productivity of the group and discourage nonfacilitative behaviors (Lieberman, 1989). Norms facilitate goal achievement because they provide the needed predictability for effective group functioning. For example, think of how a class group would operate if there were no rules governing how members communicate with each other. If an instructor did not set the agenda and provide expectations for student behavior, the class would be bedlam. In a therapy group, there is an unspoken assumption that the leader will not let the discussion become hurtful to individual members. All groups have rules governing the behaviors the group will and

will not tolerate. Such rules reflect the expectations of individual group members concerning the way members of the group will conduct themselves. Some norms are universal standards and others are specific to a particular group.

Universal Norms

Some behavioral standards are common to all successful structured groups. Confidentiality, the willingness to share information and provide feedback, and attendance at group meetings are universal norms essential for group survival. Unless group members can trust that personal information revealed in the group will not be shared outside the group setting, the necessary trust will not develop. If the leader must share any information with others for the welfare of the members, this condition should be known to the group before the information is shared. Without a commitment of attendance from its members, a group becomes an unstable means of promoting dialogue and action. Thus, regular attendance is an expectation in most groups and repeated unexcused absences are not acceptable. Since the effectiveness of the group depends on the verbal contributions of its members, verbal dialogue is a general standard of behavior.

Group-Specific Norms

Group-specific norms emerge from the interpersonal needs of group members and the identified goals of the group. Examples of norms emerging from the combined expectations, values, and needs of group members include the degree of risk taking, decision making, toleration of humor and anger, focus on task or process, and level of leader control. For instance, some groups are characterized by blunt provocations designed to strip away a person's defenses, forcing members to confront their feelings. In other groups, confrontations are presented with tact and sensitivity.

Group members initially look to their leader to model important norms. As the group develops its own identity, members assume a more active role in defining and modifying behavioral standards. Once formed, norms are difficult to change even though circumstances no longer warrant their existence. Exercise 12–2 will help you develop a deeper understanding of group norms.

EXERCISE 12–2
Identifying Norms

Purpose: To help identify norms operating in groups.

Time: 20 minutes

Directions:
1. Divide a piece of paper into three columns.
2. In the first column, put the norms you think exist in your class or work group. In the second column, put the norms you think exist in your family. Examples of norms might be: no one gets angry, decisions are made by consensus, assertive behaviors are valued, missed sessions and lateness are not tolerated.
3. Share your norms with the group, first related to the school or work group and then to the family. Place this information in the third column.

Discussion:
Discussion could focus on the following questions:
1. Were there many similarities between the norms you think exist in your school or work group and those others in the same group had on their list?
2. Were there any "universal" norms on either of your lists?
3. Were you surprised either by some of the norms you put down when you thought about it or with those of your classmates?
4. Did you or other members in the group feel a need to refine or discuss the meaning of the norms on your list?
5. How difficult was it to determine implicit norms operating in the group?

Cohesiveness

Cohesiveness refers to "the degree of positive attachment and investment (involvement, belongingness, importance) that members have for the group" (Yalom, 1985). Yalom refers to cohesiveness as the "we" value a group holds for its members. People develop a greater commitment to group goals and are willing to work harder to achieve them when they value other group members and want to be a part of the group. Group attraction can develop from the appeal of other group members, the significance of the group task, or the values and goals held by the group. Feeling a sense of belonging in group situations closely parallels the sense of mutuality and rapport that develops in successful one-to-one therapeutic relationships (Budman et al., 1989).

Cohesiveness is fostered by norms that encourage the open expression of feelings, acceptance, and mutual support. Feeling valued by others stimulates self-disclosure and a willingness to take interpersonal risks. Group members are more willing to reveal their innermost thoughts, feelings, and fears. Stressing teamwork and working through conflict as necessary parts of group dynamics are interventions the leader can use to encourage cohesiveness.

If members are to value their group participation, it is critical for the leader to credit the group as a whole for goal accomplishment and teamwork in public as well as in private. Nothing is more destructive to group cohesiveness than having the leader claim full credit for goal achievement. The leader and other members should also acknowledge the outstanding efforts of individual members. Members with low status in the group are particularly appreciative of praise from other group members and the leader. Caring for each other and a team approach are strong evidence of cohesiveness (Corey and Corey, 1987). Communication principles that enhance the development of cohesiveness are found in Box 12–2. Research suggests that cohesive groups experience more personal satisfaction with goal achievement and that members of such groups are more likely to join other group relationships (Brilhart and Galanes, 1989).

Group Think

It is possible for a group to become too cohesive. *"Group think"* is experienced when loyalty to the

1. Group tasks are within the membership's range of ability and expertise.
2. Comments and responses are nonevaluative; they are focused on behaviors rather than on personal characteristics.
3. The leader points out group accomplishments and acknowledges member contributions.
4. The leader is empathetic and teaches members how to give feedback.
6. The leader sanctions creative tension as necessary to goal achievement.

group and approval by other group members become so important that members are afraid to express conflicting ideas and opinions. The group exerts pressure on members to act as one voice. Critical thinking and realistic appraisal of issues get lost (Janis, 1971; Rosenblum, 1982). Group think deludes a group into making serious errors in judgment. In the process of rationalizing the correctness of their decision making, groups characterized by group think dehumanize others. Members who disagree with the uncritically accepted proposal are discounted or ignored. Input is not sought from people who might disagree, even if they might be affected by the decision. This usually is a serious oversight because nonparticipants are likely to sabotage a decision in which they had no part. Group

think, taken to an extreme, can result in breaking the law, as evidenced in the Watergate scandal in which a president's desire to get reelected was allowed to override the ethical and legal rights of his opponents. The symptoms of group think are outlined in Box 12-3.

Role Positions

People assume roles in groups that directly and indirectly influence their communication and the responses of others. A person's role position in the group corresponds to the status, power, and internal image other members in the group have of the member. Chosen role behaviors become standardized over time. Group members usually have trouble breaking away from roles they have been cast in, despite their best efforts. For example, people will look to the "helper" group member for advice even when that person lacks expertise or needs the group's help herself. Other times a role position is projected onto a particular group member representing a hidden agenda or unresolved issue for the group as a whole, rather than the characteristics of the member involved. If one member is being scapegoated, ignored, deferred to, or consistently idealized by all other group members, chances are that similar group behaviors or issues the group does not want to deal with are being projected onto that member.

1. Invulnerability:	Strong feeling that nothing can interfere with proposal or decisions; minimizing or ignoring danger signals.	
2. Rationalization:	Developing a unified justification about success; gathering only positive evidence without looking seriously at limitations.	
3. Morality:	Unquestioned sense of morality without considering the ethical consequences of decisions or impact on people affected by them.	
4. Stereotypes:	Nonmembers are viewed as weak, nonessential stake holders, stupid or evil. No effort is made to include or consider their position.	
5. Pressure:	Individual members who disagree with decision are eliminated, ignored, ridiculed, or silenced through social pressures from real opposition.	
6. Self-censorship:	Individual members do not express their misgivings during the crucial discussion phase.	
7. Unanimity:	There is an assumed consensus with little basis in reality.	
8. Mindguards:	Members who have opposing information protect the leader and other group members from hearing information in conflict with the groupthink decision.	

Adapted with permission from Janis I (1971). Groupthink. Psychology Today Magazine 44–46, 74 (November). Copyright © 1971 (Sussex Publishers, Inc).

Exercise 12–3 considers group role position expectations.

Power Bases in Groups

In groups, power and influence refer to the relative rank or position individual group members hold— the amount of interpersonal leverage and control one member has over another. Well-developed group structure consists of obvious ranking, interdependent roles, formalized patterns of interaction, and subgroups (Sarri and Galinsky, 1974).

An important rule associated with group power, which some people overlook, is that a per-

---

EXERCISE 12–3
Headbands: Group Role Expectations

Purpose:
1. To experience the pressures of role expectations.
2. To demonstrate the effects of role expectations on individual behavior in a group.
3. To explore the effects of role pressures on total group performance.

Time: Approximately 45 minutes

Directions:
1. Break the group up into a smaller unit of 10 to 15 members. In a large group, a small group perform while the remaining members observe.
2. Make up mailing labels or headbands that can be attached or tied around the heads of the participants. Each headband is lettered with directions on how the other members should respond to the role. Examples:

   Comedian: Laugh at me.
   Expert: Ask my advice.
   Important Person: Defer to me.
   Stupid: Sneer at me.
   Insignificant: Ignore me.
   Loser: Pity me.
   Boss: Obey me.
   Helpless: Support me.

3. Place a headband on each member in such a way that the member cannot read his or her own label, but the other members can see it easily.
4. Provide a topic for discussion—for example, why the members chose nursing, the women's movement—and instruct each member to interact with the others in a way that is natural for him or her. Don't role-play but be yourself. React to each member who speaks by following the instructions on the speaker's headband. You are not to tell each other what the headbands say, but simply to react to them.
5. After about 20 minutes, the facilitator halts the activity and directs each member to guess what his or her headband says and then to take it off and read it.

Discussion:
Initiate a discussion, including any members who observed the activity. Possible questions are:
1. What were some of the problems of trying to "be yourself" under conditions of group role pressure?
2. How did it feel to be consistently misinterpreted by the group—to have them laugh when you were trying to be serious, or to have them ignore you when you were trying to make a point?
3. Did you find yourself changing your behavior in reaction to the group treatment of you, withdrawing when they ignored you, acting confident when they treated you with respect, giving orders when they deferred to you?

Adapted from Pfeiffer J, Jones J (1977). A Handbook of Structured Experiences for Human Relations Training, vol. VI. LaJolla, CA, University Associates Publishers. With permission.

BOX 12–4
Power Bases in Groups

Reward power: Exists when one or more members of a group believe another member of the group has the power to dispense rewards or remove negative consequences.

Coercive power: Exists when one or more members of a group believe another member of the group has the power to dispense punishment or remove positive consequences.

Legitimate power: Exists when one or more members believe that another member possesses that power by virtue of rank, culture, delegation, or appointment.

Referent power: Exists when one or more members admire or desire to imitate another member.

Expert power: Exists when one or more members perceive that another member has the expertise and knowledge they lack.

---

son can influence the group only when conforming to it (Jacobson, 1989). Group members expect a person of power to respect the norms of the group. A sure way to lose power is to lack understanding of the group norms and to try to impose a solution on group members. Box 12–4 identifies power bases commonly found in groups (Sullivan and Decker, 1992).

To some extent, the degree of status one enjoys in a group corresponds to the external status or authority an individual possesses outside the group, particularly in work groups. Some group members, because of the force of their personalities, emerge as dominant forces in a group. More often power is implicitly given to the group members who best clarify the needs of the other group members and/or move the group toward goal achievement. These are not always the group members making the most statements. A person can make few but very meaningful comments. What seems important is the ability to reflect and deliver the dominant thinking of a group in a concise, direct manner.

CASE EXAMPLE

Al is a powerful leader in a job search support group. Although he makes few comments, he has an excellent understanding of and sensitivity to the needs of individual members. When these are violated, Al speaks up and the group listens. His observations are always on target, and he has a referent power base clearly as powerful as that of the more verbal group facilitators.

Role Functions

Role functions differ from the positional roles group members assume. They are defined as "more or less coherent and unified systems of behavior directed towards goals that both satisfy personal needs and maintain group values" (Goldberg and Goldberg, 1973). Every group has task and maintenance role functions that different members assume to facilitate goal achievement (*task functions*) and to foster the emotional life of the group (*maintenance functions*) (Bennis and Shephard, 1948).

A healthy balance between task and maintenance functions increases group productivity. When task functions predominate to the exclusion of maintenance functions, member satisfaction and personal commitment to the goal are at risk. On the other hand, groups in which maintenance functions override task functions do not always reach their goals. Group life flourishes, but little is accomplished. Members don't confront controversial issues, and the creative tension needed for successful group growth doesn't occur. Without meaningful task accomplishment, a group at some point ceases to exist. Without commitment and a sense of caring, group members are less motivated to achieve group goals. Within a given group, a person may assume several different roles. Contrast involvement in groups where attention is given to member needs with that in groups which disregard member needs and values. Usually some members assume more of the task functions and others more of the maintenance functions. Task and maintenance role functions found in most successful small groups are given in Box 12–5. Exercise 12–4 gives practice in identifying task and maintenance functions.

Bennis and Shephard (1948) also identify nonfunctional role functions in a group. Referred to as self-roles, a person fulfills self-needs at the expense of other member needs, group values, and goal achievement. Self-roles detract from the group's work and compromise goal achievement by taking time away from group issues and creating discomfort among group members. Nonfunctional self-roles are identified in Box 12–6.

Leadership

Leadership is defined as "interpersonal influence, exercised in situations and directed through the

Task Functions: behaviors relevant to the attainment of group goals

Initiating: Identifies tasks or goals; defines group problem; suggests relevant strategies for solving problem.

Seeks Information or Opinion: Requests facts from other members; asks other members for opinions; seeks suggestions or ideas for task accomplishment.

Gives Information or Opinion: Offers facts to other members; provides useful information about group concerns.

Clarifies, Elaborates: Interprets ideas or suggestions placed before group; paraphrases key ideas; defines terms; adds information.

Summarizes: Pulls related ideas together; restates key ideas; offers a group solution or suggestion for other members to accept or reject.

Consensus Taking: Checks to see if group has reached a conclusion; asks group to test a possible decision.

Group Maintenance Tasks: behaviors that help the group maintain harmonious working relationships

Harmonizing: Attempts to reconcile disagreements; helps members reduce conflict and explore differences in a constructive manner.

Gate Keeping: Helps keep communication channels open; points out commonalities in remarks; suggests approaches that permit greater sharing.

Encouraging: Indicates by words and body language unconditional acceptance of others; agrees with contributions of other group members; is warm, friendly, and responsive to other group members.

Compromising: Admits mistakes; offers a concession when appropriate; modifies position in the interest of group cohesion.

Standard Setting: Calls for the group to reassess or confirm implicit and explicit group norms when appropriate.

Every group needs both types of functions and needs to work out a satisfactory balance of task and maintenance activity.

After Rogers C (1972). The process of the basic encounter group. *In* Diedrich R, Dye HA (eds.) (1972), Group Procedures: Purposes, Processes and Outcomes. Boston, Houghton Mifflin.

communication process, toward the attainment of a specified goal or goals" (Tannenbaum, Wechsler, and Massarik, 1988). Two basic assumptions support the function of group leadership: (1) Group leaders have a significant influence on group process, and (2) most problems in groups can be avoided or reworked productively if the leader is aware and responsive to the needs of individual group members, including the needs of the leader. Effective leadership requires adequate preparation, professional leadership attitudes and behavior,

responsible selection of clients, and use of a responsible scientific rationale for determining a specific group approach.

Additionally, effective leaders are good listeners. They observe nonverbal as well as verbal communications and are able to convey warmth and understanding. Effective leaders are able to adapt their leadership style to fit the changing needs of the group. Finally, effective group leaders are committed to the group goals and to supporting the integrity of group members as equal partners in meeting these goals.

Fortunately, leadership behaviors can be learned. Effective group leaders have a clear understanding of their skills and limitations. Such knowledge allows the nurse to choose to explore new roles or to use previously untapped skills. You may be aware of how you interact in groups, but perhaps you have not taken the time to look at how you view yourself in the leadership role.

Types of Leaders

A group leader may be appointed or elected to the position. Or the leader can emerge from the group membership. This type of leader is classified as an emergent leader and is perceived by other group members as powerful and often having equal status

Aggressor:	Criticizes or blames others. Personally attacks other members. Uses sarcasm and hostility in interactions.
Blocker:	Instantly rejects ideas or argues an idea to death. Cites tangential ideas and opinions. Obstructs decision making.
Joker:	Disrupts work of the group by constantly joking and refusing to take group task seriously.
Avoider:	Whispers to others, daydreams, doodles, acts indifferent and passive.
Self-Confessor:	Uses the group to express personal views and feelings unrelated to group task.
Recognition Seeker:	Seeks attention by excessive talking, trying to gain leader's favor, expressing extreme ideas, or demonstrating peculiar behavior.

Developed from Benne KD, Sheats P (1948). Functional roles of group members. Journal of Social Issues 4(2):41–49.

EXERCISE 12–4

Task versus Maintenance Functions

Purpose: To help you identify task versus maintenance functions.

Time: 1 hour

Directions:
1. Break up into groups of eight students each.
2. Choose a topic to discuss—for example, how you would restructure the nursing program; nursing and the women's movement; the value of a group experience; nursing as a profession.
3. Two students should volunteer to be the observers.
4. The students discuss the topics for 30 minutes, with observers using the initial of each student and the grid below to mark with a tick [///] the number of times each student uses a task or maintenance function.
5. Following completion of the group interaction, each observer shares his or her observations with the other group members.

Task Functions

Initiating _____

Information seeking _____

Clarifying _____

Consensus _____

Testing _____

Summarizing _____

_____

_____

Maintenance Functions

Encouraging _____

Expressing _____

Group feeling _____

Harmonizing _____

Compromising _____

Gate-keeping _____

Setting standards _____

Discussion:
1. Was there an adequate balance between task and maintenance activity?
2. What roles did different members assume?
3. Were the two observers in agreement as to members' assumptions of task versus maintenance functions? If there were discrepancies, what do you think contributed to their occurrence?
4. What did you learn from this exercise?

with the designated leader. When the emergent leader recognizes and respects the authority of the designated leader, the group dynamics are enhanced. But when the emergent leader sabotages the group goals or attempts to displace the legitimate leader, group dynamics get sidetracked by a power struggle. Ideally, group leadership is a shared function of all group members, with many emergent

EXERCISE 12–5
Clarifying Personal Leadership Role Preferences

Purpose: To help you focus on how you personally experience the leadership role.

Time: 20 minutes

Directions:
Answer the following questions briefly:
1. What do you enjoy most about the leadership role?
2. What do you like least about the leadership role?
3. What skills do you bring to the leadership role?
4. What are the differences in your functioning as a group member and as a group leader?

Discussion:
1. What types of transferable skills did you find you bring to the leadership role? For example, are you an oldest child, did you organize a play group, did you teach swimming to retarded children in high school, are you a member of a large family?
2. Were some of the uncomfortable feelings "universal" for a majority of the group?
3. What skills would you need to develop in order to feel comfortable as a group leader?
4. What did you learn about yourself from doing this exercise?

leaders and with each member contributing to the overall functioning of the group (Brilhart and Galanes, 1989). Exercise 12–5 is designed to help you develop an understanding of the leadership role.

Decision Making

The final factor that influences group dynamics is the type of group decision-making process employed. Decision making is more of an issue in work groups than in therapeutic, educational, or support groups. Group decision making often yields a better product than individual solutions for three reasons: (1) The knowledge, skills, and resources of all participants are available to influ-

ence the solution; group members build on one another's ideas. (2) Since there are so many different perspectives available in group thinking, it is more likely that positive and negative consequences of each solution will be considered. (3) If the decision is to be implemented by a group rather than an individual, including those affected by the solution in the decision-making process ensures ownership and greater likelihood of compliance. Each decision-making approach will have different consequences for the group. Common approaches to group decision making are defined in Box 12–7.

GROUP PROCESS

Group process refers to the identifiable structural development of a group that is needed for a group to mature. Groups follow progressive stages of development that parallel the developmental stages of individual relationships. Each phase of group development has its own set of tasks that build and expand on the work of previous phases. Phases overlap, and the group can return to an earlier stage of development as it faces crises or membership changes.

Theories of group development are useful in orienting nurses to the complexity of group communication. The phases of groups as they are conceptualized by different group theorists are presented in Box 12–8. Tuckman's (1965) theory of small

---

BOX 12–7
Approaches to Decision Making

Default: Members cannot agree on a decision, so no decision is consciously made by the members.
Majority: The majority of members agree to the decision, but the decision does not necessarily have the support of all members.
Consensus: All members participate in the decision-making process and are willing to support the decision.
Unanimous: All members participate in the decision-making process and agree on the decision.
Minority: One or more strong members of the group make the decision. The majority does not agree with the decision but lacks the courage to say so.

BOX 12–8
Phases in Group Development

	Forming	Storming	Norming	Performing			Adjourning
Tuckman	Forming	Storming	Norming	Performing			Adjourning
Sarri and Galinsky	Origin Phase	Formative Phase	Intermediate Phase	Revision Phase	Intermediate Phase II	Maturation Phase	Termination
Bennis and Shepard	Dependence (Authority Relations) a—dependence–flight b—counterdependence–flight c—resolution–catharsis			Interdependence (Personal Relations) d—enchantment–flight e—disenchantment–flight f—consensual validation			
Yalom	*Early Formative* — Orientation Hesitant Participation Search for Meaning		Conflict Dominance Rebellion	Development of Cohesion	*Advanced Group* — Recurrent Problems a—subgrouping b—self-disclosure c—conflict		Termination
Bach (analytic approach)	Members test out group situation.	Look to conductor and center hopes on him.	Regression—playing out family roles.	Role playing becomes more fanciful.	*Stormy and Emotionally Intense* — Emotional discharge results.	Take more serious view of selves as group. See structure and function.	Deep analytic interpretations.
Schultz	Inclusion	Control	Affection				
Gibbs — Four Modes of Activity	Acceptance	Data Flow	Goal	Control			

BOX 12–9
Characteristics of Effective and Ineffective Groups

Effective Groups	*Ineffective Groups*
1. Goals are clearly identified and collaboratively developed.	1. Goals are vague or imposed on the group without discussion.
2. Open, goal-directed communication of feelings and ideas is encouraged.	2. Communication is guarded: Feelings are not always given attention.
3. Power is equally shared and rotates among members, depending on ability and group needs.	3. Power resides in the leader or is delegated with little regard to member needs. It is not shared.
4. Decision making is flexible and adapted to group needs.	4. Decision making occurs with little or no consultation. Consensus is expected rather than negotiated based on data.
5. Controversy is viewed as healthy because it builds member involvement and creates stronger solutions.	5. Controversy and open conflict are not tolerated.
6. There is a healthy balance between task and maintenance role functioning.	6. One-sided focus on task or maintenance role functions to the exclusion of the complementary function.
7. Individual contributions are acknowledged and respected. Diversity is encouraged.	7. Individual resources are not utilized. Conformity, the "company man," is rewarded. Diversity is not respected.
8. Interpersonal effectiveness, innovation, and problem-solving adequacy are evident.	8. Problem-solving abilities, morale, and interpersonal effectiveness are low and undervalued.

---

group development provides an uncomplicated theoretical framework for implementing groups. This model is used as the theoretical framework for small-group communication in this text.

Characteristics of effective and ineffective groups are presented in Box 12–9. Group process influences group dynamics. The timing and nature of verbal interventions require a knowledge of normal group development. For example, expecting a newly formed group to move directly into problem resolution without first going through the necessary introductory stages of building trust can cause needless frustration and conflict. The leader can recognize the conflict emerging in early stages of group development as a normal and necessary stage rather than as resistance on the part of individual members. Viewed in this way, the interventions are likely to be compassionate and productive.

APPLICATIONS

SIMILARITIES AND DIFFERENCES BETWEEN GROUP AND INDIVIDUAL COMMUNICATION

Group communication shares many of the characteristics of individual communication. The acceptance, respect, and understanding needed in individual relationships are essential components of effective group communication. Similar communication strategies of using open-ended questions, reflecting, paraphrasing, asking for clarification, linking, and summarizing are also important in group communication. Minimal cues in the form of eye contact with speakers and other group members, leaning forward, nodding, and smiling encourage sharing in groups. Allowing for pauses when it looks as though people are thinking is particularly important in groups. Usually it is anxiety provoking but worthwhile to wait. Pauses serve a similar purpose of bracketing information and allowing think time. The group leader can use a variety of listening responses to respond to a client's statements, each of which can elicit a different focus.

CASE EXAMPLE

Group member: I hate my work. No matter how hard I try, I can't please my boss. I'd quit tomorrow if I could.

Leader: I'm not sure I quite understand your situation; could you tell me more about it? (*Asking for clarification*)

Leader: From what you say, it sounds as though you are feeling pretty desperate. (*Reflecting*)

Leader: You're so unhappy with what is going on at work that you are thinking of quitting? (*Paraphrasing*)

As in individual relationships, the nurse links ideas with feelings and periodically summarizes member contributions, but there is an important distinction. Instead of linking ideas with feelings, the leader links common themes of two or more members.

CASE EXAMPLE

Member: I feel like giving up. I've tried to do everything right, and I still can't seem to get good grades in my classes.

Leader: I wonder if the discouragement you are feeling is similar to Mary's disenchantment with her job and Bill's desire to throw in the towel on his marriage.

Periodically, the leader summarizes or asks members to summarize the group's activities. For example,

"Today it seems as though we covered a lot of ground in finding useful strategies to reduce stress."

"Which ideas seemed most relevant to you?"

"Would someone in the group like to summarize what we discussed today?"

"Given today's discussion, I'd like to go around the room and ask each of you what you plan to do in the next week to facilitate your job search."

"We're almost out of time; I wonder if any of you have any final comments you'd like to make."

There are also important differences between individual and group communication strategies. More people are involved in a group communication process, so transactions are more complex. Each member brings to the group a different set of perspectives, perceptions of reality, communication styles, and personal agendas. This makes it harder to talk and to understand others in a group conversation. Although people talk informally in natural groups without self-consciousness, expressing oneself in a formal group makes a person wary. Taking risks to express oneself fully is potentially more frightening simply because of the possibility of multiple responses. The desired *communication flow is from member to member rather than from nurse leader to client.* Instead of the leader responding to a member, the leader might ask other group members for their reaction.

BOX 12–10
Suggestions for Giving Feedback

Summary of Suggestions for Giving Feedback

1. Be specific and direct.
2. Support comments with evidence.
3. Separate the issue from the person.
4. "Sandwich" negative messages between positive ones.
5. Pose the situation as a mutual problem.
6. Mitigate or soften negative messages to avoid overload.
7. Timing: Deliver feedback close to occurrence.
8. Manner of delivery
   a. Assertive, dynamic.
   b. Trustworthy, fair, and credible.
   c. Relaxed and responsive.
   d. Preserve public image of recipient.

From Haslett B, Ogilvie J (1988). Feedback processes in task groups. *In* Cathcart R, Samovar L (eds.) (1988), Small Group Communication: A Reader. (5th ed.). Dubuque, IA, William C. Brown, p. 397. Copyright © 1988 Wm. C. Brown Communications, Inc., Dubuque, Iowa. All rights reserved. Reprinted by permission.

CASE EXAMPLE

Member: I was really upset with last week's meeting because I didn't feel we made any progress. Everyone complained, but no one had a solution.

Leader: Would anyone like to respond to what Martha just said?

Once more information is available, the group members and leader can address the issues in a problem-solving manner. Principles of giving feedback to group members parallel those described in Chapter 10. A summary of suggestions for group communication feedback is presented in Box 12–10.

LEADER TASKS IN THE LIFE CYCLE OF A GROUP

Figure 12–3 depicts the life cycle of groups. Below are descriptions of the tasks.

Pregroup Phase

Aligning Purpose and Membership

Before the group begins, the group leader considers the following questions to provide direction in determining the most effective structural framework for the group.

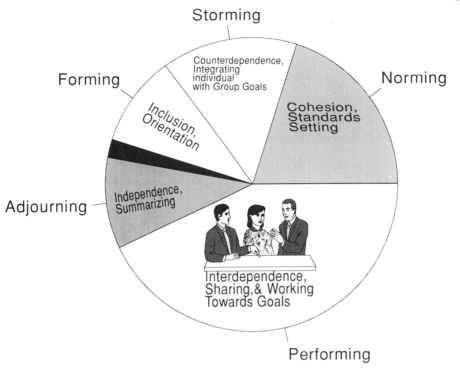

Figure 12–3 The Life Cycle of Groups

1. What is the purpose of the group?

Group leaders plan each session from beginning to end. It is important for the leader to have a clear idea of the focus of the group (Jacobs, Harvill, and Mason, 1986). The group's purpose gives direction to the establishment of group goals, the structure needed to attain identified goals, and the development of norms congruent with the group's purpose. Knowing that the group is to have an educational, therapeutic, support, task, or committee focus helps the leader plan realistically. Intervention strategies for a group with an educational or support purpose, for example, are quite different from those of a therapeutic group.

2. What are the goals of the group?

While the purpose of the group provides direction for the focus of the group, the group goal gives information about the outcome or result the group hopes to attain through its efforts. Group goals need to be achievable, measurable, and within the capabilities of group membership.

Identifying the group goals helps the leader determine the time frame and type of membership needed to achieve the group objectives. Having a goal helps members stay on course and offers a sound rationale for holding the group.

3. How will participating in a particular group help the prospective group member?

In effective groups, members feel ownership and experience personal growth or satisfaction as a result. Understanding the benefits of group membership helps the leader match individual with group interests. Groups in which members feel they personally get something out of their participation are perceived as having more value.

The leader needs to decide whether the group will have a closed or an open membership and whether the group goals are better achieved with a homogeneous or heterogeneous membership. *Closed groups* have a defined membership with an expectation of regular attendance. Most psychotherapy groups fall into this category. In an open group, the only criterion for group membership is a personal investment in the goals of the group. Individuals may come and go depending on their needs. Norms are of necessity much looser. *Open groups* do not have a defined membership; they provide more immediate direct information and practical advice. Most support groups in the community fall into this category. *Homogeneous groups* have a common denominator pertaining to all members of the group. Research indicates that such groups benefit clients who are coping with issues of exclusive importance to a particular group—a women's group focused on women's issues, for example (Prehn and Thomas, 1990). Commonalities may include a symptom, a diagnostic category, or a personal characteristic. Alcoholics Anonymous, ostomy clubs, Compassionate Friends, Alzheimer's disease family support groups, and consciousness-raising groups for men and women are familiar examples of homogeneous groups. By contrast, a *heterogeneous group* may represent a wide diversity of human experience and problems. Most psychotherapy and insight-oriented personal growth groups have a heterogeneous membership (Bertcher and Maple, 1985).

4. What capabilities does the client require to participate in a particular group?

Group members need to have the ability to function effectively in any given group. They need to have the requisite personal and cognitive characteristics and in some cases the expertise to make meaningful contributions. Clients with serious verbal difficulties, significant memory deficits, or limited tolerance for cooperative behaviors do best in group situations specially geared to meet their needs. Awareness of individual social responses and functional ability may indicate that one type of group situation is preferable to another for different individuals. "Patient mix difficult for the group" was the most frequently mentioned perceived barrier to nurse-conducted groups in a study completed by Van Servellen et al. (1991).

On the other hand, if the social distance and differences in functional capabilities among members are not extreme, the leader has several alternatives. One is to admit two members who demonstrate a similar "different" trait; another is to pair the leader temporarily with the "different" member to facilitate the process of acceptance. Using different methods to arrive at a common

goal can become a norm. When viewed as part of the work of the group, the working through of contradictory approaches can enrich the resources of the group and the quality of the solution.

5. What is my role as a nurse leader in the group, and what knowledge and skills are required to function in such a role?

Beginning practitioners with a knowledge of group dynamics can lead discussions, educational sessions, and some types of activity groups. Additional training and supervision are needed to lead a psychotherapy group effectively. Educational group leaders need to have expertise on the topic for discussion. Self-awareness of values, possible biases, and interpersonal limitations are important qualifications for all group leaders.

Creating the Appropriate Group Environment

Structuring the group experience requires thought. The group should be conducted in a quiet, open space, apart from the mainstream of activity. The room should be neither too hot nor too cold and large enough to accommodate all participants comfortably. Holding meetings in the same room each time fosters continuity and trust. Complete privacy and freedom from interruptions are key considerations. A sign on the door indicating the group is in session prevents unwelcome intrusions.

Seats should be comfortable and arranged in a circle so that each member has clear access to the facial expressions and nonverbal cues that accompany the communications of the members. Face-to-face contact is needed for optimum discussion in group sessions. The number of sessions, time of day, and frequency of meetings depend on the type of group and the group goals. For example, a work group might meet twice a month, whereas a therapy group might meet on a weekly basis. Support groups meet as frequently as once a week or as infrequently as once a month. An educational group might meet for one to eight sessions and then disband.

Although the length of a group session may vary, most groups meet for 60 to 90 minutes on a regular basis. Meeting times should be established so that members can attend on a regular basis. Having a time that doesn't conflict with the members' other obligations and that is conveniently scheduled enhances group participation, becoming a routine in the person's life instead of something the individual has to think about. Participants should be informed regularly of meeting times, and well in advance. If others are involved with the participants' scheduling activities, they should be in on the planning. Groups that begin and end on time help create an atmosphere of trust and predictabilty.

Determining Appropriate Size

The purpose and goals of the group will influence the number of members needed. In general, therapy and personal growth groups consist of six to eight members. With this number of people there is sufficient time and space to express feelings and get feedback. The group is large enough to contain a diversity of opinions and ideas, yet small enough to permit connection with all of the other members. Educational groups are traditionally larger. Groups with 12 to 15 members are common. Although there is some opportunity for group interaction and feedback, lively communication among members is less than it is in smaller groups.

The size of the group directly affects the level and amount of interaction (Bertcher, 1987). Generally, groups should not have fewer than five members. With fewer than five members, interaction is limited and tends to be leader focused. If one or more members are absent, the group interaction can become intense and uncomfortable for the remaining members, or the group can cease to exist until all members are in attendance. Since a primary purpose of engaging in group relationships is to gain a variety of ideas and viewpoints, groups with limited membership curtail collaborative problem solving.

Conducting a Pregroup Interview

Before a client joins the group, the leader meets with the prospective member. The purpose of this meeting is to explain the goals of the group, assess the client's suitability for placement in the group, and structure an opportunity for the client to ask questions. Interaction with a group of strangers is a frightening prospect for many people. Having the leader outline the goals of the group, describe the kind of commitment needed, and give a thumbnail sketch of other clients in the group is reassuring to many clients.

In the interview, the nurse observes the client's communication style and anticipates assets and limitations related to group participation. The description of the group and of its members is kept short and simple. The nurse asks potential clients what they hope to get out of the group experience and the kinds of issues they wish to explore. Using this approach, the nurse has a better idea of client expectations and is better able to correct misperceptions. The leader allows ample time for questions and comments.

Forming Phase

In the initial stages of the group, the leader takes a more visibly active role than he or she does later in the group's development, when other group members share the responsibility for the functioning of the group. At first, there are many people to keep track of, and the norms governing group behavior have yet to be established. Each person has a mental image of the group that may or may not be based in reality. Over time this mental image will become a shared representation, but when the group has just formed, members experience a lot of anxiety (Jacobson, 1989).

In the initial phase of the group, the basic need of members is *acceptance*. Time and effort must be given to developing commitment and trust before the actual work of the group takes place. A leader who is firm, fair, consistent, and warm is most likely to carry the group successfully through the forming phase. Unfolding of individual characteristics and the need to find common threads seem to be important aspects of beginning group life, which cannot be short-changed or circumvented without having a serious impact on the evolving effectiveness of the group (Yalom, 1985).

Establishing the Group Contract

It is up to the leader to create a favorable group climate by describing how the group will function. Initially, the focus is on establishing a workable group contract. The contract establishes preliminary commitments to accomplishing group goals. It specifies the time and place of meetings, the nature of the group interaction, and expectations of members with respect to behavior. In a straightforward manner, the leader identifies behavioral norms, such as confidentiality, attendance, and mutual respect (Corey and Corey, 1990). Other more specific group norms are negotiated later as needs arise. From the beginning, nurse leaders model an attitude of caring, objectivity, and integrity in their communication with group members.

Developing Trust

During the initial group meetings, participants are inclined to engage in superficial, provisional communication. Trust is at a surface level, and members tend to enact their social roles as individuals as they attempt to define the aims and procedures of the group. Regardless of the importance of the identified task, the emphasis in the beginning is on getting to know other group members, their interpersonal boundaries, and their basic orientation to the sharing of responsibility, collaborative decision making, and control. Here are some common initial questions of members:

> "Will I be accepted for who I am as a person in this group?"
> "Can I really say what I feel, what happens if I am honest with my feelings?"
> "Will I be expected to perform, or can I just be myself in this group?"
> "Am I enough like the other members to feel comfortable participating?"
> "Can I count on the leader to establish norms that respect my individuality?"

The leader plays an important role in helping members develop trust in one another. If the individuals do not know each other, the leader can ask the members to introduce themselves and give a little of their background or their reason for coming to the group. Either the leader or the person who looks most at ease starts. This can be followed by a general leading question if appropriate to the group focus. "As we begin, I would like to ask each of you, 'What does (stress, having a baby, a diagnosis of cancer) mean to you?'" Or, "I'm sure everyone here has a different mental image of what a therapy group is like. I wonder if you would be willing to share your perceptions." Find-

ing others have the same fears and perceptions decreases anxiety.

The group leader identifies the purpose and goals of the group and allows ample time for questions. Even though members may know the purpose ahead of time, taking the time to verbalize the purpose allows group members to hear it in the same way. Sometimes members' responses and questions provide important information to individual group members as well as to the group's leader.

Next, the leader clarifies how the group will be conducted and what the group can expect from the leader and other members in achieving group goals. Knowing what to expect helps to reduce anxiety.

CASE EXAMPLE

Nurse (prenatal group): I will be giving you information about taking the best care of yourself before the baby comes and what to expect during labor and delivery. This is a special time, and the more you know about yourself and your baby, the more you will get out of the group experience. It is very important that you ask questions and provide your ideas as we go along.

Clients need to be educated about the nature of the group process and the behaviors required to derive the most from the group experience. As with most other relationships, people tend to get out of a group relationship what they put into it.

Fostering Mutual Identification

Identification is an important element in the formation of bonds (Eibl-Eibesfeldt, 1975). Confirmation of similarities occurs through interpersonal expressions of interest, active listening, and empathy flowing among the participants. Identification is the foundation of the emotional encounter. One way of encouraging identification is to ask members to share their expectations.

CASE EXAMPLE

Leader: It's useful at the start of a group to have an idea of what each of you would like to get out of the group. I'd like to start with Jack and ask what each of you hopes to get out of being here.

This strategy helps the group develop a level of openness, allowing members to feel that the other group members are like themselves. It also gives the leader an opportunity to correct misperceptions about group goals and to set a positive tone for the group. As members develop a growing group identification, content and process issues tend to carry over from one group session to another. There is a developing sense of continuity within the group, and the group begins to assume more active responsibility for its own functioning. Leadership becomes a shared commitment.

Storming Phase

Storming is a transitional stage in group development, occurring after participants feel comfortable with the format of the meetings and feel enough interpersonal safety and autonomy to expose their feelings. Although this stage is uncomfortable, it leads to the development of group norms. Members use testing behaviors to elicit boundaries, communication styles, and personal reactions from other members and from the leader. Such behaviors might include disagreeing—for example, with the group format, the topics for discussion, the best ways to achieve group goals, and certain member contributions as compared with other member offerings.

Issues related to members taking responsibility for task and maintenance functions are most significant during the storming and norming stages of group development. Calling attention to the work the group has accomplished and praising the involvement and participation of members emphasizes the relationship between the task and the maintenance functions. The leader might suggest commonalities in different member contributions by paraphrasing their contributions or using encouragers to stimulate further communication on a topic. Statements such as, "That is a good point," "That comment is right on target with the next issue we need to take up," and "Thank you for clarifying," acknowledge the role functions of different members.

It is important for the leader to act as a nonanxious presence during the transitional stage and to avoid becoming defensive. The leader models effective group behaviors and works with the group to reach compromises supportive of group goals.

CASE EXAMPLE

Leader: As I understand it, you agree with John that he should take his medication when he needs it, but you don't think he is paying enough attention to the times when his symptoms are getting out of control—is that correct?

In this way, the participants are challenged to express differences, and an appropriate way to word statements of disagreement is demonstrated. Focusing on the positive comments of members and linking the constructive themes of members are effective modeling behaviors. To this end such statements might be: "I wonder if others in the group share Bob's reservations"; "How would other group members respond to what Bob is saying?" Looking in the direction of positive group members as the statements are made also encourages member response. It is important for the group leader to remain nonreactive and to redirect provocative remarks back to their maker or to the group; for example, "Bill, I wonder if you might be able to tell us a little more about how you personally feel about this project without bringing anyone else into it."

If a member monopolizes the conversation, the leader can respectfully acknowledge the person's comment and refocus the issue within the group. "I appreciate your thoughts, but I think it would be important to hear from other people as well. What do you think about this, Jane?" or, "That sounds like a strong position on _____. I'm wondering if others agree or disagree."

Members who test through sexually provocative, overly flattering, or insulting remarks need to have limits set promptly: "That behavior isn't appropriate in the group. Our purpose as a group is to help each other, and your behavior is preventing that from happening." Resolution of this stage may be seen in the willingness of members to take stands on their personal preferences without being defensive and in accepting the comments of other members. Gradually the group will begin to seek compromises: "I think we should consider our first proposal"; or, "Maybe we should consider a number of options before we decide on this." When such comments are made, the group is ready to establish group norms, which are needed for the group to reach its goals.

Norming Phase

Once power and control issues are resolved, feedback becomes more spontaneous and more open. Group members begin to share more responsibility for the leadership of the group. Out of the conflict and new-found cooperation, behavioral standards emerge that will help the group achieve its task. Group members exchange more personal information about each other and begin to think more about the task at hand. Common agreement develops about the behavioral standards expected if the group is to achieve its goals. Individual goals become aligned with group goals.

Performing Phase

Most of the group's work is accomplished in the performing phase. Cohesiveness develops to a stronger degree, so that the group is freed to work on issues as they relate to the accomplishment of group goals. Working together on a project or participating in another person's personal growth allows members to experience one another's personal strengths and the collective caring of the group. As a result, there is an esprit de corps and a possibility of affirmation. *Affirmation* is an abstract feeling that "takes place through relations with others based on validation, tenderness, cherishing and respect on a reciprocal basis" (McGuire and Fairbanks, 1977). Knowing one is valued and the nature of that value is generally a momentary experience, unexpected and certainly unconventional. Experienced emotionally rather than intellectually, one has an awareness of oneself in relation to others that cannot be solicited actively. Affirmation usually occurs in a way one never would have anticipated, yet it normally exceeds one's fondest expectations. Of all the possibilities that can happen in a group, affirmation of self is the one most valued by group members.

Termination Phase (Adjourning)

The final phase of group development is termination or adjournment. Closure is encouraged as members express their feelings about one another as significant group members. Each member can do this in turn, perhaps ending with the leader, who adds his or her own personal observations and feelings. Any concerns the group may have about an individual member or suggestions for future growth can be stated, and there is a constructive purpose in making such statements. By waiting until the group ends to share closing comments, the leader has an opportunity to soften or clarify previous comments, to connect cognitive and feeling elements, and to summarize the group experience. The leader needs to remind members that the norm of confidentiality does not end with the completion of the group. Exercise 12–6 considers closure issues.

EXERCISE 12–6
Group Closure, Expressing Affection

Purpose: To experience summarizing your feelings about each other.

Time: 45 minutes

Directions:
1. Focus your attention on the group member next to you, and think about what you like about the person, how you see him or her in the group, and what you might wish for that person as a member of the group.
2. After five minutes, your instructor will ask you to tell the person next to you to use the three themes in making a statement about the person. For example, "The thing I most like about you in the group is . . ."; "To me you represent the . . . in the group"; and so on.
3. When all of the group members have had a turn, discussion may focus on the following.

Discussion:
1. How difficult was it to capture the person's meaning in one statement?
2. How did you experience telling someone about your response to him or her in the group?
3. How did it feel being the group member receiving the message?
4. What did you learn about yourself form doing this exercise?
5. What implications does this exercise have for future interactions in group relationships?

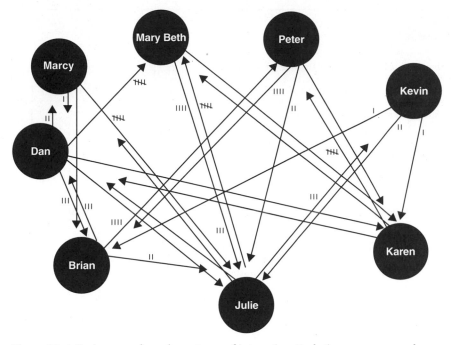

Figure 12–4 Sociograms show the patterns of interaction: Each time a person speaks, an arrow is drawn to the intended receiver of the message.

Evaluating Group Communication

Two of the most common ways of evaluating group communication are the sociogram and the Bales Interaction Scale. A sociogram is a diagram that shows the seating arrangement of member participants, the number of comments made directly and indirectly by each member, the persons to whom the comments are directed, and who responds to whom. The sociogram informs the group who the most important contributors were, who was the recipient of the most comments, and who did not participate (Fig. 12–4). This tool, however, cannot evaluate the group climate, the quality of member contributions, or the role functions of different members. The Bales Interaction Scale is used to analyze the types of contributions members make and provides information about group quality (Box 12–11).

TYPES OF GROUPS

Health care groups are categorized according to their purpose or functional design as therapeutic, activity, support, or educational groups. Applica-

tions of group communication principles to work groups are described in Chapter 22. Although the same basic group principles of communication are followed in each of these groups, the group type determines the focus.

Therapeutic Groups

"Therapeutic as it applies to group relationships doesn't always mean having to do with treatment of emotional and behavioral disorders but rather having as a broad purpose increasing people's knowledge of themselves and others" (Corey and Corey, 1987). Thus, support groups for mentally healthy individuals who are seeking personal growth or emotional support are considered in the broad category of therapeutic groups.

The factors in therapeutic groups most valued by clients across a number of research studies include "self-responsibility, catharsis, universality, altruism, group cohesiveness, self-understanding, and instillation of hope" (Hoge and McLoughlin, 1991). In a group, a client can feel a deep sense of identification with other members who are dealing with issues that are similar to the one that concerns

BOX 12–11
Bales Interaction Process Analysis

Social–Emotional Area: Positive	A	1.	**Shows solidarity,** raises others' status, gives help, rewards:
		2.	**Shows tension release,** jokes, laughs, shows satisfaction:
		3.	**Shows agreement,** shows passive acceptance, understands, concurs, complies:
Task Area: Neutral	B	4.	**Gives suggestion,** direction, implying autonomy for other:
		5.	**Gives opinion,** evaluation, analysis, expresses feeling, wish:
		6.	**Gives information,** orientation, repeats, clarifies, confirms:
	C	7.	**Asks for information,** orientation, repetition, confirmation:
		8.	**Asks for opinion,** evaluation, analysis, expression of feeling:
		9.	**Asks for suggestion,** direction, possible ways of action:
Social–Emotional Area: Negative	D	10.	**Disagrees,** shows passive rejection, formality, withholds help:
		11.	**Shows tension,** asks for help, withdraws out of field:
		12.	**Shows antagonism,** deflates others' status, defends or asserts self:

KEY a. Problems of Communication   A. Positive Reactions
     b. Problems of Evaluation   B. Attempted Answers
     c. Problems of Control   C. Questions
     d. Problems of Decision   D. Negative Reactions
     e. Problems of Tension Reduction
     f. Problems of Reintegration

From Bales RF (1950). Interaction. Process Analysis. Cambridge, MA, Addison-Wesley, p. 9. Reprinted by permission of the author.

the client. The group becomes a valued resource (*cohesiveness*). The social contact and support that clients experience with other group members who are in the same predicament as they are and who have the same supposedly unacceptable feelings provide a different perspective of self that simply is not available in a one-to-one interpersonal relationship (Kreidler and Carlson, 1991). Within a natural, safe setting the person can hear and see from the experiences of others that he or she is not unique or alone, that difficulties can be resolved. Feeling understood by peers who are struggling with similar issues (*universality*) helps people gradually shed the tremendous emotional and social isolation that is occasioned by the feeling that their experiences are unique and that others don't have such limited personal resources or can't understand their emotional pain (White, 1987). Having a regular, safe place to talk about problems helps. As a woman undergoing chemotherapy expressed it:

> I'm hopeful that this treatment will work, but I'm also dealing with the fact that I might not make it. But I can't talk with my husband because he doesn't want to see me cry. Mom has had enough. I have to keep a stiff upper lip with my friends and children because they can't handle my talking about dying. They think I'm giving up. I'm not, but I need to talk about it with someone who understands. I have no one to turn to. . . . This group is my lifeline.

Therapeutic groups offer a structured format that encourages a person to experience his or her natural healing potential (*instillation of hope*). Others in the group reinforce the client's capacity for growth and healthy resources (Kreidler and England, 1990). Generally, other group members are more optimistic about a client's personal capabilities than the client is. When six other people are supportive and understanding, and even more important, when they think there are solutions a client may have overlooked, it is difficult to deny the warmth and obvious caring that can foster hope. Sharing intimate feelings with one another (*catharsis*), coupled with the respect others have for the worth and uniqueness of the individual, strengthens personal resources (*self-responsibility*) and stimulates creative solutions to a problem.

Therapeutic groups also provide reality testing. People under stress lose perspective. The tendency is to take a single incident and view it as the only explanation of self-concept. Loss of perspective compromises effective problem solving because the problem seems too big to manage. In groups a member's global statements are usually scrutinized by other group members. Group members rarely accept universal statements at face value, so that the client is encouraged to reframe unrealistic self-appraisal.

CASE EXAMPLE

Client: I have been worthless since I had this heart attack. I can't do anything anymore.

This is a global statement that represents a pervading feeling but reveals little else about the remaining capabilities of the individual. It probably isn't true that the person has no assets that can help to reestablish identity.

In a group, others might challenge the validity of this client's statement.

Nurse: I can appreciate that the shock of having a heart attack can leave you feeling off balance, but I wonder how others see your situation.

Generally, other group members will give the client specific feedback which offers insights the client hasn't considered. Coming from peers in similar circumstances, the feedback has a special credibility. After discussion, the client might develop a more specific problem-centered statement (*self-understanding*):

Client: Six weeks ago, I had a heart attack. I feel worthless because my activities are restricted.

Now that the problem has manageable boundaries, the group can help the person identify underrecognized skills and develop specific strategies to keep morale up and make needed adjustments in lifestyle. Global statements and the use of absolutes ("You always . . .," "I never . . .") are reframed through the sensitive questioning and practical support of other group members.

Structured groups simulate actual life experience in microcosm (Slater, 1966). Through the group experience clients learn how others perceive them. And by finding that others have similar concerns, they also learn coping skills that can be transferred to real-life situations (Echternacht, 1984). Clients begin to experience parts of themselves, either heretofore unknown or unacknowledged, for the first time as they are encountered and responded to by others in a group (Prehn and Thomas, 1990).

When situations can't be changed, therapeutic groups help clients accept that reality and move on with their lives. They empower clients, providing needed emotional reinforcement and comfort for clients through the supportive framework of caring words and caring actions (Dobrof et al., 1990). A hidden benefit of the therapeutic group experience is the opportunity for clients to experience giving as well as receiving help from others. There is a satisfaction in helping others that enhances self-esteem (*altruism*). Finding value as a resource and making a difference in someone else's life is particularly beneficial for clients who in the throes of their own misfortune feel they have little to offer others (Murphy, 1975).

Examples of Therapeutic Groups

PSYCHOTHERAPY

Group psychotherapy is a treatment modality suitable for people in crisis, for clients experiencing problems in daily functioning and for the regressed psychotic client, with the aim of achieving a higher level of mental health. In a number of studies clients ranked their group therapy as one of the most valuable components of their treatment protocol (Hoge and McLoughlin, 1991).

The goals of psychotherapy directly relate to personal growth and the modification of maladaptive interpersonal behaviors. Clients are expected verbally to share personal feelings, develop insights about personal behaviors, and practice new and more productive interpersonal responses. Psychotherapy groups proliferate in outpatient mental health centers as a primary form of treatment for many clients and are used in inpatient settings for treatment of the seriously mentally ill.

Applications with Psychotic Clients. Nurses frequently engage in group psychotherapy with clients who are experiencing major psychiatric illness. Since they frequently spend the most time with the psychotic client, they are in an excellent position to develop effective, formal group relationships with them and to understand their painful conflicts. For the hospitalized psychotic client, life becomes incomprehensible, without meaning. Group therapy offers a safe place for exploring the client's natural healing processes. The client can re-experience life differently through the eyes of the nurse leader and the conversations that take place in the group.

Many seriously ill clients have never experienced being perceived as having value. Receiving affirmation from others that they are worthwhile and are capable of being reflective and of making significant changes in their lives reinforces personal responsibility. Clients begin to trust first the group and then themselves as they develop a better sense of reality and begin to cope with problems (Birckhead, 1984).

Leading a group with psychotic members is anxiety provoking. The leader needs to take an active role and a proactive approach. At each session the nurse may need to remind group members individually of the meeting. It may appear to the leader that psychotic clients are not willing to attend. More often this is not the case; their seeming reluctance is part of the passivity that characterizes psychotic clients in interpersonal situations. Holding the group session in the same room at the same time is particularly important for the psychotic client, who relies on structural cues despite seeming oblivious to them.

A flexible, proactive leadership approach is needed. Spontaneous sharing among group members is not the rule, at least in the early stages of group development. If a topic is not forthcoming from the group, the leader can introduce a relevant, concrete, problem-centered topic and elicit discussion about how group members view the issue or have handled a similar problem. Patience,

using minimal encouragers, and helping people feel comfortable by acknowledging each and every contribution help. Over time, the conversation will increase. Offering refreshments in the group session is appropriate with regressed clients because it represents another form of nurturance that enhances socialization (Echternacht, 1984).

A primary goal of the leader in group psychotherapy with clients suffering from a major psychiatric illness is to understand each person as a unique human being with needs disguised as symptoms. If the person chooses to use delusions, repetitive questions, or schizophrenic images in speaking, the nurse can try to uncover the underlying theme and translate it into understandable language. Sometimes other members will translate the message if called upon by the nurse leader. The leader might say to the group, "I wonder if anyone in the group can help us understand better what John is trying to say." At other times the leader decodes the message: "I wonder if your fear that the martians are coming and will destroy you has anything to do with your parents' visit tomorrow?" Changes in physical appearance are noted. For example, one client, after being told she was attractive, appeared at the next meeting wearing makeup.

Change does not occur rapidly with the psychotic client, nor is the progression linear. As with any chronic illness, there are setbacks and remissions of symptoms. Understanding that this is a dynamic of the illness and not a resistant response to group interaction is essential. It is important to recognize how difficult it is for the psychotic client to tolerate close interaction—and how necessary it is to do so if the client is to succeed in the outside environment. With patience and a genuine regard for the personhood of each client, the nurse can treat inevitable regressions as temporary setbacks capable of being reversed. Group therapy is an extremely important support for psychotic clients, offering hope for people who mostly cannot express their need for it. Watching the client's humanness emerge is very rewarding.

Because the demands of leadership are so intense with psychotic clients, co-leadership is recommended. Co-therapists can share the group process interventions, offset negative transference from group members, and provide useful feedback to each other In addition, co-therapy provides additional opportunities for modeling cooperative behaviors in healthy relationships, so frequently missing in the psychotic client's interpersonal experience. If there is more than one leader, every group session should be processed immediately following its completion.

APPLICATIONS WITH ADOLESCENTS

Groups are an important treatment modality for adolescents, taking advantage of their normal developmental needs. Adolescents hospitalized with either physical or emotional disorders cope with critical developmental tasks simultaneously with their disorders. Since peer relations are so important, groups offer individuals a unique opportunity to deal with their problems and insecurities as well as the physical, psychological, and cognitive changes that accompany adolescence. Informal "rap sessions," held after critical incidents or deaths on the ward, use the natural mechanism of peer interaction to defuse potentially overwhelming emotional situations for the adolescent. In adolescent groups, there is a crucial need to provide structure and ensure consistency. By establishing ground rules and firmly setting limits, nurses can provide a useful testing ground for adolescents to move through this stage of development. Groups for adolescents can help clients develop the capacity to:

1. Delay gratification.
2. Tolerate anxiety, frustration, and ambiguity.
3. Develop stronger cognitive, interpersonal, and communication skills, such as problem solving, respecting others, and directing feelings toward the appropriate person.
4. Deal with ambivalence about separating from parents.
5. Cope with bodily changes and the implications of illness.
6. Establish one's identity.
7. Recognize and accept the need for peer relations.

One example of group interventions with teenagers involved providing positive affirmations by peers (Rosenstock and McLaughlin, 1982). Positive group norms required clients to make positive statements about themselves and others. Negative comments were not allowed, and partici-

pants had to acknowledge compliments. The results indicated that with this approach group participants improved social skills and developed higher self-esteem and leadership capabilities.

Groups in Long-Term Settings

At the other end of life's developmental spectrum are specially designed group programs for the frail elderly. Because of the limited likelihood of discharge from long-term facilities, many clients consider such places their home. Groups offer a wide range of useful possibilities to assist elderly clients.

A balance of stimuli is needed to arouse but not overwhelm the elderly client. When making referrals or organizing such groups, the nurse should match the purpose of the group with the client's level of functional ability. For example, groups aimed at increasing insight would not be appropriate or helpful for clients who are confused. Here are some of the different therapeutic groups available to the elderly.

Reality-Orientation Groups

Used most often with the confused elderly client, reality-orientation groups help clients maintain contact with the environment and reduce confusion about time, place, and person. Such groups are usually held each day for approximately a half hour, and the focus of the discussion is on the immediate environment; when possible the group is led by the same person. The group should not be seen as an isolated activity: What occurs in the group needs to be reinforced throughout the 24-hour period. Visual props such as clocks, calendars, bulletin boards, pictures of items, and names placed on items help clients increase awareness and reduce confusion (Burnside, 1981).

Resocialization Groups

Because of their step-by-step structure, resocialization groups are quite useful for withdrawn clients who must begin meeting new interpersonal expectations for social interaction. Resocialization groups focus on providing a simple social setting for clients to experience basic social skills. For example, a group might settle around a table with silverware and simple foods. The nurse would provide modeling and guidance to make basic conversational requests for food.

Resocialization groups are used with clients who might not be able to get involved with a remotivation group but who need companionship and involvement with others. Improvement of social skills contributes to an improved sense of self-esteem. The senses and cognitive abilities may diminish in the elderly. Basic needs for companionship, interpersonal relationships, and a place where one is accepted and understood remain the same throughout the lifespan.

Remotivation Groups

Remotivation groups have a more directed focus. They are helpful in counteracting the isolation and apathy resulting from long-term institutionalization. Remotivation groups are deliberately designed to stimulate thinking about activities required for everyday life.

Originally developed by Dorothy Hoskins Smith for use with chronic mental patients, the remotivation technique represents an effort to reach the "unwounded areas of the patient's personality, i.e., those areas and interests that have remained healthy" (Long, 1970). More recently, the approach has been used with some types of withdrawn elderly clients. Groups, which are composed of 10 to 15 members, cover such objective topics as the way plants or trees grow or consist of a reading of poetry. Visual props engage the participant and stimulate more responses. Remotivation groups are led by nurses, nursing students, and nonprofessional staff in nursing homes and mental hospitals. The steps, presented in Box 12–12, are easy to follow, and the project is rewarding to those nurses willing to take the time. Burnside (1978, 1981) is an excellent resource, offering useful guidelines for nurses interested in group work with the elderly.

Reminiscence Groups

Reminiscence groups offer powerful sources of self-esteem for the elderly who are cognitively intact. These groups are insight oriented and require cognitive functional ability. Kovach (1991) describes reminiscence as "a cognitive process of recalling events from the past that are personally significant and reality based." Sharing past achievements with others in a group helps the per-

---

BOX 12–12
Steps for Conducting Remotivation Groups

1. Provide an accepting environment and greet each member by name.
2. Offer a bridge to reality by discussing topics of interest, such as news items and historical items.
3. Develop topic with group members through the use of questions, props, or visual aids.
4. Encourage members to discuss the topic in relation to themselves.
5. Express verbal appreciation to members for their contributions and plan the following session.

---

son remember personal life experiences that can be integrated into the individual's current self-concept. The knowledge that one has lived a meaningful life and has been loving and loved enhances self-esteem.

Nurses sometimes worry that the recalled memories will be unpleasant. Sometimes the memories are indeed bothersome or anxiety provoking, but the reminiscence group can help the individual rework in a positive way unresolved issues from the past and integrate them into the present reality. Research also supports the fact that for most people reminiscences are pleasant and ego enhancing (Haight, 1988; Hyland and Ackerman, 1988). Topics most likely to stimulate positive self-esteem include those that confirm personal meaning, and those which validate personal capabilities and strengths (Kovach, 1991).

The leader's role in a reminiscence group focuses on isolating themes, clarifying points, and sparking further reflections. The reminiscence group helps isolated people discover one another in a different way through an experience jointly constructed by its members. Members create for themselves a shared reality by revealing to one another what life has meant and can be for them. Exposing vulnerable parts of the self in a structured format and having it accepted as valued increases the sense of belonging that we all need for emotional survival. In an effective group, members as well as the leader move from "knowing" the person to "being" with the person.

Therapeutic Activity Groups

Activity groups are often overlooked as a legitimate form of therapeutic group, yet they account for the majority of nurse-led group modalities in psychiatric inpatient settings (Van Servellen et al., 1991). More frequently found in extended care, mental health, or rehabilitation health care settings than in acute care or community hospitals, they offer clients a variety of tangible ways to express the self through action and creative activity rather than through words. The nurse may function as group leader or as a support in encouraging client participation.

1. *Occupational therapy groups* offer the client the opportunity to accomplish tasks that enhance self-esteem. Group activities may allow clients to work on individual projects or to participate with others in learning life skills. Examples are a cooking or activities of daily living group. Other clients go to the OT area to make such items as ceramics or leather-tooled objects. Tasks are selected for their therapeutic value as well as for client interest. Life-skills groups use a problem-solving approach to interpersonal situations. Through modeling and role-playing techniques, the group assists clients in improvement of self-esteem, social interaction skills, assertive behavior, and locus of control.

2. *Recreational therapy groups* provide opportunities to plan and carry out activities that bring enjoyment and pleasure. Leisure activities release energy and provide a social format for learning interpersonal skills. Some people never learned how to build needed leisure activities into their lives.

3. *Dance therapy groups,* originally developed by Marion Chase, are a form of group therapy for clients who may have difficulty with verbal communication or need to experience their bodies in a different way. Participants experience movement in a safe environment. Because some of the movements are done in concert with others, there is companionship without demands. Physical movement shared with others often prompts verbal communication about its meaning.

4. *Art therapy groups* encourage clients to reveal feelings through drawing or painting. Such groups can focus on individual artwork, which is then described by each member, or on a combined group effort in the form of a mural. Psychological interpretations of artwork require advanced prepara-

tion in art therapy, but nurses can assist by modeling health behaviors that can be useful to the entire group. Often clients will be able to reveal feelings through expression of color and abstract forms that they initially cannot talk about verbally.

5. *Poetry and bibliotherapy groups* select readings of interest and invite clients to respond to literary works. One or more members first read the work aloud, and then the group explores the meaning of the work. Sluder (1990) describes an expressive therapy group for the elderly in which the nurse leader first read free verse poems and then invited the clients to compose group poems around feelings such as love or hate. Members were asked to describe the feeling in a few words, and the contributions of each member were recorded. This activity was followed by clients writing free verse poems and reading them in the group. In the process of developing their poetry, clients got in touch with their personal creativity.

6. *Exercise therapy groups* can be used by the nurse to stimulate body movement and group interaction. Usually the nurse models the exercise behaviors, either with or without accompanying music. Talking about how the exercise feels and experiencing the interplay between mind and body sometimes leads to new client insights. Music seems to enhance the process, providing a sense of festivity.

Self-Help Groups

Self-help and support groups provide emotional and practical support to clients and their families who are experiencing chronic illness, crisis situations, or the ill health of a family member. The functions of support groups are presented in Box 12–13. Community support groups are led informally by group members rather than professionals, although frequently a health professional acts as an adviser. A social action group may sponsor the meeting and arrange for the meeting place. One or more persons assume responsibility for convening the meetings, which are generally open to the public and free of charge. By contrast with therapy groups, the focus is on coping skills related to the purposes of the group. Members attend when they

BOX 12–13
Examples of Mutual-Aid Support Groups in the Community

Alcoholics Anonymous
Al-Anon
Adult Children of Alcoholics
Anorexia nervosa and bulimia support groups
Chemically Dependent Anonymous
Chronic Pain Outreach
Compassionate Friends (bereaved parents of dead children)
Emotions Anonymous
Make Today Count
Men to End Spouse Abuse
Narcotics Anonymous
Neurotics Anonymous
On Our Own
Overeaters Anonymous
United Ostomy Association
Parents Anonymous (Parents of child-abuse victims)
Parents Club of Children with Asthma
Seasons: Suicide Bereavement
Threshold: Alliance for the Mentally Ill
Tough Love (parents of teenagers)

only criterion for membership is having the identified problem that forms the rationale for the group's existence. Nurses are encouraged to contact support group networks in their community to become informed of the countless groups available to clients and their families (see Exercise 12–7).

Nurses frequently lead such groups on the unit. Examples of support groups for family members are Alzheimer's disease support groups for family caregivers, aftercare groups for families of former clients who are having emotional difficulties, and bereavement groups. Support groups for persons with cancer, mental disorders, arthritis, and learning disabilities are also available. A suggested format for leading a support group is presented in Box 12–14.

Educational Groups

Educational groups are used in community and hospital settings to help clients develop skills in taking care of themselves. They also provide families of clients with serious or chronic illness with the knowledge and skills they need to care for their loved ones.

wish to and are not penalized for nonattendance. Support groups rarely have a formal ending, and group membership is not conditional on personality characteristics or interpersonal suitability. The

BOX 12–14

Sample Format for Leaders of Support Groups	Sample of Statements
1. Introduce self.	"I am Christy Atkins, a staff nurse on the unit, and I am going to be your group facilitator tonight."
2. Explain purpose of the group.	"Our goal in having the group is to provide a place for family members to get support from each other and to provide practical information to families caring for Alzheimer victims."
3. Identify norms.	"We have three basic rules in this group. a. We respect each others' feelings. b. We don't preach or tell you how to do something. c. The meetings are confidential; everything of a personal nature stays in this room."
4. Ask each member to identify self and something about his or her situation.	"I'd like to go around the room and ask each of you to tell us your name and something about your situation."
5. Link common themes.	"It seems as if feeling powerless and out of control is a common theme tonight. What strategies have you found help you to feel more in control?"
6. Allow time for informal networking (optional).	Providing a 10-minute break with or without refreshments allows members to talk informally with each other.
7. Provide closure.	"Now I'd like to go around the room and ask each of you to identify one thing you will do in the next week for yourself to help you feel more in control."

EXERCISE 12–7
Learning about Support Groups

Purpose: To provide direct information about support groups in the community.

Time: Homework assignment.

Procedure:
1. Contact a support group in your community. (Ideally, students will choose different support groups so that a wide variety of groups is shared.)
2. Identify yourself as a nursing student and ask for information about the support group, the time and frequency of meetings, the purpose and focus of the group, how a client joins the group, the types of services provided, who sponsors the group, issues the group might discuss, and fee schedules.
3. Write a two-paragraph report including the information in (2), and describe your experience in asking for the support group information.

Discussion:
1. How easy was it for you to obtain information?
2. Were you surprised by any of the informants' answers?
3. If you were a client, would the support group you chose to investigate meet your needs?
4. What did you learn from doing this exercise that might be useful in your nursing practice?

Educational groups are reality based and focus on the present situation. They also are time-limited group applications; for example, the group might be held as four one-hour sessions over a two-week period or as an eight-week, two-hour seminar. If the educational process consists of more than one session, clients should enter at the first session (Hoover and Parnell, 1984).

Examples of primary prevention groups are childbirth education, parenting, stress reduction, and professional support groups for nurses working in critical-care settings. Suitable adolescent groups include those that deal with values clarification, health education, and sex education, as well as groups to increase coping skills, such as avoiding peer pressure to use drugs (Griffith, 1986).

Medication groups are an excellent example of educational group formats used in hospitals. Clients are taught effective ways to carry out a therapeutic medication regime while learning about their disorders. They learn about the disease process, fluctuations in the course of the illness that may occur because of new adaptations, and ways to self-regulate medication. Nurses who have a basic understanding of group dynamics can effectively lead groups, teaching clients about the side effects of medications.

Educational groups in health care settings can be used to support the competency and self-esteem of families living with a chronically ill member. Dincin's (1978) work with families of psychiatric clients involved with Thresholds, a psychiatric rehabilitation agency, is an excellent example of an ongoing group with a supportive-educative focus. Groups were structured to meet weekly for 12 weeks. Instead of focusing on the parents' psychopathology, emphasis was placed on the parents' involvement with Threshold members. Groups concentrated on such topics as helping parents to accept their child's illness, dealing with guilt feelings that prevented parents from setting limits for their adult children or that caused them to overprotect them, and assisting children to cope with the developmental task of separating from home.

Some of the interventions took the form of homework, with the expectation that parents would report to the group something pleasurable they did for themselves between sessions. In addition, parents examined and changed expectations about their children's achievement level. Also encouraged was attainment of financial independence, such as public assistance for the Threshold member, and the need for consistent medication in much the same way a diabetic requires insulin.

Discussion Groups

In professional education, discussion groups are used for a variety of purposes. Group discussions increase the student's experiential understanding of professional and work-related issues. By con-

BOX 12–15
Elements of Successful Discussion Groups

Element	Rationale
Careful preparation	Thoughtful agenda and assignment establish a direction for the discussion and the expected contribution of each member.
Informed participants	Each member should come prepared so that all members are communicating at relatively the same level of information and so that each is contributing equally.
Shared leadership	Each member is responsible for encouraging the participation of more silent members and for adhering to the agenda.
Relevant questions	Focused questions keep the discussion moving toward the meeting objectives.
Useful feedback	Thoughtful feedback maintains the momentum of the discussion by reflecting different perspectives of topics raised and confirming or questioning others' views.

trast with other types of groups, the discussion topic is known by the participants beforehand, and preparation is expected. Effectively implemented, group discussion offers the student an opportunity to learn as much from peer contributions as from the instructor.

Certain guidelines are of central importance in developing functional goals for group discussion. Careful preparation, formulating relevant questions, and using feedback ensure that personal learning needs are met. Functional elements appropriate to discussion groups are found in Box 12–15.

A lively discussion is predicated on the assumption that all participants are entering the group as informed participants. In the professional discussion group, *every* member needs to participate. A temporary lack of understanding should not be an excuse for nonparticipation. Sometimes the failure to understand material or certain parts of the dialogue is just as important to the learning process as understanding material thoroughly. If the content were easily understood without discussion, it would be easier to obtain the information from another source.

Group leadership is divided equally among the group members. Discussion groups in which only a few members actively participate are disheartening to group members and are limited in learning potential. Since the primary purpose of a discussion group is to promote the learning of all group members, other members are charged with the responsibility of encouraging the participation of more silent members. Allowing enough interpersonal space for dialogue to occur and asking for but not demanding the reluctant member's opinion encourages communication.

Ironically, silent members are more uncomfortable than their more verbal peers in discussion groups. They often wish they could contribute, but they can't. Sometimes it is helpful for the leader to suggest privately that the silent member make one contribution per meeting. There is no advantage in being silent. People get their needs met only when they become apparent. Otherwise it is a hit-or-miss approach of trying to guess the meaning of the silent member's nonparticipation.

A balance between verbal contributions and active listening produces the most beneficial learning effects. Sometimes when more verbal participants keep quiet the more reticent group member begins to speak. It is just as important to learn when to stop talking as it is to present material. Cooperation, not competition, needs to be developed as a conscious group norm in all discussion groups. Characteristics of effective and inffective listening habits in discussion groups are found in Box 12–16.

Discussion groups offer a unique opportunity for participants to practice the art of making a skilled oral presentation. Although one may stumble verbally as an active group member if not accustomed to oral presentations, the skills involved in giving a thoughtful and thought-provoking oral presentation can be used in a variety of group-process situations. In supervisory positions, the ability to present ideas clearly and convincingly to others is a key requirement.

Discussion-group topics use prepared data and group-generated material. New information is integrated with more established data. This new information requires the client to synthesize data into a relevant whole rather than simply parroting major themes and topics. Prior to the end of each meeting the leader or a group member should summarize the major themes developed from the content material.

Human Relations Training Groups

Human relations training groups integrate principles of group discussion with experiential learning. They promote the affective as well as cognitive learning of communication skills (Klein et al., 1989). Communication skills one can know only intellectually without actual experience are prac-

ticed in a controlled environment. Purposefully examining personal communication issues and style in a controlled learning setting broadens interpersonal perspective and provides the nurse with more communication strategies in working with clients. The leader of a human relations training group should have advanced training and education in psychosocial and group dynamics.

Although personal growth and self-awareness often occur as a result of increased knowledge and skill development, this is not their purpose. Converting an educational group into a therapeutic encounter represents an abuse of an educational group format. The leader should limit self-disclosure unrelated to the topics under discussion and refocus the group on the topic. Other leadership functions include establishing an interpersonal environment in which participants feel free to express their ideas and feelings related to the topic without fear of censure and a thorough knowledge of the topic under discussion. Respecting the privacy of individual members and linking individual

---

BOX 12–16
Characteristics of Effective and Ineffective Listening Habits in Discussion Groups

10 Keys to Effective Listening	The Bad Listener	The Good Listener
1. Find areas of interest.	Tunes out dry subjects.	Opportunizes; asks, "What's in it for me?"
2. Judge content, not delivery.	Tunes out if delivery is poor.	Judges content, skips over delivery errors.
3. Hold your fire.	Tends to enter into argument.	Doesn't judge until comprehension is complete.
4. Listen for ideas.	Listens for facts.	Listens for central themes.
5. Be flexible.	Takes intensive notes using only one system.	Takes fewer notes. Uses 4 or 5 different systems, depending on speaker.
6. Work at listening.	Shows no energy output. Fakes attention.	Works hard, exhibits active body state.
7. Resist distractions.	Is easily distracted.	Fights or avoids distractions, tolerates bad habits, knows how to concentrate.
8. Exercise your mind.	Resists difficult expository material; seeks light, recreational material.	Uses heavier material as exercise for the mind.
9. Keep your mind open.	Reacts to emotional words.	Interprets color words; does not get hung up on them.
10. Capitalize on face—*thought* is faster than *speech*.	Tends to daydream with slow speakers.	Challenges, anticipates, mentally summarizes, weighs the evidence, listens between the lines to tone of voice.

Sperry Corporation (1988). Your listening profile. *In* Cathcart R, Samovar L (eds.) (1988), Small Group Communication: A Reader (5th ed.). Dubuque, IA: William C. Brown, p. 382. Reprinted with permission of Unisys Corporation.

contributions that clarify and support different aspects of the discussion topic increase group cohesiveness and productivity.

SUMMARY

This chapter represents an adaptation of the communication process in interpersonal relationships. Building on the concepts developed in earlier chapters, Chapter 12 looks at the ways in which a group experience enhances the client's capabilities to meet therapeutic self-care demands, provides meaning, and is personally affirming. The rationale for providing a group experience for clients is described. Factors influencing group dynamics include individual member characteristics: motivation, functional similarity, and leadership style. Group concepts related to group dynamics consist of purpose, norms, cohesiveness, roles, and role functions. Communication variables such as clarifying, paraphasing, linking, and summarizing build and expand on techniques used in individual relationships.

Group processes refer to the structural phases of group development. Common to each theoretical model is an initial period of forming tentative group relationships and of developing a sense of alliance among members. Communication is tentative and based on stereotypes. This phase is followed by a conflictual period during which issues of power and control are addressed by group members. During the conflict phase, members get to know each other as unique individuals and sometimes discover marked differences in problem-solving styles. This phase of group development helps members reconcile differences and moves the group toward the establishment of group goals and commitment.

Successful resolution of the conflict phase creates interdependence and shared roles. Individual goals become group goals. Behavioral standards are formed that will guide the group toward goal accomplishment. The group becomes a "safe" environment in which to work and express feelings. Once this occurs most of the group's task is accomplished during the working phase. Feelings of warmth, caring, and intimacy follow; members feel affirmed and valued. Finally, when the group task is completed to the satisfaction of the individual members, or of the group as a whole, the group enters a termination phase.

Responsible selection of clients, establishment of goals that foster respect and caring, and relationship strategies are stressed. Applications of different types of groups—therapeutic, support, educational, and work groups—are described.

REFERENCES

Abrahams J (1973). *In* Goldberg C (ed.) (1973), The Human Circle. Chicago, Nelson Hall.

Bach G (1954). Intensive Group Psychotherapy. New York, Ronald Press.

Basford P (1990). How to organize brainstorming. Nursing Times 86(14):63.

Bennis W, Shepherd H (1948). Functional roles of group members. Journal of Social Issues 4(2):41–49.

Bennis W, Shepherd H (1956). A theory of group development. Human Relations 9:415.

Bertcher H (1987). Effective group membership. Social Work with Groups 10(2):57–67.

Bertcher H, Maple F (1985). Elements and issues in group composition. *In* Sundel M, Glasser S, Vinter R (eds.) (1985), Individual Change through Small Groups. New York, Free Press.

Birckhead L (1984). The nurse as leader: Group psychotherapy with psychotic patients. Journal of Psychosocial Nursing 22(6):24–30.

Brilhart J, Galanes G (1989). Effective Group Discussion (6th ed.). Dubuque, IA, William C. Brown.

Budman S, Soldz S, Demby A, Feldstein M, Springer T, Davis M (1989). Cohesion, alliance and outcome in group psychotherapy. Psychiatry 52:339–350.

Burnside I (ed.) (1978). Working with the Elderly: Group Processes and Techniques. North Scituate, MA, Duxbury.

Burnside IM (1981). Nursing and the Aged (2nd ed.). New York, McGraw-Hill.

Cathcart R, Samovar L (1988). Small Group Communication: A Reader (5th ed.). Dubuque, IA: William C. Brown.

Corey G, Corey M (1987). Groups: Process and Practice (2nd ed.). Monterey, CA, Brooks/Cole.

Corey G, Corey M (1990). Groups: Process and Practice (3rd ed.) Monterey, CA, Brooks/Cole.

Diedrich R, Dye HA (eds.) (1972). Group Procedures: Purposes, Processes and Outcomes. Boston, Houghton Mifflin.

Dincin J, Selleck V, Steicker S (1978). Restructuring parental attitudes—working with parents of the adult mentally ill. Schizophrenia Bulletin 4:597.

Dobrof J, Umpierre M, Rocha L, Silverton M (1990).

Group work in a primary care medical setting. Health and Social Work 15(1):32–37.

Echternact M (1984). Day treatment transition groups: Helping outpatients stay out. Journal of Psychosocial Nursing 22(10):11–16.

Eibl-Eibesfeldt I (1975). Ethology: The Biology of Behavior. New York, Holt, Rinehart and Winston.

Fiedler F (1967). A Theory of Leadership Effectiveness. New York, McGraw-Hill.

Gibbs J (1964). Climate for trust formation. *In* Bradford L, Gibbs J, Benne K (eds.) (1964), T-Group Theory and Laboratory Method. New York, Wiley.

Goldberg C, Goldberg M (1967). The Human Circle. Chicago, Nelson-Hall.

Griffith LW (1986). Group work with children and adolescents. *In* Janosik EH, Phipps LB (eds.) (1986), Life Cycle Group Work in Nursing. Monterey, CA, Wadsworth.

Haight B (1988). The therapeutic role of a structured life review process in homebound elderly subjects. Journal of Gerontology 43(2):40–44.

Hershey P, Blanchard K (1972). Management of Organizational Behavior: Utilizing Human Resources (2nd ed.). New York: Prentice-Hall.

Hoge M, McLoughlin K (1991). Group psychotherapy in acute treatment settings: Theory and technique. Hospital and Community Psychiatry 42(2): 153–157.

Hoover R, Parnell P (1984). An inpatient educational group on stress and coping. Journal of Psychosocial Nursing 22(6):17–22.

Hurwitz H, Zander A, Hymovitch M (1985). *In* Howe M, Schwartzberg S (eds.) (1985), A Functional Approach to Group Work in Occupational Therapy. Philadelphia, Lippincott.

Hyland D, Ackerman A (1988). Reminiscence and autobiographical memory in the study of the personal past. Journal of Gerontology 43(2):35–39.

Jacobs E, Harvill R, Mason R (1986). Group Counseling: Strategies and Skills. Pacific Grove, CA, Brooks Cole.

Jacobson L (1989). The group as an object in the cultural field. International Journal of Group Psychotherapy 39(4):475–497.

Janis I (1971). Groupthink. Psychology Today 5:43–46, 74–76.

Janis I (1982). Groupthink: Psychological Studies of Policy Decisions and Fiascos (2nd ed.). Boston, MA, Houghton Mifflin.

Janosik EH, Miller JR (1982). Group work with the elderly. *In* Janosik EH, Phipps LB (eds.) (1982), Life Cycle Group Work in Nursing. Monterey, CA, Wadsworth.

Johnson D, Hohnson F (1975). Joining Together: Group Theory and Group Skills. Englewood Cliffs, NJ, Prentice-Hall.

Klein E, Stone W, Correa M, Astrachan J, Kossek E (1989). Dimensions of experiential learning at group relations conferences. Social Psychiatry and Psychiatric Epidemiology 24:241–248.

Kovach C (1991). Reminiscence: Exploring the origins, processes, and consequences. Nursing Forum 26(3):14–19.

Kreidler MC, Carlson RE (1991). Breaking the incest cycle: The group as a surrogate family. Journal of Psychosocial Nursing and Mental Health Services 29(4):28–32.

Kreidler M, England DB (1990). Empowerment through group support: Adult women who are survivors of incest. Journal of Family Violence 5(1):35–42.

Lewin K (1951). Field Theory in Social Sciences. New York, Harper & Row.

Lieberman M (1989). Group properties and outcomes: A study of group norms in self-help groups for widows and widowers. International Journal of Group Psychotherapy 39(2):191–207.

Long R (1970). Remotivation—Fact or Artifact. No. 151. Washington, DC, American Psychiatric Association.

McGuire MR, Fairbanks LA (eds.) (1977). Ethological Psychiatry. New York, Grune & Stratton.

Meichenbaum D, Price R, Phares E, McCormick N, Hyde J (1989). Exploring Choices: The Psychology of Adjustment. Glenview, IL, Scott, Foresman.

Murphy G (1975). *In* Rosenbaum M, Berger M (eds.) (1975), Group Psychotherapy and Group Function. New York, Basic Books.

Pelletier LR (1983). Interpersonal communications task group. Journal of Psychiatric Nursing and Mental Health Services 21(9):33–36.

Pfeiffer J, Jones J (1977). A Handbook of Structured Experiences for Human Relations Training (vol. VI). LaJolla, CA, University Associates Publishers.

Prehn R, Thomas P (1990). Does it make a difference? The effect of a women's issues group on female psychiatric inpatients. Journal of Psychosocial Nursing 28(11):34–38.

Rogers C (1972). The process of the basic encounter group. *In* Diedrich R, Dye HA (eds.) (1972), Group Procedures: Purposes, Processes and Outcomes. Boston, Houghton Mifflin.

Rosenblum EH (1982). Groupthink: The peril of group cohesiveness. Journal of Nursing Administration 12.

Rosenstock HA, McLaughlin M (1982). Positive group efficacy in adolescent treatment. Journal of Clinical Psychiatry 43:58.

Rutan J, Groves J (1989). Making society's groups more therapeutic. International Journal of Group Psychotherapy 39(1):3–15.

Sarri R, Galinsky M (1974). A conceptual framework for group development. *In* Glasser P, Sarri R, Vinter R (eds.) (1974), Individual Change through Small Groups. New York, Free Press.

Sheafor RO (1991). Productive work groups in complex hospital units. Journal of Nursing Administration 21(5): 25–30.

Schultz W (1960). FIRO: A Three-Dimensional Theory of Interpersonal Behavior. New York, Holt, Rinehart and Winston.

Schultz W (1967). Joy: Expanding Human Awareness. New York, Grove Press.

Slater P (1966). Microcosm. New York, Wiley.

Sluder H (1990). The write way: Using poetry for self disclosure. Journal of Psychosocial Nursing 28(7): 26–28.

Sullivan E, Decker P (1992). Effective Management in Nursing (3rd ed.). Redwood City, CA, Addison-Wesley.

Tannenbaum R, Wechsler I, Massarik F (1988). Leadership: A frame of reference. In Cathcart R, Samovar L (eds.) (1988), Small Group Communication (5th ed.). Dubuque, IA, William C. Brown.

Tuckman B (1965). Developmental sequence in small groups. Psychological Bulletin 63:384.

Van Servellen G, Poster E, Ryan J, Allen J (1991). Nurse-led group modalities in a psychiatric inpatient setting: A program evaluation. Archives of Psychiatric Nursing 5(3):128–136.

White EM (1987). Effective inpatient groups: Challenges and rewards. Archives of Psychiatric Nursing 1(6):422–428.

Yalom I (1985). The Theory and Practice of Group Psychotherapy (3rd ed.). New York: Basic Books.

SUGGESTED READINGS

Cartwright D, Zander A (eds.) (1968). Group Dynamics: Research and Theory (3rd ed.). New York, Harper & Row.

Davis L (1984). Essential components of group work with black Americans. Social Work with Groups 7:97.

Gavin C (1985a). Practice with task-centered groups. In Fortune A (ed.) (1985), Task Centered Practice with Groups and Families. New York, Springer.

Gavin C (1985b). Resocialization: Group work in social control and correctional settings. In Conyne R (ed.) (1985), The Group Worker's Handbook: Varieties of Group Experience. Springfield, IL, Charles C Thomas.

Gazda G (1978). Group Counseling: A Developmental Approach (2nd ed.). Boston, Allyn & Bacon.

Griffith LW (1982). Group work with children and adolescents. In Janosik EH, Phipps LB (eds.) (1982), Life Cycle Group Work in Nursing. Monterey, CA, Wadsworth.

Hare, A (1962). Handbook of Small Group Research. Glencoe, IL, Free Press.

Janosik EH, Miller JR (1982). Group work with the elderly. In Janosik EH, Phipps LB (eds.) (1982), Life Cycle Group Work in Nursing. Monterey, CA, Wadsworth.

Marley MS (1980). The making of a group. Journal of Gerontological Nursing 6:275.

McGrath J (1984). Groups: Interaction and Performance. Englewood Cliffs, NJ, Prentice-Hall.

Maslow A (1975). Quoted in Yalom I (1975), The Theory and Practice of Group Psychotherapy (2nd ed.). New York, Basic Books.

Shepherd C. Small Groups: Some Sociological Perspectives. Scranton, PA, Chandler Publishing Co., 1964.

Slater P (1955). Role differentiation in small groups. American Sociology Review 20:300.

Stogdill R (1974). Handbook of Leadership: A Survey of Theory and Research. New York, Free Press.

Zander A (1982). Making Groups Effective. San Francisco, Jossey Bass.

Communicating with Families

MARCIA COOLEY

OBJECTIVES

At the end of the chapter, the student will be able to:

1. Define and describe family.

2. Identify theoretical frameworks used to study family communication and family dynamics.

3. Apply the nursing process in caring for the family as client.

4. Identify selected communication strategies to use in interacting with families.

I know I'm hot tempered like my father, but still I believe it's important to remember relatives' birthdays with cards the way my mother always did. My interest in world affairs comes from her, but I learned from my father how to unwind from gardening. His pride in a paycheck made me want always to have one of my own. Her pride in a tastefully furnished home gave me a yen for interior decorating.

McBride, 1976

Chapter 13 addresses communication issues specific to families and presents an overview of some of the common problems nurses encounter as they communicate with families. The chapter offers basic strategies to help nurses reach out with the sensitivity and care families look for and need in health care situations.

From the moment a person enters a family through birth or adoption, his or her patterns of thought, feelings, and actions are shaped by the family. Significant family members guide the person's ideas, influence his or her decisions, and interpret the personal meaning of the social culture. In fact, some family therapists believe that "the family of origin is the most powerful force in organizing and framing later life experiences and choices" (Framo, 1992, p. 128). Like them, hate them, or ignore them, families are the single most important variable in our early development. Later, people join with others to create new family groups, but while they may learn other patterns of thinking and acting from their significant others, family values and patterns continue to influence their lives.

Concepts of family have been described in a great variety of ways. Although researchers, psychologists, and teachers have been writing about family involvement in health care for many decades, only in the last half century has family communication become a relevant force in the nurse–client relationship. Nurses interact with families in many areas of practice. Whether obtaining an adequate assessment, accompanying a patient to surgery, or enlisting the family to support the coping of an ill member, nurses often find themselves relating to the family as much as to the identified client. Sometimes the entire family becomes the client as nurses expand their ideas of practice and appropriate units of care. Understanding family communication and learning how to communicate with families is different and more demanding than communicating with individuals. Whereas most nursing education focuses on dealing with an individual client, the nurse needs to add family communication to her repertoire of nursing skills.

BASIC CONCEPTS

DEFINITION

Whall (1990) defines *family* as "a self-identified group of two or more individuals whose association is characterized by special terms, who may or may not be related by bloodlines or law, but who function in such a way that they consider themselves to be a family" (p. 52). The family is the earliest and most important place where people learn about how to relate to others and to the world around them. Communication is important for survival. It helps family members get what they need within the family unit and to negotiate the larger community environment. The family provides the initial and most significant environment in which one can learn about one's worth and value to others, how and when to express and act on feelings, how to get one's needs met, and how to get others to understand what one is trying to convey.

Family Structure

Structure refers to the way a family is organized. Over the life of a family, structure does not remain exactly the same, although a certain structural continuity is maintained. Many family structures are somewhat determined by the family form or type of family. The common idea of a traditional American family living in a household with mother, father, and two children is outdated and to some extent was always a myth. Current family types are varied and changing rapidly. Box 13–1 presents some different types of families. Knowing about differences in family structure helps the nurse plan the most effective strategies. For example, in single-parent families, major issues can include conflicts around visits from noncustodial parents, achieving

BOX 13–1
Types of Family Units

Nuclear: A father and mother, with a child, living together but apart from both sets of their parents.

Extended: Three generations living together, including married bothers and sisters and their families.

Three-generational: Any combination of first-, second-, and third-generation members living within a household.

Dyad: Husband and wife or other couple living alone without children.

Single-parent: Divorced, never-married, separated, or widowed male or female and at least one child. Most single-parent families are headed by women.

Stepparent: One or both spouses are divorced or widowed and remarry into a family with at least one child.

Blended or **reconstituted:**   A combination of two families with children from one or both families and sometimes children of the newly married couple.

Single adult living alone: An increasingly common occurrence for the never-married, divorced, or widowed.

Cohabiting: An unmarried couple living together.

No-kin: A group of at least two people sharing a relationship and exchanging support who have no legal or blood tie to each other.

Compound: One man (or woman) with several spouses.

Gay: A homosexual couple living together with or without children.

Commune: More than one monogamous couple sharing resources.

Group marriage: All individuals are "married" to one another and are considered parents of all the children.

develop their own set of distinct rules for role relationships and boundaries, for administering discipline, and for resolving conflicts (Exercise 13–1).

Family Function

Function can be defined to include family activities such as protecting, socializing, working, or reproducing. It can mean an activity assigned to a certain person with a particular status and role—such as the breadwinner function or the child care function. However, most often *family function* means a measure of normality or health that occurs as a result of adaptation to stress.

Family functioning is viewed on a continuum. When using the words "functional" or "dysfunctional," one can get caught in thinking of family functioning as good or bad. All families fall on a continuum ranging from optimal functioning to disintegration as a family unit. Bowen (1989) describes families as more or less healthy according to their level of differentiation and the amount of anxiety that is present in the family. Psychologically healthy families should have moderate degrees of cohesion, coordination, and adaptability in most family functions.

The primary premise of communications theory is *the more dysfunctional the communication, the more dysfunctional the family.* Certain symptoms among family members are seen as indicators of underlying disturbances in family process. For example, a child who is not attending school may be sending a message that something is wrong in the family. The symptom bearer is communicating the distress in the family. Early observations of interaction among family members led to some important components of the communication theory. Family communication patterns were closely tied to the functioning of the family unit. When communication was open and clear, family functioning tended to be successful. Dysfunctional communication tended to parallel problems in functioning within the family as well as in interacting with others outside the family unit.

Current debates focus on the changing (and some would say deteriorating) American family. The important thing to remember is that for optimal family functioning, the structure and process must be healthy enough to allow the family to function. However, no one structure, process, or

nonblaming, direct communication with the noncustodial partner, ambiguity about discipline, and who should have the authority to make decisions affecting the children's lives. Some of these issues are not relevant in intact two-parent families. Children of divorced parents may feel conflict about pleasing both sets of parents or may try to pit one parent against the other for their personal gain. It often is difficult for divorced parents to refrain from making negative comments about their ex-partners to their children. Health care decision making in single-parent families marked by conflict may have to take into account more than one set of circumstances and role relationships in arriving at what is best for the child.

Stepparent families have a different set of dynamics than traditional two-parent families. Partners in the newly established family have to

EXERCISE 13–1
Family Communication Styles

Purpose: To observe families who interact in different ways.

Time: To be done outside of class.

Directions:
1. Spend some time in a public place where family groups are likely to pass by: a park, the grocery store, a shopping mall, a museum. Try to observe at least five families interacting for several minutes.
2. After each family has left the area, record what you observed concerning:
   a. A description of the interaction.
   b. Who talks to whom.
   c. Who has the power or leadership role.
   d. How you imagine people felt about themselves after the interaction.
   e. Patterns that seemed to be present.
   f. How decisions are made.
   g. The affective or emotional tone of the conversation.

Discussion:
1. Were you surprised at the differences in family communication styles?
2. Does the setting or purpose of the interaction affect the communication?
3. Does the age of the children or the type of family structure seem to affect the family's style of communication?
4. Was the power in the family held by an appropriate person or people?
5. What effect does style or emotional tone have on self-esteem?
6. How is what you observed different from or similar to the way your family communicates?

type of function is proposed here as the right one: There are many variations within these dimensions that can lead to healthy families.

Family Process

A process is a phenomenon that occurs over a period of time. The term "process" implies change, but within every change there are often patterns and connections with events in the past that are likely to recur. These patterns communicate meanings to family members about the world and their place in it.

Family communication is a *transactional* process in which meanings are created and shared with others. Human beings react to other people and situations on the basis of the meanings the people and events have for them. These meanings are derived from the social interactions one has with others. Meanings can change as one interprets and redefines interactions as time goes on. (Blumer, 1969). Family members continually create shared meanings as their interactions unfold over time. For example, for one family the sharing of a meal may

be an expression of support and family unity. If a family member receives a message that the meal will not be shared, he or she may view the message as a wish to pull away from the family. However, over time the meaning of such a communication might change as family members become increasingly busy and unavailable for a common meal.

Because family communication takes place within enduring relationships, the relational aspects of communication become more important than in other types of communication. Communication not only conveys a message, it provides information about family relationships in terms of power, affection, and control. Family communication is a type of relational communication in which the messages define and redefine relationships (Parks, 1977). For example, if a child balks about doing chores and the mother says, "That's okay, I'll do that for you," the message that is communicated is that the child is in the protection or care of the mother. If the mother instead says, "I'll help you learn how to do this," the message that is communicated is that the child is capable of caring for self with some help.

This symbolic interaction (Burgess, 1926) is perhaps most clearly demonstrated in the process of child development as a child learns about himself and his position and status in the world. It is also appropriate for family interactions. For example, in every marriage many actions become regulated through symbols and shared meanings that define situations and the relationship between spouses. Playing the part of the "competent husband" or "comforting wife" may consume many of the interactions in the marriage.

In the midst of enduring relationships within family systems, styles and forms of communication develop that become patterns which are repeated over and over. These patterns can be identified as interaction sequences that have typical starting points and follow a predictable sequence of interaction (Watzlawick, Beavin, and Jackson, 1967). Rules are developed within a family that help to guide the interaction and define the function of the sequences within the larger family context. Typically, members of the family know their place within the pattern and jump in at the appropriate place whenever the sequence starts. Some patterns can be helpful to the family, such as a pattern that nurtures or offers support. Others can be destructive, such as a pattern in which one member consistently loses a negotiation session (Exercise 13–2).

Many people define family process as the predictable and repetitive interaction patterns of families. For example, Mother always watches Johnnie's behavior very closely. Johnnie gets upset with her attention and complains to Dad. Dad goes to Mom and complains that she is too harsh with Johnnie. Mom backs off for a while but soon resumes her attention. One could observe these types of interactions in small groups such as mother–child, spouse–spouse, mother–child–father, and so on, or in "triangles" within the family .

The tracking of these processes sprang from communications theory. Communications theory, based on systems theory, was used widely by early family therapists. The theory views communications as the primary tool for working with families in clinical settings. It developed out of work done in California by Jackson, Watzlawick, Haley, Beaven, and Satir. These researchers are known primarily through work with double-bind communication in schizophrenic families.

A *double-bind communication* is a communication that sends two conflicting messages at once. For example, a mother who says, "Come here, I love you" to a child, yet remains rigid and cold when the child approaches is sending conflicting messages. Not only is the child in a double bind because he or she is unable to respond to both messages, but the communication usually includes an unspoken message: "Don't comment on how incongruent this communication is."

Early theories on family communication suggested that any family member's behavior, no

---

EXERCISE 13–2
Family Structures and Interaction Patterns

Purpose: To help students see the wide variation in family structures and process.

Time: 45 minutes

Procedure:
1. Interview a family that is different in structure and process from your own. Describe this family in terms of structure, function, process, and communication, and identify the ways in which this family differs from your own.

Discussion:
1. In what ways was the family you chose different from and similar to your own family?
2. How would you account for the differences?
3. How do you think these differences would affect the responses of the family you chose to a health care crisis?
4. What would you identify as the primary stresses and problems, from a developmental perspective, that would affect the family you chose if a family member got ill at this time?

matter how "crazy," could be understood if one understood the family's communication rules. Some people interpreted this to mean that psychological illnesses were the family's "fault." Current family communications therapy is usually proactive, encouraging preventive education about healthy family communication and conflict management. Today the focus is also on exploring the appropriate expression of negative and positive emotions and its effect on dependent members, spouses, self-esteem, and family satisfaction. While current family communications theory disagrees somewhat with early premises, the early work in this area has provided the basis for understanding family communication.

FAMILY COMMUNICATION

The ability to communicate effectively is essential to all aspects of family functioning because communication is an integral part of daily living. Healthy communication helps the family to carry out its functions, to meet the needs of individual members, and to move toward achieving its goals (Clemen-Stone, Eigsti, and McGuire, 1991). *Family communication* is the transactional process of sharing information and creating meanings within a family system. It is the key element that binds the family together as a whole as it attempts to fulfill its functions. Some of the principles of family communication are:

1. It is impossible not to communicate. Since any verbal or nonverbal behavior includes a message, even silence is communication.
2. Communication has several levels. On one level, the content or literal meaning of the message is communicated: "I want you to go to the store" On another level, information about intimacy, power, or conflict is transmitted. This is the message called metacommunication. "I want you to go to the store" can be said intending to communicate power, helplessness, intimacy, conflict, or many other messages about the relationship between the communicators.
3. Communication implies an exchange of information. Within a family these interactions become patterns that are predictable and repeated. For example, in one family

the only way to start a discussion about a problem may be to express affection first. Whenever the father says to the mother, "Gee, you're great, Mom . . ." the whole family knows that a discussion is to follow. Because behavior patterns tend to repeat themselves, they appear again and again.

4. In families, power and affection are demonstrated in predictable and sequential interactions. For example, in one family the only way to complain about something may be for the mother to talk to the son, who will then talk to the father. This communication may always be done in a derogatory way so that the father is blamed for what is happening.
5. All communication interchanges are either symmetrical or complementary depending upon whether they are based on equality or difference. *Symmetrical exchanges* are interactions in which each person has equal power and the exchanges mirror each other: "Do you want to go to the movies, Honey?" and she replies, "Yes, I'd like that." In contrast, *complementary exchanges* involve unequal distribution of power: "I would like to go to the movies," and she replies, "Okay, I will get ready." Symmetrical and complementary exchanges demonstrate family values, roles, and power.
6. In functional families, communication is usually:
   a. A tool to help children learn about the environment.
   b. A way to communicate rules about how people in the family should think and act.
   c. A tool for conflict resolution.
   d. A tool for nurturing and for the development of self-esteem.
   e. A way to transmit cultural values, traditions, and rituals.

Functional Communication

Healthy communication is the cornerstone of effective family functioning. For *functional communication* to occur, both the content and relational aspects of the message must be clearly and directly sent and received. The message must be clear enough that the receiver is able to understand both the content, or literal meaning, of the

Young children learn the family rules for communication from their parents.

message and the relational aspects, or emotional commands, implied within the message. Functional communication is based on valid assumptions that are supported by evidence and confirmed through feedback. Prerequisites of fully functional communication are trust in the other's intention and a firm sense of self. Each person uses "I" statements and takes full responsibility for his or her part of the conversation.

Dysfunctional Communication

In general, *dysfunctional communication* tends to occur in families in which some or all family members suffer from chronically low self-esteem. Certain family values and characteristics of family communication styles contribute to the dysfunctional sending and receiving of messages. For example, some families have very strong family values that pressure members into agreeing with each other totally. A shared or unified opinion is the only acceptable one in this type of family. Differences are viewed as threatening because they

may lead to conflict (a peace–agree family) or because they increase awareness that people are separate individuals. Other families may operate using "family myths," which are shared distorted ideas about the way the world or the family operates. For example, "Our family is better than other families and is above obeying societal rules." Another example is, "If we don't stick together as a family, we will never survive." Sometimes families have secrets, real or exaggerated events, that they do not want others to know about. In families with a secret usually all members know the secret or at least have some awareness that there is one, and communication about certain issues is distorted or closed. Families with these types of values often have strong unwritten rules that govern the way members should interact. These values and the resulting communications restrict the individuality and growth of family members.

At times certain characteristics of family members will alter family communication. Individuals who are narcissistic or self-centered will expect all decisions and family events to revolve around them. This focus on one's own needs to the exclusion of those of others communicates the message, "You are less important, less worthy, or less powerful than I am." Lack of empathy is another characteristic of a family member that alters family communication. Empathy means being able to understand another's experiences and emotional reactions both cognitively and affectively. A person who is not empathetic is also not able to recognize the impact of his own behavior on the thoughts and feelings of others. Lack of empathy and other immature personality characteristics tend to devalue certain members and contribute to an atmosphere of tension and unhappiness.

Dysfunctional communication usually includes the use of *assumptions*, with the speaker taking for granted that he or she knows what the receiver is feeling or thinking and that the receiver understands the sender's message. *Dysfunctional sending* occurs when part or all of the message fails to express the truth, or it is expressed in such a way that the receiver experiences it as a personal attack. In either case responding to the message is difficult. *Speaking for the other* occurs when one family member assumes that he or she knows what the other member wants without validating it. For example, a mother might say to a teacher, "Billy's father and I think that will be a good idea." Use of *generalizations* is another trap in family communication: "You're always messy" or, "You never listen to me."

Unclear expression of feelings sends the feelings underground or leads to resentment and hurt. For example, *sarcasm, silent resentment,* or *expression of hurt as anger* communicates a negative emotion but uncleanly and indirectly. Communications that contain messages that are *judgmental* are also dysfunctional. "You should" do this implies that the sender knows what is good and anything else is bad.

Other sender communications that are dysfunctional include *covert requests* or the *inability to express needs*. These include complaints and unexpressed needs for help. For example, a mother wishes her daughter would come for a visit and finally invents a reason that the daughter must come. When she does, however, the mother feels resentment because the daughter didn't do it of her own will.

Dysfunctional Receiving

A *dysfunctional receiver* leads to a breakdown in communication. The receiver may *fail to listen, disqualify* what is sent, *respond with negativity,* or *fail to validate* the message. Disqualification involves failure to attend to the important parts of the message, such as evading the important issue or making a response that is tangential to the conversation. A "yes but" message sends a message that the receiver disagrees with the message but doesn't want to say so directly. Negativity includes being defensive, insulting, attacking, or rebuffing. ("Tell me again how I get to the car dealer's"; or, "I'm not going to repeat myself.") Failing to validate or to explore the meaning of a message, giving advice prematurely, and cutting off communication terminates the message that is sent and leads to unclear communication and negative feelings.

Comparison of Family and Individual Communication

Communication between individuals and among family members is similar. With families communication is also a process involving a message, a sender, a receiver, and feedback. The interactions will proceed through certain stages, including engagement, a working phase, and a termination phase. The nurse uses the nursing process to help establish therapeutic relationships with families just as he or she does with individuals. However, incorporating family values and mutuality into the care-planning process is more important if the nurse expects to empower the family to participate in the care. Also, families are unique, just as individuals are.

However, there are also differences between the ways a nurse interacts with families and with individuals. Because of the nature of families, nurses can examine family structure and function from a systems, developmental, or interactional perspective. Having a comprehensive understanding of the way families operate is necessary for the nurse to be able to work with them effectively. How are families alike and different? All living systems need some sort of organization and pattern to function. Families also have this organization as they operate as a system. Families change in predictable ways as they grow and develop over the life cycle. We also know that the family will develop a signature coping style as it attempts to adapt to new demands and external stresses. Many people use a framework of structure, function, and process to describe the complex nature of families.

THEORETICAL FRAMEWORKS

Thinking about a family as a system is such a common approach that many other approaches actually combine their way of thinking about families with a systems perspective. Von Bertalanffy (1968) describes certain principles applicable to all systems in his General Systems Theory. Some of them are:

1. A system is a unit in which the *whole* is greater than the sum of its parts.
2. Certain *rules* govern the operation of such systems.
3. Every system has a *boundary* that is somewhat open or closed.
4. Boundaries allow exchange of information and resources into (*inputs*) and outside (*outputs*) the system.
5. *Communication* and feedback mechanisms between parts of the system are important in the function of the system.

6. *Circular causality* helps to explain what is happening better than linear causality. A change in one part of the system leads to change in the whole system.

7. Systems operate on the principle of *equifinality*; that is, the same end point can be reached from a number of starting points.

8. Systems appear to have a purpose, which is often the avoidance of *entropy* or complete randomness and disorganization.

9. Systems are made up of *subsystems* and are themselves parts of *suprasystems.* Bowen's family systems theory incorporates many of these general concepts into a theoretical framework for studying multigenerational transmission of ways of relating in families. His theory is used widely by nurses for examining family communication.

Bowen's Systems Theory

Bowen's systems framework looks at families as groups of people organized in a system. Thinking in a systems way means understanding the family as a unit that interacts and cooperates to achieve goals. A family is more than the collection of its individual members. It has an identity and energy all its own. Bowen (1985) describes family process as a multigenerational transmission process by which family ways of behaving and communicating are passed from generation to generation.

Family rules, such as "family comes first," "education is the only way to success," "hard work pays off," "the only real way to relax is to drink alcohol," "appearances are the only thing that counts," can operate so strongly within a family that an individual member is sacrificed for the sake of the family. When family members buy into these maxims without considering whether they have relevance for themselves as individuals and partners in new relationships, their communication tends to be "less flexible, less adaptable, and more emotionally dependent on those about them" (Bowen, 1985, p. 362).

A primary goal of family systems therapy is to help a person realize that it is healthy to become more self-differentiated and less reactive in relating to family and others. *Self-differentiation* is a term used to describe the capacity to stay involved in one's family without losing one's identity.

Bowen (1985) believes that "the level of differentiation is the degree to which oneself fuses or merges with another self in a close emotional relationship" (p. 200). Without self-differentiation, a person interacts with others outside the family system in much the same way he or she does with family members.

A systems perspective recognizes that change in one part of the system affects the entire family. For example, the alcoholic has the drinking problem, but the problem usually becomes the organizing principle in the family. When the alcoholic stops drinking, other family members don't know how to behave. Because the system has the tendency to want to stay the same (*morphostasis*), the family usually attempts to resist the change even if it is a helpful one. Nurses who are planning interventions with families, then, must consider the resistance and implications for the entire system.

Suppose a family with a disabled child is not complying with the treatments that need to be given daily. Planning an intervention that encourages the mother to spend more time doing these treatments might help the disabled child, but it might take her away from tasks that need to be accomplished for her other children. The goal of viewing families as an interconnected system makes nursing care more difficult to plan and perform, but in the final analysis it is a more accurate and time efficient way to think about families.

Families have boundaries that serve to separate them from the environment. These boundaries have different permeabilities, with some more open and others more closed to the environment. Some families allow information and resources to pass back and forth freely, whereas others shut off this exchange and attempt to deal with issues inside the family. When stress is present in an open system, it can result in adaptation and growth of the individuals. In a closed family system, stress coincides with maladaptation, distorted perceptions and feelings, and less capable individuals. Part of the role of the nurse may be to help the family open its boundaries to allow it to receive the support and information it needs to grow and adapt.

Triangles are a critical element in Bowen's theory. They are present in every family. A *triangle* is a three-person emotional system that begins when there is tension between two members. A third person or object is brought in to stabilize the two-person relationship. For example, the mother feels that the father is not paying enough attention to her. She calls her son at college on a daily basis and complains that she is very lonely. The father never hears of her discontent, but the son feels resentful that he is expected to fill the gap. The father feels bitter because he thinks his wife prefers talking with their son than with him. Always in a triangle are unspoken feelings that need to be addressed with the odd man out in the triangle. Typically, in any triangle two people are close and the third person is in a more distant position. One side of the triangle usually includes conflict or emotional tension. Attempting to map the primary or most influential triangles in the family is a part of describing the family relationships.

Duvall's Developmental Framework

Another way of looking at families is through a developmental framework. Families are not static but change from contact to contact. According to Emily Duvall (1958), families are primarily formed to promote the growth and development of their members. The family as a unit engages in a developmental process of growth, aging, and change over its lifespan. As the family confronts various *stages* of the life cycle, *developmental tasks* must be achieved if the stage is to be negotiated successfully. If the tasks are not achieved at specific times due to stress, crises, lack of resources, or unhealthy family structure and process, they may never be completely achieved. The better equipped a family is to meet its tasks, the more successful is family development.

Duvall (1958) outlined eight stages of the family life cycle and the specific tasks to be accomplished in each stage. Family stages, as presented in Box 13–2, are defined by the age of the oldest child. For example, a family that has two children aged six and two would be considered a school-age family. In the cycle of family development, the transition from one stage to the next is the critical period. The ease with which a family progresses through these critical phases is determined to some extent by the completion of earlier tasks. For example, a family in the launching stage typically has a young adult who is preparing to leave home.

The family in this stage must successfully release the young adult, maintain a supportive home base, and reestablish the relationships and structure within the family to adjust to the missing member. The transition is easier if the family has successfully completed earlier transitions.

Duvall (1958, p. 336) also identified nine family developmental tasks that span the family life cycle. She suggests that the family must be able to establish and maintain:

1. An independent home.
2. Satisfactory ways of getting and spending money.
3. Mutually acceptable patterns in division of labor.
4. Continuity of mutually satisfying sexual relationships.
5. An open system of communication.
6. Workable relationships with relatives.
7. Ways of interacting with the larger social community.
8. Competency in childbearing and child-rearing.
9. A workable philosophy of life.

Although Duvall's ideas provide a structured and logical way of looking at family life, her framework tends to view all families as nuclear, and she assumes that every family will experience the birth and eventual release of children. This portrait of family life does not represent many modern families. Others, such as Carter and McGoldrick (1980), have expanded these ideas to include younger siblings and single-parent and three-generational families. For many families, for example, the time the youngest child leaves home is often a time when increased responsibilities for elderly parents arise. Currently, many adult children are returning home after college for economic reasons, creating stressors that did not exist before.

Duvall's theoretical framework is particularly useful in assessing the types of normal developmental stressors families face at different points in the lifespan. Developmental milestones tell the nurse about possible concerns and suggest ways to adapt interventions to meet the needs of families experiencing them. Recognizing developmental crises and providing information that helps the family to normalize the crisis is helpful.

BOX 13–2
Duvall's Eight-Stage Family Life Cycle and Family Developmental Tasks

State Family Life Cycle Stage	*Family Development Tasks*
I. Beginning families (married couples without children)	• Establishing a mutually satisfying marriage. • Adjusting to pregnancy and the promise of parenthood. • Fitting into the kin network.
II. Childbearing families (oldest child birth through 30 months)	• Having, adjusting to, and encouraging the development of infants. • Establishing a satisfying home for both parents and infant(s).
III. Families with preschool children (oldest child 2½ to 6 years of age)	• Adapting to the critical needs and interests of preschool children in stimulating, growth-promoting ways. • Coping with energy depletion and lack of privacy as parents.
IV. Families with school-age children (oldest child 6 to 13 years of age)	• Fitting into the community of school-age families in constructive ways. • Encouraging children's educational achievement.
V. Families with teenagers (oldest child 13 to 20 years of age)	• Balancing freedom with responsibility as teenagers mature and emancipate themselves. • Establishing postparental interests and careers as growing parents.
VI. Families launching young adults (first child leaving home through last child leaving home)	• Releasing young adults into work, college, marriage with appropriate rituals and assistance. • Maintaining a supportive home base.
VII. Middle-aged parents (empty nest to retirement)	• Rebuilding the marriage relationship. • Maintaining kin ties with older and younger generations.
VIII. Family during retirement and aging (retirement to death of both spouses)	• Adjusting to retirement. • Closing the family home or adapting it to aging. • Coping with bereavement and living alone.

From Duvall EM (1977). Marriage and Family Development. Philadelphia, Lippincott, pp. 144, 179. Reprinted by permission of J. B. Lippincott Company.

Satir's Interactional Model

Virginia Satir, a communication theorist, emphasizes the messages about self-esteem communicated within families. Her books *Peoplemaking* (1972) and *Conjoint Family Therapy* (1983) provide interesting exercises and reading for those who want to learn more about family communication. Satir (1971) says that families can be understood by looking at three factors: (1) who speaks, (2) who speaks for whom, and (3) who speaks attributing blame or credit to another. From her point of view, the behavior of any family member is entirely appropriate and understandable in terms of the rules of that family's system. To understand any one person, then, one must understand the rules of the individual's family system.

Just as each person has a unique style of interacting and communicating with others, so does each family develop its own communication style. While these styles can vary greatly, there is evidence that some ways of communicating within families are more functional than others. In general, a family system that (1) accommodates the growth needs of each family member, (2) includes methods for achieving satisfactory joint outcomes, and (3) includes ways for using the outside world to expand and change itself is a functional family (Satir, 1971).

Satir (1983) suggests that healthy communication is *open, clear, direct,* and *congruent.* Healthy families have developed successful ways to *negotiate conflict* and send messages that affirm others' worth and that *promote self-esteem.* Communication that is healthy is termed *leveling*. This communication style is "real responding" that is integrated, flowing, and alive as it appropriately addresses a situation. Leveling is in direct contrast to dysfunctional communication styles.

Open. Both sender and receiver are open to the behavioral interaction, to the affect or emotion that accompanies the communication, and to the content of the message, even if that content is sensitive or personal.

Clear. Messages are simply and unambiguously stated. There is clarity of thought, organization of ideas, and accuracy and completeness of facts. The information is sent and received with some precision.

Direct. Messages are directed toward the person involved without going through negotiations or stand-ins. Family members talk to the person who needs to receive the message rather than around or about him or her. People know who is sending the message and for whom the message is intended.

Congruent. The behavioral messages that accompany the content match the information contained in the message and the feeling of the sender. Behavioral messages are often more meaningful than the verbal content. These double-level messages are transmitted when the voice says one thing and the rest of the person is saying something else.

Satir (1972) describes five dysfunctional ways people communicate when they are under stress. She notes that the dysfunctional sender cannot clearly state or clarify the message or may not be receptive to feedback.

Placating refers to a mode of communication that entails agreeing with what is being said even if one does not inwardly desire to do so. The placator is trying to please others and does not share personal feelings and reactions.

Blaming is a way to detour the acceptance of responsibility for one's actions or feelings by attributing them to another. It is a way to assure that one retains or acquires power by not accepting any blame oneself.

EXERCISE 13–3
Satir's Family Communication Exercise

Purpose: To demonstrate the personal and interpersonal impact of five types of family communication.

Time: Approximately 60 minutes; to be done in class.

Directions:
The students in the class should divide into groups of four to form "families." A mother, a father, an oldest child, and a youngest child are chosen for each family. The students are reminded of the five different styles of communication: *computing, placating, distracting, blaming,* and *leveling.* After reviewing these styles, each family has the task to "plan where you will go and what you will do on your vacation." This planning will be done five separate times using each of the five communication styles once. Spend five minutes discussing the problem while acting out each family style. Short debriefing sessions should occur after each role play. Family members will want to try a different style in each of the different situations. In the final situation, leveling, all the members must use this style for the communication to be effective.

Discussion:
1. Which of the communication styles did you prefer to use? Can you recognize your "typical" communication style?
2. Which styles seemed to generate the most discomfort? Was there a difference between generation of negative emotion and simple lack of problem solving?
3. Besides leveling, which style seemed to move the family toward a solution to the task? Are the dysfunctional styles sometimes useful? In what ways would they be detrimental for the family over the long term?
4. Did it matter if the communication style was used by an adult or a child? In what way did the role and the communication style interact?
5. How could families learn to use leveling most of the time? How does one influence this in one's own family?

Superreasonable refers to intellectualization or rationalization during an interaction. The person tends to act like a computer rather than a person with a range of feelings and emotional reactions.

Irrelevant refers to another way of detouring the conversation around important issues. These issues will often elicit conflict, but irrelevant content tends to restrict problem solving or dealing directly with the real issue.

Incongruent describes communication in which feelings and content do not match. The person says one thing, but the receiver is aware that the feeling that is present means something else (Exercise 13–3).

Theories of Family Coping

Families coping with stress were first studied by early researchers who looked at the impact of environmental stressors such as the Depression, unemployment, and separation during World War II (Angell, 1936; Burgess, 1926; Caven and Ranck, 1938; Hill, 1949; and Koos, 1946). Hill's work in 1949 led to the formulation of the A-B-C-X (crisis) model of family coping. *A* (the event), which interacts with *B* (resources), interacts with *C* (the definition the family makes of the event) to produce *X* (the crisis). He suggests that the family starts on a roller-coaster course of adjustment involving disorganization, recovery, and a subsequent level of reorganization. McCubbin, Cauble, and Patterson (1982) extended this work. They propose the double A-B-C-X model of family stress and adaptation. This model adds the concepts of *pileup* of demands, *family system resources,* and *postcrisis* behavior (Fig. 13–1).

McCubbin views family as a system. McCubbin's model says that for successful coping to occur, several pieces of family life must be maintained simultaneously: internal conditions for family organization and communication, promotion of member independence and self-esteem, maintenance of family bonds of coherence and unity, development of social supports within the community, and control of the impact of the stressor on the family unit.

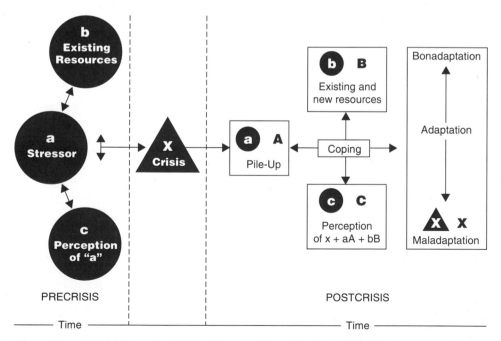

Figure 13–1 The Double A-B-C-X Model. From McCubbin H, Cauble AE, Patterson J (1982). Family Stress, Coping, and Social Support. Springfield, IL, Charles C Thomas, p. 46. Courtesy of Charles C Thomas, Publishers.

Nurses working with families who are called upon to cope with stress can use these ideas to help guide their interactions. The understanding that family coping is a process that changes over time can be communicated to the family as it is helped to make decisions. What feels like a crisis at one point in time will eventually turn into familiar behaviors and adjustments. Families and individual members use different coping styles or behaviors to deal with the stress. No one style is best. The key to helping families cope is the perceptions the family has of the event. Families who can view the stress in a positive way, such as seeing it as a challenge, do better than families who perceive the stressor to be an insoluble problem or a terrible threat.

APPLICATIONS

ASSESSMENT

Illness is usually a family event rather than an individual one. Assessment of relevant family experiences provides a way of understanding the client within his or her social context. The nurse has the opportunity to understand the family's perception of the health problem or need, which may or may not be quite different from that of the client. Additionally, the family's willingness and capacity to develop options that are helpful in resolving the health care concern are of major importance.

The nurse may want to collect identifying information or demographic data about the family. Collecting data about the family's physical environment, such as the presence of accident hazards, for example, in terms of window screens, plumbing, or cooking facilities, may help the nurse plan care that matches or supplements family resources and identify potential health problems. Community resources and facilities available to the family should also be noted. Box 13–3 (pp. 310–311) displays a sample family assessment tool developed by nursing students.

Tools for Assessing the Family Unit

While it is helpful to assess families in smaller pieces, these assessments do not capture the nature of the family as a whole. Families have unique identities that can't be understood when one thinks about only the pieces. The familiar adage "the whole is greater than the sum of its parts" means there is something more to a family than simply adding characteristics of individual members. Parameters that are often assessed include family processes, roles, communication, division of labor, decision making, boundaries, styles of problem solving, and coping abilities. Some widely used family assessment tools are discussed below.

Genograms. A *genogram* is a format for drawing a family tree that records information about family members and their relationships for at least three generations (McGoldrick and Gerson, 1985). Genograms make it easier for a clinician to keep in mind the family members, patterns, and significant events that are important in the family's care. The picture of the family that is presented on the genogram helps the observer think about the family systemically and over time. Sometimes when a larger picture is presented, connections between events and relationships become clearer and can be viewed in a more objective way.

The genogram is an assessment tool that can be useful throughout the contact with the family. At some point it may also be used as a therapeutic tool where information is interpreted and used to help individuals define the way they would like to operate within the group. Whereas the helper may fall into thinking that he or she knows what the family should do, interpretations that come from family members themselves are usually more accurate and useful for bringing about change.

Typically, the genogram is constructed in the first or a very early session and revised as new information becomes available. There are three parts to genogram construction: (1) mapping the family structure, (2) recording family information, and (3) delineating family relationships.

A diagram of family members placed in each generation is drawn using horizontal and vertical lines. Symbols used to represent pregnancies, miscarriages, marriages, deaths, and so on, are presented in Figure 13–2. Males are placed on the left of the horizontal line and females on the right. Birth order is represented by placing the oldest sibling on the far left and progressing toward the right. In the case of multiple marriages, the earliest is placed on the left with the most recent on the right.

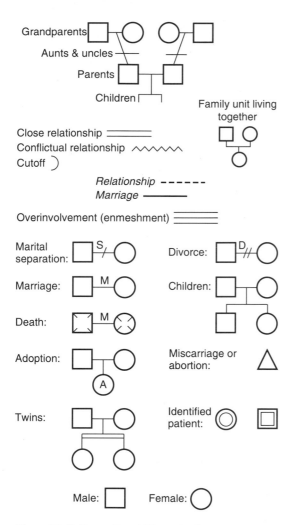

Figure 13–2 Generational Diagramming

tionship patterns can be quite complex and are inferred from observations and from family members' comments and analyses. An example of a family genogram is presented in Figure 13–3 (p. 312).

Genograms serve several other functions. The process of collecting and recording information for the construction of a genogram serves as a way for the interviewer and family to connect in a personal but emotionally safe way. It also provides the interviewer with information about how the members of the family think about family problems and interact with other members. Beginning to record information on a genogram can serve to detoxify issues or reduce anxiety about the family problem. During the process people are required to think, organize, and present facts. The helper joins the family and helps to normalize and reframe problems so that they are viewed in a larger context. This type of interaction helps someone to step back and think about an issue in a calmer way. Exercise 13–4 (p. 313) provides practice with developing a family genogram.

Family Diagrams

Another way of diagramming family life events and patterns is found in Figure 13–4 (p. 314). Horizontal events occur in the present and include such milestones as marriage, illness, or the birth of a baby. Family patterns that occur through multigenerational transmission are represented as vertical lines. They may be patterns of early death, marriage at an early age, high educational level, and so on. This diagram is useful in looking at how the family history and concurrent life events interact with the current health concern.

Family Maps

A family map is a tool that originated with structural/functional family therapists. They began to observe the structure and interaction of families in therapeutic situations and to map families in order to understand their hierarchies, roles, and power centers. After an interview in which the family is observed in an interactive situation, a map is drawn that details the *subsystems* and *boundaries* between subsystems and interactive patterns such as *coalitions, conflict,* and *detouring.*

Family information that is usually helpful includes ages, birth and death dates, geographical location, occupations, and educational levels. Critical family events and transitions such as moves, marriages, divorces, losses, and successes are recorded. Family members' physical, emotional, and social problems or illnesses are identified. A chronology or time line of family events is often useful to help people see relationships between events and behavior changes.

Observing and describing family relationships is the stage that is the most crucial and often most helpful to the family, but it is often ignored. Rela-

BOX 13–3
Family Assessment for Client Entering Cardiac Rehabilitation

Family Assessment

Coping/Stress

Who lives with you? _____

_____

How do you handle stress? _____

_____

Have you have any recent changes in your life? (job, move, marital status, loss) _____

_____

Whom do you rely on for emotional support? _____

_____

Who relies on you for emotional support? _____

_____

How does your illness affect your family members/significant other?

_____

Are there any health concerns of other family members? _____

_____

If so, how does this affect you? _____

_____

Communication/Decision Making

How would you describe the communication pattern in your family? _____

_____

How does your family address issues/concerns? _____

_____

Can you identify strengths/weaknesses within the family? _____

_____

How do the strengths/weaknesses affect you? _____

_____

Are family members supportive of each other? _____

_____

How are decisions that affect the entire family made? _____

_____

How are decisions implemented? _____

_____

Role

What is your role in the family? _____

_____

Can you describe the roles of other family members? _____

_____

Value Beliefs

What is your ethnic/cultural background? _____

What is your religious background? _____

Are there any particular cultural/religious healing practices that you participate in? _____

_____

Leisure Activities

Do you participate in any organized social activities? _____

What leisure activities you participate in? _____

Do you anticipate any difficulty with continuing these activities?

_____

If so, how will you make the appropriate adjustments? _____

_____

Do you have a regular exercise regimen? _____

Environmental Characteristics

Do you live in a rural, suburban or urban area? _____

What type of dwelling do you live in? _____

Are there stairs in your home? _____

Where is the bathroom? _____

Are the facilities adequate to meet your needs? _____

If not, what adjustments will be needed? _____

How do you plan to make those adjustments? _____

Are there any community services provided to you at home? (explain)

_____

Are there community resources available in your area? _____

_____

Do you have any other concerns at this time? _____

Is there anything that we have omitted? _____

Signature _____ (must be completed by RN) Date/Time _____

Developed by Conrad J, Williamson J, Mignardi, D (1993). University of Maryland School of Nursing.

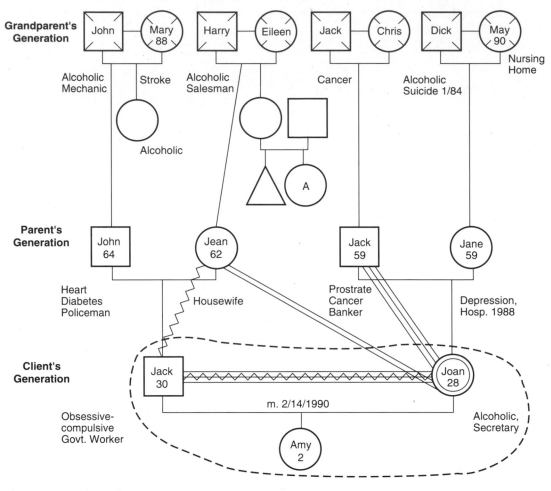

Grandparent's Generation

John — Mary 88

Harry — Eileen

Jack — Chris

Dick — May 90 — Nursing Home

Alcoholic Mechanic   Stroke   Alcoholic Salesman   Cancer   Alcoholic Suicide 1/84

Alcoholic

A

Parent's Generation

John 64   Jean 62   Jack 59   Jane 59

Heart Diabetes Policeman   Housewife   Prostrate Cancer Banker   Depression, Hosp. 1988

Client's Generation

Jack 30   Joan 28

m. 2/14/1990

Obsessive-compulsive Govt. Worker   Alcoholic, Secretary

Amy 2

Figure 13–3 Basic Family Genogram

A healthy family will demonstrate age-appropriate subsystems. Power will reside with parents, and children will have the nurturant guidance they need to grow. Spousal subsystems will have a clear identity. Boundaries between subsystems will be clear and permeable. Diffuse boundaries allow too much confusion as members move back and forth without clear definition of roles. Rigid boundaries serve to shut off necessary interaction and discourage flexibility and adaptiveness. Interactive patterns tend to repeat themselves and provide information about who will communicate and what that communication might be like.

Recognizing Families at Risk

Not all families act in the best interests of their members. Abuse of family members, violence, substance abuse, neglect, and dysfunction are on the increase as families become more and more stressed while trying to cope with the demands of today's world. The nurse must also be able to recognize families who are providing unsafe environments for their members. Referring families to professionals able to deal with these complex problems and notifying protective service authorities when necessary are other roles of nurses who work with families.

EXERCISE 13–4
Student Family Genogram

Purpose: To provide practice in the development of a genogram.

Time: Approximately 15 to 30 minutes for the interview; 30 minutes to diagram.

Directions:
To be done out of class as a telephone interview with a parent or other family member.
1. Interview a family member knowledgeable about the history of your family and its members. Choose a family member who knows about the family and might be willing to explore these issues with you.
2. Draw a genogram that includes the relatives' names and family position for three generations (to your grandparents' generation). Draw a graph with yourself and siblings at the bottom of the page, with each level above representing a preceding generation. Use circles to indicate females and squares to denote males. Other symbols may be used to indicate deceased members, divorces, separations, stillbirths, and so on.
3. Collect the facts of the family to enter on the genogram. These include birth, death, and marriage dates, occupations, geographical locations, major illnesses and symptoms, and other data pertinent to the facts of this family.
4. Collect information about the interpersonal process of the family. Who is close to whom? Who is distant? Who is in conflict? Was anyone blamed for family problems or labeled as the black sheep? Who is the family hero? Where are the lines of communication and interaction? Is there anyone who is cut off (extremely distant) from the family? What seem to be the themes that elicit strong reactions among family members?
5. In a small-group session, discuss the setting and types of questions you used to obtain the information. What were the reactions of the family members who were asked to help you collect and organize the information? What difficulties did you encounter? Did you find yourself looking at the family in a different way than before?

Because family relationships and communicating with families challenge the nurse, understanding both how families work and some important ways to modify communication with families are essential to good nursing practice. This chapter explains some of those processes and provides the nurse with techniques to use to interact with families more skillfully and more effectively.

Obtaining Client Data from the Family

There are many situations in which the individual is unable to provide accurate information or in which the information obtained from the family provides a more complete picture. In some situations, such as a client who is unconscious or has an altered mental status, the family may be the only source of data. To plan effective care, it is also crucial for the nurse to gain an understanding of the entire context in which a person lives. For example, nursing interventions will differ for a client whose family is very supportive and for one whose family is unavailable and has few resources during the experience of recovering from surgery.

In any family, there is no such thing as completely functional or completely dysfunctional communication. The communication is usually a mixture of the two and so may be viewed on a continuum from healthy to less healthy communication.

The Family Interview

Interviewing families can be more difficult than interviewing an individual client. For a nurse not familiar with this situation, it can be intimidating. After all, the family has been together for a long time and has a history together that gives even the most dysfunctional family strength and a collective power. On the other hand, interviewing families can be a rich source of information and a path to establishing relationships that are fulfilling and meaningful for both the nurse and family members.

Families might first be seen in the hospital,

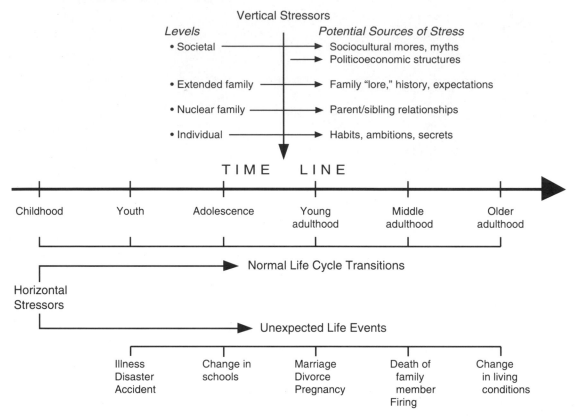

Figure 13–4 Learning Activity. Develop a comprehensive assessment of your family composed of the following elements: three-generational family genogram, and identification of vertical and horizontal stressors.

clinic, community setting, or in their own home. Seeing families in their own environment is preferable, of course, because the nurse can observe firsthand the physical and environmental conditions as well as the way the family members act with each other on their own turf. Ideally, the nurse will plan the first meeting to include an explanation of his or her role with the family and what the initial meeting will cover. Many nurses prefer to come to the meeting prepared, with an idea of what the family concerns are and the types of connections the family has had with health care institutions in the past. Knowing the members of the family, their ages, and their recent health care issues is a good start to the first visit. Many nurses will attempt to prepare themselves by collecting as much information as they can about the family and by phoning or writing the family ahead of time to gain some sense of

their concerns. Exercise 13–5 helps focus on the nurse's role with family issues.

Clarifying Purpose. The first meeting usually needs to be an information-gathering session. For most families, the issues that are of concern are too complex to be dealt with in one meeting. Letting the family know at the outset that the visit will be a time to gather information and to define their concerns is important so that realistic expectations of the visit can be kept.

Clarifying Boundaries. The nurse will want to be clear about the boundaries of the nursing encounters. How much time will be spent and when? Where will the interview take place? Who will be present? Are there conditions that are unacceptable to either nurse or family that must be spelled

EXERCISE 13–5
Questionnaire

1. Do you remember a situation in dealing with a client's family in which you felt it was a positive experience? What characteristics of that interaction made you feel this way? _____

_____

_____

_____

2. Do you remember a situation in dealing with a client's family in which you felt it was a negative experience? What characteristics of that interaction made you feel this way? _____

_____

_____

_____

out? For instance, it is common in some cities for nurses to encounter families in which drugs or guns are part of daily life. If this is suspected, the nurse should have some plan about her presence within this home.

Engaging the Family. Everyone has been in an interpersonal situation in which things just don't seem to "click." For the nurse–family relationship to be successful, there must be some connection between the nurse and the family that encourages the family to want to continue the relationship. This usually happens when the nurse can communicate respect and empathy to the family. Families know when the nurse is sincere in her demonstrations of acceptance and regard for family values. The nurse who really likes working with families in the community will be able to communicate this to families when he or she is not anxious. Families who feel they can trust a nurse will respond by letting the nurse into their private family world.

Setting Limits. For inexperienced nurses the desire to have families appreciate them and cooperate with them can backfire. Families may test what the nurse is willing to do or may be so overwhelmed and looking for help that they make inappropriate or unrealistic demands. Sometimes families ask for time, money, rides, or assistance with tasks that they could do themselves. Sometimes families are just so emotionally distraught that they seek

relief from their uncomfortable feelings by placing unrealistic hopes on the nurse. The nurse tries to develop a relationship with a family that inspires their trust. Agreeing to demands that are unrealistic or uncomfortable for the nurse will eventually erode that relationship. Starting at the very first contact nurses need to learn to be comfortable identifying and stating their limits to the family.

Planning

Once a family assessment has been completed, the nurse analyzes the data and summarizes the family's needs. Sometimes individuals within the family are the target of nursing interventions. At other times the whole family may be the focus of the nurse's care. There are NANDA diagnoses that specifically address the needs of the family as a unit. These diagnoses deal with alterations or potential problems in family process and family coping. Box 13–4 describes the major defining characteristics of the family diagnoses in detail. The reader may want to note the defining characteristics that specifically deal with ineffectual family communication and related processes.

Working with a family requires that the nurse be aware of the importance of mutual goal setting. Priorities are determined by gaining a sense of what the family defines to be important. Sometimes the family's perception of the problems or its determination of priorities is very different from

---

BOX 13–4
Major Defining Characteristics of Family Diagnoses

Family Processes, Altered

The state in which a family that normally functions effectively experiences a dysfunction. Families with this family diagnosis are families in which the family system or family members are described as follows:

1. Unable to meet physical needs of members.
2. Unable to meet emotional needs of members.
3. Unable to meet spiritual needs of members.
4. Parents do not demonstrate respect for each other's views on child-rearing practices.
5. Family members unable to express or accept wide range of feelings.
6. Family members unable to express or accept feelings of other members.
7. Unable to meet security needs of its members.
8. Unable to relate to each other for mutual growth and maturation.
9. Uninvolved in community activities.
10. Unable to accept or receive help appropriately.
11. Rigid in function and roles.
12. Not demonstrating respect for individuality and autonomy of its members.
13. Unable to adapt to change or deal with traumatic experiences constructively.
14. Failing to accomplish current or past developmental tasks.
15. Unhealthy decision-making process.
16. Fail to send and receive clear messages.
17. Boundary maintenance is inappropriate.
18. Inappropriate or poorly communicated family rules, rituals, or symbols exist.
19. Unexamined family myths exist.
20. Family has inappropriate level and direction of energy.

Family Coping, Ineffective; Compromised and Disabling

Compromised: insufficient, ineffective, or compromised support, comfort, assistance, or encouragement usually by a supportive primary person (family member or close friend). Client may need support to manage or master adaptive tasks related to his or her health challenge.
Disabling: behavior of significant person (family member or other primary person) that disables his or her own capacities and the client's capacities to effectively address tasks essential to either person's adaptation to the health challenge.

I. Compromised
   A. Subjective
      1. Client expresses or confirms a concern or complaint about significant other's response to his or her health problem.
      2. Significant person describes preoccupation with personal reactions (e.g., fear, guilt, anticipatory grief, anxiety) to client's illness, disability, or situational or developmental crisis.
      3. Significant person describes or confirms inadequate understanding or knowledge base that interferes with effective assistive or supportive behavior.
   B. Objective
      1. Significant person attempts assistive or supportive behavior with less than satisfactory results.
      2. Significant person withdraws or enters into limited or temporary personal communication with the client at the time of need.
      3. Significant person displays protective behavior disproportionate to the client's abilities or need for autonomy.
II. Disabling
   A. Neglectful care of the client in regard to basic human needs or treatment of illness.
   B. Distortion of reality regarding the client's health problem, including extreme denial.
   C. Intolerance.
   D. Rejection.
   E. Abandonment.
   F. Desertion.
   G. Carrying out usual routines, disregarding client's needs.
   H. Psychosomaticism.
   I. Taking on illness signs of client.
   J. Decisions and actions by family that are detrimental to economic or social well-being.
   K. Agitation, depressions, aggression, hostility.
   L. Impaired restructuring of meaningful life for self, impaired individualization, prolonged overconcern for client.
   M. Neglectful relationship with other family members.
   N. Client development of helpless, inactive dependence.

the nurse's determination. Empowering a family eventually to help itself (Dunst, Trivette, and Deal, p. 198) requires that the nurse negotiate a plan of care that first addresses the family priorities.

Setting realistic and achievable goals helps to ensure that the family will be able to accomplish them and retain some sense of mastery and self-efficacy about the process. Taking little steps that are achievable is preferred to taking giant steps that misjudge what the family can realistically do and so never get accomplished.

The nursing role may vary depending on the setting and the skill and experience of the nurse. In most settings, the nurse focuses on facilitating and role modeling healthy family communication, helping the family solve problems, linking the family with other parts of the health care system, providing information, and supporting and strengthening family coping. More experienced nurses may act as counselors or therapists for families experiencing more intense problems in family dynamics. The nurse must be clear about his or her role and effectively communicate that role and its limitations to the family.

Nursing Interventions with Families

Family communication theory provides the nurse with principles to use when offering nursing care, especially in assessing and intervening with families. The nurse's role is a combination of helping the family become aware of its communication and using family communication principles to guide his or her own interactions. Some of the ways nurses intervene with families include helping family systems change, educating and problem solving during developmental crises, supporting family coping, enlisting the aid of family members in caring for family members, and helping family members coordinate resources.

The nurse doesn't enter into the family system but acts more as a feedback mechanism to help the family adjust itself. The therapeutic principle that underlies all nursing interventions involves changing the rules that currently govern family communication. The goal of nursing interventions is creation of a family system that allows for the growth of all members. Once the family is assessed and a family diagnosis is determined, the nurse begins to plan care with the family. How this care is implemented is determined not only by the needs of the family but also by the skill and experience the nurse brings to the situation. Some nurses are comfortable attempting to incorporate communication principles into their interactions with families. Many nurses are able to help families solve problems and attach to resources in ways that maintain their functioning during times of stress. Nurses with more training are able to influence the family in ways that can help to change family dynamics so that members can move to a healthier state.

Helping Family Systems Change. Family systems tend to want to remain the way they are rather than change into something new, but change can occur. Change occurs most often when at least one member of the system, often a person who is the most free from constraints and has some power in the family, makes a change in his or her way of functioning within the family. In this way of thinking interventions for families are not directed at the member who is ill, injured, or at risk but at the members who are strongest and most able to change. This means the nurse will plan and target interventions with the members in the system who have some freedom and strength to carry out the interventions. A nurse who is working with a family caring for an aging mother may choose to spend more of her time with a daughter-in-law who has indicated a willingness to help rather than the aging mother or her ill spouse who is having difficulty himself. Family interventions include the entire family, working through the strength rather than the weakness.

Nurses interacting with families need to be aware of the character of a particular family's boundaries to plan more accurately how the family will use resources outside itself. Helping a family to become aware of information from the environment and to use what is available from outside itself often promotes family health.

Educating and Problem Solving during Developmental Crises

Families traditionally care for their members during times of life transitions such as pregnancies, births, marriages, and deaths. Whereas most families come to the situation with an expectation of what they will be doing, they often need support or education when they are experiencing new developmental challenges. Everyone knows that a new baby will demand that the family make some adjustments. However, it's not until the baby actually arrives that the family may realize it needs information or ideas about how to rearrange the activities of daily living. When more than one crisis occurs simultaneously, for example, the birth of a child with a congenital problem, the family who appeared to be prepared may need additional resources to cope with the pile-up of demands.

A nurse who is aware of developmental family theory will attempt to locate the family within a stage in the life cycle and to assess the family's knowledge of the current developmental demands, the strategies it is using to meet these demands, and its success in meeting them. Some families need information about the "usual" course that can be expected. Others may benefit from interventions that help them arrange some balance between the developmental demands and other demands such as illness, a job loss, or scarce family resources. Sometimes in families with an ill member the needs of a healthy child get lost in the shuffle. The goal is to enable the family to accomplish its function for all its members, not just the ones who are ill or otherwise in the forefront.

Supporting Family Coping

Each family has a different style of coping that may or may not be helpful in time of stress. At the beginning of any contact, helping the family maintain its present coping style is the best route. It is a style that has been useful to the family in the past, and it deserves to be tried out in this situation. Helping the family understand the implications of the pile-up of demands that leads to crisis helps members think about their situation and to realize that it is time limited.

The family's perception of the event will greatly influence the outcome. For example, one family in which the father has lost his job may think of the loss as a challenge and an opportunity to move to a new location. Another family may be able to see only the negative consequences, such as the lost income and the anxiety that will result. Pointing out alternative perceptions of the event (reframing) may help the family members view the stress in a way that will activate them.

Sometimes the family's style of coping is not useful in a situation. Suppose that the way one family copes is to look to the mother for all their support and the mother is the one who is ill. When the nurse and the family determine that the present style of coping is not working, then alternative solutions can be sought. The nurse can encourage the family to develop new ways of coping or can list alternatives and allow the family to choose coping styles that might be useful to them.

By listening empathetically as family members describe the stress and losses they are experiencing, by showing interest in the coping strategies that have and have not worked and in the community resources that did not prove useful, the nurse can help the family see how it has reorganized itself around the stressful situation. Starting with the family's information about itself, the nurse often is able to help members reframe a situation so that there is a healthier balance between self-needs and those created by the current stressors (Modricin and Robison, 1991).

Providing emotional support is, of course, crucial to helping families cope. An empathetic nurse is one who can be in contact with the whole family, even the ones who would typically remain distant. Of course, remaining aware of one's own values and staying calm and thoughtful can be very helpful to a family in crisis.

Not only are families a resource to the health team during a client illness, the family may also become the focus of care. As family members experience changes in family roles and family dynamics and begin to appreciate the loss a crisis or an illness can bring, many family members need help in coping with the situation. The nurse becomes a facilitator who can help the family strengthen its coping strategies. The nurse is in the position of offering emotional support and helping the family solve problems during the crisis.

Loos and Bell (1990) note four explicit needs that families of critically ill clients experience: (1) relief of anxiety, (2) information, (3) to be with and helpful to the client, and (4) to alter and adjust to new roles. They suggest use of circular questioning, as shown in Box 13–5, as a way of helping clients develop the self-awareness needed to meet each of these needs.

Enlisting the Aid of the Family for Care of an Ill Member

Other family members are often the identified caregivers for the ill members. At times the family member is homebound, and family members may need to offer all the care or coordinate it with health professionals. In other situations the ill member is more able to care for self but may need to enlist family support when changes are required in diet, activity, and so on. The nurse is the primary agent for coordinating and teaching this

---

BOX 13–5
Sample Circular Questions for the Family of the Critically Ill

Need for Relief of Anxiety

- Difference Questions:
  Who will be most relieved when father wakes up/gets better?
  Who is most anxious/fearful about the illness?
  What is the worst thing that could happen because of father's illness?
  What is most helpful to mother to relieve her anxiety?
  Is mother more anxious now or when she heard about son's accident?
- Behavioral Effect Questions:
  How does your mother show she is anxious?
  What do you do when your mother cries?
- Triadic Questions:
  What does your brother do to help mother relieve her anxiety?
- Hypothetical Questions:
  If the children stayed with you, would you be more or less anxious?
  If you went home, would you be more or less anxious?

Need for Information

- Difference Questions:
  Who finds the information most helpful?
  Who best understands what the doctors have explained to you?
  When a new member of the family needs to be told about the patient—who explains best?
  How do you understand what the doctors have told you?
  How is your understanding different from your mother's?

- Hypothetical Questions:
  If you chose to ask for more information, who could you ask?
  If you asked for more information, who would be most helpful?

Need to Be with and Helpful to the Patient

- Difference Questions:
  Who finds most comfort in being near the patient?
  Who is most uncomfortable at the bedside?
- Behavioral Effect Questions:
  How does your mother show she is uncomfortable?
  What does your brother do to avoid going to the bedside?
  How do you make sense of your brother not going to the bedside?
- Hypothetical Questions:
  If you could do one thing to help, what would it be?
- Triadic Questions:
  If mother wanted to help father while he is a patient, what do you think she could do?

Need to Alter and Adjust to New Roles

- Difference Questions:
  Now that mother is ill: Who is best at disciplining the children? Who is best taking care of the house? Who is closest to mother?
- Behavioral Effect Questions:
  How do they show they are close?
  How does dad/brother/sister help now that mother is in the hospital?
- Hypothetical Questions:
  If son/daughter were more helpful, what would they do?

From Loos F, Bell J (1990). Circular questions: A family interviewing strategy. Dimensions of Critical Care Nursing 9(1):49. Reprinted by permission of J. B. Lippincott, Philadelphia.

health care. Sometimes, however, the family members themselves need care. For example, many female caregivers themselves end up ill or resentful, having sacrificed satisfaction of their own needs to care for others in the family. The nurse needs to help the family recognize its limitations and hidden strengths and maintain a balance of health for all members.

Helping Families Coordinate Resources

Most families need some help coordinating resources. For the family with inadequate resources, the nurse will help the family supplement their own. Other families may have plenty of financial and instrumental resources but need help finding their way through the maze of the health care system. Providing information and linking families to available resources is a frequent role of the nurse.

Evaluating Nurse–Family Interactions

Evaluation is the appraisal step of the nursing process in which judgments are made about the value of the care offered. Evaluation may include an estimation of the effectiveness of the nursing care, the quality of the nurse–family interactions, changes in the family's state that may require modification or termination of the care plan, and the family's response to the interventions.

Evaluation as a part of the nursing process does not start and stop at specific times but should begin during the planning stage when appropriate outcomes are established. Continuing simultaneously with implementation, evaluation provides the nurse and family with timely data to make decisions about the client's care.

More specifically, however, the nurse should be aware of the quality of the nurse–family interactions to be able to make judgments about the contributions of family members to the care outcomes. It is possible that a care plan could be formulated that looks promising and realistically is appropriate. Without the vehicle of an effective nurse–family relationship to implement the plan, however, the efforts have been wasted. With any family interaction, the nurse will want to ask:

- Did I clarify my purpose and the boundaries of the meeting at the beginning?
- Did the family understand why I was there and what we would attempt to do together?
- After observing the way the family arrived at and started the interaction, what did family members tell me (nonverbally) about what they needed at that time?
- Did it seem that I was engaged with each and every member of the family? Were there any members who were not involved or who were not made to feel important to the interaction?
- How clearly could I see and describe the communication patterns within this family?
- What did I observe that gave me feedback about the family's perception and emotional response to the interaction?
- In what ways did I seek feedback to validate the accurate reception of my messages and my reception of the family's messages?
- Was there any way I should have modified my verbal or nonverbal communication with this family?

COMMUNICATION STRATEGIES

As nurses become more skilled and take on expanded roles, many are finding themselves in the role of family therapist or coach. Nurses with advanced training and education are recognized increasingly as primary clinicians for many families. Families with disturbances in the way they operate should be referred to someone who is trained to counsel them. Changing family dynamics is not a quick or simple assignment, but it is one that many nurses are incorporating into their practices.

Observation

The nurse using communications principles with families first examines the family's style of communication. Families have certain rules that govern the way they communicate. Their patterns of interaction repeat themselves and can be used as a source of information about family communication and members' relationships with one another. The nurse will want to observe what kinds of messages people in the family receive about themselves as people and about the problem at hand. Whereas the goals of healthy communication are open (members discuss events with each other rather than engage in circuitous ways of transmitting the information), honest (members feel free to say what they think and feel), direct (members go directly to the person involved rather than communicate through another), and congruent (verbal messages match internal feelings), the family may not be able to communicate in these ways.

Tailoring the Intervention to the Family Dynamics

On some occasions it may be appropriate to help the family alter its communication style; in other circumstances the nurse may choose to alter interventions to match the family communication style. For example, if a family has a rule that all communication goes through Dad, the nurse may initially choose to communicate with the family in this way. Exercise 13–6 presents a case study for reflection on family issues.

Even if the situation is not one that is conducive to changing family communication, the nurse can alter the situation by being careful of his or her own communication. Taking steps to ensure that communication is direct, open, honest, and congruent accurately sends information to the family and increases the chance that the family will perceive it accurately. The nurse may sometimes intervene most effectively simply by being a role model of an effective communicator. Sometimes the nurse's "meta" position, or her ability to be outside the family and observe more accurately what goes on, enables her to transmit information about family communication patterns that family members cannot observe. All family members deserve communication from the health care system that recognizes their importance and worth as individuals. How the nurse communicates to each member may be as important as what he or she chooses to say.

Encouraging Self-Awareness

Helping each family member become more aware of self and of his or her impact on others in the family is a primary objective. Techniques for doing this include role playing various positions or situations with some accompanying discussion of what that position feels like and about its con-

tinued use in the family. More skilled techniques that have been used by communications therapists include sculpting, in which a family situation is analyzed using spatial relationships of family members. Role reversals, such as parent–child reversals or spouse reversals, help family members experience another member's position.

Clarification of Rules

The nurse is in the position as an outside observer to observe rules the family may not be aware of. These rules may have to do with the expression of emotion, a family secret, avoidance of conflict, or maintenance of family equilibrium. However, the strongest rule that inhibits family growth is a rule that it is not all right to be different from the family. Helping the family become aware of its rules, clarifying what it wants the rules to be, and learning to replace implicit (embedded) with explicit (open and clear) communication helps the family grow.

Reframing

Reframing or relabeling is a way to look at both positive and negative aspects of a situation or communication. Usually this involves turning a negative perception into a positive one. The process helps people become aware of others' points of view and helps promote member self-esteem. It detours the blaming process and often shakes up the situation just enough for the family to begin trying something different. For example, a mother who criticizes her daughter's grades may be encouraged to reframe her statements to indicate her concern about how grades can affect her daughter's future.

Giving Corrective Feedback

Corrective feedback is used in a neutral way by the nurse who takes the position of an informed observer. Role modeling appropriate communication is the first priority in corrective feedback, because even if you are not directly telling the family what you want, family members will be able to infer it from your behavior. Talking to all members, not responding to someone who speaks for another member but addressing that person

EXERCISE 13–6
Case Study

Mr. Z., aged 43, was chairing a board meeting of his large, successful manufacturing corporation when he developed shortness of breath, dizziness, and a crushing, vicelike pain in his chest. An ambulance was called, and he was taken to the medical center. Subsequently he was admitted to the coronary care unit with a diagnosis of impending myocardial infarction.

Mr. Z. is married, with three children: Steve, aged 14; Sean, aged 12; and Lisa, aged 8. he is the president and majority stockholder of his company. He had no previous history of cardiovascular problems, although his father died at the age of 38 of a massive coronary occlusion. His oldest brother died at the age of 42 from the same condition, and his other brother, still living, became a semi-invalid after suffering two heart attacks—one at the age of 44 and the other at the age of 47.

Mr. Z. was tall, slim, suntanned, and very athletic. He swam daily, jogged every morning for 30 minutes, played golf regularly, and was an avid sailor who participated in every yacht regatta, usually winning. He is very health conscious and has had annual physical checkups, watches his diet, and quit smoking to avoid possible damage to his heart. He has been determined to avoid dying young or becoming an invalid like his brother.

When he was admitted to the coronary care unit, he was conscious. Though in a great deal of pain, he seemed determined to control his own fate. While in the unit he was an exceedingly difficult patient, a trial to the nursing staff and his physician. He constantly watched and listened to everything going on around him and demanded complete explanations about any procedure, equipment, or medication he received. He would sleep in brief naps, and only when he was totally exhausted. Despite his obvious tension and anxiety, his condition stabilized. The damage to his heart was considered minimal, and his prognosis was good. As the pain diminished, he began asking when he could go home and when he could go back to work. He was impatient to be moved to a private room so that he could conduct some of his business by telephone.

When Mrs. Z. visited she approached the nursing staff with questions regarding Mr. Z.'s condition, usually asking the same question several times in different ways. She also asked why she was not being "told everything."

Interactions between Mr. Z. and Mrs. Z. were noted by the staff as Mr. Z. telling Mrs. Z. a list of things she needed to do. Very little intimate contact was noted.

Mr. Z. denied having any anxiety or concerns about his condition, although his behavior contradicted his denial. Mrs. Z. would agree with Mr. Z. when questioned in his company.

After reviewing the previous case study, be prepared to discuss the following:

1. What questions would you ask the client and family to obtain data regarding their adaptation to crisis?

_____

_____

2. What cognitive nursing diagnosis would apply with this case study? _____

_____

_____

3. What nursing interventions are appropriate to interact with this client and his family? _____

_____

_____

4. How would you plan to transmit the information to the family? _____

_____

_____

_____

Developed by Conrad J (1993). University of Maryland School of Nursing.

directly, modeling clear and direct communication, demonstrating techniques for getting feedback, and taking risks to deal openly with negative feelings are all examples of ways the nurse can provide this feedback. Sometimes actual comments such as challenging generalizations ("always" and "never") or assumptions ("you assumed that he knew what you meant?") can be provided in ways that are nonthreatening and eventually perceived by the family as helpful information.

Terminating with Families

All things come to an end, and so will the nurse's interaction with the family. Whether the interaction has been very brief or whether the nurse has seen the family for a long time, the nurse will want to work toward everyone's leaving the encounter with a clear sense of what has happened and with hope that the family's progress will continue into the future.

Chapters 4 and 8 in this book describe the termination process in detail. For families, however, there are specific issues to consider. Many nurses establish a contract with a family at the beginning of the interaction. The nurse may want to inquire, "Did the family and the nurse understand the nature of the contract? At the end of the encounter was there some discussion of whether or not it was fulfilled? Did we summarize the progress toward goals in such a way that all family members left the encounter with a sense of knowing what had happened and what was gained?" Leaving the family with a sense of what was accomplished is important and may help family members see progress that was obscure to them.

If nurses are committed to the value of improving communication skills, they will hope to leave the family with a better sense of how family members communicate and perhaps with more communication skill than they had before interaction with the nurse. The nurse might ask, "Did the family members become more aware of their communication styles during our interactions? Did they learn new, more effective ways of relating to each other?"

Family needs may not have been met completely during the nursing encounter. Referrals, continuing the contact with another health professional, or family education about when to contact the health system may be needed. The nurse

should ask, "What information needs to go to others about this family or for this family? Did we decide who would communicate this information and when?"

And, finally, the nurse needs to assess the personal behaviors that influenced the relationship. Appraising self and using that information to adjust one's communication and interpersonal style can be growth producing for future contacts. The nurse will ask, "What feedback did family members give me about the way I communicated with them? In what ways did this interaction promote the growth and self-esteem of each member, including myself?"

Understanding the principles underlying family communication and learning to use them can be helpful in interactions with families. The nurse who can use open, honest, clear, direct, and congruent communication will be a better communicator, a better nurse, and probably a more effective and satisfied person. Exercise 13–7 provides experience with evaluating nurse–family interactions.

SUMMARY

Chapter 13 provides an overview of family communication. Family is defined as "a self-identified group of two or more individuals whose association is characterized by special terms, who may or may not be related by bloodlines or law, but who function in such a way that they consider themselves to be a family." Families have a structure, defined as the way in which members are organized. Family function refers to the roles people take in their families, and family process describes the communication that takes place within the family. Family frameworks identified in the chapter include Bowen's family systems theory, Duvall's developmental model, and Satir's interactional model. McCubbin's model of family coping is discussed.

The genogram is a primary assessment tool used to help families describe multigenerational transmission of family patterns. NANDA nursing diagnoses related to family communication and coping form the foundation for nursing interventions.

The nurse doesn't enter into the family system but acts more as a feedback mechanism to help the family adjust itself. Families of the critically ill need (1) relief of anxiety, (2) information, (3) to be with and helpful to the client, and (4) to alter

EXERCISE 13–7
Evaluating Nurse–Family Communication

Purpose: To help the nurse evaluate and improve his or her communication with families.

Time: Approximately 30 minutes for the family interview; 15 minutes to analyze and discuss.

Directions:
Set up an interview with a family that has volunteered to help you with this assignment. Ask the family to discuss with you a real-life problem in the family. Be prepared for the session by writing down a goal and some questions to ask the family. Ask the family's cooperation in helping you improve your communication. After the session has been conducted, ask the family members to answer these questions:
1. Did the interviewer clarify the purpose and time limits of the meeting at the beginning?
2. Did you understand the purpose and what you were supposed to do in the meeting?
3. How did the meeting begin? What was each person doing as the meeting started?
4. Did you feel involved in the discussion? Was anyone left out?
5. Did the interviewer make you feel that what you were saying was important and that he or she valued your opinion?
6. Can you identify any feelings or emotional reactions that occurred during the discussion? How did the interviewer respond to them?
7. Did the interviewer ever ask you to validate or clarify his or her ideas of what was happening?
8. Do you have any suggestions to help this person improve communication with a family group?

and adjust to new roles. Circular questioning helps families develop the type of self-awareness they require to meet these four basic needs. Other strategies involve observation, role-modeling communication, and support of the family's efforts to cope.

REFERENCES

Angell R (1936). The Family Encounters the Depression. New York, Scribner.

Beck RL (1987). The genogram as process. American Journal of Family Therapy 15(4):343–351.

Blumer H (1969). Symbolic Interactionism: Perspectives and method. Englewood Cliffs, NJ, Prentice-Hall.

Bowen M (1985). Family Therapy in Clinical Practice. Northvale, NJ, Jason Aronson.

Burgess EW (1926). The family as a unit of interacting personalities. The Family 7(3):3–9.

Cain A (1980). Assessment of family structure. In Miller JR, Janosik E (eds.) (1980), Family-Focused Care. New York, McGraw-Hill, pp. 115–131.

Carter E, McGoldrick M (1980). The Family Life Cycle: A Framework for Family Therapy. New York, Gardner Press.

Caven RS, Ranck KH (1938). The Family and the Depression. Chicago, University of Chicago Press.

Clemen-Stone S, Eigsti DG, McGuire SL (1991). Comprehensive Family and Community Health Nursing. St. Louis, Mosby Yearbook.

Dunst C, Trivette C, Deal A (1988). Enabling and Empowering Families. Cambridge, MA, Brookline Books.

Duvall E (1957). Family Development. Philadelphia, Lippincott.

Duvall E (1958). Marriage and Family Development. Philadelphia, Lippincott.

Framo JL (1992). Family of Origin Therapy: An Intergenerational Approach. New York, Bruner/Mazel.

Hill R (1949). Families under Stress. New York, Harper & Row.

Koos EL (1946). Families in Trouble. New York, King's Crown Press.

Loos F, Bell J (1990). Circular questions: A family interviewing strategy. Dimensions of Critical Care Nursing 9(1):46–53.

McBride A (1976). A Married Feminist. New York, Harper & Row.

McCubbin H, Cauble AE, Patterson J (1982). Family Stress, Coping, and Social Support. Springfield, IL, Charles C Thomas.

McGoldrick M, Carter E (1982). The family life cycle. In F. Walsh (ed.), Normal Family Processes. New York, Guilford Press.

McGoldrick M, Gerson R (1985). Genogram in Family Assessment. New York, Norton.

Modricin MJ, Robison J (1991). Parents of children

with emotional disorders: Issues for consideration and practice. Community Mental Health Journal 27(4):281–292.

Parks MO (1977). Relational communication: Theory and research. Human Communication Research 3:372–381.

Rolloff ME, Miller GR (1987). Interpersonal Processes: New Directions in Communication Research. Newbury Park, CA, Sage Publications.

Satir V (1971). Symptomology: A family production. *In* Howells J (ed.) (1971), Theory and Practice of Family Psychiatry. New York, Bruner/Mazel, pp. 663–670.

Satir V (1972). Peoplemaking. Palo Alto, CA, Science and Behavior Books.

Satir V (1983). Conjoint Family Therapy (3rd ed.). Palo Alto, CA, Science and Behavior Books.

Slater S, Mencher J (1991). The lesbian family life cycle: A contextual approach. American Journal of Orthopsychiatry 61(3):372–382.

Von Bertalanffy L (1968). General Systems Theory. New York, George Braziller.

Watzlawick P, Beavin JH, Jackson DD (1967). Pragmatics of Human Communication. New York, Norton.

Whall A (1990). The family as the unit of care in nursing: A historical review. *In* Ismeurt R, Arnold E, Carson V (eds.) (1990), Readings: Concepts Fundamental to Nursing. Springhouse, PA, Springhouse Corp.

Wright, LM, Leahey M (1984). Nurses and Families: A Guide to Family Assessment and Intervention. Philadelphia, Davis.

Zerkwith JV (1991). A family caregiving model for public health nursing. Nursing Outlook. Sept./Oct. 1991, pp. 213–217.

SUGGESTED READING

Bowen M (1978). Family Therapy in Clinical Practice. New York, Jason Aronson.

Burr W, Hill R, Nye F, Reiss I (eds.) (1979). Contemporary Theories about the Family. New York, Free Press.

Caudle P, Grover S (1992). Care of the family client. *In* Clark MJ (ed.) (1992), Nursing in the Community. Appleton & Lange, pp. 394–419.

Combrinck-Graham L (1985). A developmental model for family systems. Family Process 24(2):139–150.

Ervin NE, Chen SC (1986). Evaluation of family and community health nursing practice. *In* Logan B, Dawkins C (eds.) (1986), Family-Centered Nursing in the Community. Reading, MA, Addison-Wesley, pp. 354–371.

Friedman MM (1992). Family Nursing: Theory and Assessment (3rd ed.). Norwalk, CT, Appleton-Century-Crofts.

Garfinkel I, McLanahan SS (1986). Single Mothers and Their Children: A New American Dilemma. Washington, DC, Urban Institute Press.

Hall JE, Weaver BR (1974). Nursing of Families in Crisis. Philadelphia, Lippincott.

Hurley PM (1982). Family assessment: Systems theory and the genogram. Children's Health Care 10(3): 76–82.

Karpel M (1986). Family Resources: The Hidden Partner in Family Therapy. New York, Guilford Press.

McCubbin HI, Cauble AE, Patterson JM (1982). Family Stress, Coping, and Social Support. Springfield, IL, Charles C Thomas.

McCubbin M (1984). Nursing assessment of parental coping with cystic fibrosis. Western Journal of Nursing Research 6(4):407–421.

Miller JR, Janosik EH (1980). Family-Focused Care. New York, McGraw-Hill.

Miller SR, Winstead-Fry P (1982). Family Systems Theory in Nursing Practice. Reston, VA, Reston Publishing Co.

Nye FI, Berardo FE (1981). Emerging Conceptual Frameworks in Family Analysis. New York, Praeger.

Piercy FP, Sprenkle DH (1986). Family Therapy Sourcebook. New York, Guilford Press.

Rausch HL, Grief AC, Nugent J (1979). Communication in couples and families. *In* Burr W, Hill R, Nye FI, Riess I (eds.) (1979), Contemporary Theories about the Family. New York, Free Press, pp. 468–489.

Riskin J, Faunce E (1972). An evaluative review of family interaction research. Family Process 11(4):365–411.

Skolnik AS, Skolnick JH (1986). Family in Transition. Boston, Little, Brown.

Sussman M, Steinmetz S (1987). Handbook of Marriage and the Family. New York, Plenum Press.

Turner JG, Chavigny KH (1988). Community Health Nursing: An Epidemiological Perspective through the Nursing Process. Philadelphia, Lippincott.

Walsh F (1982). Normal Family Processes. New York, Guilford Press.

Wood NF, Yates BC, Primomo J (1989). Supporting families during chronic illness. Image: Journal of Nursing Scholarship 21(1):46–50.

Wright LM, Leahey M (1984). Nurses and Families: A Guide to Family Assessment and Intervention. Philadelphia, Davis.

Chapter 14

Resolving Conflict in Relationships

KATHLEEN BOGGS

OUTLINE

Basic Concepts

THE NATURE OF CONFLICT

UNDERSTANDING PERSONAL RESPONSES IN CONFLICT
    SITUATIONS
ASSESSING THE PRESENCE OF CONFLICT IN THE
      NURSE–CLIENT RELATIONSHIP
TYPES OF CONFLICT: INTRAPERSONAL VERSUS
      INTERPERSONAL
    Escalation of intrapersonal and interpersonal conflict
    Interpersonal sources of conflict

FUNCTIONAL USES OF CONFLICT
DYSFUNCTIONAL CONFLICT
BEHAVIORAL RESPONSES USED TO RESOLVE CONFLICT
THE NATURE OF ASSERTIVE BEHAVIOR

Applications

NURSING STRATEGIES TO ENHANCE CONFLICT RESOLUTION
DEFUSING INTRAPERSONAL CONFLICT

DEVELOPING ASSERTIVE SKILLS
CLIENT ENCOUNTERS WITH ANGRY OR DIFFICULT CLIENTS

Summary

OBJECTIVES

At the end of the chapter, the student will be able to:

1. Define conflict and contrast the functional with the dysfunctional role of conflict in a therapeutic relationship.
2. Recognize and describe personal style of response to conflict situations.

3. Discriminate among passive, assertive, and aggressive responses to conflict situations.

4. Specify the characteristics of assertive communication.

5. Identify four components of an assertive response and formulate sample assertive responses.
6. Identify appropriate assertive responses and specific nursing strategies to promote conflict resolution in relationships.

Creative confrontation is a struggle between persons who are engaged in a dispute or controversy and who remain together, face to face, until acceptance, respect for differences, and love emerge; even though the persons may be at odds with the issue, they are no longer at odds with each other.

Clark Moustakis, 1974

In every relationship, there are times when the participants experience negative feelings about a situation or about each other. The clear, direct communication needed for the nurse–client relationship is difficult enough to accomplish in nonconflictual situations. In controversial situations, it becomes even harder because one's ego is linked with the conflict itself as well as with the choices of behavioral resolution. This chapter emphasizes awareness of the dynamics associated with conflicts and the skills needed for successful resolution.

Knowing how to respond to emotions, our own as well as those of others, allows the nurse to use attitudes and emotive behavioral responses as a positive force rather than a negative one. Nurses frequently find themselves in dramatic situations in which a calm, collected response is required. To listen and to respond creatively to intense emotion when the nurse's first impulse is to withdraw or to retaliate demands a high level of skill. It requires self-knowledge, self-control, and empathy for what the client may be experiencing. It is difficult to remain cool under attack, and yet the nurse's willingness to stay with the client through the fires of heartfelt anger may be more meaningful than any other response the nurse might give to the client. Both nursing students and practicing nurses need to learn (assertive) negotiating skills that will allow them to deal constructively with conflict (de Torynay, 1990).

BASIC CONCEPTS

THE NATURE OF CONFLICT

Webster's Dictionary defines **conflict** as a "mental struggle, resulting from incompatible or opposing needs, drives, wishes or internal demands; a hostile encounter." Conflicts in a therapeutic relationship are normal and inevitable, just as they are in every other type of relationship. No two individuals will ever view the same situation in precisely the same way, nor will they always be in complete accord as to how the situation should be handled.

Conflictual feelings serve as an interpersonal alarm in a relationship, offering a warning that something either within ourselves or within a given situation is amiss and needs closer attention. They exist for a reason and are always worthy of our consideration of their potential effects on the relationship.

All conflicts have certain things in common: a concrete *content issue,* which may or may not be based on reality, and *process issues,* which may be opposing, abstract feelings about the meaning or consequences of making a decision. It is immaterial, at least initially, whether the content issues or associated feelings related to the conflict make realistic sense to the nurse. They are a part of the client's subjective experience and, as such, they need to be addressed. They feel very real to the client. In a broader sense, every interpersonal conflict always involves both people in a relationship because of its potential impact on achieving relationship goals. For example, in a conflict between a nurse and supervisor, inappropriate behavior or responses may impair chances of job success (Davidhizar, 1991).

Most people experience conflict as an uncomfortable phenomenon in which there are opposing, disquieting, or intense feelings about specific persons, things, situations, experiences, possible consequences, or tasks. The actual feelings surrounding the conflictual issue vary in intensity from individual to individual and from situation to situation. Previous experiences with similar conflict situations, the acceptability of the issue to significant others in the client's life, the client's current physical, cognitive, and emotional level of well-being, as well as the subjective meaning of the issue and possible consequences for the client, all play a role.

For example, a client may have great difficulty asking appropriate questions of the physician regarding treatment or prognosis but experience no problem asking similar questions of the nurse or family. The reasons for the discrepancy in comfort level may relate to previous experiences with this physician or perceived authority figures in

---

BOX 14–1
The Stages of Conflict

1. Latent conflict, in which disparities exist.
2. Perceived conflict, in which disparities are recognized.
3. Felt conflict, in which feelings (such as anger) erupt.
4. Overt conflict, in which feelings are acted out in observed behaviors.
5. Resolution, in which the outcome is known to all participants.

From Booth, 1985.

---

general. The client may be responding to anticipated fears about the type of information the physician might give. It may have little to do with the actual persons involved.

Some individuals can quite readily express strong feelings of anger to strangers but not to family. Still others experience tremendous difficulty with even the mildest expression of negative feelings. For each individual, the stimulus and the response to conflict may be quite different. However, as Pederson and colleagues note (1990), all conflict has the potential to be creative (functional) in that it has the ability to arouse motivation to solve a problem that may otherwise go unattended (Box 14–1).

Example

Two women who gave birth this morning are moved to a semiprivate room on the postpartum floor. Ms. A. is 19, likes loud music, and is feeling fine. Her roommate, Mrs. B., is 36, has four children at home and wants to rest as much as possible (latent). The music and visitors to Ms. A. repeatedly wake up Mrs. B. (perceived), who yells at them (overt). The nurse arranges to transfer Mrs. B. to an unoccupied room (resolution).

UNDERSTANDING PERSONAL RESPONSES IN CONFLICT SITUATIONS

Conflicts frequently arise between nurse and client within the course of the relationship. If the nurse identifies the presence of an interpersonal conflict in a relationship, it becomes the nurse's responsibility to work to resolve it. Interpersonal conflicts block the relationship process. Energy is transferred to conflict issues instead of being used to build the relationship. To accomplish conflict resolution, nurses first need to have a clear understanding of their own personal response patterns to conflict and know what situations are most likely to trigger conflictual feelings within themselves.

No one is equally effective in all situations. This is a given. Sometimes you can walk into an interpersonal situation and know almost immediately that you will be accepted. In other situations, you are vaguely aware of feeling awkward and unable to say anything meaningful (or so you feel). Still other interpersonal experiences make you feel so uncomfortable that you want to avoid them at all costs. Personal style and past experiences influence the typical responses to conflict situations. Some general responses include:

- Withdrawing from the conflict (avoidance).
- Using false reassurance to smooth over the conflict.
- Giving in, compromising.
- Suppressing the conflict in a dictatorial manner.
- Acknowledging the conflict and involving all parties in resolving it (integrative problem solving).

Most interpersonal conflicts involve some threat to the nurse or client's sense of control or represent a threat to one's self-esteem. For example, no one likes to be criticized. Negative reactions might include anger, rationalization, or blaming others (Davidhizar, 1991). Sometimes, despite the negative impact on our lives, the loss of self-esteem, and the personal upset, we continue to maintain the status quo. Our present behavior patterns appear safe because they are familiar. Trying a new behavior pattern means taking a risk with no guarantee that the consequences will prove any more satisfying. What most of us really want to do is change others or our environments so that we can continue our patterns of behavior with less anxiety. Usually it seems easier to change the behavior of others than to change our own. This is a myth that frequently leads to more frustration for the nurse.

It is important for the nurse to realize that intellectually clients may want to change, but emotionally the troublesome behavior may seem integral to the self. Clients must feel that it is in their best interests emotionally to change behaviors, and they must be able to feel that such change is also the goal of the nurse. As nurses, we affect the behavior of our clients in positive or negative ways through our actions. Awareness of how we cope with conflict is the first step in learning assertiveness strategies.

Nurses often have different attitudes toward the existence of conflict and respond to conflict differently, although the underlying feelings generated by conflict situations may be quite similar. Common emotional responses to conflict, listed in Exercise 14–1, include anger, embarrassment, and anxiety. We are socially conditioned by our past to respond to interpersonal conflict in certain ways. For some, this shaping has been a positive experience; for others, it has not been a productive experience. Fortunately, assertiveness and other skills essential to conflict resolution are behaviors that any nurse can master.

ASSESSING THE PRESENCE OF CONFLICT IN THE NURSE–CLIENT RELATIONSHIP

Evidence of the presence of conflict may be *overt*—that is, observable in the client's behavior and expressed verbally. The conflict issues may be identified, expressed, and allowed to reach resolution; constructive changes may take place. The relationship progresses and deepens. But, more often, conflict is covert and not so clear-cut. The conflict issues are hidden or buried among distracting feelings or tangential issues. The client talks about one issue, but talking doesn't seem to help, and the issue does not seem to get resolved. The client continues to be angry or anxious. Often the first clue to the existence of a conflict situation occurs when the client or the nurse becomes aware of a generalized sense of personal uneasiness. Frequently the reasons for this feeling are not clear. In a covert conflict situation, the conflict acts as a hindrance to the progress of the relationship and the ultimate treatment goals. The conflict usually cannot be resolved until the issues can be put out on the table and explored.

Subtle behavioral manifestations of covert conflict might include any of the following: a reduced effort by the client to engage in the process of self-understanding or self-care; frequent misunderstanding or misinterpretation of the nurse's words; behaviors that are out of character for the client; and extremes of behavior, such as excessive anger or undue praise for the nurse. For example, when the client seems unusually demanding, has a seemingly insatiable need for the nurse's attention, or is unable to tolerate reasonable delays in having needs met, the problem may be anxiety stemming from conflictual feelings.

A client who previously was very involved in self-care and interested in seeking alternative solutions to health problems and who suddenly loses interest or becomes angry at the nurse or the treatment process may be expressing conflictual feelings in an indirect manner. Flattering the nurse is often an unconscious attempt by the client to avoid confronting conflict with treatment or relationship issues. The nurse at this stage of knowledge about the conflict needs to pay attention to his or her own behaviors and feelings as well as those of the client. See Exercise 14–2 for practice in defining conflict issues.

Sometimes the feelings themselves become the major issue, so that valid parts of the original conflict issue are obscured. There is complete focus on only one aspect of the content issue. The larger context is discounted or denied. Feelings that become confused with the content can become a major obstacle to the development of the relationship. When clients relate to the emotional feelings aroused by the conflict instead of to the primary issue, conflict can escalate. Secondary issues develop that may have little to do with the original conflict. Furthermore, the failure to differentiate the emotional components of a conflict from the substance of a conflict issue may have behavioral consequences for the relationship long after the original conflict issues have been settled. At best, such conflict clouds communication and makes it more difficult to respond appropriately. At worst, a defensive surface shell results from not responding appropriately to the client's negative feelings. The relationship can become virtually impossible. Usually conflictual feelings have to be put into words and related to the issue at hand before the client can understand the meaning of the conflict. In some instances, feelings have to be decoded before they can be explored. Consider yourself as the nurse in this situation.

EXERCISE 14–1
Personal Responses to Conflict

Purpose: Before you can cope successfully with conflict in nurse–client relationships, you need to have a beginning understanding of how you most often respond to conflict situations, what types of feeling states and behaviors they create within you, and what types of interpersonal situations are more likely to create difficulty for you. The purpose of this exercise is to increase awareness of how you respond in conflict situations and of what in the situations—people involved, status, age, previous experience, lack of experience, place—contribute to your sense of discomfort.

Time: 20 minutes

Directions:
Break up into small groups of two or three participants. Think of two conflict situations that you would feel comfortable sharing with the group—one you handled well and the other that you wished you had handled differently.

Part I:
The following feelings are common correlates of interpersonal conflict situations that many people say they have experienced in conflict situations they haven't handled well:

anger	defensiveness	exclusion	manipulation
annoyance	deflation	frustration	obsequiousness
antagonism	devaluation	hostility	outmaneuvering
anxiousness	disappointment	humiliation	quarrelsomeness
bitterness	discountedness	incompleteness	resentment
caught off guard	embarrassment	inferiority	superiority
competitiveness	emptiness	intimidation	uneasiness
criticism	exasperation	intrusion	vengefulness

Although these feelings generally are not ones we may be especially proud of, they are a part of the human experience. By acknowledging their existence within ourselves, we usually have more choice about how we will handle them.

Using the words above to stimulate images of situations you actually have experienced, describe, as concretely as possible:
1. The details of the situation. How did it develop? What were the content issues? Was the conflict expressed in words or nonverbally? Who were the persons involved, and where did the interaction take place?

CASE STUDY

Situation: Mr. J. is scheduled for surgery at 8 A.M. tomorrow. As the student nurse assigned to take care of him, you have been told that he was admitted to the hospital three hours ago, and he has been examined by the house resident. The anesthesia department has been notified of the client's arrival. His blood work and urine have been sent to the laboratory. As you enter his room and introduce yourself, you notice that Mr. J. is sitting on the edge of his bed and that he appears tense and angry.

Client: I wish people would just leave me alone. Nobody has come in and told me about my surgery tomorrow. I don't know what I'm supposed to do, just lay around here and rot, I guess.

At this point, you probably can sense the presence of conflictual feelings, but it is unclear whether the emotions being expressed relate to anxiety over the surgery or to anger over some real or imagined invasion of privacy because of the necessary lab tests and physical exam. The client might also be annoyed by you or by lack of information from his surgeon. Or he may feel the need to know that hospital personnel see him as a person and care about his feelings. Before the nurse can respond empathetically to the client's feelings, his feelings will have to be decoded.

Nurse (in a concerned tone of voice): You seem really upset. It's rough being in the hospital, isn't it?

EXERCISE 14–1 (Continued)

2. What you were feeling prior to experiencing the conflict. Did this situation stir up any images of previous conflictual situations? How would you describe the intensity of your feelings?
3. Why was the situation particularly uncomfortable for you?

1. _____
   _____

2. _____
   _____

3. _____
   _____

Part II:
Now think of a conflict situation that you felt you handled well. Using (1), (2), and (3) from Part I, apply the same process to this situation. Be very specific in describing the behaviors you used to cope with this situation.

1. _____
   _____

2. _____
   _____

3. _____
   _____

Part III:
Discuss: in what ways these situations were different. How were your responses different in this situation? What were the differences in outcome? What was your level of satisfaction? If you could redo your behaviors in the first interaction, what would you do differently?

Share your experiences with members of your dyad or triad. Note the commonalities of feeling experiences that prevent us from acting assertively when it clearly is in our best interests to do so. Identify behaviors that were different in the more successful conflict situation.

Variations: This exercise may be done as a homework assignment.

Notice that the nurse's reply is nonevaluative and tentative. The nurse does not suggest specific feelings beyond those the client has shared, yet there is an implicit request for the client to validate the nurse's perception of his feelings and to link the feelings with concrete issues. Verbal as well as nonverbal cues are included in the nurse's reply. Concern is expressed through the nurse's tone of voice and words. The content focus relates to the client's predominant feeling tone, since this is the part of the conflict the client has chosen to share with the nurse. It is important for the nurse to remain a nonanxious presence for the client—to realize that client resistance is at some level a way to maintain personal stability and homeostasis, even though objectively it may appear counterproductive to the relationship.

TYPES OF CONFLICT: INTRAPERSONAL VERSUS INTERPERSONAL

A conflict can be internal or *intrapersonal*—that is, it can represent two or more opposing feelings about a situation, person, or idea *within* a particular individual—or the conflict may be *interpersonal*. Interpersonal conflicts signify a difference in approach, feelings, or ideas occurring *between* two or more people.

EXERCISE 14–2
Defining Conflict Issues

Purpose: To help students begin to organize information and identify problem definitions in interpersonal conflict situations. Unless there is agreement about the nature of a conflict issue, effective problem solving cannot occur. In every conflict situation, it is important to look for the specific behaviors (including words, tone, posture, facial expression), feeling impressions (including words, tone, intensity, facial expression), and need (expressed verbally or through actions).

Time: 10 minutes each

Directions:
In the following three situations, the first example is completed as a guide In situations (1) and (2), identify the behaviors, feeling impressions, and needs that the client is expressing and suggest a nursing action.

Example:

> Mrs. A., an Indian client, doesn't speak much English. She just had her baby by Cesarean section, and it is expected that she will remain in the hospital for at least four days. Her husband tells the nurse that Mrs. A. wants to breast-feed, but she has decided to wait until she goes home to begin because she will be more comfortable there and she wants privacy. The nurse knows that breast-feeding will be more successful if it is initiated soon after birth.

Behaviors: Client's husband states she wants to breast-feed but doesn't wish to start before going home. Wife is not initiating breast-feeding in the hospital.

Nursing Inference:

Assess meaning of behaviors. Indirectly the client is expressing physical discomfort, possible insecurity, and awkwardness about breast-feeding. She may also be acting in accordance with cultural norms of her country or family.

Assess underlying needs. Safety and security. Mrs. A. probably will not be motivated to attempt breast-feeding until she feels safe and secure in her home environment.

Decide what action is best: Provide family support and guarantee total privacy for feeding.

Situation 1

> Mrs. S. is returned to the unit from surgery following a radical mastectomy. The doctor's orders call for her to ambulate, cough, and deep breathe and to encourage her to use her arm as much as possible in self-care activities. Mrs. S. asks the nurse in a very annoyed tone, "Why do I have to do this? You can see that it is difficult for me. Why can't you help me?"

Behaviors: _____

_____

_____

Nursing Inference:

Assess meaning of behavior. _____

_____

Assess underlying needs. _____

_____

_____

Suggested Nursing Action: _____

EXERCISE 14–2 *(Continued)*

Situation 2

Mr. C. is a 31-year-old client who was recently diagnosed with terminal cancer of the pancreas. He answers the nurse's questions with monosyllables and turns his head away. When the nurse questions him, he says in a low voice: "There is no hope. They're going to keep me here until I die. Can't you give me my medication more often than every three hours—I'm going to die anyway."

Behaviors: _____

_____

_____

Nursing Inference:

Assess meaning of behavior. _____

_____

Assess underlying needs. _____

_____

_____

Suggested Nursing Action: _____

Escalation of Intrapersonal and Interpersonal Conflict

Depending on the type of feedback received, an intrapersonal conflict can take on interpersonal dimensions. In the case presented below, the mother initially experiences an intrapersonal or intrapsychic conflict. The wished-for perfect baby has not happened, and her personal ambivalence related to accepting or coping with her infant's defect is expressed indirectly through her partial noncompliant behavior. If the nurse interprets the client's behavior incorrectly as poor mothering and acts in a manner that reflects this attitude, the basically intrapersonal conflict can become interpersonal.

CASE STUDY

A mother with her first infant is informed soon after delivery that her baby has a small cleft palate. The physician explains the infant's condition in detail and answers the mother's questions. The mother requests rooming in and seems genuinely interested in the baby. Each time the nurse enters the client's room, the mother complains that her infant doesn't seem hungry and states how difficult it is to feed the baby. Although the nurse spends a great deal of time with them teaching the mother the special techniques necessary to feed the infant, and the mother seems interested at the time, she seems unable or unwilling to follow any of the nurse's suggestions when she is by herself. Later, the nurse finds out that the mother has been asking her roommate to feed her infant.

This client appears to be asking for guidance and to be resisting what is offered. While she may simply need further instruction in technique, the presence of an underlying intrapersonal conflict is worth investigating. Before proceeding further with client teaching, it is important for the nurse to find out how competent the mother perceives herself to be in the mothering role, what the reality of having a less than perfect baby means to her, and what her fears are about caring for an infant with this particular type of defect. Until the nature of the underlying feelings is identified and connected with the behaviors, client teaching is likely to have limited success.

Intrapersonal conflicts frequently escalate into interpersonal conflicts if they are not viewed as objective pieces of data. The intrapersonal conflict for this client can develop into an interpersonal conflict with the nurse if, through verbal or nonverbal messages, the nurse conveys disapproval of the mother's lack of consistency in feeding behavior. This development can occur either because of the nurse's own feelings of how mothers ought to behave or because of the erroneous notion that cognitive knowledge of technique is more important than dealing with emotional issues.

Cognitive information and emotion are integral to client behavior. Seeking to understand the meaning of an intrapersonal conflict to a client from his or her perspective reframes the experience. In this situation, for example, a client strength would be the mother's ability and willingness to express her uncomfortable feelings so that they can be addressed. Even though the mother may be unclear about the origin or nature of her feelings, reframing the issues in this way builds on strengths instead of personal deficits. Both the client and the nurse become learner and expert in the interpersonal situation. They teach each other; the client provides more specific input about her fears and the nature of the conflict, and the nurse provides acceptance of the client's right to have all types of feelings. Together they seek a solution based on the pooling of their individual resources. Material, power, and information are shared in ways that are meaningful to both participants in the therapeutic relationship.

Interpersonal Sources of Conflict

Sometimes in the therapeutic relationship the conflict arises from demands of the relationship that the nurse cannot meet without compromising role responsibilities or self-values.

Interpersonal sources of conflict for the nurse that frequently occur in the clinical area include one or more of the following:

- Being asked to do something you know would be irresponsible or unsafe.
- Having your feelings or opinions ridiculed or discounted.
- Being pressured to give more time or attention than you are able to give.
- Having the client shift responsibility for care or decision making to you.
- Being asked to give more information than you feel comfortable sharing.

- Negotiating expectations and setting limits with high-status clients, aggressive clients, confused elderly clients, or noncompliant adolescent clients.
- Maintaining a sense of self in the face of client hostility, sexual overtures, or personal attack.
- Wanting to do things the usual old way versus trying something new and different.

When the source of conflict is interpersonal, the nurse needs to think through the possible causes of the conflict as well as his or her own feelings about it and respond appropriately, even if the response is a deliberate choice not to respond verbally. Interpersonal conflicts usually leave residual feelings that reappear unexpectedly and affect the nurse's ability to respond realistically and responsibly in future interactions.

FUNCTIONAL USES OF CONFLICT

Traditionally, conflict was viewed as a destructive force to be eliminated or as an inevitable part of relationships that needed to be minimized (Booth, 1985). Current thinking holds that conflict can serve either a functional or a dysfunctional role in relationships. In fact, conflict is now thought to be an inevitable part of today's changing health care environment (Jones, Bushardt, and Cadenhead, 1990). The critical factor is the willingness to explore the nature of the conflict and mutually to discover ways to resolve it. Whereas the reality of many circumstances cannot be changed, the ways of looking at almost anything and of responding to it are limited only by motivation and the creative problem-solving abilities of the participants.

Despite the uncomfortable feelings that conflicts create within and among people, the existence of such feelings can have a positive value. They provide an important opportunity for interpersonal growth. The intensity of emotions inherent in a conflict potentially can be the catalyst for a deeper, more meaningful relationship. In a constructive way, a conflict can be the stimulus for highly creative problem solving in a relationship. Conflicts have been known to unfreeze interaction and to help participants shed destructive ideas about themselves and others in a relationship.

Conflict becomes manageable when the issues can be stated clearly—when they accurately reflect an individual's inner experience. Successfully handled, conflict allows the expression of strongly held ideas or feelings that otherwise might not become known. Until the true feelings or ideas of an individual are brought out into the open and made available for discussion, it is difficult to work with them with any degree of success.

Establishing a framework for acceptable behaviors within a relationship increases the security and ease of communication. As participants successfully confront the conflict situation, they develop a deeper understanding about the nature of stumbling blocks in the relationship. They get more accurate information about the types of strategies needed to correct them. Negative habit patterns can be assessed and reworked. Energy devoted to defending the self can be released for more productive use.

The relationship becomes more trustworthy. The sense of trust comes from the knowledge that another person *cares* enough to stay through the expression of very strong feelings and doesn't appear to be destroyed by the presence of conflictual feelings that seem potentially overwhelming to the person experiencing them. This trust creates a safe space to feel that all emotions have a place in the relationship—that the existence of the feelings will be acceptable, even though acting on them may not be acceptable.

Having a thought or feeling is not the same as acting on it, yet many people confuse the two. Furthermore, it is very common for individuals to have two decidedly different feelings, thoughts, or viewpoints about the same issue. For many, this possibility comes as a surprise.

Conflict can be a shared experience that heightens both stability and sensitivity in a relationship. This emotional climate allows new learning about the self. Box 14–2 lists rights and responsibilities in conflict situations. Generalized patterns of behavior often undergo significant change as a result of the struggle encountered in resolving a conflict. The actual content of a specific conflict is less important than how the conflict is resolved. In a manageable conflict, choices are made between alternatives, and the relationship may be strengthened. A conflict situation has both *content* and *process*.

DYSFUNCTIONAL CONFLICT

There are several identifiable elements that may occur in *dysfunctional conflict:* Information is withheld, feelings are expressed too strongly, the conflict is obscured by a double message, feelings are denied or projected onto others; conflicts are not resolved, so issues build up.

Nonproductive conflicts are characterized by intensity of emotional expression, misperceptions, and distancing in the relationship. The problem occurs when the emotions or differences in motivation cause an individual to distort or ignore part or all of the content portion of a conflict situation. This difficulty can originate in either the speaker or the listener. Conflict that is detrimental to the goals of a relationship can happen whenever the communication lines are unclear or indirect. Some information is withheld (or is missing by design) from one or more of the participants involved. The interaction seems incomplete and tends to leave emotional scars. At least one of the participants must guess at what is really going on in the mind of the other participant in the interaction.

In other dysfunctional conflicts the feelings are stated accurately, but they are expressed too strongly. The verbal tone or word used to express the feelings or issues is so intense that the other

---

BOX 14–2
Personal Rights and Responsibilities
in Conflict Situations

I have the right to respect from other people as a unique human being.
I have the responsibility to respect the human rights of others.

I have the right to make my own decisions.
I have the responsibility to allow others to make their own decisions.

I have the right to have feelings.
I have the responsibility to express those feelings in ways that do not violate the rights of others.

I have the right to make mistakes.
I have the responsibility to accept full accountability for my mistakes.

I have the right to decide how I will act.
I have the responsibility to act in ways that will not be harmful to myself or to others.

I have the right to my own opinions.
I have the responsibility to respect the rights of others to hold opinions different from mine.

individual literally cannot respond to the legitimate content issues, being too caught up in the metacommunication. When voice projection is either very loud or very intense, the listener may feel attacked even when the speaker does not intend attack. The automatic response of the listener to feeling attacked is usually defensive. Consequently, communication breaks down.

The opposite extreme also can happen. Sometimes very important conflictual issues are couched in laughter, meek expressions, or such tentative tones that the listener fails to grasp their importance or conflictual nature. A double message is given. The words are saying one thing, but the facial expression, body position, and voice tone are implying something quite different. Whenever the level of intensity with which the conflict is expressed is either too much or too little, the listener does not obtain enough information to act appropriately. The relationship becomes less trustworthy because it is hard for participants to know what to expect from it.

Emotions sustain the life of the conflict. Since feelings do not obey the laws of logic, any objective, logical discussion that dwells only on the content issues is not likely to be effective. Often feelings do not make complete objective sense.

In some instances participants may be too embarrassed to admit to conflictual feelings and either project them onto the environment or deny that they feel them. Strong feelings that should have been owned and expressed are left unsaid and kept inside. When such denial occurs, the relationship suffers. Win–lose or lose–lose interpersonal positions are created, resulting in lowered self-esteem for one or both participants. The dialogue within the individual is seen only in behaviors, which are less easily understood and subject to misinterpretation unless validated.

In contrast to the communication that takes place when conflict plays a functional role in the relationship, the outcomes provide little sense of satisfaction or accomplishment. The feelings of resentment related to unfinished business tend to have a build-up effect in future encounters. They may be forgiven, but they are rarely forgotten. Unresolved interpersonal conflict always interferes with the central purposes of a relationship. Special attention must be given to the disruptive forces that threaten nurse–client relationships, since the therapeutic alliance usually becomes the primary support for promoting desired behavioral changes in the client.

Since conflict resolution by its very nature demands a shift in thinking on the part of one or both participants in the relationship, understanding the types and meanings of behavioral responses to conflict situations is a necessary component of the nurse's assessment in conflict situations.

BEHAVIORAL RESPONSES USED TO RESOLVE CONFLICT

The first step in conflict resolution is to identify the conflict issues and the emotional feelings associated with the conflict. Knowledge of one's own typical past response patterns is useful. Typical behaviors used to resolve conflict can be defensive (aggressive, passive, or passive-aggressive) in nature, or they can serve to define the self (assertive behaviors). These behaviors all reflect a response of the self to the presence of conflict in a relationship (Exercise 14–3).

In making an *aggressive response,* the individual acts to defend the self, to deflect the emotional impact of the perceived threat to the self through personal attack, blaming, or an extreme reaction to a tangential issue in the conflict. Aggression has been described as a blind impulse to self-affirmation, to the expression of all the elements of one's being, without any discrimination and choice, without any concern for the consequences, without any consideration for others (Ferrucci, 1982). The tone is defensive, and the feelings generated in the other person are those of anger and resentment.

Passive responses to conflict are designed to protect the self against feeling the full emotional pressure of the perceived threat by refusing to engage actively in the interpersonal process of resolving the conflict. The emotional tone outwardly is much quieter, but the feelings generated in the other person are frustration and loss of respect.

For some people passive response to conflict may reflect a lack of experience in developing successful response behaviors to use in conflict situations. Some people don't disclose their true feelings about a situation because they never learned how or have never experienced positive consequences from doing so. For others, the current behavior pattern or conflict situation actually plays a functional role in their lives or in the lives of family members. Conflicts are used in some families as a

EXERCISE 14–3
Behavioral Responses to Interpersonal Conflict

Purpose: To help students experience the feelings associated with responses to conflict.

Time: 45 minutes

Situation:

A newly employed staff nurse is routinely assigned to care for the most critically ill clients, yet her work load is the same as that of other nurses on the floor. In her two-month evaluation conference with her manager, the nurse receives less than satisfactory ratings on "ability to complete work on time."

Directions:
Choose a partner. Using the behaviors suggested in Box 14–2, take turns role playing a response. Pause between response positions to reflect on the feelings generated by being in that position. After each person has had a turn, the class should discuss the common feelings: what your body felt like, which communication position felt most comfortable, and why.

way to distance others or as the primary mechanism to connect emotionally with each other.

Included in a passive response category is the use of *passive-aggressive behaviors.* The person appears to be a cooperative partner in planning or implementing needed changes to achieve mutually defined health goals, but agreed-upon strategies or goals seem to change about without any negotiation or analysis. On the surface, the person's behavior appears cooperative, but goals are not achieved, the strategies to achieve them are not collaborative, and problem-solving efforts to resolve the conflict seem to backfire. There is verbal acquiescence without exposing any real feelings. At the same time, actions are used that sabotage or discredit the strategies needed to achieve goals. Often the verbal messages and nonverbal actions represent opposite polarities.

As the nurse in such a situation, you may find yourself thinking, "Was I really there? That isn't what I thought I said," or, "How did this happen? This isn't what I thought we agreed upon." Whenever you are reasonably certain that you were clear in your own communication but you seem to be making no progress, chances are that you are dealing with a passive-aggressive response to conflict. The client is indirectly expressing antagonism toward some aspect of the planned interventions as a way of protecting himself against the perceived onslaught of conflictual feelings. The focus of the antagonism may be the nurse who raises uncomfortable issues; it may be some aspect of the proposed interventions for resolving the conflict; it

may also be the consequences of goal achievement. Almost always, the antagonism is unconscious, and the individual seems genuinely surprised when questions are raised about discrepancies between verbal agreement with the nurse and subsequent client actions.

THE NATURE OF ASSERTIVE BEHAVIOR

The most satisfactory way to resolve an interpersonal conflict is through use of integrative problem solving. Skills needed include the use of confrontation and the use of assertive behaviors. *Assertive behavior* is defined as setting goals, acting on these goals in a clear and consistent manner, and taking responsibility for the consequences of those actions. The assertive nurse is able to stand up for the rights of others as well as for his or her own rights.

According to Angel and Petronko (1983, 1987), the two goals of assertiveness are (1) to stand up for your personal rights without infringing on the rights of others and (2) to reduce anxiety, which often prevents us from behaving assertively. Table 14–1 compares some of the differences in basic characteristics among passive, assertive, and aggressive responses to conflict situations.

Assertive behaviors range from making a simple, direct, and honest statement about one's beliefs to taking a very strong, confrontational stand about what will and will not be tolerated in the relationship. Assertive responses contain "I" statements that take responsibility. This behavior

TABLE 14–1
Differences in Characteristic Interpersonal Responses to Conflict

	Nonassertive	*Assertive*	*Aggressive*
Goal of response	To protect the self.	To define the self.	To defend the self.
Type of response actions	Indifferent or nonresponsive, automatic.	Neutral or empathetic, genuine.	Judgmental or evaluative; impulsive.
Mechanism of action	Indirect and vague communication.	Direct, honest, firm communication.	Emotional and projective communication.
Self-image interaction	Diminishes sense of self-worth; potentiates inferior position in relationship.	Enhances equal worth in relationship.	Acts as an antagonist to relationship and potentiates defensive behavior in partner.
Effect on self	Feelings of being discounted, emotionally pressured.	Feelings of self-esteem; rational and fair.	Feelings of loss of control, guilt; irrational and exploitative.
Request for change	Hidden bargaining for change.	Asking for change.	Making a demand for change.
Reaction to conflict	Underreaction.	Collaborative interaction.	Overreaction.
Effect on personal rights	Discounts personal rights.	Respects personal rights of self and others.	Discounts rights of others.
Effect on position in relationship	Inferior position: lose–lose.	Equal position: win–win.	Superior position: win–lose.
Content of verbal conflict issues	Nonexistent or tangential.	Descriptive.	Interpretive.

is in contrast to aggressive behavior, which has a goal of dominating while suppressing the other person's rights. Aggressive responses often consist of "you" statements that fix blame and undue responsibility on the other person.

In former times, many individuals, especially women, were socialized to withdraw rather than use assertiveness to cope with unpleasant situations (Kennedy et al., 1990). Since nearly 96 percent of nurses currently are women, gender socialization exerts a significant effect on interpersonal relationship styles. Assertiveness is a learned behavior that has not typically been a component of traditional female socialization. More typically, passivity has been stereotyped as a feminine characteristic. Unfortunately, studies show that this personality characteristic in a professional nurse is related to lower levels of autonomy (Schutzenhofer, 1992). *Passive behavior* is defined as a response that denies our own rights in order to avoid conflict. An example is remaining silent and not responding to a client's demands for narcotics every four hours when he displays no signs of pain out of fear he might report you to his physician. Or passivity can be evidenced by the acceptance of a negative,

unfair comment, without any further discussion of the impact the comment had on you.

Assertiveness needs to be practiced to be learned (Exercise 14–4). Effective nursing encompasses the mastery of assertive behavior (Box 14–3). Continued patterns of nonassertive responses have adverse psychological effects on the nurse and a negative influence on the standard of care the nurse delivers (McCanton and Hargie, 1990).

APPLICATIONS

NURSING STRATEGIES TO ENHANCE CONFLICT RESOLUTION

Strategies that have been found to be useful in conflict resolution are described here. Successful use of these strategies varies with the skill level of the participants and the nature of the situation. Mastery takes practice.

Prepare for the Encounter. Careful preparation often makes the difference between being successful and failing to assert yourself when necessary. In

EXERCISE 14–4
Responding Assertively

Purpose: To help you define your position in a conflict situation in an assertive manner.

Time: 1 hour

Directions:
Think of three interpersonal situations in which you wished you had acted more assertively. What behaviors would you alter? For each of these situations, specify how you would relate in an assertive manner. (*Example:* Your employer schedules you to work overtime *or* your teacher incorrectly gives you a lower grade than earned. *Sample response:* I would tell my boss that I had exams at school and I wasn't going to be able to continue to work every weekend.)

1. _____

2. _____

3. _____

   If you are like most people, you find it difficult to express yourself clearly about your position in conflict situations. Sometimes you may not recognize that you are involved in a conflict situation until the situation is well under way.

Discussion:
1. What were some of the variables that made it difficult for you to express yourself assertively?
2. As you listen to other students' responses, what common themes emerge?
3. How could you use this information in your professional responses to conflict?

discussing assertive communication, Flanagan (1990, p. 49) notes that for communication to be effective, it must be carefully thought out in terms of certain basic questions:

- *Purpose:* What is the purpose or objective of this information? What is the central idea, the one most important statement to be made?
- *Organization:* What are the major points to be shared? in what order?

- *Content:* Is the information to be shared complete? Does it convey who, what, where, when, why, and how?
- *Word choice:* Has careful consideration been given to the choice of words?

If you wish to be successful, you must consider not only what is important to you in the discussion but also what is important to the other person. Bear in mind the other person's frame of reference when acting assertively. The following clinical example illustrates this idea.

BOX 14–3
Characteristics Associated with the Development of Assertive Behaviors

- Use strategies that respect the rights of self and others.
- Express your own position, using "I" statements.
- Make clear statements.
- Speak in a firm tone, using moderate pitch.
- Assume responsibility for personal feelings and wants.
- Make sure verbal and nonverbal messages are congruent.
- Address only issues related to the present conflict.
- Structure responses to be tactful and show awareness of the client's frame of reference.
- Understand that undesired behaviors, not feelings, attitudes, and motivations, are the focus for change.

CASE STUDY

Mr. R. is an 80-year-old bachelor who lives alone. He has always been considered a proud and stately gentleman. He has a sister, 84 years old, who lives in Florida. His only other living relatives, a nephew and his wife, also live in another state. He recently changed his will, excluding his relatives, and he refuses to eat. When his neighbor brings in food he eats it, but he won't fix anything for himself. He tells his neighbor that he wants to die and that he read in the paper about a man who was able to die in 60 days by not eating. As the visiting nurse assigned to his area, you have been asked to make a home visit and assess the situation.

The issue in this case example is not one of food intake alone. For the nurse to talk about the reasons it is important for the client to eat or to express a point of view in this conflict immediately upon arriving is not likely to be successful. The client's behavior suggests that he feels there is little to be gained by living any longer. His actions suggest further that he feels lonely and may be angry with his relatives. Once you correctly ascertain his needs and identify the specific issues, you may be able to help Mr. R. resolve his intrapersonal conflict. His wish to die may not be absolute or final because he eats when food is prepared by his neighbor, and he has not yet taken a deliberate, aggressive move to end his life. Each of these factors needs to be assessed and validated with the client before an accurate nursing diagnosis can be made (Exercise 14–5).

Organize Information. Organizing your information and validating the appropriateness of your intervention with another knowledgeable person who is not directly involved in the process is useful. Sometimes, it is wise to rehearse out loud what you are going to say.

Manage One's Own Anxiety. If you experience stage fright before engaging in a conflict situation that calls for an assertive response, know that you are in good company. Most people experience some variation of a physical response when taking interpersonal risks. Before you actually enter the client's room, take a few deep breaths. Inhale deeply, counting to yourself, 1–2–3. Hold your breath for a count of two and exhale, counting again, 1–2–3–4, slowly. Fortify yourself with positive statements—for example, "I have a right to respect." Usually anticipation is far worse than the reality.

Time the Encounter. Timing can be critical in responding assertively to a conflict situation. Conflictual situations lead to varying degrees of energy depletion. Once fatigue sets in, the value of any assertive behavior on your part may be diminished. Select a time when the client or colleague is most likely to be receptive. (When would Mr. R. be most receptive?)

You might accompany your assertive statement with comfort measures, such as arranging the table attractively. Nonverbal support of verbal statements adds strength to the meaning of the communication.

Timing is also important if an individual is very angry. The key to assertive behavior is *choice.* Sometimes it is better to allow ventilation of some "emotional steam" before engaging in conversation. In this case, the assertive thing to do is to choose silence accompanied by a calm, relaxed body posture and eye contact. These nonverbal actions convey acceptance of feeling and a desire to understand. Validating the anger and reframing the emotion as adaptive is useful. Comments such as, "I'm sorry you are feeling so upset" recognize the significance of the emotion being expressed without enlarging the frame of reference beyond what is being expressed.

Take One Issue at a Time and Focus on the Present. It is always best to start with one issue at a time. Success breeds success. Focus on the present issue, since the past cannot be changed. Limiting your discussion to one topic issue at a time enhances the chance of success. It usually is impossible to resolve a conflict that is multidimensional in nature with one solution. By breaking the problem down into simple steps, automatic responses are avoided, and enough time is allowed for a clear understanding.

EXERCISE 14–5
Becoming Assertive

Purpose: To help you practice assertive responses.

Time: 10 minutes, with a 5-minute discussion.

Directions:
Role play Mr. R's case situation (see text) in groups of three, with one student taking the role of the client, one the role of the nurse, and the third the role of the observer. Compare the results of the different approaches.

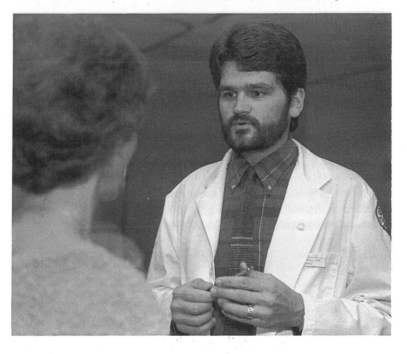

Reaching a common understanding of the problem in a direct, tactful manner is the first step in conflict resolution. (Courtesy of the University of North Carolina at Charlotte College of Nursing)

In the case example just given, the nurse might paraphrase the client's words, reflect the meaning back to the client, and validate the accuracy of the meaning of the feeling. Once the issues have been delineated clearly, the steps needed for resolution may appear quite simple. As one issue gets resolved, others may disappear of their own accord or take on a different perspective. At the very least, a sense of mutuality develops because both parties become actively involved in the process of resolving the conflict, and the client is assured of the nurse's interest. At times, however, the conflict is such that a behavioral change is needed before the conflict can be fully resolved.

Make a Request for a Behavior Change. Asking someone for a needed behavior change is handled best when the request takes into consideration the person's developmental stage, cultural and value orientation, and other life factors likely to be affected by the change. The person's level of readiness to explore alternative options also needs to be considered. Additionally, for an ill client, level of self-care as well as outside support systems are factors. To approach the task without this information is risky and haphazard.

There obviously will be situations in which such a thorough assessment is not possible, but each of these variables affects the success of the confrontation. For example, a client with dementia who makes a pass at a nurse may simply be expressing a need for affection in much the same way that a small child does; this behavior needs a loving touch rather than a reprimand. A 30-year-old client with all his cognitive faculties who makes a similar pass needs a more confrontational response.

Often what appears to be an inappropriate response in our culture is a highly acceptable way of interacting in a different culture. For example, some clients experience conflict related to taking pain medication. In the cultures of these clients, pain is supposed to be endured with a stoicism that is incompatible with reality. It is often necessary to help such clients express their discomfort when it occurs and to give them guidelines as well as explicit permission to develop a different behavior. It is easier for the client to take such medication when he can assure the family that the nurse said he needed to take it. By focusing on the behavior required to meet the client's physical needs, the nurse bypasses placing a value on the rightness or wrongness of the behavior. Refer to other chapters for a more detailed discussion of cultural differences that can create conflict.

Client readiness is vital. The behavior may need to be confronted, but the manner in which the confrontation is approached and the amount of preparation or groundwork that has been done beforehand is a determinant of success. Know specifically the behavior you wish to have the client change. Make sure that the client is capable physically and emotionally of changing the behavior.

Evaluate the Conflict Resolution. Evaluation of the degree to which an interpersonal conflict has been resolved depends somewhat on the nature of the conflict. Sometimes a conflict cannot be resolved in a short period of time, but the willingness to persevere is a good indicator of a potentially successful outcome. Accepting small goals is useful when large goal attainment is not possible. The ideal interactive process is one in which a climate of openness and trust leads to an increase in communication in the form of feedback and increased problem solving (Jones, Bushardt, and Cadenhead, 1990).

For a client perhaps the strongest indicator of conflict resolution is the degree to which he or she is actively engaged in activities aimed at accomplishing tasks associated with treatment goals. Two questions you as the nurse might want to address if modifications are necessary are:

1. What is the best method for establishing an environment most conducive to conflict resolution? What else needs to be considered?
2. What self-care behaviors can be expected of the client if these changes are made? They need to be stated in ways that are measurable.

Both the nurse and the client benefit from conflict resolution. The nurse gains because successful resolution permits the therapeutic relationship to develop further to meet treatment goals and increases his or her personal sense of confidence and self-esteem. The client achieves a clearer understanding of the actions needed to resolve intrapersonal or interpersonal conflicts as well as a unique opportunity to explore alternative solutions for coping with difficult interpersonal situations.

DEFUSING INTRAPERSONAL CONFLICT

Intrapersonal conflicts develop out of ambivalent or opposing feelings within an individual. The client with a myocardial infarction who insists on conducting business from the bedside probably feels conflicted about the restraints placed on his or her activities, as does the diabetic client who sneaks off to the food vending machine for a hamburger.

There are times when the conflictual feelings also begin intrapersonally within the nurse—for example, in working with parents of an abused child or treating a foul-mouthed alcoholic client in the emergency room. Such situations often stir up strong feelings of anger or resentment. When the conflict is judged to be intrapersonal in nature, nurses may need to help themselves defuse destructive emotions before proceeding further. The following are interventions the nurse can use to defuse interpersonal conflict in a potentially destructive interaction:

1. Identify the presence of an emotionally tense situation.
2. Talk the situation through with someone.
3. Provide a neutral, accepting environment.
4. Take appropriate action to reduce tension.
5. Evaluate the effectiveness of the strategies.
6. Generalize behavioral approaches to other situations.

For the nurse, the first step in coping with difficult emotional responses is to recognize their presence and to assess the appropriateness of expressing emotion in the situation. If expressing the emotion doesn't fit the circumstances, one must deliberately remain unruffled when every natural instinct argues against it. Ambivalence, described as two opposing ideas or feelings related to any life situation or relationship coexisting within the same individual, is a relatively common phenomenon.

It is not the responsibility of the nurse to help a client resolve all intrapersonal conflicts—only those that occur within the context of the immediate clinical situation and threaten to sabotage the goals of the therapeutic relationship. Longstanding intrapsychic or sudden acute conflicts require more experience and clinical expertise to resolve. In such cases, the nurse identifies the presence of possible conflict, refers the client to the appropriate resource, communicates with the personnel chosen, and supports the client's participation.

Identify Potential Conflict Situations. The initial interpersonal strategy used to help clients reduce strong emotion to a workable level is to provide a neutral, accepting interpersonal environment. Within this context, the nurse can acknowledge the client's emotion as a necessary component of adaptation to life. The nurse conveys acceptance of the individual's legitimate right to have any feeling. Telling a client, "I'm not surprised that you are angry about . . ." or simply stating, "I'm sorry you are hurting so much" acknowledges the presence of an uncomfortable emotion in the client, conveys an attitude of acceptance, and encourages the client to express the feeling and the circumstances generating the emotion. Once a feeling can be put into words, it becomes manageable because it has concrete boundaries.

Talk About It. The second step in defusing the strength of an emotion is to talk the emotion through with someone. Unlike complaining, the purpose of talking the emotion through is to help the person get in touch with all of his or her personal feelings surrounding the incident. For the client, this someone is often the nurse. For the nurse, this might be a nursing supervisor or a trusted colleague. If one client seems to produce certain negative emotional reactions on a nursing unit, the emotional responses may need the direct attention of all staff on the unit.

Use Tension-Reducing Actions. The third phase is to take action. The specific needs expressed by the emotion suggest the actions that might help the client come to terms with the consequences of the emotion. This responsibility might take the form of getting more information or of taking some concrete risks to change behaviors that sabotage the goals of the relationship. Sometimes the most effective action is simply to listen.

In psychiatric settings, going for a walk or to the gym to use the punching bag, taking a warm bath, and writing are neutralizing interventions the nurse can suggest to control a client's initial anxiety behaviors. Stepping in before the client's behaviors escalate to the point where they are no longer under the client's conscious control can defuse an emotionally tense situation. If the client is so consumed by emotion that he or she constitutes a danger to himself or others and talking is futile, the nurse should allow a significant amount of physical space and face the client, but avoid backing the client into a corner. The nurse should speak in a low, calm tone to the client and move slowly to the nurses' station. Many hospitals and psychiatric units have a "code blue" that is used to summon trained help.

Evaluate. The final step in the process is to evaluate the effectiveness of responses to emotions and to generalize the experience of confronting difficult emotions to other situations. Each step in the process may need to be taken more than once and refined or revised as circumstances dictate.

DEVELOPING ASSERTIVE SKILLS

Demonstrate Respect. Responsible assertive statements are made in ways that don't violate the rights of others and don't diminish their standing. They are conveyed by a relaxed but attentive posture, a calm, friendly tone of voice, and the use of appropriate eye contact.

Use "I" Statements. Assertive or self-expressive statements that begin with "I" suggest that the person making the statement accepts full personal responsibility for his or her own feelings and position in relation to the presence of conflict. It is not necessary to justify your position unless the added message clarifies or adds essential information (Smythe, 1990).

Statements that begin with "You" sound accusatory and always represent an assumption because it is impossible to know exactly, without validation, why someone acts in a certain way. Since such statements usually point a finger and imply a judgment, they are responded to defensively by most people.

"We" statements should be used only when you really mean to look at an issue collaboratively. Thus, the statement, "Perhaps, we both need to look at this issue a little closer" may be appropriate in certain situations, whereas the statement,

"Perhaps we shouldn't get so angry when things don't work out the way we think they should" is a condescending statement, thinly disguised as a collaborative statement. What is really being expressed is the expectation that both parties should handle the conflict in one way—my way.

Make Clear Statements. Statements, rather than questions, set the stage for assertive responses to conflict. When questions are used, "How" questions are more useful because they are neutral in nature, they seek more information, and they imply a collaborative effort. Questions that begin with "Why" ask for an explanation or an evaluation of behavior and often put the other person on the defensive. It is always important to state the situation clearly, describe events or expectations objectively, and use a strong, firm, yet tactful manner. The following case example shows how a nurse can use the three levels of assertive behaviors in meeting client needs in a hospital situation without compromising his or her own needs for respect and dignity.

CASE STUDY

Situation: Mr. G. is a 35-year-old company executive who has been hospitalized with a myocardial infarction. He has been acting seductively toward some of the young nurses, but he seems to be giving Miss O. an especially hard time.

Client: Come on in, honey, I've been waiting for you.

Nurse (using appropriate facial expression and eye contact, and replying in a firm, clear voice): Mr. G., I would rather you called me Miss O'Hara.

Client: Aw, come on now, honey. I don't get to have much fun around here. What's the difference what I call you?

Nurse: I feel that it does make a difference, and I would like you to call me Miss O'Hara.

Client: Oh, you're no fun at all. Why do you have to be so serious?

Nurse: Mr. G., you're right. I am serious about some things, and being called by my name and title is one of them. I would prefer that you call me Miss O'Hara. I would like to work with you, however, and it might be important to explore the ways in which this hospitalization is hampering your natural desire to have fun.

In this interaction, the nurse's position is defined several times using successively stronger statements before the shift can be made to refocus on underlying client needs. Notice that even in the final encounter, however, the nurse labels the behavior, *not* the client, as unacceptable. Persistence is an essential feature when first attempts at assertiveness appear too limited. If you find, after a careful appraisal of an interpersonal encounter, that a client's behavior is infringing on your rights as a human being, it is not only desirable but also essential that the issues be addressed directly in a tactful manner. If you don't, it is quite likely that the undesirable behavior will continue until you are no longer willing to put up with it.

Delivery Style: Use of Pitch and Tone. The amount of force employed in delivery of an assertive statement depends on the nature of the conflict situation as well as on the amount of confrontation needed to resolve the conflict successfully. Starting with the least amount of assertiveness required to meet the demands of the situation conserves energy and doesn't get the nurse into the bind of overkill. It is not necessary to use all of one's resources at one time or to express ideas strongly when this type of response isn't needed. You can sometimes lose your effectiveness by becoming long-winded in your explanation when only a simple statement of rights or intent is needed. Long explanations detract from the true impact of the spoken message. Getting to the main point quickly and saying what needs to be said in the simplest, most concrete way cuts down on the possibility of misinterpretation. This approach increases the probability that the communication will be constructively received.

Pitch and tone of voice contribute to another person's interpretation of the meaning of your assertive message. A soft, hesitant, passive presentation can undermine an assertive message as much as vocalizing the message in a harsh, hostile, and aggressive tone. A firm but moderate presentation often is as effective as content in conveying the message. (Exercise 14–6).

Own Personal Feelings. At the other end of the spectrum are behaviors that cause conflictual feelings. For example, clients may have opinions about such issues as abortion, parenting techniques, and homosexuality that differ markedly from those of the nurse. The client has the right to hold such opinions, even if the nurse cannot agree with them philosophically.

Part of an initial assessment of the nature of an

EXERCISE 14–6
Pitching the Assertive Message

Directions:
List the five vocal pitches commonly used in conversation: whisper, soft tone with hesitant delivery, moderate tone and firm delivery, loud tone with agitated delivery, screaming. Place enough individual slips of paper in a hat so that every student in class can draw one. Divide into groups of six or seven and have each student take a turn drawing and demonstrating the tone while the others in the group try to identify correctly which person is giving the assertive message. Discuss how tone affects the perception of a message's content.

Time: 5 minutes

Contributed by Saretha Boggs.

interpersonal conflict situation includes a differentiation of the nurse's intrapersonal contribution to the conflict from that of the client's. It is not wrong for nurses to have strong conflictual feelings about taking care of clients with different lifestyles and values as long as nurses acknowledge their personal views and allow clients the right to their own choices.

Use Congruent Messages. Another feature of an assertive behavioral response is that the verbal and nonverbal components of the message match. The facial expression, gestures, body posture, and voice tone that accompany the verbal message add nonverbal support to the nurse's words. Messages of importance or of anger may be misunderstood or ignored if they are delivered in a timid fashion or are accompanied by a big smile. Likewise, the choice of words should complement the intended message of the speaker.

If any behavior is incongruent with the intent of the message, it is likely that the message will be misinterpreted. Such misinterpretations may obstruct the developing relationship. For example, in the clinical situation just presented, had the nurse delivered the same message in a timid manner or seemed unsure of her position in her choice of words, it is almost predictable that Mr. G. would have continued to show disrespect to the nurse, and the underlying dynamics that created the conflict would not have been addressed.

Focus on the Present. The focus of assertive responses should always be on the *present*. Since it

is impossible to do anything about the past except to learn from it, and the future is never completely predictable, the present is the only reality in which we have much decision-making power as to how we shall act.

To be classified as assertive, the behavior must reflect deliberate *choice*. It is not always necessary to use words in order to be assertive. Sometimes it is better to listen quietly to what someone has to say, to think carefully about the message, and to plan to come back later when the person is in a more receptive frame of mind. Assertive communication is open, direct, honest, and appropriate to the interpersonal demands of the situation.

To be assertive in the face of an emotionally charged situation demands thought, energy, and commitment. Assertiveness also requires the use of common sense, self-awareness, knowledge, tact, humor, respect, and a sense of perspective. Although there is no guarantee that the use of assertive behaviors will produce desired interpersonal goals, the chances of a successful outcome are increased because the information flow is optimally honest, direct, and firm. Often the use of assertiveness brings about changes in ways that could not have been anticipated. Changes occur because the nurse offers a new resource in the form of objective feedback with no strings attached. Within a nurse–client relationship the nurse's definition of self, in relation to conflict issues, leaves room for the client to experience the conflict directly, to exercise the right of making a personal judgment based on an accurate appraisal of individual needs, and to determine the best possible action in line with those needs.

Structure Your Response. In mastering assertive responses, it may be helpful initially to use the four steps of an assertive response first presented by Angel and Petronko (1983, p. 27), who also provide the following example:

1. Express empathy: "I understand that _____"; "I hear you saying _____."
2. Describe your feelings or the situation: "I feel that _____"; "This situation seems to me to be _____."
3. State expectations: "I want _____"; "What is required by the situation is _____."
4. List consequences: "If you do this then _____ will happen" (state positive outcome); "If you don't do this, then _____ will happen" (state negative outcome).

For example, the nurse might:

1. Express empathy: "I understand that things are difficult at home."
2. Describe feelings or the situation: "But your eight-year-old daughter has expressed a lot of anxiety, saying, 'I can't learn to give my own insulin shots.'"
3. State expectations: "It is necessary for you to be here tomorrow when the diabetic teaching nurse comes so you can learn how to give injections and your daughter can too with your support."
4. List consequences: "If you get here on time, we can be finished and get her discharged in time for her birthday on Friday."

CLINICAL ENCOUNTERS WITH ANGRY OR DIFFICULT CLIENTS

Every nurse encounters clients who refuse to comply with the treatment plan, who exhibit hostile behaviors toward the staff, perhaps eventually withdrawing from any positive interaction with the nurse. As Maynard (1994) notes, there are numerous nonverbal clues to anger, including clenched jaws or fists, turning away, "forgetting" or being late for appointments, and refusing to maintain eye contact. Verbal cues by a client may, of course, include use of an angry tone of voice, but they may also be disguised as witty sarcasm and condescending or insulting remarks. In order to become comfortable in dealing with client anger, the nurse must first become aware of his or

---

BOX 14–4
Potential Approaches for Dealing with Anxious or Difficult Clients

1. Education—explain all options, with outcomes.
2. Develop a nursing care plan: involve patient in care and set goals; review and re-evaluate whether nurse and client have same goals; focus on mutual goals and progress.
3. Use incentives and withdrawal of privileges to modify unacceptable behavior.
4. Use medical and nonmedical interventions to decrease anxiety (medicine, touch, relaxation—guided imagery).
5. Set limits, give family permission to rest, to leave, and so on.
6. Promote trust by providing immediate feedback.

---

her own reactions to anger so that the nurse does not threaten or reject the individual expressing anger (Box 14–4). Successful interventions include the following:

1. Identify anger by helping the client to recognize his or her own anger by pointing out cues and attempting to validate them with the client. *Example:* "I notice you are clenching your fists and talking more loudly than usual. These are some things people do when they are feeling angry. Are you feeling angry now?" (Maynard, 1994, developed from Maynard and Chitty, 1971).
2. Give permission for anger (*Example:* "Everyone gets angry at this" and, "It's natural to be angry in these circumstances.")
3. Help the client own the angry feelings by getting the client to verbalize things that make him or her angry. Perhaps suggest a hypothetical situation.
4. Realistically analyze the current situation that is disturbing the client.
5. Assist the client in developing a plan to deal with the situation. (*Example:* The nurse could use techniques such as role playing to help the client express anger appropriately—for example, using "I" statements such as "I feel angry" rather than "You make me angry.") Bringing behavior up to a verbal level should help alleviate the need for other acting out/destructive behaviors.

An additional strategy available for helping nurses cope with difficult nurse–client interaction situa-

EXERCISE 14–7
Staff Focused Consultation

Directions: Read the case study about Mr. P. and identify four strategies based on this staff-focused consultation.

Time: 3 minutes.

1. _____
2. _____
3. _____
4. _____

Analysis of Effective Staff-Level Interventions
In this case study, once the manager became aware of the difficulty the staff was having coping with Mr. P. strategies to help staff included the following:

- Arranging a *group meeting* of caregivers who were responsible for the client.
- Using a *consultant.*
- *Ventilating feelings*—with a focus on their own reactions and feelings, not on complaints about the client's behavior.
- *Elevating awareness* of their own *feelings* of anger and other emotions, showing that these are common reactions exhibited by several nurses in the group.
- Developing increased awareness among staff of the *cause* of the client's unacceptable behavior.
- Developing a plan for handling the client's unacceptable behavior—perhaps behavior-modification strategies.
- Obtaining consensus (for all shifts to use).
- Committing the plan to writing.

tions is the staff-focused consultation, illustrated in the following situation.

CASE STUDY

Mr. P., aged 29, has been employed for six years as a construction worker. Four weeks ago, while operating a forklift, he was struck by a train, leaving him a paraplegic. After two weeks in intensive care, he was transferred to a neurological unit. When staff members attempt to provide physical care, such as changing his position or getting him up in a chair, Mr. P. throws things, curses angrily, and sometimes spits at the nurses. Staff members become very upset; several nurses have requested assignment changes. Some staff members try bribing him with food to encourage good behavior; others threaten to apply restraints. The manager schedules a behavioral consultation meeting with a psychiatric nurse/clinical specialist. The immediate goal of this staff conference is to bring staff feelings out into the open, to facilitate increased awareness of the staff's behavioral responses when confronted with this client's behavior.

The outcome goal is to use a problem-solving approach to develop a behavioral care plan, so that all staff members respond to Mr. P. in a consistent manner.

Students are particularly prone to feel rebuffed when they first encounter negative feedback from a client. Support from staff, instructor, and peers, coupled with efforts to understand the underlying reasons and the client's feelings, help the student resist the trap of avoiding the relationship (Lerner and Byrne, 1991). To develop these ideas further, do Exercise 14–7.

SUMMARY

Conflict represents a hostile encounter or a mental struggle between two opposing thoughts, feelings, or needs. It can be intrapersonal in nature—deriving from within a particular individual—or interpersonal, when it represents a clash between two or more people.

All conflicts have certain things in common; a concrete content issue and a process of expression. Expressions of passionate feelings about the issue may occur. Generally, intrapersonal conflicts stimulate feelings of emotional discomfort. A neutral, supportive interpersonal environment helps reduce emotions to a workable level. Other strategies to defuse strong emotion include talking the emotion through with someone and temporarily reducing stress through the use of distraction or additional information.

Most interpersonal conflicts involve some threat to one's sense of power to control an interpersonal situation or to ways of thinking about the self. Giving up ineffective behavior patterns in conflict situations is difficult because such patterns are generally perceived as safer since they are familiar.

Conflictual feelings usually have to be put into words and related to the issue at hand before the meaning of the conflict becomes understandable. When the source of conflict is interpersonal in nature, before making a response the nurse needs to think through the possible causes of the conflict as well as his or her own feelings about it.

Usually behavioral responses to conflict situations fall into one of three categories: Aggressive or passive behaviors usually are defensive in nature, whereas assertive behaviors are used to define rather than defend the self. Assertive behaviors range from making a simple statement, directly and honestly, about one's beliefs to taking a very strong, confrontational stand about what will and will not be tolerated.

REFERENCES

Angel G, Petronko DK (1983, 1987). Developing the New Assertive Nurse: Essentials for Advancement. New York, Springer.

Booth R (1985). Conflict and conflict management. *In* Mason DJ, Talbot SW (eds.) (1985), Political Action Handbook for Nurses. Menlo Park, CA, Addison-Wesley.

Davidhizar R (1991). Impressing the boss who criticizes you. Advances in Clinical Care Nursing 6(2):39–41.

de Torynay R (1990). Helping students deal with controversy. Journal of Nursing Education 29(4):149.

Evans S (1991). Conflict resolution: A strategy for growth. Heart and Lung: Journal of Critical Care 20(2):20A, 22A, 24A.

Ferrucci P (1982). What We May Be. Los Angeles, Jeremy P. Tarcher.

Flanagan L (1990). Survival Skills in the Workplace: What Every Nurse Should Know. Kansas City, MO, ANA.

Harmon S (1991). Giving constructive criticism with aplomb. Medical Laboratory Observer (March), pp. 24–27.

Jones MA, Bushardt SC, Cadenhead G (1990). A paradigm for effective resolution of interpersonal conflict. Nursing Management 21(2):64B, 64F–64K.

Kennedy CW, Camden C, Timmerman (1990). Relationships among perceived supervisor communication, nurse morale and sociocultural variables. Nursing Admnistration Quarterly 14(4):38–46.

Lerner H, Byrne MW (1991). Helping nursing students communicate with high-risk families. Nursing and Health Care 12(2):98–101.

Maynard C (1994). Private communication. Based on content published in Maynard C, Chitty L (1971), Dealing with anger: Guidelines for nursing intervention. Journal of Psychiatric Nursing and Mental Health Services 17(36), June.

McCanton PJ, Hargie O (1990). Assessing assertive behavior in student nurses: A comparison of assertive measures. Journal of Advanced Nursing 15(12):1370–1376.

McKay RAC, Hughes J, Carver EJ (1990). Empathy in the Helping Relationship. New York, Springer.

Moustakis C (1974). Finding Yourself, Finding Others. Englewood Cliffs, NJ, Prentice-Hall.

Pederson C, Duckett L, Maruyama G (1990). Using structured controversy to promote ethical decision making. Journal of Nursing Education 20(4):150–157.

Schutzenhofer KK (1992). Nursing education and professional autonomy. Reflections, Winter, p. 7.

Smythe E (1990). Surviving Nursing. Menlo Park, CA, Addison-Wesley.

SUGGESTED READINGS

Alberti R, Emmons M (1990). A Guide to Assertive Living. San Luis Obispo, CA, Impact Press.

Bach G, Goldberg H (1989). Creative Aggression. New York, Doubleday.

Bloom L, Coburn K, Pearlman J (1980). The New Assertive Woman. New York, Delacorte Press.

Bower S, Bower G (1991). Asserting Yourself: A Practical Guide for Positive Change. Reading, MA, Addison-Wesley.

Chenevert M (1988). Special Techniques in Assertiveness Training for Women in the Health Professions. St. Louis, Mosby.

Fisher R, Ury W (1991). Getting to Yes: Negotiating Agreement without Giving In. Boston, Houghton-Mifflin.

Hamilton J, Kiefer M (1986). Survival Skills for the New Nurse. Philadelphia, Lippincott.

Harragan B (1989). Corporate Gamesmanship. New York, Warner Books.

Kramer M (1974). Reality Shock: Why Nurses Leave Nursing. St. Louis, Mosby.

Lange A, Jakubowski P (1976). Responsible Assertive Behavior. Champaign, IL, Research Press.

McKay M, Davis M, Fanning P (1983). Messages: The Communication Book. Oakland, CA, New Harbinger Publications.

Raudsepp E (1991). Six ways to becoming more assertive. Nursing 91 21(3):112–116.

Remer R, DeMesquita P (1990). Teaching and learning the skills of interpersonal confrontation. *In* Cahn DD (ed.) (1990), Intimates in Conflict: A Communication Perspective. Hillsdale, NJ, Erlbaum.

Wolfe D, et al. (1985). Interpersonal conflict: Strategies and guidelines for resolution. Journal of the American Rec Association 56(2):18–22.

Chapter 15

Health Promotion and Client Learning Needs

ELIZABETH ARNOLD

OBJECTIVES

At the end of the chapter, the student will be able to:

1. Define health promotion.
2. Contrast motivational frameworks in health promotion.
3. Describe the three domains of learning.

4. Identify factors related to a client's readiness to learn.

5. Describe factors related to a client's ability to learn.

6. Discuss the role of self-awareness in health promotion.

You cannot teach a man anything, you can only help him discover it within himself

Galileo

Chapters 15 and 16 focus on health teaching as a special form of communication in the nurse–client relationship. This chapter introduces students to concepts of health promotion and client assessment as the basis for health teaching. Included in the chapter are theoretical models related to how people think about their health and what motivates them to engage with health service providers to promote, maintain, and restore their health and well-being. Factors related to the client's readiness and ability to learn help the nurse understand the teaching-learning process from the client's perspective. In Chapter 16, the emphasis changes to the nurse's role in implementing health teaching in professional relationships with clients and their families. Understanding the role of creative tension and the interplay in nurse–client perspectives is key to successful health teaching in the nurse–client relationship.

Health promotion requires a concentrated form of communication in the nurse–client relationship, building on therapeutic communication strategies presented in other chapters. Implementation of health–promotion strategies is content specific. By contrast with more free-flowing therapeutic conversations, the nurse includes special information the client needs to know as the primary focus of a teaching conversation. Relationship goals and objectives specifically relate to learning a new skill, developing knowledge, or changing attitudes. Learning outcomes require a specific change in behavior as a result of defined training, practice, and experiences.

BASIC CONCEPTS

DEFINITION

Healthy People 2000 notes, "Responding effectively to the health challenges of the 1990's will require a clear understanding of the health-related threats and opportunities facing all Americans" (DHHS, 1991, p. 9). The current direction of health care in the United States has a health-maintenance rather than a disease-oriented focus. Health maintenance emphasizes health-promotion activities and actions to restore the health of individuals.

Health-promotion strategies are aimed at helping people modify their lifestyles and make personal choices to improve their health prospects and quality of life. Box 15–1 lists areas identified by the U.S. Department of Health and Human Services as the priority areas for healthy people. As health care becomes more community based, the professional nurse is the natural one to play a key role in implementing health teaching related to these issues.

Health is identified as one of the four core elements of professional nursing. There are many definitions of health, ranging on a continuum from absence of physiological and psychosocial symptoms to the concept of wellness. The concept

---

BOX 15–1
Healthy People 2000: **Priority Areas**

Health Promotion

1. Physical activity and fitness
2. Nutrition
3. Tobacco
4. Alcohol and other drugs
5. Family planning
6. Mental health and mental disorders
7. Violent and abusive behavior
8. Educational and community-based programs

Health Protection

9. Unintentional injuries
10. Occupational safety and health
11. Environmental health
12. Food and drug safety
13. Oral health

Preventive Services

14. Maternal and infant health
15. Heart disease and stroke
16. Cancer
17. Diabetes and chronic disabling conditions
18. HIV infection
19. Sexually transmitted diseases
20. Immunization and infectious diseases

Strategies to Meeet Objectives

21. Professional and access issues in clinical preventive services
22. Development of surveillance and data systems to track progress

of wellness consists of attitudes supporting a lifestyle of balance and well-being in six personal dimensions: intellectual, physical, emotional, social, occupational, and spiritual (Chandler, Holden, and Kolander, 1992; Omizo, Omizo, and d'Andrea, 1992). Well-being is a subjective experience, always defined by the client, with its meaning validated by the nurse. To achieve the overall goal of optimal well-being needed for a health-promotion lifestyle, the nurse uses teaching formats related to maintenance of health, prevention of illness, restoration of health, coping with impaired functioning, and rehabilitation.

Health is measured by a variety of standards. The *medical or clinical model* considers health to be the absence of signs and symptoms of disease or injury. The *role performance model* evaluates functioning and work performance behaviors as the benchmark of health. *Adaptive models* of health consider the self-care coping strategies a client uses to adapt to physical and emotional changes as the measure of health. A fourth standard by which health is measured is called the *eudaemonistic model* (Smith, 1987). This model incorporates characteristics from the other three models and includes movement toward self-fulfillment. Maslow's hierarchy of needs model, beginning with biological integrity and moving toward self-actualization, is a good example of the eudaemonistic model of health (Rawnsley, 1992). Conceptual models of health have a direct effect on health teaching activities. The more comprehensive the health model, the more is required of the health teaching process.

Walker, Sechrist, and Perder (1987) describe a health-promotion lifestyle as "a multi-dimensional pattern of self-initiated actions and perceptions that serve to maintain or enhance the level of wellness, self-actualization and fulfillment of the individual" (p. 77). The goal of health teaching is more than simply preventing or minimizing the effects of illness or injury. Rather, it is self-directed well-being for the client. Self-direction is synonymous with client autonomy in selecting health care options that fit the person as well as the situation. Jones and Meleis (1993) characterize health as empowerment, a contextualized definition of health in which the nurse helps clients use a critical thinking process to resolve their health problems and acts as an advocate in facilitating access to those resources most likely to support their health and well-being.

MOTIVATIONAL FRAMEWORKS

Motivational frameworks, such as the health-belief and health-promotion models, inform the nurse about factors within an individual client or family that can affect the teaching-learning process.

Health-Belief Model

The health-belief model, originally developed by Lewin and his associates, focuses on three elements: (1) perceived susceptibility to a health threat or the medical and social ramifications of the health threat; (2) meaningful health concern about the seriousness of the health threat; and (3) the belief that certain actions would be able to reduce the perceived health threat at a reasonable cost (Fleury, 1992). Each of these elements can motivate or discline learner participation in the learning process.

The likelihood of action depends on whether the perceived benefits of taking health care action outweigh perceived barriers to obtaining preventive care. Barriers can include ease of access, cost, extent of life change required, and fear of pain or discomfort. Intuitively, it makes sense to presume that if a person thinks something will harm him, that person is more willing to participate in learning how to take steps to avoid the harm. This is not always the case. If the person foresees no immediate danger, he or she does not always perceive the reality that the danger can happen to him. For example, a person may have an acute awareness that walking will help diminish the effects of osteoporosis. But it is easier to maintain a sedentary life, and the threat of a chronic disease in later life is not enough to stimulate preventive care.

Despite limitations, the health-belief model informs the nurse about the context of the client's cultural and environmental background, as well as the client's self-concept and internal value system factors that influence readiness to learn and the types of teaching strategies. An example of the health-belief model applied to breast cancer prevention is presented in Figure 15–1. Exercise 15–1 provides practice with applying the health-belief model to common health problems.

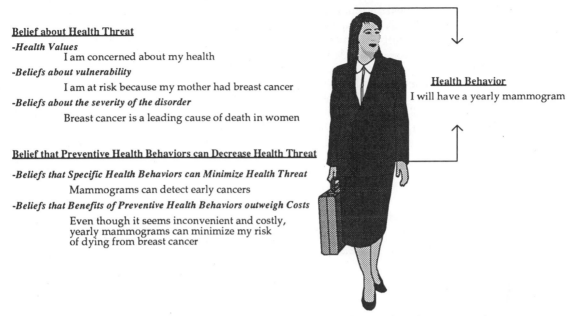

Belief about Health Threat

-Health Values

        I am concerned about my health

-Beliefs about vulnerability

        I am at risk because my mother had breast cancer

-Beliefs about the severity of the disorder

        Breast cancer is a leading cause of death in women

Health Behavior

I will have a yearly mammogram

Belief that Preventive Health Behaviors can Decrease Health Threat

-Beliefs that Specific Health Behaviors can Minimize Health Threat

        Mammograms can detect early cancers

-Beliefs that Benefits of Preventive Health Behaviors outweigh Costs

        Even though it seems inconvenient and costly, yearly mammograms can minimize my risk of dying from breast cancer

Figure 15–1 Example of Health-Belief Model Applied to the Health Behavior of Yearly Mammograms

Health-Promotion Model

Pender's (1987) health-promotion model is a more complex descriptive model, intended to complement rather than displace other health models by emphasizing movement toward a positive valuing of health and well-being. This model is basically a self-actualizing model designed to help clients acknowledge and take responsibility for achieving the highest level of well-being possi-

---

EXERCISE 15–1
The Health-Belief Model and Common Health Problems

Purpose: To help students gain experience with use of the health-belief model.

Time: May be done as a homework assignment.

Procedure:
1. Using the health care model as a guide, interview a person with a health care problem.
2. Record the person's answers and develop a diagram of the health care model using the person's answers.
3. Comment on the individual perceptions, modifying factors, and cues to action you found in the client data to determine the likelihood of taking recommended preventive health actions.

Discussion:
1. Were you surprised at the client's knowledge about the target health problem or interpretation of the meaning of it?
2. As you compare your client's answers with those of your classmates, do any common themes emerge?
3. How could you use the information you gained from your client and from doing this exercise in future practice?

ble. Modifying variables are linked with cognitive perceptual factors, which are recognized as "the primary motivational mechanisms for acquisition and maintenance of health-promoting behaviors" (p. 60). A person's definition of health, perceptions of health status, benefits, and barriers to health-promoting behaviors strengthen or weaken interest in engaging in health-promoting behaviors. Examples of modifying factors are schools that require immunizations, family experiences with a disorder or preventive measures, and interpersonal reminders, such as a family member's experience with the health care system, the mass

media, and ethnic approval. These factors act as "cues to action" in seeking health care. Figure 15–2 presents Pender's health-promotion model.

DOMAINS OF LEARNING

Learning takes place in three distinct yet often highly interrelated areas: cognitive, affective and psychomotor learning (Fig. 15–3). *Cognitive learning* refers to knowledge obtained from information a person did not have before. Knowledge is obtained from watching others, reading, and listening to experts. Cognitive knowledge also is part

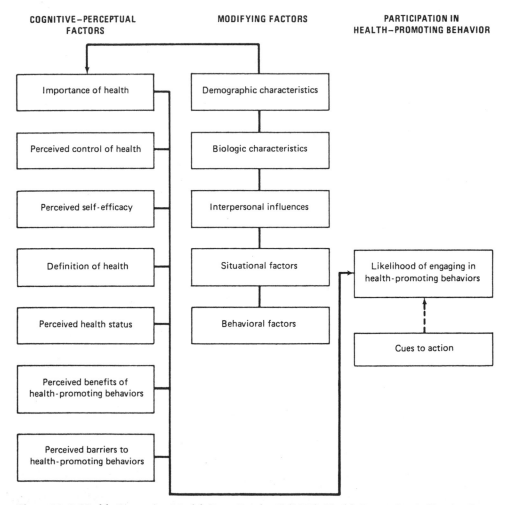

Figure 15–2 Health-Promotion Model. From Pender N (1987). Health Promotion in Nursing Practice. Norwalk, CT, Appleton Lange, p. 58.

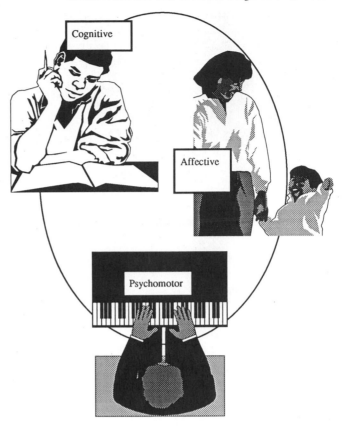

Figure 15–3 Domains of Learning

of developing a skill or changing an attitude. When people practice a skill, they also develop "knowledge" about the factors that contribute to success and the actions that need to be avoided. Attitude changes always include cognitive information the person lacked previously about a situation or person.

Affective learning refers to changes in attitude that inform and direct behaviors. Changing attitudes takes time and involves experiential learning. Affective learning is a more direct, personalized form of knowing. Through experiences of and different exposure to knowledge, people change their beliefs and perceptual views of the world. For example, Mara has a stereotyped view of Hispanic people. Her mother distrusts Hispanic people and has told her that Hispanic people are low class and lack initiative. Without having had exposure to Hispanic people, Mara's ideas reflect her mother's teaching and bear very little resemblance to reality. Her college roommate is His-

panic. As the roommates exchange experiences, they develop a shared history, quite different from Mara's experience. Mara finds that her roommate is not so different from herself. Her roommate comes from a socioeconomic background similar to her own and is one of the best students in the class. Mara's knowledge and attitude toward Hispanic people change dramatically. She has learned affectively a different set of data that contradict her previous learning and that create for her a different set of attitudes and beliefs.

Psychomotor learning refers to learning a skill. Learning psychomotor skills involves taking knowledge and applying it with "hands on." Skills are mastered through practice and feedback. Performing the skill over and over again allows the learner to become proficient as the skill becomes a natural part of the person's life. A person can learn only so much from reading about an activity or watching others. "Doing it," receiving feedback, and practicing is the only process by which one can master a

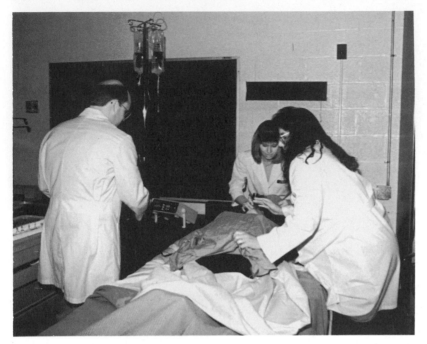

Figure 15–4 "Doing it," receiving feedback, and practicing again is the only process by which one can master a psychomotor skill.

psychomotor skill (Fig. 15–4). Making mistakes in learning a new skill may be just as instructive as doing the activity correctly the first time.

PREVENTIVE HEALTH EDUCATION

In the document *Healthy People 2000,* prevention is defined broadly as "a culture, or a way of thinking and being, that actively promotes responsible behavior and the adoption of lifestyles that are maximally conducive to good health" (DHHS, 1991, p. v). Preventive health education is designed to teach people how to promote and maintain their highest level of wellness through increased self-understanding and improved self-care.

Health teaching plays an important role in all three aspects of health promotion, labeled as primary, secondary, and tertiary prevention. *Primary prevention* is concerned with wellness behaviors of people who are basically healthy and interested in developing lifestyle health behaviors to remain healthy. It is defined as activities taken to preclude illness or to prevent the natural course of illness from occurring. The nurse teaches clients how to avoid health-related problems in their particular age, cultural, or social group. Examples include prenatal clinics, parenting courses, stress manage-

ment programs, teaching about the normal process of aging, and education about AIDS or ways to avoid drug involvement. Guidance about seat belt safety, disaster preparedness, and accident prevention are instances of primary prevention that may save many lives. Primary prevention related to the spiritual dimension centers on stressing the importance of love, relating, and forgiveness in significant relationships.

Secondary prevention involves actions to promote early diagnosis of symptoms, and treatment after the onset of the disease. The purpose of secondary preventive teaching programs is to catch health problems early and to minimize their effects on a person's lifestyle. The nurse teaches clients preventive actions to reduce the risk of social and physical problems associated with age, culture, and physical or emotional illness. Examples include mammograms, parent education, and glaucoma, diabetes, respiratory, and blood pressure screenings. Strategies to reduce the effects of burnout and to find new meaning in suffering are useful actions associated with the spiritual dimension. Important secondary teaching programs aim at helping clients and their families cope with the effects on lifestyle of cancer, diabetes, and other chronic diseases. The impact of health problems on sexuality, smoking, family relationships, and role changes are all content teaching areas found in secondary preventive teaching programs. With secondary prevention strategies, the nurse helps clients develop the appropriate attitudes and beliefs for engaging in early detection and seeking treatment of disease. Identifying high-risk populations and providing the necessary educative/supportive interventions provide cues for action in seeking appropriate health care.

Tertiary prevention describes rehabilitation strategies designed to minimize the handicapping effects of a disease. The goals of tertiary prevention are the same as those of other preventive teaching programs: to help clients achieve the highest level of wellness possible. Tertiary prevention has a similar design, but the seriousness of the client's condition distinguishes it from secondary preventive teaching programs. In tertiary prevention, client education can play as critical a role as medication or surgery in the treatment process. Examples of tertiary preventive education include teaching a cancer victim about chemotherapy, helping a stroke victim with bladder retraining to avoid infection, and teaching a client to cope effectively with the necessary adjustments a serious physical, social, or emotional illness imposes. Increasingly, clients must become knowledgeable about medication dosage and side effects, therapeutic protocols, signs and symptoms of illness, diet, and self-monitoring strategies. In a time of diminishing resources, with DRGs, earlier discharges, and decreasing health care resources available in the community, skilled health teaching is particularly important. Compliance with the prescribed treatment regimen depends heavily on health teaching strategies to motivate and direct client efforts. Individual and group formats provide the client with needed information and emotional support to implement necessary treatment.

LEARNING AND RELATIONSHIPS

The best teaching takes place in relationships. Understanding is a mutual process occurring between people, just as it is with other forms of communication. When most people think of their own learning, they typically find that their most satisfying learning experiences took place in a learning environment in which they felt accepted and valued. Their remembering of content almost always contains recall of interactions with a teacher or mentor who believed in them, supported their self-integrity, and enhanced their self-worth. Conversely, memories of negative learning experiences often include having felt disconfirmed as a person. Exercise 15–2 emphasizes the important role of relationships in health teaching.

EXERCISE 15–2
Significant Learning Experiences

Purpose: To identify elements that make for successful learning experiences.

Time: 45 minutes

Procedure:
Write a short paragraph about a significant learning situation in which you:
1. Identify the most significant learning situation you have experienced. Use the situation that comes to mind first.
2. Describe the learning outcomes you achieved, e.g., developed a skill, gained an insight, changed behavior, learned some new information, learned something about yourself.
3. Describe the activities and circumstances that contributed to making this learning situation so significant.

Discussion:
Use a chalkboard or flip chart to record student themes and activities in the significant learning situation.
1. Were you surprised at the situation that you chose for this exercise? in what ways?
2. In what ways were the activities and circumstances contributing to making this learning situation memorable similar or different from those of others in your group?
3. What previously held assumptions/values were challenged or reaffirmed by this learning situation?
4. What did you learn from doing this exercise that you could use in your nursing practice?

Clients speak of the health teaching they received as one of the most important elements in their care. Manning (1992), in characterizing the nurses she "will never forget" during her hospitalization, describes its meaning to her: "There was Nadine who was an excellent pre-operative teacher. She was the first person who clearly explained what a bladder augmentation entailed. She described different tubes I'd have and the purpose of each. When I returned from surgery, she helped me cope with my body image by teaching me how to use my bladder and by being a compassionate listener" (p. 47).

APPLICATIONS

Perhaps the most relevant part of Carl Rogers' (1969) client-centered teaching is his insistence that the teacher must start where the learner is and structure the learning process to support the learner's natural desire to learn. Learners differ in their abilities, intellectual curiosity, motivation for learning, learning styles, and rate of learning. Learner variables important in the teaching-learning process generally fall into two categories: *readiness to learn* and *ability to learn.* These factors may exist in combination or as isolated characteristics. Whereas the nurse can readily help people who want to learn, there are limitations to what can be achieved in a learning situation when the learner is unwilling or unable to learn. Finding ways to engage clients in the learning process is the first step in planning effective teaching interventions.

READINESS TO LEARN

Part of the teaching-learning process includes an accurate assessment of the client's readiness to learn and nursing strategies to enhance the possibility of readiness. Benjamin Hoff (1987) tells the story of a stranger who asked him for directions to a certain street. In response, he pointed to the street and gave the stranger very explicit instructions on how to get there. Shortly thereafter, he noticed the stranger going in the opposite direction. When he told him he was going in the wrong direction, the stranger told him: "Yes, I know, I'm not quite ready yet."

So it is with clients. Teaching cannot begin

BOX 15–2
Factors That Influence Learning Readiness

Physical	Pain, fatigue, diasability, sensory deprivation
Psychological	Motivation, attitude, belief about health and illness, emotional response to illness
Intellectual	Literacy, ability to comprehend
Socioeconomic/ cultural	Ethnicity, religious beliefs, health values, family roles and relationships, support structures, financial concerns, home environment

From Ruzicki D (1989). Realistically meeting the educational needs of hospitalized acute and short-stay patients. Nursing Clinics of North America. 24(3):631. Reprinted with the permission of W. B. Saunders Company, Philadelphia.

---

until the client is teachable (Antai-Otong, 1989). The teachable moment takes place when the learner feels that there is a need to know the information and has the capacity to learn it. Clients have to become aware of a problem in need of change and demonstrate commitment to changing it (Prochaska, Diclemente, and Norcross, 1992). Factors affecting learning readiness are identified in Box 15–2.

Motivation

Motivation is a basic part of learner readiness. Without it the learner and teacher have an almost insurmountable task. It is like trying to start a car with no gas. The driver can push the car, but it won't move on its own. Without client motivation, the nurse can "push," but the learner, like the car, will make very little movement. Before implementing teaching strategies related to content, the nurse must help the client see a need to learn the required information. Bandura (1987) identifies three sets of motivating factors: physical motivators, social incentives, and cognitive motivators.

Physical motivators are those internal and external circumstances stimulating a person to learn as a way of avoiding physical discomfort. Anticipation of a possible discomfort can be just as strong a motivator as remembering a past physical discomfort. For example, Elizabeth O'Brien's parents both died of heart disease. Elizabeth, at age 52, is at risk for developing heart disease herself. In addition to her genetic loading for heart disease, she is overweight, and blood studies reveal high cholesterol. Elizabeth has started to watch her diet and has decided to have regular checkups to forestall heart disease. On the other hand, a client's failure to comprehend the connection between lifestyle and physical symptoms may result in the client's inability to hear instructions or to comply with treatment protocols despite adequate teaching. A client may agree wholeheartedly with a nurse that smoking is bad and is likely to cause a second heart attack but continue to smoke. In his mind, it is impossible for him even to contemplate giving up smoking. His mind set precludes learning until he can see the connection between giving up cigarettes and avoiding painful symptoms. The nurse can use physical motivators to help clients recognize natural limitations in their current situations and how changes in their lifestyle coupled with knowledge about their conditions can make their problems more manageable.

The second set of motivators identified by Bandura (1987) are *social incentives.* Approval and disapproval of others who potentially have the power to reward or punish have significant motivating power for many people. The greater the possible consequences on a person's life of taking one path versus another, the stronger the power of the social incentive.

Social incentives as motivators can work in the following way. Praise and encouragement increase self-esteem and give the client reason to continue learning. But social incentives also can decrease motivation. Although an individual client may learn required behaviors, a spouse or parent may encourage the client to resume a former role and discount the need for appropriate medications and diet. The client is caught in the conflict of trying to follow what has been learned and of pleasing the significant other at the same time. The other extreme, the significant other who becomes so protective and responsible for the client's behavior that the client "forgets" what has been learned, also occurs. Consideration needs to be given to the personality traits of the individual and family relationships and their attitudes and values, as well as to the actual information needed.

Bandura (1987) refers to the third set of motivators as *cognitive motivators.* These are internal thought processes by which people cognitively develop goals and employ their minds to reach those goals. Cognitive motivators can function as positive reinforcers to achieve goals or act as barriers to make needed changes.

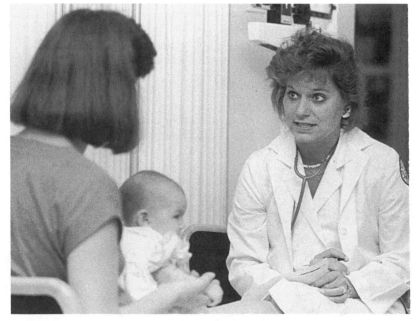

Assessing the client's readiness to learn is the first step in effective health-promotion activities. (Courtesy of the University of North Carolina at Charlotte College of Nursing)

Most changes create a cognitive dissonance between what was and what is. In health care, the change usually is not in a positive direction. Wanting something to happen will not make it happen. Changes in health status frequently dictate permanent changes in the client's lifestyle and self-perceptions. Clients with newly diagnosed chronic conditions have to change their attitudes and develop a new set of behaviors as they explore a variety of new information and beliefs. This is a difficult process for many clients, who secretly entertain the fantasy that they will be able to resume their former lives and that their bodies and functions will be the same. A variation of the role of cognitive motivators is found in clients who may want to learn but who have serious doubts about their ability or that of significant caregivers to implement the treatment protocol fully. Care-givers may have similar reservations about their competence to carry out treatments in the home without ongoing support (Exercise 15–3).

Nursing Interventions with Unmotivated Clients

Health teaching offers an unique opportunity to expand the self-concept, but it is not always viewed that way. Old patterns are hard to break. The fear of destroying old familiar patterns may be particularly strong when the new patterns designed to take its place are unknown or uncertain. Solving a problem and learning new information often require a person to uncover parts of self the individual has previously avoided or wishes to continue to avoid. For example, the alcoholic doesn't want to give up the drinking buddies or symptom

---

EXERCISE 15–3
Facilitating Readiness

1. Patrick drinks four to six beers every evening. Last year he lost his job. He has a troubled marriage and few friends. Patrick does not consider himself an alcoholic and blames his chaotic marriage for his need to drink. There is a strong family history of alcoholism.

    What kinds of information might help Patrick want to learn more about his condition? _____

    _____

2. Lily has just learned she has breast cancer. Although there is a good chance that surgery and chemotherapy will help her, she is scared to commit to the process and has even talked about taking her life.

    What kinds of health teaching strategies and information might help Lily become ready to learn

    about her condition? _____

    _____

3. Shawn has just been diagnosed as having epilepsy. He is ashamed to tell his friends and teachers about his condition. Shawn is considering breaking up with his girlfriend because of his newly diagnosed illness.

    How would you use health teaching to help Shawn cope more effectively with his illness? _____

    _____

4. Marilyn, a 14-year-old, has been admitted to the hospital with a bleeding ulcer. She has never been seriously ill before. Marilyn has never been in the hospital before, even to visit a friend. She is scared and refuses to cooperate with her nurses.

    What kinds of information and support might help Marilyn cope more effectively with her current cir-

    cumstances? _____

    _____

relief experienced with drinking. An independent person may not want to accept temporary or permanent reliance on others. The nurse has an ethical obligation to provide enough information for the client to make a reasonable decision. Usually this is in the form of a teaching conversation about the consequences of different treatment options. Framing comments in ways that respect the client's concerns is critical for acceptance.

Sample Statement:

NURSE: I know that you really think you can manage yourself at home. But most people really need some rehabilitation after this stroke to help them regain their strength. If you go home now without the rehabilitation, you may be shortchanging yourself by not taking the time to develop the skills you need to be independent at home.

This strategy does not directly challenge the client's conviction that she is capable of independent living or force the client to accept the nurse's conclusions. The nurse's comments start where the client is and give the client relevant information about the consequences of treatment versus non-treatment, including the nurse's professional judgment about the best way to proceed. If the client is a rational agent and capable of decision making, the decision about treatment remains with the client (Gauthier, 1993).

It is not always easy to detect cognitive resistance to learning new behaviors. The client may be seeking support and reassurance without any real intent to change important lifestyle behaviors. Other clients see no purpose in living with a major disability and resent the nurse who tries to involve them in coping more successfully with it. It is difficult to appreciate the need for learning new behaviors if the client can't see any reason for achieving the outcome. Sometimes the nurse can reframe objective information in a more personalized way.

Sample Statement:

NURSE: I'm a little worried that you are continuing to smoke because it does affect your breathing. There is nothing you can do about the damage to your lungs that is already there, but if you stop smoking it can help preserve the healthy tissue you still have, and you won't have as much trouble breathing. I bet your grandson would appreciate it if you could breathe better and be able to play with him.

The nurse can help clients clarify what cannot be changed and what is possible to change through one's own efforts. This can be coupled strategically with helping the client find a "purpose" in changing his behavior such as breathing better or being able to play with his grandson. Once the client becomes an active agent in his own learning process, content teaching can begin.

When the nurse perceives an unwillingness on the part of the learner to participate, there is a tendency to want to pressure the learner out of the resistance. When this occurs, the nurse needs to look carefully at what is happening between client and nurse, including the strategies the nurse is using. The nurse needs to stop and explore with the client, using nonevaluative language, the possible barriers to the learning process.

Sample Statement:

NURSE: I notice that we don't seem to be making much headway in applying what you are learning about dietary changes required by your high cholesterol. I wonder if there are some issues that we have not addressed that may be getting in the way.

Having the client's response as the basis for discussion, the nurse can work with the client to consider what needs to be different and can help the client put boundaries on the concerns in more realistic terms. The simple process of talking through concerns with the nurse and then with significant others unmasks fears and negative energy that can get in the way of effective learning.

Psychological Barriers to Learning

Clients can teach nurses a lot about learning and health teaching. With all new learning, there are high points and soft spots. Soft spots are thought of as resistance or as noncompliance. They may be simply areas in need of further exploration and restructuring of teaching strategies. For each client, the emotional barrier may be a little different. Typically, health teaching is done with clients who are trying to adjust to recent and problematic life events, often accompanied by personal rejection, compromised body function, loss of a job, or the end of an intimate relationship. They must make major life decisions at the worst possible time and under the worst possible conditions. The emotional fallout from these situations has a significant bearing on the learning process. Nurses need to remember that learning is never smooth or linear in its development. Rather than challenge the client's learning pattern, the nurse needs to understand it and incorporate it into new opportunities for learning. This is the art of health teaching.

Previous Knowledge and Experience

Closely linked to culture, and often intertwined with it, are previous knowledge and experiences of the client that make the client less able to engage in a traditional learning process. Each learning situation has a past as well as a present reality. Past experience, perceptual associations, and talking with others about symptoms prior to official health teaching have provided the client with a set of assumptions and knowledge that must be factored into the teaching process. Previous knowledge, while often an asset, can present barriers and confusion for the client in learning new information.

The client's understanding, attitudes, and previous experiences related to the topic or issues requiring teaching interventions can be erroneous and even life threatening. For example, in a study of low-income, inner-city pregnant women, most of whom had had no prenatal care, the women were receiving ongoing teaching from friends and relatives. Some of the information was valid, but other information (such as the belief that a pregnant woman should not have intercourse or take a bath because she will drown the baby) was wrong. Inducing labor if the baby is overdue by taking large doses of laxatives or jumping off stairs are potentially unsafe health practices (St. Claire and Anderson, 1989). The nurse needs to know not only what information the client has received but also whom the client looks to and respects for health teaching purposes. Focusing on accurate information without destroying the credibility of well-meaning and influential informal health teachers in the client's life is part of the art of health teaching. It is important, even if the information given through informal networks is wrong, to avoid injuring the reputation of the person who gave the client the information. Nothing is served by questioning the integrity or knowledge of a culturally identified helper in the client's environment. Instead, the nurse might say,

Sample Statement

NURSE: There have been some new findings that I think you might be interested in. The most current thinking suggests that _____ works well in situations like this.

In this way, the nurse can introduce a different way of thinking without challenging the person identified in the client's mind as expert.

Assessment and inclusion of previous learning continue throughout the teaching process. This allows the nurse to make the teaching meaningful to the client and relevant to changes in the client's condition. As the client's condition worsens or becomes stable, the teaching content and strategies necessarily change. For example, one family facing an unexpected diagnosis of cancer or stroke may need information about the condition and the care and treatment involved. Another family in the same situation may need to deal with their grief and the normal reactions of shock, disbelief, denial, and anger before they are ready to hear about the condition and the different treatment options. Some families are overwhelmed by a sense of loss. Unexpected threats to health or life force individuals and their families to consider their own vulnerability and to acknowledge the possible loss of vital family members.

Personal Meanings

For most people, illness and injury create losses that may render a person temporarily unable to learn because of what they mean psychologically. Different from anxiety, personal reactions to changes in health status present unique emotional responses to the present situation as well as projections about the future. Self-concept, issues of dependency, and role performance influence the client's emotional capacity to absorb cognitive data.

Changes in the health status of significant others can affect the client's willingness or ability to learn. Many clients have depended on others for direction and for overseeing treatment. When these supports are no longer available, through death or incapacity, the client may lack not only motivation but the skills to know how to learn or what is expected.

CASE EXAMPLE

Edward Flanigan, an 82-year-old recent widower, has diabetes. There is no evidence of memory problems, but there are some significant emotional components to his current health care needs. All his life his wife pampered him. Although Edward administered his insulin daily, his wife reminded him to take it and saw to it that he followed his diabetic diet. Now that his wife is dead, Edward takes no interest in controlling his diabetes. The home care nurse who visits him on a regular basis is discouraged because despite careful instruction, and seeming comprehension, Edward appears unwilling to follow the prescribed diabetic diet and is not consistent in taking his medication. Predictably, he goes into diabetic crisis. His family worries about him, but he is unwilling to consider leaving his home of 42 years.

In this case, the nurse learned that his wife assumed all responsibility for Edward. She paid the bills, monitored his diet, and prepared all his meals. Edward did not know how to cook, and he had never gone grocery shopping in over 45 years of marriage. The learning needs of this client are complicated by emotional issues of loss, change, and dependency needs. Edward could function and maintain his health as long as he could rely on his wife for support. This support is no longer available to him.

Although it was difficult for this nurse to understand how a grown, educated man might not know how to go to the grocery store or prepare his own food, dependency on others happens, and it affects how a client responds to health teaching about diet. Teaching objectives might incorporate helping Edward to understand and accept the normal process of grieving and include referral to supportive resources in his crisis situation. Helping him expand his social support system and consider alternative ways to meet his health and dependency needs would be a critical component of his teaching care plan. He might need instruction about grocery shopping, cooking, or Meals on Wheels in order to implement a diet teaching plan. Considering Edward's unique learning needs from a holistic, caring, as well as educational, perspective might make a difference in Edward's ability to learn and in his readiness to take responsibility for self-care. As can be seen in Edward's case, the needs and the most appropriate supports to achieve client goals differ with each client.

A simple way to find out the client's perceptions and attitudes is simply to ask the client and family what they already know about the topic or what they associate with it. This is important information about personal fears, expectations, and what is important to the client. The more obvious the links between previous experiences and the new knowledge, the deeper the learning (Glover and Bruning, 1990).

In the learning situation, the competent nurse might help the client and family develop a common understanding of the client's illness and explore the meaning of noncompliance. Is the client able, without the consistent support of a significant other, to learn and take responsibility for self-care? Will the nurse have to help the client cope with changes in self-image and identity prior to or concurrently with providing concrete information? The sensitivity of the nurse in accurately perceiving the unique and immediate learning needs, so strongly intertwined with the emotional meaning of the health need, will facilitate the learning process.

Active Involvement of the Learner

Active involvement is necessary for most learning. Think about the differences between classes in which you are passive and those in which you are expected to be actively involved. Instructors who provide practical examples and invite participation from the class generally hold student interest more than those who simply lecture.

Most people learn best when they engage more than one sense in the learning process. Practical learning takes place through doing. People feel a sense of pride and accomplishment from having successfully mastered active hands-on involvement with something they weren't quite sure they could accomplish. The same thing happens in health promotion. A highly participatory learning format with the opportunity to try out new behaviors is far more effective than giving simple instructions to a client or family—or doing it for them because it is easier and faster to do so. Health-promotion strategies require a sensitive appraisal and choice of strategy, unique in every case, and matched to the relevant needs of the individual, family, or group:

CASE EXAMPLE

Soon Mrs. Hixon began learning how to dress herself. At first she took an hour to complete this task. But with guidance and practice, she eventually dressed herself in 25 minutes. Even so, I practically had to sit on my hands as I watched her struggle. I could have done it so much faster for her, but she had to learn, and I had to let her (Collier, 1992, p. 63).

Active learning also requires critical decisions to determine the extent to which family members are to be involved either in a supportive role or as the primary recipients of the teaching process. For example, the family or caregiver would be involved as a primary unit in certain cultures, with children, and with clients who have sensory or cognitive deficits. Content presentations to these family members would be the same as that given to the client if the client were able to assume full responsibility for self-care.

On the other hand, family members take supportive roles in cases involving teenagers, clients in crisis, elderly clients with intact cognitive abilities, and those with a depressive disorder that compromises concentration. The difference in content and strategies for these family members would center on what they needed to know to support the learner. They may or may not need detailed content given to the client; they do need information about strategies to enable their loved one to take responsibility for self-care management.

Strategies to encourage active involvement of the client might include self-monitoring strategies, such as recording eating patterns or thoughts and feelings surrounding anxiety attacks. Information and anticipatory guidance about what to expect when the client goes home and early warning signs of complications or potential problems are given to family members as well as clients. Return demonstrations are essential components of any psychomotor learning because performance errors can be corrected on the spot.

Physical Barriers to Learning

Sometimes the client's condition precludes teaching. A client in pain cannot focus on anything else.

A client emerging from the shock of a difficult diagnosis may require teaching in small segments or postponement of serious teaching sessions until the physical problems are under better control.

Certain physical conditions make health teaching difficult. Nausea, weakness, or speech or motor impairments may make it difficult for the client to maintain concentration. Medications or the period of disorientation after a diagnostic test or surgical procedure can influence the level of the client's ability to participate in learning. A careful assessment will usually reveal when the client's physical or emotional condition is a barrier to learning.

Concurrent health care problems that could interfere with the goals or process of teaching are important pieces of data that influence what can and should be taught. For example, an exercise program might be useful for an overweight person, but if the client also has a cardiac condition or other problem that would limit activity, this information has a direct impact on the goals and strategies of the intervention.

ABILITY TO LEARN

Many clients are ready to learn, but they are not able to learn with traditional learning formats. Assessment of the client's ability to learn and accommodating the learning format to the learner's unique characteristics makes a difference. If the client can't understand what is being taught, learning does not take place. Clients give up or "tune out," not because they don't want to know the information but because they lack the skills to obtain and assimilate it. Many psychological, physiological, intellectual, and emotional factors affect a client's capacity to learn new information and ways of behaving.

Attentional Set

Attentional set refers to the capacity of a person to attend to the learning process and the extent to which the person is distracted by other factors in the environment. Clients cannot pay attention when they are in pain. In times of stress, the client's attentional set may be limited by anxiety. A client in the acute phase of an illness needs additional reinforcement and repetition of key concepts. As described in Chapter 5, a person's perceptual field narrows in times of acute anxiety.

The anxiety associated with crisis can be used productively, provided it is not extreme. Mezirow and associates (1990) note that crisis and life transitions provide a format for the most significant adult learning. Attention is likely to be at its peak during these times. Crisis learning is particularly effective with many homeless and Medicaid clients, who do not voluntarily seek health care at any other time. Health teaching for these clients should be immediate, practical, designed to resolve the crisis situation, and carefully organized to maximize client attention.

Everyone has his or her own optimal attention span. Some people learn better with short segments, whereas others prefer to learn all of the material and break it down later. Scheduling shorter sessions with time in between to process information helps prevent sensory overload (Demuth, 1989). This is particularly true in health teaching of the elderly. Too much information in too short a time breeds frustration for the elderly client who needs extra time to process and integrate information.

To appreciate the significance of allowing processing time to prevent sensory overload, compare your own level of interest, attention, and learning during the last hour of class on a heavy lecture day with that during the first hours. Chances are your attention has diminished by the last hour of class. A simple strategy that helps break up learning segments is to change the pace by inserting an activity, visual aid, or discussion point.

Low Literacy

Low literacy is not the same as low intelligence, although frequently people confuse the two. There is an assumption that educationally disadvantaged or functionally illiterate people are less responsible learners. But just because a person is educated doesn't mean the person will be more ready to assume responsibility for changing difficult behaviors than a less educated individual. Nor does it mean that an illiterate person cannot learn.

A persistent stigma about low literacy and learning disabilities exists even though there shouldn't be one. For this reason many people try to hide the fact that they can't read or don't know the meaning of complex words. They fake their inability to understand by appearing to agree with the educator and by not asking questions.

Using symbols and images the client is familiar with helps overcome the barriers of low literacy. Simple, concrete words convey the same message as more sophisticated language. For example, one client referred to testing his urine for diabetes as "testing for sugar in the piss." This language had meaning for him. Describing diabetes in abstract terms would have little relevance for this client, who would have difficulty following and participating in the learning process. Taking the time to understand the client's use of words and phrases provides the nurse with words and ideas that can be used as building blocks in helping the client understand difficult health-related concepts. Otherwise the client may misunderstand what the nurse is saying.

CASE EXAMPLE

The discharge nurse said to a new mother, "Now you know to watch the baby's stools to be sure they're normal. You do know what normal stools look like, don't you?" The mother replied, "Oh, yeah, sure, . . . I've got four of them in my kitchen" (Doak et al., 1991).

The nurse should keep instructions as simple as possible, presenting ideas in an uncomplicated, step-by-step format. Familiar words supplemented by commonplace pictures provide an extra sensory input for the client and improve retention. Drawings and photographs provide additional cues, allowing clients to understand meanings they would be unable to grasp through words alone (Fig. 15–5).

Use the literal meanings of words rather than nonliteral terminology. "Call the doctor if you run into trouble" may not mean that the client will call the physician if symptoms develop unless the precise reasons for calling the doctor are described and understood. A better direction would be, "Call the doctor on Monday if you still have pain or swelling in your knee." These same instructions, written exactly as they were spoken, act as a reminder once the person leaves the actual teaching situation.

In addition to using simple words and literal interpretations, it is important always to use the

Eating Fruit for Dessert is Good!

YES

Eating Cake for Dessert is Bad

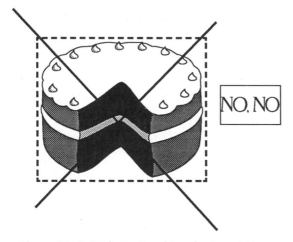

NO, NO

Figure 15–5 Diabetic Teaching for Low-Literacy Clients: Example of Teaching Aids

same words to describe the same thing. For example, if you use "insulin" in one instance and "medicine" or "drug" later to describe the same medication, the client may become confused.

Logical sequencing of content is particularly important in teaching the low-literacy client. Doak (1991) suggests thinking about the order of a teaching session from the client's perspective and advocates the following series of questions as a framework for instruction about medication:

"What do I take?"
"How much do I take?"
"When do I take it?"
"What will it do for me?"
"What do I do if I get a side effect?"

By selecting related pieces of data and structuring them into informational chunks, the client can remember the information better through association even if one fact is forgotten. Whenever possible, link new tasks and information with what the client already knows. This strategy, important with all clients, is particularly advantageous with the low-literacy client. It takes advantage of previous learning and helps reinforce self-esteem by reminding the client of competencies learned in the process of instruction.

When technical words are necessary for clients to communicate about their condition with other health professionals, clients need direct instruction about appropriate words to use. As with the culturally diverse client, keeping sentences short and precise and using active verbs helps clients understand what is being taught. Box 15–3 provides guidelines for the nurse in teaching low-literacy clients.

Learning Disabilities

The learning-disabled client may require adaptation of normal teaching strategies to learn new material. Learning disability is defined as "impairment in one or more aspects of a broad range of functional areas comprising such processes as attention, memory, visual perception, receptive

---

BOX 15–3
Guidelines for Teaching Low-Literacy Clients

1. Teach the *smallest amount* possible to do the job.
2. Make your point as vividly as you can. (Use visual aids and examples for emphasis.)
3. Incorporate as many senses as possible in the learning process.
4. Have the client *restate* and demonstrate the information.
5. Review repeatedly.

Adapted from Doak CC, Doak LG, Root JH (1985). Tips on teaching patients. *In* Doak CC, Doak LG, Root JH (1985), Teaching Patients with Low Literacy Skills. Philadelphia, Lippincott, p. 4. Reprinted with the permission of J. B. Lippincott Company, Philadelphia.

language, expressive language, motor output and higher order conceptualization" (Levine, 1980, p. 312). The concept of learning disability covers a wide range of learning handicaps ranging from severe impairment of learning potential in many functional areas to mild disability in one area and marked excellence in others. Learning disabilities affect self-concept and self-esteem. They also influence social interactions and the interpretation of critical life events. Clients with learning disabilities need special consideration in health teaching.

Nurses should be aware that a learning-disabled client possibly has a history of feelings of failure or frustration. As in any other teaching situation, communication skills such as empathy and sincere interest are used to establish a sense of rapport.

Problems in processing communications may occur anywhere in the communication process, starting with the intake and processing of sensory data and ending with the construction and delivery of relevant responses (Figure 15–6). Problems in the *encoding* aspect of the communication process

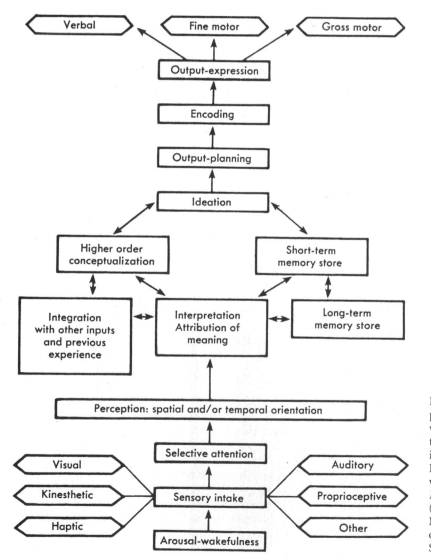

Figure 15–6 Problems in processing can occur anywhere in the communication process for the learning-disabled client. From Levine M (1980). The Child with Learning Disabilities. *In* Scheiner A, Abroms L (eds.) (1980), The Practical Management of the Developmentally Disabled Child. St. Louis, Mosby.

could occur in idea formulation, in the process of encoding the idea into language symbols, in the memory, or in the motorneurological mechanics used in speaking or writing. Problems in the *decoding* process may involve impairment in the integration of stimuli in the brain or in the ability to translate sensory information into an idea. Accurate assessment of the client's learning needs is useful because the strategies used to health teach vary with the nature of the learning disability. Information about the type of learning disability helps the nurse avoid the kind of content the client has difficulty processing. For example, the client may have difficulty with numbers but not with word concepts. Concrete concepts may present little difficulty, but abstract or symbolic material may require great effort to process. Some clients have trouble reproducing a word or picture from memory but experience little difficulty recognizing written words and symbols in picture format. Other clients have problems with written materials but have normal auditory processing skills for the words they hear. Fine-motor deficits can present as eye–hand coordination problems that can become an issue with psychomotor learning requirements. Poor retention of multiple-step instructions, confusion about time relationships, and sequencing difficulties can be problems for some learning-disabled clients. In each case the nurse's approach should convey understanding of the client's deficits. Supporting the client's strengths, using a mode of delivery the client can understand, and providing additional time for processing are key to successful instruction of the learning-disabled client.

Many learning-disabled clients have above average intelligence but need additional time to process information. Learning disabilities get worse in high-stimuli environments and in anxiety-provoking situations. Learning-disabled clients respond best to very small group or one-to-one teaching formats. The environment in which information is presented can be structured to limit distractions. New information is best presented in small units, using easily understood vocabulary and visual aides to make concepts "concrete." Choosing learning materials to compensate for client deficiencies and reinforce strengths, frequent positive reinforcement, and a strong, informed advocacy for the learning-disabled client help make the learning situation manageable.

Developmental Level

Health-maintenance strategies ideally start in childhood. Clients are at all levels of the learning spectrum with regard to their social, emotional, and cognitive development, and development is not always age related. Developmental level affects both teaching stategies and subject content. The developmental concepts presented in Chapters 1 and 18 are important guides for the nurse in choosing the most appropriate teaching strategies for children.

Teaching strategies should incorporate a small child's immediate experience whenever possible. For example, in teaching preschoolers to swim, one instructor used an example of blowing up a balloon to help them understand how to breathe under water. One child did this easily because it was a part of her experience at home. The other preschooler seemed at a loss. In the next class, a substitute teacher taught the same concept using the example of blowing out a candle. This time the situation was reversed for the two children: The child who could not grasp the idea the first time was able to use the example of the candle and perform the teaching task. The other child experienced difficulty because she did not have a similar experience with blowing out candles. Parents can provide useful information about the child's immediate life experiences and use of words in relating to them. Vocabulary words of importance can be recorded on the chart as well for use by other health personnel.

School-aged children struggling with Erikson's stage of industry have an interest in building competencies. Focusing teaching on the development of competency, whether physical, psychological, or cognitive, takes advantage of the child's natural stage of development. Children of this age are eager to learn about better ways of taking care of themselves. Box 15–4 presents an application of a teaching sequence for school-aged children.

Andragogy refers to the "art and science of helping adults learn" (Knowles, 1980). According to Knowles, adult learners favor a problem-focused approach to learning. They are interested in learning skills and knowledge that will help them master life problems. Self-directedness is a key component of the adult teaching-learning process. Adults like to be in control of their learning process. They

BOX 15–4
Application: Nutrition Class for Fifth-Graders

1. Ask children to identify their favorite foods.
2. Present factual information about the pyramid.
3. Ask the children to tell their peers about the foods they eat and to identify the food groups to which they belong.
4. Give each child a diet worksheet to record his or her food intake for the next week; encourage the children to select foods from each food level.

appreciate structure and advance organizers, but only as structures within which they can create their own sense of how the learning will apply in their lives. To facilitate the process, the nurse might use the following overview: "Today, I am going to give you some information about food groups and specific quantities you will need to know about in controlling your diabetes. Then we can see how you might be able to incorporate this information into menu planning, given your work schedule and family eating habits." It is up to the adult client to help the nurse determine how these necessary changes in diet will be integrated into the client's current lifestyle. Learning is likely to be successful only if the adult client can reassess a problem or situation and move to a position of taking action.

Individual responsibility through taking action and reflecting on the consequences ensures ownership and stimulates learning in the adult client. One way to test the validity of this statement is to consider how you learn to be a nurse. For example, although theory and simulated learning are important, neither is recognized by most students as the essence of the learning process. Learning remains academic until students have the opportunity actually to practice skills and put theory into action.

The adult's orientation to learning is *life centered*. Adult learners need to be able to see the practicality of what they are learning. They can discriminate between essential information and irrelevant data. Many adult learners are insulted when the nurse does not seem to know the difference. The adult client expects the nurse to inquire about previous life experience and to incorporate this knowledge into the teaching plan. Experience is a rich resource that can be used wisely in planning nursing interventions. Box 15–5 describes the

natural learning process elements required for adult learners.

Elderly clients learn as well as younger clients if the material is presented in ways that acknowledge their different developmental learning needs. They respond best to learning formats that integrate knowledge from the past, involve the use of more than one sense, and are practical. Content relevant to the person's health and related to the current condition is more likely to hold the elder's attention. Most elderly clients appreciate recognition of their long years of experience in choosing content. The elderly learner responds best in a learning milieu in which the nurse faces the client when talking and speaks clearly and slowly in a low-pitched voice.

The nurse needs to allow for the additional reaction time elderly clients need (Kick, 1989; Kim, 1986). Sufficient time to practice and frequent praise encourage elderly clients to take an active role in their learning process. Frequent, shorter learning sessions are better than long formats.

The elderly client may have difficulty with some psychomotor tasks—for example, removing bottle caps or filling syringes—because of dexterity loss. Pride may prevent the client from revealing this to the nurse. Assuming that elderly clients lack the capacity to understand the instructions is a common error. Health care providers often direct instruction to the elderly client's younger companion even when the client has no cognitive impairment. This action disconfirms the elderly

BOX 15–5
Learning as a Natural Process

- We cannot teach another person directly; we can only facilitate his learning.
- A person learns significantly only those things which he perceives as being involved in the maintenance of, or enhancement of, the structure of self.
- Experience that is perceived as inconsistent with self can only be assimilated if the current organization of self is relaxed and expanded to include it.
- The educational situation that most effectively promotes significant learning is one in which the threat to the self of the learner is reduced to a minimum.

From Knowles M (1990). The Adult Learner: A Neglected Species, pp. 32–33. Copyright © 1990 by Gulf Publishing Company, Houston, TX. Used with permission. All rights reserved.

BOX 15–6
Recommended Teaching Strategies at Different Developmental Levels

Developmental Level	Recommended Teaching Strategies
Preschool	Allow child to touch and play with safe equipment.
	Relate teaching to child's immediate experience.
	Use child's vocabulary whenever possible.
	Involve parents in teaching.
School age	Give factual information in simple, concrete terms.
	Focus teaching on developing competency.
	Use simple drawings, models to emphasize points.
	Answer questions honestly and factually.
Adolescent	Can use metaphors and analogies in teaching.
	Give choices and multiple perspectives.
	Incorporate the client's norm group values, personal identity issues in teaching strategies.
Adult	Involve client as an active partner in learning process.
	Encourage self-directed learning.
	Keep content and strategies relevant and practical.
	Incorporate previous life experience into teaching.
Elderly	Incorporate previous life experience into teaching.
	Accommodate for sensory and dexterity deficits.
	Use short, frequent learning sessions.
	Use praise liberally.

---

client and diminishes self-worth. The sensitive nurse observes the client before implementing teaching and gears teaching strategies to meet the individual learning needs of each elderly client. Box 15–6 presents teaching strategies for use with clients at different developmental levels.

Culture

Culture adds to the complexity of the teaching-learning process in health care. Culturally, learners come from many different value systems with different beliefs, interaction styles, and language backgrounds. Language barriers can make learning virtually impossible for a client. Pictures, the use of dictionaries, and the help of translators may be necessary supports to the learning process.

Incorporating the client's cultural beliefs about health into the teaching promotes better acceptance. Such beliefs include assumptions about health and illness, the causes of and treatments for different types of illnesses, and traditionally accepted health actions or practices to prevent or treat illness. For each ethnic group the perspectives differ (Spector, 1989).

Appropriate client education for culturally diverse clients should include both the client and the client's social support system (Tripp-Reimer, 1989). In many cultures the family assumes a primary role in the care of the client even when the client is physically and emotionally capable of self-care. All parties needing information, especially those expected to support the learning process of the client, should be included from the outset in developing a realistic teaching plan, as well as in implementing and evaluating the plan. Otherwise the teaching plan may be sabotaged when the client goes home.

Incorporating cultural ways of knowing and supports into the learning process increases client motivation and participation. The culturally sensitive nurse develops a knowledge of the preferred communication style of different cultural groups and uses this knowledge in choosing teaching strategies. For example, Native Americans like stories. Their oral tradition of telling stories is a primary means of teaching that the nurse can use as a teaching methodology. Box 15–7 presents guidelines for teaching the culturally diverse client.

SELF-AWARENESS

The nurse has an ethical and legal responsibility in health teaching to maintain the appropriate expertise and interpersonal sensitivity to client needs

BOX 15–7
Suggested Strategies for Teaching the Culturally Diverse Client

1. Speak slowly (plan the teaching session to last at least twice as long as a typical session).
2. Make the sentence structure simple (use active, not passive, voice; use a straight forward subject–verb pattern).
3. Avoid technical terms (for example, use "heart" rather than "cardiac"), professional jargon, and American idioms ("red tape").
4. Provide instructional material in the *same* sequence in which the patient should carry out the plan.
5. Do not assume you have been understood. Ask the patient to explain the protocol; optimally, if appropriate, obtain a return demonstration.

From Tripp-Reimer T, Afifi LA (1989). Cross cultural perspectives on patient teaching. Nursing Clinics of North America 24(3):615. Reprinted with the permission of W. B. Saunders Company, Philadelphia.

required for effective learning. Equally important is the need to understand the complexity of the teaching process in health care and to appreciate one's role as health educator. There are as many perceptual realities as there are persons. The nature of those realities makes each learning experience and the resources the client has to commit to the process different (Rogers, 1969).

Interpersonal competence, based on self-awareness, is essential to effective health teaching. It is easy enough to remain engaged and to provide interesting teaching formats for the self-directed, highly motivated learner. But it takes energy and imagination to impart hope to clients, to stimulate their emotions and interest when they see little reason to participate in learning about self-care management. It is discouraging for the nurse when the client feels helpless and doesn't want to change, or participates with little change in outcome. There is a tendency to feel rejected when a client doesn't value our information and betrayed when the outcomes don't match the effort the nurse has put into teaching the client. When these feelings occur, it is important to detach one's ego from achieving perfect success and to reflect on one's own motivations and investment in the process.

Health promotion is a mutual interpersonal process. The nurse is responsible for the health teaching. The client assumes responsibility for the outcome. At all times the nurse respects the client's autonomy. Some clients want symptom relief, whereas others want more in-depth teaching. The desired level of change ultimately is up to the client. At the same time, the nurse has an ethical responsibility to provide appropriate health teaching, and the right to hope that if the information is not used now, perhaps later it will be.

SUMMARY

Teaching for health promotion is a more concentrated form of therapeutic communication. Two theoretical frameworks, the health-belief model and the health-promotion model, are important in understanding the readiness of the client to participate in health-enhancing activities. Preventive health education is designed to teach people how to promote and maintain their highest level of wellness. Three types of health prevention—primary, secondary, and tertiary—are described. Effective preventive education starts where the client is and builds on the client's knowledge base and perceptual understandings. Learning takes place in three distinct yet often highly interrelated areas: cognitive, affective, and psychomotor. Learner variables, important as the foundation of client education, generally fall into two categories: assessment of the client's readiness to learn and assessment of the client's capacity to learn. Personal and community factors such as physical condition, literacy, culture, emotional context, interpersonal dynamics, and previous experience influence learning. Self-awareness and critical reflection of experiences, important in other aspects of the nurse–client relationship, continue to be significant elements for the nurse in teaching conversations with clients. Nurses participate routinely in community health-promotion and disease-prevention activities. They are a major resource in helping clients understand their illnesses and represent a primary intervention in assisting clients to develop effective ways of coping with illness. Helping clients achieve optimal wellness is the primary goal of all health teaching.

REFERENCES

Antai-Otong D (1989). Concerns of the hospitalized and community psychiatric client. Nursing Clinics of North America 24(3):665.

Bandura A (1987). Human agency in social cognitive theory. American Psychologist 44:1175–1184.

Buckwater KC, Kerfoot KM (1982). Teaching patients self-care: A critical aspect of psychiatric discharge planning. Journal of Psychosocial Nursing and Mental Health Services 20:15.

Carlson MB (1988). Meaning Making: Therapeutic Processes in Adult Development. New York, Norton.

Chandler C, Holden J, Kolander C (1992). Counseling for spiritual wellness: Theory and practice. Journal of Counseling and Development 71:168–175.

Check JF, Wurzbach ME (1984). How elders view learning. Geriatric Nursing 1:37–39.

Collier S (1992). Mrs. Hixon was more than the C.V.A. in 251. RN '92 22(11):62–64.

Curran J, Monti P (eds.). Social Skills Training. Washington Square, NY, New York University Press, 1986.

Damarosch S (1991). General strategies for motivating people to change their behavior. Nursing Clinics of North America 26:833–843.

Demuth J (1989). Patient teaching in the ambulatory setting. Nursing Clinics of North America 24(3): 645–654.

Department of Health and Human Services (1991). Healthy People 2000. Washington, DC, Government Printing Office.

Doak CC, Doak LG, Root JH (1985). Teaching Patients with Low Literacy Skills. Philadelphia, Lippincott.

Fleury J (1992). The application of motivational theory to cardiovascular risk reduction. Journal of Advanced Nursing 229–237.

Gauthier C (1993). Philosophical foundations of respect for autonomy. Kennedy Institute of Ethics Journal 3(1):21–37.

Glover J, Bruning R (1990). Educational Psychology: Principles and Applications. (3rd ed.). Glenview, IL, Scott, Foresman.

Hoff B (1987). The Tao of Pooh. New York, Penguin Books.

Holyoak J, Koh K (1987). Surface and structural similarity in analogical transfer. Memory and Cognition. 15:332–340.

Honan S, Krsnak G, Peterson D, Torkelson R (1988). The nurse as patient educator: Perceived responsibilities and factors enhancing role development. Journal of Continuing Education in Nursing 19(1):33–37.

Jones P, Meleis A (1993). Health is empowerment. Advances in Nursing Science 15(3):1–14.

Kick E (1989). Patient teaching for elders. Nursing Clinics of North America 24(3):681–686.

Kim KK (1986). Response time and health care learning of elderly patients. Research in Nursing and Health Care 9:233–236.

Knowles M (1980). The Adult Learner: A Neglected Species (2nd ed.). Palo Alto, CA, Mayfield Publishing Co.

Levine M (1980). The child with learning disabilities. In Scheiner A, Abroms I (eds.) (1980), The Practical Management of the Developmentally Disabled Child. St. Louis, Mosby.

Lockhart EJ (1990). Communicating with Kids: A Practical Guide to the Forgotten Language. Frederick, MD, Undercurrents Press.

Manning S (1992). The nurses I'll never forget. RN '92 22(8):47.

Mezirow J, et al. (1990). Fostering Critical Reflection in Adulthood: A Guide to Transformative and Emancipatory Learning. San Francisco, Jossey-Bass.

Omizo M, Omizo S, d'Andrea M (1992). Promoting wellness among elementary school children. Journal of Counseling and Development 71(3):194–198.

Overholser JC (1988). Clinical utility of the Socratic method. In Stout C (ed.) (1988), Annals of Clinical Research. DesPlaines, IL, Forest Institute, pp 1–7.

Pavlish C (1987). A model for situational patient teaching. Journal of Continuing Education in Nursing 18(5):163–167.

Pease RA (1984). Praise elders to help them learn. Journal of Gerontological Nursing 11:16–20.

Pender N (1987). Health Promotion in Nursing Practice (2nd ed.). Norwalk, CT, Appleton & Lange.

Pender N, Walker S, Sechrist K (1990). Predicting health promoting life styles in the work place. Nursing Research 38:326.

Peterson MC, Hollloway RL, Solberg LI (1987). Assessment by patients of their health education needs. Family Practice Research 6:158–164.

Prochaska J, Diclemente C, Norcross J (1992). In search of how people change: Applications to addictive behaviors. American Psychologist 47(9):1102–1114.

Rawnsley M (1992). Brief psychotherapy for persons with recurrent cancer: A holistic practice model. Advances in Nursing Science 5(1):69–76.

Redmond BK (1988). The Process of Patient Education (6th ed.). St. Louis, Mosby.

Rogers C (1969). Freedom to Learn: A View of What Education Might Become. Columbus, OH, Merrill.

Ruzicki D (1989). Realistically meeting the educational needs of hospitalized acute and short-stay patients. Nursing Clinics of North America 24(3):629.

Severson De Muth J (1989). Patient teaching in the ambulatory setting. Nursing Clinics of North America 24(3):645.

Smith CE (1987). Patient Education: Nurses in Partnership with Other Health Professionals. Orlando, FL, Grune & Stratton.

Spector RE (1989). Heritage consistency: A predictor of health beliefs and practices. Recent Advances in Nursing (23):23–35.

St. Claire P, Anderson N (1989). Social network advice during pregnancy: Myths, misinformation and sound counsel. Birth 16(3):103–107.

Tilly JD, Gregor FM, Thiessen V (1987). The nurse's role in patient education: Incongruent perceptions among nurses and patients. Journal of Advanced Nursing 12:291–301.

Tripp-Reimer T, Afifi LA (1989). Cross-cultural perspectives on patient teaching. Nursing Clinics of North America 24(3):613–619.

Walker SN, Sechrist KR, Perder NJ (1987). The health promoting lifestyle profile: Development and psychometric properties. Nursing Research 36:76–81.

Williams MT (1991). Creating a positive impact on the health and well-being of children and families through education. Journal of Pediatric Nursing 6(1):72–73.

SUGGESTED READINGS

Arenson J (1988). Discharge teaching in the NICU: The changing needs of NICU graduates and their families. Neonatal Network 6:29–39, 47–52.

Baker K, Kuhlmann T, Magliaro B (1989). Homeward bound: Discharge teaching for parents of newborns with special needs. Nursing Clinics of North America 24(3):655.

Steele J, Ruzicki D (1987). An evaluation of the effectiveness of cardiac teaching during hospitalization. Heart and Lung 16(3):306–311.

Whiteside SE (1983). Patient education: Effectiveness of medications programs for psychiatric patients. Journal of Psychosocial Nursing and Mental Health Services 21:16–21.

Chapter 16

Health Teaching in the Nurse–Client Relationship

ELIZABETH ARNOLD

OBJECTIVES

At the end of the chapter, the student will be able to:

1. Define health teaching and describe the role of the nurse.

2. Contrast selected theoretical frameworks used in health teaching.

3. Identify different types of formats found in health teaching.

4. Use the nursing process to develop, implement, and evaluate a teaching care plan.

5. Specify teaching strategies relevant to health teaching.

6. Describe applications in different care settings.

*When adults teach and learn in one another's company, they find them-
selves engaging in a challenging, passionate, and creative activity. The acts
of teaching and learning—and the creation and alteration of our beliefs,
values, actions, relationships, and social forms that result from this—are
ways in which we realize our humanity.*

Brookfield, 1986

This chapter presents an overview of the development, implementation, and evaluation of health teaching in the nurse–client relationship. Each teaching conversation develops its own unique character because of the participants involved. Yet most effective teaching conversations conducted by nurses also follow a similar plan of organization and development. Just as therapeutic communication is more than talking in other aspects of the nurse–client relationship, health teaching as a special form of communication requires more than simply providing cognitive data to clients and their families. This chapter provides useful guidelines for health teaching with clients and their families in a variety of health care situations.

BASIC CONCEPTS

DEFINITION

Health teaching is defined as a flexible, person-oriented process in which the helping person provides information and support to clients with a variety of health-related learning needs. In the nurse–client relationship the teaching process is characterized as content-specific communications with knowledgeable health professionals related to the health and self-care needs of the client. Health teaching is a creative interpersonal experience. It is distinguished from other forms of teaching by its person-oriented relationship.

Although teaching has many definitions, most of them do not address the complexity of the teaching process in health care. They fail to include the multiple communication factors and decisions required of the nurse who teaches clients in health care situations. For example, the "learner" in a health care setting can be a client, the client's family, a caregiver, or a significant other. Each person involved in learning about the care of one client may require different content and teaching strategies. Whereas most teaching situations require that the students enter with a similar level of education

and knowledge, health teaching must be designed to meet the learning needs of individuals from diverse socioeconomic, educational, and experiential backgrounds. In no other teaching circumstances is an educator called upon to meet simultaneously such a diversity of learning needs. For example, a Ph.D. and a low-literacy client may have the same medical condition and similar needs for health teaching. In providing relevant health teaching, the nurse will have to use very different teaching approaches to achieve successful outcomes with each client. Everything about the learning environment, including expected outcomes, teaching strategies, involvement of others, and even the content needs to reflect these unique learning needs. Integrating the emotional and tangible, practical supports needed to meet the challenges of the learning situation is just as important as the actual information given to clients and those intimately involved with client care. A teaching conversation may be brief or may extend over several sessions. The purposes of teaching conversations are to:

- Identify relevant health care needs.
- Furnish emotional and cognitive support during the learning process.
- Provide new models for functioning in different ways. Health teaching conversations follow the format of the nursing process and require a specific knowledge base, self-awareness, and a good understanding of teaching-learning principles.

HEALTH TEACHING AS A PROFESSIONAL NURSING ROLE

Health teaching is an essential component of the professional nurse role (Creasia and Parker, 1991). Professional nursing standards, developed by the American Nurses Association, specifically relate to health teaching. They call for nursing actions that provide for "client/patient participation in health promotion, maintenance and restoration," specifying that "the nurse assists clients, families, and groups to achieve satisfying and productive patterns of living through health teaching" (ANA, 1982). Moreover, almost every nursing intervention has a health teaching component.

Most state nurse practice acts mandate health teaching as an independent professional nursing function. Third-party reimbursement for Medicare defines health teaching as a skilled nursing intervention. Included in the code of ethics for nurses is the formal statement, "The nurse participates in the profession's efforts to protect the public from misinformation and misrepresentation and to maintain the integrity of nursing" (ANA, 1985). It is impossible to be an effective nurse without developing skills in health teaching.

Health teaching begins in the community and becomes an integral part of each client's care plan from the moment the client enters the hospital. Hospitals issue directives about clients' right to education and full participation in their treatment. For example, statements such as, "Clients have the right to have reasonable informed participation in their health care treatment" and, "Clients have the right to learn about their medical condition, plans for treatment and anticipated outcomes" are part of the admission information given in writing to each client (Crawford Long Memorial Hospital, 1992). The nurse plays a primary role in providing this information.

As health care delivery systems in the 1990s move from a hospital-based to a community-focused delivery system, health teaching will receive even greater emphasis as a cost-containment measure. Our current health care delivery system requires a new form of communication in health teaching, one that is meaningful and relevant to an increasingly diverse client population.

Health Teaching and Informed Consent

Health teaching about the client's illness and potential options is a primary element in informed consent. *Informed consent* means that clients fully understand what is happening or is about to happen in their health care and knowingly consent to that care. It is not unusual for clients, however, to have incomplete information about what they consent to in writing (Redmond, 1988). Educating clients about informed consent is an ethical responsibility of the nurse, who often is in the best position to judge the amount of disclosure and individualized health teaching necessary. Failure to provide clients with essential education on which to base decisions about their health care can be interpreted as negligence and can lead to legal action against the nurse.

Multiple Roles in Health Teaching

Change, restructuring, development of new perspectives, and problem solving become the focus in health teaching, demanding a type of teaching that is much broader than simply imparting information. In health teaching, the nurse cannot solve the clients' problems but can only help them achieve greater self-understanding and coping skills in meeting their health care needs. The nurse acts as a facilitator, information provider, and collaborator in health-promotion and prevention activities.

As a *guide,* the nurse helps clients to reconstruct a new knowledge base that places clients more in charge of their health care. Personal interactions between nurse and client recognize differences in client values and learning needs and strive to develop a common understanding of what will be meaningful to the client. In every successful learning experience, the learner must be in charge of his or her own being and creativity.

As an *information provider,* the nurse helps clients become more aware of why, what, and how they can learn to take better care of themselves. The nurse acts as a knowledgeable resource to help the client think through choices and develop different perspectives, providing information and making referrals based on client needs.

As a *partner in learning,* the nurse collaborates with the client to identify perceptions and to take actions that maintain or enhance optimal well-being. Both partners have responsibilities and data to bring to the learning situation. The client knows more about his or her body, internal perceptions, feelings, beliefs, and values. The nurse has a different knowledge base built on data from many sources. Through the nurse–client relationship, clients begin to challenge old unworkable ideas and habits, transform unproductive understandings and actions, and act on new perspectives.

THEORETICAL FRAMEWORKS

Although there are many learning models applicable to teaching, three models, person centered, critical thinking, and behavioral, have particular relevance for health teaching.

Person-Centered Health Teaching

Carl Rogers' person-centered learning is a particularly useful model in creating an environment for health education that focuses on the client. Rogers believes education is represented best as a complex and dynamic relationship between teacher and student. Not simply a cognitive process, learning involves the whole person. There is a unity of thought and feeling that is necessary for effective learning. Rogers (1983) describes learning as a natural, inherent human process that people want to engage in because it helps them actualize their human potential. The teacher acts as a guide and monitors the student's progress in learning the content, making sure that what is learned is factually and strategically correct. The learning climate stresses respect for and among students and between student and teacher. Teaching involves engaging students as active partners in the learning process and helping students take responsibility for their own learning. To do this, nurses in the teaching role must respond consistently to the student's needs and use the student's motivation, experiences, abilities, interests, and skills as the foundation for learning new material. There is no single right way to teach, and the routine application of standard teaching procedures is not acceptable. Teaching methodologies vary from situation to situation as the teacher strives to make new content comprehensible and interesting to the students. Self-disclosure appropriate to the situation and the relationship add to the human quality of the teaching experience.

Critical Thinking

Critical thinking provides a cognitive learning structure for making good decisions. This cognitive process works equally well with nurses and clients who are capable of abstract processing. Critical thinking has received more attention in recent years, and in 1991 it became an NLN behavioral outcome expected of all students enrolled in undergraduate nursing programs. Basically a reflective process with cognitive and emotional components, *critical thinking* offers a framework for problem solving by which persons can identify and analyze the assumptions underlying the actions, decisions, values, and judgments of themselves and others (Brookfield, 1986). Included in the process of critical thinking is careful examination of all the circumstances contributing to the development and maintenance of a health care situation.

Critical thinking skills have three functions (Mezirow and associates, 1990):

- To guide actions.
- To give coherence to the unfamiliar.
- To reassess the justification for what is already known.

Critical thinking is based on the premise that it is as important to learn *how* to learn as it is to learn about specific content. Knowing where to look for information saves time and empowers people when answers are not readily forthcoming.

As a reflective process, critical thinking is particularly useful in deciphering the meaning of the unknown and uncertain reality. Faced with the unknown, people sometimes willlingly accept a simplistic explanation of problems and how to resolve them. Or they give up because they feel there is no answer. Highly competent people become temporarily immobilized, losing touch with their abilities and the problem-solving strategies they have used countless times in other situations. They are unable to use previous information or to sort out details that could help them develop a more creative solution in the face of crisis. Here the nurse can help guide the client through a seemingly incomprehensible maze of details through informal teaching and guidance. Critical thinking, with the help of appropriate questioning, helps clients make thoughtful decisions based on the information available.

Critical thinking involves looking at a situation from many different perspectives. The purpose of using a critical thinking approach is to bring knowledge already possessed into the client's conscious awareness and to help the client reason through difficult problems. Using a critical thinking approach, the client is able to identify structural similarities across data that may appear quite different on the surface. New situational data become familiar through connections with things that are already known.

Critical thinking strategies make use of analogies and metaphors to help clients consider the universal elements of similar predicaments in different areas (Holyoak and Koh, 1987). For example, the common metaphor, "If you give a man a fish, you feed him for a day, but if you teach him how to fish, you feed him for life" is a word image for the concepts in the teaching-learning process presented in this chapter. Analogies may be used, such as "Think about how difficult it was for you to learn to ride a bicycle. Now that you know how to ride it, you don't worry about it because it is an automatic skill. The anxiety you are experiencing in learning how to give yourself insulin is similar. It will decrease with practice, and it will become an automatic part of your life." By using a reflective process, clients are able to generalize the problem-solving process beyond a specific situation.

Critical thinking can help clients restructure a problem so that it is amenable to change. By playing an active role in exploring a difficult problem and in developing the most reasonable solution, the client sharpens reasoning skills. The nurse, in implementing this strategy, uses factual evidence and systematic questioning integrated with a problem-solving approach. Critical thinking encourages the participant to weigh the risks and benefits of each proposed solution. The process of critical thinking analyzes the likelihood of success, the amount of effort needed to perform a task, the people the client needs to involve, and how to get the most benefit out of a chosen solution as part of reasoning through difficult problems.

Critical thinking is a creative, flexible process. An open, inquisitive mind about people, problems, and solutions becomes part of the framing habit characteristic of a critical thinking approach to difficult problems. The critical thinker develops the capacity to imagine entirely different and creative ways of thinking about and acting in a wide variety of life situations. Imagination in critical thinking processes differs from intuitive thinking in that it is a disciplined cognitive process combined with analysis and synthesis of real data. The

critical thinker is as aware of potential pitfalls and limitations in thinking as of real possiblities in the situation.

Critical thinking in nursing practice is particularly important because the nurse must form critical decisions based on incomplete data. Most decisions in nursing practice are not clear-cut, similar to one another, or applicable to all situations. The purpose of introducing a critical thinking approach as part of the teaching process is to bring knowledge already possessed into the nurse's conscious awareness so it can be used to develop a reasoned approach to the current health problem. The nurse uses critical thinking skills to compile different pieces of data into a comprehensive, holistic portrait of the client.

In clinical practice, nurses use critical thinking skills to *analyze* data and to *synthesize* this information into a meaningful whole. Assessment observations of behavior, client statements, lab tests, and the comments of others intimately involved with the client's care form the basis for analyzable data. In analyzing the data, the nurse breaks the data apart for closer examination and identifies relevant relationships among the different pieces of data. These clinical impressions are integrated with one another using a reasoning process referred to as synthesis. Synthesis skills integrate empirical, intuitive, personal, and aesthetic ways of knowing about data into a meaningful whole, from which one can draw logical conclusions. Use of a reflective journal (see Exercise 16–1 provides a tool for critically thinking about important incidents in nursing practice.

Behavioral Models

Many people look at behavioral models of learning with suspicion. The reality is that we use behavioral concepts in many aspects of our lives as learning supports. For example, most course syllabi contain specific guidelines expressed in behavioral terms. If the student meets established standards of behavior, the student receives a passing grade as a reward. Some socialized behaviors of males and females are taught behaviorally, that is, by the reactions a child receives from parents and significant others. It still is more acceptable for boys to be aggressive; little girls are not rewarded for being

EXERCISE 16–1
Guidelines for Reflective Journals
This exercise may be completed as a one-time experiential learning exercise, or it may be used over a semester.

Definition:
Reflection is "the process of reviewing one's repertoire of clinical experience and knowledge to invent novel approaches to complex clinical problems. Reflection also provides data for self-examination and increases learning from experience" (Saylor, 1990, p. 8.).

Purpose:
The capacity to examine one's actions, thoughts, and feelings about professional practice is of particular significance in the development of professional attitudes. Reflective journals allow students to raise important questions, reflect on activities and progress, and consider new approaches and resources.

Procedure: Your *first* journal entry should be a short narrative reflecting on the persons, circumstances, situations, and values that drew you to consider nursing as a profession.

In *subsequent* weeks, or as a one-time learning experience, your journal entry should focus on your educational experience and address the following questions.

- What was the most significant experience I had this week? The experience can be an incident, an encounter, or a discovery about self, client, nursing professor, nursing profession.
- In what ways was it important?
- What questions did it raise for me personally? as a professional?
- How could I use what I learned from this experience in my nursing practice?

Discussion:
1. What makes an incident significant for a person?
2. How do people learn from critical incidents in their lives?
3. In what ways did you use critical thinking to develop the meaning of this incident?
4. In what ways can you use this exercise in future nursing practice?

aggressive. In the work setting, paychecks, performance appraisals, and disciplinary actions similarly influence learned behaviors. A behaviorist, however, would use a behavioral approach as the predominant teaching methodology.

Behavioral approaches favor a structured learning format. A behaviorist focuses on the learner's *behavior*. Feelings about the learning situation and the relationship between teacher and learner do not receive attention. Learning occurs by linking the behavior with the associated response through reinforcing rewards and punishments.

Originally developed by Thorndike and refined by Skinner (1971), the behaviorist approach believes that, given a stimulus in the environment, the learner responds. Taking this natural phenomenon as a basic concept, the behaviorist approach deliberately pairs stimuli and consequences to produce certain responses in the learner. Change results from stimulus–response conditioning. *Con-*

ditioning occurs when the learner repeatedly observes new behavior and the resulting consequences and begins to associate the two elements with each other. Early experiments with animals found that when an animal received an electrical shock when it went into a certain part of its cage, the animal "learned" to avoid going into that section. The behavioral response became so automatic that the animal continued the avoidance behavior even after the shock was no longer applied.

Although sometimes viewed as a mechanistic learning strategy, behavioral approaches prove highly effective with individuals who are unable to process needed instruction cognitively and with clients who are unmotivated. Children, adolescents, and mentally retarded and seriously mentally ill clients, all requiring skills training for very different reasons, respond better to behavioral learning strategies than to cognitive learning approaches (Curran and Monti, 1986).

Behavioral Concepts

Reinforcement

Learner responses are strengthened or weakened through reinforcement. *Reinforcement* refers to the consequences of performing identified behaviors. Skinner (1983) defines positive reinforcers as "any event that increases the probability of a response" and negative reinforcers as "any event that decreases the probability of a response." Adaptive behaviors are positively reinforced; maladaptive behaviors are weakened or extinguished through negative reinforcement. Learning is strengthened each time a positive response is received or the individual avoids a negative consequence. As the desired response is reinforced, it becomes more natural for the learner to perform the behavior, which in turn increases the frequency and consistency of the response. Through repeated practice and modeling, an individual begins to internalize and personalize the desired behavioral change. Behaviors are weakened when they are either ignored or associated with a punishment. Reinforcers should always be made contingent on successful performance of desired behavior.

Although reinforcement can be either positive or negative, positive reinforcement is more effective in most learning situations. *Positive reinforcement* is a reward of some kind for performing desired actions. Rewards can be tangible in the form of candy and privileges or they can be socially reinforcing such as praise or a smile. *Negative reinforcement* occurs when the withdrawal of a stimulus strengthens the tendency to behave in a certain way—for example, being able to eat in the cafeteria instead of on the unit. Negative reinforcers are used more frequently to extinguish undesirable social behaviors such as aggressiveness. Punishment as a reinforcer consists of presenting a negative consequence for undesired behavior—for example, denying of privileges or time outs. When using punishment to influence behavior, it is important to apply it with careful thought to its impact on the client and to avoid comments that blame or that can be perceived as sarcasm, scolding, or ridicule. Otherwise the client is likely to focus on the abrasive comment rather than on the punishment in relation to his or her behavior. Behaviors also are "extinguished," or eliminated, by ignoring their existence. The nurse can overlook certain behaviors and respond only to those that are desirable. Usually this process is slower than using specific reinforcers (Box 16–1).

The *Premack Principle* says that reinforcers should be of value to the client. It also is important that they be consistent with unit resources and policy. To be effective, the reinforcement should be small enough to satisfy, and not large enough to disincline the client to pursue earning more rewards for learning. For example, one or two M & M candies are more effective than a handful. Initially, this may seem to the nurse as insufficient reward, but it works better than larger rewards. Reinforcement immediately following successful performance is more effective initially in establishing the desired response. Once the

---

BOX 16–1
Types of Reinforcement

Concept	Purpose	Example
Positive reinforcer	Increases probability of behavior through reward.	Stars on a board, smiling, verbal praise, candy, tokens to purchase items.
Negative reinforcer	Increases probability of behavior by removing aversive consequence,	Restoring privileges when client performs desired behavior.
Punishment	Decreases behavior by presenting a negative consequence or removing a positive one.	Time outs, denial of privileges.
Extinguishing	Decreases behavior by ignoring it.	Disregards undesired behavior and ignores the person when behavior is performed.

behavior is learned, new content and accompanying reinforcement are needed. Behavioral methodologies require interest and progressive incentives to accomplish new behaviors in addition to the relationship between the stimulus and reinforcer. For example, the student would quickly lose interest in a curriculum that did not progressively challenge the learners to accomplish more sophisticated tasks, regardless of the rewards offered.

Modeling

Modeling refers to learning by observing another person performing a behavior. Nurses "model" behaviors both unconsciously and consciously in their normal conduct of nursing activities as well as in actual teaching situations. Bathing an infant, feeding an older person, and talking to a scared child in front of significant caregivers provide opportunities for informal teaching through modeling.

Shaping

Changing a person's behavior (learning response) is called *shaping.* To shape means to guide the appropriate behaviors. Reinforcement variables affecting shaping include timing, amount, and frequency of positive reinforcement. Generally, positive reinforcement given directly after the desired behaviors occur is most effective. Small amounts of reinforcement increase or shape the behavior in the desired direction.

Shaping as a behavioral strategy to increase learning is a common occurrence in our lives. The grades students receive in this course, the approval or disapproval of an instructor, written comments on care plans and papers, all help shape student behaviors by providing positive or negative reinforcement of their learning. In health care, encouraging client efforts reinforces learning and shapes future attempts.

Implementing a Behavioral Approach

To implement a behavioral approach, the nurse conducts a careful descriptive analysis of behaviors in need of change. These data form a baseline against which improvements can be measured. Examples of baseline behaviors might be the num-

ber of times a client fails to dress himself, participates in unit activities, makes a comment in group therapy, and "cheats" on his diet. Each behavior is described as a single behavior unit. The next step in the process is to define the problem in explicit behavioral terms. For example, "The client does not dress himself" or, "The client does not attend any unit activities." Once the nurse defines the problem in behavioral terms, it is important to share the findings with the client. Even if the client appears unable to comprehend fully or to appreciate the significance of the behavior in need of change, the nurse should take this action. A behavioral approach requires the cooperation of the client and a mutual understanding of the problem on the part of the nurse and the client. Active listening skills will alert the nurse to any concerns or barriers to implementation.

The next part of the process is identifying the behaviors necessary for the solution. Behavioral tasks are defined in specific, measurable, and achievable terms. Complex problem behaviors are broken down into simpler definitions, beginning with the simplest and most likely behavior to stimulate client interest. With some clients there is considerable input and negotiation related to the behavioral steps needed to meet goals. When this is not possible because of the client's condition or resistance, the nurse identifies the tasks in sequential order. The nurse defines specific consequences, positive and negative, for behavioral responses. Obviously the chosen reinforcers should be of value to the learner.

Once these steps are complete, the nurse establishes a learning contract with the client. With some clients the contract is written. The agreement describes the behavioral changes that are to occur, any conditions under which they are to occur, the reinforcement schedule, and the time frame. The learning contract serves as a formal commitment to the learning process. As behaviors change and problems are resolved, the contract may be rewritten for higher-level behaviors. Contracts spell out the responsibilities of each party and the consequences if behaviors are implemented or, in the case of undesired behaviors, persist.

At the beginning of each teaching session the nurse clearly outlines expected behaviors and the associated tangible or social reward the client can expect from completing them. If a homework assignment is given, the nurse reviews it with the client at the beginning of the session.

Training using a behavioral model can be broken down into simpler modules, designed so that the skills taught in new modules expand on skills previously taught. This strategy builds confidence and enhances self-esteem as the client achieves mastery over certain behaviors. The pride of accomplishing a task, receiving approval from others, and personally experiencing reinforcement of interpersonal skills has the added benefit of providing the participant with a different, more positive sense of self. Simple building steps also move the learner from the familiar to the unfamiliar.

Throughout the learning process the nurse rewards the client for each instance of expected behavior. Only positive efforts receive acknowledgment. It is important not to criticize the client because criticism reduces self-esteem. Furthermore, for some clients criticism may represent a form of reinforcement because they are receiving attention for their bad behavior. For some clients, criticism may be more important than the designated reinforcer. Instead, the client would be told, "This (skill) needs a little more work." One advantage of a behavioral approach is that it never considers the client as bad or unworthy.

CASE EXAMPLE

Peggy Braddock, a student nurse, was working with a seriously mentally ill client suffering with diabetes. All types of strategies were used to help the client take responsibility for collecting and testing her urine. Regardless of whether she was punished or pushed into performing these activities, the client remained resistant. To avoid taking her insulin injections, the client would take urine from the toilets or would simply refuse to produce a urine sample. Peggy decided to use a behavioral approach with her. She observed that the client liked sweets. Consequently, the reward she chose was artificially sweetened Jell-O cubes. To earn a Jell-O cube, the client had to bring her urine to Peggy. After some initial testing of Peggy's resolve to give the cubes only for appropriate behavior, the client began bringing her urine on a regular basis. Once this behavior was firmly established, Peggy began to teach the client how to give her own insulin. The reward remained the same. Peggy also used the time she spent with the client to build trust and acceptance. She wrote her plan in the Kardex, and other nurses used the same systematic approach with the client. Over time the client took full responsibility for testing her urine and for administering her own insulin.

Exercise 16–2 is designed to provide experience working with some of the common elements of a behavioral learning approach.

EXERCISE 16–2
Using a Behavioral Approach

Purpose: To help students gain an appreciation of the behavioral approach in the learning process.

Time: 45 minutes; the written part of the assignment may be done outside class.

Procedure:
Think about a relationship you have with one or more people that you would like to improve. The person you choose may be a friend, teacher, supervisor, peer worker, parent, or sibling.
1. Set a goal for improving that relationship.
2. Develop a problem statement as the basis for establishing your goal.
3. Identify the behaviors that will indicate you have achieved your goal.
4. Identify the specific behaviors you will have to perform in order to accomplish your goal.
5. Identify the personal strengths you will use to accomplish your goal.
6. Identify potential barriers to achieving your goal.
7. In groups of four or five students, present your goal-setting agenda, and solicit feedback.

Discussion:
1. Do any of your peers have ideas or information that might help you reach your goals?
2. Are there any common themes, strengths, or behaviors related to goal setting that are found across student groups?
3. What did you learn about yourself that might be useful in helping clients develop goals, using a behavioral approach?

TYPES OF FORMATS

Most health teaching is accomplished in one of three formats: informal one-to-one relationships, formal structured group sessions, and family conferences. The media provide mass health teaching, particularly in primary prevention, such as safe sex and drug abuse prevention commercials. Written instructions, videotapes, and informational pamphlets provide supplemental health teaching. Occasionally they are used when a helping professional is not available to provide the necessary instruction.

The process of health teaching involves informal as well as formal teaching strategies. Informal teaching takes place throughout the nurse–client relationship—in one-on-one teaching sessions and spontaneous family conferences. Individualized health care instructions allow people to feel more confident in caring for themselves in the hospital and community. With formal teaching strategies, the nurse uses a more structured format, usually in a group setting. The nurse may conduct scheduled teaching groups related to health care issues, for example, in medication and rehabilitation discharge groups. Many conferences incorporate formal and informal teaching strategies for providing families with information they will need to help the client recover and for answering the many questions families have about their loved ones in the clinical setting.

APPLICATIONS

CONSTRUCTING A TEACHING PLAN

Assessment

In the nurse's mind and in the questions asked of the client, the nurse structures a data base related to what the client is ready and able to learn. This information determines the staging of content and teaching interventions needed to help the client achieve mastery and well-being.

Conducting an Assessment Interview

An often missed advantage of taking time to do a good assessment is that from the start it actively engages the client. Checking out how much the client already knows aids the nurse in knowing the appropriate level and amount of knowledge the client needs to have as a participant and agent of self-care management.

Every assessment begins with an introduction. Even clients who seem unresponsive should be given the courtesy of knowing who is speaking to them and for what purpose. Following the introduction, the nurse makes a statement about the reason for asking questions and how they relate to the goals of the proposed health teaching. Otherwise the client may interpret the nurse's questions as intrusive.

> NURSE: There is some information that will be useful for you to know before you go home, but first I'd like to ask you a few questions that will help me better understand your needs.

The nurse gives the client permission to ask questions, and by introducing the idea that most people do have questions, the client feels freer to question data or ask for more explanation.

> NURSE: Many people have questions that come to mind when they are asked these questions. If you have any questions or thoughts about anything I am telling you, I would be glad to respond to them.

Confidentiality in health teaching situations is just as important as it is in other aspects of the nurse–client relationship. Clients and their families need to know that their private thoughts, feelings, and experiences will be shared only with the health professionals who are directly involved in the client's care. They need direct assurance that they or their contributions will not be talked about outside the teaching sessions.

In health teaching the nurse always begins by assessing the client's understanding of the issues. It is important to know if you are dealing with the right problem. Probing the learner's assumptions is an essential aspect of the assessment process. Assumptions represent interpreted realities of cause and effect relationships. For example, the client who believes that any drugs taken into the body are harmful will have a hard time learning about the insulin injection he needs to take every day. The client who thinks that if one tablet to relieve pain is good, two must be better, may not understand the need to take only one pill every four hours. Assumptions about the outcomes of health teaching are equally important. People are not cured as a result of health teaching. Realistic dialogue about what health teaching can and cannot do enhances cooperation.

A framework for the kinds of information the nurse will use as baseline data might include the following:

> What is happening in the client's life related to this situation?
> What does the client already know about his or her condition and treatment?
> In what ways is the client affected?
> In what ways are those intimately involved with the client affected?
> Is the client willing to take personal responsibility for seeking solutions?
> What goals would the client like to achieve?
> What will the client need to do in order to achieve those goals?
> What resources are available to the client and family that might affect the learning process?
> What barriers to learning exist?

The nurse analyzes the assessment data to determine gaps in knowledge or skills the client needs to function more effectively and the most suitable teaching strategies to accomplish learning goals. If others need to be included in the teaching process, this will become apparent to the nurse as he or she carefully asks questions about the ways the persons who are intimately involved with the client are affected by or will participate in the client's care. Attitudes present themselves as comments about how the current situation is affecting self and others.

It is best in a health assessment interview to begin with the least threatening questions and to move to more sensitive topics after establishing rapport with the client. For example, the nurse might first ask for information having to do with demographics. This would be followed by questions related to the client's perception of the current situation and its impact on his or her life. Sample questions might be as follows:

> "What has this illness been like for you?"
> "Have you had any previous experiences or heard any information about other people with similar health problems?"
> "Can you tell me what your doctor has told you about your treatment?"

Active listening and careful observation of the client's body language validate the information the client has provided or serve as food for further thought. It is important to get a clear sense of the whole—what is the nature of the client's learning needs, and what is needed to help the client achieve optimal well-being. Sometimes clients demonstrate impatience, anger, and disrespect when they are asked certain questions. This response usually represents a need that the nurse–client relationship has not met. The client may be scared and ambivalent about learning the facts. Above all, however, the client is entitled to respect and a caring attitude throughout the interview.

Assessment of the interest and involvement of family and friends is also important. Many highly effective teaching interventions do not produce the desired outcomes because the family does not really understand or fully support the client's efforts to change destructive lifestyle patterns. Successful implementation of a teaching plan includes evaluating the client's relationship with family and interpersonal networks, the family's general patterns of health care behaviors, expectations for the client, and knowledge of the client's condition. Health teaching with small children, confused adults, and clients whose severe physical handicaps affect their capacity to act as their own agents necessarily includes signicant caregivers from the onset.

At the conclusion of the assessment interview, it is important for the nurse to summarize important points. This strategy not only helps the client identify critical factors that are relevant to the learning process but also serves to validate any misinformation the nurse may have about the assessment data that has been collected.

In addition to the basic questions that guide the nurse throughout the health teaching process, the nurse can assess critical learning needs at time of discharge by focusing on the following questions (Rankin and Stallings-Duffy, 1991, p. 169):

1. What potential problems are likely to prevent a safe discharge?
2. What potential problems are likely to cause complications or readmission?
3. What prior kowledge or experience does the patient and family have with this problem?
4. What skills and equipment are needed to manage the problem at home?

Exercise 16–3 provides practice with collecting assessment data as a basis for establishing nursing diagnoses in health teaching.

EXERCISE 16–3
Role Play of an Assessment Interview

Purpose: To develop an appreciation for the many aspects of an assessment interview.

Time: 1 hour

Procedure:
1. Recall an experience that you, a member of your family, a friend, or an acquaintance had with an illness, requiring health treatment, that you would be willing to share with your class group. You should have enough information about the person to assume the general characteristics of the situation.
2. Using the factors identified in Chapter 15, role play the person you chose.
3. Pick a partner, and role play the part of the person as if you were a client.
4. Your partner should take on the role of the interviewer and use the questioning guidelines in the assessment interview to develop an appropriate assessment from the role play. (20 minutes)
5. Reverse the process with your partner so that each participant has an opportunity to experience each role. (20 minutes)

Discussion:
1. Which was the harder role to take, that of client or interviewer?
2. Were you surprised at any of the information that emerged?
3. After doing this exercise, what pieces of information do you think are most relevant?
4. What kinds of nursing diagnoses could you develop from this assessment information?
5. What implications for future nursing practice do you see from doing this exercise?

Developing a Nursing Diagnosis

Developing a specific nursing diagnosis as the foundation for health teaching helps direct the focus of the teaching that is to follow. A knowledge deficit obviously is one of the most salient reasons for implementing teaching interventions, but the deficit must be specifically identified so that the teaching process can be planned accordingly. It is as important for the nurse to know the reason for the deficit as it is to know the actual content of the knowledge deficit. Smith (1987) notes that nurses often teach too much detail about the fine medical or scientific points of a condition and too little about the side effects of medication, self-care management, and coping strategies. This situation occurs when the nature of the knowledge deficit is assumed rather than developed with the client.

The nursing diagnosis specifies whether the knowledge deficit is related to lack of exposure or experience, cultural values, misinformation, lack of interest or motivation, organic deficits, unfamiliarity with support resources in the community, or lack of confidence in the health care system. A knowledge deficit related to a lack of knowledge about signs and symptoms of hyper/hypoglycemia requires different content and strategies from a nursing diagnosis of "Knowledge deficit, related to how to prefill syringes and administer insulin."

Ineffective coping by individuals or families that is rooted in inadequate social or problem-solving skills responds to teaching interventions. Again, the nurse needs to know more about the the origin of ineffective coping skills. Potential for injury or violence, anxiety, noncompliance, alterations in parenting or family process, impaired home maintenance management, and self-care deficits are other examples of nursing diagnoses requiring health teaching interventions (Redmond and Thomas, 1985).

Planning

Developing Teaching Goals

Learning goals need to be clearly stated and appropriate to the client's condition, resources, and developmental and educational level (Redmond, 1988). Whenever possible, the client should have autonomy in choosing learning goals. In developing relevant goals, the nurse focuses on what the client and family want to know about a topic, as well as what they need to know. Health teaching goals should be comprehensive enough to provide needed information, yet narrow enough to be

BOX 16–2
Guidelines for Developing Effective Goals and Objectives

Goals and objectives:
- Should be linked to the nursing diagnosis.
- Should be specific and defined as measurable, behavioral outcomes.
- Should have a time frame specified for achievement.
- Should represent a plan of action for achieving identified outcomes.
- Should show a logical progression of actions with established priorities.
- Should be reviewed periodically and modified as conditions warrant.

achievable. Included in the development of outcome goals is a broad statement about what the client needs to achieve maximum health potential. "Expected outcome is dietary control of diabetes by time of discharge, 60 days" or, "The client will maintain a diastolic blood pressure below 90." The communication and relationship skills presented in previous chapters should guide the nurse and client in choosing goals that are realistic, adequate to meet the needs of the situation, within the client's capability, measurable, and able to be met

within a reasonable amount of time. Box 16–2 summarizes guidelines to use in the development of effective health teaching goals and objectives.

Part of an effective goal-setting process is the development of realistic ideas about how the client will achieve the goals chosen. For example, it may not be possible for a client, because of finances, motivation, learning, or resistance of others, to achieve what the nurse would like to see the client accomplish. Setting realistic goals prevents disappointment on the part of both nurse and client. Exercise 16–4 provides experience with developing relevant behavioral goals.

Establishing Priorities

It is important to establish what the client *needs* to know versus what it would be *nice* for the client to know (Rankin and Stallings-Duffy, 1991). If there is sufficient time, the teaching can be comprehensive and cover all bases. This is not always possible in critical care, in which practical considerations require the nurse to focus only on the most essential information. Consider the time element, age, experience, and condition of the client in deter-

EXERCISE 16–4
Developing Behavioral Goals

Purpose: To provide practical experience with developing teaching goals.

Time: 45 minutes

Procedure:
Establish a nursing diagnosis related to health teaching and a teaching goal that supports the diagnosis in each of the following situations:
1. Jimmy is a 15-year-old adolescent who has been admitted to a mental health unit with disorders associated with impulse control and conduct. He wants to lie on his bed and read Steven King novels. He refuses to attend unit therapy activities.
2. Maria, a 19-year-old single woman, is in the clinic for the first time because of cramping. She is seven months pregnant, and she has had no prenatal care.
3. Jennifer is overweight and desperately wants to lose weight. However, she can't walk past the refrigerator without stopping, and she finds it difficult to resist the snack machines at work. She wants a plan to help her lose weight and resist her impulses to eat.

Discussion:
1. What factors did you have to consider in developing the most appropriate diagnosis and teaching goals for each client?
2. In considering the diagnosis and teaching goals for each situation, what common themes did you find?
3. What differences in each situation contributed to variations in diagnosis and teaching goals? What contributed to these differences?
4. In what ways can you use the information in this exercise in your future nursing practice?

mining crucial elements. Key points should be written for future reinforcement of learning. In identifying critical information, consider strategies as well as content. For example, children should be given general information without going into detail, whereas adults usually want details. Clients who are from certain cultural groups require additional learning time. Clients who are experiencing a procedure for the first time need to have more detailed information than clients who require only follow-up information. In crisis situations the information given should be concrete and to the point and should be repeated. If time is limited, focusing on a specific topic is better than trying to cover a global subject.

Define the critical points you want to cover. Identify points the client and the client's family need to know and can use concretely in their situation. Everything else should be treated as extraneous data.

Incomplete information, on the other hand, can be dangerous. For example, a nurse instructed an 85-year-old man to keep his arm in an upright position following a treatment procedure. The nurse neglected to tell him that he could release his arm once the needle was securely in place. The man called his wife at 5 A.M. the next day to tell her he didn't think he could hold his arm in that position any longer. The man had been awake all night, his arm felt numb, and he was at his wits' end because of incomplete health teaching. It is better to overestimate what needs to be taught than to miss details.

Developing Measurable Objectives

Objectives describe the tasks needed to accomplish identified goals. They should be achievable, measurable, and related to specific health outcomes. To determine if an objective is achievable, consider the client's level of experience, educational level, resources, and motivation. Then define the specific learning objectives needed to achieve the health goal. The objectives, like the terminal health goal, should relate to the nursing diagnosis. For example, the nursing diagnosis might read, "Knowledge deficit related to diabetic diet." The expected outcome might be, "Dietary control of diabetes by time of discharge in 60 days." Each related learning objective should describe a single learning task.

Including the time frame by which each objective should be achieved reinforces commitment. Examples of learning objectives related to diet in diabetes control might include the following:

- The client will identify the purpose of a diabetic diet by the end of the first teaching session.
- The client will identify appropriate foods and serving sizes allowed on a diabetic diet by the end of the second teaching session.
- The client will demonstrate actions for urine testing for sugar at home by the third teaching session.
- The client will identify foods to avoid on the diabetic diet and the rationale for compliance by the fourth teaching session.
- The client will describe symptoms and actions to take for hyperglycemia and hypoglycemia by the end of the fifth teaching session.
- The client will develop a food plan for one week by discharge in two weeks.

Structuring the Environment

Suitable environmental conditions for health teaching are similar to those needed for other types of nurse–client interactions. The type of teaching format determines the most appropriate setting. Freedom from distractions is important regardless of the setting. It is difficult to pay attention when other conversations are taking place in the room or can be heard as a dull rumble from the next room. Teaching sessions conducted in a quiet, well-lighted area stress the importance of the learning endeavor. If health teaching is done in the home, all of those involved in the health care of the client should be included. Small children need to be cared for elsewhere, and the phone should not become a distraction. Stating these conditions before the teaching session begins prevents misunderstandings and unnecessary disturbances.

In hospital situations the client frequently is in bed or sitting in a chair. The learning environment is relatively informal, with the nurse actively involved in interpersonal contact with the client at eye level. Enough space for equipment and demonstration is critical.

Formal group teaching and family conferences should be structured in a space large enough to accommodate all participants. Ventilation is a component of the environment that can seriously restrict the learning process. A hot, stuffy room causes people to become drowsy. A room that is too cold interferes with concentration. Comfortable seating is necessary. Everyone involved should be able to hear and see the instructor. The client should be able to see all of the equipment and visual aids without strain. Space to practice and equipment to take notes give people a sense of purpose.

It is important to arrive a little early to set up the room. If the teaching plan calls for use of equipment or flip charts for visual aids, they need to be available and in working order. Nothing is more disconcerting than to be unable to integrate teaching aids and props into the discussion. Consistency and planning help provide a structured environmental framework for the teaching process and decrease instructor anxiety. Should the equipment not work, it is better to eliminate the planned teaching aid completely than to spend a portion of the teaching session trying to fix it.

Timing

Timing is essential in structuring the learning environment. As stated in Chapter 15, learning takes place only when the learner is ready. The client's condition or emotional attitudes may temporarily preclude teaching. Allowing the client enough time to process difficult data or to ventilate troublesome emotions may be critical before health teaching can begin. It is futile to engage in a serious teaching process when the client is unreceptive. This does not mean that the nurse abandons the teaching project, but simply that the "stage" must be set before the "play" can begin.

Timing governs what is to be taught. How much time is needed to learn this particular skill or body of knowledge? Complicated and essential skills need blocks of time and repeated practice with feedback. More time is needed for attitudinal changes. The elderly client may need more time than the younger client. Difficult concepts may need to be broken down into smaller segments, requiring a greater time allocation.

Timing also incorporates the time constraints of the nurse. In many settings it may be possible to give only "survival content" (Barr, 1989). If this is the case, the nurse needs to structure the learning session to include the key elements: What is the minimum information the client needs to know, and what kinds of activities are absolutely essential for the client and family to have knowledge of in meeting client health care needs? Health teaching can never be eliminated because the nurse lacks time, but it can be streamlined. Scheduling a definite block of time for teaching to occur is essential in high-paced health care situations. Otherwise other duties will always receive higher priority.

Timing is also a matter of sensitivity and compassion. What does the client need now? Not all teaching requires massive amounts of time. Simple, spontaneous health teaching takes minutes, yet it can be as effective as more formal teaching sessions. Careful observation of the client can prompt the nurse to use the moment to health teach. For example, in *Heartsounds,* the wife of a heart client provides a poignant example:

> A nurse came in while he was eating dinner. "Dr. Lear," she said, "after angiography the patients always seem to have the same complaints, and I thought you might want to know about them. It might help." (This was a good nurse. I didn't know it then, because I didn't know how scared he was. But later I understood that this was a damned good nurse.) "Thanks, it would help," he said. "It's mostly two things. The first is, they say that during the test, they feel a tremendous rush. It's very suddern and it can be scary."
>
> . . . Now he told the nurse, "Okay, the flush. And what's the other thing?"
>
> "It's . . . well, they say that at a certain point, they feel as though they are about to die. But that feeling passes quickly." He thanked her again. He was very grateful. (Lear, 1980)

Later, during the actual procedure, Dr. Lear remembers the nurse's words and finds comfort:

> Easy. Easy. You're supposed to feel this way. This is precisely what the nurse described. The moment you feel you are dying. (Lear, 1980)

This teaching intervention probably took less than two minutes, yet it was perceived by the client and his wife as extremely beneficial and healing. There are countless opportunities for this type of health teaching in clinical practice if the nurse consciously looks for them.

Timing considers the client's energy level and other factors. Certain times of the day are more favorable for learning. For many people, there is a dip in energy late in the evening or after lunch. This is not a good time for teaching. If possible, the client should choose the best time for health teaching. When this is not possible, the nurse needs to make every attempt to pick times when energy levels are high, the client is not distracted by other things, it is not visiting time, and the client is out of pain. Some people learn better in the morning; others are more alert in early evening. Careful observation of the client will help determine the most appropriate times for learning. Consider when the client is more talkative and interested in what is going on. A good time for formal one-to-one health teaching may be right after the client has showered or had a bed bath. The client is likely to feel relaxed and trusting of the nurse's interest.

Timing and length of sessions are important issues for learners handicapped by memory deficits, lack of insight, poor judgment, and limited problem-solving abilities. They respond best to a learning environment in which the content is presented in a consistent, concrete, and patient manner, with clear and frequent cues to action. Providing sufficient time to practice and offering encouragement frequently help elderly clients who have difficulty learning in sophisticated, fast-paced environments (Brillhart and Stewart, 1989; Check and Wurzbach, 1984).

Timing takes into account the need for trust. The nurse must take the time to establish a non-threatening interpersonal climate in which the client can feel comfortable. Teaching without feeling the interest of the nurse is instructional but not necessarily heard by the client. The client who feels the nurse has genuine interest in the person as well as the process is more likely to listen to instruction and accept reliable feedback. All of the factors identified in Box 16–3 are important aspects of timing in health teaching.

Selecting Appropriate Content

Essential content in all teaching plans includes information about the health care problem, risk factors, and self-care skills the client will need to manage at home. Attitudes that will affect the

---

> **BOX 16–3**
> **Factors Involved in Timing**
>
> Client readiness.
> Time needed to learn skill or body of knowledge.
> Possible need for attitude change by client.
> Time contraints of nurse.
> Client priorities about information or skill.
> Client's energy level.
> Atmosphere of trust.

---

client's adjustment and compliance with treatment require attention. Unless the nurse includes in patient education effective teaching strategies that meet the individualized needs of the client, the needed changes in behavior may not occur (Smith, 1987).

In addition to selecting appropriate content relevant to the personal, developmental, and cultural learning needs of the client, the nurse should consider the impact on the client of the subject being taught. Some topics are more acceptable and more easily learned than others. Is the content complicated or likely to make the client uncomfortable? If so, the nurse must be able to organize it in such a way that the client can relate to it. Clients learn more effectively when they understand the goals of the learning session and when the content helps them connect new knowledge to what they already know. Advance organizers, consisting of cue words related to more complex data, help clients anticipate and respond to more complex information in their own minds.

Most teaching in health care settings is not a one-time event because usually not everything can be taught in one session. People need to have time to process new information and to think about it. Questions that did not occur during the teaching session arise during this thinking period. In selecting appropriate content, the nurse needs to have an overall picture of the connections between past, current, and future content. The content needs to be organized so that the client can logically follow its progression. In developing content, the nurse should have an internal dialogue that continually asks, "What happens next?"

To make content comprehensible to the client is an art. Part of the nurse's role as educator is to help the client establish a relationship with the content and become actively involved in learning it. Content that builds on the person's experiences, abilities, interests, motivation, and skills is more likely to engage the learner's attention. Attention to the reading level of clients helps ensure that the pamphlet can be read. Clients with perceptual difficulty or an inability to speak can sometimes respond to picture boards and line drawings. Large print pamphlets and audiotapes are learning aids for those with sight problems (Smith, 1987).

Selecting Appropriate Teaching Methods

No one teaching strategy can meet the needs of all clients. Recognizing distinctive differences in client learning needs is critical in choosing the most appropriate teaching strategies. Moreover, the nurse often continually has to adjust teaching strategies to meet client needs as their medical conditions change. Preoperation teaching strategies should differ from those used immediately after the operation. The amount of information given, the pace of the teaching, and the level of learner involvement necessarily reflect the client's physical condition and learning needs in each time frame (Fig. 16–1).

The nature of the subject matter itself often forms the rationale for selecting one teaching method over another. For example, the strategies used to teach a client how to give insulin would be quite different from those used to instruct a person about the nature of diabetes or to recognize the signs and symptoms of hyperglycemia.

Instructional strategies should be appropriate to the learning needs of the client and clearly linked to the goals of the lesson. There are many ways the nurse can meet these requirements. For example, the nurse can provide one-to-one instructional or coaching sessions, family conferences, or group sessions on various topics. The nurse has the responsibility to make sure that what is learned is factually and procedurally correct. It is important for the nurse to monitor the client's understanding of the content through a variety of means. Providing feedback and adjusting content as needed help the nurse use instructional time more effectively.

The client's preferred learning style also affects the selection of teaching strategies. Characteristics of learning activity preferences incorporating the NLP priniciples presented in Chapter 9 are given in Box 16–4.

It is best to use a variety of teaching strategies to meet different learning needs. For example, mothers respond positively to posters showing normal infant features and development because they can see as well as hear that head molding and skin rashes are typical.

Implementation

A key element to successful health teaching is an enthusiastic presentation that demonstrates a thorough knowledge of the subject matter, a keen

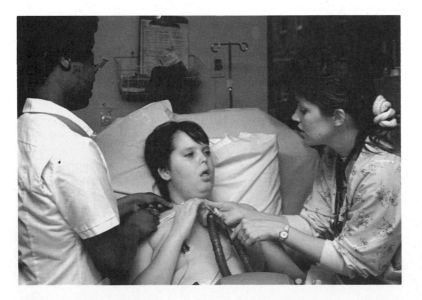

Figure 16–1 Teaching should reflect the client's physical condition and learning needs. (Courtesy of the University of Maryland Medical System)

BOX 16–4
Characteristics of Different Learning Styles

Visual	*Auditory*	*Kinesic*
Learns best by seeing.	Learns best with verbal instructions.	Learns best by doing.
Likes to watch demonstrations.		Hands-on involvement.
Organizes thoughts by writing them down.	Likes to walk things through.	Needs action and likes to touch, feel.
Needs detail.	Detail not as important.	Loses interest with detailed instructions.
Looks around; examines situation.	Talks about situation—pros, cons.	Tries things out.

understanding of the client's learning needs, and a genuine interest in the client. Effective teaching involves a healthy exchange of information plus an opportunity to ask questions and to receive feedback. Purposeful learning requires that the learner be actively involved in the process and that both participants value the opportunity to learn more about themselves.

Sequencing the Learning Experience

Sequencing the information in a logical way provides a guide for the learner to follow that makes sense and makes information easier to comprehend. Presentations in which ideas logically relate to one another are more effective. It is confusing to include too many ideas in a statement, particularly if they do not relate well to each other.

The nurse sets the stage for the learning process by giving the client and family a simple overview of what will be taught and why the information will be important to them. This is followed by the body of the content. If the material is extensive, it can be broken down into smaller learning segments. For example, diabetic teaching might be addressed as five topics to include:

- Basic pathophysiology of diabetes.
- Diet.
- Pharmacology and drug administration.
- Recognition and treatment of hyper/hypoglycemia.
- Care of skin and feet.

It is important to allow enough time for questions. A strong closing that summarizes major points reinforces the learning process. Exercise 16–5 provides practice with developing a mini-teaching plan.

Evaluation

Documentation of the health teaching and learning outcomes is essential. The Joint Commission of Health Care Organizations (JCHCO) requires documentation of patient teaching. Accurate and thorough charting of the learning process is critical. Notes about the initial assessment should be detailed, comprehensive, and objective. Included in the documentation should be assessment data, the nursing diagnosis, objectives, teaching strategies, actions taken, and outcomes. For example, the nursing documentation for health teaching about diabetic control might include the following:

> 12/15/92 Blood glucose check normal. Vital signs stable. Client on insulin for 10 years; has difficulty prefilling syringes. Lives with son who works. Nursing diagnosis: Knowledge deficit related to prefilling syringes. Nurse prefilled syringes, wrote out med schedule, and discussed in detail with client. Client receptive to medication instruction, but may have difficulty with insulin prefill secondary to poor vision. Instructed client on medications, signs and symptoms to report to MD, diet and safety measures. Spoke with son regarding medication supervision. M. Haggerty, RN

Note in this example how observations of learner needs and learner responses must be documented carefully. The nurse records subjective as well as objective learner responses. Outcomes should relate to the nursing diagnosis and identified objectives. In this example the nurse's actions are an accurate assessment of the client's unique learning needs, and referrals are documented.

Accurate documentation also serves another critical purpose in health teaching. It helps ensure continuity and prevents duplication of teaching efforts. The client's record becomes a vehicle of

EXERCISE 16–5
Developing Teaching Plans

Purpose: To provide practice with developing teaching plans.

Time: May be done as a homework exercise.

Procedure:
1. Develop a mini-teaching plan for one of the client situations listed below.
2. Use guidelines presented in Chapters 15 and 16 in the development of your teaching plan.
3. Include the following data: a brief statement of client learning needs, a list of related nursing diagnoses in order of priority. For one nursing diagnosis, develop a long-term goal, short-term learning objectives, a teaching time frame, content to be covered, teaching strategies, and methods of evaluation.

Situations
1. Jim Dolan feels stressed and is requesting health teaching on stress management and relaxation techniques.
2. Adrienne Parker is a newly diagnosed diabetic. Her grandfather had diabetes.
3. Vera Carter is scheduled to have an appendectory in the morning.
4. Marion Hill just gave birth to her first child. She wants to breast-feed her infant, but she doesn't think she has enough milk.
5. Barbara Scott wants to lose weight.

communication, informing other health care workers what has been taught and what areas need to be addressed in future teaching sessions. This is important for two reasons. First, the client can lose interest or become confused when the same information is repeated or is given in such a different way that the client is unsure which is "the right information." Second, since many insurance carriers will not pay for parallel teaching, nurses need to share their teaching with other members of the interdisciplinary health team. This helps to avoid additional costs for the client and prevent complicating the client's life with insurance company questions about claim information.

SUGGESTED TEACHING STRATEGIES

Proceeding from Simple to Complex

People learn best when there is a logical flow and building of information from simple to complex. Information that builds on previous knowledge and experience is even better. For example, taking a blood pressure, giving an injection, and engaging a client in conversation are routine for a senior nursing student. For the beginning student, they can be overwhelming. Think what it would be like if the complex tasks a senior nursing student performs were not preceded by development of simpler skills first. The same holds true for client learning.

Repeating Key Concepts

To implement a successful teaching plan, the nurse must provide the client with appropriate supports to learn the desired material. Review new information frequently. If possible, have more than one session for each learning segment. Although it may feel redundant, repeating yourself and restating key elements help the client process material by going over it in his mind. Allowing extra time for the client to talk about and do return demonstrations of tasks reinforces learning.

Another strategy is to ask the client to repeat the instructions in his own words and to describe for the nurse the actions that need to be taken if the instructions cannot be followed exactly or fail to produce the desired effect. Asking the client to repeat as you go along reinforces each piece of information and eliminates the problem of delivering a comprehensive teaching plan only to discover that the client lost your train of thought after the first few sentences.

Giving Frequent Feedback

Feedback is a continuous process in health teaching. Giving feedback about learning performance informs clients about their progress and points the way to further learning. As students, it is easy to appreciate the importance of feedback in the learning process. Think what it would be like if you did not receive performance evaluations regularly and had no comments on your written work. Research draws a similar conclusion. In a research study of factors considered necessary to a successful patient teaching program on medications, clients identified feedback as an essential element (Mullen and Green, 1985) .

To be effective, teaching feedback should be descriptive, not evaluative. It is important to provide the client with feedback about those things the person does well as much as about the behaviors that need modification. Having the nurse validate behaviors that facilitate, support, or improve his or her actions can help a person learn just as much as descriptive feedback on negative actions. One way of doing this is to describe all of the behaviors that contributed to an outcome rather than selectively choosing only those in need of alteration. Focused on the client's behavior rather than the person, feedback should concern only those behaviors capable of being modified and related to health teaching.

Effective feedback is honest and based on concrete data. It is important to differentiate between observational data, or those behaviors that could be observed or heard by anyone, and personal interpretations or conclusions. Focus on the "what" and not the "why" of behaviors. Determining motivation is a guessing game. Many clients respond better to teaching feedback that allows them to explore alternatives rather than a direct solution. The nurse's solution, brilliant though it may be, may not work for a client because the problem, as the client perceives it, is different. Other times the client and nurse view a problem similarly, but the client is aware of flaws in the nurse's proposal that would make it difficult for the client to implement it. When the nurse offers a feedback solution that is not tentative or designed to stimulate further discussion, it diminishes the autonomy of the other person.

Feedback given as soon as possible after observation is more likely to be accurately reported, and hence more readily accepted by the client. Behavioral statements on a continuum (i.e., "You need a little more practice" or, "You are able to draw up the medication OK, but you need a little more work with selecting sites") are more effective than absolute statements such as, "You still are not doing this correctly." Exercise 16–6 provides practice with giving teaching feedbacks.

There also are many forms of indirect feedback to reinforce learning. For example, nodding, smil-

---

EXERCISE 16–6
Giving Teaching Feedback

Purpose: To give students perspective and experience in giving usable feedback.

Time: 45 minutes

Procedure:
Divide the class into working groups of three or four students.
1. Give a three-minute sketch of some aspect of your current learning situation that you find difficult—for example, writing a paper, speaking in class, coordinating study schedules, or studying certain material.
2. Each person in turn offers one piece of usable, informative feedback to the presenter. In making suggestions, use the guidelines on feedback given in this chapter.
3. Feedback suggestions are placed on a flip chart or chalkboard.

Discussion:
1. What were your thoughts and feelings about the feedback you heard in relation to resolving the problem you presented to the group?
2. What were your thoughts and feelings in giving feedback to each presenter?
3. Was it harder to give feedback in some cases than in others? in what ways?
4. What common themes emerged in your group?
5. In what ways can you use the self-exploration about feedback in this exercise in teaching conversations with clients?

ing, sharing information about the process and experiences of others are all ways of indirectly reinforcing learning. Acknowledging the contributions of participants in group learning provides encouragement for active participation. Repeating client statements and actions that can be used by the individual as well as other members in group learning helps reiterate key concepts. Another way of providing feedback indirectly is by encouraging clients to keep a diary or journal of their progress. This is a self-directed way of monitoring progress that the client can use after the formal teaching sessions end. Journals also are useful as a foundation that both nurse and client can use for follow-up discussions. Sometimes clients are able to write what they cannot bring themselves to say in a face-to-face conversation. Once written, the material seems easier to discuss.

Linking Ideas

Sometimes the reason people don't understand instructions is that the nurse fails to make the necessary transitions that link one idea to another. Johnson notes that "being complete and specific seems so obvious, but often people do not communicate the frame of reference they are using, the assumptions they are making, the intentions they have in communicating or the leaps in thinking they are making" (quoted in Flanagan, 1990). Directions may seem simple and obvious to the nurse, but clients may have difficulty with elementary material simply because the information is new to them. Transition statements can help the client see how the ideas fit together.

Example
Statement A

> NURSE: The doctor wants you to take a half a pill for the first week and increase the dose to a full pill after the first week. You should call him if you experience any side effects such as nausea or headaches.

Statement B

> NURSE: This medication works well for most people, but some people tolerate it better than others. The doctor would like you to take a half a pill for the first week so that your system has a chance to adapt to it and the doctor can see how you are

responding before you take the full dose. If you have no side effects, he would like you to increase the dose to a full pill after the first week. The most common side effects are nausea or headaches. They don't occur with most people, but each person's response to medication is a little different. He would like you to call him if you notice these side effects.

Although the second statement takes a little longer, it includes clear transitions between ideas that will make it easier for the client to remember the instructions. Including the transitions helps the client to see the rationale for the change in dosage, and because it seems logical there is a greater probability of compliance.

If the material is abstract or difficult to understand, defining the terms and linking the words with specific examples helps make the transition. Although the nurse uses appropriate language and may be quite clear in presenting information, a concrete example helps fix the idea in the client's mind. Again, think of your own learning process and how having concrete examples makes the learning come alive for you.

Coaching the Client

Webster's Ninth New Collegiate Dictionary defines *coaching* as "instructing or training, for example, of a player in fundamental rules and strategies of a game." Clients in health care settings need coaching through unfamiliar and often painful procedures. Coaching is particularly effective in helping clients achieve mastery in self-care and control over potentially frightening processes. In most cases, the nurse will teach problem-solving skills by "coaching" the client.

Coaching involves a number of skills presented in this chapter, which are displayed in Figure 16–2. It is a teaching strategy that fully respects the client's autonomy in developing appropriate solutions because the client is always in charge of the pace and direction of the learning. In addition to giving appropriate information, coaching involves taking the client step by step through the procedure or activities. It is a mutual dialogue in which clients also make suggestions about their care.

Essential components of the coaching process are helping the client to take the primary responsibility for actions to achieve health goals and

Figure 16–2 The Nurse's Role in Coaching Clients

explaining what to expect. To coach a client successfully, the nurse must know and appreciate the client as an individual. This helps the nurse to know what information the client needs and how best to guide a particular client in taking charge of a situation. Sometimes the coaching a client needs relates to negotiating a complex health care system or developing better ways to get personal needs met. In many cases, successful coaching involves helping the client understand the political factor and how to negotiate it as well as actual information. The secret of successful coaching is to provide enough information to help the client take the next step. Self-directed adult clients can make effective use of this coaching strategy. It would not be appropriate, however, for a small child or a learner who is not self-directed. Exercise 16–7 provides practice with coaching as a teaching strategy.

EXERCISE 16–7
Coaching Exercise
Identify the steps you would use to coach clients in each of the following situations. Use Figure 16–2 as a guide to develop your plan.
1. A client returning from surgery with pain medication, ordered as needed.
2. A client newly admitted to a cardiac care unit.
3. A client with a newly inserted IV for antibiotic medications.
4. A child and his parents coming for a preoperative visit to the hospital before surgery.
Share your suggestions with your classmates.

Discussion:
1. What were some of the different coaching strategies you used with each of these clients?
2. In what ways were your coaching strategies similar to or unlike those of your classmates?
3. How could you use the information you gained from this exercise to improve the quality of your helping?

Using Clear Language

Language has the potential to distort meaning as well as to clarify it. In health education the language used to convey meaning is critical to understanding. It is important to remember that many words have several meanings. For example, the word "cold" can refer to temperature, an illness, an emotional tone, or a missed opportunity. Providing information with abstract and vague language leaves the learner wondering what the nurse really meant. For example, "Call the doctor if you have any problems" can mean many different things. "Problems" can refer to side effects of the medication, a return of symptoms, problems with family acceptance, changed relationships, and even alterations in self-concept. The best way to provide information and instructions is to use behavioral descriptions.

To be clear, the nurse's instructions should include:

- Who is involved.
- The specific behaviors.
- The exact circumstances.

Using a behavioral description format allows the nurse to identify whether the client alone is involved, the precise nature of the problem or instructions, and in what circumstances the behavior occurs or needs to occur. Examples of clear statements the nurse might use include these:

"If you should develop a headache or feel dizzy in the next 24 hours, call the emergency room doctor."

"You may find that you feel as though you want to take a drink when you are out of the hospital. If this occurs, you should call the hospital number immediately."

Using Visual Aids

Visual aids are useful tools, but they should be viewed as supplemental and not as the primary mode of instruction. They help imprint concepts in people's minds through concrete visual images. Simple images and few words work better than more complex visual aids (Huntsman and Binger, 1981). The visual images should complement and reinforce the words. Visual aids are particularly relevant in explaining complex anatomy. For example, the nurse might show a client a skeleton model to explain a collapsed disc. A chart or model showing the heart might help another client understand the anatomy and physiology of a heart disorder. Cartoons can show a relationship concept more clearly than words alone (Fig. 16–3).

Films and videotapes are especially useful in teaching clients with limited reading skills. Following the film or videotape discussion with the nurse helps correct misinterpretations and emphasize pertinent points.

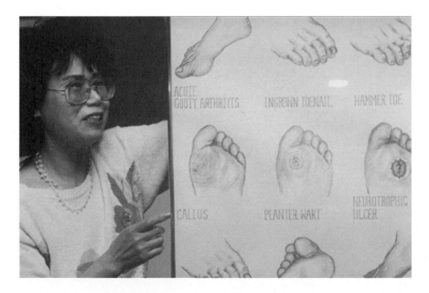

Visual aids provide concrete images that help a client remember essential information. (Courtesy of the University of Maryland School of Nursing)

Figure 16–3 Cartoons can show a relationship concept more clearly than words alone. PEANUTS reprinted by permission of UFS, Inc.

Using Advance Organizers

Another way of sequencing and organizing material is the use of a *mnemonic,* defined as a key letter, word, or phrase to help organize important ideas. For example, the nurse might use the word "diabetes" to help a client remember key concepts about diabetes.

- D = Diet.
- I = Infections.
- A = Administering medication.
- B = Basic pathophysiology.
- E = Eating schedules.
- T = Treatment for hyper/hypoglycemia.
- E = Exercise.
- S = Symptom recognition.

Each letter stands for one of the concepts needed for comprehensive diabetic education. Taken together, the client has a useful tool for remembering *all* of the important concepts. A mnemonic can be letters of the alphabet, places, words—in fact, any associations that have personal or group meanings for the persons developing them. Nursing students can use mnenomics to help them remember key points. The word association fosters identification in much the same way that linking new information to previously learned information does. For example, the 4 Fs (fat, forty, female, family history) can help students remember risk factors for gall bladder disorder. The basic food pyramid provides a way of categorizing food groups everyone needs to include in the diet for good nutrition. Developing mnenomics can be fun and creative. Exercise 16–8 provides an oppor-

tunity to see the value of mnemonics in learning content.

TEACHING APPLICATIONS IN DIFFERENT SETTINGS

Group Presentations

Preparation and practice can ensure that your presentation is clear, concise, and well spoken. Practice giving the information in a natural manner, particularly if the information is emotionally laden for you, the client, or both. If your teaching includes visual aids or equipment, developing an ease with incorporating them into your teaching process will make it easier and you will appear more confident.

In a group presentation, you also will need to establish rapport with your audience. This means being receptive to the learner's style, making courteous observations, and initiating discussion appropriately. A quote at the beginning that captures the meaning of the presentation or a humorous opening gets the audience's attention. It is important to make eye contact immediately and to continue to do so throughout the teaching session. Extension of eye contact to all participants communicates acceptance and inclusion. General content statements are strengthened by the careful use of specific examples. Citing a specific problem and the ways another person dealt with it gives general statements credibility. Repeating key points and summarizing them again at the conclusion of the session will reinforce learning.

To be a good teacher one must also be a good

EXERCISE 16–8
Using Advance Organizers as a Teaching Strategy

Purpose: To help students understand the value of verbal cues (advance organizers) in health teaching.

Time: 30 minutes

Procedure:
1. Identify a segment of course content you need to know or a skill you need to learn and develop a mnemonic to organize and help you remember it.
2. Write down the verbal cue and explicitly what it stands for in helping you remember important information.
3. Share your results with your classmates in the group.

Discussion:
1. In what ways was it easy or difficult for you to develop your mnemonic?
2. What benefits or difficulties do you envision in using it?
3. Do mnemonics work better for some types of information than others?
4. In what ways can you use the insights you gained in your future nursing practice?

listener. Asking questions confidently and thoughtfully as they relate to your understanding of participant circumstances conveys interest in the client's learning needs. Giving answers that are direct and clear reinforces the presentation. It is important for the nurse to anticipate questions and be on the alert for blank looks.

No matter how good a teacher you are, you will from time to time experience the "blank look." When this occurs it is appropriate to ask, "Does anyone have any questions about what I just said?" or "This content is difficult to grasp; I wonder if you have any questions or concerns about what I have said so far?"

If you don't know the answer to a question, it is important not to bluff or offer incomplete informa-

tion. It is appropriate to say, "That is a good question. I don't have the answer to it at this moment, but I will get back to you with the answer." Sometimes in a group presentation another person will have the required information and with encouragement will share it. Group formats offer a rich learning resource in the thoughts and experiences of other members.

Follow-up pamphlets and written instructions can provide additional reinforcement. Making sure the information is accurate and complete, easy to understand, and logical is essential. Sometimes it is useful to have a nonprofessional who is unfamiliar with the topic review written instructions for clarity and logic before using them with clients. Asking clients for feedback also helps. Exercise 16–9 provides an opportunity to practice health teaching in a group setting.

Family Conferences

Family conferences are used as teaching sessions during discharge planning. Topics commonly covered in discharge planning include information about the nature of the illness or injury, a summary of individual progress in meeting treatment goals, and information about care of the client once the client leaves the hospital. Reinforcement of teaching about medications and referrals to community health and support groups are also a part of the teaching session. For example, there may have to be some modifications in medication

EXERCISE 16–9
Group Health Teaching

Purpose: To provide practice with presenting a health topic in a group setting.

1. Plan a 15–20-minute health presentation on a health topic of interest to you, including teaching aids and methods for evaluation.

Suggested Topics

Nutrition	Drinking and driving
High blood pressure	Dental care
Weight control	Mammograms
Safe sex	

2. Present your topic to your class group.

schedules to fit individual and family lifestyles. The family should have ample opportunity to ask questions and to have them answered completely and honestly. Written instructions and a postdischarge phone number support learning and provide necessary transitional support for client and family (Cagan and Meier, 1983) .

Health Teaching in the Home

As health care moves to community-based care, with a case mix of unstable, acutely ill home care clients and constrained funding for community home-based care, skilled health teaching becomes an increasingly important component of health care delivery. Although the principles of health teaching remain the same, regardless of setting, implemention requires modification in home care settings (Johnson and Jackson, 1989). Teaching outcomes for clients in their homes relate to increased knowledge, increased functioning, and better self-care management. In addition to content knowledge about the client's condition, the nurse must have a working knowledge of community resources. An understanding of Medicare, Medicaid, and other insurance, including regulations, required documentation, and reimbursement schedules, is factored into the management of health care teaching in home health care.

The community health/home care nurse works alone. Consequently, there is a need for creativity as well as competence in providing health teaching. The nurse must be able to select from a number of existing resources and create new ones through novel uses of family and community support systems.

In home care the nurse is a guest in the client's home. Part of the teaching assessment includes appraisal of the home environment, family supports, and resources as well as client needs. Teaching aids and strategies available in the hospital setting may have to be set aside and the reality of the client's environment incorporated into the health teaching. But in many ways the home offers a teaching laboratory unparalleled in the hospital. The nurse can actually "see" the improvisations in equipment and technique that are possible in the home environment. Family members may have ideas that the nurse would not have thought of, which can make care easier. It is more natural for

the client to replicate teaching in the environment in which it was initially taught.

The nurse should call before going to the client's home. This is common courtesy, and it protects the nurse's time if the client is going to be out. The tools of the trade are housed in a bag the nurse carries into the home. Before setting the bag down on a table, the nurse should spread a clean paper to protect both the client's table and the bag. It is important for the nurse to talk clients through procedures and dressing changes in much the same way as was done in the hospital. The nurse models appropriate behaviors, for example, washing her hands in the bathroom sink before touching the client. Simple strategies, such as not washing one's hands in the kitchen sink where food is prepared, encourage the client to do likewise.

Teaching in home care settings is rewarding. Frequently the nurse is the client's only visitor. Other family members often display a curiosity and willingness to be a part of the learning group, particularly if nurses actively use their knowledge of the home environment to make suggestions about needed modifications.

Teaching in home care has to be short term and comprehensive since most insurance companies will provide third-party reimbursement only for intermittent, episodic care. Nurses need to plan teaching realistically so that it can be delivered in the shortest time possible. Content needs to reflect specific information the client and family need to provide immediate effective care for the client—*nothing more and nothing less.* Sometimes it is tempting to include everything the learner needs to know. Since there are so many regulations regarding the length and scope of skilled nursing interventions imposed by third-party reimbursement guidelines, the nurse needs to pay careful attention to health teaching content and formats.

SUMMARY

Chapter 16 describes the nurse's role in health teaching. Three theoretical frameworks, client-centered teaching, critical thinking, and behavioral approaches, guide the nurse in implementing health teaching. The nursing process provides an organizing structure. Assessment for purposes of constructing a teaching plan centers on three areas: What does the client already know? What is important for the client to know? What is the client ready to know? Essential content in all teaching plans includes information about the health care problem, risk factors, and self-care skills needed to manage at home. No one teaching strategy can meet the needs of all individual clients. The learning needs of the client will help define relevant teaching strategies. Several teaching strategies, such as coaching, use of mnemonics, and visual aids, are described. Repetition of key concepts and frequent feedback make the difference between simple instruction and teaching that informs. Documentation of the learning process is essential. The client's record becomes a vehicle of communication, informing other health care workers what has been taught and what areas need to be addressed in future teaching sessions.

REFERENCES

American Nurses Association (1982). Professional Nursing Standards. New York, National League for Nursing.

American Nurses Association (1985). Professional Code of Ethics. New York, National League for Nursing.

Barr W (1989). Teaching patients with life-threatening illnesses. Nursing Clinics of North America 24(3):639.

Brillhart B, Stewart A (1989). Education as the key to rehabilitation. Nursing Clinics of North America. 24(3):675.

Brookfield S (1986). Understanding and Facilitating Adult Learning. San Francisco, Jossey Bass.

Cagan J, Meier P (1983). Evaluation of a discharge planning tool for use with families of high risk infants. Journal of Obstetrical, Gynecological and Neonatal Nursing 12:275–281.

Check JF, Wurzbach ME (1984). How elders view learning. Geriatric Nursing 1:37–39.

Collier S (1992). Mrs. Hixon was more than the C.V.A. in 251. RN '92 62–64.

Crawford Long Memorial Hospital (1992). Patient Rights Statement. Atlanta, GA, Crawford Long Hospital pamphlet.

Creasia J, Parker B (1991). Foundations of Professional Nursing Practice. St. Louis, Mosby.

Curran J, Monti P (ed.) (1986). Social Skills Training. Washington Square, NY, New York University Press.

Flanagan L (1990). Survival Skills in the Workplace: What Every Nurse Should Know. Kansas City, MO, American Nurses Association.

Holyoak J, Koh K (1987). Surface and structural similarity in analogical transfer. Memory and Cognition 15:332–340.

Huntsman A, Binger J (1981). Communicating Effectively. Wakefield, MA, Nursing Resources.

Johnson, quoted in Flanagan L (1990). Survival Skills in the Workplace: What Every Nurse Should Know. Kansas City, MO, American Nurses Association.

Johnson E, Jackson J (1989). Teaching the home care client. Nursing Clinics of North America. 24(3): 687–693.

Lear MW (1980). Heartsounds. New York, Pocket Books (Simon & Schuster), pp. 120–121.

Mezirow J, and associates (1990). Fostering Critical Reflection in Adulthood: A Guide to Transformative and Emancipatory Learning. San Francisco, Jossey Bass.

Mullen P, Green L (1985). Meta-analysis points the way toward more effective teaching. Promotion of Health. 6:6–8.

Rankin SH, Stallings-Duffy KL (1991). Patient Education: Issues, Principles and Guidelines. Philadelphia, Lippincott.

Redmond BK (1988). The Process of Patient Education (6th ed.). St. Louis, Mosby.

Redmond BK, Thomas S (1985). Patient teaching. In Bulchek G, McCloskey J (eds.) (1985), Nursing Interventions. Philadelphia, W. B. Saunders.

Rogers C (1983). Freedom to Learn for the '80's. Columbus OH: Merrill.

Saylor CR (1990). Reflection and professional education: Art, science and competency. Nurse Educator 15(2):8–11.

Skinner BF (1971). Beyond Freedom and Dignity. New York, Knopf.

Smith CE (1987). Patient Education: Nurses in Partnership with Other Health Professionals. Orlando, FL, Grune & Stratton.

Webster's Ninth New Collegiate Dictionary (1985). Springfield, MA, Merriam-Webster.

SUGGESTED READINGS

Buckwater KC, Kerfoot KM (1982). Teaching patients self-care: A critical aspect of psychiatric discharge planning. Journal of Psychosocial Nursing and Mental Health Services. 20:15.

Honan S, Krsnak G, Peterson D, Torkelson R (1988). The nurse as patient educator: Perceived responsibilities and factors enhancing role development. Journal of Continuing Education in Nursing, 19(1):33–37.

Jimenez R. Educating minorities about AIDS: Challenges and strategies. Family and Community Health. 10(3):115–125.

Kick E (1989). Patient teaching for elders. Nursing Clinics of North America. 24(3):681–686.

Kim KK (1986). Response time and health care learning of elderly patients. Research in Nursing and Health Care. 9:233–236.

Pavlish C (1987). A model for situational patient teaching. Journal of Continuing Education in Nursing. 18(5):163–167.

Pease RA (1984). Praise elders to help them learn. Journal of Gerontological Nursing. 11:16–20.

Ruzicki D (1989). Realistically meeting the educational needs of hospitalized acute and short-stay patients. Nursing Clinics of North America. 24(3):629.

Severson De Muth J (1989). Patient teaching in the ambulatory setting. Nursing Clinics of North America. 24(3):645.

PART IV

RESPONDING TO SPECIAL NEEDS

Chapter 17

Communicating with Clients Experiencing Communication Deficits

ELIZABETH ARNOLD • KATHLEEN BOGGS

OUTLINE

Basic Concepts

TYPES OF DEFICITS
    Hearing loss
    Blindness
    Speech and language deficits
    Serious mental illness
    Environmental deprivation

Applications

COMMUNICATION STRATEGIES WITH:
    Hearing loss
    Blind clients
    Deaf/blind clients
    Clients having speech and language difficulty
    Seriously mentally ill clients
    Clients experiencing environmental deprivation

Summary

OBJECTIVES

At the end of the chapter, the student will be able to:

1. Identify common communication deficits.

2. Describe nursing strategies for communicating with clients experiencing communication deficits.

As Hubert Humphrey was fond of saying, the moral test of a society is how well it treats people in the dawn of life (children), people in the twilight of life (the elderly), and people in the shadows of life (the poor, the sick, the handicapped). We in the field of communication still have far to go in our contribution to these groups.

Thompson, 1984

This chapter presents an overview of the more common communication deficits and suggests communication strategies to use in working with clients experiencing them. Interactions with clients experiencing communication deficits require modifications of general therapeutic communication strategies used in nurse–client relationships. Communication deficits can arise from sensory deprivation related to temporary mobility and environmental limitations in an ICU (Fig. 17–1) or from more permanent physical handicaps such as hearing loss, blindness, and aphasia. Clients with serious mental disorders have a different type of communication deficit, resulting from a malfunctioning of the neurotransmitters that normally transmit and make sense out of messages in the brain.

Social isolation, impaired coping, and low self-esteem accompany the client's inability to receive or express language signals from the milieu. The emotional impact of these disabilities reflects the degree of severity of the deficits and the coping skills of the client. At the same time, it is important for the nurse to remember that two individuals can be equally impaired but not equally dis-

abled. People compensate for their impairment in different ways. The social, psychological, and behavioral context in which a communication handicap develops accounts for some of the differences in the ways people handle their disability.

BASIC CONCEPTS

TYPES OF DEFICITS

Hearing Loss

Hearing, an essential part of the communication process, is needed to receive messages and transmit them for decoding. It is the means by which a person is alerted to changes in the environment and is able to respond effectively to them. The listener in the communication process hears not only the words but also the speaker's vocal pitch, loudness, and intricate inflections accompanying the verbalization. Subtle variations can completely change the sense of the communication. Combined with the sounds, intensity, and organization of the verbal symbols, they allow the client to perceive and interpret the meaning of the sender's

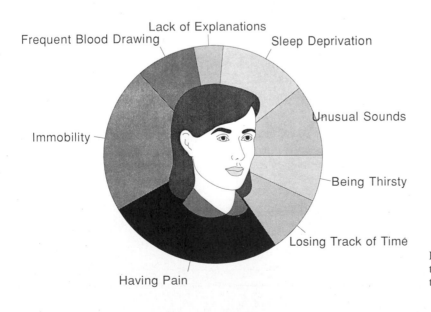

Frequent Blood Drawing

Lack of Explanations

Sleep Deprivation

Unusual Sounds

Immobility

Being Thirsty

Losing Track of Time

Having Pain

Figure 17–1 Situational Factors Affecting Client Responses to Critical Care Units

message. When this channel of communication is compromised through injury, illness, or the aging process, the client is at an enormous disadvantage in relationships with others. The extent of the loss is not always appreciated because the person looks normal, and the effects of partial hearing loss are not always readily apparent. Deprived of a primary means of receiving signals from the environment, clients with hearing loss frequently withdraw from relationships.

Blindness

Whereas hearing loss cuts out the verbal parts of messages, blindness eliminates visual nonverbal cues that accompany the message. Because the client can actively participate in the communication process in ways the deaf client cannot, it is natural to assume that communication is less difficult for the blind client. Unfortunately, this assumption is not true. Vision is an important sense used by clients to decode the meaning of messages. People watch the sender's facial expression and gestures for clues about interpreting the meaning of the message. All of the nonverbal cues that accompany speech communication, such as facial expression, nodding, and leaning toward the client, are lost to the blind client. Since the client cannot see their faces or observe their nonverbal signals, nurses need to use words to express what the client cannot see in the message.

Speech and Language Deficits

Clients who have speech and language deficits resulting from neurological trauma present a different type of communication problem. Normal communication allows a person to perceive and interact with the world in an organized and systematic manner. People use language to express self needs and to control environmental events. Language is the system people rely on to represent what they know about the world. When the ability to process and express language is disrupted, many areas of functioning are assaulted simultaneously. Aphasia, defined as a neurological linguistic deficit, produces a sudden alteration of communication that invariably has an impact on the sense of self. The person is intimately affected by feelings of loss and social isolation imposed by

the communication impairment. Some of the reactions of self and others occur not as reactions to the disabling condition itself but as responses to the meaning of the deficit. For example, it is not uncommon for employers and family members to wonder if the client with a stroke has intellectual impairment as well as language impairment. Whereas for some clients this is the case, clients with mild neurological disruptions simply need more cognitive processing time. Changes in self-image occasioned by physical changes, the uncertain recovery course and outcome of strokes, shifts in family roles, and the disruption of free-flowing verbal interaction among family members make the loss of functional communication particularly agonizing for clients. The inability to talk about these profound changes in one's lifestyle increases the client's feelings of social isolation and fear. Even more important than verbal interaction with the aphasic client is the attitude the nurse brings to the interaction. When the nurse is sensitive to these concerns and is able to express them, clients report feeling supported and reassured.

Aphasia represents a speech-language pathology that is most frequently associated with neurological trauma to the brain. Aphasia can present as primarily an expressive or receptive disorder. The client with expressive aphasia can understand what is being said but cannot express thoughts or feelings in words. Receptive aphasia creates difficulties in receiving and processing written and oral messages. With *global aphasia,* the client has difficulty with both expressive language and reception of messages.

Serious Mental Illness

The communication deficits found in clients with serious mental dysfunctions are related to their psychiatric disorders. Psychotic clients have intact sensory channels, but they cannot process and respond appropriately to what they hear, see, smell, or touch. The most serious communication difficulties are found in clients with autism (a childhood disorder characterized by a profound inability to communicate) and schizophrenia. Alterations in the biochemical neurotransmitters in the brain that normally conduct messages between nerve cells and help orchestrate the person's response to the external environment tangle messages and distort meanings. It is beyond the scope of this text to discuss in detail the psychotic client's communication deficits or the most appropriate strategies to use in communicating with this client. Such coverage is found in the many excellent psychiatric nursing texts available to the student. It is appropriate here, however, to appreciate the profound thought disintegration and communication problems psychotic clients face and to suggest basic guidelines for interacting with them.

The psychotic client usually presents with a poverty of speech and limited content. Speech appears blocked, reflecting disturbed patterns of perception, thought, emotions, and motivation. The client demonstrates a lack of vocal inflection and unchanging facial expression, which makes it difficult for anyone to really understand the underlying message. Many clients display illogical thinking processes in the form of illusions, hallucinations, and delusions. Common words assume new meanings known only to the person experiencing them. The client thinks concretely and is unable to make abstract connections between ideas. Words and ideas are loosely connected and difficult to follow. Spontaneous movement is decreased, and the schizophrenic client exhibits inappropriate affect or appears nonresponsive to conversation. What the client hears may be overshadowed by the client's mental disorder, resulting in pervasive distorted perceptions.

Environmental Deprivation

Communication is particularly important in nursing situations characterized by sensory deprivation, physical immobility, and limited environmental stimuli. In the emergency room as well as on the intensive care unit (ICU), perceptions and dialogue are limited by the nature of the unit and by the unstable nature of the conditions precipitating admission. Yet even in the most hi-tech setting, the potential for caring remains an underlying theme (Ray, 1987).

For the most part, the client is kept physically immobile, so that by default the relationship with the critical care nurse often becomes the most important one to the client. Nurses who show concern for the client as a person and who have a sensitive awareness of what the client may be experiencing in a strange environment help the client maintain a sense of self in a bewildering situation. A nurse who is with the client psychologically as well as physically helps the client develop meaning from the current situation.

Temporary, reversible changes in cognitive equilibrium occur because there are few organizing structures to anchor the client. Such clients, surrounded by hi-tech equipment, usually find themselves in settings in which there are no gender distinctions, privacy is at an minimum, and there isn't even a window from which to view the outside world. The immediate environment is unfamiliar, circumscribed, upsetting, and punctuated with strange sounds. Medical emergencies are the rule rather than the exception, and the client's usual support system is excluded except for brief visits. It is often difficult for the client to differentiate noises and equipment as important or insignificant. Everything seems equal and strange. As Cooper (1993) points out, the ICU "is not the ordinary world of human experience." The lack of familiar landmarks and varied stimuli in a hospital special care unit (the ICU, labor room, or emergency room, for instance) limits a person's ability to use environmental cues to direct behavior. Moreover, clients usually are frightened, in pain, and unable to communicate easily with others. Barriers to communication can also include the client's inability to respond in a conversation, usually because of intubation or sedation.

Research indicates that the subsequent gradual decline of cognitive abilities and the absence of interpersonal stimulation are related. Clients with normal intellectual capacity can appear dull, uninterested, and lacking in problem-solving abilities if they don't have frequent interpersonal stimulation.

APPLICATIONS

COMMUNICATIONS STRATEGIES WITH:

Hearing Loss

Assessment of the effects of auditory sensory loss should include the age of onset and the severity. Hearing loss that occurs after the development of speech means that the client has access to word symbols and language skills. Deafness in children can cause developmental delays, which may need

EXERCISE 17–1
Loss of Sensory Function in Geriatric Clients

Purpose: To assist you to get in touch with the feelings often experienced by older adults as they lose sensory function. If the younger individual is able to "walk in the older person's shoes," he or she will be more sensitive to the losses and needs created by those losses in the older person.

Time: 20 minutes

Directions:
1. Divide yourselves into three groups.
2. Group A, place cotton balls in your ears. Group B, place a plastic bag over your eyes. Group C, place cotton balls in your ears and cover your eyes with a plastic bag.
3. A student from Group B should be approached by a student from Group A. The student from Group B is to talk to the student from Group A, using a whispered voice. The Group A student is to verify the message heard with the student who spoke. The student from Group B is then to identify the student from Group A.
4. The students in Group C are expected to identify at least one person in the group and describe to that person what he or she is wearing. Each student who does not do the description is to make a statement to the other person and have that individual reveal what he or she was told.
5. Having identified and conversed with each other, hold hands or remain next to each other and remove the plastic bags and cotton balls (to facilitate verification of what was heard and described).

Discussion:
1. How did the loss you experienced make you feel?
2. Were you comfortable performing the function expected of you with your limitation?
3. What do you think could have been done to make you feel less handicapped?
4. How did you feel when your "normal" level of functioning was restored?
5. How would you feel if you knew the loss you just stimulated was to be permanent?
6. What impact can you project this experience might have on your future interactions with older individuals with such sensory losses.

Glenn BJ, R.N., Ed.D, Member, State Health Coordinating Council—Acute Care Committee, and Assistant Professor, University of North Carolina, Charlotte, 1993.

to be taken into account in planning the most appropriate communication strategies (Jaffe and Luterman, 1980). Clues to hearing loss occur when clients appear unresponsive to sound or respond only when the speaker is directly facing them.

The deaf client uses visual cues to compensate for the loss of hearing. Clients with partial hearing loss can use verbal cues if speakers position themselves directly in front of them. Facial expressions and gestures that reinforce the verbal content are helpful. Partially deaf clients respond best to well-articulated words spoken in a moderate, even tone.

The nurse should ask clients if they use a hearing aid and if it is working properly. Use of auditory amplifiers in the form of hearing aids and telephone attachments counterbalance certain types of hearing loss. Frequently clients have hearing aids but fail to use them. Common reasons for not wearing them include poor fit and difficulty

with inserting them correctly. Other people complain that the hearing aid amplifies all sounds indiscriminately, not just the voices of people in conversation, and they find this distracting. Exercises 17–1 and 17–2 will help you understand what it's like to have a hearing deficit.

Specific strategies to maximize the quality of the communication process might include the following:

1. Stand or sit so that you face the client and the client can see your facial expression and mouthing of words. Communicate in a well-lighted room.
2. Use gestures and speak distinctly without exaggerating words.
3. Write important ideas and allow the client the same option to increase the chances of communication.

EXERCISE 17–2
Hearing Loss Exercise

Purpose: To help raise consciousness regarding hearing as a channel of communication and experience the loss of hearing function.

Time: 15 minutes

Directions:
1. Watch the first fifteen minutes of a television show with the sound turned off. All students should watch the same show—for example, the 6 o'clock news report or a rerun of a situation comedy. Write down what you think was said during this time period. Your instructor will either tape or listen to the broadcast.
2. Share your observations of the television show and describe for each other in turn what went on.
3. Following completion of the exercise, the instructor will summarize what actually happened in the broadcast or show the videotape

Discussion:
1. Were perceptual differences noted in how each student interpreted the show? If so, what implications do you think these differences have in working with deaf clients?
2. How frustrating was it for you to watch the show without sound? How did it make you feel?
3. What could the characters in the show have done to make it easier for you to receive information without sound?
4. What did you learn about yourself from doing this exercise?

4. Help elderly clients adjust hearing aids. Lacking fine motor dexterity, the elderly client may not be able to insert aids to amplify hearing.
5. Allow more time to communicate information.
6. Become familiar with the client's communication pattern, likes, and dislikes.

An intermediary, such as a family member who knows sign language, may be needed to facilitate communication.

Blind Clients

It is important to use words as you approach the blind client. Speaking to a client from behind sometimes startles the client who can't see signals from the sender that indicate a wish to converse. It also is helpful to mention your name as you enter the client's room. This helps the client know who is there. Even people who are partially blind appreciate hearing the name of the person to whom they are speaking, because otherwise they may have to guess. The blind person experiences the world as full of shadows and lacking in detail.

It is important during the conversation to remember that because blind clients lack visual cues, they rely more heavily on vocal tones to interpret messages. The nurse needs to use words to supply additional information to counterbalance the missing visual cues. For example, a blind elderly client commented to the student nurse that she felt the student was uncomfortable talking with her and perhaps didn't like her. Not being able to see the student, she interpreted the hesitant uneasiness in the student's voice as evidence that the student did not wish to be with her. The student agreed with the client that she was quite uncomfortable but didn't explain further. Had the client been able to see the apprehensive body posture of the student, she would have realized that the student was quite shy and might have been ill at ease with *any* interpersonal relationship. It was a serious, but not necessarily a fatal error in communication. In such a situation, the student might have clarified the reasons for her discomfort and the relationship could have moved forward. Unfortunately, she did not do this, and the client was left feeling that her emotions were inconsequential, inappropriate, or misunderstood. She stood disconfirmed.

The social isolation experienced by blind clients can be profound, yet the need for human contact remains as important as ever. Touching the client lightly *as* you speak alerts the client to your presence. Voice tones and pauses that reinforce the verbal content are helpful. The client needs to be informed when the nurse is leaving the room. Compensatory interventions for the blind include a plentiful assortment of auditory and tactile stimuli such as books on tape and in braille and music.

When a blind client is being introduced to a new environmental setting, the nurse should orient the client by describing the size of the room and the position of the furniture and equipment. If other people are present, the nurse should inform the client of their presence by naming each one. A good communication strategy is to ask the other people in the room to introduce themselves to the client. In this way the client gains an appreciation for their voice configurations. Sometimes there is a tendency to speak with a blind client in a louder than usual voice or to enunciate words in an exaggerated manner. This exaggeration is unnecessary and is perceived by some clients as condescending or insensitive to the nature of the handicap. Voice tones should be kept natural. Exercise 17–3 will give you a sense of what it's like to be visually impaired.

The blind client needs guidance in moving around in unfamiliar surroundings. One way of preserving the client's autonomy is to offer your arm to the client instead of taking the client's arm. Verbal notation of steps and changes in movement as they are about to appear help the client successfully navigate new places and differences in terrain successfully. The client will be less socially isolated if the nurse helps him or her maintain contact and involvement with as much of the environment as the client's capabilities will allow.

Deaf/Blind Clients

The deaf/blind client presents a special communication challenge to the nurse, but many of the strategies described above can be used in combination to facilitate communication. Methods of communication used by these clients include reading/writing in braille and use of American sign language. While these skills are not common among nurses, several other techniques can be used by any nurse to communicate with the deaf/blind client. Capital letters can be printed in the client's palm. Touch becomes very important. The nurse can help the client touch and feel the position of different items in a room. Walking deaf/blind clients around their environment allows for sensory knowledge that otherwise would be inaccessible to them.

The *Optacon* is a reading device that converts printed letters into a vibration which can be felt by

---

EXERCISE 17–3
Experiencing What It Is Like to Be Blind

Purpose: To help students understand what it is like to be blind.

Time: 45 minutes

Procedure:
1. Have students pair up. One student should be blindfolded.
2. The other student should guide the "blind" student on a walk around the campus.
3. During the walk, the student guide should converse with the "blind" student about the route they are taking.
4. The students should return to the classroom after 15 minutes and reverse roles for a second 15-minute walk.

Discussion:
1. What did it feel like to be temporarily blind?
2. In what ways was the student guide helpful and considerate of your handicap?
3. What actions did you wish your student guide had taken that would have made the walk easier?
4. What trust issues arose for you as a result of being dependent on another person?
5. In what ways can you use the learning from this exercise in your nursing practice?

the deaf/blind client. The *Tellatouch* is a portable machine into which the nurse types a message that emerges in braille.

As with the other clients discussed in this chapter, a primary nursing goal is to maximize the client's independence. Armstrong (1991) provides the following suggestions for helping the deaf/blind client:

1. Let the person know when you approach by a simple touch, and always indicate when you are leaving.
2. Make positive use of any means of communication available.
3. Develop and use your own special sign to identify yourself to the client.
4. Encourage the client to verbalize speech, even if the person uses only a few words or the words are difficult to understand at first.
5. Keep the client informed.
6. Use touch and close physical proximity while you are with the client; give the person something substantial to touch in your absence.
7. Do not lead or hold the client's arm when walking; instead, allow the person to take your arm.
8. Develop and use signals to indicate changes in pace or direction while walking.

Clients Having Speech and Language Difficulty

Assessment of the type of aphasia aids the nurse in selecting the most appropriate intervention. Expressive language problems are evidenced in an inability to find words or to associate ideas with accurate word symbols. In some instances, the client can find the right word if given enough time and support. Other clients have difficulty organizing their words into meaningful sentences or describing the sequence of events. Clients with receptive communication deficits have trouble following directions, reading information, and writing. They hear the words but have difficulty classifying data or relating data to previous knowledge. Common properties of familiar items are not connected. This inability limits short-term memory and is sometimes misinterpreted as a short-term memory deficit associated with dementia. These clients appreciate the nurse who helps them supply the missing connections. Clients who lose both expressive and receptive communication abilities have global aphasia. Even though they appear not to understand, the nurse should explain in very simple terms what is happening. Using multiple modalities such as touch, gestures, eye movements, squeezing of the hand etc. can improve chances of communication and should be attempted.

Clients with speech and language deficits become frustrated when they are not understood and may refuse to repeat themselves. The level of concentration required by the nurse to capture every word and its meaning is tiring. Clients fatigue easily and need short, positive sessions to reinforce their efforts. Otherwise they may become nonverbal as a way of regaining energy and composure. Difficulties in communication are compounded when appropriate comprehension skills are compromised. This is evidenced when the client is unable to make the connections betwen objects and events and has difficulty understanding the meanings of social situations.

When the capacity to communicate through words is lost through illness or injury, the client must learn different ways to compensate for normal speech production skills. Any language skills that are preserved should be exploited. Other means of communication can be used, such as pointing, gesturing, using pictures, and repeating phrases. Sounds and eye movements can develop into unique communication systems between nurse and client.

Flexibility and accurate assessment of learning needs are keys to developing the most effective teaching strategies with aphasic clients. For example, Collier (1992, p. 63) describes an aphasic client's initial reluctance to participate in self-care teaching and the strategies the nurses used to engage the client.

> Mrs. Hixon seemed determined to ignore us. When we tried to get her to work with us, her reply was an emphatic "No, no, no!" . . . We agreed to try two things. First, we'd carefully explain to Mrs. Hixon everything we were going to do and how she could help us. We wanted her to understand that we weren't just doing things *to* her, but *with* her. Second, we'd speak to her as an adult. When a patient is aphasic, a caregiver can easily slip into feeling she's also deaf and possibly mentally retarded. This isn't true, and although we made a point of speaking clearly and in short sentences, we still spoke to her as adult to adult and in a normal tone of voice.

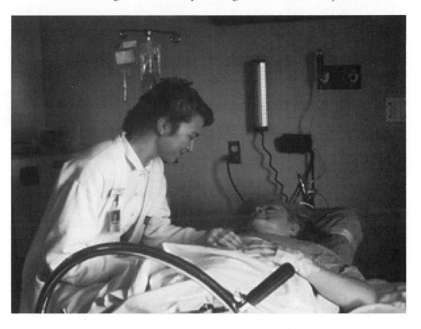

Touch, eye movements, and sounds can be used to communicate with clients experiencing aphasia. (Courtesy of the University of Maryland School of Nursing)

Over time, Mrs. Hixon developed trust in her nurses, allowing them to involve her as a partner in her health care.

Specific communication strategies to assist the client with speech and language dificulties can include the following:

1. Avoid prolonged, continuous conversations; instead use frequent, short talks.
2. When clients falter in written or oral expression, supply needed compensatory support.
3. Praise efforts to communicate and make learning new ways to communicate a creative game.
4. Provide regular mental stimulation in a nontaxing way.
5. Help clients focus on the faculties still available to them for communication.
6. Allow extra time for delays in cognitive processing of information.
7. Encourage the client to practice what is learned in speech therapy.

If the client is able to use short phrases and simple sentences, this should be encouraged. It doesn't matter if the sentence doesn't make complete grammatical sense or is expressed in a halting way. The important thing is that the client is communicating and the communication is under- standable. Anything the nurse can do to encourage and support verbal expressive abilities is useful. If the client is in speech therapy, the nurse can be an important source of support. Exposure to varied social environments without the pressure to talk helps the client with a communication deficit remain connected. The nurse can point out familiar objects as they tour the immediate environment on foot or with the client in a wheelchair.

Seriously Mentally Ill Clients

The nurse faces a formidable challenge in trying to establish a relationship with the psychotic client. The most important modifications needed in communicating with psychotic clients center on taking a more proactive approach. Rarely will the psychotic client approach the nurse directly. It is the nurse who must reach out and try different communication strategies. Patience and respect for the client are essential. The client generally responds to questions, but the answers are likely to be brief, and the client does not elaborate without further probes. Knowing this is the most common form of response helps the nurse depersonalize the impact of a response that conveys little information. Although the client appears to rebuff any social interaction, it is important to keep trying to connect. Shorter contacts with the client are preferable to longer interactions. Simple, concrete sentences and use of props and actions, such as games, magazines, going for walks, discussing simple topics, curling a client's hair, or doing the client's nails are useful ways to engage the client. Keeping in mind that the client's unresponsiveness to words, failure to make eye contact, unchanging facial expression, and monotonic voice are patterns of the disorder and not a commentary on the nurse's communication skills helps the nurse continue to engage with the client.

If the client is hallucinating or using delusions as a primary form of communication, the nurse should not challenge their validity directly. Nor should there be prolonged discussions of illogical thinking. Instead, the nurse might say, "I know that your sense that God is going to destroy the world tomorrow seems very real to you, but I don't see it that way."

Often the nurse can identify the underlying theme the client is trying to convey with the delusional statement. For example, the nurse might say to the client making the statement above, "It sounds as though you feel powerless and afraid at this moment." Listening to the client carefully and trying to make sense out of the underlying feelings models effective communication for the client and helps the nurse decode nonsensical messages. If the nurse expects the client to talk crazy, the client will oblige. But if the nurse is willing to look beyond the misleading exterior to the way the individual experiences reality and wishes to be seen by others, a different picture can emerge. A mark of the growing trust in a relationship with a psychotic client is expanded rational conversation and a willingness to remain with the nurse for increasing periods of time.

Clients Experiencing Environmental Deprivation

It isn't that the client really is forgotten, but nurses in the high-tech ICU environment often forget the client is still a psychosocial being. The human concerns of the client assume a secondary priority, receiving less attention than the more immediate physical needs. In the rush to get the client stabilized physically, communication is of poor quality,

with nurses verbalizing less often or being less sensitive to the client's behavioral cues (Turnock, 1991).

When a client is not fully alert, it is not uncommon for nurses to speak in the client's presence in ways they would not if they thought the client could fully understand what is being said. Such situations are unfortunate for two reasons—first, because hearing is the last sense to go, and clients have been able to repeat whole conversations; and, second, because the client may hear only parts of what is said and misinterpret it. A rule of thumb is *never to say anything you would not want the client to hear.*

Strategies for communicating include, in addition to a caring, compassionate attitude on the nurse's part, providing pictures or a simple object from home; orienting the client to the environment; frequently providing information about the client's condition and progress; reassuring the client that cognitive and psychological disturbances are common; giving explanations prior to procedures; and providing information about the sounds, sights, and feelings the client is experiencing. It is important to provide the client with frequent orienting cues to time and place. Meals can be labeled as breakfast, lunch, or dinner. Linking events to routines, for example, saying, "The x-ray technician will take your chest x-ray right after lunch" helps secure the client in time and space. When the client is unable or unwilling to engage in a dialogue, the nurse should continue to initiate communication in a one-way mode (Turnock, 1991).

Sample Statements

NURSE: I am going to give you your bath now. The water will feel a little warm to you. After your bath, your wife will be in to see you. She stayed in the waiting room last night because she wanted to be with you. *(No answer is necessary if the client is unable to talk, but the sound of a human voice and attention to the client's unspoken concerns can be very healing.)*

The client should be called by name. Nurses need to identify themselves and explain procedures in simple language even if the client does not appear particularly alert. Clients who are awake or even semi-alert should not be allowed to stare at a blank ceiling for extended periods of time. Changing the client's position frequently benefits the person physiologically and offers an opportunity for episodic dialogue with the nurse. The nurse is frequently in a position to broaden a client's perceptual perspectives, creating a more stimulating environment. For example, a simple animated conversation that taps into the client's world of knowledge can provide a source of ongoing emotional support because of the indirect recognition of the client's intellectual and perceptual qualities.

If the client in the ICU becomes temporarily delusional or experiences hallucinations, the nurse can use strategies similar to those employed with the psychotic client. The client is reassured if the nurse does not appear bothered by the symptoms and is able to confirm to the client that experiencing strange sensations, thoughts, and feelings is a common occurrence in the ICU.

SUMMARY

This chapter discusses the specialized communication needs of clients with communication deficits. Basic issues and applications for communicating with clients experiencing sensory loss of hearing and sight are outlined. Sensory stimulation and compensatory channels of communication are needed for clients with sensory deprivation. The mentally ill client has intact senses, but information processing and language are affected by the disorder. It is important for the nurse to develop a proactive communication approach with psychotic clients. The aphasic client has trouble expressing and/or receiving communication. Nurses can develop alternative methods of communicating with these clients. Clients in the ICU can experience a temporary distortion of reality. Such clients need frequent cues that orient them to time and place, as well as sensory stimulation.

REFERENCES

Armstrong NT (1991). Nursing care of the deaf-blind client. Insight 16(3):20–21.

Baerg KL (1991). Effective communication with autistic children. Rehabilitation Nursing 16(2):88–93.

Collier S (1992). Mrs. Hixon was more than the C.V.A. in 251. RN '92 22(11): 62–64.

Cooper M (1993). The intersection of technology and care in the ICU. Advances in Nursing Science 15(3):23–32.

Elvins R (1991). Attitudes to people with mental handicaps. Nursing Standard 5(34):29–32.

Jaffe B, Luterman D (1980). The child with a hearing loss. *In* Scheiner A, Abroms I (eds.) (1980), The Practical Management of the Developmentally Disabled Child. St. Louis, Mosby.

Ray M (1987). Technological caring: A new model in critical care. Dimensions of Critical Care Nursing 6(3):169–173.

Turnock C (1991). Communicating with patients in ICU. Nursing Standard 9(5):38–40.

SUGGESTED READINGS

Hall SS, Weatherly K (1989). Using sign language with tracheotomized infants and children. Pediatric Nursing 15(4):362–367.

Niewenhuis R (1989). Breaking the speech barrier. Nursing Times. 85(15):34–36.

Chapter 18

Communicating with Children

KATHLEEN BOGGS

OUTLINE

Basic Concepts

THE CHILD'S DEVELOPMENTAL ENVIRONMENT
    Piaget's stages

Applications

ASSESSMENT
    Regression as a form of childhood communication
INTERVENTION
COMMUNICATING WITH HOSPITALIZED CHILDREN
    Infants
    Toddlers
    Preschoolers
    School-aged children
    Adolescents
    Helpful attitudes and behaviors in communicating
      with children
INTERACTING WITH PARENTS OF ILL CHILDREN

Summary

OBJECTIVES

At the end of the chapter, the student will be able to:

1. Identify how developmental levels have an impact on the child's ability to participate in interpersonal relationships with caregivers.

2. Describe modifications in communication strategies to meet the specialized needs of children.

3. Describe interpersonal techniques needed to interact with concerned parents of ill children.

Child of the pure unclouded brow
and dreaming eyes of wonder!
Though time be fleet, and I and thou
Are half a life asunder,
Thy loving smile will surely hail
The love-gift of a fairy tale

Lewis Carroll, 1909

This chapter is designed to help the nurse recognize and apply communication concepts related to the nurse–client relationship in pediatric clinical situations. Each nursing situation represents a unique application of communication strategies. By understanding the client's cognitive, developmental, and functional level the nurse is able to select the most appropriate communication strategies.

Communicating with children at different age levels requires modifications of the skills learned in previous chapters. Developmentally, children undergo significant age-related changes in the ability to process cognitive information and in the capacity to interact effectively with the environment. To cultivate an effective therapeutic interpersonal relationship with a child, the nurse needs an understanding of feelings and thought processes from the child's perspective. Developing rapport requires that the nurse know about the interpersonal world as the child perceives it and convey honest, respect and acceptance of feelings.

BASIC CONCEPTS

Childhood is very different from adulthood. The child has fewer life experiences from which to draw and is still in the process of developing skills needed for reasoning and communicating. Erikson's concepts of ego development (see Chapter 3) and Piaget's description of the progressive development of the child's cognitive thought processes form a theoretical basis for the child-centered nursing interventions described in this chapter. Both theorists say that the child's thought processes, ways of perceiving the world, judgments, and emotional responses to life situations are qualitatively different from those of the adult. Cognitive and psychosocial development unfold according to an ordered hierarchical scheme, increasing in depth and complexity as the child matures.

THE CHILD'S DEVELOPMENTAL ENVIRONMENT

Jean Piaget's (1972) descriptions of stages of cognitive development provide a valuable contribution toward understanding the dimensions of a child's perceptions. Cognitive development and early language development are integrally related, as evidenced by the mutual nonverbal communication that occurs between infant and caretaker. Although current developmental theorists expand on Piaget's theoretical model by recognizing the effects of the parent–child relationship and a stimulating environment on developing communication abilities, his work forms the foundation for childhood cognitive development. Piaget observed cognitive development occurring in sequential stages (Box 18–1). The ages are only approximated since Piaget himself was not specific.

Piaget's Stages

In the first stage of cognitive maturation, the *sensorimotor period,* the infant explores its own body as a source of information, gradually modifying reflexive responses to include more purposeful interactions with the environment. As the infant gains more motor control, cognitive behaviors become more intentional, and the infant begins to differentiate between objects in the environment. Around eight months of age, the infant clearly is able to distinguish the primary caregiver in the environment from less familiar persons. The infant may begin to vocalize some awareness that objects may be dissimilar in nature and function. By the end of this stage, the infant is developing an understanding of symbolic thinking and thus begins to use language to communicate.

The second stage of cognitive development emerges around the age of two. In this stage, known as the *preoperational period,* the toddler is markedly egocentric, unable to see another's viewpoint, and for this reason unable to engage pro-

BOX 18–1
Stages of Cognitive Development

Age	Piaget's Stages	Characteristics	Language Development
Birth–2 years	Sensorimotor	Infant learns by manipulating objects. At birth, reflexive communication, then moves through 6 stages to reach actual thinking.	Communication largely nonverbal; vocabulary of more than 4 words by 12 months, increases to >200 words and use of short sentences before age 2.
2–6 years	Preoperational	Beginning use of symbolic thinking. Imaginative play. Masters reversibility.	Actual use of structured grammar and language to communicate. Uses pronouns. Average vocabulary >10,000 words by age 6.
7–11+ years	Concrete operations	Logical thinking. Masters use of numbers and other concrete ideas, classification, conservation, etc.	Mastery of passive tense by age 7 and complex grammatical skills by age 10.
>12+ years	Formal operations	Abstract thinking. Futuristic, takes a broader, more theoretical perspective.	Near adultlike skills.

Adapted from Piaget J (1972). The Child's Conception of the World. Savage, MD, Littlefield, Adams and Co.

ductively in interactive, cooperative play. However, there is a genuine interest in being with other children, playing alongside them in parallel play. In the preoperational stage of cognitive development, children are not able to make cognitive connections between past events and a given end result.

The preschool child is still unable to distinguish fantasy from reality, to consider another's viewpoint, or to accept the possibility of alternative options. Images are developed through concrete devices. Verbal explanations should be accompanied by opportunities for the child to use concrete, touchable objects and to play in a cooperative take-turns fashion with other children. As the child makes the transition to the concrete operational stage, there is a growing ability to categorize information and to internalize more structures into thinking about things. At the end of the preoperational period in the early elementary school years, the child begins to notice the cause-and-effect relationships in situations and is able to describe differences in objects having some similarities (Crain, 1992; Piaget, 1972).

The third stage of cognitive development, referred to as the *concrete operations period,* extends from approximately 7 to 11 years of age and beyond. The child now is capable of structural cooperative play with complex rules. Children can comprehend concepts presented in graphic detail and are beginning to appreciate the possibility of developing alternative solutions to problems. The child is able to distinguish between concrete, disparate groups of objects. Health teaching with children in this stage of cognitive development should be closely aligned with reality and presented with concrete images.

The final stage of cognitive development described by Piaget is the *formal operations period.* Starting around the age of 12 in some children and continuing through adulthood, abstract reality and logical thought processes emerge. Cooperation, collaboration, and social conscience are noted. The formal operational thinker is able to consider several alternative options at the same time and to set long-term goals. Adolescents who have developed formal operational thinking abilities are capable of making health-related judgments about their care. Whenever possible, they should be given the opportunity to exercise this right.

Wide individual differences exist in the intellectual functioning of same-age children. Variations also occur across situations, so that the child under stress or in a different environment may process information at a lower level than he or she would under normal conditions. Since two children of the same chronological age may have quite different skills as information processors, the nurse needs to assess level of functioning. Language alternatives familiar to one child because of certain life experiences may not be useful in providing health care and teaching with another. Application of nursing care to children draws heavily from Erikson's model of psychosocial development. Integrating cognitive and psychosocial developmental approaches into communication with children at different ages enhances its effectiveness.

Understanding the Hospitalized Child's Needs

Difficulties arise in adult–child communications in part because of the child's cognitive level in an early developmental stage. Children have limited social experience in interpreting subtle nuances of facial expression, inflection, and word meanings. When illness and physical or developmental disabilities occur during formative years, situational stressors are added that affect the way children perceive themselves and the environment. Hospitalized children have to contend not only with physical changes but also with significant alterations in role relationships with family and peers, separation from family, and a strange, frightening and probably hurtful environment.

Hospitalization is a situational crisis for the entire family. Any deviation from normal creates unwanted stress. The family needs to learn new interactional patterns and coping strategies that take into consideration the meaning of an illness and disability in family life. Because personal disappointments and frustrations are feelings many families are reluctant to share freely when a child is ill, important behavioral responses frequently are stifled in fathers as well as in mothers.

APPLICATIONS

ASSESSMENT

Assessing a child's reaction to hospitalization requires knowing the child's normal patterns of communication. Interactions are observed between parent and child. The child's behavioral responses to the entire interpersonal environment (including nurse and peers) are assessed. Are the child's interactions age appropriate? Are behaviors organized, or is the child unable to complete activities? Does the child act out an entire play sequence, or is such play fragmented and disorganized? Do the child's interactions with others suggest imagination and a broad repertoire of relating behaviors, or is communication devoid of possibilities? Once baseline data have been collected, the nurse plans specific communication strategies to meet the specialized needs of the child client. An overview of nursing adaptations needed to communicate effectively with children are summarized in Box 18–2.

BOX 18–2
The Role of the Nurse in Adapting Communication to Meet the Ill Child's Needs

1. Develop an understanding of age-related norms of development.
2. Convey respect and authenticity.
3. Assess and use familiar vocabulary at the child's level of understanding.
4. Assess the child's needs in relation to the immediate situation.
5. Assess the child's capacity to cope successfully with change.
6. Use nonverbal communication, alternatives to verbalization: tactile-soothing strokes, kinesthetic rocking, visual-eye contact, and reassuring facial expressions.
7. Work to develop trust through honesty and consistency in meeting the child's needs.
8. Use "transitory objects" such as familiar pictures or toys from home.
9. Interpret the child's nonverbal cues verbally to him or her.
10. Use humor and active listening to foster the relationship.
11. Increase coping skills by providing play opportunities; use creative, unstructured play, medical role play, and pantomime.
12. Instead of conversation, use some indirect age-appropriate communication techniques such as storytelling, picture drawing, creative writing.
13. Use alternative, supplementary communication devices for children with specialized needs: sign language, computer-enhanced communication programs, etc.

Regression as a Form of Childhood Communication

Hospitalization is always stressful for children, stimulating behaviors that are reminiscent of an earlier stage of development. A certain amount of normal regression is to be expected of all children entering a hospital. Common behaviors include whining, teasing other children, demanding undue attention, and withdrawal. A preschooler may begin having "toileting accidents," regressing back to the use of diapers. In most cases, the underlying dynamic is the powerlessness and inadequacy the child feels in attempting to cope with a potentially overwhelming, frightening environment.

Because children have limited life experience to draw from, they exhibit a narrower range of behaviors in coping with threat. The quiet, overly compliant child who doesn't complain may be more frightened than the child who is able to scream or cry, thereby alerting caregivers to his or her emotional response to a new and terrifying situation. To fully understand the nature of regression in normal children, the nurse needs to obtain detailed information regarding the basic behavioral responses of the family and child. Sometimes functioning that looks regressive represents a typical behavioral response for the child in most situations. A complete baseline history that includes a description of the child's usual behaviors and responses to stress, developmental milestones, and achievements offers a good counterpoint for assessing the meaning of current interpersonal behaviors.

The involvement of the family and the degree to which they respond to the stress of the hospitalized child also affect the severity and duration of the child's regressive symptoms. Labeling such behavior as a normal response to a significant change in the child's perception of self frequently reassures the parent.

INTERVENTION

Whenever possible, the nurse should communicate with language symbols familiar to the child. For example, the nursing data base for a toddler admitted to the pediatric unit should elicit specific words used for toileting, pain, etc. The parents are valuable resources in understanding the child's communication patterns and in interpreting behavioral data to their children. If possible, they should be incorporated as part of the nurse's interpersonal relationship with the child. An assessment of vocabulary and understanding is essential in fostering communications. The nurse can assist a child who is having difficulty finding the words to convey a thought by reframing what the child has said and repeating it in a slightly different way. Another strategy is to ask the parent what words the child uses to express specific health-related concerns.

The afflicted child's peers often have difficulty accepting individual differences created by health deviations. They lack the knowledge and the interpersonal sensitivity to deal with the physical changes in their friends that they don't understand, as evidenced by "bald-headed" jokes about the child receiving chemotherapy. Children with hidden disorders such as diabetes, some forms of epilepsy, or minimal brain dysfunction are particularly susceptible to interpersonal distress. For example, it may be difficult for juvenile diabetics to regulate fast-food intake when all of their friends are able to eat what they want. When peer pressure is at its peak in adolescence, a teenager with a newly diagnosed convulsive seizure disorder may find it difficult to tell peers he no longer can ride his bicycle or drive a car. Unless appropriate interpersonal support is provided by the family and nurse, such children have to cope with an indistinct assault to their self-concept all by themselves.

COMMUNICATING WITH HOSPITALIZED CHILDREN

It is easy to overestimate a child's understanding of information about his or her illness or hospitalization. Doing so results in confusion, increased anxiety, anger, or sadness (Marcus, 1988). Beyond physiological care, ill children of all ages need the love and attention they would receive at home, including stimulation to talk, listen, and play (Baerg, 1991; Parish, 1986). They have major difficulties verbalizing their true feelings about the hospitalization experience. The nurse can be a primary resource in adapting communication to meet the ill child's needs by incorporating the guidelines presented in Box 18–3 into care of the child at different ages.

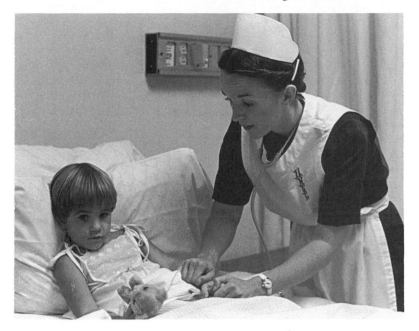

Nurses can use transitional objects and touch to communicate with small children in distress. (Courtesy of the University of North Carolina at Charlotte College of Nursing)

Infants

Assessment of the preverbal infant requires attention to cues such as tone of the cry or facial and body movements. Preverbal infants signal the nurse with physiological cues that indicate pain. In addition to the cry, the nurse observes for diaphoresis, pallor, increases in pulse and respirations, and changes in arterial oxygenation, as shown on a monitor. Effective nonpharmacological interventions include pacifiers, rocking, physical contact, and sometimes even swaddling (Page and Halvorson, 1991).

Since the infant uses sensorimotor mechanisms to receive information, the kinesthetic communication channel, tactile stimulation, and body movement are most important. Nonverbal types of communication such as touch are important tools for the pediatric nurse. Tone of voice, rocking motion, use of distraction, use of a soothing touch can be employed in addition to or in conjunction with verbal explanations. For example, a low, soothing tone and stroking are useful strategies. Face-to-face position, bending or moving to the child's eye level, maintaining eye contact, and a reassuring facial expression further help the nurse to interact with infants.

Awareness of developmental norms helps the nurse anticipate behaviors such as "stranger anxiety" exhibited by infants between 9 and 18 months. The nurse takes care to avoid startling the child. Rather than reaching to pick a child up immediately, the nurse might smile and extend a hand toward the child or caress the child's limb or back before attempting to hold the child. In this way, the nurse acknowledges the infant's inability to generalize to unfamiliar caregivers. If the child is able to talk, asking the child his or her name and pointing out a notable pleasant physical characteristic conveys the impression that the nurse sees the child client as a unique person. To a tiny child, this treatment can be synonymous with caring.

Toddlers

Almost all small children in the hospital feel some threat to their safety and security, as described in Maslow's hierarchy of needs. This basic need is exaggerated in toddlers and young children because they lack the verbal capability to articulate their needs. They also lack understanding about why they are ill. To help the child's comprehension, nurses adapt their vocabulary and style of speech by using phrases rather than long sentences

---

BOX 18–3
Key Points in Communicating with Children According to Age Group

---

Infants

Nonverbal communication is a primary mode.
Use stroking, soft touching, holding; soothe with crooning voice tone.

Kinesthetic Communication
Use motion (rocking, for example) to reassure. Allow freedom of movement, and avoid restraining where possible.
Infants are bonded to primary caregivers only. Those over eight months may display anxiety when approached by strangers.
Utilize parents to give care. Arrange for one or both parents to remain nearby.
Establish rapport with the caregiver (parent) and at first keep at least two feet between nurse and infant. Talk to and touch the infant and initially smile often.
Learn specifically how the primary caregiver provides care in terms of sleeping, bathing, and feeding, and attempt to mimic these approaches.
Always allow the mother to be within sight of her child, and vice versa.

Vision: 20/200–20/300 at Birth
Encourage the infant's caregivers (parents) to utilize a lot of intimate space interaction (8–18 inches). Mimic the same when trust is established.

Minimal Receptive Language Skills
Use a soft, slow voice tone; smile often; sit down as often as possible or stoop down so as to look less imposing.
Talk out loud in an active listening manner. Say such things as, "Mommy is here and she loves you"; "Mommy will keep you safe."

Separation Anxiety When Primary Caregiver Is Absent
Provide for kinesthetic approaches; offer self while infant is protesting (examples: stay with the child; pick the child up and rock or walk; talk to the child about Mommy and how much the child cares for Mommy and Daddy).

Short Stature
Sit down on chair, stool, or carpet to decrease posture superiority.

Toddlers

Limited Vocabulary and Verbal Skills
Make explanations brief and clear. Use the child's own vocabulary words for basic care activities. Assess (for example, use the child's words for "defecate"—"poop," "gooies," "urinate"—"pee-pee," "tinkle"). Learn and use self name of the child.

Speaks in Phrases
Rephrase the child's message in a simple, complete sentence; avoid baby talk.

Limited Vocabulary
Use vocabulary skills to get to know the primary caregiver *first* before approaching the child. For example, allow the child to see that the nurse can be a friend of Mommy.

Kinesthetic Communication
Allow ambulation where possible (toddler chairs, walkers). Pull the child in a wagon often if child cannot achieve mobility.

Struggling with Issues of Autonomy and Control
Allow the child some control (for example, say, "Do you want a half a glass or a whole glass of milk?")
Reassure the child if he or she displays some regressive behavior (example: if child wets pants, say, "We will get a dry pair of pants and let you find something fun to do").
Allow the child to express anger and to protest about his or her care (example: say, "It's OK to cry when you are angry or hurt").

Allow the child to sit up or walk as often as possible and as soon as possible after intrusive/hurtful procedures. Say, "It's all over and we can do something more fun."
Use nondirective modes, such as reflecting an aspect of appearance or temperament (example: "You smile so often") or playing with a toy and slowly coming closer to and including the child in play.

Fear of Bodily Injury
Show hands (free of hurtful items) and say, "There is nothing to hurt you. I came to play/talk."

Egocentrism
Allow child to be self-oriented and accepted. Use distraction if another child wants the same item or toy rather than expect the child to share.

Direct Questions
Use a nondirective approach. Sit down and join the parallel play of the child. Reflect messages sent by toddler (nonverbally) in a verbal and nonverbal manner. For example, say, "Yes, that toy does lots of interesting and fun things."

Separation Anxiety
Accept protesting when parent(s) leave. Hug, rock the child, and say, "You miss Mommy and Daddy! They miss you too." Play peek-a-boo games with child. Make a big deal about saying, "Now I am here."
Show an interest in one of the child's favorite toys. Say, "I wonder what it does," or the like. If the child responds with actions, reflect them back.

Continued

BOX 18–3 *(Continued)*
Key Points in Communicating with Children According to Age Group

Preschoolers

Speaks in Sentences but Is Unable to Comprehend Abstract Ideas
Use simple vocabulary; avoid lengthy explanations. Focus on the present, not the distant future; use concrete, meaningful references. For example, say, "Mommy will be back after you eat your lunch" (instead of "at one o'clock"). Use play therapy, drawings.

Unable to Tolerate Direct Eye-to-Eye Contact (Some Preschoolers)
Use some eye contact and attending posture. Sit or stoop, and use a slow, soft tone of voice.

May React Negatively and with Increased Anxiety If a Long Explanation Is Given Regarding a Painful Procedure
Complete the procedure as quickly as possible; give explanations about its purpose afterward. For example, say, "Jimmy, I'm going to give you a shot" (quickly administer the injection). "There, all done. It's OK to cry when you hurt. I'd complain, too. This medicine will make your tummy feel better."

Short Attention Span and Imaginative Stage
Explain, using imagination (puppetry, drama with dress-ups); use music.
Use play therapy: Allow the child to play with safe equipment used in treatment. Talk about the needed procedure happening to a doll or teddy bear, and state simply how it will occur and be experienced. Use sensory data: Say, for example, "The teddy bear will hear a buzzing sound."

Concrete Sense of Humor Beginning
Tell corny jokes and laugh with the child.

Continuing Need to Have Control
Provide for many choices. Say, "Do you want to get dressed now or after breakfast?"

School Age

Developing Ability to Comprehend
Include the child in concrete explanations about condition, treatment, protocols.
Use draw-a-person to identify basic knowledge the child has, and build on it.
Use some of the same words the child uses in giving explanations.
Use sensory information in giving explanations. Say, "You will smell alcohol in the cast room," for example.

In Assuming Increased Responsibility for Health Care Practices
Reinforce basic care activities in teaching.

Increased Need for Privacy
Respect privacy: Knock on the door before entering; tell the client when and for what reasons you will need to return to his or her room.

Early Adolescence

Increased Comprehension About Possible Negative Threats to Life or Body Integrity, Yet Some Difficulty in Adhering to Long-Term Goals
Verbalize issues about treatment protocols that require giving up immediate gratifications for long-term gain. Explore alternative options. For example, tell a diabetic adolescent who must give up after-school fries with friends that he or she could save two breads and four fats exchanges to have a milkshake.

Confidentiality May Be an Issue
Reassure the adolescent about the confidentiality of your discussion, but clearly state the limits of this confidentiality. If, for example, the child should talk of killing himself, this information needs to be shared with parents and staff.

Struggling to Establish Identity and Be Independent
Allow participation in decision making, wearing own clothes. Avoid an authoritarian approach when possible. Avoid a judgmental approach. Use a clarifying and qualifying approach. Actively listen. Accept regression.

Beginning to Demonstrate Abstract Thinking
Use abstract thinking, but look for nonverbal cues (puzzled face) that may indicate lack of understanding. Then clarify in more concrete terms.

Uses Colloquial Language or Street Slang
Couch your dialogue with the use of some of the client's words.

Sexual Awareness and Maturation
Offer self and a willingness to listen. Provide value-free, accurate information.

Joyce Ruth, M.S.N., R.N., University of North Carolina College of Nursing at Charlotte, 1987, 1993.

and by emphasizing or repeating words. Since the toddler has a limited vocabulary, the caretaker may need to "put into words" the feelings that the ill child is conveying nonverbally.

Evaluate the agency environment: Is it safe? Does it allow for some independence and autonomy? Communication is enhanced by agency policies that promote parent–child contact, such as unlimited visiting hours, rooming-in, or use of audio cassettes of a parent's voice. Use of familiar objects also makes the environment safer. According to Wincott (1971), transitional objects such as a teddy bear, blanket, or favorite toy remind the alone or frightened child that the security of the parental unit is still available even when the person is not physically present. In a hospital situation, transitional objects are even more important because the child is in an unfamiliar and potentially scary situation. Some hospitals have a prehospital orientation and present small children with a familiar transitional object to bring with them when they return for the actual hospitalization. Box 18–4 presents a representative nursing care problem.

Preschoolers

Throughout the preoperational period, young children tend to interpret language symbols in an exact, literal way. For example, the child who is told that he or she will be "put to sleep" during the operation tomorrow may equate this with the humane action recently taken for a pet dog who was too ill to live. These children do not request clarification of ambiguous messages, so messages can be misunderstood quite easily.

Preschool children have limited auditory recall and are unable to process auditory information quickly. They have a short attention span. Verbal communication with the preschool child should be clear, succinct, and easy to understand (Enlow and Swisher, 1986).

Prior to the age of seven, most children cannot make a clear distinction between fantasy and reality. Everything is "real," and anything strange is perceived as potentially harmful. Watching the preschooler run from the room when a monster appears on television gives the observer a keen sense of the limitations of the child's early perceptual functioning. Anything the nurse can do to

---

BOX 18–4
Representative Nursing Problem:
Dealing with an Irritable Toddler

Situation

A two-year-old boy is hospitalized for a minor surgical procedure. The mother is a single parent and unable to room-in because of family responsibilities. The father is unavailable. The toddler is very fussy and irritable when the mother is not around, crying frequently and demonstrating aggressive behaviors during caretaking activities.

Problem

Separation from mother because of hospitalization.

Nursing Diagnosis

Ineffective coping related to separation anxiety and stress of hospitalization.

Nursing Goals

Reduce stress of hospitalization related to separation anxiety and loss of consistent mothering; provide warm, secure environment.

Method of Assistance

Acting or doing for, providing developmental environment.

Interventions

1. Assign consistent substitute self-care agent who will provide warm, nurturing care.
2. Accept the child's behavior (crying, screaming) as healthy manifestations of separation anxiety; do not attempt to suppress the child's expression of anger or nonverbally communicate to the child that he is "bad" for acting this way.
3. Position self near the child while he or she is crying or angry and provide nonverbal support (touch, tactile stimulation) in order to demonstrate acceptance of the child's behavior.
4. Provide a transitional object or familiar objects from home that will comfort and soothe the child.
5. Allow liberal visiting hours so the mother may visit at her convenience.
6. Adhere to the child's home routines as much as possible during hospitalization to create a secure environment for the child.
7. Allow the child the opportunity to express anger at being "deserted" through such play activities as pounding a board with pegs, playing with large wooden spoons and nonbreakable pots, or drawing with thick crayons on paper.
8. If limits must be set to reduce aggressive behavior, make sure the limits are few in number and are consistently followed by all health care personnel.

M. Michaels, University of Maryland School of Nursing, 1987.

EXERCISE 18–1
Pediatric Nursing Procedures

Purpose: To give practice in preparing young clients for painful procedures.

Time: 15 minutes

Directions:
Timmy, age four years, is going to have a bone marrow aspiration (The insertion of a large needle into the hip is a painful procedure.)

Discussion:
Answer the following questions.
1. What essential information does Timmy need?
2. If this is a frequently repeated procedure, how can you make him feel safe before and after the procedure?
3. How soon ahead of time should you prepare him?

make the child's environment stable, real, and manageable will be helpful to the preschool client.

Since young children have a limited capacity for appreciating continuity of care, they need frequent concrete reminders to reinforce reality. Assigning the same caregiver reduces insecurity. Visiting the preschooler at the same time each day and posting family pictures are simple strategies the nurse can share with parents to reduce the child's fears of abandonment (Petrillo and Sanger, 1980). The nurse can link information to activities of daily living. For example, saying, "Your mother will come after you take your nap" rather than "at two o'clock" is much more understandable to the preschool client.

Assessment of the preschooler's ability to communicate involves a careful evaluation of the actual child's level of understanding. Children need to be assessed for misconceptions and troubling problems, preferably using free play and/or fantasy story-telling exercises. Normal developmental processes may limit understanding. Egocentrism may prevent children who have to fast before a scheduled test from understanding why they can't have a drink when they want it.

Explanations given long beforehand may not be remembered or may not allay fears. If something is going to hurt, the nurse should be forthright about it, while at the same time reassuring the child that he or she will have the appropriate support. Simple explanations reduce the child's anxiety. No child should ever be left to figure out what is happening to him or her without some type of simple explana-

tion. Exercise 18–1 can help you focus on specific communication strategies with the preschooler.

Play

The preschooler lacks a suitable vocabulary to understand fully and to express complex thoughts and feelings. Small children cannot simply be told what is going to happen to them. They lack the cognitive mechanisms for picturing what they have never experienced as an inner representation of reality. Play is an effective means by which a puzzling and sometimes painful real world can be approached. Play allows the child to create a concrete experience of something unknown and potentially frightening. By constructing a situation in play, the child is able to shape and put together the components of the situation in ways that promote recognition and make it a concrete reality. When the child can deal with things that are small or inanimate, the child masters situations that to him or her might otherwise be overwhelming. Media such as cartoons, pictures, or puppets can explain what is happening in tangible terms—for example, using a puppet to demonstrate actions and terminology. Dolls with removable cloth organs help children understand scheduled operations.

Preschoolers tend to think of their disabilities or illnesses, their separation from parents, and any painful treatments as punishment. Play can be used to help children express their feelings about an illness and to role play coping strategies. Allowing the young child to manipulate syringes, give "shots" to a doll, or put a bandage or restraint on a teddy bear's arm allows the child to act out his or her feelings. The child becomes "the aggressor." Play can be a major channel for communication in the nurse–client relationship with a young child.

Preschool children develop communication themes through their play and work through conflict situations in their own good time—the process can't be rushed. As the child develops trust in the interpersonal environment, themes are clarified and goal accomplishment becomes possible. Play materials vary with the age and developmental status of the child. Simple, large toys are used with young children, whereas more intricate playthings are used with older preschoolers. Almost any object has creative potential for play, such as clay, crayons, and paper. These articles become the modes of expression for important feelings and thoughts about problems.

Play can be the pediatric health care professional's primary tool for assessing preschool children's perceptions about their hospital experience, their anxieties and fears, and their coping ability (Parish, 1986). Preschoolers love jokes, puns, and riddles—the cornier the better. Using jokes during the physical assessment, such as, "Let me hear your lunch" or, "Golly, could that be a potato in your ear?" helps form the bonds needed for successful relationship with the preschool client.

Petrillo and Sanger (1980) propose a number of guidelines to use in implementing play as a communication strategy:

- Reflect only what the child expresses.
- Supply materials that stimulate play.
- Allow enough time without interruption
- Permit a child to play at his or her own pace.
- Determine when it is appropriate to go beyond the child's expression.
- Play for the child who cannot play for himself or herself.
- Allow direct play for the emotionally strong child.
- Be familiar with different forms of artistic materials as a medium of expression.
- Use knowledge of child growth and development as a guide to professional clinical judgment.

Box 18–5 presents a typical nursing care problem.

Storytelling

A communication strategy often used with children making the perceptual transition from preoperational to concrete operational thinking is the use of story plots. Gardner (1986) describes a mutual storytelling technique in which the caregiver helps a child to tell a story. The nurse asks the child if he or she would like to help make up a story. If the child is a little reluctant, the nurse may begin. For example, the nurse might say, "I'll start the story, and when I point my finger at you, you say exactly what comes into your mind at that time. Okay, let's start. Once upon a time—a long, long time ago—in a distant land—far, far away— there lived a . . ." The nurse then points to the child to fill in the blank. Whatever the word is, the nurse uses it to connect with another statement followed by pointing again for the child's response. During the story, the child may be asked to supply additional characteristics or to expand descriptions by identifying motivations.

The nurse then analyzes the themes presented by the child, which usually reveal important feelings. Is the story fearful? Are the characters scary or pleasing? At the end of the story, the child is asked to indicate what lesson might be learned from the story. If the child seems a little reluctant to give a moral to the story, the nurse might suggest that all stories have something that can be learned from them. The child should be praised for telling the story. The next step in the process is for nurses to ask themselves, "What would be a healthier resolution or a more mature adaptation than the one used by the child?" The nurse could suggest an alternative ending or plot. In the nurse's version of the story, the characters and other details remain the same initially, but the story contains a more positive solution or suggests alternative answers to problems. The object of mutual storytelling is to offer the child an opportunity to explore different alternatives in a neutral communication process with a helping person. Exercise 18–2 provides an opportunity to experiment with a mutual storytelling strategy.

Health teaching with preschool and school-aged children should be realistic and concrete for maximum effectiveness. The child becomes absorbed in being a part of the action of a story

BOX 18–5
Representative Nursing Problem:
Dealing with a Fearful Preschooler

Situation	*Intervention*
While climbing a tree in his backyard, John Allen, 4½ years old, falls and breaks his left femur. He is hospitalized for four to six weeks of traction prior to application of a hip spica cast. During routine morning care, John tells you he was a naughty boy for climbing the tree and now he's being punished. He goes on to say, "If I don't do everything the nurses tell me to do, then this big hairy monster will sneak in during the night and break my other leg."	1. Maintain mutual respect while talking to the child by not ridiculing or belittling his fears or perceptions. 2. Use reflection to determine what he has been told about the accident, what his parents' reactions were, and so forth. 3. Respond to the feeling tone of what the child is saying rather than content; help him understand what he is feeling (fear, anger, helplessness) rather than why he is feeling that way.

Problem

The child perceives the broken leg and subsequent hospitalization as punishment for climbing the tree.

Nursing Diagnosis

Ineffective coping related to hospitalization and threats to body integrity due to immature cognitive structures and simplistic, "magical" view of morality.

Nursing Goals

Reduce the stress of hospitalization and increase the child's sense of control; reduce threats to body integrity.

Method of Assistance

Acting or doing for the child: providing a developmental environment.

4. Talk slowly and casually; don't overwhelm or frighten him with lengthy explanations; when appropriate, reassure him that no one is to blame.
5. Assign a primary nurse or consistent caregiver to ensure continuity of care and to provide a sense of security for the child.
6. Encourage the parents to visit frequently and even become involved in the child's care; such involvement will tell the child his parents are concerned and care about him.
7. Utilizing the concept of storytelling, have the child make up a story about a particular event or show him a picture of an event and have him describe what is happening.
8. Because 4½-year-olds enjoy manipulative or constructive play, provide toys that require being put together or even "fixed"; provide materials for making a cast and have the child "fix" a doll's broken leg; have the child tell you how the doll's leg was broken.
9. Provide a night light in his room and discuss all the different things that scare monsters—lights, for example.

M. Michaels, University of Maryland School of Nursing, 1987.

with details and tangible connections made between concepts. Attempts to present abstract ideas without concrete applications are not likely to be understood by children in this age group.

School-Aged Children

As children move into concrete operational thinking, they begin to internalize the reasons for illness: Illness is caused by germs, or you have cavities because you ate too much candy or didn't brush your teeth. Use Exercise 18–3 to reformulate medical technology into age-appropriate expressions.

Taking responsibility for oneself increases with age. In later childhood, most children become better able to work verbally with the nurse. It still is important to prepare responses carefully and to

anticipate problems, but the child is capable of expressing feelings and ventilating frustration more directly through words.

Assessment of the child's cognitive level of understanding continues to be essential; the nurse searches for concrete examples the child can relate to rather than giving abstract examples the school-aged child cannot comprehend. If children are to learn from a model, they must see the model doing the skill to be learned. School-aged children thrive on explanations of how their bodies work and enjoy active participation in understanding the scientific rationales for their treatment. School-aged children and adolescents should themselves become the primary source of information needed by the nurse (Enlow and Swisher, 1986). Parental input may be used for validation.

EXERCISE 18–2
Using a Mutual Storytelling Technique

Purpose: To give practical experience with the mutual storytelling technique.

Time: 20 minutes

Directions:
1. Use the mutual storytelling process described in the text with a five-to-eight-year-old child in your neighborhood.
2. Write down the story the child told and suggest alternate endings.
3. Share your stories with each other in turn during the next class period.

Discussion
1. How difficult was it for you to engage the child? If you had trouble, what alternate actions would you incorporate in using the technique again?
2. Were you surprised at the story the child produced? If so, in what ways?
3. What did you learn about the child when using this technique?
4. What conclusions might you draw from hearing the other students relate their experiences about the use of this technique? In what situations was it most effective? Least effective?
5. What did you learn about yourself as a helping person in using this technique?

Sample Answer:
Nurse: Once upon a time in a land far away, there lived a . . .
Child: dragon
Nurse: a dragon who ate . . .
Child: carrots.
Nurse: The dragon ate carrots and slept . . .
Child: in a cave.
Nurse: One day he left the cave to go out and find many sweet carrots to eat, but as he walked along he ran into a . . .
Child: bike.
Nurse: He was afraid of the bike and so he . . .
Child: kicked it and ran away.
Nurse: After he ran away, is there any more to the story? . . .
Child (upset): He got hit with a stick.
Nurse: What is the message to this story? What does it tell us? . . .
Child: about running away not to be punished.

Communication Strategies

Audiovisual aids can enhance communication. Reading material geared to the child's level of understanding may supplement verbal explanations. Details about what the child will hear, see, smell, and feel are important. Diagrams can be used to help provide simple, accurate scientific information. As the early school-aged child develops the manual control and cognitive ability to render thoughts and emotions figuratively, expressive art can be a useful method to convey feelings and to open up communication (Parish, 1986). The older school-aged child or adolescent might best convey feelings by writing a poem, a short story, or a letter. This written material can assist the nurse in understanding hidden thoughts or emotions. Williams (1987) suggests that self photographs are an innovative shortcut to developing meaningful talk sessions with emotionally disturbed children.

Mutuality in Decision Making

Children of this age need to be involved in discussions of their illness and in planning for their care. Explanations giving the rationale for care are useful. Involving the child in decision making may decrease fears about the illness, the treatment, or the effect on family life. Use of videotapes and written materials geared to the child's level may be useful in involving the child in the management phase of care. Lewis, Pantell, and Sharp (1991) note that while children often are included in data gathering, there is a tendency to exclude them from management and diagnostic information. In this study, when children were included in discussions of medical recommendations, the children were more satisfied with their care and recalled more information.

Adolescents

An understanding of adolescence and the intensity of the search for identity is essential for the nurse working with teenagers. The adolescent vacillates between childhood and adulthood. Adolescence is a time of life when one is emotionally vulnerable; it may be characterized by rapidly changing moods or fantasies of great experiences. The ambivalence of the adolescent period gets expressed through withdrawal, rebellion, loss of motivation, and irritability. All of these behaviors are normal in varying degrees as teenagers examine and experiment with values and standards that will have personal meaning to them. However, identity issues become more difficult to resolve when the normal opportunities for physical independence, privacy, and social contacts are com-

promised by illness or handicaps. Sick or well, every adolescent has questions about his or her body as it develops, as well as about sexuality. The same longings and desires are present in the handicapped or ill teenager as in other youth. Problems may be greater for ill teens because the natural outlets for their expression with peers often are curtailed either by the disorder or by the hospitalization. Use of peer groups, adolescent lounges (separate from the small children's play room), and a phone in the rooms, as well as provisions for wearing one's own clothes, "fixing up" hair, or attending hospital school may help the teen adjust to hospitalization. When the developmental identity crisis becomes too uncomfortable, adolescents may project their fury and frustration onto family or staff. Identifying the adolescent's rage as a normal response to a difficult situation can be very reassuring.

Assessment of the adolescent should occur in a private setting. Attention to the client's interpersonal comfort and space are factors that will have a tremendous impact on the quality of the interaction. To the teenager, the nurse represents an authority figure. The need for compassionate concern and genuine interest by another is perhaps greater during adolescence than at other times in the lifespan. Often lacking the verbal skills of adults, yet wishing to appear in control, adolescents do well with direct questions. Questions of a relatively innocuous nature are used first to allow the teenager enough space to check the validity of his or her reactions to the nurse. Assessment of cognitive level would involve finding out about the ability to make long-term plans. Areas of psychosocial functioning that need to be assessed include the following:

1. Level of self-care responsibility.
2. Quality of relationships with significant others—family and peers, including health practices such as safe sex for those who are sexually active.
3. Self-concept, body image, and personal identity as well as perceptions of threats to self.
4. Threats to developmental integration of body functions such as may occur with an ostomy.
5. Age-appropriate interpersonal and cognitive functioning.

Communication Strategies

Adolescents respond best to multiple use of sensory modalities. If an adolescent client has difficulty relating or cognitively comprehending in one sphere, use of another modality may be appropriate. For example, a student nurse became quite frustrated during the course of her relationship with a 17-year-old adolescent on a psychiatric unit. Despite a genuine desire to engage him in a therapeutic alliance and the appropriate use of verbal strategies, the client wasn't talkative. Attempts to get to know him on a verbal level seemed to increase rather than decrease his anxiety. The nurse correctly inferred from the client's inability to put feelings into words and his tendency to focus on the more concrete aspects of an experience that, despite his age, this adolescent's individualized needs dictated a more tangible approach. Knowing that the client likes cars, the nursing student brought in an automotive magazine. Together they looked at the magazine; the publication soon became their special interpersonal vehicle for communication, bridging the gap between the client's inner reality and his ability to express himself verbally in a meaningful way. Feelings about cars gradually generalized to verbal expressions about other situations, and the adolescent rather quickly began describing his life dreams, disappointments and attitudes about himself. When the student nurse left the unit, he asked to keep the magazine and frequently spoke of her with fondness. A simple recognition of his awkwardness in verbal communication and use of another tool to facilitate the relationship had a positive effect. A knowledge of the child's level of cognitive development helps the nurse apply communication principles while recognizing the uniqueness of the client's individualized needs.

Limit Setting

Behavior problems in adolescents present a special challenge to the nurse. Clear communication of expectations, treatment protocols, and hospital rules is of value. By adolescence, children usually have the necessary skills and intellectual capabilities to make many decisions about their health care. Adolescents should be allowed to act on their own behalf in making choices and judgments

about their functioning. At the same time, the adolescent still needs limits on behavior. Although limit setting is an issue for all children, it assumes special importance in adolescence, where, of necessity, it becomes a more collaborative experience.

All children need to know their boundaries, even sick children. Limits define the boundaries of acceptable behaviors in a relationship. Initially determined by the parents or the nurse, limits can be developed mutually as an important part of the relationship as the child matures and becomes capable of abstract, logical reasoning. Limit setting should be educational rather than punitive in form and implementation.

Order is essential on any unit. On the pediatric unit, it is particularly important because the child has less internal control over behavior, as well as less conceptual and ego ability to consider possible alternatives to problem behaviors. Because the child client has not developed the capacity to act fully as an agent in his or her self-care, the nurse and parents serve as advocates. Interpersonal relationships with children are more effective when limits and expectations are clear, firm, and consistent, with a certain degree of tolerance for minor infractions. Firmness is a refusal to give in to the undue demands of the child or to indulge the child in every whim. Determining consequences beforehand makes necessary limit setting less reactive. The child is able to make a choice about doing or not doing a behavior and gains a stronger sense of control. Determining consequences has a positive value in that it provides the child with a model for handling frustrating situations in a more adult manner (see Box 18–6).

Once the conflict is resolved and the child has accepted the consequences of his or her behavior, the child should be given an opportunity to discuss

---

BOX 18–6
Guidelines for Developing Workable Consequences for Unacceptable Behavior

Effective consequences are:
- Logical and fit the situation.
- Applied in a matter-of-fact manner without lengthy discussion.
- Situation centered rather than person centered.
- Applied immediately after the transgression.

attitudes and feelings that led up to the need for limits as well as his or her reaction to the limits set.

Although communication about limits is necessary for the survival of the relationship, it needs to be balanced with time for interaction that is pleasant and positive. Sometimes with children who need limits frequently, discussion of the restrictions are the only conversations that take place between nurse and client. When this is noted, nurses might ask themselves what feelings the child might be expressing through his or her actions. Putting into words the feelings that are being acted out helps children trust the nurse's competence and concern. Usually it is necessary for the entire staff to share this responsibility. Box 18–7 presents a step-by-step proposal for setting limits within the context of the nurse–client relationship.

Helpful Attitudes and Behaviors in Communicating with Children

Active Listening

Listening to what a child is trying to tell you is essential for successful communication with any child, but it is even more important when the child is hospitalized and coping with a world that he or she can neither understand nor describe. Knowing what a child really needs and values is the heart of successful interpersonal relationships in health care settings. The process of active listening is more subtle in some ways than it is with adults. It takes form initially from watching the behaviors of children as they play and interact with their environments. As a child's vocabulary increases and the capacity to engage emotionally with others through words and actions develops, listening becomes a more verbally interactive process. It begins to approximate more closely the communication process that occurs between adults—with one important difference. Since the world of the child perceptually is composed of concrete understandings, the nurse's feedback and informational messages should coincide with the child's developmental level. Buscaglia (1986) describes the type of listening needed, in a poem by an anonymous writer.

> When I ask you to listen and you start giving me advice, you have not done what I asked.
> When I ask you to listen to me and you feel you

have to do something to solve my problem, you have failed me, strange as that may seem.

> Listen! All that I asked was that you listen, not talk or do—just hear me.
> When you do something for me that I can or need to do for myself, you contribute to my fear and inadequacy.
> But when you accept as a simple fact I do feel what I feel, no matter how irrational, then I can quit trying to convince you and get about this business of understanding what is behind this irrational feeling.
> And when that's clear, the answers are obvious and I don't need advice.
> Irrational feelings make sense when we understand what's behind them.
> So, please listen and just hear me.
> And if you want to talk, wait a minute for your turn—and I'll listen to you.

Working with children is rewarding, hard work that sometimes must be evaluated indirectly. For instance, a primary-care nurse who had worked very hard with a 13-year-old girl over a six-month period that the girl was on a bone marrow trans-

---

BOX 18–7
Outline of a Limit-Setting Plan

1. Have the child describe his behavior.
   Key: Evaluate realistically.
2. Encourage the child to assess his behavior—is it helpful for others and himself?
   Key: Evaluate realistically.
3. Encourage the child to develop an alternative plan for governing his behavior.
   Key: Set reasonable goals.
4. Have the child sign a statement about his plan.
   Key: Commitment to goals.
5. At the end of the appropriate time period, have the child assess his performance.
   Key: Evaluate realistically.
6. Provide positive reinforcement for those aspects of performance that were successful.*
   Key: Evaluate realistically.
7. Encourage the child to make a positive statement about his performance.
   Key: Teach self-praise.

*If the child's performance does not meet the criteria set in the plan, return to step (3) and assist the child in modifying the plan so that success is more possible. If, on the other hand, the child's performance was successful, help him to develop a more ambitious plan (e.g., for a longer time period or for a larger set of behaviors).

From Felker D (1974). Building Positive Self-Concepts. Minneapolis, MN: Burgess Publishing. Reprinted with permission.

plant unit felt bad that upon discharge the girl declined to acknowledge the relationship had any meaning for her. She was glad to be going home and stated, "I never want to see any of you people again." However, just before leaving, the nurse found her sobbing on her bed. No words were spoken, but the child threw her arms around her nurse and clung to her for comfort. For this nurse, the child's expression of grief was an acknowledgment of the meaning of the relationship. With children, even those who are verbal, communication meanings are often implied through behavior rather than verbally communicated under stress.

Authenticity

Life crises, sometimes in the form of illness, are an inevitable part of life. Many parents and health professionals deceive children about procedures, illness, or hospitalization in the mistaken belief that children will be overwhelmed by the truth. Just the opposite is true. Children, like adults, can cope with most stressors as long as they are presented in a manner children can understand and if the children have sufficient time and support from the environment to cope with the sources of stress. In fact, very ill children often are a source of inspiration to the adults working with them because of their courage in facing the truth about themselves and dealing with it constructively. A nurse should never allow any individual, even a parent, to threaten a child. For example, many a parent has been heard to say, "You be good or I'll have the nurse give you a shot."

Children respect honest expression of emotions in adults. Being real with children is a crucial factor in the development of a therapeutic relationship.

CASE EXAMPLE

An older student nurse, with a family of her own, was following a family in the community in which the mother had terminal cancer. There were three children in the family, and the identified client of the student was a 13-year-old boy. He was abnormally quiet, and it was difficult to draw him out. Halfway through the semester, the boy's father died unexpectedly of a heart attack. When the boy and student nurse next met, the nurse asked the boy if there was anything special that had happened between father and son that the boy would remember about his father. The boy replied that the day before his father's death, he had received a letter of acceptance to the same school his father had attended, and he had shared this with his father. He said his father was very proud that he had gotten in. The student nurse could feel her eyes fill as the boy revealed himself to her in this special way. Her sharing of honest emotion was a significant turning point in what became a very important relationship for both participants. It was a moment of shared meaning for both of them, and from that time on, the needed common ground for communication existed.

Being real does not mean being overly familiar. Trying to interact with older children and adolescents as if the nurse is their buddy, trying to get down to their level, is confusing to the client when, as a professional caregiver, the nurse has to perform uncomfortable procedures. What the child wants is an emotionally available, calm, caring, competent resource who can protect, care about, and, above all, listen to him or her.

Conveying Respect

It is easy for adults to impose their own wishes on a child. Respecting a child's right to feel and to express his or her feelings appropriately is important. Providing truthful answers is a hallmark of respect. Confidentiality needs to be maintained unless the nurse judges that revealing information is necessary to prevent harm to the child or adolescent. In such cases, the child needs to be advised of the disclosure.

INTERACTING WITH PARENTS OF ILL CHILDREN

The child depends heavily on the sensitivity of the nurse to include the family. The nurse is often called upon to act as the child's advocate in giving parents helpful information and anticipatory guidance about the health care and developmental needs of their child (Dixon and Stein, 1987).

Parents' participation in the care of their child and active involvement in decision making regarding the youngster's treatment ensures a more stable environment for the child. Every parent is entitled to a full explanation of the child's disability and treatment. Because the parents usually assume responsibility for the child's care after they leave the hospital, it is essential to encourage active involvement from the very beginning of treatment. Many parents look to the nurse for guidance and support in this process.

Parents frequently have questions about discussing their child's illness or disability with others. Telling siblings and friends the truth is important. For one thing, it provides a role model for the siblings to follow in answering the curious questions of their friends. Issues such as overprotectiveness, discipline, time out for parents to replenish commitment and energy, and the quality and quantity of interactions with the hospitalized child have a powerful impact on the child's growth and development.

More frustrating to nurses are parents who are critical of the nurse's interventions, displacing the anger they feel about their own powerlessness to control the often devastating circumstances surrounding their child's affliction (Box 18–8). The nurse may be tempted to become defensive or sarcastic or simply to dismiss the comments of the parent as irrational. But a more helpful, empathetic response would be momentarily to place oneself in the parents' shoes and to consider what

---

BOX 18–8
Representative Nursing Problem:
Dealing with a Frightened Parent

Situation

During report, the night nurse relates an incident that occurred between Mrs. Smith, the mother of an eight-year-old admitted for possible acute lymphocytic leukemia, and the night supervisor. Mrs. Smith told the supervisor that her son was receiving poor care from the nurses and that they frequently ignored her and refused to answer her questions. While you are making rounds following the report, Mrs. Smith corners you outside her son's room and begins to tell you about all the things that went wrong during the night. She goes on to say, "If you people think I'm going to stand around and allow my son to be treated this way, you are sadly mistaken."

Problem

Frustration and anger due to a sense of powerlessness and fear related to the son's possible diagnosis.

Nursing Diagnosis

Ineffective coping related to hospitalization of son and possible diagnosis of leukemia.

Nursing Goals

Increase the mother's sense of control and problem-solving capabilities; help the mother develop adaptive coping behaviors.

Method of Assistance

Guiding; supporting; providing developmental environment.

Interventions

1. Actively listen to the client's concerns with as much objectivity as possible; maintain eye contact with the client; use minimal verbal activity, allowing the client the opportunity to express her concerns and fears freely.
2. Use reflective questioning to determine the client's level of understanding and the extent of information obtained from health team members.
3. Listen for repetitive words or phrases that may serve to identify problem areas or provide insight into fears and concerns.
4. Reassure the mother when appropriate that her child's hospitalization is indeed frightening and it's all right to be scared; remember to demonstrate interest in the client as a person; use listening responses such as, "It must be hard not knowing the results of all these tests," to create an atmosphere of concern.
5. Avoid communication blocks, such as giving false reassurance, telling the client what to do, or ignoring the concerns. Such behavior effectively cuts off therapeutic communication.
6. Keep the client continually informed regarding her child's progress.
7. Involve the client in her son's care; do not overwhelm her or make her feel she has to do this; watch for cues that tell you she is ready "to do more."
8. Acknowledge the impact this illness may have on the family; involve the health team in identifying ways to reduce the client's fears and provide for continuity in the type of information presented to her and to other family members.
9. Assign a primary nurse to care for the client's son and serve as a resource to the client. Identify support systems in the community that might provide help and support to the client.

M. Michaels, University of Maryland School of Nursing, 1987.

BOX 18–9
Guidelines for Communicating with Parents

Present complex information in informational chunks.
Repeat information and allow plenty of time for questions.
Keep parents continually informed of progress and changes in condition
Involve parents in determining goals; anticipate possible reactions and difficulties.
Discuss problems with parents directly and honestly.
Explore all alternative options with parents.
Share knowledge of community supports; help parents role play responses to others.
Acknowledge the impact of the illness on finances, on emotions, and especially on the family, including siblings.
Use other staff for support in personally coping with the emotional drain created by working with very ill children and their parents.

the issues might be. Asking the parents what information they have or might need, simply listening in a nondefensive way, and allowing the parents to ventilate some of their frustrations facilitates the possibility of dialogue about the underlying feelings. Here the listening strategies given in Chapter 10 are helpful. Sometimes a listening response that acknowledges the legitimacy of the parent's feeling is helpful: "I'm sorry that you feel so bad" or, "It must be difficult for you to see your child in such pain." These simple comments acknowledge the very real anguish parents experience in health care situations having few palatable options. If at all possible, parental ventilation of feeling should occur in a private setting, apart from the child's hearing. It is very upsetting to children to experience splitting in the parent–nurse relationship. Guidelines for communicating with parents are presented in Box 18–9.

SUMMARY

Working with children requires patience, imagination, and creative applications of therapeutic communication strategies. Children's ability to understand and communicate with nurses is to a large extent influenced by their cognitive developmental level and by limited life experiences. Nurses need to develop an understanding of feelings and thought processes from the child's perspective, and communication strategies with children should reflect these understandings. Various strategies for communicating with children of different ages are suggested, as are strategies for communicating with their parents. A marvelous characteristic of children is how well they respond to caregivers who make an effort to understand their needs and take the time to relate to them.

REFERENCES

Baerg KL (1991). Effective communication with autistic children. Rehabilitation Nursing 16(2):88–93.

Barrett R (1991). Culture and Conduct: An Excursion in Anthropology (2nd ed.). Belmont, CA, Wadsworth.

Brammer L (1988). The Helping Relationship: Process and Skills (4th ed.). Englewood Cliffs, NJ, Prentice Hall.

Buscaglia L (1986). Loving Each Other: The Challenge of Human Relationships. Thorofare, NJ, Charles B. Slack.

Carroll L (1909). Through the Looking Glass and What Alice Found There. New York, Dodge Publishing Co., Introduction.

Crain W (1992). Theories of Development: Concepts and Application (3rd ed.). Englewood Cliffs, NJ, Prentice Hall.

Dixon S, Stein M (1987). Encounters with Children. Chicago, Year Book Publishers.

Enlow A, Swisher S (1986). Interviewing and Patient Care (3rd ed.). New York, Oxford.

Erikson EH (1963). Childhood and Society. New York, Norton.

Gardner R (1986). Therapeutic Communication with Children (2nd ed.). New York, Science Books.

Hall SS, Weatherly K (1989). Using sign language with tracheotomized infants and children. Pediatric Nursing 15(4):362–367.

Ikeda A (1971). A cry of loneliness. American Journal of Nursing 73.

Johnson D (1986). Reaching Out (3rd ed.). Englewood Cliffs, NJ, Prentice-Hall.

Lewis CC, Pantell RH, Sharp L (1991). Increasing patient knowledge, satisfaction, and involvement: Randomized trial of a communication intervention. Pediatrics 88(2):351–358.

Marcus DM (1988). Manifestations of the therapeutic alliance in children and adolescents. Child and Adolescent Social Work 5(2):71–83.

Niewenhuis R (1989). Breaking the speech barrier. Nursing Times 85(15):34–36.

Page GG, Halvorson M (1991). Pediatric nurses: The assessment and control of pain in preverbal infants. Journal of Pediatric Nursing 6(2):99–106.

Parish L (1986). Communicating with hospitalized children. Canadian Nurse 82(1):21–24.

Petrillo M, Sanger S (1980). Emotional Care of Hospitalized Children (2nd ed.). Philadelphia, Lippincott.

Piaget J (1972). The Child's Conception of the World. Savage, MD, Littlefield, Adams and Co.

Spees, CM (1991). Knowledge of medical terminology among clients and families. Image 23(4):225–229.

Tesser A, Forehand R (1991). Adolescent functioning: Communication and the buffering of parental anger. Journal of Social and Clinical Psychology 10(2):152–175.

Thompson TL (1984). The invisible helping hand: The role of communication in the health and social service professions. Communication Quarterly 32(2):148–163.

Williams BE (1987). Reaching adolescents through portraiture photography. Child and Youth Care Quarterly 16(4):241–245.

Williams J (1991). Meaningful dialogue, Nursing Times 87(4):52–53.

Wincott D (1971). Playing and Reality. London, Tavistock.

SUGGESTED READINGS

Badger TA, Jones E (1990). Deaf and hearing children's conceptions of the body interior. Pediatric Nursing 16(2):201–204.

Beal CR, Belgrad SL (1990). The development of message evaluation skills in young children. Child Development 61:705–712.

Eland JM (1990). Pain in children. Nursing Clinics of North America 25(4):871–884.

Giger JN, Davidhizar R (1990). Transcultural nursing assessment: A method for advancing nursing practice. International Nursing Review 37(1):199–202.

Hansen B, Evans M (1981). Preparing a child for procedures. MCN 6:392.

Inman CE. Analysed interaction in a children's oncology clinic: The child's view and parents' opinion of the effect of medical encounters. Journal of Advanced Nursing 16:782–793.

Nugent KE (1989). Routine care: Promoting development in hospitalized infants. MCN 5(14):318–321.

Communicating with Older Adults

JUDITH W. RYAN

OBJECTIVES

At the end of the chapter, the student will be able to:

1. Identify age-related physical, cognitive, and psychosocial/environmental changes that can affect communication.
2. Identify two theoretical frameworks used with the older adult client.

3. Discuss appropriate assessment strategies and related nursing interventions.

4. Describe blocks to communication with the older adult.

5. Specify communication strategies for use in long-term care of the older adult.

6. Describe communication strategies to use with clients demonstrating cognitive impairment.

Chapter 19 focuses on communication strategies used in the nurse–client relationship with the older adult. The term "older adult" encompasses persons 65 and older. By the year 2030, projections are that this age group will encompass 22 percent of the U.S. population (USDHHS, 1991). This population represents a highly diverse group of people with a corresponding variety of past and present experiences and interests. Although this time period in a person's life is sometimes viewed as marking the end of a productive life, its meaning varies substantially to those who experience it. The purpose of including this chapter in a text about interpersonal relationships and communication skills is to heighten the student's awareness of the specialized relationship needs of the older adult.

Today's society increasingly demands that health care take into consideration the quality of life afforded clients (Steinbach, 1992). This is particularly true with geriatric health care. As direct providers of care to older adults in their homes, in hospitals, and in nursing homes, nurses are held accountable for defining standards of care for the older adult, and increasingly, for delivering appropriate psychosocial care to this segment of our population. Older adults experience a gradual deterioration of their functional abilities, making them more in need of the services of professional nurses. Normal social supports dwindle as a result of death or illness. Communication becomes a major determinant of success in health-promotion, health teaching, and compliance health care issues (Burke and Sherman, 1993).

To understand the principles of communication as they relate to relationships with older adults requires a clear understanding of the uniqueness of older persons. The stereotypical image of the older adult is that of a homogeneous, somewhat frail, not very mentally competent population. Nothing could be further from reality. There is no time in life when people are more different from each other than in later life. Consider the behavior of a group of 2-year-olds, 16-year-olds, or 30-year-olds. The persons within these groups behave much more similarly than a group of 75-year-olds. The world of older adults is as diverse as the individuals who make up this population. Older adults vary greatly in capabilities, interests, and capacities for relationships. Whereas some are frail and have reduced intellectual function due to disease, others retain a high level of physical and intellectual function until their death.

In the past, and currently in some cultures, the older adult was revered and acknowledged as the keeper of wisdom. The transmission of knowledge and tradition from generation to generation was primarily through word of mouth. The older generation served a valuable function in teaching the younger generation the ways of life. Because fewer people lived to advanced years, their unique contribution to society was considered special. As society has evolved and the printed word has become the primary transmitter of knowledge, the need for, and value of, the older adult has diminished. In addition, with more people living to advanced years, the novelty of their existence is gone. Advances in technology and medicine have

Age-related changes for healthy adults are minimal.

435

also increased the numbers of older persons who survive with significant disease and limitation, thereby putting a strain on society and the health care system.

BASIC CONCEPTS

The significant problems in communication that many nurses experience with older adults arise first from the societal discrimination and stereotyping that occurs. The second problem has to do with understanding the nature of the physical changes that take place in older adults and dealing with the sensory losses that occur with normal aging. Hearing, and secondarily, vision changes both contribute to alterations in developing therapeutic relationships. About one third of adults over 65 years have enough hearing impairment so that their social interactions are adversely affected (Mills, 1985). The third dimension of communication difficulties flows from psychosocial changes in the older adult's environment, which limit availability of social support and normal interpersonal stimuli.

PHYSICAL CHANGES IN NORMAL AGING

As a person ages, a number of physical changes occur, all of which can affect self-concept, self-esteem, and communication ability. Although in many instances the impact of these physical changes can be modified with diet, exercise, and a positive attitude, they nevertheless occur with regularity in everyone. This general physical deterioration, which everyone experiences to a greater or lesser degree, increases vulnerability to illnesses such as cancer, cardiovascular and respiratory disorders, and degenerative bone loss. The older adult will undergo diminished acuity of vision and hearing, sensory losses, vascular changes in all organ systems, and diminished vitality in muscle strength and muscle tone. The skin loses its elasticity and develops wrinkles. Menopausal and degenerative joint changes remind the older adult of the age-specific changes in body system functioning. The shifts in body fat that accompany the aging process change body contours in ways that rarely are embraced with gratitude. All of these physical changes affect body image. Many of these factors narrow previous physical functional ability. Self-concepts undergo reevaluation directly related to the significance these changes hold for each person. For most people, age-related changes are perceived as having a negative value.

AGE-RELATED CHANGES IN COGNITION

Age-related changes in cognition for healthy adults are minimal. The healthy older adult is incorrectly viewed by society as someone who is fuzzy thinking, forgetful, and heading toward dementia. For the healthy older adult, nothing could be further from reality. Without the ravages of disease, the older adult has no loss of intelligence at all but may require more time in completing verbal tasks or in retrieving information from long-term memory (Byrd, 1986; McIntyre and Craik, 1987; Petros, Zehr, and Chabot, 1983). In addition, older adults are less likely to make guesses when they are presented with ambiguous testing items in mental status exams or respond less well if they are under time pressure to perform. Therefore, communication with healthy older adults does not require special modification based on changes in their cognition. Allowing a little extra time for processing may be all that is required for successful communication.

For approximately 5 percent of the population over the age of 65, and 20 percent of those who reach the age of 80, however, there are abnormal cognitive changes. Associated with age-related dementias that are profound and progressive, these conditions are referred to as Alzheimer's disease and related dementias. Dementia is characterized by memory loss, personality changes, and a deterioration in intellectual functioning that affects every aspect of the victim's life. Although age related, the dementias are not part of the normal process of aging. The nurse can play a vital role in helping clients and their families to seek appropriate diagnosis and treatment. This is important because a small percentage of dementias are caused by organic problems, such as drug toxicity, metabolic disorders, and depression, and can be reversed with treatment.

PSYCHOSOCIAL AND ENVIRONMENTAL CHANGES

Communication is affected by the environment. As people grow older, they are more likely to suffer multiple losses of people, activities, and functions that were very important to them. Berezin (1980) notes that "the older one becomes, the more losses he sustains" (p. 22). Occupational changes in the form of retirement can have the dual impact of significantly changing a person's lifestyle, both financially and as a source of meaning. Living on a fixed income can be difficult for many people because it limits a person's options. Emotional energy that used to find expression in work, friendships, and creative activities may lose its earlier intensity as the familiar landmarks in a life tapestry are altered by age. For people who have placed a high value on their achievement in a job, there can be a perceived loss of status and self-esteem. Losses of people significant to the older adult occur with increasing regularity—through death of friends and family and adult children moving away. Any one of these factors may affect the ability of the older adult to maintain independent living because functional ability decreases and the need for assistance increases. Zetzel (1980) suggests that loss and grief must be considered an essential companion of the aging process.

Depression is a common finding in the older adult, and age is one of the strongest risk factors for suicide among white males (Waters and Goodman, 1990). The client may express a decreased capacity for mastery in many areas of his or her life, feelings of helplessness, and a loss of self-esteem. In its more severe forms, there is a loss of purpose and sense of identity. Whenever the nurse senses from the client that there is a loss of emotional energy in life and feelings of desolation about a client's situation, the nurse needs to get more information. A life without purpose is a life without meaning, and all people need to feel that their lives have meaning. Statements indicating a need for further exploration include:

"What good am I, anymore?"
"I have no role."
"What is the meaning of it all?"
"I just need a friend or someone who cares about me."
"I can't do any of the things I used to do."
"I wish I were dead."

Somatization of vague physical complaints also is cause for concern. Because age is such an important risk factor for suicide, statements reflecting helplessness and hopelessness should never be taken lightly.

Older clients face many negative situational stressors, but they also carry a lifetime of strengths that can be temporarily forgotten. Whereas deficits are real and must be acknowledged, it is the client strengths that form the basis for planning and interventions. In considering the relevance of client strengths, ask yourself the following question: How is it that many people are able to cope successfully with the aging process? Despite significant physical and psychological losses, they are able to act as important role models of how life might be lived and to share their wisdom with others. As noted in Cicero's *De Senectute (On Old Age):* "Old age, especially when honoured, has influence so great that it is of more value than all the pleasures of early manhood" (quoted in Berezin, 1980, p. 39). Generally, people who have demonstrated resiliency in tackling life's difficult issues during earlier stages of their lives will continue to do so as they face the tasks of aging. Exercise 19–1 can help you understand the value of resiliency as an adaptive mechanism in promoting well-being.

THEORETICAL FRAMEWORKS

Erik Erikson

Erikson's (1982) model of psychosocial development can be used in the assessment of the older adult's health care needs. Erikson portrays the psychosocial maturational crisis of old age as that of ego integrity versus ego despair. Ego integrity relates to the capacity of older clients to look back on their lives with a deep sense of satisfaction and their willingness to let the next generation carry on their legacy. Threads from all of life's previous psychosocial crises, trust, autonomy, purpose, competence, identity, intimacy, and generativity will resurface during this period. The extent to which these crises were successfully resolved in the past influence their impact in the present. The mature adult must recognize that his or her life is unique and that it, and the people in it, had to occur in their own particular way. By reason of having lived a full life, the older adult has developed judgment and wisdom.

Empowerment is a particularly useful concept to use as the basis for intervention. Sometimes in the throes of reverses of life, the older adult loses sight of a proven track record of coping skills. The nurse can help clients get in touch with their ability to create their own path in old age, as they have

EXERCISE 19–1
Psychosocial Strengths and Resiliency

Purpose: To promote an understanding of psychosocial strengths in life accomplishment.

Time: Discussion 1 hour, interview 30 minutes

Procedure
1. Interview an older adult (60 years or older) who, in your opinion, has had a fulfilling life. Ask the person to describe a few of his or her most satisfying achievements, and what he or she did to accomplish them. Do the same for a few of the person's most challenging moments. The interview should be taped or written immediately following the interview.
2. In a written format, reflect on this person's comments and your ideas of what strengths this person had that allowed him or her to achieve a sense of well-being and to value his or her accomplishments.

Discussion
1. On a blackboard or flip chart, identify the accomplishments that people have identified. Classify them as work related or people related.
2. Were you surprised at any of the older adult's responses to the question about most satisfying experiences? Most challenging experiences?
3. What common themes emerged in the overall class responses that speak to the lived experience of an adult?
4. Using the information from (1) and your written notes on the strengths this person possesses, identify the strengths the older adult identified on the same blackboard or flip chart. Follow the directions for (2) and (3).
5. How can you apply what you learned from doing this exercise in your future nursing practice?

done in other situations. Ego despair is defined as the failure of a person to accept one's life as appropriate and meaningful. It can be temporary, lifted by a more realistic appraisal of one's life, or permanent, leading to feelings of emotional desolation, bitterness, and hostility.

Abraham Maslow

Another theoretical framework used in assessing the needs of the older adult and directing appropriate interventions is that of Maslow. The needs of the older adult are superimposed on Maslow's hierarchy of needs, as identified in Figure 19–1.

APPLICATIONS

The assessment of older adults should focus on their level of functioning rather than on chronological age, especially since the span of old age covers 30 plus years. Functional level is a far more accurate indicator of the client's issues and relationship needs. Functional abilities in the older adult can range from vigorous, active, and independent to frail and highly dependent, with serious physical, cognitive, psychological, and sensory deficits (Waters and Goodman, 1990).

ASSESSING SENSORY DEFICITS

Because sensory deficits can have a direct impact on communication, they are of initial concern.

Hearing

Hearing loss associated with normal aging begins after age 50 and is due to loss of hair cells (which are not replaced) in the organ of Corti in the inner ear. This change leads initially to a loss in the ability to hear high-frequency sounds (e.g., *f, s, th, sh, ch*) and is called *presbycusis.* Later the loss includes the sounds of the explosive consonants (*b, t, p, k, d*), whereas the lower-frequency sounds of vowels are preserved longer. Older adults also have difficulty especially in perceiving sounds against background noises and in understanding fast-paced speech. The most understandable speech for older adults is about 125 words per minute (McCroskey and Kasten, 1982).

Problems	Symptoms		Needs	Interventions
Social clocks Self-fulfilling prophecies Routinized life	Apathy Rigidity Boredom Ennui	**Self-actualization**	Self-expression New situations Self-transcendence Stimulation	Creative pursuits Meditation Reflection Fantasy Teaching/learning Relaxation
Social devaluation Lack of role Meaninglessness Little autonomy	Delusions Paranoia Depression Anger Indecisiveness	**Self-esteem**	Control Success To be needed	Reminiscing Control of money Activate latent interests Allow to help others Identify legacy
Displacement Losses	Depression Hallucinations Alienation Loneliness	**Belonging**	Territory Friends Family Group affiliation Philosophy Confidante	Significant objects Pets, plants Soap opera families Touch group participation Listening Fictive kin
Sensory losses Limited mobility Translocation	Illusions Hallucinations Confusion Compulsions Obsessions Fear/anxiety	**Safety and security**	Safe environment Sensory accouterments Mobility	Familiar routines Spaced stimulation Explanations Environmental cues
Homeostatic resilience Poor nutrition Medications Income Subclinical disease Pain	Confusion Depression Fear Anxiety Disorientation	**Biologic integrity**	Food Shelter Sex Rest Body integrity Comfort	Adequate resources Knowledge of medications Conservation of energy Napping Small, frequent meals Choices of food

Figure 19–1 Maslow's Hierarchy of Needs Applied to the Assessment of Older Adult Clients. From Ebersole P, Hess P (1990). Toward Healthy Aging. St. Louis, Mosby.

Therapeutic Strategies to Use with Hearing Changes

In addition to the strategies suggested in Chapter 17 for the hearing impaired, several strategies can be used to improve communication with an older adult who has age-related partial hearing loss. Nurses should do the following:

- Determine if hearing is better in one ear, and then direct speech to that side.
- Help elderly clients adjust hearing aids. Lacking fine-motor dexterity, the elderly client may not be able to insert aids to amplify hearing.
- Speak distinctly in a normal voice.
- Address the person by name before beginning to speak.
- Do not speak rapidly; about 125 words a minute is best.
- If your voice is high pitched, lower it.
- If the older adult does not understand, use different words when repeating the message.
- Face the older adult so he or she can use facial expression and/or lip reading to enhance comprehension. For example, humor is often communicated by subtle facial expressions.
- Use gestures and facial expression to expand the meaning of the message.
- Do not talk with your hands in front of

your mouth or with food or gum in the mouth.
- Keep background noises to a minimum (e.g., turn down the radio or TV set when talking).
- Obtain feedback periodically to monitor what the person hears.

It is important to remember that the older adult who does not hear well is not cognitively deficient. With a little attention paid to modifying communication with the hearing-impaired older adult, there is no reason why the relationship should be any different from one with a client who does not have this disability.

Vision

Vision decreases as people grow older. Colors lose their vividness, and images can be blurred. Loss of vision can affect a person's ability to perform everyday activities, including dressing, preparing meals, taking medication, driving or using other transportation, handling the checkbook, and using the telephone. It also affects functional ability to engage in many hobbies or leisure activities, such as reading, doing handwork, and watching television. In short, a decrease in visual function almost invariably affects an individual's ability to function autonomously. The nurse can play a vital role in supporting the independence of the visually impaired client by taking a few simple actions.

Strategies to Use with the Visually Impaired

- If the older adult is also visually impaired, have eyeglasses in place to enhance ability to discern visual cues.
- Identify yourself by name when you enter the room or initiate conversation.
- Stand in front of the client and use head movements.
- Verbally explain every written piece of information, allowing time for the client to ask questions. Do not assume that because the person appears to be reading a document that it has been read accurately. Ask questions to determine the level of comprehension.
- Appropriate lighting and other visual aids can enhance vision.
- Remove any hazards, such as obstructed pathways or glares from lighting.

- Use words to describe landmarks and where you are taking the client.

Exercise 19–2 is designed to help you understand the impact of physical impairments on communication.

ASSESSING AND RESPONDING TO PSYCHOSOCIAL NEEDS

Beginning with the Client's Story

Assessment of the older adult always begins with the client's story. It is important to see and hear what is happening from the older person's perspective (Waters and Goodman, 1990). In this way, value-laden psychosocial issues, such as independence, fears about being a burden, role changes, and vulnerability, can be brought to the surface.

CASE EXAMPLE

Nurse: You seem concerned that your stroke will have a major impact on your life.
Client: Yes, I am. I'm an old woman now, and I don't want to be a burden to my family.
Nurse: In what ways do you think you might be a burden?
Client: Well, I obviously can't move around as I did. I can't go back to doing what I used to do, but that doesn't mean I'm ready for a nursing home.
Nurse: What were some of the things you used to do?
Client: Well, I raised three children, and they're all married now with good jobs. That's hard to do in this day and age. I did a lot for the church. I held a job as a secretary for 32 years, and I got several awards for my work.
Nurse: It sounds as though you were very productive and were able to cope with a lot of things. You are right that this time in your life is different. It isn't possible to do the things you did previously, but you have a proven track record of coping with life. What you have given to your family is important, but it also is important to allow them to give some things to you. It can be very meaningful to them and to you. Let's think about some ways you can make your life more satisfying and as rewarding as it has been in the past.

In this dialogue, the nurse listens carefully to what the older adult is expressing and uses this information to help the client reframe problems as challenges to be addressed in the present. Successful past achievements can be used as tools to help the client face necessary transitions and take con-

EXERCISE 19–2
What Is It Like to Experience Physical Decline?

Purpose: To promote an understanding of the effects of physical decline on the activities of daily living.

Time: 45 minutes

Procedure
1. Put cotton in your ears, dry rice in your shoes, gloves on your hands, and smear a pair of glasses with a very thin coat of Vaseline. Use tie shoes and loosely tie your shoelaces together.
2. With a partner take a short walk and carry on a conversation about what you are experiencing. Now try to open a jar and manipulate objects.

Discussion
1. What does it feel like to have diminished functional ability?
2. In what ways did your feelings about yourself change?
3. How do you think your experience will affect your appreciation and response to the older adult?

trol of his or her life. Helping the client identify sources of social support, personal resources, and coping strategies can alter the impact of physical and emotional stressors associated with age-related transitions. Exercise 19–3 provides a glimpse into the life stories of the older adult.

A mental status exam for the older adult can be much more productive if the nurse takes the time to modify its content in the simple manner identified in Box 19–1.

Using a Proactive Approach

For many reasons, the older adult needs the nurse to assume initial responsibility for directing the interview in the initial stages of the relationship. At first, new situations can cause transitory confusion for many older adults. Knowing what to expect helps decrease anxiety. Many clients are aware of the stereotypes associated with aging and are reluctant to expose themselves as inadequate in any way. They also are aware of the *YAVIS syndrome* (the tendency of physicians and other health care providers to want to treat the young, attractive, verbal, intelligent, and successful client) and to ignore or minimize the health care needs of people who do not fall into this category (Butler, 1975). In fact, some health care providers have large signs in their offices explicitly stating they do not accept new Medicare patients. For all of these

EXERCISE 19–3
Hearing the Story of the Older Adults in One's Family

Purpose: To promote an understanding of the older adult

Time: Discussion 1 hour, interview 45 minutes

Procedure
1. Interview an older adult in your family (minimum age 60). If there are no older adults in your family, interview a family friend whose lifestyle is similar to your family's.
2. Ask this person to describe what growing up was like for them, what is different today from the way it was when they were your age, what are the important values that they have held, and whether there have been any changes in them. Ask this person what advice they would give you, based on their experience, about how to achieve satisfaction in life.

Discussion
1. Were you surprised at any of the answers the older adult gave you?
2. What are some common themes you and your classmates found related to values and the type of advice the older adult gave each of you?
3. What implications do the findings from this exercise have for your future nursing practice?

BOX 19–1
Mental Status Exam for the Older Adult

---

1. Establish rapport with client and gain client's trust and acceptance before mental status examination.
2. Rule out possibility of sensory deficits (especially hearing and visual losses) before mental status examination.
3. Rule out possibility of toxic effects accruing from medication and drug dependencies before mental status examination.
4. Assess the presence, if any, of agitation, acute anxiety, and depression resulting from recent stressful events before mental status examination.
5. Assess client's retention and recall by using information, experiences, and events that have been known to have registered.
6. Test client's memory for events by selecting events that are of considerable interest and significance to the elderly client.
7. Memory of recent events should be tested by asking client to recall events that occurred in the past 8 to 24 hours (e.g., name of visitors; important event of the day).
8. Memory of more remote events may be evaluated by asking client to recall dates of important past events (birthday, anniversary date, age) and names of persons who had considerable significance for the client.

9. An independent assessment should be obtained from the client's family of the extent of the client's motivation and interest in the surroundings before the mental status examination.
10. Assessment of client's capacity for basic self-care tasks should be done before the mental status examination.
11. The nature of cognitive tasks expected of the client in the mental status examination must make allowance for the limited educational attainment of some clients and also for the impoverished nature of the client's current environment.
12. Questions of understanding, recall, and integration of materials in the mental status examination must definitely take into account the life style, cultural bias, and previous interests of the elderly client.
13. Elderly clients should not be expected to engage in psychological tests that involve prolonged capacity for memory and attention.
14. Mental status tests should be supplemented by the use of other psychologic tests involving observation of behavioral symptoms of the elderly client.
15. Careful assessment of mental status should be conducted over a longer time to preclude the possibility of off-days or client's distress on a given testing day.

From Fry PS (1986). Depression, Stress and Adaptations in the Elderly: Psychological Assessment and Intervention. Rockville, MD, Aspen Publishers, Inc., p. 62.

---

reasons, a warm, informative, proactive approach initially helps the older client feel more at ease and enhances the development of trust.

The older adult appreciates having the nurse provide structure to the history-taking interview by explaining the reasons for it and the outline of what it will involve. The I–Thou position stressed in earlier chapters is used to enhance connectedness. Questions that the older adult perceives as relevant and that follow a logical sequence are likely to hold the client's interest. Having an opportunity to talk about oneself can be extremely beneficial.

Of equal importance is the sensitivity of the nurse to the unexpressed fears of the older adult. Often the client has a strong concern that in accepting external or professional services, there is a loss of independence. In the client's mind, accepting help is the first step toward the nursing home. Consequently, the older adult may minimize difficulties. The nurse may need to assess environmental supports directly and should always bear in mind the possible association in the older adult's mind between accepting any help and independent living. For example, an older adult in cardiac rehabilitation told his nurse that he had a bedside commode and no stairs in his home. When the nurse visited the home, there was no commode, and the client's home had a significant number of stairs. He told the nurse that he was afraid she would take steps to change his living arrangements if these facts were known.

Promoting Client Autonomy

The nurse plays a critical role in helping older adults maintain their autonomy. For many clients, being independent means that they are still in charge of their lives. It is easy for the nurse to confuse the fact that an older adult appears frail, with an inability to function. As the nurse assists the client to clarify values, make choices, and take action, a stronger understanding of the unique needs and strengths of the client emerges. An open-ended approach to understanding the client as a person is helpful to both nurse and client. Often in relating their life story and exploring options relevant to the current situation with the nurse, older clients are able to step back and look at the present in a more positive way.

CASE EXAMPLE

Nurse: Mr. Matturo, it sounds as if being in charge of your life is very important to you.

Client: Yes, it is. I grew up on a farm and was always taught that I should pull my own weight. You have to on a farm. I've lived my entire life that way. I've never asked anyone for anything.

Nurse: I can hear how important that is to you. What else has been important?

Client: Well, I was a marine sergeant in World War II, and I led many a platoon into battle. My men depended on me, and I never let them down. My wife says I've been a good provider, and I've always taught my children to value honor and the simple way of life.

Nurse: It sounds as though you have led a very interesting and productive life. Tell me more about what you mean by honor and the simple way of life.

As the client expresses important information about values and life experiences, previous coping strategies can be identified. At the end of the dialogue, the nurse might summarize what the client has expressed, and say to the client, "Do you think you might be able to use any of these life skills now?" It is easier for the client to imagine possible coping skills when they are linked to principles of coping in the past. The precise actions may be quite different, but the problem-solving process may be quite similar. With this line of open-ended questioning, the nurse uses the client's story as the baseline for planning and implementing nursing care. That care is individualized and sensitive to the older adult's needs and values.

To whatever extent possible, the client should be given the opportunity to take responsibility and participate in goal setting and decision making. This simple emphasis on client autonomy in planning appropriate interventions reinforces the client's self-esteem. Developing action plans and providing support for the client in implementing them enhances self-esteem and promotes self-control. Cases in which changes in the life situation are not within the client's control should be handled honestly but matter of factly. For example, the nurse might say, "I'm really sorry that you are being transferred to the nursing home. I know it must be hard for you to accept."

Acting as the Client's Advocate

The nurse plays an important role as advocate with the older adult client. When there is a breakdown in the client's ability to meet essential needs, sometimes they can be addressed with some very simple environmental modifications and referrals. It is important to engage the client in actively exploring appropriate environmental supports, for example, homemaker services, leisure activities, and home nursing support. Introducing the need for external supports, however, without first building rapport and helping the client establish a sense of his or her personal strengths is likely to be counterproductive. Framing suggestions for external supports in terms of helping the older adult maintain independent living as long as possible often works with clients who are reluctant to use them.

Advocating for the client with the family also is important. Seen from the client's eyes in this poem, the dilemma of allowing the older adult both enough freedom and enough protection is eloquently described:

My children are coming today. They mean well. But they worry.

They think I should have a railing in the hall. A telephone in the kitchen. They want someone to come in when I take a bath. They really don't like my living alone.

Help me to be grateful for their concern. And help them to understand that I have to do what I can as long as I can.

They're right when they say there are risks. I might fall. I might leave the stove on. But there is no real challenge, no possibility of triumph, no real aliveness without risk.

When they were young and climbed trees and rode bicycles and went away to camp, I was terrified, but I let them go.

Because to hold them would have hurt them.

Now our roles are reversed. Help them see.

Keep me from being grim or stubborn about it. But don't let them smother me.

Groups are an important source of social support for the older active adult. They help restore hope and reestablish a sense of personal worth. The model of empowerment, described in Chapter 5, and the wide variety of groups available for the older adult, described in Chapter 12, offer hope to clients by helping them receive needed emotional support and providing guidance to select the most appropriate tools. It becomes easier with support to mobilize resources in the environment that will assist an individual in developing a different productive way of being in old age.

BLOCKS TO COMMUNICATION

There are a few special considerations or cautions that are relevant when communicating with older adults. Whereas these can be problems across the lifespan, they seem more prevalent in interactions with older persons. It is very easy to impede communication with any of the following:

Offering Cliché Reassurances

For example, an older man says, "I just got back from burying my wife; she was sick with cancer a long time." Communication-blocking responses might be, "Well, at least her suffering is over" or, "In time your grief will lessen." These are not particularly helpful comments, and they certainly do not promote a response from the client. In addition, they do not contribute to an assessment of the impact of this situation on the client. A better option might be, "How are you doing?" or, "I have some time, would you like to talk?"

Giving Advice

Telling an older adult what to do in a given situation rather than exploring the options available is a common block to communication—for example, "With your bad arthritis you really do need to start a walking program or you will start to lose function." A better response might be, "With your bad arthritis, I worry about your losing your mobility. What kinds of things do you do to stay physically active?"

Answering Your Own Questions

Sometimes older adults require more time to hear and understand the communication, so that their responses are not as rapidly forthcoming as with younger persons. For example, "Which do you want—tomato, orange, or apple juice?" may be quickly followed by, "I guess you would like apple juice" if a response from the older adult did not come fast enough. Another example of not waiting for an answer is, "How would you describe your chest pain?" which is too quickly followed by, "Is it sharp, dull, pricking, or aching?" The older adult should be allowed the additional few seconds to determine an answer ("It's burning") before the question is made "multiple choice." This provides a much better data-gathering approach when the cognitively intact older adult is allowed to use his or her own words to describe a problem or concern rather than having the caregiver provide the terminology.

Giving Excessive Praise or Reprimands

Often giving effusive praise can be detrimental because it blocks most responses except "thank you." For example, "You have done a wonderfully fantastic job in organizing your medications" does not readily allow the older adult to ask questions or raise a concern about some aspect of what has been done. A better response might be to recognize the accomplishment and ask if there are any remaining concerns about the medications. Also, reprimanding or scolding the older adult can be demeaning as well as a block to communication. For example, "Haven't you finished your lunch yet? You are the slowest one on the unit. What am I going to do with you?" could be more appropriately managed by identifying that this person eats slowly and perhaps could benefit from getting meals first.

Defending Against a Complaint

Many older adults have no difficulty in criticizing their environment or treatment by others, and it is often to the nurse that this criticism is verbalized. For example, "No one answered my call light last night, and I almost fell going to the bathroom by myself" may elicit a defensive response such as, "The unit was really busy last night. We had two admissions." A better approach is to determine what underlies the comment. Is the older adult afraid of being alone, of falling, or of something else? A better response might be, "What was happening with you last night?"

Using Parenting Approaches or Behaviors

When nurses use such approaches older adults may be embarrassed or feel demeaned. It is treating them like children, using terms such as "honey," "sweetie," or "doll" rather than asking them the names by which they would like to be addressed. Additionally, the nurse may answer for the older adult when someone asks the person a question. For example, the chaplain asks an older woman, "How are you doing today?" and the nurse answers for her, "Oh, she is just fine." There is a simple rule to follow when communicating with older adults: The older adult *is* an adult and should be acknowledged as such and related to in an adult manner.

COMMUNICATION STRATEGIES IN LONG-TERM CARE SETTINGS

The rigid lifestyle imposed by many long-term care facilities reinforces clients' awareness of their diminished capacity to care for themselves independently and to choose voluntary activities that have meaning to them. It is difficult to avoid feeling like an object of care rather than a person in such situations. Yet people with intact cognitive abilities in nursing homes have the same need for touching, playful teasing, outings, and other activities that most of us take for granted as ways to maintain self-esteem and happiness. Older adult clients have the same need as their younger counterparts for an individualized nursing response that takes into consideration their unique characteristics. Maintaining self-esteem is key to helping clients retain ego integrity as their physical senses diminish and their life choices decrease in quantity. The quality of the later years depends on being able to maintain hope, to have an identity, and to be valued and loved by others. The nurse plays a central role in helping clients preserve their sense of personhood by creating a nursing environment that is supportive of clients' independence and that promotes quality of life for older adult clients.

Liukkonen (1993) reports that many older adults in long-term facilities suffer from loneliness and long for someone simply to listen to them. Older adults who are institutionalized in hospitals or nursing homes often appreciate short, frequent conversations. Like everyone else, the need to be acknowledged is paramount to the older client's sense of self-esteem. Examined from an older client's perspective, the way in which the social isolation and loneliness experienced in a nursing home could be diminished is presented in the following poem:

A Cry of Loneliness

Outside my window there's only smog . . .
A row of buildings,
A never ending crowd.
Sometimes I wish someone would see me . . .
But here I sit, alone, endlessly.
Four walls surround me,
Four neutral colored walls.
Outside there are corridors
Of endless halls.
Other people are with me,
But they don't care . . .
As far as they're concerned,
I'm not there.
There is a time in the day,
It may sound silly,
When all my troubles go away.
One nurse, one smiling friendly nurse,
Stops in, stops in to say,
"And how are you today?"
The other nurses are nice
In their sterile clinical way,
But they never utter that same
"How are you today?"
She floods my room with light
The seemingly inner one,
And tho' she attends to others
And their endless chores to be done,
She makes me feel special
Like I'm the only one.*

*From Ikeda (1971). A cry of loneliness. American Journal of Nursing 73.

Continuity of care with one primary caregiver helps foster the development of a nurse–client relationship with the older adult client. It helps reduce the sense of confusion many older people experience when confronted with different caregivers (Teresi et. al., 1993) and provides a safe, comfortable environment in which the nurse is able to get to know the individual client, gaining both trust and respect.

Dealing with Memories and Reminiscences

It is not uncommon for healthy older persons to share the memories from youth, or earlier days, with those who are around. Whereas this is a meaningful way in which older adults review their life in an attempt to establish meaning and reconcile conflicts and disappointments (Butler, 1963), it can also be frustrating for the people who have heard the stories a hundred times and so turn off or avoid interacting with the persons. Rather than responding with, "Oh my, here he goes again with that Model T story," it is better to respond to the story and enter it with the older adult to learn more about why it has special relevance or meaning. It is an opportunity to gain insight into the person, who he or she was, what aspirations and dreams were fulfilled or unfulfilled, what contributions are valued, and what goals are yet to be attained. Reminiscing also has been demonstrated to increase self-esteem, mood, morale, and socialization (Lappe, 1987).

Several suggestions have been made by Cox and Waller (1987) in connection with responding to the reminiscences of the older person:

1. *Ask exploring questions.* In the Model T story, one might ask, "What made you buy that car?" or, "How did you get the money to buy it?"
2. *Use the memory as a bridge to other information.* "What other types of cars did you have after that?" "Were you usually the one in your social group who had the car—where would you go?"
3. *Find a cue for a question within frequently heard stories.* "Cars seem very important to you. What was it like for you when you had to give up driving last year?"
4. *Practice ways to tell the person that you have heard the story before.* (This should be done only if the repetition occurs within the same conversation, or close to it.) "Oh yes, I remember the Model T episode when you drove the car into the Madison County reservoir. What other unusual or amusing things happened to you during your life?"

When Couples Enter Long-Term Care

Erikson identifies "loss of a significant other" as an important factor in the geriatric client's life. For many couples who have lived together for 30 or 40 years, the prospect of being separated is intolerable. The nurse faces a special challenge when husband and wife enter a long-term facility together. Frequently they have very different needs. For example, the husband who has suffered a stroke requires complete nursing care, whereas the wife is not incapacitated physically, but desires to be with her husband as much as possible. One partner may reside in the nursing unit and the other in independent or assisted-living quarters. They still have a need for each other's companionship, yet they display different communication needs. Sensitivity and a proactive approach that helps the older couple honor their commitment to each another can be extremely important in ensuring their quality of life. No greater human gift can be given than that which supports the personhood and human commitments of one person to another. The following strategies can be used to support the communication needs of partners living in the nursing home:

1. Get to know the couple's routine. If possible, complete the routine for a partner when the spouse is unable to do this—for example, take the partner for a walk. This relieves the spouse's anxiety and promotes the belief that the partner is receiving the care the spouse ordinarily would provide.
2. Provide social activities that can involve both partners.
3. Develop ways to allow married couples to share and to remain in close contact with each other.
4. Acknowledge and reinforce the contributions of one spouse caring for the other.
5. Give the more independent spouse "time off" to regroup, and provide frequent information.
6. Treat both partners as integral parts of the health care team, and offer additional emotional support as the dependent spouse's health diminishes (Hoogendijk and Brooke, 1991).

These strategies, with obvious modifications, are also helpful with adult children of dementia victims. It is not unusual for the "sandwich generation" to feel a keen responsibility to care for the cognitively impaired parent and to feel torn between that responsibility and taking care of their own children. Sometimes the nurse needs to give permission to the caregiver to take a break. When this permission is accompanied by a genuine reassurance that the loved one will be cared for and that the caregiver is an important member of the health team, the advantageous results for the cognitively impaired client and family members can be startling.

A related aspect of care with the older adult is sexuality. For some reason we in our society assume that older persons no longer feel sexual. Consequently, older adults have little opportunity to discuss this often very important dimension of self with a knowledgeable health professional. Issues such as how to respond to one's spouse in the early stages of a dementia when he or she still seeks marital relations, what to do with sexual feelings that can no longer be gratified, and whether it is appropriate to have sexual feelings and desires over age 65, often never get discussed. The nurse can play an important role in bringing these issues up as relevant topics for discussion. In doing so, the nurse can help clients or family members resolve unnecessary guilt and embarrassment about having very normal personal feelings.

Role Modeling

Role modeling is an aspect of care that indirectly affects the interpersonal relationships older adults have with their caregivers. Since ancillary personnel often constitute the largest group of primary caregivers in long-term care settings, it is particularly important for professional nurses, who frequently supervise them, to serve as positive role models. This means that the professional nurse needs to be actively involved with older adult clients and willing to share observations with other personnel. People learn not only what is taught but also what is "caught," in the form of attitudes toward the older adult. Although as students you may not think that ancillary personnel are paying attention to you, they are very much aware of how you interact with clients. If professional attitudes are positive and supportive, they influence positively the care a nurse's aide gives to clients. If the nurse treats the client as an object, why should the nurse's aide, who looks to the professional nurse as an important role model, do anything different?

COMMUNICATION STRATEGIES WITH THE COGNITIVELY IMPAIRED ADULT

It is important to assess cognitive function in an older adult early in the communication process. Some older adults with moderately severe communication deficits retain all of their intellectual abilities. It is not unusual to find an older adult in a dementia day care center who earns a perfect score on a mental status exam but who manifests marked depression and minimal communication and therefore has been inappropriately placed in day care rather than having the depression treated. Also, the deaf older adult presents significant communication problems but may very likely be intellectually intact.

Other older adults retain enough of their sensory functions to communicate effectively, but the means of processing information, learning, and responding become dysfunctional. Most communication deficits associated with memory loss are cumulative and progressive. Unfortunately, in the early stages environmental conflicts may be heightened because of the older adult's seemingly normal superficial verbal behaviors. Only when one tries to engage the older adult in a deeper conversation does the degree of communication deficit become apparent. For example, the client may say, "I'm feeling great; Martha and I visited the grandchildren, and we had a great time." But when asked what he actually did on the visit, he may be unable to answer with any real detail. Because dementia victims can express themselves clearly in superficial conversation, there is a sense that the communication ability is still present. To some extent it is, but it is a profoundly narrower range of language behavior and meanings.

In a more advanced loss of cognition, the older adult is unable to express complete thoughts. He or she has difficulty finding the words to use, and sentences are unfinished. The dementia victim, unable to continue, stops in mid-sentence, or continues with phrases that have little to do with the intended meaning. In such cases the nurse can help by filling in the missing words, smiling, supplying the logical meaning, and then asking the client if this is what he or she meant. Another strategy is to almost finish a sentence and have the client supply the last word. In fact, anything to help reduce the client's anxiety about groping for thoughts that do not come helps the person continue. To appreciate how the cognitively impaired client feels, think of a time when you were not able to retrieve a word or fact because of anxiety. The more you try to retrieve the information, the harder it becomes. Having another person compassionately give a boost by providing a verbal cue often jogs the process of remembering.

Another communication difficulty is *apraxia,* defined as the loss of the ability to take purposeful action even when the muscles, senses, and vocabulary seem intact. This condition causes a person to appear to register on a command, but then to act in ways that suggest he or she has little understanding of what transpired verbally. When the cognitively impaired adult fails to follow through on the agreed-upon action, the nurse may interpret the behavior as uncooperative or obstinate. Talking the client through a procedure, step by step, providing additional cues, and allowing additional time for processing information reduce the person's anxiety and improve performance.

Reminiscence

Relationships with older adults with mild to moderate cognitive disability can take advantage of the simple fact that remote memory (recall of past events) is retained longer than memory for recent events. Asking older adults about their past life experiences often serves as a way to connect verbally with those who might have difficulty telling you what they had for breakfast two hours ago. A memory is a gift to the nurse from someone who is sharing part of himself or herself and who might have little or nothing else to give (Ebersole and Hess, 1990). For some reason, once older adults with mild memory deficits begin to reminisce about their past, communication flows more freely and retention of messages is stronger. Mentally impaired persons become more verbal and will even assist others in remembering events when in a reminiscence group (Baker, 1985). The nurse can act as an advocate in learning about the dementia victim's needs, expressed as past occurrences, and can translate them into current requirements for care.

Repetition and Instructions

The nurse should have additional means of communicating with older adults experiencing memory loss. It is very appropriate to address the older adult by his or her name several times before beginning the communication. This approach can be useful in focusing the older adult's attention on what is coming next. By selecting a simple, relevant thought from a stream of loosely connected ideas, the nurse permits the conversation to continue, often to the visible relief of the impaired dementia victim. Restating ideas, using the same words and sequence, are simple communication strategies that allow a conversation to continue.

By speaking in simple sentences, repeating phrases, and giving directions one at a time, the nurse enables the older adult to use his or her remaining capabilities. For example, asking the older adult to make a cup of coffee might be beyond his comprehension. But breaking the request down into smaller steps—"Open the cupboard," "Open the drawer," "Take out a spoon," "Close the drawer," "Open the jar of instant coffee," and so on—may make the activity possible, and thus reinforce self-esteem.

Use of Touch

Gaining eye contact and using touch are also helpful to maintain focus. The use of appropriate touch with the cognitively impaired can be a helpful tool, but its applicability must be determined on an individual basis. For some people, being touched increases their agitation and confusion, whereas for others being touched is a calming and welcome action.

Nurses should be sensitive to their own style of touching: how it is done, to whom, when, and why. The older adults least likely to experience touch from nurses are men—and those who have severe cognitive impairment (Watson, 1975).

There is also a hierarchy of places on the body to touch. The least threatening and private areas of the body are the hands, shoulders, back, and arms. Although the thigh and face are relatively personal parts of the body, they are frequently selected when touching older adults. These areas should not be chosen as sites for touching dementia victims at the beginning of the nurse–client relationship but may be appropriate after rapport has been established.

Use of Multiple Modalities

Using more than one sense in communication facilitates the process. For example, touching the hand with the hair brush in it and saying, "Now use the brush to fix your hair" provides an additional focus for the older adult. Knowing, when helping a dementia victim groom and dress, that stiffening can occur due to an automatic neurological response and that this manifestation is not due to a resistive and rejecting person enables the nurse to be more sensitive to the older adult. Sometimes, waiting 15 minutes and trying again can be a productive option.

Use of Distraction for Disruptive Behaviors

Since older adults with memory loss lack the cognitive ability to develop alternatives, they can have what appears to be temper tantrums in response to real or perceived frustration. These tantrums are called *catastrophic reactions* and represent a completely disorganized set of responses. They are often difficult for the nurse to comprehend or manage. Usually there is something in the immediate environment that precipitates the reaction, but fatigue, overstimulation, misinterpretations, and inability to meet expectations may also be contributing factors. The emotion may be appropriate even if its behavioral manifestation is not. In these situations, the nurse can use distraction to move the older adult away from the offending stimuli in the environment or to diffuse the troublesome feeling through postponement. For example, the nurse might say to the older adult, "We will do that later; right now, let us go out on the porch," while gently leading the person away. Direct confrontation and an appeal for more civilized behavior usually serve to escalate rather than diminish the episode.

Often there are warning signs of an impending catastrophic reaction—such as restlessness, refusals, or general uncooperativeness; by redirecting the dementia victim, the outburst may be avoided. It is important for the nurse to model the appropriate responses to this behavior and to explain to the family members and staff what is happening and what to do to prevent or address it.

SAMPLE CLINICAL SITUATION

PROBLEM: An 86-year-old woman exhibits disturbed attention and confusion.

NURSING DIAGNOSIS: Inadequate coping related to organic memory loss.

NURSING GOALS: Minimize factors that contribute to dysattention.

NURSING APPROACH: Compensatory and supportive.

METHOD OF ASSISTANCE: Guiding, supporting, providing an understanding environment

NURSING INTERVENTIONS:

1. Look directly at the client when talking.
2. Call the client by name several times.
3. Position self in the client's line of vision.
4. Rest hands on the client's hands.
5. Give clear, simple directions in a step-by-step manner.
6. Direct conversation toward concrete, familiar objects.
7. If attention lapses, let the client rest a few minutes before trying to regain his or her attention.
8. Provide simple activities that will encourage purposeful action.
9. Repeat messages slowly, calmly, and patiently until she shows some sign of comprehension.
10. Vary the words to fit the client's ability to comprehend.
11. Modify the environmental stimuli that affect attention.
12. Assist the family to understand that inattention and failure to respond is due to her inability to process information cognitively.

The evaluation of the effectiveness, appropriateness, and efficiency of the nursing actions with the dementia victim does not occur through words, as it does with other nurse–client relationships. Behaviors of the client in which agitation is reduced, cooperation is obtained, and the client responds positively to the caregiver are indicators of effective nursing interventions and successful outcomes.

SUMMARY

Chapter 19 emphasizes the use of therapeutic communication skills with older adult clients. To understand the principles of communication as they relate to relationships with older adults requires a clear understanding of the uniqueness of older persons.

Older adults vary greatly in capabilities, interests, and capacities for relationships. Whereas some are frail, with reduction of intellectual function due to disease, others retain a high level of physical and intellectual functioning until their death. Technological advances and better nutrition have reduced mortality rates, increased the lifespan, and correspondingly increased the number of older adults who now require health care. Communication difficulties can occur because of changes in sensory and cognitive functioning in the older adult as well as because of significant changes in social support systems. The nurse can provide the older adult client with a therapeutic environment that supports the client's independence and that helps the client compensate for failing physical, cognitive, and emotional functioning. Strategies such as reminiscing, encouraging spousal support, and treating the older adult client with dignity are proposed. A care plan for the cognitively impaired client is presented. As a primary provider of long-term care, the nurse is in a unique role to support and meet the communication needs of the older adult client.

REFERENCES

Baker, N (1985). Reminiscing in group therapy for self-worth. Journal of Gerontological Nursing 11:21.

Berezin M (1980). Psychodynamic considerations of aging and the aged: An overview. In Steury S, Blank M (1980). Readings in Psychotherapy with Older People. Washington, DC, U.S. Department of Health and Human Services.

Burke M, Sherman S (eds.) (1993), Gerontological Nursing: Issues and Opportunities for the Twenty First Century. New York, National League for Nursing Press.

Butler, R (1963). Life review: An interpretation of reminiscences in the aged. Psychiatry 26:65.

Butler R (1975). Why Survive? Being Old in America. New York, Harper & Row.

Byrd, M (1986). The effects of previously acquired knowledge on memory for textual information. International Journal of Aging and Human Development 24(3):231.

Cox, BJ, Waller L (1987). Communicating with the Older Adult. St. Louis, Catholic Health Association of the United States.

Ebersole P, Hess P (1990). Toward Healthy Aging: Human Needs and Nursing Response (3rd ed.). St. Louis, Mosby.

Erikson E (1982). The Life Cycle Completed. New York, Norton.

Fry PS (1986). Depression, Stress and Adaptations in the Elderly: Psychological Assessment and Intervention. Rockville, MD, Aspen Publishers, Inc.

Hoogendijk L, Brooke V (1991). After all these years: Help couples living in a nursing home keep the spark alive. Geriatric Nursing September/October 247.

Ikeda (1971). A cry of loneliness. American Journal of Nursing 73.

Lappe J (1987). Reminiscing: The life review therapy. Journal of Gerontological Nursing 13:12.

Liukkonen A (1993). The content of nurses' oral shift reports in homes for older adult people. Journal of Advanced Nursing 1095–1100.

Maclay E (1977). Green Winter: Celebrations of Old Age. New York, Reader's Digest Press.

McCroskey RL, Kasten RN (1982). Temporal factors and the aging auditory system. Ear Hear 3:124–127.

McIntyre J, Craik F (1987). Age differences in memory for item and source information. Canadian Journal of Psychology 41:175.

Mills R (1985). The auditory system. In Pathy, MSJ (ed.), Principles and Practice of Geriatric Medicine, (6th ed.). London, Wiley, pp. 841–854.

Petros TV, Zehr HD, Chabot RJ (1983). Adult age differences in accessing and retrieving information from long-term memory. Journal of Gerontology 38:589.

Steinbach U (1992). Social networks, institutionalization, and mortality among older adult people in the United States. Journal of Gerontology 47(4): 183–190.

Teresi J, Homes D, Benenson E, Monaco C, Barrett V, Ramirez M, Koren M (1993). A primary care nursing model in long-term care facilities: Evaluation of impact on affect, behavior and socialization. Gerontologist 33(5):667–674.

Waters E, Goodman J (1990). Empowering Older Adults: Practical Strategies for Counselors. San Francisco, Jossey-Bass.

Watson W (1975). The meaning of touch: Gerontological nursing. Journal of Communication 25:104–112.

U.S. Department of Health and Human Services (1991). Healthy People 2000. Washington, DC, Public Health Service.

Zetzel E (1980). The dynamics of the metaphysiology of the aging process. In Steury S, Blank M (1980), Readings in Psychotherapy with Older People. Washington, DC, U.S. Department of Health and Human Services.

Chapter 20

Communicating with Clients in Stressful Situations

ELIZABETH ARNOLD

OBJECTIVES

At the end of the chapter, the student will be able to:

1. Define stress and sources of stress.

2. Identify selected theoretical frameworks of stress and coping.

3. Identify factors influencing the impact of stress.

4. Specify the relationship between stress and disease.
5. Identify expressions of grief.

6. Identify basic concepts of coping.

7. Apply the nursing process to the care of clients in stressful situations.

8. Identify strategies for burnout prevention.

I knew I was being childish; still I acted terribly. I insulted nurses and doctors, repeatedly questioned their judgment . . . basically acted like a jerk. If only someone could have realized what was happening to me.

Bluhm, 1987

The purpose of this chapter is to provide the student nurse with a foundation for understanding basic concepts of stress and coping in the nurse–client relationship. Interacting with clients in stressful situations is a challenge nurses meet on a regular basis in nursing practice. Families and clients entering any health care situation experience a wide range of emotions that shield both normal and abnormal anxiety. The nurse frequently is the first point of contact as well as the most accessible health professional for clients and their families in any health care situation. It is to the nurse that the client and family turn in times of stress, not only for information and care but also for understanding and reassurance as a fellow human being.

Some stressors in health care can be modified within a problem-solving framework. Other stressors in the clinical setting cannot be changed. They defy rational explanation. Unchangeable stressors such as a terminal illness, chronic pain, death of a person or the end of a relationship, and serious injury may require acceptance, a constructive outlook, and strategies to maintain self-esteem in the face of overwhelming, unfair, and irreversible stressful circumstances. Helping a person explore new directions and develop a different perspective can be just as important as the more traditional problem-solving strategies used to cope with stress (Lazarus and Folkman, 1984). In health care situations, making difficult decisions under less than ideal circumstances is the rule rather than the exception.

Assessment of the effects of stressors on clients and their families helps the nurse identify appropriate nursing diagnoses and plan effective interventions. This chapter offers a framework for understanding the nature of stress and proposes guidelines for responding constructively to clients who experience stress with expected and unexpected changes in their lives. Learning effective coping and stress-management strategies enables the nurse to communicate effectively in stressful health care situations ranging from health promotion to care of the terminally ill. By learning to care for others experiencing stress, the nurse can apply similar concepts to his or her own life. One cannot give from an empty cupboard.

BASIC CONCEPTS

DEFINITION

Stress can be defined as a physiological and psychological response to the presence of a stressor. It is a simple term used to describe a complex phenomenon. Selye (1982) notes that "Everybody knows what stress is, and nobody knows what it is." Some people refer to stress as an external condition or stimulus, "the stress of nursing school, the stress of an illness, a visit to the in-laws," for example. Other people regard stress as a person's internal physiological response to a perceived or actual threat to self (a stress response). A third way of looking at stress is as a transaction between the stressor and the individual experiencing it. With this approach, the outcome depends on (1) how an individual appraises the meaning of a stressor and (2) whether the person feels that appropriate coping responses and social support systems are available.

A *stressor* is any demand, situation, internal stimulus, or circumstance that threatens a person's personal security and balance. A person's sense of personal security and balance is referred to as **homeostasis,** or **dynamic equilibrium.** When a person feels centered and personally secure, the person experiences "dynamic equilibrium," or a homeostatic state. People respond to stressors in their lives with troublesome feelings of strain, tension, and anxiety. These inner tensions disrupt homeostasis, leading to other physiological changes and possible permanent damage to body, mind, and spirit.

Sources of Stress

Sources of stress can be physiological, psychological, social, or spiritual in nature. Physiological stressors include illness, aging, injury, heat, cold, or pain. Psychological stressors are as varied as the people experiencing them, including loss of a job, death of a friend or pet, getting married or divorced, being a single parent, moving away from home, and feeling role overload or value conflicts. Spiritual stressors are linked with physical or psychological stressors and emerge from within, in the form of a loss of purpose or meaning or a questioning of religious values. For example, role overload, extreme pain, or a change in organizational culture can call into question the meaning of one's contributions or the presence of a higher power. Men and women experience stressors differently and characteristically respond differently, but the physiological experience of inner strain is similar, and stress invariably causes a reappraisal of self-concepts (Gadzella et al, 1991). A person's environmental context, including language, ethnohistory, religion, social support, cultural values, and economic and educational factors affect his or her presentation of stress (Leininger, 1990).

Hospitalization creates stress. Entering a health care situation in and of itself creates varying levels of psychological and physical stress. Clients and their families don't know what to expect or how to respond in an unfamiliar setting. Pain coupled with worries about health, work, or social relationships heighten the impact of each stressor. Fear of the unknown—surgery, outcomes, prognosis, medical procedures and treatments, pain management—creates tremendous anxiety for clients. Individual identity gets lost with the donning of the short hospital gown and a wrist band. Physical discomfort, strange noises and lights, interruptions and unfamiliar people asking personal questions, and strange equipment heighten the drama. Unanticipated events and circumstances that one cannot control increase stress. For example, unexpected side effects from a medication or pain that doesn't respond to medication increase stress levels because the client feels things are not progressing as they should (McCaffery and Beebe, 1989). With experience, *the nurse can anticipate stress reactions and inquire about important client feelings*. The nurse is a valuable resource in providing measures of support and information to clients and their families in stressful situations.

THEORETICAL MODELS OF STRESS

Stress as a Stimulus

As a stimulus, stress covers a wide range of situations, including those in which there is a stimulus deficit (the absence of expected stimulation), intense stimulation, or unrelenting stimulation.

Any change in a life situation or relationship stimulates a stress reaction. Regardless of whether the change was sought, most people respond to changes in their lives with a physical reaction, confusion, and feelings of being overwhelmed. Since life situations and relationships are in flux for almost everyone, ranging from family structure, unexpected illness or catastrophe to career, role identity, and social changes, stress is inevitable. The extent to which a transition, change, or crisis alters a person's lifestyle and personal relationships affects the level of stress it creates for that person. Stressors requiring a significant change in the life style of the individual have a greater impact, as do cumulative stresses that occur within a short period of time (Steptoe and Matthews, 1984).

Stress arouses powerful emotional reactions ranging from exhilaration, anxiety, anger, frustration, and disbelief to sadness and functional immobilization (Emmons, 1991; Epstein and Katz, 1992). Physically, a person responds to prolonged or intense stress with physiological symptoms. In 1967, Holmes and Rahe generated a list of 43 potential life events capable of stimulating a stress reaction and subsequent physical illness. According to the Holmes and Rahe model, certain predictable life events create a stress stimulus that activates a nonspecific vulnerability to developing physical illness. Each life event stressor is given a numerical score. Their research suggests that experiencing a significant number of stressors over a short period of time fairly predictably leads to physical illness. The higher the life events scale score, the more likely the person is to experience severe distress and perhaps develop a stress-induced physical illness. The Holmes and Rahe Life Events Scale (1967) (see Box 20–1) is used by nurse researchers as an instrument for empirical evidence of a correlation between critical life events and subsequent illness. Although the scale has been criticized for trying to capture a major concept with a single measure, 25 years later it remains one of the most widely used measurement tools of the links between mind and body in understanding the development of stress reactions. Exercise 20–1 is designed as a clinical application of the model.

Nonevents in a person's life can have just as severe an impact on a person's stress level as an actual situation—not being promoted or not con-

BOX 20–1
The Social Readjustment Rating Scale

Forty-three common life events are listed in the order of their importance found in the research of Holmes and Rahe (1967). Total score predicts likelihood of developing a serious illness within the next two years. Scores more than 300 indicate a high probability (80 percent) of developing a serious illness within the next few years. Scores between 150 and 300 have a 51 percent probability, and scores less than 150 within a year have a 37 percent probability of developing a major physical or psychological illness.

Life Event	Your Value Score	Life Event	Your Value Score
1. Death of spouse	100 ____	23. Son or daughter leaving home	29 ____
2. Divorce	73 ____	24. Trouble with in-laws	29 ____
3. Marital separation	65 ____	25. Outstanding personal achievement	28 ____
4. Jail term	63 ____	26. Spouse begins or stops work	26 ____
5. Death of a close family member	63 ____	27. Starting or finishing school	26 ____
6. Personal injury or illness	53 ____	28. Change in living conditions	25 ____
7. Marriage	50 ____	29. Revision of personal habits	24 ____
8. Fired at work	47 ____	30. Trouble with boss	23 ____
9. Marital reconciliation	45 ____	31. Change in work hours, conditions	20 ____
10. Retirement	45 ____	32. Change in residence	20 ____
11. Change in family member's health	44 ____	33. Change in schools	20 ____
12. Pregnancy	40 ____	34. Change in recreation	19 ____
13. Sex difficulties	39 ____	35. Change in church activities	19 ____
14. Addition to family	39 ____	36. Change in social activities	18 ____
15. Business readjustment	39 ____	37. Mortgage or loan under $10,000	17 ____
16. Change in financial state	38 ____	38. Change in sleeping habits	16 ____
17. Death of close friend	37 ____	39. Change in number of family get-togethers	15 ____
18. Change to different line of work	36 ____	40. Change in eating habits	15 ____
19. Change in number of arguments with spouse	35 ____	41. Vacation	13 ____
20. Mortgage over $10,000	31 ____	42. Christmas	12 ____
21. Foreclosure of mortgage or loan	30 ____	43. Minor violation of law	11 ____
22. Change in work responsibilities	29 ____		Total ____

From Holmes TH, Rohe RH (1967). The social readjustment rating scale. Journal of Psychosomatic Research 11:213–218. The scale gives complete wording of the items. Reprinted with the permission of Pergamon Press, Ltd, Oxford, England.

ceiving a child, for example. For many people, the stress of a nonevent can be even more painful because nonhappenings may not be obvious to anyone else other than the person feeling the stress. Most people don't feel as comfortable talking about being passed over for promotion or not being able to conceive a child as they do about sharing a visible illness or job stress.

Stress as a Physical Response

The concept of stress as a generalized response to environmental demands was first described by Hans Selye in 1936. Selye's model is basically a biological model of the stress reaction. His research found that a person's body reacts in a predictable manner to any stressor regardless of its nature. According to Selye (1982) the *stress response* is a term used to describe a nonspecific physiological response to the pressures affecting an individual during the course of daily living.

Not all stress is dangerous. A certain amount of anxiety and stress facilitates productivity, increasing personal involvement and satisfaction. In fact, life would be quite boring with no stress. It is unlikely most people would get out of bed without feeling a certain amount of tension about anticipated activities. Selye uses the term *eustress* to describe a milder level of stress that acts as a positive stress response with protective and adaptive functions. The increased stress a person feels in completing a project with a deadline is an example of eustress. As a person capitalizes on the additional physiological stress response, he or she actu-

EXERCISE 20–1
Assessing Stress as a Stimulus

Purpose: To provide practice with understanding stress from a stimulus perspective

Procedure: Analyze the following case example and identify factors using the Holmes and Rahe Life Events Scale, with the case example as the basis for data analysis.

> Sally Byrd's father was diagnosed as having Alzheimer's disease a year ago. Her mother, who has been the primary caregiver, recently broke her hip. Her father is ineligible for Medicaid, yet they do not have enough money to pay for the care he needs. Sally's husband fears he will be laid off from his job within the next few months. Her three teen-aged sons are normal teenagers who demand her attention and time. As the only child of her aging parents, Sally sees no alternative but to bring her parents to live with her, temporarily and perhaps permanently. If she does assume this responsibility, Sally can expect to experience a significant change in her role, her family routines, and even in her relationships with other family members. The cumulative stressors of her father's chronic disorder, her mother's illness, and her husband's potential job loss create a complex crisis situation for Sally and her family.

Critical Thinking Questions for Discussion:
Using the Holmes and Rahe Life Events Scale (see Box 20–1), how would you rate Sally's level of stress? What individual, family, and environmental factors would you have to consider in planning care? If you were the nurse in this situation, how would you intervene to help Sally and her family reduce the impact of multiple stressors?

ally can feel a sense of exhilaration in meeting the deadline.

General Adaptation Syndrome

More intense and prolonged levels of stress can produce *distress,* a stress response capable of creating permanent pathological changes and even death. Selye (1956, 1982) hypothesized that the body tries to respond and compensate for stress through a series of physiologically adaptive changes referred to as the General Adaptation Syndrome (GAS). This biological stress syndrome, diagramed in Figure 20–1, occurs in three phases. First, the body institutes an initial *alarm* phase, evidenced in changes in the sympathetic nervous system and hormonal secretions of the adrenal glands. These neuroendocrine changes cause physical alterations that are designed to mobilize energy resources for action. There is an increase in norepinephrine followed by a return to normal levels. To appreciate the significance of the initial alarm reaction, think of the immediate physiological response you have when the car in front of you stops unexpectedly and you think you might hit it. You feel a physiological rush of adrenaline, which causes increased breathing, muscle tension, and accelerated heart rate. These sensations subside after you realize you are no longer in danger. You then feel momentarily drained and limp as you realize you are not going to hit the car.

The state of alarm cannot exist indefinitely so the body tries to adapt to the presence of the stress agent. Selye refers to this stage of the GAS as the *resistance phase.* With chronic exposure to stress, other hormonal and chemical changes attempt to stabilize the physical response to the stress agent. The body has finite resources that over time become depleted and establish permanent alterations in brain and body chemistry. Such metabolic changes can influence the development or advance the progression of stress-related chronic diseases such as peptic ulcer, high blood pressure, asthma, heart disease, and mental disorders (Leidy, 1989).

There is a positive side to the resistance phase that can aid in reducing stress. Physiologically, the body develops a chemical substance referred to as endorphins to maintain homeostasis. Snyder (1977) first described endorphins as naturally occurring internal opiate substances that develop in response to a brain stimulus. They bear a resem-

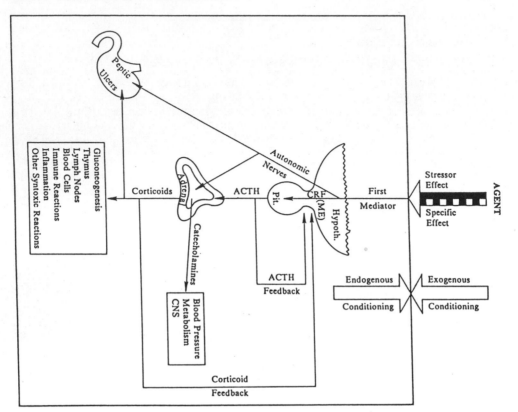

Figure 20–1 Model of the General Adaptation Syndrome (GAS)

Stage I: Alarm Reaction. Characterized by a hypervigilant state, general mobilization of the body's somatic defense mechanisms, discharge of hormones affecting neurotransmitters, enlargement of adrenal cortex and lymphatic system.

State II: State of Resistance. Occurs with continued exposure to stressful agent. An adaptive phase in which the body tries to regain equilibrium. Hormonal and chemical changes help the person restore function. Body produces endorphins, substance related to ACTH with antistress effects, shrinkage of adrenal cortex.

Stage III: State of Exhaustion. Occurs when the body's adaptability is no longer sufficient to respond to the stress. Enlargement dysfunction of lymphatic structures; loss of adaptability and exhaustion can result in death. Depletion of adaptive hormones.

Reprinted with the permission of The Free Press, an imprint of Simon & Schuster, from *Handbook of Stress: Theoretical and Clinical Aspects,* Leo Goldberger and Shlomo Breznitz, editors. Copyright © 1982 by The Free Press.

blance to the effects of morphine in stimulating good feelings in some people (Emrich, 1981). Physical exercise, sexual activity and brief stress increase the production of endorphins. Prolonged or recurrent stress, however, depletes endorphin production (McCaffery and Beebe, 1989). Knowledge of the role of endorphins in stress management is helpful. Exercising and large muscle activity increase the production of endorphins, causing a lowering of blood pressure, heart rate, and buffering the unhealthy effects of stress. To test this assumption, try an aerobics class or a daily swim and see if you feel less tense and more energetic. Like any other stress-management strategy, consistency and a regular routine enhance its effectiveness. With stress-reducing strategies and social support, a person can recover from the stress stronger physically and psychologically. Without intervention, the physical response can continue to intensify.

Over time the body becomes unable to respond effectively to excessive or prolonged stress. When this occurs, a state of exhaustion ensues, in which the body literally gives up the fight. The *exhaus-*

tion phase characteristically presents as symptoms of serious mental disorganization and physical collapse. This final physiological response to a stress agent can end in death if the demands continue to exceed the person's resources. Even when the body is able to return to a previous state of resistance and adaptability, residual effects and possible irreversible damage can alter the immune system permanently. The major criticism of Selye's theory is that it fails to take into consideration environmental and personal factors influencing the adaptive process.

Stress as a Transaction

The classic cognitive appraisal model of Lazarus and Folkman (1984) is particularly helpful in understanding the concept of stress as a transactional process rather than simply as a physiological state or outcome. By contrast with Selye's physiological model, Lazarus conceptualizes stress from a cognitive appraisal perspective, taking into consideration individual differences in how people interpret and respond to stressful situations.

From a transactional perspective, Lazarus (1966) defines stress as "a generic term for the whole area of problems that includes the stimuli producing stress reactions, the reactions themselves and the various intervening processes." For stress to occur, there must be a dynamic relationship between a (stressor) situation or circumstance in the environment and the individual experiencing the stressor. The appraisal of the stressor and the person's ability to resolve it are critical components of that relationship.

Primary and Secondary Appraisals

In the Lazarus stress model, the emphasis is on personal judgments critical to the development of the stress reaction. There are two levels of appraisal, primary and secondary, that will influence the development of a stress response. The first level focuses on the event itself. How a person perceives the stressor (primary appraisal) influences how the person will respond to it. Stressors perceived as a major threat to the self-concept or satisfying relationships with family and friends elicit a stronger stress response than those that do not have a direct impact on a person's sense of self and significant relationships. Emotional arousal occurs in response to events experienced as a personal threat to homeostasis, an acceptable self-image, and good relationships with family and friends. Figure 20–2 provides a visual description of the process.

Once emotional arousal occurs, a person automatically switches to a second form of appraisal focusing on the availability and adequacy of personal coping skills. Included in this secondary appraisal of the situation is the person's perception of his or her resources and external supports to handle the stressor. Interpersonal support, information, and tangible resources provided during this appraisal period will make a difference in the development of the stress response.

Stress Is a Subjective Experience

Lazarus contends that stress is a subjective experience, and consequently an objective stressor may or may not create a stressful situation for a given person. Whereas a certain set of circumstances can be overwhelmingly stressful for one person, another person can cope with the same set of circumstances without significant distress (Lazarus and Folkman, 1984). Two college freshmen, for example, may experience their first semester away from home quite differently. For one student, the experience may be a challenging and growth-producing adventure. The other student may feel extremely confused and frightened. How each student personally perceives the meaning of the stressor will influence its impact. Personal coping behaviors (previous experiences, ability to make friends, cognitive maturity) are secondary appraisal variables that can intensify or reduce the impact of the stressor. Changing the circumstances even slightly can affect the secondary appraisal. For example, having a supportive roommate and frequent care packages from home can reduce the impact of the stressor for the student who is lonely and unsure during the first semester of college.

FACTORS INFLUENCING THE IMPACT OF STRESS

Magnitude of the Stressor

The objective magnitude of the stressor affects the impact it has on an individual. Losing a child or a spouse unexpectedly, having one's home and valued belongings totally destroyed by fire or hurricane, and suffering a significantly disfiguring facial

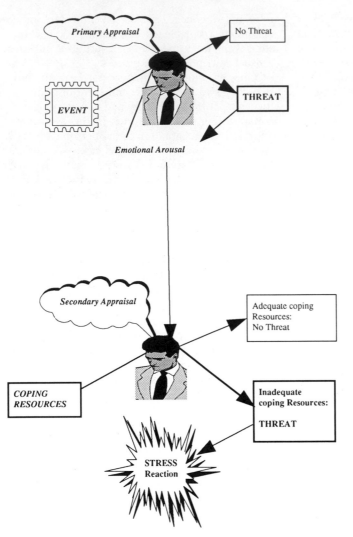

Figure 20–2 Primary and Secondary Appraisal in Stress Reactions

injury are examples of stressors that can create lifelong stress for most people.

Meaning of the Stressor

The perceptual meaning of the stressor has just as much effect on a person as the actual magnitude of the stress (Fig. 20–3). Personal interpretations of a stressful event are as varied as the persons affected by them. Individual differences in personality affect the impact of a stressor. High self-esteem and a strong sense of personal identity buffer stress interpretations. Sources of identity strength such as education, occupational level, aspirations, religion, and cultural supports partially account for differences in coping resources. The relationship one has can affect the perception of a stressor. Being criticized by your boss or a valued friend has greater impact than receiving similar criticism from a stranger.

The meaning of a stressor can be altered temporarily with self-talk and other emotionally based defensive maneuvers (Lazarus and Folkman, 1984). Self-talk statements such as, "I decided that's not my problem," "I'm surprised to find that I don't miss Jack as much as I thought I would," or, "This radiation has had no impact on my life; I still play tennis every day" allow a person

Figure 20–3 The Client's Perception of the Crisis Event Is As Important As the Actual Event. © 1994; reprinted courtesy of Bunny Hoest and Parade Magazine.

to minimize the impact and modify the meaning of stressors. Other coping strategies such as selective attention, ego defense mechanisms, and avoidance change the meaning of a stressor by allowing only certain portions of it into awareness or by transforming the meaning and refocusing negative energy onto another object or person.

Number of Stressors

The number of stressors a person experiences within a time period influences the impact of the current stressor. Logically, this makes sense; a person is a finite being with a certain amount of personal resiliency and resources. When these personal reserves are exceeded, the person becomes increasingly unable to respond. The accumulated stress becomes a chronic condition, making the individual more susceptible to experiencing new stressors with greater intensity. Another dimension of the number of stressors is the number and quality of stressors concurrently operating in the family. Frequently these can have a ripple effect in increasing the stress for a single family member, even though the person is not directly involved in the family crisis.

Developmental Level

A person's developmental level influences the impact of the stressor. For example, death of a parent is highly traumatic for any child, but par-

ticularly so during the years four to six and during early adolescence when the child psychosocially is more vulnerable to separation issues and budding identity changes. Aging clients may not have the same cognitive flexibility or physical stamina to cope with multiple stressors that they experienced at an earlier age. On the other hand, elders may have developed a coping perspective that their younger colleagues may lack.

Availability of Social Support

In a number of research studies, social support is identified as an important buffer, capable of reducing stress. *Social support* consists of all of the social environmental factors that contribute to a person's sense of well-being (Edens, Larkin, and Abel, 1992). Social support has both direct and buffering effects. Direct effects help a person make decisions enhancing the development of a positive self-concept. Indirect buffering effects act as interpersonal shock absorbers. They help the client reduce the level of stress by providing social and practical resources needed to make the stressor less threatening (November et al., 1992). Community sources of social support include most support groups, senior citizens, church groups, and camps for handicapped children.

Sharing stressful situations with another person helps put boundaries on the stressor (Davis et al., 1992). Support systems need not be restricted to people who are relatives, close at hand, or good at listening. When clients or families experience stress they may need a wide range of professional and supportive services. Support systems can include people with common interests, community agencies and therapists, local support groups, and social service groups that can be depended upon to moderate the wear and tear influences of chronic stress on mind, body, and spirit. The simple act of talking about one's stress helps a person think through its meaning and allows the opportunity for developing constructive coping strategies. The emotional support a person receives strengthens the individual's personal resources and lessens the burden (Felsten, 1991).

Previous Life Experiences with Similar Stressors

Previous experience with similar stressors can prove helpful or can intensify the stressor for an individual. If the person has been successful in coping with a similar stressor, coping strategies used in the original circumstances can be applied to the current situation. The person with a history of resolving stress successfully has confidence that his or her personal resources will be sufficient to relieve the current stress. On the other hand, having had previous experience with similar stressors can increase the intensity of the current stressor. For example, a person laid off from work for the third time in as many years may experience the current layoff in a much more profound way than would be the case if this were the first layoff.

RELATIONSHIP OF STRESS AND DISEASE

Extensive research on the topic suggests that stress increases vulnerability to illness. Physical symptoms of stress are well known and cover a wide range of possibilities. Sleep disturbances, changes in eating patterns, headaches, stomach and bowel disturbances, heart palpitations, perspiration, muscle tightness, feelings of lightheadedness, back pain, fatigue, and skin eruptions are well-recognized physiological indicators of stress-related responses.

Stress affects the immune system. It is implicated as a primary contributing factor in stress related disorders such as hypertension, headaches,

heart attacks, Graves' disease, ulcers, colitis, HIV infections, and arthritis (Ben-Schlomo and Chaturvedi, 1992; Gelent and Hochman, 1992; Niaura and Goldstein, 1992; Perry, Fishman, and Jacobsberg, 1992; Thompson et al., 1992). Figure 20–4 displays some of the disorders associated with acute and chronic stress. Although stress does not cause the disorder directly in most instances, it acts as a risk factor by compromising a person's immunologic status. Knowledge about the role of stress is still far from being fully understood, but there is no question that it plays an important role in a person's physiological makeup and response to the environment (Schafer and Fals-Stewart, 1991). Furthermore, psychological and physiological stress-reducing strategies can prevent or diminish the effects of stress-induced illness (Burchfield, 1985; Steptoe, 1991).

HOW STRESS GETS EXPRESSED

Temporary, acute psychological stress in health care settings finds expression in anxiety, hostility, denial, grief, and depression. During times of stress, it is more difficult to ask for help or to express thoughts and feelings clearly. A common reaction is anger. People say things they don't mean and wouldn't dream of saying in ordinary circumstances. A person experiencing stress, in looking for reasons for its occurrence and by assigning blame or guilt, is likely to antagonize those persons in the environment who are best able to help.

Anxiety

The word "anxiety" derives from the Latin root *angere,* "to cause anguish or distress." Anxiety in stressful situations makes the experience more painful and compounds feelings of powerlessness in a threatening environment. Heightened anxiety reduces a person's ability to reflect on situations objectively. It becomes increasingly difficult to envision possibilities, weigh options, make choices, and take action. Unlike fear, which has a direct, identifiable source of discomfort, anxiety is diffuse. The experience of anxiety may be out of proportion to the stimulus and often is not traced readily to any identifiable cause.

People experiencing anxiety as a response to

Figure 20–4 Physical Effects of Chronic Stress

stress have many emotions simultaneously—anger, grief, shame, embarrassment, dread, dismay—which may be difficult to sort out emotionally. At times, the anxiety is expressed directly in nervousness, pacing, inability to concentrate, or insomnia. Or it can be felt but not expressed as "emotional numbness," images of impending doom, feelings of going crazy, and destructive fantasies.

The consistent nonanxious presence of the nurse as a source of support is the most helpful intervention. Giving the family progress reports, being available to answer questions, and letting the client and family know who is available to respond to their needs and how to contact the nurse are simple interventions that keep a client and family from becoming more anxious (Hull, 1991; Rushton, 1990). It is important to include every family member in discussions and to provide practical information about community resources. Knowledge and acceptance are powerful antidotes to stress expressed as anxiety.

Hostility

Nobody is completely rational in times of stress. It is easier to be verbally hostile than to admit feeling totally overwhelmed and powerless. The client or family expresses dissatisfaction with the nursing care, the food, visiting hours, nonfunctional equipment—anything, and everything. Family members angrily blame each other for an injury, blame the physician for operating—or not operating—on a loved one, and criticize the nurse for not responding quickly enough. If the nurse can recognize the origin of the hostility and see it as a cry for help in coping with escalating stress, it is possible to defuse the stress before it gets out of control. Verbal hostility can be deflected by being open to the expression of negative feelings, accepting ownership of mistakes, and supporting the hostile person without necessarily condoning the behavior. Exercise 20–2 is designed to help you appreciate the close relationship between anxiety and anger.

EXERCISE 20–2
The Relationship between Anger and Anxiety

Purpose: To help students appreciate the links between anger and anxiety and how anger is triggered.

Time: 25 minutes

Procedure:
1. Think of a time when you were really angry. It need not be a significant event or one that would necessarily make anyone else angry.
2. Identify your thoughts, feelings, and behavior in separate columns of a table you construct. For example, what were the thoughts that went through your head when you were feeling this anger? What were your physical and emotional responses to this experience? Write down words or phrases to express what you were feeling at the time. How did you respond when you were angry?
3. Identify what was going on with you prior to experiencing the anger. Sometimes it is not the event itself but your feelings prior to the incident that make the event the straw that breaks the camel's back.
4. Identify underlying threats to your self-concept in the situation—for example, you were not treated with respect; your opinion was discounted; you lost status; you were rejected; you feared the unknown.

Discussion:
1. In what ways were your answers similar and different from those of your classmates?
2. In what ways did anxiety and threat to the self-concept play a role in the development of the anger response? What percentage of your anger related to the actual event and to what percentage to self-concept?
3. In what ways did you see anger as a multidetermined behavioral response to threats to self-concept?
4. Did doing this exercise change any of your ideas about how you might handle your feelings and behavior in a similar situation?
5. What are the common threads in the events that made people in your group angry?
6. In what ways could experiential knowledge of the close association between anger and anxiety be helpful in your nursing practice?

CASE EXAMPLE

Client: I don't see any point in talking to you. You can't bring Jenny back, and I don't want what you have to offer me now.

Nurse: (in a calm, low voice and slowly): You're right, Don, I can't bring Jenny back, but what I can offer you is a chance to talk about a very tragic and frightening situation for you. My experience is that this can prove to be healing.

It is important for the nurse to remember that stress can get transformed into hostility or a demandingness without the person being aware that the underlying emotion is anxiety. In times of stress the nurse needs to consider that (1) hostility is a temporary emotional response displaced on you. It has nothing to do with you personally. You simply happen to be the most likely target because you are available; you are the one most involved with the care of the loved one, and you are unlikely to retaliate. (2) The experience of a serious illness is always an emotional as well as an intellectual event for families, who are emotionally connected to the client (Bluhm, 1987). Emotional understandings differ from intellectual understandings. People can understand intellectually why the nurse is acting in certain ways and what is happening to their loved one. But their emotional understanding may be quite different. When there is a discrepancy between cognitive and emotional understanding, anger is a frequent common denominator. For example, even though Mother is 95 and the family knows intellectually that death is imminent, the emotional remembrance of her is as someone they don't want to lose just yet. The emotional understanding of the situation may take precedence over the intellectual facts. Family members may be angry at the physician or other family members for the decision to let her die without heroic measures. Helping the family accept the fact that there is no way to avoid making very difficult life and death decisions, and supporting them in their decision making is supportive.

Anger projected on the nearest target, the nurse as primary caregiver, threatens the nurse's energy and commitment. Turning frustration, despair, anger, and feelings of being overwhelmed into constructive, meaningful cooperation is not easy. Yet in every stressful and crisis situation, what the person or family yearns for most is understanding, healing, and human intimacy (Dossey, 1991). What every client and family expects from the nurse is a person who will perceive their pain and confusion and help them to decode the behaviors, feelings, and thoughts that distort reality.

Most important is the nurse's willingness to acknowledge and validate a person's right to be angry about situations beyond his or her control as long as it doesn't compromise the rights of others (Bluhm, 1987). For example, the nurse can listen calmly and suggest ways in which the client's concerns can be addressed. If client or family expectations are unrealistic or unable to be met in the current situation, alternative explanations and suggestions reduce anxiety and allow further discussion.

> CLIENT: I'm paying a lot of money here and no one is willing to help me. The nursing care is terrible, and I just have to lie here in pain with no one to help me.
>
> NURSE: I'm sorry you are feeling so bad. Could you tell me a little more specifically what's going on with you, and maybe we can try to do something a little differently to help you.

The nurse first acknowledges the feelings of the client. Her second statement asks for more information and encourages the client to enter a mutual partnership in correcting the problem. The client feels heard even if the issue cannot be totally resolved as the client wishes. More helpful guidelines for helping clients diffuse their anger are presented in Chapter 14. Strategies to use in situations when hostility escalates into violence are described in Chapter 21.

Grief

The word "bereavement" derives from the Latin, to be robbed. Grief develops as a normal psychological response to the loss of something or someone significant to an individual. The loss of a person can occur death or through separation. Bowlby's (1961) study of children and later adults demonstrated the acute grief reactions associated with the loss of a significant person. Even temporary losses can provoke a grief reaction. The loss of a part of self can accompany loss of a body part, loss of a role, or loss of a physical function such as memory or bladder control. Many losses carry symbolic meanings that intensify the actual loss, such as the loss of identity a job provides. When a child dies, the role of parent is lost. Many parents speak of losing a part of themselves when they lose a child.

The nurse needs to be aware of the multilayered dimensions of grief work (Sanders, 1989). Factors affecting grief as a response to stress include previous attachment history and the quality of the attachment, previous losses, the developmental age of the griever, the emotional complexity of the relationship, and the availability of social networks. A person who has experienced secure relationships is more likely to be able to express his or her feelings and to cope with grief in later life. On the other hand, if the grieving person has had previous, unresolved losses, the current loss may reactivate feelings about past losses. Obviously, the stronger the emotional attachment to a person, role, or body part, the more intense the grief. Similarly, the loss of open, honest relationships are easier to grieve. Relationships characterized by ambivalent, angry, denied, or idealized feelings require a more complicated grieving process because one ultimately must address the unresolved feelings in addition to mourning the loss. Exercise 20–3 allows you to consider your own attitudes about grieving.

Lindemann's (1944) classic description of grief reactions following a fire at a nightclub in Boston in which almost 500 people died still serves as a major source of information about the grieving process. He proposed that grief is a normal reaction to a loss and that if normal grieving does not occur, the person is vulnerable to the development of psychopathology. He viewed pathological grief as an exaggeration of the normal process. According to Lindemann (1944, p. 141): "Common to all is the following syndrome: sensations of somatic distress occurring in waves lasting from 20 minutes to an hour at a time, a feeling of tightness in the throat, choking with shortness of breath, need

EXERCISE 20–3
Attitudes toward and Beliefs about Grief and Bereavement

To help you identify your attitudes about grief, respond to the following questions by using the initials *A* (agree), *NS* (not sure), or *D* (disagree).

_____Grieving becomes more difficult when people "give in" to their sorrow.
_____Having many sympathetic people around tends to prolong grief.
_____Grieving for more than one year becomes abnormal.
_____Bereavement is an opportunity for people to mature as well as a time of suffering.
_____Grief is as powerful as love in shaping attitudes and behavior.
_____Grief left unexpressed goes underground to reappear later.
_____People never fully recover from the damage of major losses.
_____Some people do not need to grieve, even after a serious loss.
_____People can make their grieving "better" or "worse" by the way they choose to live during bereavement.
_____A person's grief is abnormal when she or he sees or hears the dead person.
_____An adult's renewed interest in someone of the opposite sex is a sure sign that bereavement has abated.
_____A mother's loss of a young child is the most difficult grief of all to experience.
_____Religious beliefs profoundly affect the way bereavement is expressed.
_____Children should be shielded as much as possible from the effects of a death.
_____Children up to adolescent years grieve differently than do adults.

Questions About Grief
Please complete the following sentences. It is up to you to decide whether you will share your responses with your teacher.

1. What frightens me the most about grief is _____.

2. The aspect of grief I am most uncertain (or most confused) about is _____.

3. When it comes to the subject of grief, the opinion that I have that most people disagree with is

_____.

4. On the subject of grief and bereavement, what I would like to know more about is _____.

Dershimer RA (1990). Counseling the Bereaved. New York, Pergamon Press, pp. 129–131. Copyright © 1990 by Allyn and Bacon. Reprinted by permission.

for sighing, and an empty feeling in the abdomen, lack of muscular power and an intense subjective distress described as tension or mental pain."

Later, Engel (1972) described a sequence of events that characterize the grieving process. The first stage, *shock and disbelief,* starts with a visceral response to the loss. As one person described it, "It felt as though there was a great distance between me and everyone else, as if I was cocooned in cotton wool. Literally numb with shock; no tears, no feelings, just absolute numbness" (Lendrum and Syme, 1992, pp. 24–25)." Denial frequently is seen in the first stage. Statements such as, "He's a strong boy, I know he is going to make it," even though the child is on a respirator and is not expected to live, or, "I just had Johnnie to the doctor last week and he didn't say anything about leukemia" are examples. This initial disbelief is protective as an emotional buffer against a powerful assault to the integrity of the self. It does not mean that the client or family has no perception of what is happening, or is delusional. It simply is an ego defense against a reality that will take time to absorb. Getting the family or client to accept the reality of the situation is counterproductive at this point. Perhaps the most helpful response the nurse can make is to acknowledge what the client is experiencing and to suggest that there is no logical explanation for why it happened.

It also is important to find out what purpose

the denial is serving and to assess the extent to which it compromises treatment. Time is not always of the essence. If there is no immediate jeopardy of treatment, it is best to support the person's right to process it in his or her own way. While the nurse should not reinforce the denial, neither should the hope that accompanies the denial be immediately squelched. An appropriate initial response to expressions of denial might be, "This must be very difficult for you to absorb. Can you tell me what you are experiencing right now as you think about . . . ?" This response allows the client to put concerns into words and offers clues about the role denial plays in the current situation.

If the client tells the nurse, "I think I'm losing my mind," which is a frequent occurrence, the nurse might respond, "Many people feel that way. You are not losing your mind. What really is happening is that you are feeling disoriented because of the sudden and unbelievable nature of what is happening here. Can you identify what worries you the most?" By acknowledging the legitimacy of the client's feelings and labeling the nature of it, the nurse reinforces the client's self-integrity and begins to help the client put boundaries on the anxiety by identifying important concerns.

Engel refers to the second stage as *developing awareness.* During this phase, there is an urge to recover the lost person or part of self. The response to the loss is acted out through crying, irritability, and outrage. The grieving person may report seeing or hearing the presence of the lost person or may sense his or her presence through the smell of a flower. Clients who have lost body parts physically feel the sensations or pain in the missed limb. These are not hallucinations brought about by biological misfiring of neurotransmitters. Clients can be reassured that these are normal feelings brought about by thoughts of the missed person or part of self.

CASE EXAMPLE

Client: Sometimes when I'm driving home from work, I can actually hear Nancy talking to me. It's eerie, but it feels so real. Am I going crazy?

Nurse: Mary, when people have suffered a loss of someone very significant to them, they often do think they hear or see them. It can be very frightening and disorienting, but it really is a very normal response to a powerful loss of someone special.

During the *reinstititution phase,* a person begins the recovery process by acknowledging the reality of the loss. Spiritual beliefs and the support of friends help provide an initial sense of acceptance. Nurses can encourage involvement by inquiring about religious rituals.

The fourth stage of the grieving process, *resolving the loss,* is characterized by a withdrawal from others in order to regain strength and sort out important feelings. The danger during this period is that the grieving person will damage relationships with significant people who don't understand his or her need to withdraw. It is important to caution the grieving client not to make major life decisions at this point and to share the observation that many people try to sever relationships with important people in their lives following a serious loss. The nurse can also support the client's significant others by sharing the same observation and encouraging them to remain in contact with the grieving person.

The *idealization* phase is characterized by the ability to abstract those qualities and values that were fundamentally significant about the person or lost object. Meaning is given to the loss because of the legacy that has been left behind. This enables the grieving person to put the loss in perspective. It is a necessary step in the process of rebuilding a world in which the lost object does not dominate but, rather, is integrated into it. At this stage, the grieving person feels more in control and can move toward reestablishing bonds with others. Simos (1979, p. 45) advises that, "The task of mourning is completed when a personality reorganization takes place, through which the old self and the new self now without that which has been lost are integrated. . . . Healthy grieving should end with new avenues for creative living."

Grieving is a slow process. A normal grief response can last from one to three years with gradual symptom reduction. Even though life seems to be back to normal, a chance scene or remarks continue to stir memories. Missing the person can be intense on the anniversary of the death. Clients appreciate the nurse who verbalizes this. Many people, including the client, believe that grieving is a short-term six-week process and that people should get on with their lives once the funeral is over.

Multiple losses take longer to resolve. The most

helpful intervention is to focus on one relationship at a time instead of trying to address the losses together. To do the latter can be overwhelming to the client. It also is important to put the cumulative effects of the loss into words so that the client does not allow himself or others to be deluded into thinking multiple loss is the same phenomenon as a single loss. Most people who suffer multiple losses require professional assistance to help them sort out the complexity of their feelings.

Anticipatory Grief

Anticipatory grief initially was described by Lindeman as an emotional response that occurs before the actual loss. It has many of the characteristics of an actual grief reaction with some notable exceptions. With anticipatory grief there is always the hope that the loss which one anticipates will not occur. The constellation of feelings, sorrow or anger over the projected loss, and ambivalence—wishing it would happen soon and simultaneously dreading the finality of the loss—make the grieving process more unstable. People find themselves torn between remaining faithful to the client and needing to start a new life for themselves. There is no way to complete the grieving process.

CASE EXAMPLE

Marge was married to Albert for 43 years. She was a good and loving wife, but Albert was diagnosed with Alzheimer's disease five years ago. He is in a nursing home and can no longer communicate. The doctor told Marge that his disease is progressing rapidly and he most likely will die within the next few years. Marge just turned 60. She has been living with this disorder since she was 55 and would like to have a life of her own. She misses Albert and feels guilty because she has the "other feelings, of wishing he would die so that she can get on with her life, and feeling cheated out of a life she deserves."

Grieving in Children

Children grieve too. But frequently adults assume the depth of their grief is less or that they should be spared participating in the full knowledge of what has happened. Most children know something is dreadfully wrong even if they don't voice their concerns. For example, a young woman of 30 spoke of going with her grandmother to the emergency room and of her grandmother's subsequent death when she was nine years old. Her parents minimized her feelings and didn't allow her to see her dead grandmother in the hospital bed. As an adult, this woman experiences acute anxiety every time she enters a hospital. Her memory of her grandmother's sudden death springs to her mind as if it happened yesterday. If she had had the chance to process it and to ask questions, she might not have this reaction.

Dying children often are aware that they are terminal, but feel so socially isolated that they are unable to express their grief and depression (Stephenson, 1985). They don't want to upset their parents or siblings. When they have been given false information or reassurance, they don't know what to believe because their intuition and body symptoms don't compute with the information they are receiving from people they trust. This can compound their stress.

Children express their grief according to their stage of development and established family patterns. Although it is particularly difficult to tell a child what is really going on, all children need to have their questions answered simply and honestly, taking into account their stage of development. Since parents often are so consumed with their own grief, the nurse becomes important in helping the child identify important feelings and making sure that they do not get buried. Asking children open-ended questions about what they know about their illness and how they think they are doing prompts them to voice significant fears and concerns. The nurse also might ask the child how people important in his or her life—parents, grandparents, and siblings—think they are doing. Small children can be encouraged to express their feelings through drawings and manipulating doll figures.

Special Issues for the Frail Elderly

At the other end of the lifespan are the frail elderly who have lost hope. For many, particularly those without a consistent social support system, their grieving is different. It is experienced as a prolonged, meaningless existence in a body that no longer responds to their commands and with the loss of almost all that matters—friends, family, and work. The frail elderly frequently mourn the social death they experience, and instead of fearing physical death they long for it. Theirs is a chronic stress, unrelieved by the presence of a social support system that their younger counterparts have at their disposal. The nurse is in a unique position to help frail elderly clients fill this gap.

Complicated Grief

A reactive depression represents a more complicated grief response to stress in which the intensity of the grief reaction does not subside. Physically, stress symptoms appear as sleep and appetite disturbances, fatigue, stomach or chest pains, and poor concentration. Overactivity without a sense of loss, withdrawal from friends and relatives, hostility and mistrust of others, and involvement in self-destructive relationships and activities are some of the overreactions people experience after a loss (Lindemann, 1944). Emotionally, a person may feel sad, experience irritation at inconsequential situations, and feel empty or hopeless. It is hard for a person experiencing depressive symptoms to have a future orientation. There seem to be few options worth considering, and energies are directed inward.

To assess for symptoms of complicated grief, the nurse might ask questions such as, "Do you find that you are able to go to sleep, but wake up at 3 or 4 A.M. and find it difficult to fall asleep again?" "Have you had a recent weight loss?" "Is it harder to concentrate at work?" A person who is not dieting and experiences a 10-pound weight loss over a six-month period probably is experiencing depression. A sleep pattern of falling asleep and waking too early without being able to resume sleep and an inability to concentrate are cardinal symptoms of depression. The nurse can ask the client directly about feelings of sadness, guilt, and emptiness, including the question, "Have you felt bad enough to harm yourself in any way?" Unresolved grief usually requires the skills of an advanced practitioner. Clients should be referred immediately when the nurse makes a determination that the normal grieving process is abnormally delayed, absent, prolonged, or too intense.

Hidden Stressors

Practical, social, and financial considerations are indistinct problems that create significant stress for a client in health care settings. They often get missed because they occur within the framework of a diagnosed physical illness. For example, a diagnosis of cancer can stimulate questions of mortality even if it is caught in an early stage. The person receiving the diagnosis is never the same. Each physical exam or questionable symptom arouses thoughts of a recurrence of the disease, even when there is nothing to warrant such a conclusion. By verbalizing the existence of such questions for many people, the nurse can help the client address concerns that are not readily apparent.

Nurses who are reluctant to ask questions about personal relationships as they relate to the client's illness or to probe emotionally tinged subjects such as sexual or occupational adjustment are doing their clients a disservice. Although it is difficult to answer questions like, "Have I got cancer" or, "Will this surgery make me impotent" or, "Am I going to die?" the client deserves an honest answer. Usually it is useful to ask the client what prompted the question and to have a good idea of the client's level of knowledge before answering. The answer can be tentative and should reflect the nurse's level of knowledge about the client as well as the condition.

Questions about how the person will experience reentry into the work force after a disfiguring, mental or lengthy illness frequently never get asked. People are embarrassed to ask them, or they may feel the issues are inconsequential because the person is over the worst parts of the experience. Yet reentry and acceptance questions are legitimate concerns of the client, and they create hidden stress.

Family members' hidden stress gets expressed through self-questioning, such as, "How will I manage?" "Was it my fault?" "Could I have done more?" These questions strike close to the core of a person's self-concept. They remain unexpressed because to articulate them would be overwhelming, or they might be perceived as "selfish" or irrelevant. The nurse who is astute enough to pick up on the family's stress can prompt discussion of these hidden fears. For example, the nurse might say to the wife of a recent paraplegic, "Seeing your husband like this must be a terrible shock. I would think you might be wondering how in the world you are going to live with John immobilized like this." This type of statement allows the client to describe the unexpressed thought and make sense of her current situation.

CONCEPTS OF COPING

Lazarus defines **coping** as "constantly changing cognitive and behavioral efforts to manage specific external and/or internal demands that are appraised as taxing or exceeding the resources of the person" (Lazarus and Folkman, 1984). Coping includes a person's immediate management of stress as well more long-term efforts to adapt to difficult and stressful circumstances. Coping strategies may be conscious or unconscious, negative as well as positive. People learn coping strategies from their parents, peers, and the particular circumstances life presents to them.

Pearlin and Schooler (1978) in their classic work on coping, define *coping* as "the concept used to refer to any response to external life strains that serves to prevent, avoid or control emotional distress." They identify three types of coping strategies people use to deal with stressful situations: (1) strategies to change the stressful situation, (2) strategies that change the meaning of the stressor, and (3) strategies to help the person relax enough to take the stress in stride. Usually they work best as interrelated tasks. The more versatile and flexible a person's coping strategies are, the more likely a person is able to manage life's challenges. People with a wide variety of life opportunities and supportive people in their lives have an advantage over those who lack them. A person, like a hothouse plant, benefits from gradual exposure to different environments and circumstances. Inadequate coping strategies can reflect a life in which a person has not had to respond to danger and lacks the necessary skills to do so. Exercise 20–4 helps you examine coping strategies.

Defensive Coping Strategies

People use conscious and unconscious methods to change the meaning of a situation in their minds. Knowledge of defensive coping strategies helps the nurse assess client coping skills. Although most people use unconscious ego defense mechanisms in difficult situations, such mechanisms are useful only as a temporary coping strategy for tension reduction. Their value is limited because they serve as a form of self-deception or reality distortion (Lazarus and Folkman, 1984).

Ego defense mechanisms work unconsciously to protect a person from intolerable anxiety by (1) distorting a threat, (2) substituting another reality, or (3) completely blocking out the threat to self through denial. As a short-term strategy, they may prove beneficial. People need time to absorb the meaning of a serious stressor.

CASE EXAMPLE

Lynn was diagnosed as having a high cholesterol count and was advised to go on a low-fat diet. Her friends notice no change in her diet, and Lynn says she sees no reason to modify it. Lynn says she sees no purpose in going on a low-fat diet because "it's all in the genes." Both her parents had high cholesterol, and she claims there is nothing she can do about it, even though the physician has advised her differently.

EXERCISE 20–4
Coping Exercise

Purpose: To help students experience the wide range of adaptive and maladaptive coping strategies.

Time: 45 minutes

Procedure:
1. Identify all of the ways in which you handle stressful situations.
2. List three personal strategies that you have used successfully in coping with stress.
3. List one personal coping strategy that did not work, and identify your perceptions of the reasons it was inadequate or insufficient to reduce your stress level.
4. List different coping strategies identified by students on a chalkboard or flip chart.

Discussion:
1. What common themes did you find in the ways people handle stress?
2. Were you surprised at the number and variety of ways in which people handle stress?
3. What new coping strategy might you use to reduce your stress level?
4. Are there any circumstances that increase or decrease your automatic reactions to stress?

Lynn's denial is a defense against feeling that she will die like her parents from heart disease.

Defense mechanisms are separated into two categories. Anxiety-reducing defenses are used to help people adapt more successfully to their stressful environment. Included in this category are defenses such as compensation, identification, and sublimation. The other category of defense mechanisms is anxiety postponement. Defenses that put off the full experience of anxiety include denial, displacement, projection, reaction formation, rationalization, repression, and undoing. Box 20–2 presents definitions and clinical examples of common defense mechanisms.

Freud (1940) believed that a person will ignore or repress powerful emotional feelings that threaten the self-concept. For example, many people have little memory for difficult parts of their childhood. Repression is also used to push unacceptable, hostile, selfish, and sexual feelings out of awareness. Embarrassing behaviors that are illogical and undesired by a person will continue to emerge unexpectedly in relationships until the real problems and anxieties are unmasked and resolved. Over time ego

---

BOX 20–2
Ego Defense Mechanisms

Ego Defense Mechanism	*Clinical Example*
Regression: Returning to an earlier, more primitive form of behavior in the face of a threat to self-esteem.	Julie was completely toilet trained by two years. When her younger brother was born, she began wetting her pants and wanting a pacifier at night.
Repression: Unconscious forgetting of parts or all of an experience.	Elizabeth has just lost her job. Her friends would not know from her behavior that she has any anxiety about it. She continues to spend money as if she were still getting a paycheck.
Denial: Unconscious refusal to allow painful facts, feelings, or perceptions into awareness.	Bill Marshall has had a massive heart attack. His physician advises him to exercise with caution. Bill continues to jog six miles a day.
Rationalization: Offering a plausible explanation for unacceptable behavior.	Annmarie tells her friends she is not an alcoholic even though she has blackouts, because she drinks only on weekends and when she is not working.
Projection: Attributing unacceptable feelings, facts, behaviors, or attitudes to others. Usually expressed as blame.	Ruby has just received a critical performance evaluation from her supervisor. She tells her friends that her supervisor doesn't like her and feels competitive with her.
Displacement: Redirecting feelings onto an object or person considered less of a threat than the original object or person.	Mrs. Jones took Mary to the doctor for bronchitis. She is not satisfied with the doctor's explanation and feels he was condescending but says nothing. When she gets to the nurse's desk to make the next appointment, she yells at her for not having the prescription ready and taking too much time to make the next appointment.
Intellectualization: Unconscious focusing on only the intellectual and not the emotional aspects of a situation or circumstance.	Johnnie has been badly hurt in a car accident. There is reason to believe he will not survive surgery. His father, waiting for his son to return to the ICU, asks the nurse many questions about the equipment and philosophizes about the meaning of life and death.
Reaction formation: Unconscious assuming of traits opposite of undesirable behaviors.	John has a strong family history of alcoholism on both sides. He abstains from liquor and is known in the community as an advocate of prohibition.
Sublimation: Redirecting socially unacceptable unconscious thoughts and feelings into socially approved outlets.	Bob has a lot of aggressive tendencies. He decided to become a butcher and thoroughly enjoys his work.
Undoing: Verbal expression or actions representing one feeling, followed by expression of the direct opposite.	Barbara criticizes her subordinate, Carol, before a large group of people. Later, she sees Carol on the street and tells her how important she is to the organization.

defense mechanisms act as a smokescreen to action and prevent a more problem-focused resolution of difficult issues. They can become so much a part of a person's communication system that almost all dialogue can be described as defensive. Carried to an extreme, they become defining characteristics of major psychiatric illnesses. Figure 20–5 shows the different levels of an ego defense mechanism leading to ego disintegration.

Emotional responses to chronic stress can cripple and destroy relationships. Persistent attempts to manage stress by denying, distorting, and postponing reality promote regression to less mature problem solving. Regression in one or more areas of a person's life eventually can lead to serious ego rupture in the form of major psychiatric illness. As a serious psychological response to stress, ego defense mechanisms break down and the ego begins to disintegrate.

The biological component of unrelieved stress can trigger a major psychiatric illness. As neurotransmitters misfire in response to a stressor, thoughts can become disorganized, and primitive destructive feelings can overwhelm the psychotic client. Impulses and feelings are acted out in ways that make a person dangerous to self and others. Partial or complete ego rupture results. Unrelieved high anxiety can result in assaultive behavior, suicide, panic attacks, psychotic behavior, or the intense catastrophic reactions of dementia clients.

Most people favor certain defense mechanisms over others. An individual's choice of defense mechanisms tends to be consistent with the individual's overall personality makeup. For example, denial and rationalization are favorite defense mechanisms of drug-dependent clients and their families. The drug-dependent client frequently denies there is a problem—for example, "I drink only wine and only with meals," despite the fact that "meals" include breakfast, lunch, snacks, and dinner. Or he rationalizes his drinking: "If I had a decent relationship with my wife, I wouldn't drink." A paranoid person is more likely to use projection as a primary defense against anxiety: "The reason I'm in this mental hospital is that my husband set me up so he could have other women in the house and I wouldn't know about it." Eventually, however, everyone needs to confront conflicting impulses and feelings directly in order to resolve stressors in their lives.

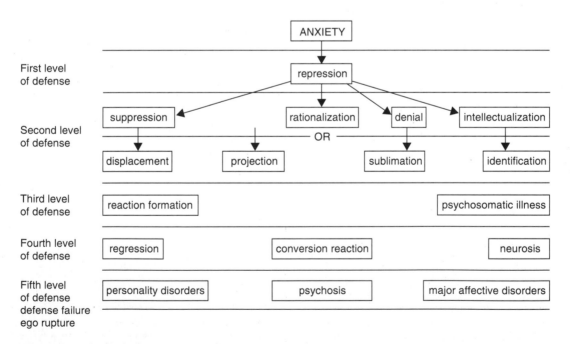

Figure 20–5 Ego Defense Mechanism—Levels of Complexity

APPLICATIONS

NURSING PROCESS

Assessment

The first step in assessment is to uncover the factors within the client, family, and environment that contribute to the crisis. Stressful situations affect the whole person, but generally are perceived in one of three ways: (1) as a threat to the person's self-integrity or well-being, (2) as a loss of something important to the person's well-being and self-esteem, or (3) as a challenge. If the nurse can assess the person's perception of a stressful situation accurately, then the nurse's response can appropriately mirror the client's experience. For example, stress perceived as a threat stimulates anxiety, whereas the predominant expression of stress as a loss presents as depression and grief. The strategies the nurse would use to help each of these clients reduce their stress would differ. In the first case, the nurse would help the client take actions to reduce the threat and might suggest stress-management techniques. But in the second case, the nurse would help the client acknowledge the loss and work through the grieving process.

The nurse would need to assess and analyze the factors that influence the impact of stress: suddenness of onset, the magnitude of change the stressor presents, the number and meaning of concurrent stressors in the family, and the biopsychosocial status of the individual and family prior to the onset of the current situation. In addition, the nurse would need to gather data about the impact of the stress on other family members and to identify likely sources of social support. A sample assessment tool is presented in Box 20–3.

Listening to the content for relevant themes is important, but so are the communication patterns and what the family or client is not saying. The nurse would make the following observations as part of a data base: Are family members and client communicating with each other? What are the family and client's expectations? What does the family or client need from you? from each other? Is there a family spokesperson? What are the client and family's perceptions of appropriate family involvement? What are the client's cultural, religious, and family values concerning the meaning of the illness? Of critical importance in times of

---

BOX 20–3
Assessment/Intervention Tool

Assessment

A. Perception of Stressors
  1. Major stress area or health concern.
  2. Present circumstances related to usual pattern.
  3. Experienced similar problem—how was it handled?
  4. Anticipation of future consequences.
  5. Expectations of self.
  6. Expectations of caregivers.
B. Intrapersonal Factors
  1. Physical (mobility, body function).
  2. Psychosociocultural, (attitudes, values, coping patterns).
  3. Developmental (age, factors related to present situation).
  4. Spiritual belief system (hope and sustaining factors).
C. Interpersonal Factors
  1. Resources and relationship of family/significant other(s) as they relate to or influence (B).
D. Environmental Factors
  1. Resources and relationships of community as they relate to or influence (B).

Prevention as Intervention

A. Primary
  1. Classify stressor.
  2. Provide information to maintain/strengthen strengths.
  3. Support positive coping mechanisms.
  4. Educate client/family.
B. Secondary
  1. Mobilize resources.
  2. Motivate, educate, involve client in health care goals.
  3. Facilitate appropriate interventions; refer to external resources as needed.
  4. Provide information on primary prevention/intervention as needed.
C. Tertiary
  1. Attain/maintain wellness.
  2. Educate/reeducate as needed.
  3. Coordinate resources.
  4. Provide information about primary/secondary intervention.

Developed by J. Conrad, BSN, University of Maryland School of Nursing, 1993.

---

stress is the client or family's need to feel heard. Clues as to how the nurse might emotionally connect with the client or family member are discovered in the process of asking these questions.

It is useful to determine what coping strategies the client has used in the past and where the client perceives the greatest difficulty with coping. The nurse may need to be quite specific. Assessment of coping strategies used in the past may include questions such as:

- What kinds of things increase your stress?
- Are any of your activities limited by your stress level?
- What kinds of leisure activities do you engage in?
- Do you take any drugs to relieve stress?
- When you feel stressed, what are your usual methods of coping?

Naturally, the nurse would ask these questions as part of a larger conversation and would use the client's reactions as a guide to how quickly the information can be gathered.

Nursing Diagnoses

Nursing diagnoses related to coping strategies of individuals and families form an important part of the nursing assessment and planning process. Nursing diagnoses related to individual coping would be cited as, "Alteration in coping related to . . . , or powerlessness, or grieving related to. . . ." Alterations in family coping might include (1) altered family processes related to such stressors as illness or loss of a family member, unemployment, change in family roles, divorce, or (2) altered parenting, for example, the case of an ill child or child abuse.

Planning

Clients in stressful situations need assistance with regaining control and balance in their lives. Care planning should incorporate client-centered goals that recognize this need as primary. Clients who are co-participants in developing the most appropriate strategies fare the best in reducing stress. The seeds of healing are to be found within each individual. Each person needs the kind of nursing support that best recognizes and responds to his or her personalized expression of stress.

Intervention

The general guidelines the nurse can use to help clients deal with stress effectively relate to action strategies to change the situation: altering the impact of the stressor by changing its meaning and helping clients to develop of stress-management strategies to reduce the impact of stress.

Effective Strategies to Change the Situation

Stressors that are amenable to change through direct action obviously are the easiest to resolve. People use a variety of coping mechanisms—negotiation, specific actions, seeking advice, and rearranging their priorities—to develop different perspectives and modify difficult stressful situations. They often start with negotiation as their first line of defense in changing a situation. The nurse can negotiate with family members to use a different set of actions in caring for their loved one. For example, Lazarus and Folkman (1984) describe a situation with an aging client who had suffered a stroke in which this strategy was used. His behavior worsened despite his family's encouragement.

CASE EXAMPLE

After talking with the family, a provisional assessment was made that by being overprotective, the family had inadvertently deprived the client of responsibility for caring for himself and doing things around the house. This infantalizing him allowed his damaged condition to deteriorate further behaviorally. The lack of responsibility seemed to increase his mental confusion. The family was enjoined to make more demands on the client, with the result that he began to function better.

Sensitivity to situations capable of increasing a client's stress can help the client anticipate difficult situations and plan responses.

HELP CLIENTS TAKE ACTION

Taking control of one's life is perhaps the most important stress-reduction strategy. In difficult situations, this coping strategy often gets lost. Beckingham and Baumann (1990) suggest that it is not simply the identified problem but the accompanying feelings of helplessness and functional immobilization that create a stress state. The nurse initially can help the client take charge in stressful situations by reinforcing a client's identity and by respecting his or her individuality. There are several ways to do this. From the moment the client enters the health care situation, nurses can ask clients how they would like to be addressed. This is a simple intervention, but one frequently overlooked in stressful situations when so much else needs to be accomplished quickly. Orienting the client to the hospital or agency helps the client feel comfortable in the new environment. Providing information about visiting hours and the timing of tests and procedures allows family members and clients to plan and in the process gain control over at least some aspects of the hospitalization. Information given to clients and families should reflect an understanding of their background and developmental level. Obviously, the terminology used and explanations given will be different for children, for people with low literacy levels, and for a layperson as contrasted with a physician.

Strengthening the client's decision making in all aspects of the nursing process is very beneficial. Clients should be encouraged to participate in all aspects of their care planning to whatever extent possible. This simple nursing action conveys the idea that the nurse considers the client a necessary partner in successful implementation of the nursing process. Helping clients to develop a realistic plan to offset stress, dealing directly with obstacles as they emerge, and evaluating action steps help people cope with stress in a more adaptive way. During this process, it is important for the person to factor in action steps to cope with the inevitable feelings associated with the change process (Wurzbach, 1992). Knowing that any change will probably provoke feelings of uncertainty and that these feelings will pass as the person develops more familiarity with the changed expectations and activities is reassuring to clients and their family.

CASE EXAMPLE

Sam Hamilton received a diagnosis of prostatic cancer on a routine physical exam. His way of coping included getting as much information on the disease as possible. He researched the most up-to-date material on treatment options and sought the advice from physician friends as to which surgeons had the most experience with this type of surgery. As he shared his diagnosis with friends and colleagues, he found several men who had successfully survived without a cancer recurrence. Sam used the time between diagnosis and surgery to finish projects and delegate work responsibilities. He attended a support group with his wife and was able to get valuable advice on handling his emotional responses to what would happen. When the time came for his surgery, Sam was still apprehensive, but he felt as though he had done everything humanly possible to prepare for it. The actions he took prior to surgery reduced his stress.

Families feel helpless when all decisions are made by the health care team without consulting them (Abel-Boone, Dokecki, and Smith, 1989). Apart from fostering the family's self-esteem by including them in all aspects of care, family involvement is critical to client stress reduction for the following reasons: (1) the family is a constant presence in the client's life, whereas health care providers usually have more limited involvement; (2) family members know the client best and can provide valuable data that can affect the type and implementation of treatment; (3) the family will have to be intimately involved with the client's care at home; and (4) providing opportunities for family members to help promotes self-confidence and skill development (Whetsell and Larrabbee, 1988).

REPEAT INFORMATION

In stressful situations, most people experience sharply reduced powers of concentration. It is difficult for them to focus their attention. Information and directions given in the first 48 hours of an admission should be repeated because this is the time of highest stress. Providing specific information and repeating the information at different time intervals allow families and clients to cope more effectively with an illness or injury. Another strategy is to leave written instructions with the client after they have been discussed verbally. The nurse should also consider the environment in which the information is delivered. Taking the time to provide a quiet, relaxing environment for the delivery of disturbing news can make the difference between whether or not the communication is heard in almost any stressful situation.

HELP CLIENTS VENTILATE FEELINGS

In stressful situations, black and white thinking can replace normal thought processes. Care, people, and one's own participation in the stressful situation are categorized as good or bad, with little room for negotiation. Clients experiencing stress should be given the opportunity to express their feelings, thoughts, and worries. Crying, anger, and magical thinking are normal reactions to painful and frustrating situations that one cannot control. It is important not to argue with the client about the validity of the feelings but to acknowledge that such feelings are understandable in the stressful situation. "What you have experienced is extraordinarily difficult. . . . This must be devastating for you."

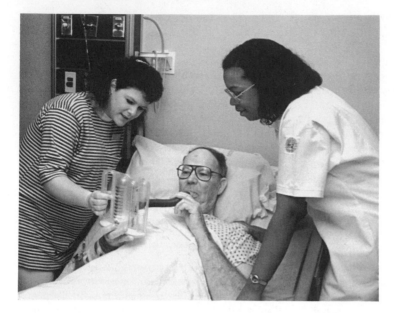

A calm approach and repetition of instructions can help clients in stressful situations relax enough to hear important instructions. (Courtesy of the University of Maryland School of Nursing)

In the process of helping clients ventilate important feelings, the nurse can suggest action the client can take to increase mastery. Allowing clients to control areas and issues that are not of critical importance to a protocol and helping clients discover the real causes of their frustration can reduce destructive acting out behaviors. Encouraging clients to take one day at a time in their expectations and recovery activities and offering suggestions of referral and concrete resources are helpful strategies the nurse can use to assist clients take needed action.

PROVIDE PRACTICAL SUGGESTIONS

When people feel stressed, their problems seem overwhelming, and normal problem-solving skills vanish into thin air. Providing simple, practical suggestions helps the client reframe a situation into a more manageable perspective. Schlossberg (1989) identifies seeking advice as an essential coping strategy for changing a situation. First, the nurse asks the client to describe the stressful situation. The act of voicing one's problem and the stress it creates to another person helps to put boundaries on the problem and to establish its validity. In the process of explaining a problem situation to another person, different facts and feelings emerge that often provide clues for a more

productive solution. The nurse from whom the ideas are sought frequently has suggestions or resources that a person in the midst of a stressful situation may not think of—how a situation might be reframed or the availability of a support group, for example. Seeking advice from someone who knows the political climate in an organization can help a person phrase a request in a way likely to receive attention. The nurse bears the responsibility to be knowledgeable as well as trustworthy in providing practical suggestions. When providing practical suggestions, the nurse can help clients define short-term goals. The ability to meet goals and set milestones in developing strategies stimulates self-confidence.

HELP CLIENTS SET PRIORITIES

Once goals are identified, the client needs to prioritize the tasks necessary to achieve them. The nurse asks the client to identify the concrete tasks needed to achieve treatment goals, including the people involved and the contacts needed. Designating the amount of time each task will take and selecting specific hours or days for each task reinforce prioritization. For example, the nurse might say, "Let's see what you need to do right now, and what can wait until tomorrow." Tasks that someone else can do and those that are nice but not essential to the achievement of goals should be eliminated or ignored. It is helpful for the client to identify a time frame for the accomplishment of each short-term goal.

Stressful situations usually represent a wake-up call that forces an individual to reassess his or her priorities. People and activities that have been taken for granted, are once again considered important. Clients need support and encouragement to rework old patterns that compromise the quality of their lives.

Priority setting also helps reduce the stresses associated with procrastination. Putting off tasks that need to be done and making necessary decisions increase stress in health care as well as personal situations. Most of the time procrastination and resulting stress occur when the client or family perceives a task or decision as potentially overwhelming. Helping a client or family think through the important elements of a stressful situation and consider which elements are critical and which components can be addressed later simplifies life for many people. Not everything is equally important or needs to be done at the same time. Yet in times of stress the client's ability to do what needs to be done first can be compromised through lack of knowledge or support. Helping clients to make lists and to rank tasks according to time allocations and importance are useful intervention strategies.

Setting a deadline improves chances of accomplishment. Deadlines should be reasonable. The most important tasks needed for goal accomplishment should be scheduled during times when the client or family has the most energy and freedom from interruptions. Some people have more energy early in the morning, whereas other people are evening persons.

BREAK TASKS INTO WORKABLE SEGMENTS

Tasks that are appropriate but too overwhelming can be divided into manageable smaller segments. For example, making funeral arrangements for a terminally ill client can be accomplished in several small steps—deciding on the funeral home, writing the obituary, contacting the funeral home, taking care of the arrangements—rather than as one "task" the client or family has to accomplish. Developing realistic goals and a concrete plan for

achieving them enhances self-confidence and an improved sense of personal security.

COACHING

Coaching can relieve stress by helping clients and their families help themselves. In the process they develop a sense of competency and mastery over at least part of their environment. For example, the nurse might suggest some strategies clients can use to distract themselves from the intensity of their predicament.

Providing guidelines for families to participate actively in the process of caring for their loved one helps dispel feelings of helplessness. Families can provide simple loving actions, such as moistening the client's lips or stroking the client's hair or hand, which can prove meaningful to both the client and the family member. The nurse may need to let the family know that it is okay to touch the client and hold his or her hand.

Clients experiencing stress often have trouble relating to other people. The nurse can help clients who have difficulty communicating with friends or family about their circumstances to begin the conversations with their significant others. Finding out the nature of the difficulty is a necessary first step. A starting point is to ask the client what he or she anticipates will be the result of sharing difficult feelings. "What is the worst thing you can imagine happening if you tell your mother (wife, child) about . . . ?" Direct suggestions in dealing with the awkwardness of others in responding to the client can make a difference in clients' willingness to share their experiences with others. Coaching as a health teaching strategy is illustrated Chapter 16.

Constructive Strategies to Change the Meaning of the Situation

When stressful circumstances cannot be changed, as in the case of a terminal illness, the birth of a defective child, or a disease process that cannot be reversed, constructive strategies to change the meaning of the situation may be the most appropriate nursing intervention.

Coping strategies to change the meaning of a situation can be ego enhancing or defensive in nature. Ego-enhancing strategies include the use of interpersonal resources. Other people can help a person reframe an experience in a more positive way. Practical advice and emotional support provide a wider variety of possible options that a person in the midst of overwhelming stress may not have considered. A strong belief system can place the meaning of a stressor in a different realm of experiencing. Ego defense mechanisms, mentioned earlier in the chapter, are used to buy time or change meanings through misinterpretation of the reality. They are counterproductive as long-term coping strategies. As a temporary strategy, they have a protective function in initially helping clients avoid painful realities until the initial shock of encountering an overwhelming stressor wears off.

UNDERSTAND THE CLIENT'S PERSPECTIVE

There is no one strategy or response the nurse can use to help clients and their families change their perception of a stressor and develop more realistic expectations of self and other health care professionals. But there are some principles that can prove helpful. First, put yourself in the client or family's position. How would you feel if you were in the same situation? It is helpful to put into words how you might feel in similar circumstances. Cautioning clients not to pass negative judgment on themselves based on one incident sometimes helps families and clients to put a stressful situation into perspective. Statements such as, "Most people would feel anxious in this situation" or, "It would be hard for anyone to have all the answers in a situation like this" remind clients and families to accept the human limitations we all possess. Empathy, extremely important in all communication, is particularly meaningful in understanding a client's behavior in stressful situations.

PROVIDE ANTICIPATORY GUIDANCE

Fear of the unknown intensifies the impact of a stressor. In stressful situations, a client's perceptions and cognitive processing abilities are strained to the limit. Because they don't understand what is happening, most people try to fill in the gaps. Misinterpretations of events and ascribing motives to other people unnecessarily intensify the client's stress. Whether a small child or an adult, elder—highly intelligent, retarded, or mentally ill—most people are unable to deal capably with events and circumstances they don't fully understand. Anticipatory guidance helps the client cope more effectively with the unknown. Exercise 20–5 provides role-playing practice in handling stressful situations.

Anticipatory guidance begins when the client enters the hospital. Getting used to the hospital and the constant intrusions accompanying admission procedures is difficult for most clients. Their expectations may be unrealistic, simply because they honestly don't know what to expect. Familiarizing the client and family to the hospital or unfamiliar procedures helps them reassess their wishes without necessarily directly challenging unrealistic expectations. This strategy has several benefits. It helps clients save face by proactively communicating realistic expectations clearly, and it establishes the credibility of the nurse as a knowledgeable, caring professional. Anticipatory guidance is particularly effective in mitigating the stress of new procedures.

Nurses can anticipate informational needs and provide information without the client having to ask for it. Every procedure the client experiences should be explained in detail, using terminology the client understands. For example, the nurse might go through the steps of a procedure with a client step by step, explaining sensations the client can expect to feel at each step. Since a person under stress is likely to misinterpret or not hear the entire communication, the nurse should take care to repeat important points at different intervals. This is particularly important with elderly clients, who have the double stress of adjusting to a change in setting as well as to the stress of an unfamiliar procedure.

Preparing family members for their first visit with a client with a visible disfigurement or deterioration and for the presence of technical apparatus is essential. For example, the nurse explains how the client looks and what they may expect. "Your father will look as though he is sleeping, but he can still hear what you are saying." Another helpful intervention is to furnish the family with an initial verbal statement: "You might want to identify yourself and tell your father you are here with him."

Physical descriptions provide the family member with a mental picture of what to expect. "In the

EXERCISE 20–5
Role Play: Handling Stressful Situations

Procedure: Use the case study as the basis for this exercise, and follow the directions below.

Case Study

Dave is a 66-year-old man with colon cancer. In the past he had a colostomy. Recently he was readmitted to your unit and had an exploratory laparotomy for small bowel obstruction. Very little can be done for him because the cancer has spread. He is in pain and he has to have a feeding tube. His family has many questions for the nurse: "Why is he vomiting?" "How come the pain medication isn't working?" "Why isn't he feeling any better than he did before the surgery?" You have just entered the client's room; his family is sitting near him, and they want to know . . . now!

1. Read the case study and have different members of your group role play the client, the nurse, the son, the daughter-in-law, and the wife. One person should act as observer.
2. Identify the factors that will need to be clarified in this situation to help the nurse provide the most appropriate intervention.
3. Using the strategies suggested in this chapter, intervene to help the client and the family reduce their anxiety.
4. Role play the situation for 10–15 minutes.

Discussion:

1. Have each player identify the interventions that were most helpful.
2. From the nurse's perspective, which parts of the client/family stress were hardest to handle?
3. How could you use what you learned from doing this exercise in your clinical practice?

accident, your son received a head injury and broke bones in his left arm and leg. His face is swollen and bruised, and he has casts on an arm and a leg." Anticipatory descriptions also can take into account the strangeness of the equipment. To a new mother visiting her premature daughter, the nurse might say, "There will be a lot of equipment and tubes attached to your baby to help her breathe and to give the nurses information about how she is doing." Offering such descriptions gives family members permission to ask questions and to become more comfortable in coping with undesired and potentially overwhelming circumstances surrounding someone they care about deeply.

OFFER SELF AS SUPPORT

In addition to anticipatory guidance about what to expect, the offer of the presence of the nurse during the initial encounter lessens the shock of a marked change in appearance or function. Sometimes the sight of a family member on a ventilator or with serious injuries overwhelms family members. Accompanying the client's family to the bedside for the first visit strengthens the family member during the initial shock of seeing their family

member in such a condition. If the client is intubated, family members should be advised that he or she will not be able to speak.

The nurse may serve as a role model on how to initiate a conversation with the very ill or comatose client: "Hello, Mr. James, I have brought your daughter in to see you." By modeling a normal greeting, the nurse indirectly encourages the family to react in their usual manner with the client. Family members also appreciate a suggestion that if they feel uncomfortable, they should feel free to leave the bedside after the initial contact and return when they feel better.

Anticipatory guidance and reassurance can come from other clients as well as from the nurse. The successful client has a credibility difficult to refute. Arranging for a client to talk with someone having a similar stressful experience is helpful. Talking with someone who has successfully adjusted and gone on with life can make all the difference for someone who feels life will never be normal again. A word of caution—always check with the other client first. Some people, even with highly successful outcomes, are not ready to talk about their problems, and confidentiality needs to be respected.

HELP CLIENTS REFRAME THE SITUATION

There are several communication strategies nurses can use to help clients reframe a situation. Knowledge of the client's concerns and response patterns will dictate which strategy or combination of strategies is most likely to defuse the stressor for the client.

A major goal in implementing this nursing intervention is to help the client or family re-examine present unrealistic expectations for self, other professionals, and the health care setting and replace them with attainable goals. It is usually useless to defend personalities or intentions. A tactful statement acknowledging the client's feeling is helpful: "It sounds as though you are pretty angry with Dr. Moore, and you may have every right to be, but I'd like to see if there is something we could come up with that might make this situation less frustrating." Such an approach accomplishes several objectives. It acknowledges feelings, but it also asks the client or family how they might work together with the nurse to make the experience more positive. It reframes the experience as one in need of resolution, and it takes the focus off nonproductive blaming that will not resolve the situation. It helps people refocus on specific productive behaviors. It helps the nurse reinforce realistic expectations, and it allows space to contradict false information without the client losing face. Most important, in most cases the client feels heard. At the same time there is a shift to looking at behaviors that reinforce realistic expectations or contradicts false information. This strategy is also helpful when the client or family blame themselves for things that are beyond their control. "If only's" are self-defeating because there is nothing anyone can do to change the past. The nurse can help the family reframe their participation in a stressful situation as one in which they acted with good intentions on the basis of the knowledge they had at the time. Family members sometimes feel better about circumstances they cannot erase when they can look at a situation with this perspective.

HELP FAMILY MEMBERS CONSERVE THEIR STRENGTH

It is not unusual for family members in critical care situations to feel that they need to be in constant attendance and to become physically and emotionally exhausted in the process. A useful strategy is to suggest that the family members take short breaks from the situation. Family members may need permission and a suggestion from the nurse to go to a movie or eat in a restaurant outside the hospital. Assuring the family that they will be called should there be any change in the client's condition may be a necessary part of the communication.

HELP CLIENTS AND FAMILIES FIND MEANING THROUGH EXTERNAL SUPPORTS

Acceptance of one's suffering may be possible only when it is viewed as part of a larger worldview. Faith can help a person buffer the effects of stress related to illness, anxiety, and fatigue. Placing a terrible and unfair stressor in the hands of a higher power allows a person relief from taking too much personal responsibility both for the stressor and for finding its resolution in a traditional way. This strategy is particularly effective with clients facing stressors that cannot be changed in other ways.

Social support is an essential component of stress management. Having contact with other human beings is a resource that most people depend on to help them reduce stress. Social support provides three distinct functions: validation, emotional support, and correction of distorted thinking. Validating the legitimacy of anger, frustration, and helplessness prevents the tunnel vision many clients experience under stress. Emotional support consists of those actions that allow a person to feel loved and cared about. It strengthens a person to realize that there are people who can be counted on and confided in. Informational support and feedback help a client correct distortions, and maintain morale.

Social support can come from the nurse as well as from significant others in the client's life. Supportive measures can include the tangible reinforcement of direct aid. The nurse is in a unique position to help clients assess the type of aid they need and the most appropriate community resources. Sometimes it is difficult for clients to find community agencies and to access their services. The more knowledgeable the nurse is about community resources, the better the client service. Exercise 20–6 is designed to help you become better acquainted with resources in your community.

EXERCISE 20–6
Community Resources for Stress Management

Purpose: To help you understand the community resources available in your community for stress management

Time: Homework assignment; class discussion 30–45 minutes.

Procedure:
1. Look in the newspaper for ideas, and contact a community agency, social services group, or support group in your community that you believe can help clients cope with a particularly stressful situations.
2. Find out how a person might access the resource, what kinds of cases are treated, what types of treatment are offered, the costs involved, and what you as a nurse can do to help people take advantage of the resource.

Discussion:
1. How did you decide which community agency to choose?
2. How difficult or easy was it to access the information about the agency?
3. What information about the community resource did you find out that surprised or perplexed you?
4. In what ways could you use this exercise in planning care for your clients?

HOLD REGULAR FAMILY CONFERENCES

Holding regularly scheduled family conferences helps reduce family stress. If at all possible, a team approach involving the nurse, physician, social worker, and chaplain can meet with the family to discuss the client's care. These conferences offer the opportunity for two-way communication between the health care team and the client. Family conferences help families feel they are partners in the care of their loved ones and provide a unique forum for giving information simultaneously to those most involved with the client's well-being. A family conference can be scheduled around any change in the client's condition or the family's ability to cope (Ceronsky, 1983).

Relaxation Strategies

Pearlin and Schooler (1978) describe a third set of coping strategies designed to lessen the intensity of the stressor on a person once the stress response has occurred. Known as mind-body therapies, transcendental meditation, progressive relaxation, or biofeedback, relaxation strategies use the mind to change the physiological impact of stress on the body. Relaxation strategies help people take stress more in stride. They provide a person with more physical energy and flexibility in responding to

stress. The purpose behind all of the mind-body therapies in stress reduction is twofold: to redirect a person away from external stressors and to refocus this outwardly directed consciousness and psychological energy inward. In the process of altering physiological reactions to stress such as blood pressure, heart rate, muscle tension, and respiratory rate, most people experience greater calm and peace of mind. Regular practice of these techniques can improve physical and emotional well-being.

TRANSCENDENTAL MEDITATION

Meditation is a strategy designed to produce an altered state of consciousness. As a way of finding inner peace and centeredness, it is a strategy dating back to early Christian times. Early mystics and holy men used the practice to obtain an altered sense of consciousness that allowed them to experience the presence of God and to transcend the stresses of daily life. In modern times meditation is used by many people to develop a sense of inner peace and tranquility.

The practice of meditation requires four essential elements: a quiet place, a passive attitude, an object or word symbol to focus on, and a comfortable position (Benson, 1975). The quiet place can be a room, a garden where one can be alone, or a place of worship. In choosing an appropriate

---

BOX 20–4
Meditation Techniques

1. Choose a quiet, calm environment with as few distractions as possible.
2. Get in a comfortable position, preferably a sitting position.
3. To shift the mind from logical, externally oriented thought, use a constant stimulus: a sound, word, phrase, or object. The eyes are closed if a repetitive sound or word is used.
4. Pay attention to the rhythm of your breathing.
5. When distracting thoughts occur they are to be discarded and attention redirected to the repetition of the word or gazing at the object. Distracting thoughts will occur and do not mean you are performing the techniques incorrectly. Don't worry about how you are doing. Redirect your focus to the constant stimulus and assume a passive attitude.

Adapted from Benson H (1975). The Relaxation Response. New York, Morrow, pp. 112–113.

---

place, the mediator should look for an environment with few external distractions.

Of the four elements, a passive attitude is the most important and the most difficult to cultivate. The mediator should deliberately rid the mind of all thoughts and distractions. Those thoughts and feelings that do emerge are ignored and allowed to pass through the mind without consciously dwelling on them. It is important to refocus on the object or word symbol and not to try consciously to banish the intruding thought. The object or word symbol chosen should be simple and easy to focus on. It can be a visual object, a particular feeling, or a repetitive word such as "one," "God," "love." When the mediator is distracted, concentrating on the chosen symbol helps clear the distraction from the mind.

The last element needed for meditation is a comfortable position. Meditation is a process requiring at least 20 minutes of concentrated time, so being in a comfortable position is essential. A sitting position with arms supported is ideal. A lying or semireclined position is not desirable because it frequently leads to sleep. The process as described by Benson (1975) is found in Box 20–4.

BIOFEEDBACK

Biofeedback is a technique that gives a person immediate and continuous information about his or her physiological responses through auditory and visual signals. Most people are unaware of their physiological activity in response to external events. Biofeedback provides an awareness of minute-by-minute changes in biological activity, providing for the subject a psychophysiological feedback loop. With this kind of information many people are able to develop control over their physiological responses to external events.

Equipment used with biofeedback include the electroencephalogram, skin temperature devices, blood pressure, measures, galvanic skin resistance measurements, and the electromyogram to measure muscle tension. Each device monitors physical information from the subject. The data are converted to visual or auditory signals that are reported back to the subject. The continuous and immediate biological feedback allows subjects to monitor and control their physiological responses.

Biofeedback techniques were developed after scientists observed physiological elevations in one or several bodily systems in response to stress. Certain people seemed highly reactive to frequent stress episodes and demonstrated stereotypic physiological responses. The scientists also noted that sustained arousal and an inability to relax easily were associated with the development of stress-linked illness.

Biofeedback has an important role in stress management for clients with chronic stress responses affecting individual body systems such as essential hypertension, migraine headaches, Raynaud's disease, and ulcerative colitis. The major disadvantages of biofeedback are the cost of the equipment, the availability of trained personnel and the complexity of the stress response in most people.

PROGRESSIVE RELAXATION

Most people cannot relax on demand. Just wanting to relax and have relief from stress is not enough (Mast, Meyer, and Urbanski, 1987). Progressive relaxation is a technique that focuses the subject's attention on conscious control of voluntary skeletal muscles. Originally developed by Jacobson, a physiologist physician, the technique consists of alternately tensing and relaxing muscle groups. The subject sits in a relaxed position in a chair with arm supports. Feet should be on the ground and legs are placed side by side. To experience the progressive relaxation technique do Exercise 20–7.

EXERCISE 20–7
Progressive Relaxation Exercise

Purpose: To help you experience the beneficial effects of progressive relaxation in reducing tension. This exercise consists of alternately tensing and relaxing voluntary skeletal muscles.

Time: 20 minutes

Procedure:
1. Sit in a comfortable chair with arm supports. Place the arms on the arm supports and sit in a comfortable upright position with legs uncrossed and feet flat on the floor.
2. Close your eyes and take ten deep breaths, concentrating on your inhaling and exhaling.
3. Your instructor or a member of the group should give the following instructions, and you should follow them exactly.

I want you to focus on your feet and to tense the muscles in your feet. Feel how that feels. Hold it, and now let go. Feel the tension leaving your feet.

And now I would like you to tense the muscles in your calves. Feel the tension in your calves and hold it. Now let go and feel the tension leaving your calves. Feel how that feels.

Now I want you to tense the muscles in your thighs. Most people do this by pressing their thighs against the chair. Feel the tension in your muscles and experience how that feels. Now release the tension and feel how that feels.

Now I would like you to feel the tension in your abdomen. Tense the muscles in your abdomen and hold it. Hold it for a few more seconds. Now release those muscles and feel how that feels.

Now I would like you to tense the muscles in your chest. The only way you can really do this is to take a very deep breath and hold it. (The guide counts to 10.) Concentrate on feeling how that feels. Now let it go and feel how that feels.

Now I would like you to tense your muscles in your hands. Clench your fist and hold it as hard as you can. Harder, harder. Now release it and feel how that feels.

Now I would like you to tense the muscles in your arms. You can do this by pressing down as hard as you can on the arm supports. Feel the tension in your arms and continue pressing. Now let go and feel how that feels.

Now I would like you to feel the tension in your shoulders. Tense your shoulders as hard as you can and hold it. Feel how that feels. Now release your shoulder muscles and feel how that feels.

Now I would like you to feel the tension in your jaw. Clench your jaw and teeth as hard as you can. Feel the tension in your jaw and hold it. Now let it go and feel the tension leave your jaw.

Now that you are in this relaxed state, keep your eyes closed and think of a time when you were really happy. Let the images and sounds surround you. Imagine yourself back in that situation. What were you thinking? What are you feeling?

Now open your eyes. Students who feel comfortable may share the images that emerged in the relaxed state.

Discussion:
1. What are your impressions in doing this exercise?
2. Do you feel more relaxed after doing the exercise?
3. If you feel differently after doing the exercise, in what ways?
4. Were you surprised at the images that emerged in your relaxed state?
5. In what ways do you think you could use this exercise in your nursing practice?

GUIDED IMAGERY

Guided imagery is a technique used frequently with other forms of interventions to help relieve the stress of pain. Imagery techniques use the subject's imagination to stimulate mental pictures in ways that alter consciousness and promote distraction from painful affects or procedures. The guide may use the relaxation techniques described above to prepare the subject for imagery. The subject is asked deliberately to image sensory mental representations of more peaceful or positive substitutes for negative feelings and stressors. Positive mental images are associated with improved functioning and reduced pain in clients suffering from intractable pain, cancer, depression, and hypertension. Techniques for using guided imagery are presented in Box 20–5.

Reducing Stress in the Caregiver

Professional nursing is a calling associated with high stress levels and potential burnout, beginning with nursing school (Davidhizar, 1991). Although the primary focus of this chapter is on interven-

---

BOX 20–5
Using Guided Imagery

Time involved: Reading time, 5 minutes; implementation time, 10 minutes.
Sample situation: Patient is in pain and probably will continue to be for about 30 to 45 minutes while you and/or others are trying to do something more to relieve his pain, e.g., obtain appropriate analgesic orders.
Possible solution: Patient may be willing to try a simple type of imagery or use his own spiritual beliefs.
Expected outcome: Patient will feel his pain is acknowledged and someone cares. He finds the sensation of pain is relieved by becoming less intense or by changing to a more acceptable sensation. Or, he merely finds the pain more tolerable because this distracts him momentarily. He may note that he feels less anxious.

Don'ts

1. Do not expect or suggest that imagery will substitute for appropriate pain, relief, e.g., adequate analgesic orders.
2. Do not attempt to present imagery for pain relief if you feel unsure or uncomfortable about it. *Or,* admit these feelings before you proceed, and explain why you think it's worth a try.
3. Do not say there is nothing else anyone can do.
4. Do not tell the patient that he must learn to cope with pain on his own. (He may learn to do this, but not in 10 minutes.)
5. Never tell the patient his pain is not as bad as he thinks.

Dos

1. Take a deep breath outside his room and relax a little yourself. Plan on spending up to 10 minutes with the patient. You are about to discuss something the patient may find strange; you need to be relaxed and confident.
2. When you enter the room tell the patient you know he hurts. Be certain that you have assured the patient that you consider his pain real, not imaginary, and that you believe it is just as intense as he says.
3. Tell the patient you are still hoping (searching) for a better alternative, but that meanwhile you would like to *offer* him the opportunity to try a technique that may ease his pain for just a little while.
4. Explain that you are going to describe a method of using concentration and imagination to help with pain for a brief time. Tell the patient that this may sound strange

and he may not want to try it. If so, that is perfectly all right, but you want to offer it just in case it turns out to be something he wants to try and finds helpful.
5. Ask the patient if he daydreams or has a good imagination, or if prayer or any kind of faith helps him with pain or illness.
   If he gives a negative reply, tell him he may be better at it than he thinks. Ask him if he remembers a bedroom from his childhood (progress to any bedroom he remembers). Ask him how many windows it had and how many doors. If he can answer with confidence, point out that this is a result of memories that are mental pictures of some sort and not a result of storing numerical information. It is one example of how people who do not even have vivid mental pictures still use their imagination, e.g., images from the past. If he cannot answer these questions, admit that you might be wrong about the appropriateness of this method for him. Ask him if he wants you to continue. If so, try either of the following.
   If he gives a positive reply to daydreaming or a good imagination, use simple symptom substitution, stressing that you are hoping that this will at least reduce unpleasant aspects of the pain for a short time. If the patient cannot concentrate well, try providing another sensation, e.g., cold, to focus on.
   If he gives a positive reply to some type of faith, use the ball of healing energy, suggesting that he substitute his personal faith for the healing energy and that this may reduce his pain.
6. Tell the patient you will return to find out if he decided to try this and if it helped. Tell the patient when you will return, but give yourself leeway. It's better to return early than late.
7. When you return, ask the patient what he decided about the imagery.
   If the patient says he did not try the imagery, tell him you appreciate his considering it.
   If it did not work, tell him you admire his willingness to try the technique, reassuring him that it does not always work.
   If it did help, tell him you do not expect him to rely on it as his only source of pain relief.
8. In all cases, continue to explore and explain other plans for pain relief.

From McCaffery M, Beebe A (1989). Pain: Clinical Manual for Nursing Practice. St. Louis, Mosby, p. 213. Reprinted with permission.

tions to reduce stress levels in clients, it is important to reflect on the nature of stress in the nurse and to provide a basis for reducing its occurrence. Many nurses leave the profession because they view this as their only option in managing the stress of caring for others. Another reason for including professional stress is the effect that low energy and buried resentments have on the quality of nursing care (Gray and Diers, 1992; Schaefer and Peterson, 1992).

Caregivers, especially nurses and those most intimately involved in the care of the seriously or chronically ill client, experience stress and burnout routinely. Caring for terminally ill, obnoxious, cognitively impaired, and out of control clients places a severe strain on the dedicated caregiver. Yet often nurses do not attend to their own level of stress or that of their co-workers (David, 1991).

THE CYCLE OF BURNOUT

Freudenberger (1985) describes a cycle of burnout symptoms leading to depression and total burnout exhaustion. The road to burnout begins insidiously with a need for perfection. Nurses who don't care about their work or invest very much of themselves in it are not candidates for burnout. Instead, the syndrome occurs in people who have excessive expectations of themselves and who feel they need to do everything right. Exercise 20–8 can help you assess your own burnout potential.

Nurses are at high risk for burnout because they care. So strong is the need to be the exemplar nurse, mother, and expert clinician that the compulsion to do the highest-quality job takes over rational thinking at the expense of health and well-being (Freudenberger, 1985). The need to be perfect doesn't allow for error. There is a story about Babe Ruth teaching a young boy how to pitch a baseball that has applicability for the professional nurse. The Babe asked the boy how he was planning to pitch the ball. The young boy answered, "I'm going to throw it with all my might and get it right where it needs to go. I'm going to give it 110 percent. But Babe Ruth had different advice: "Throw the ball with 80 percent of your might. You will need the reserve to correct for any mistakes." Nurses need the same reserve to correct for the inevitable curved balls of life.

SYMPTOMS OF BURNOUT

Physiological, emotional, and spiritual symptoms of burnout are identified in Figure 20–6. Physical symptoms in the form of increased smoking, drinking or eating, skipping meals, eating compulsively on the run, and sleep disturbances are warning signals of stress. The potential burnout victim begins to feel drained, constantly tired, "like a robot," or in a constant state of hyperarousal in which much of life seems irritating.

Intensity develops that doesn't allow the potential burnout victim to ask for help or an extension on a project. There is a feeling that no one else in the organization can do it as well or with as much dedication. Conscientiousness gets confused with the fear of losing control. It becomes increasingly difficult to delegate responsibility because others might not do a task as well. Time begins to slip away, and the nurse finds little time for self. Nor is there time for others—family or friends. Every demand on one's time seems like an intrusion. Fatigue accompanies the preoccupation for work or too many demands on one's time. Emotional pleasures become a thing of the past.

As self needs get buried in meeting the needs and demands of others, conflict develops. Rationalizations such as, "As soon as I get the unit staffed," "As soon as my kid finishes college," "As soon as I get my degree" legitimize the existence of burnout symptoms and postpone actions needed to rebalance one's life. Anxiety gets displaced in overeating, overspending, snapping at family, or avoiding friends. Insomnia during the week and utter exhaustion on the weekend or days off suggest a serious imbalance in lifestyle.

Values become distorted. Family members are forgotten or taken for granted. There is such a need to control what is happening that every other important segment of a person's value structure gets dropped or ignored. The nurse feels alone and isolated, misunderstood and unappreciated. Other people are willing to help and offer their assistance, but there is such a need for control that assistance given by others is not judged as worthy and the tasks are redone. People who once were happy to give input and assistance do not offer again when their work is rejected, reworked without explanation, or used without being credited.

EXERCISE 20–8
Burnout Assessment

Purpose: To help students understand the symptoms of burnout.

Time: 10 minutes

Procedure:
Consider your life over the past year. Complete the questionnaire by answering with a 5 if the situation is a constant occurrence, 4 if it occurs most of the time, 3 if it occurs occasionally, 2 if it has occurred once or twice during the last six months, and 1 if it is not a problem at all. Scores of 60–75 indicate burnout. Scores of 45–60 indicate you are stressed and in danger of developing burnout. Scores of 20–44 indicate a normal stress level, and scores of less than 20 suggest you are not a candidate for burnout.

1. Do you find yourself taking on other people's problems and responsibilities? _____
2. Do you feel resentful about the amount of claims on your time? _____
3. Do you find you have less time for social activities? _____
4. Have you lost your sense of humor? _____
5. Are you having trouble sleeping? _____
6. Do you find you are more impatient and less tolerant of others? _____
7. Is it difficult for you to say no? _____
8. Are the things that used to be important to you slipping away from you? _____
9. Do you feel a sense of urgency and not enough time to complete tasks? _____
10. Are you forgetting appointments, friends' birthdays? _____
11. Do you feel overwhelmed and unable to pace yourself? _____
12. Have you lost interest in sex? _____
13. Are you overeating, or have you begun to skip meals? _____
14. Is it difficult to feel enthusiastic about your work? _____
15. Do you feel it is difficult to make real contact with others? _____

Tally up your scores and compare your scores with your classmates. Nursing school is a strong breeding ground for the development of burnout (demands exceed resources). To offset the possibility of developing burnout symptoms:
1. Think about the last time you took time for yourself. If you cannot think of a time, you really need to do this exercise.
2. Identify a leisure activity that you can do during the next week to break the cycle of burnout.
3. Describe the steps you will need to take to implement the activity.
4. Identify the time period required for this activity and what other activities will need rearrangement to make it possible.
5. Describe any obstacles to implementing your activity and how you might resolve them.

Discussion:
1. Was it difficult for you to come up with an activity? If so, why?
2. Were you able to develop a logical way to implement your activity?
3. Were the activities chosen by others surprising or helpful to you in any way?
4. How might you be able to use this exercise in your future practice?

Thinking becomes clouded with the self as its only referent. Freudenberger (1985) identifies intolerance and anger as strong characteristics of this stage. There is a tendency to look at others as if they were not pulling their weight and to cancel appointments with subordinates. As one person described it:

I felt I was looking in at a party—from outside through a window. It was a little dizzying. I knew something was wrong with me but was so resentful that I pushed harder to maintain control of my actions. At work, I'd sit in meetings silently disliking everyone, thinking how bored I was, how stupid everyone sounded, how no one was recognizing how smart I was. I felt like a robot . . . (Freudenberger, 1985).

Criticism is viewed by the overworked burnout victim as divisive rather than as the creative ten-

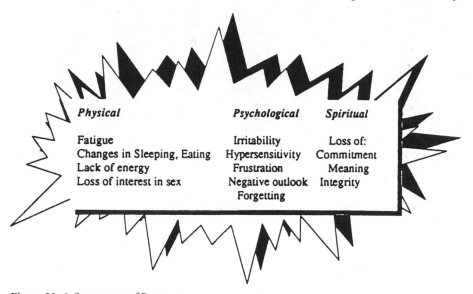

Figure 20–6 Symptoms of Burnout

sion needed in any organization for growth. Because of the growing alienation from others, judgments are subjective and not necessarily appropriate. People who could help don't offer. The sense of helplessness increases, and so does the potential for burnout exhaustion.

As the symptoms of burnout progress, there is a growing sense of unreality and disengagement from life. It seems as though no one understands or cares. Disappointment, helplessness, and rage interact, further immobilizing any type of constructive, organized actions. A robot, going through the motions with no real enjoyment of life, is a cardinal representation of the spiritual disengagement elements of the burnout cycle. Burnout is contagious, and it is important to develop strategies for burnout prevention.

BURNOUT PREVENTION

The symptoms of burnout can be reversed at any point in the continuum. Taking the steps outlined in Figure 20–7 can help prevent burnout (Arnold, 1989).

Awareness

The first step in burnout prevention is awareness. Cognitive awareness is gained by reflecting on

the nature of the stressors in one's life and by asking others for their impressions. Deliberately reflecting on the stress in your life immediately puts boundaries on it. Solutions become possible once the problem is defined appropriately. As you examine your stress behavior, note differences in the way you feel about important people in your life. To what extent have your life, your

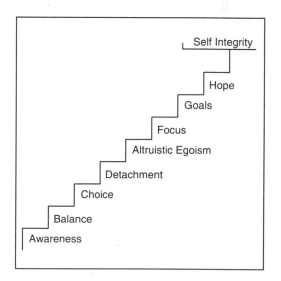

Figure 20–7 The ABC Steps to Burnout Prevention

attitudes, and your thinking become rigid or meaningless?

The other component of awareness is emotional. To what extent is your ego involved in the outcome—to what extent is it useful to have ego involvement in this project, idea, etc.? Who are you trying to please, and for what reasons? Often it is our ego involvement that gets in the way of awareness as well as the actions we could take to achieve a better balance in our lives. Think about your feelings. Talk to someone who is able to offer you the support and sensitivity you need to become aware of what is going on in your life. Take into consideration what others are telling you about your behavior.

Balance

If the answers on your questionnaire were indicative of burnout potential, your life most probably is out of balance. A healthy balance among work, family, leisure, and lifelong learning enhances personal judgments, satisfaction, and productivity. Actively scheduling time for each of these activities is the only way to achieve balance. Anything else falls short of the mark. Good intentions will never cure burnout. Only deliberate actions will provide relief.

Choice

People experiencing the burnout syndrome usually do not think they have any choice other than to keep doing what they have been doing, but life is a series of choices and negotiations. All human beings have choices, and the choices they make help create the fabric of their lives. It is important to recognize that refusing to delegate work because someone else cannot do it as well, or not going out to dinner with friends because you have too much work to do, represents a choice on your part. Making a different choice actually can enhance a person's productivity, even though this is difficult to appreciate in the throes of a burnout situation. Everyone needs emotional support to nourish the spirit.

Detachment

Detachment differs from disengagement. With disengagement, there is a withdrawal of emotional energy. Detachment allows full emotional involvement in a task or relationship, but not to the degree that it compromises the person's quality of life, values, or needs. It means focusing on a job or project to the best of one's ability. But at the end of the day at the end of the or time designated to the project, the job is dropped completely. Saying to oneself, "Sufficient for the day" is a stress-management strategy that puts boundaries on life tasks.

Emotional detachment means dropping ego involvement to the extent that it interferes with balance and integrity. The end does not always justify the means. Nothing is so important that friends, co-workers, family, and even oneself are sacrificed on the altar of achievement. When someone asked Mother Teresa how she is able to remain so energetic and hopeful in the midst of the suffering she encounters in Calcutta, she replied that it was because she did the best she could, realizing that it is important to do her best and not at all important to worry about the outcome. The outcome she couldn't control; the quality of her work she could regulate.

(Altruistic) Egoism

Potential burnout victims generally put everyone and everything ahead of themselves. Their own needs are ignored or taken for granted. Altruistic egoism simply means paying as much attention to your own personal needs as you do to the needs of others. Although this seems obvious, many people consider attention to their own needs as being selfish. Nothing is further from the truth. In the long run, a balance between self needs and the needs of others enhances the quality of care one can give to others.

Focus

Focusing full energy on one thing at a time and finishing one project before starting another have several benefits. First, it is more likely that you will enjoy each activity more. Your full attention will make for a better product. Finishing one project before starting another allows you to put a job out of your mind as you begin the next one. A powerful contributor to the development of burnout is several unfinished projects all demanding similar space in your mind.

Goals

Identifying goals that are realistic, achievable, and in line with your personal values is an excellent burnout-prevention strategy. If you want to go to New York, you don't buy a ticket to California, and vice versa. The same is true of life. Knowing where you want to go and what it takes to get there enhances your chances. It is important to know where you do want to go with your life and to have a realistic sense of what you will find when you get there. Too often people consider only the former and are disappointed when they find it is not where they really want to be!

Hope

The inner emptiness so often associated with burnout gradually disappears with the instillation of hope. There are several sources of hope a person can use. Turning troubles over to a higher power and seeking guidance, direction, and peace from external resources can stimulate hope. The despair accompanying emptiness and a sense of futility can be reversed by simply seeking out connections with others. Their advice and caring support even in one encounter can prove a powerful antidote to inner emptiness.

Integrity

Burnout always leads to some loss of personal integrity in the sense that important values are ignored or devalued. When you begin to forget who you are and to become what everyone else expects of you, you are in trouble. Reclaim yourself! Burnout can be reversed by taking responsibility for yourself, doing what you feel is important and maintaining your own personal integrity. Take the risk to be all that you are as well as all you can be!

Many of the coping strategies described earlier in the chapter for use with clients work equally well for nurses. Nurses working in high-acuity settings also find professional support groups highly effective in providing needed time to reflect on their experience and in finding nurturance from others who understand. Professional support groups and their value and function are described in Chapter 22.

SUMMARY

Chapter 20 presents a comprehensive overview of basic concepts related to stress, coping, and crisis. Stress is defined as a physiological and psychological response to the presence of a stressor. A stressor is defined as any demand, situation, internal stimulus, or circumstance threatening a person's personal security and balance. This sense of personal security and balance is referred to as homeostasis, or dynamic equilibrium. Three theoretical models of stress are presented: stress as a stimulus, stress as a physiological response, and stress as a transaction. Factors influencing the development of a stress reaction include the nature of the stressor, the personal interpretation of its meaning, the number of previous and concurrent stressors, previous experiences with similar stressors and the availability of support systems and personal coping abilities. Hidden stressors can be uncovered if a holistic approach to stress assessment is used.

Coping is defined as the concept used to refer to any response to external life strains that serves to prevent, avoid, or control emotional distress. The three types of coping strategies people use to deal with stressful situations include strategies to change the stressful situation, those that change the meaning of the stressor, and those that help the person relax enough to take the stress in stride. Accurate assessment allows the nurse flexibility in choosing the most appropriate intervention.

Burnout is a form of stress that frequently occurs in high-stress situations. To reduce the possibilities of burnout, nurses must develop awareness, balance, make appropriate choices, maintain focus, and allow time for self.

REFERENCES

Abel-Boone H, Dokecki P, Smith M (1989). Parent and health care provider communication and decision making in the intensive care nursery. Children's Health Care 18(3):133–141.

Aguilera DC (1990). Crisis Intervention: Theory and Methodology. St. Louis, Mosby Yearbook.

Arnold E (1989). Burnout as a spiritual issue. *In* Carson V (ed.) (1989), Spiritual Dimensions of Nursing Practice. Philadelphia, W.B. Saunders.

Beckingham A, Baumann A (1990). The ageing family in crisis: Assessment and decision making models. Journal of Advanced Nursing 15:782–787.

Ben-Schlomo Y, Chaturvedi N (1992). Stress and Graves' disease. Lancet 339:427.

Benson H (1975). The Relaxation Response. New York, Morrow.

Bluhm J (1987). Helping families in crisis hold on. Nursing '87. 45.

Bowlby J (1961).The process of mourning. International Journal of Psychoanalysis 42, Parts 4–5:331.

Burchfield S (ed.) (1985). Stress: Psychological and Physiological Interactions. Washington, DC, Hemisphere Publishing Corp.

Caplan G (1964). Principles of Preventive Psychiatry. New York, Basic Books.

Ceronsky C (1983). Family/staff conferences open communication, resolve problems. Hospital Progress 64(8):58–59.

David J (1991). How well do nurses care for their own? Journal of Advanced Nursing 16(8):887–888.

Davidhizar R (1991). How to stay sane as a student of nursing. Imprint 38(4):96–98.

Davis JM, Hoshiko BR, Jones S, Gosnell D (1992). The effect of a support group on grieving individuals' level of perceived support and stress. Archives of Psychiatric Nursing. 6(1):35–9.

Dossey B (1991). Awakening the inner healer. American Journal of Nursing 91(8):31–34.

Edens JL, Larkin KT, Abel J (1992). The effect of social support and physical touch on cardiovascular reactions to mental stress. Journal of Psychosomatic Research 36(4):371–81.

Emmons R (1991). Personal strivings, daily life events and psychological and physical well-being. Journal of Personality 59(3):453–72.

Emrich HM (1981). The role of endorphins in neuropsychiatry. *In* Ban TA (ed.) (1981), Modern Problems of Pharmacopsychiatry. New York, Basal.

Engel G (1972). Grief and grieving. *In* Schwartz L, Schwartz S (eds.) (1972), The Psychodynamics of Patient Care. New York, Prentice-Hall.

Epstein S, Katz L (1992). Coping ability, stress, productive load and symptoms. Journal of Personality and Social Psychology 62(5):813–825.

Felsten G (1991). Influences of situation-specific mastery beliefs and satisfaction with social support on appraisal of stress. Psychological Reports 69(2): 483–495.

Folks DG, Kinney FC (1992). The role of psychological factors in dermatologic conditions. Psychosomatics 33(1):45–54.

Freud S (1940). An outline of psychoanalysis. *In* Standard Edition, Vol. 23. London, Hogarth Press, 1964.

Freudenberger H (1980). Burnout. Garden City, NY, Anchor Books.

Freudenberger H (1985). Women's Burnout. New York, Doubleday.

Gadzella B, Ginther D, Tomcala M, Bryant G (1991). Differences between men and women on stress producers and coping strategies. Psychological Reports 69(2):561–562.

Gelent MD, Hochman JS (1992). Acute myocardial infarction triggered by emotional stress. American Journal of Cardiology 69(17):1512–1513.

Goldberger L, Breznitz S (1982). Handbook of Stress: Theoretical and Clinical Aspects. New York, Free Press.

Gray S, Diers D (1992). The effect of staff stress on patient behavior. Archives of Psychiatric Nursing 6(1):26–34.

Hoff LS (1989). People in Crisis: Understanding and Helping (2nd ed.). Menlo Park, CA, Addison-Wesley.

Holmes T, Rahe R (1967). The social readjustment rating scale. Journal of Psychosomatic Research, 11:213–218.

Hull MM (1991). Hospice nurses: Caring support for caregiving families. Cancer Nursing 14(2):63–70.

Lazarus RS (1966). Psychological Stress and the Coping Process. New York, McGraw-Hill.

Lazarus R, Folkman S (1984). Stress, Appraisal and Coping. New York, Springer.

Leidy NK (1989). A physiologic analysis of stress and chronic illness. Journal of Advanced Nursing 14:868–876.

Leininger M (1991). Culture Theory: Diversity and Universality. New York: National League for Nursing Publication 15-2402.

Lendrum S, Syme G (1992). Gift of Tears: A Practical Approach to Loss and Bereavement Counseling. New York, Tavistock/Routledge.

Lepore S, Evans G, Schneider M (1991). Dynamic role of social support in the link between chronic stress and psychological distress. Journal of Personality and Social Psychology 61(6):899–909.

Lindemann E (1944). Symptomatology and management of acute grief. American Journal of Psychiatry 101:141–148.

Maslach C (1982). Burnout—The Cost of Caring. Englewood Cliffs, NJ, Spectrum.

Mast D, Meyer J, Urbanski A (1987a). Relaxation techniques: A self-learning module for nurses. Unit I. Cancer Nursing 10:141–147.

Mast D, Meyer J, Urbanski A (1987b). Relaxation techniques: A self-learning module for nurses. Unit II. Cancer Nursing 10:217–225.

McCaffery M, Beebe A (1989). Pain: Clinical Manual for Nursing Practice. St. Louis, Mosby.

Niaura R, Goldstein MG (1992). Psychological factors affecting physical condition. Cardiovascular disease literature review. Psychosomatics 33(2):146–155.

November MT, Morris M, Litton J, Stabler B (1992). Stress buffering effect of psychological support in a diabetic camp. Diabetes Care 15(2):310–311.

Ostell A (1991). Coping, problem solving and stress: A framework for intervention strategies. British Journal of Medical Psychology 64:11–24.

Pearlin LI, Schooler C (1978). The structure of coping. Journal of Health and Social Behavior 19:2–21.

Perfetti T (1982). Montgomery County, Maryland, Crisis Center, Training Manual for Crisis Counselors.

Perry S, Fishman B, Jacobsberg L (1992). Stress and HIV infection. American Journal of Psychiatry 149(3):416–417.

Rushton CH (1990). Strategies for family centered care in the critical care setting. Pediatric Nursing 16(2):195–199.

Sanders C (1989). Grief: The Mourning After. New York, Wiley.

Schaefer K, Peterson K (1992). Effectiveness of coping strategies among critical care nurses. Dimensions of Critical Care Nursing 11(1):28–34.

Schafer J, Fals-Stewart W (1991). Issues of methodology, design and analytic procedure in psychological research on stress. British Journal of Medical Psychology 64:375–383.

Schlossberg N (1989). Overwhelmed: Coping with Life's Ups and Downs. Lexington, MA, Lexington Books.

Selye H (1956). The Stress of Life. New York, McGraw-Hill.

Selye H (1982). History and present status of the stress concept. In Goldberger L, Breznitz S (eds.) (1982), Handbook of Stress: Theoretical and Clinical Aspects. New York, Free Press.

Simos B (1979). A Time to Grieve. New York, Family Services.

Slaikeu K (1984). Crisis Intervention: A Handbook for Practice and Research. Boston: Allyn & Bacon.

Snyder SH (1977). Opiate receptors and internal opiates. Scientific American 236:44–56.

Stephenson J (1985). Death, Grief, and Mourning. New York, Free Press.

Steptoe A (1991). Invited review. The links between stress and illness. Journal of Psychosomatic Research 35(6):633–644.

Steptoe A, Matthews A (1984). Health Care and Human Behavior. Orlando, FL, Academic Press.

Terry DJ (1992). Stress, coping and coping resources as correlates of adaptation in myocardial infarction patients. British Journal of Clinical Psychology 31:215–225.

Thompson BT, Brantley PJ, Jones GN, Dyer HR, Morris JL (1992). The relation between stress and disease activity in rheumatoid arthritis. Journal of Behavioral Medicine 15(2):215–225.

Trygstad LN (1986). Stress and coping in psychiatric nursing. Journal of Psychosocial Nursing 24(10):23–27.

Wakefield M (1992). Stress control for nurses. Canadian Nurse 88(4):24–25.

Weinberger R (1991). Teaching the elderly stress reduction. Journal of Gerontological Nursing 17(10):23–27.

Whetsell M, Larrabee M (1988). Using guilt constructively in the NICU to affirm parental coping. Neonatal Network 6(4):21–27.

Wurzbach ME (1992). Assessment and intervention for certainty and uncertainty. Nursing Forum 27(2):29–35.

SUGGESTED READINGS

Abbott K (1990). Therapeutic use of play in the psychological preparation of preschool children undergoing cardiac surgery. Issues in Comprehensive Pediatric Nursing 13(4):265–277.

Andrews G, Tennant C (1978). Being upset and becoming ill: An appraisal of the relationship between life events and physical illness. Medical Journal of Australia I:324–327.

Anonymous (1992). Open learning programme: Managing stress. The stress question. (Continuing education credit.) Nursing Times 88(20):13–19.

Brandon JE, Loftin J, Curry J (1991). Role of fitness in mediating stress: A correlational exploration of stress reactivity. Journal of Perceptual and Motor Skills 73:1171–1180.

Dooley D, Catalano R (1991). Unemployment as a stressor: Findings and implications of a recent study. WHO Region Publications European Series 37:313–339.

Gay S (1991). Over the wall. American Journal of Nursing 91(8):82.

Gropper E (1992). Promoting health by promoting comfort. Nursing Forum 27(2):5–8.

Hefferin EL (1980). Life-cycle stressors: An overview of research. Family and Community Health 2(4):71.

Jin P (1992). Efficacy of Tai Chi, brisk walking, meditation and reading in reducing mental and emotional stress. Journal of Psychosomatic Research 36(4):361–370.

Johnson JE, Rice VH, Fuller SS, Endress MP (1978). Sensory information, instruction in coping strategy, and recovery from surgery. Research in Nursing and Health 1:4–17.

Johnson JE, Fuller SS, Endress MP, Rice VH (1978). Altering patients' responses to surgery: An extension and replication. Research in Nursing and Health 1:111–121.

McFarland PH, Stanton AL (1991). Preparation of children for emergency medical care: A primary prevention approach. Journal of Pediatric Psychology 16(4):489–504.

McKerron LC (1991). Dealing with the stress of caring for the dying in intensive care units: An overview. Intensive Care Nursing 7(4):219–222.

Miller T (1988). Advances in understanding the impact of stressful life events on health. Hospital and Community Psychiatry 39(6):615.

Nyamathi A, Jacoby A, Constancia P, Ruvich S (1992). Coping and adjustment of spouses of critically ill patients with cardiac disease. Heart and Lung 21(2):160–166.

Parachin VM (1991). Pressure-proof your life: Creative ways to reduce stress. Today's OR Nurse 13(12): 9–11.

Pelletier M (1992). The organ donor family members' perception of stressful stiuations during the organ donation experience. Journal of Advanced Nursing 17(1):90–97.

Perakyla A (1991). Hope work in the care of seriously ill patients. Qualitative Health Research 1(4):407–433.

Rigdon IS, Clayton BC, Diamond M (1987). Toward a theory of helpfulness for the elderly bereaved: An invitation to a new life. Advances in Nursing Science 9(2):32–43.

Russler M (1991). Multidimensional stress management in nursing education. Journal of Nursing Education 30(8):341–346.

Ryan-Wenger NM (1992). A taxonomy of children's coping strategies: A step toward theory development. American Journal of Orthopsychiatry 62(2):256–263.

Thompson SW (1991). Communication techniques for allaying anxiety and providing support for hospitalized children. Journal of Child and Adolescent Psychiatric and Mental Health Nursing 4(3): 119–122.

Wynd CA (1992). Relaxation imagery used for stress reduction in the prevention of smoking relapse. Journal of Advanced Nursing 17(3):294–302.

Communicating with Clients in Crisis

ELIZABETH ARNOLD

OBJECTIVES

At the end of the chapter, the student will be able to:

1. Define crisis and identify its characteristics in health care.
2. Identify theoretical frameworks for the study of crisis.
3. Identify two types of crises.

4. Define crisis intervention.

5. Apply the nursing process to the care of the client in crisis.

6. Describe crisis intervention applications in selected special situations.

Families come to us—the nurses—scared and seeking, at times not knowing themselves how to sort through what they fear or need most. This is often their first experience of this kind that involves a loved one.

Kleeman, 1989

Chapter 21 develops basic concepts related to crisis and crisis intervention. The concepts presented in this chapter are meant to accompany those presented in the previous chapter with special applications to crisis situations. These occur when a person's stress level in meeting life goals reaches an intolerable breaking point and creates a temporary, acute personality disorganization. Without prompt treatment, a crisis state has long-range effects on a person's mental health and consequent behaviors. Crisis intervention strategies can help prevent these effects. Included in the chapter are suggestions for coping with some of the serious crises found in health care: families in crisis, violence, suicide, and rape.

BASIC CONCEPTS

DEFINITION

Beckingham and Baumann (1990) define a *crisis* as a "sudden unanticipated or unplanned for event which necessitates immediate action to resolve the problem." A crisis situation develops when a condition or set of circumstances places an individual in a state of unbalance. It happens to individuals and families in all age, socioeconomic, and sociocultural groups. Typical crisis situations in health care settings include the following: parents of infants in the NICU, parents of children experiencing acute illness, trauma and terminally ill clients and their families, siblings of hospitalized children, children or grandchildren of critically ill clients, families of clients in nursing homes, families of clients with cancer or sudden illness, suicide threats, and violence. Each player may experience the crisis drama differently. People at the center of the crisis obviously experience it differently than those on the periphery. Family members may progress through the phases of a crisis at different rates of speed. Noting differences in each person's reaction is an important part of assessment that helps define the most appropriate interventions.

Webster's dictionary defines "crisis" as "a turning point." A crisis, as an episodic circumstance in a person's life, can have a growth-producing or a destructive effect on self-identity and functioning. The Chinese symbol for crisis has a dual meaning: danger and opportunity. In a crisis situation, the danger is that the crisis will prove so devastating that the client will not be able to function or to engage with life again in a full and meaningful way. Opportunity lies in the fact that the disruption forces one to look again at patterns of coping with life in ways that are not possible when everything is going well (Aguilera, 1994). Reworking a difficult situation and discovering one's personal strengths in the process is described by some people as a "rebirth."

CHARACTERISTICS

A crisis is time limited. Four to six weeks is the time period most people consider reasonable in resolving a crisis. This does not mean that the client or family's stress level has returned completely to normal, only that the immediate feelings of acute personality disorganization have lessened to a workable level. The time frame is used to differentiate crisis intervention as an emergency treatment from other psychological treatment.

A crisis is not the same as an illness. People in crisis are not mentally ill or disturbed. The crisis state is a normal human response to an acute emotional imbalance. People in crisis situations experience a loss or sense of loss of something important to their self-concept. Usually the person has no frame of reference for coping with the current crisis situation. Typically people experience a crisis reaction by moving through stages of *shock,* seen at the time of impact, followed by a period of *recoil* and inner turmoil as the initial shock subsides. This stage is followed by a period of *adjustment* in which a person begins to take constructive action to rebuild a shattered dream and reestablish identity.

Functional behaviors seen in crisis situations vary from the societal norm of everyday life and frequently are viewed as uncharacteristic of a person's normal personality. A person in crisis experiences disorganization and disequilibrium in one or more life areas, accompanied by feelings of fatigue, helplessness, inadequacy, and anxiety (Slaikeu, 1984). In crisis situations people display cognitive rigidity. They have trouble seeing beyond the problem or considering alternative options. Their thinking processes seem paralyzed, and they are unable to resolve problems using customary coping skills. Behaviorally, the person in crisis can display a wide spectrum of behaviors, ranging from appearing disorganized and hysterical to highly controlled emotionally or belligerent. Decision making may appear haphazard or impulsive. People in crisis, however, are more open to considering their health than they are at other times. This is the time to introduce preventive health care and to take advantage of increased interest in health care with clients who normally shy away from it.

THEORETICAL FRAMEWORKS

Lindeman's (1944) model of the grief process presented in Chapter 20 and Caplan's model of preventive psychiatry form the basis for much of the current thinking about crisis and crisis intervention. Caplan (1964) identifies four developmental phases in a crisis situation, summarized in Box 21–1. Crisis occurs when important life goals are thwarted and common methods of problem solving are insufficient to remove the obstacles in meeting them. According to Caplan, there are many possibilities for personal growth in a crisis situation. But the outcome of a crisis situation depends on what happens between the person or persons experiencing the crisis and the quality of human support the person receives to resolve the crisis. Community mental health practice relies heavily on crisis intervention as a primary treatment modality. Caplan applied the concepts of primary, secondary, and tertiary prevention to crisis intervention and viewed the nurse as a key figure in intervention.

A nursing framework for the study of crisis in clinical practice is the classic model originally developed by Aguilera and Messick (1978–1990) of balancing factors that can make a difference in the resolution of a crisis (Fig. 21–1). This model proposes that a crisis does not occur in isolation of a person's normal functioning and interpersonal environment. It exists either because of a distorted perception of a situation or because the client lacks the resources to cope successfully with it. The client's resources may be internal (beliefs or attitudes) or external (environmental supports). Strong connections between the client and other factors in the environmental context contribute to the development and resolution of a crisis, and these factors are important to assess. Exercise 21–1 provides practice using the Aguilera and Messick model.

TYPES OF CRISES

Situational Crises

Most crises in health care situations can be classified as situational. A *situational crisis* represents an external event or environmental influence perceived as harmful to the organism. It is characterized by a sudden, unexpected onset. The event can be physiological, emotional, environmental, or spiritual in nature. Loss of a limb, a car accident, rape, diagnosis of cancer, natural disasters, the death of a loved one, loss of a job, and even a job promotion or move to a new area are examples of actual and potential situational crises. In contrast to developmental crises, situational life crises strike randomly and can affect large numbers of people simultaneously.

Developmental Crises

Developmental crises arise in connection with maturational changes. Erikson's (1963–1982) theory of developmental psychosocial crises, first discussed in Chapter 3, provides a basis for understanding the role of psychosocial crises at every life stage. According to Erikson, psychosocial crises result from an incongruity between a person's interpersonal skills or strengths and the expectations of the

---

BOX 21–1
Developmental Phases in a Crisis Situation

1. Rise in tension and use of customary problem-solving strategies.
2. Coping strategies are insufficient to resolve the crisis; there is an increase in discomfort.
3. Emergency coping strategies are used: The problem is redefined, avoided, or goals are relinquished.
4. If none of the coping strategies work, tension increases, creating major personality disorganization and the crisis state.

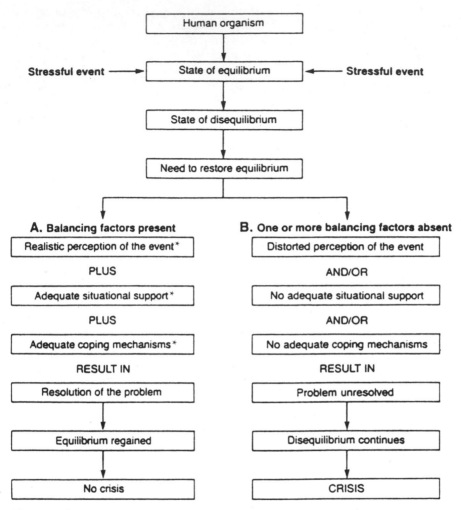

Figure 21–1 Crisis Model for Intervention. From Aguilera D (1994). Crisis Intervention: Theory and Methodology (7th ed.), p. 32. St. Louis, Mosby.

culture. Successful coping involves learning the skills and competencies to master the new cultural requirements. A developmental view of crisis takes into consideration the interpersonal challenges and stressors that occur at every life stage. Examples of developmental crisis events include conflicts with teachers or parents, unwanted pregnancy, going away to college, marriage, a first job, and caring for aging parents (Slaikeu, 1984). Each of these events calls for interpersonal resources or personal coping strengths a person may not have acquired in his or

her life, thus creating a maturational crisis for that person.

A situational crisis may be superimposed upon a developmental crisis. For example, a hysterectomy performed just prior to menopause may be a critical incident for a woman struggling with issues of her femininity and the meaning of loss of function. The restrictions of a diabetic diet, urine or blood testing, and daily insulin injections may be an intolerable situational crisis for a newly diagnosed adolescent diabetic client.

EXERCISE 21–1
Understanding the Nature of Crisis

Purpose: To help you understand the elements in the development of a crisis situation Aguilera's (1990) paradigm of the role of balancing factors is important in assessing and planning communication strategies in crisis situations.

Time: Homework assignment; class discussion 30–45 minutes.

Procedure:
1. Describe a crisis you experienced in your life. There are no right or wrong definitions of a crisis, and it doesn't matter if the crisis would be considered a crisis in someone else's life.
2. Identify how the crisis changed your roles, routines, relationships, and assumptions about yourself.
3. Apply Aguilera's model to the situation you are describing. Identify balancing factors and other relevant data as they apply to your circumstances.
4. Identify the strategies you used to cope with the crisis.
5. Describe the ways in which your personal crisis strengthened or weakened your self-concept and increased your options and your understanding of life.

CRISIS INTERVENTION

The theoretical literature is rich with information on crisis intervention and recommended nursing actions. These actions, however, must be adapted to fit each client's individual situation. Differences in cultural background, developmental level, and previous life experiences require the nurse to exercise critical thinking and reflective clinical judgment to make the intervention specific to the client's situation. Crisis intevention strategies also compel the nurse to examine personal attitudes toward difficult client behaviors so that they are better able to understand a client in crisis and can respond humanely to life's most serious challenges.

Crisis intervention is defined as "the systematic application of problem-solving techniques, based on crisis theory, designed to help the client move through the crisis process as swiftly and as painlessly as possible and thereby achieve at least the same level of psychological comfort as he or she experienced before the crisis" (Kus, 1985). Treatment strategies represent a relatively inexpensive, brief treatment model almost exclusively focused on immediate problem solving and the restoration of an individual to a precrisis state functional level. Crisis intervention strategies are designed to help clients achieve a deeper level of understanding and acceptance. The process of acceptance is not a single event. It represents a stage of adjustment arrived at through the support of the nurse and the strengthening of the personal resources of the client and family (Bluhm, 1987)

A crisis situation in a nonpsychiatric health care setting usually is obvious and can be addressed more easily because of the hospital structure. As health care moves steadily into the community, nurses are encountering serious crisis situations in home health care and in occupational health and school health situations that are not as obvious, and not as easily addressed. The nurse has a special advantage, however, in mobilizing primary and secondary prevention inteventions to help families identify and treat episodic situations before they escalate into crisis proportions. For example, a bereavement support intervention following a classmate's suicide or anticipatory guidance and referral for a dying client can minimize the effect of an acute crisis or prevent it from happening. Informal teaching of parenting skills can help prevent child abuse.

APPLICATIONS

NURSING PROCESS

Assessment

Assess Client Safety

The first assessment in any crisis situation is of the client's current danger potential. A crisis by definition is a state of imbalance. The person feels overwhelmed and unable to cope with the crisis circumstances in particular and with life in general. In a state of crisis, people do things they

Stage	Client Behavior	Nurse Actions
1. Environmental trigger	Stress response	Encourage ventilation: avoid challenge, speak calmly, clearly, offer alternative.
2. Escalation period	Movement toward loss of control	Take control: maintain safe distance, acknowledge behavior, medicate if appropriate, remove to quiet area, "show force" if necessary.
3. Crisis period	Emotional/physical discharge	Apply external control: implement emergency protocol, initiate confinement, give focused intensive care.
4. Recovery	Cool down	Reassure: support, no retaliation; encourage to discuss behavior and alternatives; release when in control; assess reaction to release; assist in reentry toward environment; conduct sessions for staff to process all areas of incident.
5. Postcrisis and letdown	Reconciliatory	Demonstrate acceptance while continuing clarification of unit standards and expectations.

Figure 21–2 Guidelines for Choosing Intervention with Different Stages of Aggressive Behavior in the Emergency Department. From Steele RL (1993). Staff attitudes toward seclusion and restraint: Anything new? Perspectives in Psychiatric Care 29(3):28, 1993. Reprinted with the permission of Nursecom, Inc.

ordinarily wouldn't consider, including causing physical harm to themselves or others. Suicide and violence are psychiatric emergencies that present regularly in the emergency departments in most hospitals.

The nurse needs to evaluate the client's mental status and level of emotional decompensation. Is the client capable at this time of participating in crisis intervention? Clients who are psychotic, under the influence of drugs, organically impaired, or temporarily out of control cannot provide a logical, sequential description of their problem, even with the nurse's help. At the time, they are incapable of understanding the psychological motivations behind their problematic behavior. Clients in crisis whose condition is complicated by organic impairment involving drugs require immediate triage to stabilize their condition before interviewing can be productive. Instead of an in-depth assessment interview, attention is given to providing immediate medical intervention and support. Figure 21–2 provides guidelines. Family members or the person accompanying the client often can provide some of the background related to the current crisis state.

Define the Crisis Problem

Initially, the goal of the crisis interview is to help the client develop a workable understanding of the crisis problem, its origins, and the tasks needed to resolve it (Hobbs, 1984; Mitchell, 1977). The nurse needs to explore the client's feelings and reactions about the crisis and help the client identify the precipitating event(s) leading up to it. Since the client's perception of the crisis event is critical to its understanding, inquiry about the crisis event should focus on the client's own words concerning what happened. The client frequently will tell the nurse who is involved, what happened, and when it happened. Less frequently the client speaks about his or her feelings about what happened until prompted by the nurse. It is appropriate to inquire how the client is feeling at the present time and to ask directly, "What does this crisis mean to you?"

Careful inquiry into the feelings of significant others about the crisis situation, history, and duration of the problem and general information about the client, including any past psychiatric history, follows. For example, the nurse might ask the client, "How do you see what has happened affecting your present relationships?" "In what ways do you see your current situation affecting your future?" Each of these questions allows the nurse to explore the personal meaning of an objective crisis from the client's perspective. An accurate perception of the crisis event and its probable consequences has a significant effect on the client's attempts to resolve it. The more realistic the perception, the easier it is to develop appropriate strategies to resolve the crisis.

Solicit Relevant Past History

Information about what led up to the crisis and any past experiences with similar situations provides the nurse with additional data about coping responses that might be used in the present situation. Questions the nurse might ask include, "Has anything similar happened in the past?" "How did you handle it?" "What was helpful to you in resolving this problem in the past?" Of particular importance is evidence of previous suicide attempts, drug use, or major psychiatric illness. The nurse asks questions about medications and previous treatment for medical and psychiatric disorders. The history helps the nurse anticipate potential reactions. For example, a woman's husband is admitted to the coronary care unit with an acute myocardial infarction. Her father died of heart disease when she was 12 years old. This previous experience with a similar problem will intensify the current crisis for her. The same is true for another client with a different twist. This man is recently divorced. His mother had stomach cancer two years ago, and his sister was recently diagnosed with breast cancer. His youngest child will start college in the fall. Although he has handled all of these crises without undue stress, he falls apart when his father is admitted to the coronary unit. The cumulative losses have become one too many. In both cases, relevant past history plays an important role in the client's appraisal of the events and personal coping ability.

People who have coped well in the past, who have demonstrated resiliency and creativity in other aspects of their lives, are more likely to weather a crisis satisfactorily. Clients with few interpersonal and cognitive resources need more external supports to survive. Knowledge about interpersonal deficits such as poor self-image, lack of friends, marital conflicts, and poor motivation can help the nurse understand the types of help a particular client may need. Does the client have a steady job? How has the person coped with other problems? Has the client used available services, networks, and social support systems? Each of these considerations provides the nurse with important information about the client's personal ability to develop realistic options for the present situation and the types of compensatory supports the client needs.

Having knowledge of the coping strategies a person has used in the past to reduce tension is relevant. For example, aerobics or bible study are realistic options as tension reducers, especially if the client has used them in the past. Questions the nurse might ask include: "What do you usually do when you have a problem?" "To whom do you turn when you have a difficult problem?" If the client seems immobilized and unable to give an answer about usual coping strategies, the nurse can offer prompts such as, "Some people talk to their friends, bang walls, pray, go to a bar, withdraw. . . ." Usually with a verbal prompt and encouragement, the person will identify characteristic coping mechanisms.

Identify Recent Changes in Client Behaviors

Another key issue is change. Any deviation from previous functioning is important. The nurse needs to assess whether the current crisis has just occurred, and whether it occurred suddenly or is an intensification of previous functioning. Questions the nurse would ask include, "How long have you had the current symptoms?" and, "In what way has this crisis affected your ability to function?" Through these questions the nurse is able to assess the client's current functioning compared to his or her behavior prior to the crisis. Family members can be helpful in verifying data and in adding new information.

Recognize Personal Strengths

In a time of crisis, there is a tendency for both nurse and client to focus on what is wrong without balancing this information with what is right about the client. It is just as important for the nurse to develop information about what aspects of a person's life are working well as it is to focus on those that are not functioning well at the moment (Aguilera, 1990). Having a job, having supportive family and friends, and having a strong church community are important buffers of stress in crisis situations (Exercise 21–2). It is possible to incorporate them into the current care plan if they are known. Personal strengths might include a deep faith, good problem-solving skills, and past interpersonal success.

EXERCISE 21–2
Personal Support Systems

Purpose: To help students appreciate the breadth and importance of personal support systems in stressful situations.

Time: 30 minutes. May be done as a homework assignment and shared in class.

Procedure:
All of us have support systems we can use in times of stress, such as church, friends, family, coworkers, clubs, and recreational groups.
1. Identify a support person or system you could or do use in terms of stress.
2. What does this personal support person do for you—e.g., listen without judgment; provide honest, objective feedback; challenge you to think; broaden your perspective; give unconditional support; share your perceptions, etc.? List everything you can think of.
3. What factors go into choosing your personal support system—e.g., availability, expertise, perception of support, etc.—and which is the most important factor?
4. How did you develop your personal support system?

Discussion:
1. What types of support systems were most commonly used by class or group members?
2. What were the most common reasons for selecting a support person or system?
3. After doing this exercise, what strategies would you advise for enlarging a personal support system?
4. What applications do you see in this exercise for your nursing practice?

Distinguish Applicable Environmental Factors

Factors in the environment, such as availability of resources and other life responsibilities, can intensify a crisis for individuals and their families. For example, consider the situation of this mother. Her two-year-old was recently diagnosed with leukemia. She lives 75 miles from the nearest hospital, and her other children range in age from four to ten. The crisis of having a child suffering with a potentially fatal disease is compounded by environmental constraints that do not allow her free access to her child. In other situations, factors such as legal charges, financial concerns, and marital or co-existing mental problems can intensify almost any psychosocial crisis. Developing information about these variables can help the nurse identify the most appropriate resources in the present crisis situation.

Identify Social Supports and Community Resources

Just as the environment is capable of intensifying a crisis for individuals and their families, it also has resources that can be mobilized to resolve it. A healthy, supportive family is without peer in the resolution of almost any crisis. Friends and support groups provide practical advice and reaffirm a person's worth during the period of personal questioning that accompanies a crisis. The nurse needs to know what family and social support systems the client has available to help resolve the current crisis. Questions the nurse can ask about family and social supports are presented in Box 21–2.

Neighborhood and agency resources can provide the client with needed supports. An impor-

---

BOX 21–2
Questions about Family Support

"Does the client have close family ties?"
"Does the client have close friends?"
"Is the client a member in a social organization (church, social club, etc.)?"
"Who currently is the most important person in the client's life?"
"What is the impact of the crisis event on the client's social relationships (spouse, children, friends, etc.)?"
"Who in the social network can be approached to help the client work through the crisis?"
"Who in the client's network might hinder successful crisis resolution?"

Slaikeu K (1984). Crisis Intervention: A Handbook for Practice and Research. Boston, Allyn & Bacon, pp. 130–132. Used with permission.

tant piece of information is whether or not the client is willing to use outside resources, and if so, which ones. For example, it may not be a lack of knowledge that prevents Rose from seeking welfare as a way of stabilizing her financial situation, but rather her feelings about the meaning of being on welfare. If being on welfare is considered shameful, it is unlikely Rose will choose it as a viable option unless she can change her feelings about it. Antidepressant medication could help Louis cope with his present crisis and longstanding depression, but he thinks of medication as a "crutch" that will affect his functioning. He would never consider it as an option.

Planning

Once the nursing assessment is complete, the nurse selects relevant nursing diagnoses to reflect the direction of the intervention. Sample nursing diagnoses are presented in Box 21–3.

Intervention

The role of the nurse in crisis intervention is intense, time limited, action oriented, and goal directed to a greater degree than it is in most conventional therapeutic relationships with clients. In the early stages of crisis, people need to be listened to rather than to be given much information. It is a period of enormous emotional turmoil, and people can absorb very little compared to their usual capabilities. Yet a crisis can represent a turning point in the client's and family's life.

Concepts and principles of communication discussed in previous chapters also apply to crisis situations, but they are modified to meet the special communication needs of the client in crisis.

BOX 21–3
Sample Nursing Diagnoses

Grieving related to perinatal loss as evidenced by inability to sleep and constant crying.

Ineffective coping related to job loss as evidenced by suicide attempt.

Anxiety related to rape as evidenced by fear, emotional disorganization, and restlessness.

Ineffective family coping related to son's accident, as evidenced by inability to work and expressed desire to dissolve marriage.

The goals of crisis intervention are to help the client gradually to accept the reality of his or her current situation and to develop new and different ways of coping with it. The nurse acts as advocate, resource, partner, and guide in the crisis intervention. An important part of the crisis intervention process is helping the client mobilize personal resources and use support resources effectively (Hoff, 1991).

Application of a Model of Intervention

A three-stage model of intervention that involves engaging the client, exploring the problem, and developing alternatives through creative problem solving is designed to mobilize clients and their families in emergency situations (Perfetti, 1982). This model offers the client the additional interpersonal structure needed in crisis situations.

1. ENGAGING THE CLIENT

The first step in the process of crisis intervention is engaging the client. The setting is important. The area for the interview should be a quiet one, free from distraction where the nurse and client/family can hear each other (Bluhm, 1987). If the client or family member(s) appear particularly upset, it may be appropriate to have more than one person conduct the interview. One health professional should be designated as the primary contact person. This strategy has several benefits. It allows the family to develop a relationship with a primary caregiver who can serve as a needed contact for questions and problem solving. It cuts down on the possibility of conflicting information. It allows the nurse to become well acquainted with the client's problem and to act as a therapeutic partner in resolution of the crisis.

Therapeutic goals in the initial stages of a crisis are to reduce the intensity of the crisis and to help the client feel supported in a time of great emotional turmoil. Most clients in crisis look to the helping person to structure the interaction. The concepts of empathy, authenticity, immediacy, and active listening are very important with clients in crisis, but they need to be focused explicitly on understanding the crisis as a critical event in the client's life. Here are some guidelines for communicating with the client in crisis during the engagement phase.

Be Specific. Don't ask irrelevant questions. Respond to the client in brief, concise sentences, and don't explain a lot initially. Let the client tell you what he or she is experiencing. Listen for both facts and feelings, and use reflective statements to develop a complete picture of the crisis situation. When either facts or feelings are missing, attempt to bring the missing component into the conversation—for example, "I'm clear that you feel responsible for the baby falling down the stairs, but you say your husband was in the same area. What was he doing when the accident happened?"

Pace the Discussion. Follow the client's description; don't let the client get ahead of you. Ask for clarification so that you understand the client's situation as completely as possible, but don't anticipate the story. Summarize content from time to time so that both parties arrive at the same place simultaneously. It is important that the nurse present a calm, controlled presence and allow the unfolding of emotions and story as the client is experiencing it (Kleeman, 1989). Sometimes this is difficult when the nurse feels overwhelmed by the implications of the crisis and the other persons affected by the crisis event seem oblivious to its impact. For example, the nurse might know that a client brought to the trauma unit has a bleak prognosis, but the family needs time to arrive at this conclusion on its own. The nurse needs to be there psychologically for the client and client's family, offering realistic support while respecting their need to understand the meaning of the crisis in their own way and within their own time frame.

Reinforce Strengths. Point out the client's strengths as you observe them, and acknowledge the client's ability to respond constructively to a difficult situation. Ask the client how he or she handled difficult situations in the past. For example, although a current loss is experienced as catastrophic, the client may have coped successfully with other losses in the past. Recalling these events can offer hope to the client that the current crisis can also be resolved.

Stay with the Topic. Refocus when the client changes the subject, introduces irrelevant material, or seems to be going around in circles. Refocusing can be done by asking the client if there is a relationship between the new material and the crisis situation, by making an appropriate connection between the content offered and the original stated problem, or by making a comment about the primary problem. Refocusing needs to be done tactfully, with statements such as:

"We need to find out a little more about your immediate situation."
"I think we can help you best if we can understand what led up to this crisis and what its impact is on your life right now."
"How has this crisis (name it) affected your family life, friendships, physical health?"
"I wonder if you could tell me a little more about what led up to this crisis."

2. Exploring the Problem

Help the Client Identify Critical Elements. During the second stage of nursing intervention, the nurse helps the client explore the immediate parts of the problem in greater depth. This process lets the client reframe the crisis event and provides the nurse with an opportunity to define the problem clearly and to clarify it in his or her own mind. Breaking down issues of concern into smaller elements makes the possibility of developing a realistic solution more workable.

The dialogue should remain focused on the crisis situation. Keeping clients centered on the precipitating crisis event is sometimes difficult but very necessary. Tangential subjects, even though they may prove interesting, serve only as distractions and allow clients to postpone taking deliberate action on their own behalf. Such inactivity is counterproductive to the resolution of the crisis. Clients need to think about what the issues are related to the particular problem and what the meaning of the event is or could be in the larger scheme of their lives.

A useful technique is to help the client attach feelings to specific events—for example, "Because you think your son is using drugs [precipitating event], you feel helpless and confused, and it seems you don't know what to do next [client reaction]." The more precise the exploration and redefinition of the problem, the more likely the client will choose the goals and objectives most appropriate to resolve the problem.

Provide Truth in Information. Being truthful about the client's condition and letting the client know as much as possible about progress, treatment, and the effects of treatment helps the client feel supported. Learning about the consequences of choosing different alternatives allows the client to make informed decisions and reduces the heightened anxiety that is present in every crisis situation. The words the nurse uses are important because the client is likely to misinterpret them in a time of stress. *The nurse needs to be sensitive to the amount of information the client is capable of absorbing.* Usually this is limited. Critical elements should be given slowly and repeated at intervals. Truth in information is equally important for the family. Including significant others in the discussion helps by giving the client a resource who can confirm or correct what was heard. Sufficient time should be allowed for both processing and asking questions.

Identify Recurring Themes. Usually in the course of the conversation the helping person picks up underlying themes or clues that have a connection with the precipitating problem but that lie outside the client's awareness. It is important to bring these themes to the client's conscious attention *if* doing so facilitates the intervention. The following is an example of listening to the client's message and responding to both the content (experience and thoughts) and the latent feelings in the message. *The situation and the client's manner of expression (metacommunication) will dictate the most appropriate listening response.*

CASE EXAMPLE

Client: It's my wife—she's dying. I'm afraid to go in there and see her. I can't act cheerful, and it won't do her any good to see me upset.

Nurse (responding to the content of the statement): You don't want your wife to see you're upset because she's dying?

Nurse (responding to the speaker's feelings): You're worried that you can't disguise your feelings of sadness?

Nurse (responding to the content and feelings expressed by the speaker): You're afraid of getting upset in front of your wife and unsettling her?

Help the Client Normalize Emotions. Often clients in crisis feel that their emotional reactions to a situation are abnormal because the emotions feel so strange. It is important to point out to the client that a wide array of feelings is quite normal in crisis situations and that many people in similar situations experience comparable feelings.

To a person relating a rape incident without expressing any feeling about it, the nurse might say, "You must feel so violated and angry that this happened to you." Should the client respond by saying, "I feel numb," the nurse can console the client that this "shutdown" of feelings is a common occurrence in crisis situations. Even if the client doesn't respond immediately, the linking of the event to the feelings about it helps the person in crisis recognize difficult feelings as related to a stressful event. Though it may seem obvious to the nurse, the client may be unaware of the connection. Legitimizing feelings of rage and betrayal helps the victim integrate these feelings as normal reactions to what has happened to her.

Help the Client Clarify Distortions. Distinguishing real from unrealistic fears helps clients put a crisis situation into perspective and forces them to look at what can be changed in a situation versus what cannot. It is futile and a waste of needed energy to try to change what is unchangeable in any set of circumstances. When clients present a distorted view of a situation—blaming themselves, for example—it is important to challenge the distortion and to take the blame out of the situation. For example, the mother of a premature or deformed child often blames herself for a number of reasons: she smoked; she didn't really want this baby so God is punishing her; she shouldn't have lifted anything when she was pregnant; and so forth. The nurse can help the client translate this perception into a more objective perspective by assuring the client that every crisis represents a complex group of behaviors that come together in a unique configuration. No one factor is completely responsible for the crisis, and it is important for the nurse to help the client make this distinction. Later, when the crisis has subsided, the client may want to look at one or more contributing factors that may need to be changed. But it is inappropriate to do so during the acute stages of a crisis.

3. Developing Alternatives

Crisis intervention is action oriented and goal directed toward the immediate resolution of the emergency conditions. The purpose of leading the client to decide on a future course of action to resolve the crisis is to bring closure to the crisis. Problems not related to the crisis need to handled later. In the problem-solving stage, the nurse helps the client identify a specific plan of action to cope with the crisis. It is important to explore several different action strategies because the client is forced to think through the options (Egan, 1990). Whereas the nurse may suggest a range of realistic options in crisis interventions, specific advice about important life decisions should not be offered. Obviously, direct intervention is necessary when the client presents a danger to self or others, but when this is not the case, the locus of control should remain with the client to whatever extent possible. Usually clients in crisis feel powerless and need to feel as though they have more control of their lives. Allowing choices encourages clients to take charge of their actions and to take responsibility for the consequences of their choices.

It is useful to help the client examine the consequences of proposed solutions and to break them down into small, achievable parts. Proposed solutions should fit both the problem *and* the resources of the client. Previous successful coping mechanisms are identified, with the idea that skills can be transferred from one interpersonal field to another. The family and significant others should be involved in the plan.

Part of the process includes discussing the consequences of actions. "What would happen if you choose this course of action as compared to. . . ?" "What is the worst that could happen if you decided to. . . ?" Using common sense and knowledge of human behavior as a guide for interaction, the nurse may provide some alternative actions the client has not yet considered.

Help the Client Reconstruct Meanings. Whereas the circumstances themselves cannot be altered, it is possible to recast their meaning by separating the unchangeable facts of the event from the parts that can be reworked in a more positive way. For example, the loss of an infant at childbirth is undoubtedly one of life's greatest crises. The reality of the child's death cannot be reversed, but the nurse can help the parents integrate the tragic event into their lives in a meaningful way by dressing the child in an infant shirt and diaper, wrapping it in a blanket, and encouraging the family to see the child. Even if the infant is macerated or

deformed, the external wrappings can emphasize the normal aspects of the infant, and the nurse through his or her words can emphasize the positive features. Arranging for religious support acknowledges the existence of the child and is a major source of comfort to many parents. These simple actions on the part of the nurse can significantly mitigate the distortions that inevitably accompany a catastrophic event and can change some of the negative meaning of the situation.

Establish Follow-up Mechanisms. Providing for follow-up is a necessary component of the communication process in therapeutic relationships with clients in crisis. Suggestions should be clear, concise, and simple. The client needs to develop follow-up mechanisms that are realistic and comfortable to implement.

Application of a Model of Intervention

CASE EXAMPLE

Mrs. James is a 39-year-old woman, married, with three children, ages 7, 14, and 16. She is very upset, anxious, verbal, and not sure what to do. She is seeking nursing intervention because she just discovered that her 14-year-old son is using cocaine. She discovered this when she accidently uncovered an envelope of cocaine while putting some clothes in his dresser. She has no knowledge of cocaine and its effects and fears what it might be doing to her son's health, safety, and future. Her husband tells her not to worry. This is "just a phase."

Nursing Diagnosis. Ineffective coping related to discovery of son's possession of drugs.

Intervention: Engagement. Identify and discuss client's feelings of confusion, anxiety, betrayal by son, guilt at having gone through his drawers, and the conflict over how to confront both her husband and son. She will probably exhibit anger and blame toward her son but have difficulty looking at her own actions and motivations.

Exploring the Problem

1. Explore the client's feelings and reactions (fears, concerns, anger).
2. How will other family members react?
3. What will be the reaction of the family's social network (church, neighbors, school,

and police)? Will they have an effect on the situation?

4. Will Mrs. James's relationship with her son change now?
5. If the relationship changes, in what ways?
6. How can Mrs. James handle distrust constructively? (The ways she comes up with are the alternative options.)
7. Has she developed any symptomatology as a result of the stress, such as headaches, stomach aches, or depression?
8. Will she confront her son with this information?
9. How did Mrs. James discover that her son was using drugs? when? Did she have a sense that it was going on before? for how long?
10. How does Mrs. James feel about her son now?

Exploring Alternatives

1. Explore what Mrs. James can do to reduce her anxiety.
   a. Plan for confronting son and father.
   b. Discuss limits she can realistically place on son's drug use—for example, not in the house.
2. Identify areas that Mrs. James cannot control.
3. Discuss her need to express to her son the consequences of his behavior.
4. Explore how Mrs. James can utilize the family's social network to help.

Follow-Up

1. Arrange for follow-up family therapy.
2. Refer son for drug counseling.

Exercise 21–3 gives practice in using the three-stage model of crisis intervention.

SELECTED APPLICATIONS

Families in Crisis

A family can experience a state of crisis in the face of unexpected, severe, and complex illness or injury to a family member. Usually a family has had little preparation for the event and is called upon to act in ways that may be quite unfamiliar and disruptive of its lifestyle. Bluhm (1987) suggests an image of a family in crisis as "a group of people standing together, with arms interlocked.

What happens if one family member becomes seriously ill and can no longer stand? The other family members will attempt to carry their loved one, each person shifting his weight to accommodate the additional burden" (p. 44). A crisis in the family can affect relationships, school work, activities, and parenting—all of which may need to be redefined in response to an unexpected crisis. Behaviors the nurse is likely to encounter in crisis situations include anxiety, shock, fright, denial, anger, hostility, distrust, remorse and guilt, grief, and hopelessness. Families in crisis also typically experience a great deal of anger, including anger at the client, which cannot be expressed directly. Frequently the person or family in crisis may not be ready to divulge critical concerns to another family member. For example, how do you tell someone you are angry he or she is dying? How do you tell your family you are afraid you'll never walk again when your family doesn't want to hear such news? Families and clients frequently enter into a reciprocal conspiracy of silence because each does not want to frighten the other. Or family members are afraid their anger will show, and they know intellectually that this is not fair to the family member in crisis. It may not be appropriate to air such concerns, but the nurse can take a needed proactive role by helping clients voice their concerns within the safety of the nurse–client relationship. The nurse can help family members develop meaningful ways to communicate effectively with their loved one.

The words a nurse uses with families and the manner in which information has presented has an important influence on the family in crisis. Explanations should be kept simple and to the point. Diagrams, simulations, and pictures can sometimes help families understand what is happening better than words alone. If the client is capable of understanding, all explanations given to the family should also be given to the client.

Observation of the family's physical state is important. In the face of severe shock, it may not be possible really to find out much about the current crisis until the major players have had some rest. Family members may need the nurse's permission and encouragement to take a rest.

Written information about unit rules may be read at home and used as an ongoing reference. The client should be given the phone number of a primary caregiver on the unit and should be

EXERCISE 21–3

Interacting in Crisis Situations

Purpose: To give you experience in using the three-stage model of crisis intervention.

Time: Approximately 1 hour

Directions:
1. Break up into groups of three. One student should take the role of the client and one the role of the nurse; the third functions as observer.
2. Using the role play below or others that may represent your current experience, act out your respective parts. The observer uses the counselor rating sheet to provide feedback to the nurse.

Role Play

Julie is a 23-year-old woman who has been married for three years. Her husband, Jack, is 25 and a law student. They were married when she was a senior in college. Although she graduated with a degree in social sciences, she has been unable to find work in her chosen field. As a result, she has been working full time as a secretary. Her husband worked part time as a security guard and attended school full time. During their second year of marriage, Julie unexpectedly became pregnant. Jack had to quit school to support her during her last trimester. He continued to do so two months after the baby was born.

Eventually Jack was able to return to school and Julie to work. Although the baby was a burden, they loved her and were managing. When Julie went back to work, they found a reliable babysitter who lived two doors away. Four days ago she received a call from the hospital to meet with a staff doctor with her husband. When they arrived at the hospital, they were informed by the doctor that their daughter had died at the babysitter's of sudden infant death syndrome.

Both Jack and Julie's parents came to stay with them until the baby's burial. They buried her yesterday morning, and the relatives left in the afternoon. This morning, after Jack left for work and the baby's feeding time came, Julie found herself preparing the baby's formula. She became overcome with feeling and began to cry. She also began feeling angry at her husband and family. She also felt guilty for feeling that way. She says she feels as though she is "going crazy." She can't stop thinking about the baby and has constant vivid images of her whenever she is alone. Julie is flooded with a host of emotions she is unable to identify or control.

In order to give helpful feedback to the counselor, rate his or her performance with a number from 1 (least effective) to 5 (most effective).

Rating Scale

1. Did the counselor engage the client?	5 4 3 2 1
2. Did the counselor accurately reflect the client's feeling?	5 4 3 2 1
3. Did the client appear to share sensitive emotional information with the counselor?	5 4 3 2 1
4. Did the counselor communicate openness and a nonjudgmental attitude toward the client?	5 4 3 2 1
5. Did the counselor use brief, concise sentences?	5 4 3 2 1
6. Did the counselor utilize the compound sentence when connecting emotional reactions to stressors?	5 4 3 2 1
7. Did the client and counselor establish a mutually understood definition of the problem?	5 4 3 2 1
8. Did the counselor allow the client to do most of the talking and explaining?	5 4 3 2 1
9. Was the client able to arrive at useful alternatives as a result of the interview?	5 4 3 2 1
10. Did the counselor and client plan actions the client could begin using right away?	5 4 3 2 1

Discussion:
1. What did you learn from doing this exercise?
2. What would you want to do differently as a result of this exercise when communicating with the client in crisis?
3. What was the effect of using the three-stage model of crisis intervention as a way of organizing your approach to the crisis situation?

Rating Scale developed by Perfetti T (1982).

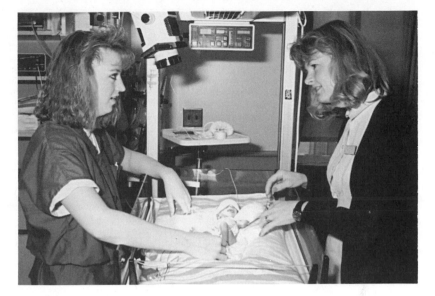

Careful coordination of the information to be shared with family members reduces confusion and allays anxiety in crisis situations. (Courtesy of the University of Maryland Hospital)

encouraged to call if he or she has questions. A simple phone call can relieve hours of potential worry.

Familes often feel confused about what they hear, particularly if they receive incomplete or contradictory information. They imagine the worst possible scenario or develop an internal image of what is happening that has little to do with reality. The nurse can advise families to designate one contact person within the family to give information to outsiders and family friends. This intervention helps reinforce the family as the primary unit for information and reduces the possibility of unnecessary or unauthorized calls to the unit. Furthermore, the more people involved in the information loop, the greater the possibility of misinformation in time of crisis.

As mentioned earlier, it is difficult for families in crisis to absorb everything they hear because they feel overwhelmed with the shock of the crisis. Informing the family of a change in their loved one's condition should be done in incremental stages, and in everyday language the client and family can understand. Many decisions the family needs to make—related to surgery, the donation of organs, the placement of the family member in an alternative treatment center, treatment choices that might be debilitating, use or discontinuance of extraordinary measures—have long-term emotional ramifications. It is important for the nurse to support the family's right to make the decision

and to offer family members honest and compassionate information so that they can make an informed decision. Discussion of the client's physical and mental condition should be presented in a matter of fact, constructive manner. Painting a highly pessimistic or overly optimistic picture should be avoided. Instead, family members can be led gently to developing their own sense of the truth. Communication strategies the nurse can use to help families in crisis are presented in Box 21–4.

Families of critically ill clients in the emergency room should be escorted to a private waiting area if one is available. Providing frequent updates and being available to answer questions at regular intervals helps reduce the family's anxiety (Puskar and Obus, 1989). If possible, a family member should be allowed to see the client, and if the client dies in the emergency room, it is appropriate to invite the family to see the body before it is dispatched to the funeral home. The nurse would accompany the family and would be available to answer any questions.

Violence

The emergency room is the first point of contact for many clients demonstrating violent behaviors in nonpsychiatric settings. Violence in health care settings represents a psychosocial emergency that can be just as critical as a medical emergency. It demands a similar type of immediate action

---

BOX 21–4
Interventions for Initial Family Responses to Crises

Anxiety, shock, fright	Giving information that is brief, concise, explicit, and concrete
	Repetition of information and frequent reinforcement—encourage families to record important facts in writing
	Ascertain comprehension by asking family to repeat back to you what information they have been given.
	Provide for and encourage or allow ventilation of feelings, even if they are extreme
	Maintain constant, nonanxious presence in the face of a highly anxious family
	Inform family as to the potential range of behaviors and feelings that are within the "norm" for crisis
	Maximize control within hospital environment, as possible
Denial	Identify what purpose denial is serving for family (e.g., is it buying them "psychological time" for future coping and mobilization of resources?)
	Evaluate appropriateness of use of denial in terms of time; denial becomes inappropriate when it inhibits the family from taking necessary actions or when it is impinging on the course of treatment
	Do not actively support denial but neither dash hopes for the future (e.g., "It must be very difficult for you to believe your son is nonresponsive and in a trauma unit")
	If denial is prolonged and dysfunctional, more direct and specific factual representation may be essential
Anger, hostility, distrust	Allow for ventilation of angry feelings, clarifying what thoughts, fears, and beliefs are behind the anger; let them know it's "OK" to be angry
	Don't personalize family's expressions of these strong emotions
	Institute family control within the hospital environment when possible (e.g., arrange for set time(s) and set person(s) to give them information in reference to the patient and answer their questions)
	Remain available to families during their venting of these emotions
	Ask families how they can take the energy in their anger and put it to positive use for themselves, for the patient, for the situation
Remorse and guilt	Do not try to "rationalize away" guilt for families
	Listen, support their expression of feeling and verbalizations (e.g., "I can understand how or why you might feel that way; however, . . .")
	Follow the "howevers" with careful, reality oriented statements or questions (e.g., "None of us can truly control another's behavior"; "Kids make their own choices despite what parents think and want"; "How successful were you when you tried to control _____'s behavior with that before?"; "So many things have happened for which there are no absolute answers")
Grief and depression	Acknowledge family's grief and depression
	Encourage them to be precise about what it is they are grieving and depressed about; give grief and depression a context
	Allow the family appropriate time for grief
	Recognize that this is an essential step for future adaptation—do not try to rush the grief process
	Remain sensitive to your own unfinished business and hence, comfort/discomfort with family's grieving and depression
Hope	Clarify with families what their hopes are, individually, and with one another
	Clarify with families what their worst fears are in reference to the situation—Are the hopes/fears congruent? realistic? unrealistic?
	Support realistic hope
	Offer gentle factual information to reframe unrealistic hope (e.g., "With the information you have or the observations you have made, do you think that is still possible?"
	Assist families in reframing unrealistic hope in some other fashion (e.g., "What do you think others will have learned from _____ if he doesn't make it?" "How do you think _____ would like for you to remember him/her?")

From Kleeman K (1989). Families in crisis due to multiple trauma. Critical Care Nursing Clinics of North America 1(1):25.

(Cahill et al., 1991). Violence also creates a crisis for the nursing staff, leaving nurses feeling shaken and unprotected if not handled quickly and in an organized manner.

Violence is physical force used by one person against another. It is a form of communication that is not always under a person's conscious power to control. Violence is associated with power and control—usually the perpetrator feels powerless or out of control, with little other recourse but violence. The client's violent behavior is an attempt to reestablish dynamic equilibrium. This is important for the nurse to remember because usually it is impossible not to have feelings about the perpetrator, and so a bad situation becomes worse. Frequently the etiology of violent behavior is organic, and the nurse is well advised to assume there is an organic component until otherwise indicated. Drugs and alcohol often are implicated. The violent client must be stabilized immediately for the protection of self and others (Puskar and Obus, 1989).

Observation of the client with potential for violence is of paramount importance. The client usually will demonstrate forewarning actions of potential violent behavior. Signs of rapid or antagonistic eye and facial movements, a hostile expression, angry gestures, change in vocal tone, pacing, and other forms of agitation are common. A recent history of violence, violence in the client's family or neighborhood, a history of substance abuse, mental retardation, problems with impulse control, and psychotic clients with delusions or hostile hallucinations are familiar contributing factors in the development of violent behaviors. It is appropriate to ask potentially violent clients directly if they feel they might lose control. Physical size can be deceptive and should never be underestimated. A one hundred pound woman can have the strength of a person twice her size because of increased adrenalin during a violent episode. Mental status, motor behavior, affect, and speech patterns offer a framework for assessment of the potentially violent client. Usually there is a combination of the indicators presented in Box 21–5.

Treatment of violent clients consists of providing a safe, nonstimulating environment. The client should be checked thoroughly for potential weapons and physically disarmed, if necessary. Obviously, prevention of violent behavior is best. Some simple strategies to reduce tension can be employed. The nurse should call the client by name and explain when and why delays are necessary in a calm, low voice. Encouraging the client to walk and to vent emotions verbally can be helpful. Sometimes the environment is overstimulating and the client calms down if taken to an area that provides less sensory input.

If uncomfortable procedures must be done on

BOX 21–5
Indicators of Potential Violence

Behavioral Categories	Suggested Indicators
Mental status	Confused
	Paranoid ideation
	Evidence of drug involvement
	Organic impairment
Motor behavior	Agitated
	Pacing
	Aggressive gestures
Speech patterns	Rapid
	Incoherent
	Menacing tones
	Verbal threats
Affect	Belligerent
	Labile

---

a client with suspected organic involvement and potential for violence, restraints can be applied temporarily before the procedure begins (Kinkle, 1993). If restraints must be applied, however, it is important to develop a plan and to have sufficient staff to implement the restraints. It is essential to maintain a calm, consistent approach and to explain the necessity of the restraints to the client even if it appears that there is little understanding of what is said. The explanation should be simple, direct, and compassionate. Box 21–6 presents some useful guidelines for communicating with a potentially violent client.

Rape

Another common crisis situation seen in the emergency room is rape. "By law, forcible rape represents the ultimate form of violation of self, second only to homicide. In this violent act, the victim surrenders autonomy, control of self, and privacy to a hostile intruder" (DHHS, 1990, p. 35). The nurse is in a front-line position to help the rape survivor regain his or her sense of self in this humiliating and overwhelming situation. Although description of the full treatment protocol for the rape survivor in the emergency department is beyond the scope of this text, there are some simple communication strategies the nurse can use.

Healthy People 2000 suggests that emergency departments set up standard protocols to identify and treat victims of violent and abusive behavior (DHHS, 1990). Priority is given to providing pri-

---

BOX 21–6
Don'ts and Dos in Dealing with the Nonorganically Impaired Violent Client

---

Don't overlook your feeling that your client is growing hostile and showing inappropriate anger.

Document your observations (even though your client has not behaved in an overtly dangerous way), and share your feelings and suspicions with the staff and the nursing administration.

Request medication p.r.n. (medication prescribed early enough and in adequate doses can help prevent violence).

Review your client's history, searching purposefully for signs of alcoholism, drug addiction, reaction to a change of medication, or a metabolic or emotional disturbance.

Don't undervalue what others (family or staff) tell you about your client's behavior in the belief that he'll be different with you or that you can handle it.

Use what the family and other staff members already know about the client: This information is significant—especially information about previous violence, about what's apt to provoke the client, and how the client behaves when provoked.

Don't continue with a treatment or interview if a client is obviously growing more and more agitated. Do not touch him or move toward him. He may misinterpret your gesture and react with physical aggression.

Ask the client why he's angry or agitated—and what's making him act this way. Also, ask him how he handles such feelings ordinarily and what others can do to help him. You want him to know that his feelings and point of view are being respected so he'll feel less powerless, less victimized. Be sure he understands that violence on his part will not be tolerated.

Don't isolate yourself with a client who has a record of or potential for violence. Don't corner yourself in a setting without a clear exit. (Elevators may prove particularly troublesome since you have no instant exit.)

Put this client in a room near the nurses' station—not at the end of a long, relatively unprotected corridor. Keep the door open when working with this client—and face him (or align yourself literally and figuratively beside him), rather than turn your back on him.

Have a security officer or male aide within immediate call if you suspect violence is imminent.

Study the contents of the client's room carefully, with an eye to what he could use to harm himself or one of the staff.

Don't disturb this client (with treatments or taking vital signs) any more than is necessary. He may need his own territory.

Arrange opportunities for physical activities if these seem to help the client siphon off his excess energies. Arrange for time out of his room, if this seems appropriate—and he agrees to it.

Don't assign a timid, inexperienced nurse to a potentially violent client.

Assign a mature, easygoing, experienced nurse to care for this client. (In this kind of powderkeg situation, it is axiomatic that there should be only one anxious person in the room: the client.)

Don't overlook the significance of gender in the assignment of a nurse to this client.

Therefore, you might want to consider assigning a male staff nurse to a female client who's potentially violent and a female nurse to a male client. Observers have learned that a woman client may be inclined to react negatively to another woman, but positively to a male staff member. This gender crossing also works for the male client, who might hesitate to strike or injure a female nurse.

Developed by Joyce Wallskog, Ph.D., R.N., Marquette University, Milwaukee, Wisconsin.

---

vacy and emotional support. This is important because often the rape victim is not considered a triage priority in the emergency room. Interventions should support the client's autonomy and control of self. Since the client cannot bathe or change her underwear prior to being examined if she intends to take legal action, it is important for the client to be taken to a private room. Rape vic-

tims should never be left alone. Clients can be so overwhelmed by the experience that it is difficult for them to talk about it. Acknowledging the difficulty and suggesting common emotional responses to rape are helpful strategies. Comments such as, "This is such a terrible assault to a person's self-integrity that many people have trouble talking about it. You may experience a range of emotions that are very normal, such as disbelief, feeling dirty, anger, wondering if you provoked it. It will take time before you feel normal again" assure the client of the legitimacy of having many conflicted feelings.

The rape survivor has several decision points in the health care setting, including whether to report the incident, which will require the collection of evidence, and whether to prosecute. The nurse's role in these decision points is that of advocate, promoting the client's self-determination and autonomy in decision making. At no time is it appropriate for the nurse to offer a personal opinion about what the client should do. But it is important to provide the client with enough information about the choices the client has and what each entails to make an informed decision.

The nurse can encourage the client to talk about the rape as an event and can use this information as the basis to help the client discuss the personal meaning of it. As the client talks about the rape, the nurse can help her identify any distortions, such as blaming herself. No matter what occurred, the client did not provoke the rape; passivity may have been the only realistic coping strategy a person could have used in this type of situation. Issues of blame are particularly relevant in how rape survivors think about "date rape" situations.

It is important to ask the client about significant others in her life and how she might tell them about the rape. The client may need considerable support in telling her family. If she chooses to talk about it with family members, the nurse can offer suggestions about time and format. Role playing and rehearsal are helpful.

During the physical examination, the nurse can provide emotional support and should talk the client through the procedure. Once the examination and evidence collection are completed, the client should have the opportunity to shower and have fresh underwear. Values and beliefs about prophylactic treatment of possible pregnancy should be explored. Without exception, the rape victim needs follow-up treatment for medical evaluation of sexually transmitted diseases and at least short-term counseling. Giving the client a written list of referrals to appropriate community resources and making a follow-up phone call a few days later underscore the nurse's recognition of the gravity of this event in a person's life.

Suicide

It is a myth that people who talk about doing harm to themselves are at less risk. Every suicidal statement, however oblique, should be taken seriously. Even if the client indicates that he is "just kidding," the fact that he has verbalized the threat places him at greater risk. The nurse also should assess whether the client basically wants to live, usually by asking the question directly. Some verbal indicators of potential suicide include statements such as: "I wish I were dead," " I don't think I can go on without . . . ," "I sometimes wish I wasn't here," or, "People should be better off without me." If a person states he cannot go on anymore, the nurse would ask for further clarification: "You say you can't go on any longer—can you tell me more about what you mean?"

With the suicidal client, the nurse would ask the following questions:

- Are you thinking of hurting yourself?
- Do you have a plan?
- What do you hope to accomplish with the suicide attempt?
- What is your support system like? Who are you able to turn to when you are in trouble?

Nonverbal indicators worthy of concern include giving away possessions, listlessness, and a depressed mood. Irrational statements, a psychotic state, drugs, alcohol, suicide gestures, and verbal threats are always matters of concern when coupled with other indicators of suicide or homicide. A sudden mood change from vegetative expressions of depression to significantly more energy and "a weight being lifted off the shoulders" should be watched carefully.

Clients will usually admit to feelings of suicide if they are having them. Having a plan, especially one that could be implemented, no support system, and distorted feelings or thoughts about what the suicide attempt would accomplish increases the risk of suicide (Slaikeu, 1984).

When any combination of these factors is present, the client should be referred immediately for psychiatric evaluation. Most clients are relieved when the nurse explains the reason for the referral. This should be done tactfully, with an emphasis on the behaviors that led the nurse to make the referral: "I'm worried that you might harm yourself because of the way you say you are feeling. You have a plan in mind and you have several of the factors that place you at high risk for suicide. I would like you to see Dr. Jones for an evaluation." The nurse should try to address any of the client's reservations while simultaneously reinforcing the idea that the client has little to lose by having the evaluation. If the client declines treatment evaluation, this should be noted with the time and date of refusal written on the chart.

People intent on hurting themselves or others have tunnel vision. In circumstances in which the nurse has reason to believe that the client is a danger to himself or others, there is a legal and moral responsibility to disclose the information to appropriate parties. Confidentiality is secondary to the goal of saving a human life. It is important, however, to inform the client about the disclosure of information, and to whom the information will be given.

SAMPLE STATEMENT

"I may need to act on your behalf until your situation is stabilized, and that includes talking with your family and other health professionals involved in your care about what we have just discussed."

The actively suicidal client should never be left alone, and all potential weapons should be confiscated. This includes mirrors, razors, glass frames, etc. The way this is done can be important to the client's feelings of self-esteem. When taking these items, the nurse should explain in a calm, compassionate manner the reason the items should not be in the client's possession and where they will be kept. The client should be assured that the items will be returned when the danger to self or others has been resolved. Most people who make a suicide attempt feel shame and embarrassment about their desire to end their lives. A major part of the intervention is directed toward helping suicidal clients better understand the reasons that led up to the suicide attempt and assisting them to develop alternative strategies. Acceptance of the client is a critical element of rapport. Helping people to reestablish a reason for living and getting others involved as a support system are critical interventions. Box 21–7 displays the level of supervision warranted by clients demonstrating suicidal behaviors.

If the circumstances are favorable and the client does not have a significant organic impairment, the nurse can establish a no-suicide contract with the client and can help the client develop a prevention plan for responding to difficult life issues. It is important to realize that the suicide contract does not wipe out the need for other assessment and intervention strategies. Also, suicide contracts are useless with clients demonstrating organic involvement, such as overtly psychotic or drug-abusing behaviors.

Debriefing for Staff Nurses

Critical incidents in health care always affect the personnel who respond to them. Without having an opportunity to process the meaning of a critical situation, the nurse is at risk for becoming a psychological casualty. The emotions are too powerful to dismiss without discussion. *Debriefing* is a crisis intervention strategy designed to help nurses process critical incidents in health care, thereby reducing the possibility of symptoms (Back, 1992). Flannery et al. (1991) note that staff members "who are given the opportunity to discuss the event immediately after it occurs often cope more effectively without long-lasting disruptions" (p. 936). The goal of a debriefing is to reduce the impact of a crisis event on professional staff and others involved in the crisis situation. A debriefing offers people an opportunity to ventilate feelings, discuss their role in the situation, develop a realistic sense of the big picture, and receive peer support.

Critical incident debriefing uses a psychoeducational format in group discussion to provide a safe place in which nurses and those intimately involved with a critical incident can talk about what happened. The debriefing generally is led by a professional specifically trained to conduct this type of strategy. Only those actively involved in the critical incident should attend the debriefing session. Everything said in the session must be kept confidential. The leader introduces the purpose of the group and invites each person to identify who they are and what happened from their perspective, including the role they played in the incident. Following the introduction, the leader might ask the participants to recall the first thing they remember thinking or feeling about the inci-

BOX 21–7
Sample of Level of Supervision Warranted by Suicidal Clients

Current checks _____

Any gestures in past 24 hours _____

Number of days of hospitalization _____

Medications available _____

Off Checks	Observation Every 30 Minutes	Observation Every 15 Minutes	Close Observation Every 5–10 Minutes	1:1 Restriction	Restraint or Seclusion
Verbalizes no suicidal ideation.	Verbalizes suicidal ideation.	Verbalizes suicidal ideation with plan and/or intent.	Sudden change in activity level . . . not chronic anxiety.	Concealing equipment that could be used to harm self with available specific plan.	Attempt made to kill self in front of staff; i.e., even 1:1 cannot resist impulse to kill self.
Congruence shown in verbal and behavioral information.	Verbalizes no plan.	No perception of support.	Unable to agree not to [attempt] suicide.	Attempt made while hospitalized to kill self.	
100% compliance with treatment plan.	Verbalizes no intention.	Little compliance with treatment plan.	Makes suicidal gesture currently.		
Has perception of support in community.	Cooperative with treatment plan.	Subjective or objective frustration.			
Verbalizes concerns on a feeling level to present nurse.	Withdrawn, low.	Anger.			
	Multiple previous attempts.	Labile affect or mood.			
	Verbalizes superficially to present nurse.	Mute or decreased amount of verbalization.			
		Avoidance of staff and others.			
		Withdrawn, high.			
		Intoxicated.			
		Impaired reality testing.			
		Hyperactive.			
		Demonstrates limited problem-solving ability.			

From Bydlow-Brown B, Billman R (1990). At risk for suicide. *In* Ismeurt R, Arnold E, Carson V (eds.) (1990), Readings in Concepts Fundamental to Nursing. Springhouse, PA, Springhouse Publishing Company, p. 267. Reprinted with permission. Copyright © 1990 Springhouse Corporation. All rights reserved.

dent. As the dialogue expands, the leader asks participants to recall the worst part of the incident and their reaction to it. Participants are asked to discuss any stress symptoms they may have related to the incident. This part of the session is followed by a consideration of psychoeducational strategies to reduce stress. Any lingering questions are answered, and the leader summarizes the high points of the critical incident debriefing for the group (Rubin, 1991).

SUMMARY

Crisis is defined as a "sudden unanticipated or unplanned for event which necessitates immediate action to resolve the problem." Theorists who pioneered the development of crisis theory and crisis intervention are Lindemann, Caplan, and Aguilera. Two types of crises were identified: developmental crises, which parallel psychosocial stages of ego development, and situational crises, which occur as unanticipated episodic events unrelated to human development. Crisis does not occur in a vacuum and must be considered within the social context in which it occurs.

Crisis intervention is a time-limited treatment that focuses only on the immediate problem and its resolution. A three-step model of intervention is proposed, including engaging the client, exploring the problem, and creative problem solving. Guidelines for communication with clients experiencing selected crisis situations, such as suicide and violence toward self or others. are identified.

REFERENCES

Aguilera D (1994). Crisis Intervention: Theory and Methodology. (7th ed.). St. Louis, Mosby.

Back K (1992). Critical incident stress management for care providers in the pediatric emergency department. Critical Care Nursing. 12(1):78–79; 82–83.

Beckingham A, Bauman A (1990). The aging family in crisis: Assessment and decision making models. Journal of Advanced Nursing 15(7):782–787.

Bluhm J (1987). Helping families in crisis hold on. Nursing '87 17(10):44–46.

Cahill C, Stuart G, Laraia M, Arana G (1991). Inpatient management of violent behavior: Nursing prevention and intervention. Issues in Mental Health Nursing 12:239–252.

Caplan G (1964). Principles of Preventive Psychiatry. New York, Basic Books.

DHHS (1990). Healthy People 2000: National Health Promotion and Disease Prevention Objectives. Washington, DC, The Department.

Erikson E (1963). Childhood and Society. New York, Norton.

Erikson E (1982). The Life Cycle Completed. New York, Norton.

Flannery R, Fulton P, Tausch J, DeLoffi A (1991). A program to help staff cope with psychological sequelae of assaults by patients. Hospital and Community Psychiatry. 42(9): 935–938.

Hobbs M (1984). Crisis intervention in theory and practice. British Journal of Medical Psychology. 57:23–34.

Hoff L (1991). People in Crisis: Understanding and Helping. Menlo Park, CA, Addison-Wesley.

Kinkle S (1993). Violence in the E.D.: How to stop it before it starts. American Journal of Nursing 93(7): 22–24.

Kleeman, K (1989). Families in crisis due to multiple trauma. Critical Care Nursing Clinics of North America 1(1):23–31.

Kus R (1985). Crisis intervention. In Bulechek G, McCloskey J (eds.) (1985), Nursing Interventions: Treatments for Nursing Diagnoses. Philadelphia, W. B. Saunders.

Mitchell CE (1977). Identifying the hazard: The key to crisis intervention. American Journal of Nursing 77:1194.

Perfetti T (1982). Training Manual for Crisis Counselors. Bethesda, MD, Montgomery County Crisis Center.

Puskar K, Obus N (1989). Management of the psychiatric emergency. Nurse Practitioner 14(7):9–18, 23, 26.

Rubin J. (1990). Critical incident stress debriefing: Helping the helpers. Journal of Emergency Nursing 16(4):255–258.

Slaikeu K (1984). Crisis Intervention: A Handbook for Practice and Research. Boston, Allyn & Bacon.

Chapter 22

Communicating with Other Health Professionals

ANN O'MARA

OBJECTIVES

At the end of the chapter the student will be able to:

1. Identify concepts in professional relationships.

2. Describe methods to handle conflict when it occurs through interpersonal negotiation.

3. Discuss methods for communicating effectively in organizational settings.

4. Apply group communication principles to work groups.

*It is not the brains that matter most, but that which guides them—
the character, the heart, generous qualities, progressive ideas.*

Fyodor Dostoyevski, 1881

Chapter 22 focuses on the development of collegial relationships with other health team members. The principles of communication used in the nurse–client relationship are broadened to include the nature of the communication process in collegial relationships. Specific bridges to communication with other health professionals, such as advocacy, collaboration, coordination, and networking, are described. Also included in the chapter are strategies to remove barriers to communication with health professionals, such as coping with offensive communication and responding to constructive criticism.

To be effective as a nursing professional, it is not enough to be deeply committed to the client. The quality of relationships in the workplace heavily influence the development of a positive work climate and cohesive collegial relationships (Flanagan, 1990). Ultimately, the workplace atmosphere will have an effect on the relationship that takes place between nurse and client even though the connection may not be readily apparent. Professional relationships provide a unique opportunity to approach client care from a holistic perspective by drawing on the expertise of various disciplines such as psychiatry, medicine, dentistry, social work, nutrition, and physical and respiratory therapy. The same thoughtful purpose, authenticity, empathy, active listening, and respect for the dignity of others that underscore successful nurse–client relationships are needed in relations with other health professionals. Caring commitment to developing constructive working relationships with other professionals gives direction, form, and substance to all nursing actions, thereby providing a recognizable pattern of professional nursing practice.

Working with others effectively in health care is a challenge. The nursing profession is in transition; nurses entering the profession need a more complex set of communication skills than was the case a decade ago. Communication with members of other health disciplines, other nurses, allied health personnel, and peers affects how nurses feel about themselves—and this has a direct, immediate impact on the quality of nursing care given to clients. The human aspect of nursing practice is what causes the nurse to feel the most joy when the inner emotional connections between self and others are truly felt; it causes nurses the most pain as they relive in their minds missed chances and failures to communicate. Communication and human relationships with all those involved in the client's care support the nurse–client relationship as the foundation of nursing practice.

BASIC CONCEPTS

ADVOCACY

Client advocacy is a professional role requiring not only self-awareness but also a broad knowledge base about the client in the health care system. *Client advocacy* can be defined as interceding or acting on behalf of the client to provide the highest quality care obtainable (Donahue, 1985). The advocacy role is not new to nursing. Nurses have always been involved in promoting the growth and development of the client as a person rather than just treating the diseased or injured part of the body. Nurses have always acted in the interests of clients who cannot act for themselves, such as children and clients who are immobilized, unconscious, or mentally disabled. Furthermore, nurses have been instrumental in giving information to clients about their health problems and in educating clients to care for themselves. More recently, however, client advocacy has received recognition as a formalized component of the professional nursing role.

The client advocate role includes, first, *informing* clients about the nature of their health problems and the choices they have in seeking to resolve or modify their health care needs with nursing intervention. This role is activated whenever the client is unable to assume responsibility for his or her health care needs. Need can arise from a lack of knowledge or skills or from a cognitive, emotional, or financial base. The nurse's role is to help the client gather information and learn the behaviors necessary to execute the chosen option.

Second, the advocacy role is one of *support* when the client has been informed, has made reasoned choices, and must implement them. The client's right to choose health care options is a new phenomenon. It recognizes the client's inherent right to make decisions for self and to take individual responsibility for a chosen decision. The advocacy role requires the nurse to view the client as an equal partner in resolving the client's health care needs. To fulfill this role, the nurse is respectful of client choices, even when the decisions reached are not what the nurse would recommend for the client.

Types of Advocacy (Box 22–1)

Anticipatory guidance is a form of primary prevention. Helping the client foresee and predict potential difficulties decreases the client's stress. For example, respite care is needed at regular intervals in families with severely ill children or elderly family members. Having no relief from caretaking activities fosters the development of strained family relations and potential client abuse. This need should be anticipated for families of clients with sustained handicaps or chronic illness.

For teenage mothers, poverty, inadequate housing, and lack of privacy make it difficult to reach out for needed help as these young women make the transition to motherhood. The adolescent single parent with little financial support usually needs the Women, Infants, Children program to supply formula and a referral to social services for follow-up. Providing information about ways to obtain public support services can help an adolescent mother meet her child's basic needs. Children with developmental disabilities benefit if the nurse explains to the parents motor development in infants. Each of these simple nursing actions acts to improve the client or family member's capacity to cope and care. Other forms of anticipatory guidance are seen in parent education and prenatal classes, in which the upcoming childbirth

experience and parent–child issues are constructed and discussed in advance of their actual developmental presence.

In the clinical setting, the nurse acts as a role model for appropriate behaviors. For example, the nurse can be a role model to a new mother by talking with the infant and smiling and handling the baby in a supportive way. Setting limits in a kind but firm way with toddlers often helps family members focus on minimizing stress and achieving simple, constructive goals in the clinical setting. Asking the child age-appropriate questions in the presence of the parents models an interpersonal approach to clients that the parents may find quite useful. Modeling behaviors combined with anticipatory guidelines for coping with behavioral changes and caretaking strategies help eliminate a sense of confusion and self-doubt.

Referral is an important component of client advocacy. Health-related problems are multidimensional and require the services of more than one health discipline. Frequently the nurse provides educational support as well as specific client data to other health professionals. This educational support provides a context in which the client's problems become more understandable. Support may focus on the client's needs, nursing interventions, or information about the client's family. An interdisciplinary approach to client care in which all members of the health team pool their expertise to develop a workable care plan ensures comprehensive treatment. By clearly articulating client needs from a number of perspectives, each health team member acts as an educational resource to the client as well as to other health professionals.

Steps in the Advocacy Process

The nurse, as the client's advocate, uses a four-step informational process, as presented in Box 22–2. The nurse's power base in advocacy is relevant knowledge and information. Basically, the nurse needs to be aware of personal and professional ethics, values, and prejudices. "One needs to have a good knowledge and understanding of personal views on how human beings relate to each other in a framework or philosophy of fairness" (Kohnke, 1982). For example, if the nurse thinks of elderly clients as helpless and equates aging with being

---

BOX 22–1
Types of Advocacy

Anticipatory guidance.
Role modeling.
Educational support.
Professional direction and collaboration.
Primary prevention.
Mobilization of community resources.

BOX 22–2
Informational Steps in Client Advocacy

Knowledge of the personally held values of nurse and client.

Awareness of treatment and of professional and personal goals.

Information about professional nursing, environmental, and interpersonal protocols and of the bureaucratic structure of the organizational work system.

Knowledge of potential power or recognition needs that could compromise the integrity of the client advocacy process.

---

taken care of, then the nurse will be likely to "take charge" of all client health activities, even those the client is still capable of performing with little or no assistance. In this situation, personal values have gotten in the way of individualized professional nursing values associated with client advocacy.

Self-awareness is important. Nurses should have a firm understanding of their personal as well as their professional goals in nursing situations. Frequently both goals are unstated and remain a part of the blind self until they are called into conscious awareness by circumstance. For example, the nurse may have an unstated personal goal of wanting to be liked by every client or an unspoken professional goal of never making a mistake in the delivery of clinical nursing care. Each implied goal will have as much effect on the nurse's interpersonal behaviors with clients and coworkers as a stated professional goal of wanting to learn the latest tracheal suctioning technique.

Understanding the System

To be successful as client advocates, nurses also need to know the environmental, interpersonal, and bureaucratic system within which they work. For example, how do all the units—nursing and hospital administration, the medical staff, and other health system disciplines—relate to one another, and how does the system relate to the community at large? It is important to understand how the communication flow filters through the different systems. Usually a combination of formal and informal communication with other staff is necessary for complete understanding.

The professional nurse can gain some of this knowledge by observing how communication is passed from person to person and by asking many

questions. Knowing how the various units are influenced by outside pressures such as politics, financial constraints, consumer groups, and regulatory agencies is as important as knowing who is in charge and who is influential in facilitating change. All of these understandings add to the nurse's power base in effecting change on the client's behalf. With this knowledge base, the nurse is in a position to inform and assist the client in making the most of health care choices with the least amount of effort.

Finally, the nurse needs to recognize personal power needs that stem from his or her personal insecurities and to analyze how those needs affect professional relationships with clients. To a greater or lesser extent, everyone has power needs and insecurities. The important thing is to recognize their presence. Keep in mind as you do Exercise 22–1 that real interpersonal power comes from having an adequate knowledge base coupled with the courage to take interpersonal risks when the situation requires it.

Assessment

Client advocacy is designed to help the client overcome feelings of helplessness and powerlessness in the hospital or health care treatment setting. Questions might center on the following: (1) What does the client feel is the most pressing problem? (2) What aspects of the problem might be a good place to start? (3) What supports—family, minister, rabbi, social services—are in place? (4) What health or social services is the client familiar with or resistant to considering? Clinical aspects to consider related to self-concept in helping clients reestablish personal control in their lives are body image, changes or losses in self-control, knowledge deficits, identity changes inflicted by the illness or injury, and circumstances in the client's history that may have an effect on the current capacity for self-care (Smith, 1985). Powerlessness can be decreased through anticipatory guidance, role playing, modeling behaviors, education, and mobilization of community resources on the client's behalf.

Planning

When a problem situation is identified, the nurse acts quickly to mobilize the necessary resources. Consultations are requested. The client or responsible family member is involved in the process of

EXERCISE 22–1
The Nature of Power Needs

Purpose: To generate thoughts about the nature of power needs.

Time: 1 hour; may be done as a homework assignment.

Directions:
1. Let each statement below stimulate a memory of a clinical situation.
2. On paper, describe that situation and the outcome. If the outcome on analysis seems to boost a sense of power or of knowing better than the client, try to formulate another potential outcome in which the client is more equal.
3. Look at the new outcome and ask how difficult promoting that outcome would be.
4. Go back to the definition of client advocacy and review the outcome response in light of that definition. Is the professional responsibility of providing high-quality nursing care being carried out?
    a. A lot of times I try to get people to do what I want. I might get defensive or upset if the client disagreed with what I wanted to do or did not follow my directions.
    b. I believe there is a balance in client interviews between my participation and the client's.
    c. I could feel angry when working with a resistant or stubborn client.
    d. I can see that I might be tempted to get some of my own ideology across to the client.
    e. Sometimes, I feel impatient with clients who have a different way of looking at the world than I do.
    f. I know there are times when I am reluctant to have another nurse take care of my client, especially if the other nurse's style differs from mine.
    g. Sometimes I feel rejecting or intolerant of clients whose values and lifestyle are very different from mine.
    h. It is hard for me to avoid trying to convince clients I am right.

Adapted from Brammer L (1979). The Helping Relationship. Englewood Cliffs, NJ, Prentice-Hall.

defining the problem and assuming as much responsibility as possible. Sometimes the nurse serves as dual advocate for the client and a family member. In a child-abuse situation, for example, the nurse needs to act as an advocate of the child by taking the steps necessary to provide a protective and safe environment for the child, but the nurse must also be an advocate of the parents by referring them to appropriate community resources and helping them develop different methods for coping with situational stressors. As advocate for both client and family, the nurse is a role model for behaviors tht foster a relationship of mutual respect. Once the nurse and client can meet as equal and complementary partners in promoting the interests of the client in health care situations, advocacy becomes an intimate part of the nursing process. Oda (1991) describes the role of the school nurse, often perceived as an irrelevant one, as critical to assisting children and their families into the health care system. It is not uncommon for the school nurse to encounter children who, because of their socioeconomic background, have received inadequate immunizations, are suffering the conse-quences of inadequate nutrition, and are victims of inappropriate parenting. Access to health care services that can begin to meet these problems can be accomplished by the school nurse.

Implementation

Another component of the advocacy role is to help the client become a self advocate. More recently this process has been referred to as *empowerment* (a model of which is found in Chapter 5). Empowerment requires a certain degree of assertiveness on the part of the nurse. Gibson (1991) describes the process as assisting individuals to assert control over the factors affecting their lives. By maximizing clients' independence and minimizing their dependence, nurses are engaging in partnerships with their clients. If a nurse has difficulty being assertive, then the client can hardly be expected to learn assertive interpersonal skills and instead will pick up on the nurse's sense of inferiority and inability to use self in the accomplishment of health-promotion goals. Watching the nurse falter and avoid needed confrontations, the client may feel even less powerful and less able to take a stand on important health care issues. Additionally, the nurse should recognize when to speak for the client and when to encourage the client to speak up. In general, encouraging clients to take as much responsibility as possible to speak on their own behalf is more ego enhancing and leads to a higher level of self-esteem.

Finally, as client advocate, the nurse is seen as the client's protector. Client advocacy by nurses is becoming a legitimate role concept, used in the legal system in malpractice and negligence cases. A nurse who does nothing is generally held more liable than one who tries to do something within the scope of nursing practice and fails. Cushing (1985) notes that "as nursing evolves so too will the law, no doubt continuing to clarify the definition of the nurse as protector of the patient." The law is particularly interested in client advocacy as it relates to the presence of inadequate or improper medical care of the nurse's client. Therefore, not only must nurses be knowledgeable, they must also be willing and able to assert their knowledge in situations involving poor medical management of a client.

EXERCISE 22–2
Client Advocate Role Play

Purpose: To understand the nurse advocacy role in difficult and conflictual clinical situations.

Time: 1 hour

Directions:
1. Read the clinical situation below and answer the questions, writing down your answers.
2. Have one of the students play the role of the client and another play the role of the nurse.
3. Look at the answers previously written to the questions, and see if there are any changes you would like to make after the role-playing.
4. Finally, make up a situation and give it to your colleague with the same questions. Role play the situation with your colleague, this time taking the role of the client.

Situation:

A 65-year-old man has been a client on the medical unit for 10 days, and you are assigned to care for him for the next four days. Diagnostic workup and tests reveal that he has cancer of the larynx. Surgery is indicated and has been scheduled. The doctor discusses his diagnosis and prognosis with him in your presence.

During the next two days, the client becomes increasingly withdrawn and introspective. Subsequently, he requests to speak with you and the physician. He states that he does not wish to have any surgery performed, no medication given, that he "has lived a good life" and would like you and the health team to accept his decision to die. He asks that no tube feedings be given or IVs be administered. He asks that you cooperate and support his wishes.

Questions:
1. What would your reaction be in this situation?
2. What does the statement "death with dignity" mean to you?
3. Do you think the client has the right to refuse treatment that may be life sustaining?
4. What nursing care should you provide for this man as he continues to refuse food and fluids (keeping in mind that the client is an equal partner in his care)?
5. What conflicts does this situation pose for you? How would you see yourself dealing with them?
6. How can you as a nurse respect the integrity of a client's decision when it conflicts with promoting maximum client health functions?
7. Does the client's age influence your acceptance of his decision?
8. How will you support the client when faced with other health-care professionals who disapprove of the client's decision?
9. What risks will you be taking in supporting the client?

Adapted from Uusral D (1978). Values clarification in nursing: Application to practice. American Journal of Nursing 78:2058.

Asserting one's knowledge, however, should not be confused with usurping the client's decision-making power. Advocacy is not paternalism. The elderly have often been viewed as a group reluctant to decide their health care outcomes. Kjervik (1990) warns nurses not to misinterpret this reluctance as the client's decision to confer his or her decision-making power on health care professionals. Instead, the nurse's responsibility in this situation is to work with the client to identify and select an advocate, independent of the health care system, who will preserve the client's autonomy.

Client advocacy acts as a connective link between ethics and the law. Providing appropriate information that allows a client to make an informed choice conforms to client's rights under the law, and supporting the client's right to make a decision that may or may not be compatible with the nurse's recommendation indicates an ethical commitment to ensure the client's self-determination (Kohnke, 1982). Exercise 22–2 provides a clinical situation in which the nurse's advocacy role is in conflict with traditional nursing and medical advice.

Evaluation

The need for client advocacy can develop in any phase of the nurse–client relationship, but it is a particularly valuable resource when ordinary means of providing information and support fail to meet the client's need. Usually the collective product developed from client-advocacy activity expands far beyond the original thoughts and motivations of individual participants in the process.

COLLABORATION

Collaboration is an essential component of the professional nursing role in today's social world. Never before has the potential for conflict become so visible in the health care system. As society redefines every citizen's right to health, more and sicker clients are demanding higher-quality services in spite of declining resources. Society also is struggling to redefine gender role behaviors. Although some of these changes are viewed as necessary and good in that they encourage greater equality, conflicts can emerge. Stereotyped feminine characteristics such as passivity have given way to greater assertiveness and autonomy in the way women present themselves (Schutzenhofer, 1992). Perhaps the greatest challenge is with physician–nurse relationships because the professional health care alliance has changed from a traditional notion of the nurse as "handmaiden to the physician" to a concept of the nurse as an autonomous professional who collaborates with the physician

Collaboration is an essential component of the professional nursing role. (Courtesy of the University of Maryland School of Nursing)

to maximize client health goals. Physician–nurse conflicts go both ways. Evans (1991) cites overt examples of "physician bashing" within the nursing profession, suggesting that there is generalized conflict between these health providers resulting in a we/they situation.

With tightening fiscal resources and greater specialization, health care professionals frequently have "turf battles" regarding who can provide what services (Evans, 1991). Collaboration offers a means of communication among different members of the interdisciplinary health care team.

Definition

Collaboration has been described by Macht (1978) as follows: In collaboration, whether work is focused on a client or on the development and operation of a program, two or more people work together to solve a common problem and share responsibility for the process and outcome. By combining efforts and sharing professional assets, a broader spectrum of information can be pooled to design a comprehensive care plan for the client (Kalafatich, 1986).

It is essential to the development of a collaborative relationship that each discipline understand and appreciate the other's role so that nurses and physicians do not have expectations of each other based on stereotyped beliefs. Subtle evidence of a relational behavior that typecasts the nurse in a subservient role would be the archaic practice of physicians calling the nurse by his or her first name while at the same time expecting the nurse to address the physician by title and last name.

Understanding one another's role needs and responsibilities begins in the educational system. Often, health care professionals receive their professional education and training in isolation from one another. Providing interprofessional courses and an informal forum where nurses and physicians in training can share their role-related expertise would help clarify expectations of one another, lending emphasis to the importance of a collaborative strategy in providing high-quality client care.

Achieving an interprofessional understanding with one another does influence the quality of client care. A recent research project found that "if you are a patient in an intensive-care unit, your life may depend on the communication that passes between the physicians and the nurses who care for you" (Knaus et al., 1986).

Study results indicated that the highest quality care occurred in hospital settings associated with (1) the most comprehensive nursing education system; (2) the greatest number of clinical specialists to orient and develop staff; (3) clinical protocols on the unit that define independent nursing responsibilities; and (4) routine interprofessional conferences in which discussions of client care and coordination of staff responsibilities occur. Conversely, the worst client care occurred in hospital settings in which there were no policies for communication among health disciplines and no coordination of staff capabilities and clinical demands.

The concept of collaboration is a new one. It means working simultaneously at a new relationship with one another and with the client. This new relationship requires that nurses, physicians, and client communicate effectively with one another and view one another as coming from different perspectives but as having an important joint influence on client care. The physician brings a specialized body of knowledge to bear on a diseased or injured part in need of health care resolution, whereas the nurse often represents the creative force in health care by helping a client integrate the medical information and new learning necessary to cope with health-related changes in self-concept. Both share a responsibility to ensure different aspects of holistic, safe, effective, and compassionate care for clients.

Everyone profits from this alliance. The physician's work load is decreased as the nurse assumes a more independent role and responsibility for certain areas of health care. Relieved of some of the legal liability and emotional and technical obligations of being the primary health care resource for the client, the physician is then able to provide more comprehensive, direct health care services to clients. Physicians can incorporate the observations of competent nurses in their professional deliberations and delivery of health care.

Sharing information and ideas with another health care professional who has more direct access to client care is an important and worthwhile exercise leading to trust and mutual respect. With a nursing perspective, the nurse provides a holistic assessment of health care issues and important information about how likely the client is to accept medical treatment protocols. Because of the nature of their professional responsibilities, nurses are frequently in a better position to help clients explore different options and to plan creatively the most effective approach. A collegial relationship means not only that the client gets better care but that the nurse finds the experience of collaboration personally and professionally affirming (Mauksch, 1981).

COORDINATION

Coordination is closely related to collaboration, the difference being that with collaboration there may be more joint direct interaction with a client. In coordination, two or more people provide services to a client or program separately and inform each other of their activities. They attempt to "synchronize their actions and develop ways of preventing non-constructive overlap, duplication or counterproductive action as they work to provide separate but related services" (Macht, 1978). At times a careful assessment of the nature of the client's adaptive or self-care requirements reveals a need beyond the scope of the nurse's professional practice or level of experience. The nurse needs to identify the health care professional who can best serve the client's need and to contact that person.

To make an appropriate referral, the nurse should have a good sense of personal or professional limitations and an adequate understanding of health, human services, and community resources. Having a knowledge about referral sources allows the nurse to match the client's needs and preferences with the best resource. Some referral source factors to be considered include compatibility with the client's expressed need, financial resources, accessibility (time as well as place), and ease of contact. Ease of contact and financial considerations sometimes are forgotten elements in coordination efforts, much to the detriment of the client's welfare.

Questions the nurse might ask include, What are the services like? Does the agency have a sliding fee scale? What are the hours of service? How does the client contact the agency? and Does the client need an appointment? How would the client get there? Some of these questions may seem quite basic, and yet for the person in need of health care or human services the answers can be crucial to client compliance efforts. Exercise 22–3 gives practice in exploring community resources.

Once the referral source has been identified,

EXERCISE 22–3
Community Resources

Purpose: To help you assess different types of health, human services, and community resources.

Time: To be done as a homework exercise. Class discussion, 1 hour.

Directions:
1. Contact a health or human services resource of your choosing in the community. The questions cited in the discussion section below can be used to elicit information.
2. Write down such information as telephone number, address, person to contact and bring it to class.
3. Take turns presenting your findings. You'll appreciate having the resource information presented in class; write it down for future reference.

Discussion:
1. How did you choose your resource?
2. Where did you find your initial information about it—Yellow Pages, from a friend, or your own experience?
3. How easy was it to get in touch with someone who could give you relevant information about the resource? Were you treated with courtesy and respect? If not, why not? Is there anything you would do differently?
4. What is the fee structure in the agency—sliding scale?
5. Are there any restrictions on the allowable number of client visits?
6. Is the service resource accessible by public transportation, or are there any provisions for transportation?
7. Are there any other questions you might have asked, based on your experience of contacting the resource?

the nurse should personally contact the source. The purpose of a direct contact is twofold: to establish a good working relationship with a variety of referral resources and to develop a mutually acceptable method for handling referrals (Donahue, 1985).

NETWORKING

A concept closely related to collaboration and coordination is that of *networking.* This is a form of peer collaboration whereby individuals take advantage of making and using contacts (Kennedy, 1986). It is a reciprocal process that validates the nurse's peers as valuable sources of information and reaffirms the individual nurse as a valuable source. As with the previously mentioned roles of collaboration, advocacy, etc., networking is a relatively new role for the professional nurse. In other professions networking is an essential component in building professional relationships and ultimately advancing one's status within the profession.

When engaged in networking, nurses are making contacts with peers from as close as the nursing unit on the floor below to as far away as a professional conference 500 miles distant. By making contacts, nurses are communicating their expertise and sharing their ideas in a particular area of the profession at the same time as they are gathering information from their contacts. This give and take of information is often the bridge in networking with peers. For example, oncology nurses often exchange ideas about the best approach to relief of side effects from chemotherapy and radiation therapy. Extensive networking among oncology nurses was the impetus for the formation of the Oncology Nursing Society. Networking and collaboration will become increasingly important as advanced practice nurses become an active voice in health care reform.

Professional Rights

All health professionals, including nurses, have rights as well as significant responsibilities in interprofessional relationships with colleagues. Here are the rights nursing professionals have in nursing practice (Chevenent, 1978, p. 53):

1. You have a right to be treated with respect.
2. You have a right to a reasonable work load.
3. You have the right to an equitable wage.
4. You have the right to determine your own reasonable priorities.
5. You have the right to ask for what you want, as long it doesn't interfere with the rights of others.
6. You have the right to refuse unreasonable requests without making excuses or feeling guilty.
7. You have the right to make mistakes and be responsible for them.
8. You have the right to give and receive information as a health professional.
9. You have the right to act in the best interest of the client as long as it isn't in conflict with agency policy and respects the rights of others involved in the client's care.
10. You have the right to be human.

Acting responsibly in nursing practice situations requires a willingness to go the extra step in establishing good working relations with professional colleagues, to try different interpersonal communication strategies, and to push on in the face of adversity. Persistence and a good sense of humor are essential characteristics of honest interpersonal relationships with peers, reflecting a dual professional commitment to self and others.

Rights carry with them corresponding responsibilities. Often rightful acceptance of responsibilities fosters the automatic granting of rights by the other person. Think about your professional collegial relationships and your dual professional commitment to self and others. Now go back to the professional values identified in Chapter 1 and reexamine the components of professionalism. Each of those components is basically a professional responsibility. Add your ideas for rights next to those responsibilities. Exchange ideas of professional rights and responsibilities with others.

APPLICATIONS

CONFLICT RESOLUTION

The relationship between doctor and nurse is still under negotiation. Change is slow, and some physicians still regard themselves as the only legitimate authority in health care, seeing the professional nurse as an accessory. An attitude that excludes the nurse as a professional partner in health care promotion benefits no one and needs to be challenged.

Other interpersonal sources of conflict for the nurse that frequently occur in the clinical area include one or more of the following:

- Being asked to do something you know would be irresponsible or unsafe.
- Having your feelings or opinions ridiculed or discounted.
- Being pressured to give more time or attention than you are able to give.
- Being asked to give more information than you feel comfortable sharing.
- Maintaining a sense of self in the face of hostility or sexual harassment.

When the source of conflict is interpersonal, the nurse needs to think through the possible causes of the conflict as well as his or her own feelings about it and respond appropriately, even if the response is a deliberate choice not to respond verbally. Interpersonal conflicts that are not dealt with leave residual feelings that reappear unexpectedly and affect the nurse's ability to respond realistically and responsibly in future interactions.

As nurses assume the professional responsibility for coordinating treatment protocols, it is often their role to initiate the discussions about difficult relational issues in the holistic care of their clients (Hamilton and Kiefer, 1986). Although conflict is inevitable, it is not necessarily detrimental to productivity and job satisfaction. Successful resolution often has a positive effect on both outcomes. Thus the primary goal in dealing with workplace conflict is to find a high-quality, mutually acceptable solution, a win-win strategy. This involves a willingness to confront and manage conflict, efforts to develop a mutual understanding of messages, and commitment to solutions acceptable to all parties (Bertinasco, 1990). In many instances, a different type of relationship can be developed through the use of conflict-management communication techniques. Using purposeful strategies to defuse a negative interaction, the nurse reframes a clinical situation as a cooperative process in which the health goals and *not* the status relations of the health care providers become the focal object. Steps in the conflict-resolution process are presented in Box 22–3.

A clear idea of the outcome one wishes to achieve is a necessary first step in the process. It is important to do your homework by getting all relevant information about the specific issues involved and about the client's behavioral responses to a health care issue before engaging in negotiation. Having some idea of what issues might be relevant from the other person's perspective provides important information about the best interpersonal approach to use.

BOX 22–3
Steps to Promote Health Goals and Defuse Status Quarrels among Health Care Workers

- Have an objective or a goal clearly in mind.
- Set the stage for collaborative communication.
- State your position clearly.
- Identify the key points.
- Be willing to develop alternative solutions in which all parties can meet essential needs.
- Depersonalize conflict situations.
- Maintain respect for the values and dignity of both parties in the relationship.

Among the most commonly identified conflict-resolution strategies, *confrontation* has been found to be the most effective (Jones, Bushardt, and Cadenhead, 1990). In order to use confrontation in a productive manner, Jones et al. prescribe four essential steps: (1) identify as many concerns as possible from both parties; (2) clarify assumptions; (3) identify the real issue being confronted; and (4) work collaboratively through a problem-solving process to find a solution that satisfies both parties. Exercise 22–4 provides a clinical situation in which the staff's behavior is creating a conflict on the unit.

Knowing your own interpersonal communication strengths and weaknesses as well of those of the other participants is equally important in developing the most appropriate communication strategies. Some people respond better when they have written or oral information prior to the discussion so they can come prepared. Other people react well to more spontaneous, on-the-spot interactions. The same is true of decision making. Some people need time to absorb the meaning of a situation before coming to a decision, whereas others like to come to decisions at the time of the dialogue. One way of processing and responding to situations is not necessarily better than another, but knowing the characteristics of the other party is an important strength in resolving conflict situations.

Often the professional may not know the communication strengths and weaknesses of the other

EXERCISE 22–4
Applying Principles of Confrontation

Purpose: To help you understand the importance of using specific principles of confrontation to resolve a conflict.

Time: 15 minutes for exercise; 10 minutes for group discussion.

Directions:
1. Divide the class into two groups: A is the day shift (7A.M.–7P.M.), and B is the night shift (7P.M.–7A.M.).
2. The following case study is an example of some problems between the night and day shifts resulting in mistrust and general tension between the two groups. After reading the case study, each group is to utilize Jones, Bushardt, and Cadenhead's (1990) first three principles, as identified in the text (identify concerns, clarify assumptions, identify real issue). The two groups then share their concerns, assumptions, and what they believe to be the real issue. Finally, both groups are to apply the fourth principle, collaboratively identifying a solution(s) that satisfies both groups.

Case Study

The night shift's (group B) responsibilities include completing as many bedbaths as possible and the taping report as close to change of shift (7A.M.) as possible. The day shift (group A) finds that very few, if any, of the bedbaths are completed and that the taped report is usually done around 5 A.M., reflecting very few of the client changes that occurred between 5 A.M. and 7 A.M..

The day shift is angry with the night shift, feeling they are not contributing their fair share of the work load. The night shift feels the day shift doesn't understand their responsibilities; they believe they are contributing more than their fair share of the work load.

individual; then it is best to allow some time for the individual to process the information. Few situations are true emergencies that need to be settled immediately. The confronter should allow the recipient to respond later to the issues that are raised. An appropriate way to diffuse the notion of immediacy might be, "Let me get back to you when you have had some time to think about what we've talked about today."

If the individual being confronted is forced or coerced into an immediate response, conflict resolution is likely to be less effective.

It is even appropriate to write key points on a 3 by 5 card for reference in emotionally tense confrontations. Sometimes this strategy helps the nurse stay focused on the main issue when emotions threaten to prelude direct confrontation or dilute the impact of the issues to be negotiated. Another tactic that stimulates self-confidence is to discuss the issue with a trusted colleague on the unit or with a valued supervisor beforehand to gain a broader perspective. Interpersonal power is increased by an accurate knowledge of the scope of practice boundaries imposed by the institution, as well as those of other health providers. Unfortunately, although confrontation frequently is the most effective strategy, it is not the most frequently employed. Cavanagh's (1988) study of 64 ICU nurses revealed that avoidance or withdrawal were most frequently utilized, suggesting a lack of assertiveness among this small sample.

Setting the stage for goal negotiations is an important part of the process. In the first few minutes, convey the attitude that a major objective of the interaction from your perspective is a better understanding of the issues surrounding the current conflict and a real desire for a relationship. Through words and actions the nurse needs to demonstrate that the desire is genuine. Discussion should begin with either a statement of the commonalities of purpose or the points of agreement about the issue, for example, "I thoroughly agree Mr. Smith will do much better at home. However, we need to contact social services and make a home care referral before we actually discharge him; otherwise he will be right back in the hospital again." *Points of disagreement should always follow rather than precede points of agreement.* Empathy and a genuine desire to understand the issues from the other's perspective enhance communication and the likelihood of a successful resolution.

Sometimes there are issues about which the other person feels so strongly that discussion is impossible. Frequently the person's ego is too intimately involved with the situation or personal goals. Knowing what issues are within one's power to change and what issues cannot be changed helps the nurse to discern the more important and relevant goals and issues for dialogue. Success with a few objectives generally is more productive than attempting to change all of another's deeply held convictions in one or two sessions. Emotional as well as objective data are included in problem analysis, since they often represent the most important component of the conflict issue.

During conflict negotiation, it is important to remain flexible, yet not to yield on important, essential dimensions of the issue. Sometimes it is difficult to listen carefully to the other person's position without automatically formulating your next point or response, but it is important to keep an open mind and to examine the issue from a number of perspectives prior to selecting alternative options. The communication process should not be prematurely concluded. The process of open, flexible communication can be facilitated by using paraphrases and clarifying statements that encourage further disclosure.

Sample Comments

- "If you did that, what would you see as the outcome?"
- "So then are you saying that in your opinion, this should. . . ?"
- "Are you saying, then, that. . . ?"

Likewise, reflection phrases are used to gather information about the feelings accompanying the manifest content of the message.

- "It sounds as if you would be quite disappointed if . . ."
- "I would imagine it must be quite disconcerting to even think that something like . . . could happen."

It also is appropriate to use open-ended questions and attending behaviors in gathering more data. The more information you have, the more likely it is that the solution will represent the needs of both parties. Finally, no matter how reasoned your personal solution to the problem, unless there is common ground to support ideas, change is unlikely to occur.

Solutions taking into consideration the needs and human dignity of all parties are more likely to be considered as viable alternatives. Backing another health professional into a psychological corner by using intimidation, coercion, or blaming simply is counterproductive. More often than not, solutions developed through such tactics never get implemented. Usually a number of reasons are found for this phenomenon, but the basic issues have to do with how the problem was originally defined and the control issues that were never really dealt with in the problem-solving discussion.

Essential to the implementation of confrontation strategies are full disclosure and discussion before decisions are made. Both parties must be allowed the opportunity to discuss ideas, concerns, and reasons while searching for proper ways to reach the agreed-upon goals (Jones, Bushardt, and Cadenhead, 1990). Whenever people feel that the solution has been predetermined and they have had little input into the outcome, they may feel manipulated and angry. Taking an unrealistic stand with the implicit intent of giving up some of what you really didn't want usually is unworkable over time. It destroys credibility once the manipulative nature of the strategy is uncovered. Furthermore, it stands in the way of a truly creative resolution of the problem. Often the final solution derived through fair negotiation is better than the one arrived at alone by the nurse, the physician, and the client or other health care provider.

NEGOTIATING WITH AUTHORITY FIGURES

Negotiating can be even more threatening with a nursing supervisor or an instructor who has direct line authority because these people have some control over the future of the staff nurse or student. Usually a poor relationship with a supervisor is tolerated but not shared with peers for fear of damaging the peers' view of oneself, or of peers reporting what was said to the supervisor for their own advantage. Not being able to discuss the relationship with colleagues often distorts what is really happening. Many times the frustration gets played out with the client as the nurse sabotages the supervisor's directives for improved clinical care.

Supervision implies a shared responsibility in the overall professional goal of providing high-quality nursing care to clients. It is the wise supervisor who is able to promote a nonthreatening environment in which all of the aspects of professionalism are allowed to emerge and prosper. In a supervisor–nurse relationship conflict may arise

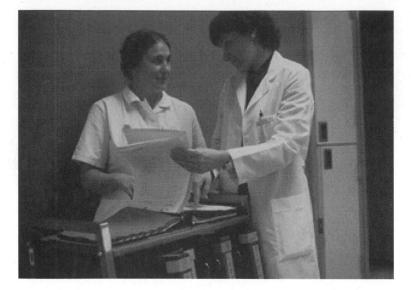

It is the wise supervisor who provides a nonthreatening environment in which professionalism can emerge (Courtesy of the University of North Carolina at Charlotte College of Nursing)

when expectations for performance are unclear or when the nurse is unable to perform at the desired level. Communication of expectations often occurs after the fact, within the context of an employee performance evaluation. Effective management requires that expectations are known from the beginning and that the nurse is advised of the need for improvement as part of an ongoing, constructive interpersonal relationship. When the supervisor must give constructive criticism, it should be given in a nonthreatening and genuinely caring manner, as presented in Box 22–4.

BOX 22–4
Steps in Giving Constructive Criticism

Steps	Sample Statement
1. Express empathy.	"I understand that things are difficult at home."
2. Describe the behavior.	"But I see that you have been late coming to work three times during this pay period."
3. State expectations.	"It is necessary for you to be here on time from now on."
4. List consequences.	"If you get here on time, we'll all start off the shift better. If you are late again, I will have to report you to the personnel department."

Receiving criticism is difficult for most people. When a supervisor gives constructive criticism, some type of response is indicated from the person receiving it. Initially, it is crucial that the conflict problem be clearly defined and acknowledged. In addition, Davidhizar (1991) recommends that the nurse:

- Defuse personal anxiety.
- Listen carefully to the criticism and paraphrase it
- Acknowledge that suggestions for improvement are taken seriously.
- Discuss the situation.
- Develop a plan for dealing with it.

In studying approaches to authority figures, you are encouraged to analyze your overall personal responses to authority, as in Exercise 22–5.

COLLABORATING WITH PEERS

The nurse–client relationship occurs within the larger context of the professional relationship with other health disciplines. How the nurse relates with other members of the health team will affect the level and nature of the interactions that transpire between nurse and client. Interpersonal conflict between health team members periodically is concealed from awareness and projected onto client behaviors.

EXERCISE 22–5
Feelings about Authority

Purpose: To recognize your feelings about authority.

Time: 1 hour; may also be done as a homework assignment and discussed in class.

Directions:
1. Lean back in your chair, close your eyes, and think of the word "authority."
2. Who is the first person that comes to mind when thinking of that word?
3. Describe how this person signifies authority to you. Next, think of an incident in which this person exerted authority and how you reacted to it.
4. After you have visualized the memory, answer the following questions.
   What were your feelings about the incident after it was over?
   What changes of feelings occurred from the start of the incident until it was over?
   Was there anything about the authority figure that reminded you of yourself?
   Was there anything about the authority figure that reminded you of someone else you once had a strong relationship with (if the memory viewed is not mother or father)?
   How could you have handled the incident more assertively?
   Can you see any patterns in yourself that might help you handle interactions with authority figures?
   What about those patterns that are not assertive?
   How could those patterns be improved to be more assertive?

Adapted from Levy R (1972). Self Revelation through Relationships. Englewood Cliffs, NJ, Prentice-Hall.

CASE EXAMPLE

On a psychiatric nursing unit, the nursing staff found Mr. Tomkins's behavior highly disruptive. At an interdisciplinary conference attended by representatives from all shifts, there was general agreement that Mr. Tomkins would spend one hour in the seclusion room each time his agitated behavior occurred. The order was written into his care plan. The plan was implemented for a week with a noticeable reduction in client symptoms. During the second week, however, Mr. Tomkins would be placed in the seclusion room for the reasons just mentioned, but the evening staff would release him after five or ten minutes if he was quiet and well behaved.

The client's agitated behavior began to escalate again, and another interdisciplinary conference was called. Although the stated focus of the dialogue was on constructive ways to help Mr. Tomkins cope with disruptive anxiety, the underlying issues related to the strong feelings of the day nursing staff that their interventions were being undermined. Equally strong was the conviction of the evening staff that they were acting in the client's best interest by letting him out of the seclusion room as soon as his behavior normalized. Until the underlying behaviors could be resolved satisfactorily at the staff level, the client continued to act out the staff's anxiety as well as his own.

Similar types of issues now and again arise when there is no input from different work shifts in developing a comprehensive nursing care plan. The shift staff may not agree with specific interventions, but instead of talking the discrepancy through in regularly scheduled staff conferences, they may act it out, unconsciously undoing the work of the other shifts. Any time there is covert conflict among nursing staff or between members of different health disciplines, it is the client who ultimately suffers the repercussions. The level of trust the client may have established in the professional relationship is compromised until the staff conflict can be resolved.

RESPONDING TO PUTDOWNS

At some time in your professional career you will run into unwarranted putdowns and destructive criticisms. Generally, they are delivered with self-defeating language and have but one intent: to decrease your status and enhance the status of the person delivering the putdown. The putdown or criticism may be handed out because the speaker is feeling inadequate or threatened. Often it has little to do with the actual behavior of the nurse to whom it is delivered. Other times the criticism may be valid, but the time and place of delivery are grossly inappropriate—in the middle of the nurses' station, for example, or in the client's presence. In either case, the automatic response of many nurses is to become defensive and embarrassed and in some way actually to begin to feel inadequate, thus allowing the speaker to project unwanted feelings onto the nurse.

Recognizing a putdown or unwarranted criticism is the first step toward dealing effectively with it. If a coworker or authority figure's comment generates defensiveness, embarrassment, and doubt about one's professional ability to perform the nursing role, it is likely that the comment represents more than just factual information about performance. If the comment made by the speaker contains legitimate information to help improve one's skill and is delivered in a private and constructive manner, it represents a learning response and cannot be considered a putdown. Learning to differentiate between the two types of communication helps the nurse to separate the "wheat from the chaff."

CASE EXAMPLE

A nurse examining a crying child's inner ears notes that the eardrums are red and reports to the head nurse that the child may have an ear infection. The head nurse responds:

A. (*learning response*): When a child is crying, the drum often swells and reddens. How about checking again when the child is calm?

B. (*putdown response*): Of course it's red when the child is crying. Didn't you learn that in nursing school? I haven't got time to answer such basic questions!

Whereas response A allows the nurse to learn useful information to incorporate into practice, response B serves to antagonize, and it is doubtful much learning takes place. What will happen is that the nurse will be more hesitant about approaching the head nurse again for clinical information. Again, it is the client who ultimately suffers.

Once a putdown is recognized as such, the nurse needs to respond verbally in an assertive manner as soon after the incident has taken place as possible. Waiting an appreciable length of time is likely to cause resentment in the nurse toward the other person, leaving the staff nurse with feelings of lost self-respect. Furthermore, it may be more difficult later for the other person to remember the details of the incident. At the same time, if the nurse's own anger, not the problem behavior, is likely to dominate the response, it is better to wait for the anger to cool a little and then to present the message in a more dignified and reasoned manner.

The process for responding to putdowns is similar to that described in Chapter 12 for conflict resolution, but the emphasis is a little different. As with all forms of conflict resolution, the nature of the relationship should be considered. Attitudes are important. If you can, look upon the incident as an opportunity to learn more about yourself in conflict situations. Respect for the value of each individual as a person should be evidenced throughout the interaction. Try to determine how to respond to this person in a productive way so that you are on speaking terms, but still get your point across. Even if you don't fully succeed in your initial tries, you probably will have learned something valuable in the process. Taking reasoned interpersonal risks is not easy, but generally it is beneficial to the personal and professional growth of the nurse. The process of response is as follows.

Address the objectionable or disrespectful behaviors first. Briefly state the behavior and its impact on you. It is important to deliver a succinct verbal message without getting lost in detail and without sounding apologetic or defensive. Do not try to give a prolonged explanation of your behavior at this point in the interaction, and do not suggest possible motivations. Instead, emphasize the specifics of the putdown behavior. Once the putdown has been dealt with, you can discuss any criticism of your own behavior on its own merits. Refer only to the behaviors identified, and don't encourage the other person to amplify the putdown.

Since putdowns often catch one by surprise, it is useful to have a standard set of opening replies ready. Examples of openers might include the following:

1. "I think it was out of line for you to criticize me in front of the client."
2. "I found your comments very disturbing and insulting."
3. "I experienced what you said as an attack that wasn't called for by my actions."
4. "I thought that was an intolerable remark."

A reply that is specific to the putdown delivered is essential. The tone of voice needs to be even and firm. In the clinical example given above, the nurse might have said to the head nurse: "My school is not an issue, and your criticism is unnecessary." Or, "It seems to me that the assessment of the child's ears, not my school, is the issue, and your superior tone is uncalled for."

An important aspect of putdowns is that they get in the way of the nurse's professional goals of providing high-quality nursing care to clients. The effect of the head nurse's response B is for both nurses to assume the reddened eardrums are from crying and not to reevaluate the child's eardrums. Feeling resentful and less sure of his or her clinical skills, the staff nurse is less likely to risk stirring up such feelings again. If fewer questions are asked, important information goes unshared. In the clinical example just cited, a possible ear infection might not be detected.

PEER NEGOTIATION

As students, you will encounter situations in which the behavior of a colleague causes a variety of unexpressed differences or disagreement because their interpretation of a situation or meaning of behavior is so different from yours. The conflict behaviors can occur as a result of differences in values, philosophical approaches to life, ways of handling problems, or lifestyle, different definitions of a problem, different goals, or alternative strategies to resolve a problem. Nevertheless, they cause friction and turn relationships from collaborative to competitive.

Resolving conflict among peers often is difficult because you are working together and in many ways are dependent upon each other for support and networking. Conflict itself, when handled properly through peer negotiation, can promote learning and a deeper appreciation for the complementary skills of a coworker. When handled improperly, conflict interferes with the nurse's professionalism and decreases the level of client care (Mallory, 1981).

Recognizing the existence of a conflict is the first step toward peer negotiation. Generally, conflict increases anxiety. When interaction with a certain peer or peer group stimulates anxious or angry feelings, the presence of conflict should be considered. Once it is determined that conflict is present, look for the basis of the conflict and label it as personal or professional. If it is personal in nature, it may not be appropriate to seek peer negotiation. It might be better to go back through the self-awareness exercises presented in previous chapters and locate the nature of the conflict through self-examination.

Sharing feelings about a conflict with others helps to reduce its intensity. It is confusing, for example, when nursing students first enter a nursing program or clinical rotation, but this confusion does not get discussed, and students frequently feel they shouldn't feel confused or uncertain. Because students face several complex interpersonal situations—class and clinical—simultaneously, they may experience loneliness and much self-doubt about their skills compared to those of their peers. These feelings are universal in human beings at the beginning of any new experience. By sharing them with one or two peers, one usually finds that others have had parallel experiences. In reviewing Exercise 22–4, think of a conflict or problem that has implications for your practice of nursing—one you would be willing to share with your peers.

Self-awareness is beneficial in assessing the meaning of a professional conflict. For instance, if the nurse's *major* response to the conflict is emotional, one can be reasonably certain the conflict raises personal feelings from a previous experience. This assumption does not negate the legitimacy of the conflict issue, but it suggests that the personal material needs to be recognized, worked through, and removed from the peer negotiation process. Concrete, observable facts related to the issue should be the focus of discussion; conflictual personal feelings should be discussed elsewhere except as they directly affect the current situation.

CASE EXAMPLE

The head nurse on the cardiac intensive care unit, Mrs. Brown, and Mrs. Smith, the head nurse on the cardiac step-down unit, were once again discussing whether to transfer Mr. O'Brien to the CICU because he was experiencing recurring shortness of breath, profuse sweating, and intermittent tachycardia. He had experienced these symptoms before his second heart attack two weeks ago. Mrs. Brown, although recognizing the transfer as in the best interest of the client, found herself saying to Mrs. Smith, "Your staff always save the client's life and get all the credit for it! My nursing staff can handle Mr. O'Brien's symptoms."

As Mr. O'Brien's symptoms continued to worsen, Mrs. Brown, analyzing her response to Mrs. Smith, realized that although there were some data to support her statements, she was really responding at some level to her teenage years when she was forced by her father to care for her elementary school–aged siblings. Although she cared for them every day, her father never acknowledged her importance as a surrogate mother or allowed her to accompany the children to school activities or doctors' appointments. He always went alone and received all of the praise for raising the children so well. Once Mrs. Brown recognized that her resentment related back to her teenage years and was not primarily related to Mrs. Smith, she was able to transfer Mr. O'Brien to the CICU.

Now that you have an opportunity to study different types of conflict, do Exercise 22–6.

DEVELOPING A SUPPORT SYSTEM

Collegial relationships are an important determinant of success as professional men and women enter nursing practice. Although there is no substitute for outcomes that demonstrate professional competence, interpersonal strategies can facilitate the process. Integrity, respect for others, dependability, a good sense of humor, and an openness to sharing with others are communication qualities people look for in developing a support system.

Forming a reliable support system to share information, ideas, and strategies with colleagues provides a collective strength to personal efforts and minimizes the possibility of misunderstanding. With problem or conflict situations, getting ideas from trusted colleagues beforehand enhances the probability of accomplishing outcomes more effectively. For example, it allows the nurse to develop and test ideas in a safe environment. Validating the appropriateness of what he or she wishes to convey and developing a practical, logical framework for the presentation helps to organize ideas so that the nurse can effectively explain important issues without getting lost in complicated details or snarled up in unrelated, fragmentary ideas.

Professional Support Groups

In nursing practice, interpersonal sharing and collaboration are an integral part of effective nursing care. But there are times the nurse feels overwhelmed with the responsibility and intense feelings associated with his or her work. For example, working with a young, terminally ill client with a family can raise important existential questions for even the most experienced nurse. Working in critical-care settings, nursing homes, and hospices with clients one knows and loves and watching them deteriorate and die despite the best possible nursing care and medical technology leads one to question one's own effectiveness, the meaning of suffering, and even one's own mortality.

On the one hand, it is easy to become hardened to such experiences or to feel that the only recourse is to leave the profession. Frequently family and friends have a limited understanding of the emotional impact of such experiences or the heart-rending toll it takes over time on the individual nurse. A professional support group, composed of individuals having similar work experience, is designed to provide emotional and cognitive support, enabling nurses to work more effectively in high-risk nursing situations.

One of the meanings of the word "comfort" is "to strengthen." In meeting the needs of others in demanding nursing situations, nurses need to take time to strengthen personal resources, and one way to do this is to seek comfort and understanding in a professional support group. Talking it through with others who can support our explorations and commitment, who can both argue and encourage the expression of conflictual feelings from a position of knowledge as well as compassion, is comforting. In professional support groups members offer themselves as resources and in return fulfill their own needs in the interaction. Giving each other guidance and thoughtful support when we need it is essential to replenish the nurse who is so busy attending to the interpersonal needs of others that there is little time to discover who he or she is as an individual in the situation (Arnold, 1989).

Special considerations needed to facilitate support groups in nursing practice and education include the following.

1. *Schedule the group at the most convenient time for participants.* Usually some times are better than others, and the staff has an awareness of the most appropriate times.
2. *Secure the cooperation of the nurse in charge of the unit, and work out details beforehand.* Enough staff should be scheduled during meeting times to allow attendance and take

EXERCISE 22–6
Barriers to Interprofessional Communication

Purpose: To help you understand the basic concepts of client advocacy, communication barriers, and peer negotiation in simulated nursing situations.

Time: 1 hour

Directions:

1. Below are four examples of situations in which interprofessional communication barriers exist. Go back and refamiliarize yourself with the concepts of professionalism, client advocacy, communication barriers, and peer negotiation.
2. Formulate a response to each example.
3. Compare your responses with those of your classmates, and discuss the implications of common and disparate answers. Sometimes, dissimilar answers provide another important dimension of a problem situation.

Case A

Dr. Tanlow interrupts Ms. Serf as she is preparing pain medication for 68-year-old Mrs. Gould. It is already 15 minutes late. Dr. Tanlow says he needs Ms. Serf immediately in Room 20C to assist with a drainage and dressing change. Knowing that Mrs. Gould, a diabetic, will respond to prolonged pain with vomiting, Ms. Serf replies she will be available to help Dr. Tanlow in 10 minutes (during which time she will have administered Mrs. Gould's pain medication). Dr. Tanlow, already on his way to Room 20C, whirls around, stating loudly, "When I say I need assistance, I mean now. I am a busy man, in case you hadn't noticed."

If you were Ms. Serf, what would be an appropriate response?

Case B

A newly hired nurse is helping a resident draw femoral blood. The nurse states that although she has never assisted with this procedure, she is thoroughly familiar with the procedure through the hospital manual. The nurse requests that if the resident should require anything different from the manual, he should tell her so. The resident responds, "You should have practiced this with someone else. I shouldn't be stuck with a neophyte. Ha Ha! Get it? Neophyte, instead of needle."

How should the nurse respond?

Case C

Mrs. Warfield, the nursing supervisor, remains on Unit C most of the evening with Mr. Whelan, who is working his first evening shift as charge nurse. Toward the end of the evening, Mr. Whelan asked Mrs. Warfield if there was a special reason she was spending so much time on the unit. Mrs. Warfield replied vaguely that she always does that with first-time charge nurses. Two days later, Mr. Whelan received a written report about his evening as charge nurse that was negative in nature and particularly critical of the fact that the supervisor had to spend so much time on Unit C. A copy of the report went to the head nurse on Unit C, and to Mr. Whelan's personnel file.

How would you respond if you were Mr. Whelan?

Case D

Mrs. Swick had been working the evening shift for eight months. When she was hired, she was promised in writing that she would be moved to a permanent day-shift assignment as soon as a replacement could be found for the evening shift. Recently, two new nurses have been hired and assigned to permanent days.

Writing a note to the supervisor brought no response; Mrs. Swick thus scheduled an appointment to discuss her schedule with her supervisor. After the appointment, her supervisor began scheduling her on days, but her new assignment requires once a month a two-day rotation to nights, a day off (which she used to sleep following her night shift) consistently followed by five straight days.

How would you approach this situation if you were Mrs. Swick?

care of inevitable emergencies. Unless there is a commitment from management, there will always be reasons other things take priority.

3. *Support groups should be conducted in an area apart from the nurses' station.* Group members need to know they will not be interrupted.

4. *Support groups should begin and end on time.* Sometimes the informal communication taking place in the group lends itself to casualness about time limits. The time constraints are a group boundary that reinforces the safety of the group relationships.

5. *Periodically the goals and rationale for meeting members needs through the support group should be evaluated.* Assuming perpetual interest and commitment without checking it out demoralizes even the best-intentioned group members.

UNDERSTANDING THE ORGANIZATIONAL SYSTEM

Whenever one works in an organization, either as student or professional, one automatically becomes a part of an organizational system with established political norms of acceptable behavior. Each organizational system defines its own chain of command and rules about social processes in professional communication. Even though your idea may be excellent, failure to understand the chain of command or an unwillingness to form the positive alliances needed to accomplish your objective dilutes the impact. For example, if your instructor has been defined as your first line of contact, then it is not in your best interest to seek out staff personnel or other students without also checking with the instructor.

Although side-stepping the identified chain of command and going to a higher or more tangential resource in the hierarchy may appear less threatening initially, the benefits of such action may not resolve the difficulty. Furthermore, the trust needed for serious discussion becomes limited. Some of the reasons for avoiding positive interactions stem from an internal circular process of faulty thinking. Because communication is viewed as part of a process, the sender and receiver act on the information received, which may or

---

BOX 22–5
Examples of Unclear Communication Processes That Block the Development of Cooperative and Receptive Influencing Skills

Low Self-Disclosure

Consequently
No one knows my real thoughts, feelings, and needs.
Consequently
I think no one cares about me or recognizes my needs.
Others see me as self-sufficient and are unaware that I have a problem.
Consequently
Others are unable to respond to my needs.

Reluctance to Delegate Tasks

Consequently
Other people think I don't believe that others can do the job as well as I can.
Consequently
The others work at a minimum level.
I don't expect or ask others to be involved.
Consequently
Other people don't volunteer to help me.
Consequently
I feel resentful and others feel undervalued and dispensable.

Making Unnecessary Demands

I expect more from others than they think is reasonable.
Consequently
I feel the others are lazy and uncommitted, and I must push harder.
Others see me as manipulative and dehumanizing.
Consequently
Others assume a low profile and don't contribute their ideas.
Consequently
Work production is mediocre.
Morale is low.
Everyone, including me, feels disempowered.

---

may not represent the reality of the situation. Examples of the circular processes that block the development of cooperative and receptive influencing skills in organizational settings are presented in Box 22–5.

GUIDELINES FOR COMMUNICATION

Often a person is not directly aware of personal communication blocks in professional relationships. Asking for feedback and engaging in self-reflection give the nurse an honest appraisal of personal communication strategies in professional situations.

Using a Focused Opening Statement

Most people will respond better when there is an opening statement giving the receiver of the message an overview of the issue to be discussed. This is given in general terms without initially getting into detailed specifics or tangential issues. Such an overview can be accomplished by using an initial focus statement capturing the essence of the communicated message. For example, a nursing student might approach an instructor to discuss problems with the development of a care plan with the focus statement, "I'd like to discuss my care plan with you—more specifically, how to individualize my behavioral objectives before I start my next care plan." This type of statement is preferable to an interpersonal approach that shows little forethought—for example, "I'm not sure what you want from me on this care plan."

Considering the Ego of the Other Person

The empathy discussed in previous chapters plays an equally important role in reciprocal communications with other professionals. It is useful to find out what the other person's communication style is like before choosing a strategy. For example, some people prefer written communication prior to verbal discussion, whereas others respond better with more informal interaction. Knowing something about the values and issues of the other person allows the nurse to tailor responses and positions with language and actions clearly recognizing the other person's concerns. It is a more subtle but extremely important element of successful professional communication.

Another aspect of ego consideration in professional dialogue is the potential emotional impact your comments about certain issues may cause in the receiver. Comments requiring a specific interpersonal change in behavior and negative commentaries on behavior can affect the self-esteem of the receiver. Even when the critical statements are valid—"You do . . ." or, "You make me feel . . ."— they should be replaced with "I" statements that define the sender's position. Otherwise, the meaning of the communication will be lost as the individual strives to defend the self against a personally felt attack.

Similarly, statements and attitudes discounting the value of the person can prevent one from achieving professional objectives. For example, verbal expressions using dogmatic language or derogatory adjectives, violating confidences, interrupting a conversation, and asking loaded or offensive questions usually diminish the other person's feelings of personal power and self-esteem. Nonverbal behaviors, such as lateness or withdrawal, serve to disconfirm the importance of the other person.

To be effective, verbal and nonverbal activities should serve a useful purpose in interprofessional dialogue. Otherwise they can and do stimulate needless hostility on the part of the receiver and, in the end, sabotage the legitimate goals of the communication. Any behavior that makes an individual feel small or less significant is counterproductive.

Keeping Your Options Open

There is power in keeping your options open in interprofessional dialogue, in not getting so locked into an either/or type of discussion. Having more than one option usually gives both the sender and receiver a greater feeling of flexibility and personal control in responding. It allows the person to respond rather than to react.

The best way to keep your options open is to consider the issue from a variety of perspectives and to *listen*. Talking situations through with an impartial, trusted colleague or mentor beforehand decreases anxiety and allows the person initiating the dialogue an opportunity to look at the issues from more than one perspective.

The second step, approaching the dialogue with an open mind about which path to take, increases the probability of developing a more satisfactory solution. Approaching a person as a mystery waiting to unfold is useful in that the final answers may be quite different from what either of you might have projected as possibilities. Finally, deliberately choosing words or behaviors that help the other person feel respected as an equal and valuable member of the health team usually strengthens the communication process.

PROFESSIONAL WORK GROUPS

Throughout a professional nursing career, nurses are involved in peer work-related groups of one kind or another. Multiple group membership is a fact of life in most organizations. Groups found in organizational settings take the form of standing committees, ad hoc task forces, and quality circles to accomplish a wide range of tasks related to the goals of the organization. The quality of health care delivery directly corresponds to effective collaboration among a wide variety of interconnecting work groups in the health care system (Cathcart and Samovar, 1988). Nurses traditionally use task and support groups for goal accomplishment in health care settings.

Work (Task) Groups

Every organization develops permanent and temporary group structures to accomplish its mission. In work groups, just as in therapy groups, there are two main elements, *content* and *process*. By contrast with therapy groups, task group content is predetermined by an assignment or charge given to the group. Work groups center their attention on a task to be accomplished or the resolution of difficult interpersonal issues specifically related to the professional work setting.

Emotional issues except as they relate to the accomplishment of group goals are not addressed. Successful groups make this distinction because a work group is not designed to be a personal growth or therapy group. Personal growth may be an important by-product of task accomplishment, but it cannot become the primary concern of the group. Failure to understand the differences between the purposes of a work group and a therapeutic group can be a disruptive side track for the group and a personally devastating experience for individual group members.

Leadership Style

Flexibility of leadership style is an essential characteristic of successful work groups. Effective leadership develops from leader characteristics, situational features, and member needs in combination with each other. Successful leadership in one group situation does not guarantee similar success in other group situations (Sullivan and Decker, 1992). Different groups require different leadership behaviors. Leadership is contingent on a proper match between a group situation and the leadership style.

There are three basic types of leadership styles found in groups: authoritarian, democratic, and laissez-faire (Brilhart and Galanes, 1989). Of the three leadership styles, the authoritarian style is the most structured.

Leaders demonstrating an *authoritarian leadership* style take full responsibility for group direction and control group interaction. Dissenting opinions are squelched. The leader makes little attempt to encourage team effort, and decision making is accomplished through authority rule. Authoritarian leadership styles work best when the group needs structure and there is limited time to reach a decision. Most mature groups resist an authoritarian leadership style.

Democratic leaders involve members in active discussion and decision making. The leader encourages open expression of feelings and ideas while providing support and encouragement. Democratic leaders are goal directed but allow flexibility in how group objectives and goals are met. In general, a democratic leadership style offers the group structure while preserving individual member autonomy. Member satisfaction is highest in groups with a democratic leadership. A variation of a democratic leadership style is a *participatory* leadership style. Here the group leader maintains final control but actively solicits and uses group member input.

The third leadership style studied is referred to as *laissez-faire.* Leaders with a laissez-faire style, although physically present, provide little or no structure and essentially abdicate their leadership responsibilities. Group members are free to decide the direction of the group interaction without leader input or structure. Groups with a laissez-faire leader are likely to be less productive and satisfying to group members.

Group Member Responsibilities

Sensitivity to group process and acceptance of personal responsibility as a group member make a person a more effective group participant. Teamwork enhances the probability of goal achievement as well as personal satisfaction with group outcomes and one's own participation (Sheafor, 1991). In a professional work-related group, each group member assumes individual responsibility for the overall functioning of the group and the achievement of group task goals. Effective professional groups need the cooperation of all members. The functional goals in a professional group cannot be dictated by others; they need to emerge from the member roles and responsibilities created in group interaction.

The primary purpose of using a group format to benefit problem resolution is to generate new ideas. A secondary purpose is to involve key individuals directly in clarifying work-related or difficult interpersonal problems and in seeking workable answers to concrete problems. Personal ownership of problem definition and change are essential to successful implementation. Exercise 22–7 is designed to help you focus on your personal involvement as a group member. Building on the assumption that each member is equally responsible for the success or failure of the achievement of the group purposes, the format in Exercise 22–7 can be used as a task or learning contract and reevaluated at the end of the group task. Using a similar format as you begin membership in a professional group clarifies the nature of the group task and enables you to take personal responsibility for your own actions and learning in a group situation.

Types of Work Groups

Permanent, ongoing task groups within an organization are referred to as *standing committees.* Standing committees establish work policies and perform many of the maintenance functions within the organization. *Quality circles* are small, temporary work groups focused on developing problem-solving and decision-making strategies to enhance the work of the organization. Usually there is an agenda circulated prior to the meeting in both group formations.

Temporary groups formed for the purpose of resolving a specific work-related problem or developing a specific project are called *ad hoc committees* or *task forces.* They serve as a temporary arm of the larger standing committee or executive group and disband once the task is completed. Although an ad hoc task force can make recommendations, final decision-making power rests with the governing body that appointed it. It is important that task forces be allowed to break up once the work is completed. Otherwise participants are reluctant to volunteer for other task forces.

Task Identification in Different Phases

Pregroup Tasks

Before the group starts, participants should have a clear idea of what the group task commitment will entail in terms of time, effort, and knowledge. Group members should have enough in common to engage in meaningful communication, a willingness to make a contribution to the group solution, and the capability to complete the task. A strong commitment to the group goal is not always a prerequisite because this may develop as part of the group process, but a commitment to engage constructively in the development of a viable solution is essential. Participants with complementary rather than the same views on task group issues ensure a more lively discussion and a potentially stronger outcome.

Ideally, group membership is limited to enough people to accomplish a given task and no more. A five- to six-person task committee is best (Basford, 1990). Less than five members leads to the development of subgroup coalitions that can sabotage the group process; more than eight members prolongs discussion and reaching consensus. Essential to the implementation of the outcome is inclusion of anyone who ultimately will be affected by the group solution.

Forming

Clear goal identification is important because the objectives and specific nature of the group problem will determine the number of members required to accomplish the task. The leader responsible for convening the group explains the group purpose and structural components—time, place, commitment—in detail. Group members take personal responsibility for clarifying and modifying group goals. A task group with vague or poorly understood goals can breed boredom or frustration, leading to power struggles and inadequate task resolution.

Norming

Member responsibilities are outlined clearly and understood by all members. In general, all data developed within the group context should be kept confidential until officially ready for publication. Otherwise the grapevine is likely to distort information and sabotage the efforts of the group.

536 //   PROFESSIONAL ISSUES

EXERCISE 22–7
Goals and Objectives in Work Groups

Purpose: To help you identify professional goals in work groups.

Time: May be done as a homework assignment and shared in class.

Directions:
Think of a real or hypothetical work group task related to a clinical or nursing education problem in need of resolution. Answer the questions below and be prepared to discuss them in class. Objectives should reflect what you personally hope to achieve as a group participant as well as what you might contribute to the overall group task. Give it some real thought so that you are clear about what you want from the experience, and what you have to give to the group.

1. Identify a general goal or goals as they relate to: _____

   Group member _____

   _____

   _____

   Group task _____

   _____

   _____

   Professional growth _____

   _____

   Supervision (if applicable) _____

   _____

2. Identify short-term objectives, or the steps needed to reach the goals identified above, as precisely as you can as they relate to the identified group goals and your own professional goals as a member of the group.

   Group member _____

   _____

   _____

   Group task _____

   _____

   _____

   Professional growth _____

   _____

   Supervision (if applicable) _____

   _____

   _____

3. Share your written goals with other members in your group, and include any relevant input from other members.

Informal communication, whether about content or process, if discussed outside the group, needs to be acknowledged in the group. This norm is essential if the needed trust is to occur.

Members need to be held accountable for regular attendance. If administrative staff are part of the group membership, it is essential that they attend every meeting. Few circumstances are more threatening to a work-related group than having a supervisor enter and exit the task group at will.

Performing

Once norms are in place, attention turns directly to the designated work of the group. Leader interventions should be consistent and well defined. The process the group would use to develop an understanding of the problem is listed below.

1. Description of relevant background and historical data.
2. Definition of problem, goal, and task objectives.
3. Feedback and refining of problem statement, goals.
4. Identification of potential resources and obstacles to goal achievement.

Exercise 22–8 provides practice with problem definition. Following identification of basic data relevant to the work of the group, the group members begin to analyze possible solutions. *Brainstorming* is a strategy used to generate ideas quickly. In addition to creating innovative ideas, brainstorming usually is a stimulating and pleasant experience for group members. Here are some guidelines for brainstorming:

1. All ideas are entertained without censure.
2. More promising ideas are tested for legitimacy.
3. Possible consequences of each idea chosen are explored.
4. Personnel and resources are identified (need for *and* availability).
5. A final group solution is developed.

Group members are partners in the brainstorming process. Each group member should feel that he or she has had a clearly defined opportunity to share in final decision making. The process of pulling diverse ideas together in a group means that each member has a clear understanding of the problem and the personal satisfaction of contributing to the group goals. Exercise 22–9 provides practice in the use of brainstorming.

Group formats are particularly useful vehicles for facilitating changes in organizational life. Sufficient time and administrative support for proposals are essential components of successful group work. Most of the failed efforts to implement change occur because of a lack of understanding of the processes needed to effect change, insufficient administrative support, unclear expectations, and

---

EXERCISE 22–8
Problem Diagnosis Exercise

Unless you can define a problem accurately, it cannot be solved. This exercise should be done individually and without consultation with other members. Think of a work-related problem in need of resolution. Define the problem in such a way that the group can work on it successfully with its current resources, i.e, current membership. Complete each question *before* going on to the next one.

1. Identify the problem you wish to work on. Describe the problem as you see it now.
2. Most problem statements can be rephrased so that they describe two things: (a) the situation as it is now and (b) the situation as you would like it to be (the ideal). Restate your problem situation in both these terms.
3. Define the changes you think you might have to make, as a member of the group, in order to make your ideal situation become reality.
4. Define the changes you think others in the group might have to be willing to make in order to make your ideal situation become reality.
5. Describe how you would envision your functioning vis-à-vis other group members to bring about an ideal situation from your perspective so that this group would be most meaningful.

EXERCISE 22–9
Brainstorming: A Family Dilemma

Purpose: To increase self-awareness and provide practical experience with the use of brainstorming as a group activity.

Time: 60 minutes

Directions:
1. Using the format on brainstorming identified in this chapter, consider the following clinical problem:

Mrs. Joan Smith is an 80-year-old woman living in Florida. Her husband recently suffered a stroke, which has affected his speech. All he is able to say to his wife is that he loves her, although he seems to understand her words to him. He is paralyzed on one side. When he tried to get out of bed, he fell and broke his hip, so he is confined to a wheelchair. No longer able to care for him, Mrs. Smith moved to Virginia to be close to her daughter, and Mr. Smith is being cared for in a nearby nursing home. She is living temporarily in her daughter's home, sleeping on the couch because her daughter has a 15-year-old boy and a 3-year-old girl occupying the bedrooms.

Mrs. Smith visits her husband every day and entertains the idea that he will get well enough that they will be able to return to Florida. She tries to be there at meal time because she thinks no one will feed him if she doesn't, and he can't eat by himself. Now that the evenings are getting darker, her daughter fears her driving after dark. She hesitates to bring up the idea of selling the house in Florida for fear it will distress her mother. Mrs. Smith is not sleeping at night and seems driven to be with her husband. Her daughter worries that her mother will collapse if she keeps up her current pace. Meanwhile the house in Florida remains empty, her mother has taken no steps to secure legal advice, and the current living situation is becoming more permanent by default.

2. Divide the group into smaller groups of three to six students depending on class size.
3. Each group should identify a spokesperson to the larger group. Use a flip chart of board to record ideas.
4. Follow the steps described in the format to generate ideas for a practical solution to the Smith family's problem. Allow 15 minutes for the first part of the exercise and 20 minutes for the brainstorming section.
5. Describe your group's solution and give the rationale for your selection.

Discussion:
1. In the larger group, each spokesperson presents the smaller group's solution to the Smith family's problem.
2. How did you group's answers compare with the answers of other groups?
3. What did you learn about the brainstorming process as a problem-solving format?
4. What was the most difficult part of the process for your group?
5. As you listen to how other groups implemented the process, what ideas came to mind?
6. How might you use this format in your nursing practice?

poor communication with those who are affected by the change. Although it is beyond the scope of this text to describe all dimensions of the organizational change process, Box 22–6 summarizes guidelines that nurses can use in groups responsible for developing changes in organizational settings.

Termination Phase

Termination in professional groups can be a group experience that all members share when the group task is accomplished and there is no further need for the group, or it can take place for one individual leaving the group. For the single individual leaving an intact group, it is important for that person to know that he or she was valued as a group member. The remaining group members need an opportunity to express their feelings of loss to and about the departing member. If the termination is unplanned and affects the work of the group, the group may need to discuss the matter further after the loss of the member.

BOX 22–6
Guidelines for Use by Groups Planning Organizational Changes

1. Clarifying Plans

Make one person responsible for implementation plans.
Formulate clear, simple, time-bound goals.
Make specific plans with milestones and outcomes.
Make plans public.
Give and solicit frequent face-to-face feedback.

2. Integrating New Practices

Limit the amount of change introduced at any one time.
Slow the change process.
Introduce the change to receptive users first.
Ensure that the rationale and procedure for change are well known.

3. Providing Education

Involve the end users and incorporate their experience.
Provide "hands-on" training whenever possible.
Design training from end users' perspectives.
Train motivated or key end users first.
Evaluate the effects of training or work practices and end-users' attitudes.

4. Fostering Ownership

Ensure that the change improves end users' ability to accomplish work.
Provide incentives for end users applying the change.
Specify milestones for getting end-user feedback.
Incorporate end-user suggestions in the implementation plans.
Publicize end-user suggestions.

5. Giving Feedback

Document and communicate the expected outcomes of the change.
Ensure frequent face-to-face feedback.
Identify clear milestones.
Make sure feedback includes the large organization.
Acknowledge key successes.

From Schoonover S, Dalziel M (1988). Developing leadership for change. *In* Cathcart R, Samovar L (eds.) (1988), Small Group Communication: A Reader (5th ed.). Dubuque, IA, William C. Brown, p. 397. Used with permission.

Usually it is better to overestimate rather than underestimate the extent of relationship in groups. Although most people will not deny that an important work-related group is ending, they frequently ignore or minimize their feelings about it. It seems harder to acknowledge that important interactions with our peers are ending than it is to admit this with our clients. As a result, it is not unusual for group members to allow one of their peers to leave without saying a genuine good-bye.

Group endings should be formal if the group has gone on for a period of time and participants have formed significant relationships with each other. A party, certificate, or opportunity to discuss the primary achievements is important. Time to express the meaning of being a part of a work-related professional group is important for individual members as well as for the group. Members can evaluate important milestones in group task accomplishment, giving time to what went wrong as well as what went right. Depending on the nature of the group, members might also evaluate the contributions of their peers and express feelings and appreciations that are more likely to go unexpressed once the group dissolves.

SUMMARY

In Chapter 22, the same principles of communication used in the nurse–client relationship are broadened to examine staff conflicts and the nature of communication among health professionals. Similar elements of thoughtful purpose, authenticity, empathy, active listening, and respect for the dignity of others that underscore successful nurse–client relationships are needed in relations with other health professionals. Building bridges to professional communication with colleagues involves concepts of collaboration, coordination, and networking. Modification of barriers to professional communication includes negotiation and conflict resolution. Self-concept changes and evolves with increasing knowledge, life-stage crises, and experiences. Self-awareness as a nursing student will be different from that of the beginning nurse. The interpersonal competencies of the new nurse will be different from those experienced by the nurse ten years later, "for the entirety of our lives we must continually assess and reassess where our responsibilities lie in the everchanging course of events" (Peck, 1978).

Work groups are an important part of organizational life. Although the focus is different from client-centered groups, work groups follow a similar pattern of growth and development.

One needs to recognize self-changes and be

able to assess how those changes influence one's professional self in collegial relationship with physicians, nursing supervisors, and peers. This chapter can be reviewed and used throughout one's nursing career because it provides self-assessment exercises and applies self-awareness strategies to enhance the quality of professional relationships. In turn, successful collegial relations strengthen the nurse–client relationship.

REFERENCES

Arnold E (1989). Burnout as a spiritual issue. *In* Carson V (1989), Spiritual Dimensions of Nursing Practice. Philadelphia, W. B. Saunders.

Baggs JG, Ryan SA (1990). ICU nurse–physician collaboration and nursing satisfaction. Nursing Economics 8:386.

Bertinasco L (1990). Strategies for resolving conflict. Health Care Supervisor 8:4, 35–39.

Brammer L (1979). The Helping Relationship. Englewood Cliffs, NJ, Prentice-Hall.

Brilhart J, Galanes G (1989). Effective Group Discussion, 6th ed. Dubuque, IA: Wm. C. Brown, Publishers.

Cathcart R, Samovar L (1988). Small Group Communication: A Reader (5th ed.). Dubuque, IA: William C. Brown.

Chenevent M (1978). Stat: Special Techniques in Assertiveness Training. St. Louis, Mosby, p. 53.

Cushing M (1985). Lessons from history: The Pickett–Guard nurse. American Journal of Nursing 10:1073–1074.

Davidhizar R (1991). Impressing the boss who criticizes you. Advances in Clinical Care 6(2):39–41.

Davidhizar R, Bowen M (1988). Confrontation: An underused nursing management technique. Health Care Supervisor 8:1, 29–34.

Donahue P (1985). Advocacy. *In* Bulechek GM et al. (eds.) (1985), Nursing Interventions. Philadelphia, W. B. Saunders.

Dostoyevski F (1881). In Steele S, Maraviglia F (eds.) (1981), Creativity in Nursing. Thorofare, NJ, Charles B. Slack.

Evans S (1991). Conflict resolution: A strategy for growth. Heart and Lung 20(2):20A, 22A, 24A.

Flanagan L (1990). Survival Skills in the Workplace: What Every Nurse Should Know. Kansas City, MO: American Nurses Association.

Gibson CH (1991). A concept analysis of empowerment. Journal of Advances in Nursing 16:354.

Hamilton J, Kiefer M (1986). Survival Skills for the New Nurse. Philadelphia, Lippincott.

Jones MA, Bushardt SC, Cadenhead G (1990). A paradigm for effective resolution of interpersonal conflict. Nursing Management, 21:64B.

Kalafatich A (1986). Nursing interfacing with nursing. *In* England D (ed.) (1986), Collaboration in Nursing. Rockville, MD, Aspen Publications.

Kennedy AH (1986). Environment for collaborative practice/professionalism. *In* England D (ed.) (1986), Collaboration in Nursing. Rockville, MD, Aspen Publications.

Kjervik DK (1990). Empowerment of the elderly. Journal of Professional Nursing 6:74.

Knaus W, Draper E, Wagner D, Zimmerman J (1986). An evaluation of outcome from intensive care in major medical centers. Annals of Internal Medicine 104:410.

Kohnke M (1982). Advocacy: Risk and Reality. St. Louis, Mosby.

Levy R (1972). Self Revelation through Relationships. Englewood Cliffs, NJ, Prentice-Hall.

Macht L (1978). Community psychiatry. *In* Nicholi M Jr. (ed.) (1978). The Harvard Guide to Modern Psychiatry. Cambridge, MA, Harvard University Press.

Mallory G (1981). Believe it or not, conflict can be healthy once you understand it and learn to manage it. Nursing '81 (Career Guide), 97.

Mauksch I (1981). Nurse–physician collaboration. A changing relationship. Journal of Nursing Administration 6:35.

Nobel KA, Rancourt R (1991). Administration and interdisciplinary conflict within nursing. Nursing Administration Quarterly. 15(4):36–42.

Oda DS (1991). The invisible nursing practice. Nursing Outlook, 39:26.

Peck MS (1978). The Road Less Traveled. New York, Simon & Schuster.

Schoonover S, Dalziel M (1988). Developing leadership for change. *In* Cathcart R, Samovar L (eds.) (1988), Small Group Communication: A Reader (5th ed.). Dubuque, IA, William C. Brown.

Schutzenhofer KK (1992). Nursing education and professional autonomy. Reflections Winter, 7.

Sheafor M (1991). Productive work groups in complex hospital units: Proposed contributions of the nurse executive. Journal of Nursing Administration 21(5):25–30.

Smith F (1985). Patient power. American Journal of Nursing 11:1260.

Sullivan E, Decker P (1992). Effective management in Nursing, 3rd ed. Redwood City, CA: Addison-Wesley.

Uusral D (1978). Values clarification in nursing: Application to practice. American Journal of Nursing 78:2058.

SUGGESTED READINGS

Albrecht K (1983). Assertiveness in nursing: Part I. American Journal of Nursing 3:424.

Albrecht K (1986). Personal Power. San Diego, CA, Shamrock Press.

Alt-White AC, Charns M, Strayer R (1983). Personal, organizational and managerial factors related to nurse–physician collaboration. Nursing Administration Quarterly, 8:8.

American Association of Colleges of Nursing (1986). Essentials of College and University Education for Professional Nursing. Final Report. Washington, DC.

American Nurses' Foundation. (1989). On Specializing in Nursing: Toward a New Empowerment.

Ashe C (1984). Are you an advocate? For patient care as well as the profession. Cancer Nursing 7:447.

Chinn P (1985). The art of criticism. Advances in Nursing Science 4:vii.

Creighton H (1984). RN advocate and the law. Nurse Manager 15:16.

Curtin L (1979). The nurse as advocate: A philosophical foundation of nursing. Advances in Nursing Science 1:1.

Donnely G (1979). When it's best not to assent: Playing advocate for your patient may serve neither of you well. RN 9:49.

Kapp M (1989). Medical empowerment of the elderly. Hastings Center Report 19:5.

Kreigh H, Perko J (1979). Psychiatric and Mental Health Nursing: A Commitment to Care and Concern. Englewood Cliffs, NJ, Prentice-Hall.

Malin N, Teasdale K (1991). Caring versus empowerment: Considerations for nursing practice. Journal of Advances in Nursing 16:657.

Rogers C (1964). Toward a modern approach to values: The valuing process in the mature person. Journal of Abnormal and Social Psychology 68:160.

Taylor S (1985). Rights and responsibilities: Nurse–patient relationships, models of moral development. Image 17:9.

Professional Documentation

KATHLEEN BOGGS

OBJECTIVES

At the end of the chapter, the student will be able to:

1. Discuss the relationship of a theory-based assessment to the nursing process and nursing diagnosis.
2. Describe and implement the essential components of a nursing assessment of an individual client.
3. Specify a relevant psychosocial nursing diagnosis.

4. Describe six charting formats.

5. Identify legal aspects of charting.
6. Discuss application of basic rules for writing professional forms of documentation.

7. Describe and analyze interactions between nurse and client in a written process recording.

> *If those who have studied the art of writing are in accord on any one point, it is on this: the surest way to arouse and hold the attention of the reader is by being specific, definite, and concrete.*
>
> Strunk and White, 1979

The process of obtaining, organizing, and conveying information to others in a written format is referred to as *documentation.* This chapter focuses on formats for the documentation of nursing care, including examples of nursing assessment, nursing diagnosis, charting methods, and other professional documentation skills. It also describes the use of interpersonal process records.

BASIC CONCEPTS

DOCUMENTING CLIENT INFORMATION FOR RECORDS

Written documentation of client care must be complete and accurate. Standards of documentation must meet the specifications of agency and professional practice regulators, third party payers, and the courts (Gryfinski and Lampe, 1990; Lampe, 1985). Nursing process has long been recognized as the basis for professional practice. As described in Chapter 2, the nursing process focuses on five nursing activities: assessment of problems, nursing diagnoses, planning of nursing care, implementation of care, and evaluation of its effectiveness. Every health care agency has its own version of forms to be filled out. For most agencies written documentation on each client includes a client history (often this data base also includes a summary list of health problems and needs), a client-centered nursing care plan (NCP), and daily records of client progress. These daily records often run to multiple pages and may include flow sheets, nursing notes, and intake and output forms (which may not become part of the permanent record), and medication records.

Developing a Data Base

Communication skills are the essential tools nurses need to compile a client data base. An intake assessment is part of the first step in the nursing process. However, assessment all too often remains a somewhat unclear concept combining elements of medical history, physical health status, and information on psychosocial functioning. A nursing data base is usually far more comprehensive than the type of information collected by physicians using a body systems format.

As nursing science developed, a variety of nurse theorists published comprehensive conceptual models of nursing practice. Each model specifies the types of data the nurse needs to collect about the client in order to provide effective care. In considering what types of data to collect when assessing the client, selection of a theory-based assessment framework provides the nurse with a guideline for exactly what type of information is needed. Even though there are wide differences among the nursing theories, each is able to provide a systematic format for nursing practice. Each theory-based model is relatively holistic in the sense that an assessment guideline derived from each would lead the nurse to collect comprehensive data dealing with physiological and psychosocial health status. Use of a theoretical model not only specifies what information is needed but it also helps the nurse organize a large number of facts into a logical pattern for consideration before implementing the other steps of the nursing process.

Figure 23–1 provides one example which can help us visualize stages of care that need documentation. Selection of a conceptual framework is a prerequisite. The next eight boxes are steps in the assessment phase of the nursing process—gathering and analyzing client information to identify a list of problems and related nursing diagnoses. These are followed by boxes representing the planning, implementation, and evaluation phases. The arrow at the bottom of the graph illustrates an essential step in the nursing process—the need to reassess or develop alternative plans and interventions when your evaluation indicates that the initial nursing plan did not work effectively.

Documentation of assessment data facilitates care by sharing client information with all those giving care to the client. The Joint Commission on Accreditation of Health Care Organizations (JCAHO), the organization that accredits many agencies, no longer requires that nurses repeat

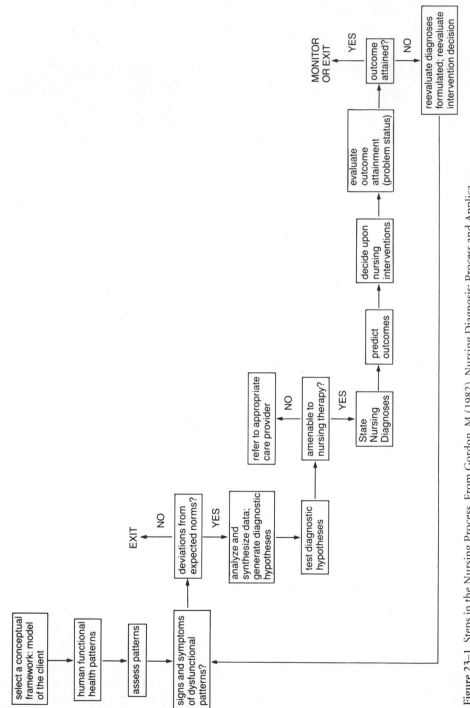

Figure 23–1 Steps in the Nursing Process. From Gordon, M (1982). Nursing Diagnosis: Process and Application. New York, McGraw-Hill Book Company, with permission from Mosby-Yearbook, St Louis, MO.

information recorded by the physician on the medical history. Documentation may consist merely of completing and updating an intake history form supplied by the agency.

The term "nursing assessment" implies that the nurse conducts a systematic inquiry into the client's past and present health status. The five assessment activities include collecting data, validating data, organizing data, identifying patterns, and communicating this assessment. If the entire agency uses the same format, paperwork is simplified. Basing this assessment on a conceptual framework developed by a nurse theorist ensures that the information-gathering phase of the client interview will be comprehensive and will proceed in an organized manner. This type of format guides the nurse and lets the nurse know what types of data to collect. The final result will be the compilation of a database containing enough information to formulate appropriate diagnoses and plan interventions. It also has the advantage of being easily understood and utilized by other nurses involved in giving care who have been oriented to use of the chosen theory-based format used by a given agency. Establishing the purpose of the data base, what information is needed, and how the information will be used helps the client respond in a more meaningful way to the short-answer questions on a database form.

Sample Application Using Orem's Theory

Table 23–1 is a sample assessment format based on Orem's self-care framework used by one group of nurses. This form emphasizes the need for the nurse to assess the client's abilities to practice self-care, since that is an important component of Orem. Self-care includes all the activities performed by the client in an effort to maintain, restore, or promote his or her own health. Self-care deficits are areas in which the client is currently unable to meet his or her own self-care needs. Once these are identified, it is the nurse's role to assist the client (wholly, partially, or through provision of emotional support and education) in meeting those needs until the client is able to do so. The brief care plan in Table 23–1 illustrates the use of one form based on a self-care framework to gather information about a client in preterm labor. The nurse elicited information about the client's biological, environmental, and social needs (universal self-care requisites) and about the needs relevant to her childbearing life stage (developmental self-care requisites). Needs associated with current alterations in health status (health deviation self-care requisites) were also documented. Since pain and anxiety associated with the current labor were noted, appropriate nursing diagnoses were formulated on the basis of these problems. A comprehensive evaluation of the client's family situation revealed other problems (deficits) that health care providers had to address prior to discharge.

Many other models with examples of assessment tools exist in the literature. Some of these articles are noted in the reference list at the end of this chapter. The most important consideration in developing any assessment format is that all care providers understand its conceptual base and that it provide sufficient information (Box 23–1). Content generic to any type of assessment is provided below. For specific communication strategies used by nurses in obtaining assessment information, the reader is advised to refer to earlier chapters for interviewing skills.

BOX 23–1
Elements of Comprehensive Client Assessment

1. Demographic information identifying the client's name, age, sex, marital status, and family constellation; primary language, occupation, social support relationships with significant others, cultural or religious preferences that might impact on care.
2. Information about prior health status (medical history).
3. Information about current problems, concerns, stressors, or alterations in current health status, as perceived by the client or client's family, for example, current comfort status. Other information about coping patterns, developmental needs, or health maintenance behaviors. Problem-solving methods are also included.
4. Objective observations by the nurse about the client's current physiological and psychosocial status, including activity level, ability to perform self-care, health needs and goals, and level of understanding of health status. This data base usually, but not always, includes information obtained from the nurse's physical examination.
5. A written list of client health problems, nursing diagnoses, or other summary of the nurse's analysis of the assessment data.

TABLE 23–1
A Client Assessment Form Based on Concepts Developed by D. Orem

Client: L.K., age 32
Medical Diagnosis: Preterm Labor (21st hospital day)
Partially Compensatory System: Client and nurse working collaboratively to meet client needs.

Assessment	Nursing Diagnosis	Goals	Nursing Orders
USCR: Universal self-care requisites NPO—IV fluids Bed rest Husband and mother close by	Diversional activity deficit related to socially restricted environment of labor room.	L.K. will respond verbally to interpersonal contacts with nurse and family.	Alert L.K. to time of day, what is occurring w/labor progress. Encourage husband and mother to stay and be of support. Explain activities and clarify any changes in environment.
DSCR: Development self-care requisites Developmental task of incorporating another member into the family. New tasks of being mother to another potential premature. Has 3 other preschool children.	Fear related to possibility of having another severely premature baby.	L.K. will communicate feelings and needs and express decreased fear and anxiety.	Establish relationship with client and allow for verbalization of fears, anxiety, anger. Facilitate husband's involvement in all relevant nursing activities.
HDSCR: Health deviation self-care requisites Emotional and physical changes during PTL pain.	Anxiety related to PTL. Alteration in comfort, pain, related to uterine contractions.	L.K. will report two positive changes in her comfort level related to decreased pain and irritability levels.	Position for comfort. Give p.r.n. pain medication as ordered. Be supportive and caring. Educate client in relaxation techniques.
TSCD: Therapeutic self-care demands Received medical care. Receiving Ritodrine HCl. Getting support from husband and mother. Used phone to talk to her other children at home. L.K. oriented to time and what was happening to her.			

Evaluation	
Related well to nurse, asked many questions, expressed confidence in physician and nurses.	L.K. stated that medication eased her pain. Also, having nurse close by and husband close for support helped with her pain.

Self-Care System	
Assets	Deficits/Environmental Set Factors
Intelligent Motivated and cooperative Husband present and supportive Positive outlook toward others Positive relationship between husband, mother Intact nuclear family Had experienced PTL previously. Knows about S.E. of ritodrine middle class SES	Has a 20-mo.-old premie at home w/ multiple complications and a gastrostomy tube. Has had a $100,000 hospital bill, still owes $5,000–$6,000. Will have 4 small children to care for at home; husband is a minister and not home very often. Mother-in-law coming to "visit" with her 3 children. Anxious about that visit.

Courtesy of Naomi East, R.N., M.S.N., University of North Carolina at Charlotte, 1987.

Problem List

Client records preferably will include a summary list of the client's health problems and care needs. In some agencies all members of the health team add to one problem list. Elsewhere nurses develop their own lists. Problems requiring medical or nursing intervention should be *prioritized* in descending order of importance. The theoretical underpinning for prioritization may vary. Maslow's hierarchy of human needs may provide a useful framework. Although often the basis is biophysiological—an ordering of problems that are most life threatening—this theory also covers psychosocial needs. The list of health problems may be written in the form of a series of nursing diagnoses, serving as a yardstick to measure therapeutic progress.

Nursing Diagnoses

Nursing diagnoses have been demonstrated to be a highly useful way of defining client problems that can be treated by nurses. Nursing diagnosis statements have become a key factor in nursing communications. Diagnoses describe actual or potential health problems that nurses, by virtue of their education and experience, are capable of treating (Gordon, 1987). They are a clinical judgment about an individual, family, or community response to health problems or life processes. They are derived from nursing practice and provide the basis for selection of nursing interventions to achieve outcomes for which the nurse is responsible (NANDA, 1992). Nursing diagnoses are a vital component of the nursing process because they describe the essence of nursing practice.

Duespohl (1986) writes that just as the nursing process provides a basis for the nursing practice, nursing diagnosis gives direction for activities of therapeutic nursing intervention. Moritz stressed the importance of the nursing diagnosis to nursing when she defined it as a label for a client condition (response to health or illness) that professional nurses are able and legally responsible to treat. Duespohl suggests that nurses apply only those diagnoses approved by the North American Nursing Diagnosis Association (NANDA). Others feel that whereas NANDA provides "life process" concepts of some wellness diagnoses, the current list of NANDA-approved diagnoses is not yet broad enough to encompass its clinical practice problems.

The partial listing of psychosocial and communications-related diagnoses provided in Table 23–2 is provided with the intent of generating enough material to allow thoughtful inquiry and application in the accompanying learning exercises. Most of the diagnoses listed have been approved by NANDA. The reader should refer to books on nursing diagnoses, some of which are listed at the end of this chapter, for complete information on the use of nursing diagnoses.

A nursing diagnosis provides information about the client to the client's nurses. It is distinct from what other health care providers are doing for the client because it delineates areas of independent nursing functions. A nursing diagnosis is not another name for a medical diagnosis since that is unnecessary and would be confusing. When the primary intervention must be initiated by a physician, the nursing actions are collaborative, secondary interventions (NAACOG, 1989). Collaborative problems are medical diagnoses about physiological problems that the nurse monitors and manages using physician-prescribed and nurse-prescribed interventions (Carpenito, 1992).

NANDA (1992) categorizes nursing diagnoses as follows:

1. *Actual diagnosis:* a state that has been clinically validated by identifying major defining characteristics.
2. *High-risk nursing diagnosis:* a state for which the client is at high risk and that is validated by the presence of risk factors. (This category replaces "potential" diagnoses.)
3. *Possible diagnosis:* a suspected problem for which additional data are needed.
4. *Wellness diagnosis:* a statement reflecting a transition to a higher level of wellness.
5. *Syndrome diagnosis:* a cluster of actual or high-risk diagnoses that are predicted to be present because of a certain event or situation. Example: Rape trauma syndrome.

The use of nursing diagnoses actually saves time by improving communication among staff members and ensuring consistent care in the writing of nursing care plans, charting nursing notes, retrieving client data, conferring with health team members, making change of shift oral reports, and communicating with community health care agencies for follow-up services (Tartaglia, 1985).

TABLE 23–2
Sample Nursing Diagnoses

Nursing diagnosis problem statement relevant to interpersonal relationships

Directions: When writing a diagnostic statement for an *actual* nursing diagnosis (which describes a human response the nurse can treat), the nurse should use the PES formula: Stating the *P*roblem, the *E*tiology, and the *S*ymptoms or signs of risk factors that validate the diagnosis. Take any of the case studies in this book and practice writing a diagnosis

Example: Impaired verbal communication related to inability to speak English as manifested by inability to follow instructions in English and verbalizing requests in Spanish (Alfaro, 1990).

Re: Interpersonal Relationships

*Altered parenting associated with . . .	Alteration in role expectations related to . . .
*Impaired social interaction associated with . . .	*Altered family processes related to . . .
*Social isolation related to . . .	*Parental role conflict associated with . . .
Decreased social support system associated with . . .	*Sexual dysfunction
*Altered role performance related to . . .	

Re: Cognitive Functioning—Sensory-Perceptual Alterations

*Visual sensory deficit associated with . . .	*Tactile sensory deficit associated with . . .
*Auditory sensory deficit associated with . . .	*Altered thought processes associated with . . .
*Kinesthetic sensory deficit associated with . . .	

Re: Coping Patterns

*Ineffective individual coping related to . . .	*Posttrauma response . . .
*Ineffective family coping: compromised . . . (specify)	*Spiritual distress . . .
*Spiritual distress related to . . .	*Anxiety about . . .
Threat to developmental task of . . . (list task or life stage, such as adolescence)	*Fear associated with . . .
	*Anticipated grieving related to loss of . . .
*Decisional conflict related to . . .	*Dysfunctional grieving related to . . .
*Impaired adjustment related to . . .	*Sleep pattern disturbance related to . . .
*Potential for violence: directed at others . . .	

Self-Perception

*Body image disturbance related to . . .	Some nurses have expressed a need to develop nursing diagnoses that reflect their evaluation of the client's positive functioning. Examples of such diagnoses might be:
*Self esteem disturbance associated with . . .	
*Alteration in self-esteem related to . . .	
*Disturbance in role performance related to . . .	*Strong drive for self-actualization associated with . . .
	*Adaptive coping associated with . . .
	*Adequate preventive health maintenance related to . . .

*NANDA-approved diagnostic category.

In analyzing assessment data to identify problems, the nurse notes deviations from expected norms or unhealthy responses and then attempts to identify their cause. By making this "nursing diagnosis," the nurse places a client in a diagnostic category for the purpose of determining the most appropriate interventions. There are three parts of a diagnostic category:

1. The terms describing the problem (the problem category label).

2. The probable cause of the problem (the etiology).

3. The defining characteristics (the major signs and symptoms that validate the diagnosis).

In writing a nursing diagnosis, the nurse needs first to list the problem or potential problem. The problem label needs to be *clear, concise,* and *specific* enough to be clinically useful. The second component of the written diagnosis is a statement about the probable etiology of the problem. If the cause of the problem can be identified and written in a clinically clear, concise fashion, it will help suggest a plan of care for each client. The problem label and etiology statement of each diagnosis are connected with words such as "related to" or "associated with." An example of such a statement might be "Alteration in parenting related to prolonged separation." A third optional component of a nursing diagnosis is specific observations or phrases that further validate and define actual identified health problems—for example, "as evidenced by infrequent visits to hospitalized client."

Currently a few problems remain for agencies using nursing diagnoses, although there has been widespread acceptance of them within the last ten years. For example, a number of nurses have expressed frustration with categorizing client problems that they have identified but that do not seem to fit easily into a standard diagnosis. Recently NANDA has accepted some diagnoses that reflect the client's positive adaptation to a situation. These are the "wellness diagnoses." Additionally, specific specialty groups are evolving adaptations of standard diagnoses to mesh with the needs identified for their types of clients. In addition to miscommunication within the nursing profession, communication difficulties have been encountered in interpreting the term "diagnosis" to members of other health care professions.

Writing nursing diagnoses takes practice. Exercises 23–1 and 23–2 are designed to provide experience in writing diagnoses that are relevant to client relationships.

Nursing Care Plan

Once client health problems are identified in the form of diagnoses, problem lists, and so on, *goals* for desired client outcomes are developed. These goals and accompanying nursing interventions or nursing orders are recorded in the client care plan. Documenting goals and interventions promotes communication among nurses so as to provide continuity of care.

CHARTING FORMATS FOR DOCUMENTING NURSING CARE

Charting is one of the most common forms of written nurse-to-other communication. All agency contact with clients is documented in some written form, such as an individual's office file, hospital chart, or clinic record. Quality care depends upon finding a complete, accurate, and easily used chart-

---

EXERCISE 23–1
Charting Nursing Diagnoses

Directions: Use the following examples to help clarify client situations that provide a direction for independent nursing interventions.

Time: 5 minutes

Example 1
Incorrect: Inability to communicate related to deafness.
Correct: Social isolation related to limitations in communication secondary to deafness, as evidenced by refusal to interact with other clients.

Questions
1. What additional information is provided in the correct diagnosis?
2. Why would the first statement be incorrect? Are all people who are deaf unable to communicate?

Example 2
Incorrect: Acute lymphocytic leukemia.
Correct: Pain during ambulation related to leukemic process as evidenced by limping, grimacing, and increased pulse.

Question
Could a nurse make any independent intervention based on the information provided by the diagnosis "Acute lymphocytic leukemia"?

EXERCISE 23–2
Developing Nursing Diagnoses

Purpose: To increase familiarity with psychosocial nursing diagnoses.

Time: 20 minutes

Directions:
1. Take each one of the standard diagnoses listed in Table 23–2 and write a second component to tailor it to a specific client you have worked with. Some examples are:
   a. Impairment of communication . . . (associated with Japanese spoken as a first language).
   b. Moderate anxiety . . . (associated with separation from kin).
   c. Impaired self-concept . . . (related to profound sensory impairment).
2. In a group or dyad discussion, compare your statements with those of other students. What can the listener tell you about the client just from reading a diagnosis written by another nurse? What is the most difficult aspect of writing diagnoses? What problems were identified that were not easily found among the listing of accepted diagnoses?

ing system. Charting practices that worked in the 1970s and 1980s may not be useful today (Iyer, 1991). Current systems are flawed; each type has advantages and disadvantages. The perfect charting system has yet to be developed.

According to Smith and Duell (1989), there are three purposes for charting: communication with the health team, provision of a permanent record for future reference (a possible legal document should litigation occur), and a record of employee performance, assisting supervisory personnel to evaluate day-by-day staff performance. Next to direct care, charting is one of the nurse's most important functions.

In 1991, JCAHO revised standards for nursing care delivery. These revised standards were designed to provide visited agencies with guidelines that would help ensure higher-quality, more cost-effective care. These standards affect broad areas of nursing practice, including documentation, by establishing criteria for charting client care. Nurses spend up to 40 percent of their time performing information-collection and processing (documentation) tasks (McHugh, 1986, p. 294). Recent literature is filled with articles advocating more streamlined forms of charting. According to JCAHO, written nursing notes no longer need to restate information listed elsewhere in the client's chart.

Traditional Narrative Charting

Narrative charting is defined as a chronological record of events happening to the client. Tradi-

tional charts used in hospitals and clinics in the past typically contained separate sections for each source from which information was obtained. For example, data from the laboratory would be found in a section of the chart marked "Lab." Likewise, information about nursing care would be in a section called "Nursing Notes." Generally, nurses using this format are expected to write nursing notes for every shift, a total of three times daily. As depicted in the following examples, narrative notes are a chronological list of the day's care.

CASE EXAMPLE:
NARRATIVE EXAMPLE 1

0700	Morning care given. Appetite good. K. Boggs, RN
0900	Medicated for complaint of dull pain in right upper quadrant of abdomen with relief. K. Boggs, RN
1100	To X-ray for chest film. K. Boggs, RN
1400	Reviewed medication information in anticipation of discharge tomorrow. Visitors in; resting comfortably, no complaints. K. Boggs, RN

Many nurses who write narrative notes have expanded this format to reflect their assessment of the client's current health status. They begin the notes for their shift by listing their physical or psychosocial assessment and summarizing the status of ongoing treatment measures.

CASE EXAMPLE:
NARRATIVE EXAMPLE 2

1600   Uncommunicative when approached by staff. Occasionally answers in monosyllables when asked direct yes–no questions. Lying in bed with sheet pulled up over head. Refused all 4 P.M. oral medication.

1800   No dinner eaten.

2100   Boyfriend arrived 10 minutes before the end of visiting hours. Walked in hall with client, who was crying and exhibited a sad facial expression.

2200   Ten-minute conversation with student nurse, during which client stated she was upset because her boyfriend wants to break up with her and was wondering whether life will be worth living without him. Psychiatric resident notified per team leader. M. Bess, SN4

Advantages: Traditional method, requiring little thought.

Disadvantages: Repetitive, time consuming, does not necessarily reflect changes in the client's primary health problems, and certainly does not follow the nursing process; does not encourage the nurse to document primary areas of concern.

Problem-Oriented Record (POR): Using SOAP Format

In the 1970s, a second charting format was developed by a physician, Dr. Weed, which was organized around the client's health problems. This format is known as the **problem oriented record (POR)**. A POR chart contains four basic sections: a data base, a list of the client's identified problems, a treatment plan, and progress notes. In the POR, a problem list is developed by the health team. The problems identified on the problem list may be a sign or symptom, an abnormal laboratory value, a risk factor, or a social or economic problem. Typically, the identified problems are medical diagnoses (Griffiths, 1989).

All health care providers in contact with the client contribute to each of the four sections. Nurses refer to the problem list and chart their observations by referring to the listed problem by number. Ideally, these progress notes are interdisciplinary, each health team member charting in the same location. However, in some agencies, the charting done by nurses is in a separate section of progress notes, "The Nurse's Progress Notes." Graphs, known as flow sheets, are utilized to record common aspects of daily client observations and care. Information about the client's progress in regard to each of his or her identified problem areas is documented only when some measurable change occurs. A specific format (called *SOAP*) is utilized to record data relevant to each problem. The first part of the four-step suggested method of documentation lists all the client's subjective comments (S) relevant to the identified problem. The second section lists all the current objective information (O) noted by the nurse. Then comes the nurse's analysis or problem assessment (A) of the client's current progress. Finally, there is a list of the nurse's intended future interventions or plans for care (P).

CASE EXAMPLE:
POR EXAMPLE 1

Problem 4: Alteration in skin integrity: decubitus related to immobility as evidenced by excoriation and drainage.

S: I think my leg looks better today. It doesn't hurt anymore when they change the dressing.

O: 4 cm × 2 cm excoriation on outer aspect of left thigh. App. 2 cm of serous drainage noted on old dressing. Sensitive to touch. Unable to note skin color due to purple staining from gentian violet treatments. Peripheral area red and puffy.

A: Less drainage than yesterday, less peripheral inflammation noted; healing decubitus.

P: Continue applications of 1/2-strength H_2O_2 and NS every 4 hrs. Apply gentian violet every 8 hrs; Cover with DSD, monitor for signs of infection. 1400: K. Boggs, RN

Advantages: Focuses on the status of the client's progress in terms of identified problems.

Disadvantages: A tendency to focus on medical diagnoses and the difficulty in maintaining interdisciplinary contributions (Lampe, 1985).

Exercise 23–3 gives practice in using the POR format.

Psychosocial problems may be documented in the same manner. Once the problem is stated, relevant client behaviors or comments should be listed as subjective data (S), nursing observations can be recorded (O), the nurse's analysis of the

EXERCISE 23–3
Utilization of Nursing Diagnosis in POR Charting Formats

Purpose: To provide practice developing a relevant nursing assessment using a POR charting format.

Time: 10 minutes

Directions: Take the sample nurse's notes provided in the section on "Traditional Narrative Charting" and convert the information to a problem-oriented format. Discuss the advantages and disadvantages of each approach.

Which documentation provides the greatest clarity? List the nursing diagnosis in each example. Discuss whether the nursing diagnosis should be assessed in the (A) section of SOAP.

problem (A) is developed as a nursing diagnosis, and current and future nursing interventions related to this specific diagnosis are listed under (P) as the plan.

Problem-Oriented Record (POR): Using PIE Format

An expanded variation of the SOAP format containing additional information about implementation interventions and evaluation of outcome is known as *SOAPIE,* or *PIE* for short. In this version charting information is as follows: (P) = the plan (goals), (I) = the interventions, and (E) = an evaluation of outcome.

CASE EXAMPLE:
POR EXAMPLE 2 (Iyer, 1991, p.50)

1/15/94	1000	S: "I have abdominal pain."
		O: Grimacing, rubbing abdomen.
		A: Abdominal pain.
		P: Medicate for pain.
		I: Demerol 75 mg, IM, RD.
		K. Boggs, RN
	1045	E: Verbalized relief of pain.
		K. Boggs, RN

Focus Charting

Focus charting is readily understood by nurses and is adaptable to many settings (Iyer, 1991). Focus charting uniquely combines the nursing care and nursing notes on the same form. It's similar to the problem-oriented record except that the "focus" doesn't have to be limited to a clinical problem— it also lists strengths. A focus may be a sign or symptom, a nursing diagnosis, a behavior, a con-

dition, a significant event, or an acute change in condition. This charting method, by listing a focus, is designed to provide a quick description of the client's current status. This is a brief statement, not a medical diagnosis, which is a statement about what is happening to the client. The SOAP is replaced by DAR—data, action and response.

The nurse charts information in columns. The left-hand column, *Data,* lists all subjective and objective assessment information, patient behaviors, patient status, and nursing observations to substantiate the problem or strength (the focus). In the next columns, *Action* lists the nursing plan and interventions and the nursing orders for the identified focus, and *Response* lists all evaluations and information indicative of the client's response to the interventions (Driedger and Dick, 1988; Lampe, 1985, 1990; Lucatonto, et al., 1991).

A nursing care plan would be in a similar format, listing the focus and then the expected client outcomes. This method is supplemented by a client data base, flow sheets, graphs for vital signs, and check lists because only relevant data are selected for documentation. The focused charting method streamlines documentation in some cases and has the advantage of capturing the critical thinking and decision-making process of the professional nurse (Driedger and Dick, 1988; Lampe, 1985, 1990).

Advantages: In one study, use of focus charting saved 90 minutes of RN time in a 24-hour period, a 36 percent reduction (Lucatonto et al., 1991), whereas another study found a 73-minute (per eight-hour shift) time savings (Griffiths, 1989).

Disadvantages: Not used by medical staff; legal questions about lack of comprehensiveness not yet widely tested in court.

CASE EXAMPLE:
FOCUS CHARTING EXAMPLE 1

Date/ Hour	Focus	Data Assessment	Action
1/15/94 0900	Social Isolation: **Withdrawn**	Refused to go to dining room for breakfast. Remained in room during music therapy group session. Answers questions in monosyllables.	Assess for discomfort Q2h *Do* spend time with client in 1:1 activity and offer to accompany client to dining room. K. Boggs, RN
1300		*Response* Interacted with nurse in constructing a puzzle and went to lunch in dining room but remains nonverbal.	*Plan* Continue to monitor behavior and spend 1:1 time with client. Arrange for phone call to parents in Italy. K. Boggs, RN

CASE EXAMPLE:
FOCUS CHARTING EXAMPLE 2
(Iyer, 1991, p. 50)

1/15/94   **Pain**   D: Grimacing, c/o burning in abdomen.
A: Demerol 75 mg, IM, Rt.D.
R: Verbalized relief of pain.
                                                L. Wilson, RN

Charting by Exception

Charting by exception is more involved than focus charting. It is based on a clear understanding of standards of care and criteria for nursing orders. This method evolved from the POR. In this type of charting, normal data are charted using checkmarks on flow sheets, with only abnormal/significant findings, called exceptions, being charted in a long-hand descriptive format. In some agencies these flow sheets containing assessment information are kept at the client's bedside, including the vital signs and intake graphic record, nursing/physician order sheet, and patient teaching records (Murphy, Belinger, and Johnson, 1988). These flow sheets include a column for recording narrative notes in the event of an abnormal finding. See Figure 23–2 for a sample flow sheet.

   Advantage: By providing a concise method for documenting routine care, nurses direct their attention to abnormal or significant findings rather than spending time detailing normal findings. Murphy, Belinger, and Johnson (1988) reported a 44 percent

decrease in RN documenting time and a 53 percent drop for the LPN (1988, p. 68), thus allowing time for evaluation of the client's progress.

Disadvantages: Requires better orientation of nursing staff, since in the current malpractice climate nurses tend to repeat flow sheet information in the "Nursing Notes" section.

Computer-Assisted Charting

In very recent years modern technology has designed *computer systems to facilitate charting.* The keeping of computer-assisted records has been implemented in some large health care systems. From the time of admission a client's records are entered and stored in a central computer. Use of a computer system is intended to facilitate access to client information. The computer system may be designed to simplify many routine functions by changing the way information flows through the health care delivery system. For example, after the client's admission to an acute-care hospital, the physician's orders are entered into the computer and can be transmitted directly to the pharmacy, the laboratory, and the nursing unit. The results of laboratory tests are available to care providers as soon as the lab technician makes an entry.

   Use of the computer facilitates the charting of nursing notes. At a video display terminal located in the nurse's station or in client care areas, each nurse enters his or her identification number and

NURSING/PHYSICIAN ORDER FLOW SHEET

DATE _____

NRSG DX	NURSING/ PHYSICIAN ORDER	12-1	12-1	12-1	12-1	12-2	12-2	12-2	12-2	12-3
#1	GI Assessment	09 ✓	13 ✓	19 ✓	23 ✓	09 — 3 loose BMs this AM	11 — hyperactive BS	18 ✓	22 ✓	10 ✓
#1	GU Assessment	09 — Vdg. frequently 50–100 cc q 1–2 hrs	13 ✓	19 ↑	23 ✓	09 — Vdg. 2–4° urine conc.	14 ↑	18 ✓	22 ✓	10 ✓
#2	Integumentary Assessment	09 — Quarter-size open, red area on coccyx— sm. amt. drng.	13 ↑	19 ↑	23 ↑	10 — No drng.	14 ↑	18 ↑	22 ↑	10 — Remains reddened, but no open areas
#2	Turn q2° (even)	08 14 ✓		22 ✓		D/C'ed				
D.O.	Kretchmar Rx to coccyx	103 0 ✓		20 30 ✓		09 ✓	21	18 ✓		10 30 ✓
#2	✓ Periph. Circ. −✓ Homan's Sign	09 ✓		20 ✓		09 ✓		19 — pedal pulses +¼ CRT>3 sec		10 ✓
#2	Amb. in hallways c̄ walker & assist of 2—document tol.					12 — done x 2 in AM— tol. well	15 — amb. x 1, no diff. both times	30 — sl. SOB exertion exertion	22 — c̄ when times	10 — up x 1— no SOB
	NURSE SIGNATURE	S. Smith, RN	S. Smith, RN	J. Doe, RN	J. Doe, RN	L. Fritz, RN	L. Fritz, RN	J. Doe, RN	J. Doe, RN	S. Smith, RN

Figure 23–2 Charting by Exception. From Murphy, Belinger, and Johnson, 1988.

Computer-assisted charting is becoming the norm for nursing documentation in the 1990s. (Courtesy of the University of North Carolina at Charlotte College of Nursing)

then enters data into the client's computer file. Most systems utilize a mouse or light pen and standard groupings or categories of client-care information. When the operator points the pen at the correct phrase displayed on the video terminal, data are entered into an individual's computer "chart." In similar fashion to word processing programs, these applications allow the nurse to display entries and make corrections before storing data in the client's permanent computer record. Since the computer has preset pathways, the nurse needs to learn the correct sequence for entering data. However, once skill is developed in using the system, computer charting considerably reduces the nurse's volume of written work (McHugh, 1986).

> *Advantages:* Reduction in work load; clarity, because all entries are typed. Paper printouts can be made anytime the nurse so desires. Up-to-the-minute care plans and medication orders are available to each nurse at the beginning of and during his or her shift. Each person, including the student nurse caring for a client, can print out his or her own copy of the current orders, plan of care, and so on. An advantage of computer-assisted charting, in addition to saving time, is that specific categories of client care are listed and may be selected. These categories act as a prompt to the nurse to ensure that the nursing notes are complete.

> *Disadvantages:* A delay may occur between administering medication and permanently recording its administration in the computer. Curran (1994) has noted problems in confidentiality. Anyone with entry to the system can access supposedly confidential client information.

Any of several charting systems is acceptable to regulators at JCAHO, but the agency must demonstrate consistency across similar units. All charting, regardless of method, must address the client's *current status* according to a prioritized needs list. Emphasis in documentation needs to be placed on charting the outcomes of care.

LEGAL ASPECTS OF CHARTING

Management literature emphasizes the need for less repetitive, less time-consuming methods of documentation that reflect the nursing process. At the same time the need for all documentation to be legally sound is strongly emphasized. Unless the care given the client is documented, the legal assumption is that the care was not given (Bergerson, 1988, Fiesta, 1991b). Malpractice settlements have approached millions of dollars for individuals whose charts failed to document safe, effective care. Aside from issues of legal liability, third-party reimbursement depends upon accurate recording of care given. Major insurance companies audit charts and contest charges not validated in the written record.

Since the purpose of the medical record is to document client care, any information that is clinically significant should be included. Any method of charting that provides comprehensive, factual information is legally acceptable. This includes graphs, checklists, and all of the types of charting discussed earlier in this chapter. "Long, narrative paragraphs should be a necessary part of charting only *infrequently* and in exceptional circumstances" (Fiesta, 1991b, p. 17).

Corrections to the medical record should be made in such a way that the incorrect information is still legible and is never obliterated. In the preferred method of correction, the nurse draws a line through the incorrect entry and adds his or her initials and the date. Additions to existing charting, even if added shortly afterward, are not a problem in the courtroom. Additions that occur after the defendant has been notified that the client is contemplating legal action are difficult to defend in court.

Table 23–3 lists some recommended "rules" for charting recommended to keep you legally safe. For further information, Fiesta (1991a) provides an excellent overview of the legal process involved in malpractice claims. Or contact ANA's Marketing Division for a copy of "Liability Prevention and You—What Nurses and Employers Need to Know."

WRITTEN COMMUNICATION WITH OTHER PROFESSIONALS

A professional nurse is called upon daily to communicate with other professionals in some type of written format. Written communication has several advantages over other forms of communication (see Box 23–2). Written text provides a potentially permanent record of information and may

TABLE 23–3
Charting "Rules"

Content

Chart promptly but never ahead of time.
Document complete care.
Document noncompliant behavior and the teaching/information you gave the client, and the reason.
When care or medicine is omitted, document action and rationale—who was notified and what was said.
Correct inaccurate entries without obliterating the mistake.

Format

Use black or blue ink.
Write legibly.
Use military time and authorized abbreviations.
Use correct spelling and grammar.
Do not leave blank spaces.

Adapted from Iyer P (1991). Thirteen charting rules. Nursing '91 (21(1): 40–44; and Iyer P (1991). Six more charting rules. Nursing '91 21(2).

diminish miscommunication. The natural tendency to distort verbal messages or forget components over time is alleviated when there are written records to refer to, particularly when the topic being discussed is complex or when the communication is directed at larger groups of people.

A number of types of written documentation may be utilized to improve communication with nurse colleagues within the agency or to supplement verbal communication mechanisms—for example, shift reports and staff meeting reports. Some examples are memos, communication books, minutes from staff meetings, and professional newsletters.

In dealing with colleagues in an organization, Claus and Bailey (1977) advise nursing leaders to improve their chances of being understood by

BOX 23–2
Guidelines for Written Communication

1. Use the format appropriate to the situation, one familiar to the individuals with whom you are communicating.
2. Use vocabulary or terminology at a level the intended recipients understand.
3. Avoid unnecessary jargon and abbreviations.
4. Be clear; use exact dates and times.
5. Use correct grammar and spelling.
6. Try to organize your message logically (introduction, rationale, content, conclusion).

combining spoken words with other forms of communication, including memos, letters, and other written messages. They identify prerequisites for effective formal communication. The sender of the message must have credibility by having demonstrated trustworthiness, positive regard for others, and consistency. The message must be composed in such a way as to be understandable to the recipients. Finally, the sender needs feedback to verify that the message was correctly interpreted.

Rules for written communication vary with the type of situation. The three principles of written communication are: be *accurate,* be *brief,* be *complete.* As with the acquisition of psychomotor skills or problem-solving skills, development of competent writing skills requires extensive practice. Most school curriculums offer many opportunities to develop and improve basic writing skills. However, many of us require additional practice with professional writing before we feel comfortable as well as proficient.

Nurses, like members of other professions, are obligated to contribute to the body of the discipline's knowledge. In part, this contribution is made through publication in professional journals.

APPLICATIONS

DOCUMENTING CLIENT INFORMATION FOR LEARNING: INTERPERSONAL PROCESS RECORDS

Frequently in a relationship interactions occur that either facilitate or hinder the progression of the relationship. Often, however, we remain unaware of exactly what we did or said that helped move us along or what it was that disrupted communication. The written *interpersonal process record* is a tool that has been utilized for many years in nursing and other human science professions to help analyze interpersonal communication.

There are three essential parts to the process record. First, a written anecdotal record is done of both the client's words and the nurse's words along with notes about their nonverbal behavior. Second, to enhance learning, a written analysis of the interaction process is done, identifying specific communication skills and interventions utilized. This analysis is an evaluation of the effectiveness of the nurse's communication skills in fostering the goals of the interaction. Through this effort the nurse can develop a better understanding of the therapeutic nature of her interpersonal interactions.

Since the goal of analyzing a process record is to promote use of more effective nursing interventions, a third component of the process is to add written suggestions for making more effective comments. The writer suggests alternative communication responses that might have better facilitated the therapeutic nature of the interaction. Focus is placed on better strategies to help the client solve problems. At the very least, analyzing a conversation can help the nurse determine which communication techniques work and which are ineffective, perhaps finding clues to psychosocial factors that influence the interaction. These may help identify any recurring communication patterns and enable the nurse to discover why certain intervention strategies didn't work.

Writing a process record is a self-study process that helps the nurse synthesize communication theory by applying concepts in a clinical situation. Over a period of time this activity leads to an increased sensitivity to one's own communication strengths and weaknesses. It may also promote an increased acceptance of one's own thoughts and feelings. It involves active participation of the learner, closely followed by an opportunity to interpret the effectiveness of the process.

Educators often recommend sharing the written process record with a more experienced professional. An objective reader is often able to discern patterns of behavior the learner does not see. The reader may also be able to help the learner develop more effective communication skills by critiquing the written record's analysis and suggesting more effective communication strategies.

Use of the written process record is an effective but time-consuming process. To obtain maximum benefit from this learning tool, the nurse needs to record a series of nurse–client interactions, conduct a self-analysis, and obtain feedback for each interaction from a reader. Confidentiality must be maintained at all times to protect the client and the therapeutic nature of the nurse–client relationship. Anonymity can be ensured on the process record by using only client initials rather than full names and by omitting identifying demographic information.

Directions for Using Process Records for Learning

To be able to review an interaction objectively, it is necessary first to record the content of the conversation. Figure 23–3, which illustrates one standard format for listing this information, may be photocopied for use. The written process record is designed to be used after the nurse has finished interacting with a client. Some experts suggest that notes be taken during the conversation. Writing while talking, however, may be extremely disruptive to the conversation as well as to the overall nurse–client relationship.

A better approach is to find a quiet, private spot as soon after the interaction as possible and to write down the content of the interaction. An example of this content is provided in columns 1

INTERPERSONAL PROCESS RECORD

Student's Name _____   Client's Initials _____
Process Record # _____   Background Information _____
Date & Time of Interaction _____   _____
Setting _____   _____

Client	Nurse	Analysis

Figure 23–3 Interpersonal Process Record

Date: 1/18/94–9:23 A.M. Intake Interview in Clinic, private exam room. Mrs. S's second visit for weight reduction.

Client	Nurse	Analysis
Hello, Ms. Foy.	Hi, Mrs. S. I brought you those booklets on dieting I promised you.	
Thank you.	I'd like to spend time today talking about them with you.	Establishing trust.
I've been on every diet published in every magazine. I gain on them all.	You have tried dieting several times before?	Tried to clarify
Yes, I've had a weight problem for five years. Diets don't help. (loud voice, sad face) I get disgusted with them after two or three weeks.	You've had trouble actually losing weight on these diets?	Paraphrased to verify
Yes, I'd like to slimmer. For years I pictured myself as a lump in a bathing suit but every time I resolve to diet, I end up stuffing myself. I always reward myself with a treat when I've had a hard day at work like I'm a big nothing . . . just a weak-willed slob. (started crying)	You find dieting discouraging. (attentive posture) (I began to feel uncomfortable when she got off into these negatives) Well, I see it upsets you. Let's review these booklets now. I have a lot to cover today.	Reflection Silence Acknowledgment of nonbehavioral feelings but changed subject. My own anxiety led me to focus on my own needs.
No comments. (avoided eye contact, slumped in chair)	Mrs. S., you look like this conversation is getting you down. Maybe we should talk about how you're feeling and discuss the exchanges later. You've mentioned that being overweight makes you feel bad about yourself. What is it about the weight that bothers you most?	Attempt to salvage discussion by refocusing on client's problem Open-ended question to facilitate communication.
I find it most depressing to fail on a diet because of the way it makes me feel, but I also can't accept not fitting into a size less than 16.	Okay, Mrs. S., I think I have a better ides of how you feel. You feel equally bad being overweight and failing to successfully lose weight on a diet. To help me better understand your usual eating patterns, I'd like you to fill out this daily record of food intake. With each meal entry, also list a rating of 1 to 10, bad to good, of how you feel. Next week when you come for your appointment, we'll go over this notebook together and look for clues to help you succeed in losing weight.	Summarization
Thanks, I'll be glad to try something constructive. Goodbye.	(I felt great!)	Summary Figured I'd really turned around a bad situation. Her mood change let me know I might be on the right track. (1) She needs to develop insight into her eating patterns. (2) Participating in the process of selecting her diet may be a more effective plan than teaching exchange groups.

Figure 23–4 A Sample Process Recording

This example illustrates beginning-level student analysis appropriate for a communications course. A more in-depth analysis would be expected of an advanced student practicing in a psychiatric clinical setting.

and 2 of Figure 23–4. Since this form is a tool for learning, space is provided for self-analysis of the therapeutic components of the interaction. Any interaction between a nurse and a client can be recorded and analyzed to learn better communication skills. As Joyce Travelbee (1971) notes, "No nurse is without some degree of skill in being able to purposefully use the communication process; neither is any nurse a communication expert in the sense that she cannot develop further skill."

A form similar to that shown in Figure 23–3 can be used to list interpersonal interactions. As listed in Box 23–3, the interpersonal process record should contain some information about the client while still protecting the client's identity, such as using the client's initials and the date of the interaction. Statements about where the interaction occurred and the environmental circumstances or personal background factors that affected the interaction are helpful. For example, an immediate preceding factor, such as medication for pain with a strong narcotic, might significantly change the way a client responds.

A complete listing should be made of all comments. Notes about tone of voice may also be made. This record should be as accurate as possible. The nurse should resist the natural inclination to edit or "improve," the comments made to the client. The list should record the conversation in the order in which it occurred. Although the nurse may forget some of the words used, he or she should strive to make as accurate a recording as possible. Since it is often difficult to recall extensive information, limit the actual interaction to be described on the process recording to 10 or 15 minutes.

Since nonverbal behaviors can significantly affect the nature of a communication, all relevant nonverbal behaviors exhibited by either the nurse or the client are also listed along with verbal responses. Of particular interest are comments about the nurse's thoughts and feelings during the interaction. The nurse should describe his or her "gut-level" responses during the course of the interaction—whether he or she felt comfortable, uncomfortable, helpless, or knowledgeable—by making comments in parentheses in column 2 of Figure 23–3.

The last column in the figure is for analysis of the content and meaning of the interaction. After careful reflection, the nurse should write his or her interpretation of each of the statements made by the client and the nurse's responses. Use of each specific communication skill should be identified along with the rationale for utilizing it and a critique of its effectiveness. Commentary about transitions in the conversation, such as the rationale for changing the subject, should be entered. A brief analysis of identified predominant emotions should be recorded in the third column, as well as any conscious and perhaps unconscious feelings held by the client or nurse during the interaction. Note the effects of client or nurse values, such as age difference or religious orientation, on the course of the conversation.

The nurse needs to make an overall summary, evaluating the process of interaction and the effectiveness of the nurse's interventions. Possible alternative interventions should be listed that, in retrospect, might have more effectively accomplished client or nurse goals for the interaction. This brief summary may also contain information about any factors or client needs noted during the interaction that might affect the future course of the client–nurse relationship. For example, noting a consistent behavior pattern of lateness may point up the need to focus on underlying feelings about the relationship.

Some of the most effective learning may occur as a result of analysis of less than perfect responses. Column 2 of Figure 23–4 clearly reveals errors made by the nurse during the course of the interaction. Many individuals have commented that some of their best learning has occurred when they "bomb." It is potentially threatening to write up comments that may not reveal ourselves in a favorable light. This is particularly true for students when an instructor reads the process record

---

BOX 23–3
Elements of Interpersonal Process Record

1. Summarize demographic and other relevant data.
2. List all comments made by client and nurse.
3. List all nonverbal behaviors and "gut-level" feelings.
4. Interpret statements and responses; identify skills used.
5. Summarize the encounter and propose alternative interventions/modifications.

EXERCISE 23–4
A Process Record

Purpose: To provide the student with practice in writing process records.

Time: 1 hour

Directions:

1. Conduct a 10-minute interaction with a client.
2. Photocopy the format in Figure 23–3 to write up the actual interaction as soon as possible following your contact with the client. Fill in any needed data about the client, time, or place of the interaction. Identify your goal for the interaction—what you intended to accomplish. Then fill out only the first two columns, listing raw data, that is, all the comments made by both the client (column 1) and the nurse (column 2) in the order in which they occurred. Some inaccuracies will naturally occur, but try to write as faithful a record as you can recollect. In parentheses, note nonverbal behaviors observed in the client or any feeling you recall that accompanied your conversation with the client.
3. After recording all the raw data, begin your analysis (column 3). Read through each exchange between you and the client (usually, initially, an exchange constitutes only one or two sentences from each of you). The analysis should be guided by the purpose doing the process recording. Essential components usually are development of communication skills and identification of client problems requiring nursing assessment and intervention.
   a. Identify each communication skill utilized.
   b. Describe your rationale for using each skill in your responses. Suggest alternative skills for areas in which the listed skill did not achieve the desired results.
   c. Describe relevant feelings not previously identified in column 2, particularly if they are related to your choice of the next intervention.
   d. Make comments about what you think went on in the process of the conversation. List any opinions, tentative interpretations, or hypotheses you can make about the recorded behavior. In particular, highlight your interpretation of the client's behavior. Apply principles from communication theory to help identify the underlying process that occurred during the interaction.
   e. Conclude with a statement summarizing those aspects in the process that seem relevant for your future interactions with the client. For example, certain inferences made from this record may need to be checked or validated with the client in your next interaction.

and makes comments on it or grades it. However, if it is established ahead of time that process records are learning tools, concerns about getting good grades may be minimized. The amount of learning will depend on the nurse's willingness to be vulnerable, especially in regard to the ability to perceive accurately deficits in his or her communication skills. A reader's critique is based not on the nurse's right or wrong answers but upon the writer's ability to analyze the interactive process correctly and insightfully to apply concepts from communications theory. Understanding that this is a learning activity and knowing that communication "errors" are an expected part of the learning process may enable the writer to avoid deliberate censoring or distortion of the data recorded. Exer-

cises 23–4 and 23–5 are provided to give practice in writing process records and to help nurses further their understanding of process records.

SUMMARY

Chapter 23 focuses on the uses of written communication in the nurse–client relationship. Documentation refers to the process of obtaining, organizing, and conveying information to others in a written format. Three areas of content are discussed: written tools utilized in developing communication skills, transcribed documentation of the nursing process, and the reporting of client information in professional records. Learning to

EXERCISE 23–5
The Interpersonal Process: Related Concepts

Purpose: To help you analyze interpersonal responses in process records. The process recording is an effective tool for developing increased awareness of process problems and use of communications skills. Alternatively, audio or video recordings may accomplish the same purpose. The following exercise may be used to supplement process records or may be used alternately with process records.

Time: 15 minutes

Directions: Answer the following questions after completing a nurse–client interaction.
1. Were your goals or objectives for the interaction achieved?
2. To what extent were they not achieved?
3. Cite evidence to document that your objective was achieved. (This is usually in the form of a behavioral change noted in the client.)
4. Identify why some goals were not achieved.
    a. Were your goals realistic?
    b. Were they mutual goals or just your goals as a nurse?
5. Were any client goals achieved or needs fulfilled?
6. What were your preconceptions or feelings prior to this interaction? To what extent did they affect the outcome of the interaction?
7. What did you learn about the client that you weren't aware of before?
8. What particular communication skills were you uncomfortable using? Which were ineffective?
9. What new nursing diagnoses or client problems did you identify after this interaction?

write process records, to chart accurately, and to provide clear written communication to other health professionals is an essential component of successful nurse–client relationships.

REFERENCES

Aguilera D (1994). Crisis Intervention: Theory and Methodology, 7th ed. St. Louis, Mosby.

Alfaro R (1990). Applying Nursing Diagnosis and Nursing Process: A Step-by-Step Guide (2nd ed.). Philadelphia, Lippincott.

Bergerson S (1988). Charting with a jury in mind. Nursing '88 (April): 51–56.

Carpenito LJ (1992). Handbook of Nursing Diagnosis. Philadelphia, W. B. Saunders.

Claus KE, Bailey JT (1977). Power and Influence in Health Care. St. Louis, Mosby.

Curran MA (1994). Private communication.

Driedger LS, Dick J (1988). Patient focused charting. Canadian Journal of Nursing Administration 1(2):20–22.

Duespohl TA (1986). Nursing Diagnosis Manual for the Well and Ill Client. Philadelphia, W. B. Saunders.

Egan G (1990). The Skilled Helper. Belmont CA: Brooks Cole.

Fiesta J (1991a). Legal procedure. Nursing Management 22(7):12–13.

Fiesta J (1991b). If it wasn't charted, it wasn't done. Nursing Management 22(8):17.

Gordon M (1987). Nursing Diagnosis: Process and Application. New York, McGraw-Hill.

Griffith J, Ignatavicius D (1986). The Writer's Handbook. Baltimore, MD, Resource Applications.

Griffiths, A (1989). Focus charting in rehabilitation. Rehabilitation Nursing 14(3):142–148.

Gryfinski JJ, Lampe SS (1990). Implementing focus charting, process and critique. Clinical Nurse Specialist, 4(4):201–205.

Iyer, PW (1991). New trends in charting. Nursing '91 21(1)48–50.

Joint Commission on Accreditation of Health Care Organizations (1991). The New Standards for Nursing Care.

Kim M (1990). Practice Guide to Nursing Diagnosis (4th ed.).

Lampe SS (1985). Focus charting: Streamlining documentation. Nursing Management 16(7):43–46.

Lampe SS (1990). Focus charting assists the nurse manager. Primary Nursing 9(5). Minneapolis, MN, Creative Nursing Management, Inc.

Lucatonto M, Petras D, Drew I, Zbuckvich I (1991). Documentation: A focus for cost savings. Journal of Nursing Administration 21(3):32–36.

McHugh ML (1986). Increasing productivity through computer communications. Dimensions of Critical Care Nursing 5(5):294–303.

Murphy J, Belinger J, Johnson B (1988). Charting by exception: Meeting the challenge of cost containment. Nursing Management 19(2):56–72.

NAACOG (1989). Nursing Diagnosis. NAACOG OGN Nursing Process Resource.

NANDA (1992). Nursing Diagnoses: Definitions and Classifications. Philadelphia, North American Nursing Diagnosis Association.

Smith S, Duell D (1989). Clinical Nursing Skills (2nd ed.). Los Altos, CA, National Nursing Review.

Strunk W, White EB (1979). The Elements of Style. New York, Macmillan.

Tartaglia MJ (1985). Nursing diagnosis: Keystone of your care plan. Nursing '85 15(34).

Travelbee, J (1971). Interpersonal Aspects of Nursing (2nd ed.). Philadelphia, Davis.

SUGGESTED READINGS

Comstock LG, Moff T (1991). Cash effective, time efficient charting. Nursing Management 22(7):44–48.

Facteau LM (1980). Self-care concepts and the care of the hospitalized child. Nursing Clinics of North America 15(145).

Harper DC (1984). Application of Orem's theoretical constructs to self-care medication behaviors in the elderly. Advances in Nursing Science 6(29).

Hartman D, Knudson J (1991). A nursing data base for initial patient assessment. Oncology Nursing Forum 18(1):125–130.

Kishi KI (1983). Communication patterns of health teaching and information recall. Nursing Research 32(230).

Lough J, Ritchie C (1988). Ritchie-Lough Charting System. Physiotherapy, 74(6):274.

Orem DE (1971). Nursing: Concepts of Practice. New York, McGraw-Hill.

Paradiso C (1985). Self-care framework: A guide for clinical application. Journal of Nephrological Nursing 2(3):139.

Runtz SE, Urtel JG (1983). Evaluating your practice via a nursing model. Nurse Practitioner 8(30).

Sorrell JM (1991). The composing processes of nursing students writing nurses' notes. Journal of Nursing Education 30(4):162–167.

Taylor SG (1991). The structures of nursing diagnosis from Orem's theory. Nursing Science Quarterly 4(1):24–32.

Zorn CR, Smith MC, Werley HH (1991). Watch your language. Nursing Outlook 39(4):183–185.

Glossary

(The number at the end of the entry indicates the chapter(s) in which the term is defined.)

Acculturation: The natural learning of cultural roles and behaviors, as with little children learning from their elders; the process by which a person learns and accepts the values of a new culture. **(6, 11)**

Achieved roles: Roles earned or bestowed on a person. **(6)**

Active intervention phase: *See* **Working phase. (4)**

Active listening: A dynamic interpersonal process whereby a person hears a message, decodes its meaning, and conveys an understanding about the meaning to the sender. **(10)**

Actual nursing diagnosis: A state that has been clinically validated by identifying major defining characteristics. **(23)**

Ad hoc committee: A temporary group formed to resolve a specific work-related problem or to develop a specific project. **(22)**

Adaptive model of health: Health as assessed by the self-care coping strategies a client uses to adapt to physical and emotional changes as the measure of health. **(15)**

Affective learning: Changes in attitude that inform and direct behaviors. **(15)**

Affirmation: An abstract feeling that takes place through relations with others based on validation, tenderness, cherishing, and respect. **(12)**

Aggressive response: A response in which the individual acts to defend the self, to deflect the emotional impact of the perceived threat to the self through personal attack, blaming, or an extreme reaction to a tangential issue. **(14)**

Alarm phase: The initial phase of the General Adaptation Syndrome (GAS) stress response, evidenced in changes in the sympathetic nervous system and in the hormonal secretions of the adrenal glands. **(20)**

Androgogy: The art and science of helping adults to learn. **(15)**

Anticipatory guidance: Helping the client foresee and predict potential difficulties. **(22)**

Anxiety: A vague, persistent sense of impending doom. **(5)**

Aphasia: A neurologic linguistic deficit; a speech-language pathology that is most frequently associated with neurologic trauma to the brain. **(17)**

Apraxia: The loss of ability or the inability to take purposeful action even when the muscles, senses, and vocabulary seem intact. **(19)**

Ascribed roles: Roles over which a person has no control, such as family position or gender. **(6)**

Assertive behavior: Setting goals, acting on these goals in a clear and consistent manner, and taking responsibility for the consequences of one's actions. **(14)**

Assimilation: A conscious learning process in which a person deliberately chooses to learn a language and expected role behaviors as a way of gaining acceptance in a dominant society. **(6)**

Attentional set: the capacity of a person to attend to the learning process and the extent to which the person is distracted by other factors in the environment. **(15)**

Authenticity: Honesty; clarity about one's own personal values, feelings, and thoughts in response to a client **(4)**

Authoritarian leadership: The style in which the leader takes full responsibility for group direction and controls group interaction. **(22)**

Autonomy: Having decision-making power; the nurse supports autonomy by leaving decision making to the client whenever possible and by supporting the client's decisions unless there is a chance of harm to the client or others. **(4)**

Bias: Generalizations representing expectations and prejudgments about people and behaviors. **(5)**

Body image: The physical dimension of self-concept; thoughts and feelings about one's physical appearance, body parts, movements, and body functions. **(3)**

Body language: A system of communication that includes facial expression, eye movements, body movements, posture, gestures, and proxemics. **(9)**

Burnout: A state in which a person's physical, psychosocial, and spiritual resources are exhausted. **(20)**

Caring: An intentional human action, characterized by commitment and a sufficient level of knowledge and skill, that allows the nurse to support the basic integrity of the person being cared for. Caring develops from a natural response to help persons in need, the knowledge that caring is a part of nursing ethics, and respect for self and others. **(5)**

Catastrophic reaction: An outburst of a dementia victim, similar to a temper tantrum, that represents a completely disorganized set of responses in reaction to real or perceived frustration. Warning signs of an impending catastrophic reaction may be restlessness, refusals, or general uncooperativeness. (19)

Charting by exception: A type of charting in which normal data are charted using check marks on flow sheets, with only abnormal/significant findings, called exceptions, being charted in a longhand descriptive format. (23)

Circular communication: A continuous, mutually interdependent activity involving interdependent communicators who reciprocally influence one another's behavior. (1)

Circular questions: Questions that are designed to explore the interpersonal context in which an illness occurs, focusing on relationships and differing responses among family members. (10)

Client advocacy: Interceding or acting on behalf of the client to provide the highest quality of care obtainable. (22)

Closed questions: Questions that can be answered with a yes, no, or one-word answer. (10)

Cognitive dissonance: The holding of two or more conflicting values at the same time. (7)

Cognitive learning: Knowledge obtained from information a person did not have before. (15)

Cognitive motivators: Internal thought processes by which people develop goals and employ their minds to reach those goals. (15)

Cohesiveness: The degree of positive attachment and investment that members have for the group. (12)

Collaboration: Two or more people working together to solve a common problem and sharing responsibility for the process and outcome. (22)

Complementary exchanges: Interactions that involve unequal distribution of power. (13)

Computer-assisted charting: Use of a computer system to facilitate access to client records. (23)

Conceived values: Values taught by one's culture that describe conceptions of the ideal. (7)

Concrete operations period: Piaget's developmental stage in which a child can play cooperatively and employ complex rules. (18)

Conditioning: The association of new behavior and resulting consequences. (16)

Confidentiality: Respect for another's privacy that involves holding and not divulging information given in confidence, except in cases of suspected abuse, commission of a crime, or threat of harm to self or others. (4, 5)

Confirming responses: Validation of the client as a person and of the client's thoughts and feelings in the context of the situation. (10)

Conflict: A mental struggle resulting from incompatible or opposing needs, drives, wishes, or internal demands; a hostile encounter. (14)

Connotation: The personalized meaning of a word or phrase. (9)

Context: A person's environment, defined as all of the intrapersonal and interpersonal circumstances influencing client behaviors. (3)

Coordination: Two or more people providing services to a client or program separately and keeping one another informed of their activities. (22)

Coping: Any response to external life strains that serves to prevent, avoid, or control emotional distress. (20)

Countertransference: Personal feelings or attitudes the helping person may feel toward a client that emerge as a reaction to the client's behavior or from the nurse's past life experiences. (1)

Covert: That which is not expressed outwardly but is hidden. (14)

Crisis: A sudden unanticipated or unplanned for event that necessitates immediate action to resolve the problem; a turning point. (21)

Crisis intervention: The systematic application of problem-solving techniques, based on crisis theory, designed to help the client move through the crisis process as swiftly and painlessly as possible and thereby achieve at least the same level of psychological comfort the client experienced before the crisis. (21)

Critical thinking: A framework for problem solving by which a person can identify and analyze the assumptions underlying the actions, decisions, values, and judgments of themselves and others. (16)

Cultural assessment: A systematic appraisal of beliefs, values, and practices conducted in order to determine the context of client needs and to tailor nursing interventions. (11)

Cultural brokering: The act of bridging, linking, or mediating between groups or persons of differing cultural backgrounds for the purpose of reducing conflict or producing change. (11)

Cultural diversity: Differences between cultural groups. (11)

Cultural relativism: The belief that cultures are neither inferior nor superior to one another and that there is no single scale for measuring the value of a culture. (11)

Culture: Collective beliefs, values, and shared understandings and patterns of behavior of a designated group of people. (11)

Curanderos: Local folk healers and herb doctors of Hispanic culture. (11)

Debriefing: A crisis-intervention strategy designed to help nurses and others process critical incidents in health care, thereby reducing the possibility of symptoms. (21)

Democratic leadership: The style in which the leader

involves members in active discussion and decision making, encouraging open expression of feelings and ideas. (22)

Denial: Unconscious refusal to allow painful facts, feelings, and perceptions into conscious awareness. (8)

Denotation: The generalized meaning assigned to a word. (9)

Distress: A stress response capable of creating permanent pathological changes and even death. (20)

Documentation: The process of obtaining, organizing, and conveying information to others in a written format. (23)

Double-bind communication: A communication that sends two conflicting messages at once. (13)

Dynamic equilibrium: *See* **Homeostasis.** (20)

Dysfunctional communication: A communication style in which messages are defensive or distorted and do not serve to inform or enhance communication between people. It usually develops as a communication pattern in families suffering from chronic low self-esteem. Differentness within the group is viewed as a threat. (13)

Dysfunctional conflict: Conflict in which information is withheld, feelings are expressed too strongly, the problem is obscured by a double message, or feelings are denied or projected onto others. (14)

Dysfunctional receiving: Communication in which a receiver fails to listen, disqualifies what is said, responds with negativity, or fails to validate the message. (13)

Dysfunctional sending: Communication that occurs when part or all of a message fails to express the truth or is expressed in such a way that the receiver experiences the message as a personal attack. (13)

Ego defense mechanisms: Conscious and unconscious coping methods used by people to change the meaning of a situation in their minds. (20)

Empathy: The capacity to understand another's world and to communicate that understanding. The ability of one person to perceive and understand another person's emotions accurately and to communicate the meaning of feelings to the other through verbal and nonverbal behaviors. (1, 5)

Empowerment: Helping a person become a self-advocate; an interpersonal process of providing the appropriate tools, resources, and environment to build, develop, and increase the ability of others to set and reach goals. (5, 22)

Environment: All the cultural, developmental, physical, and psychosocial conditions external to an individual that influence a person's perception and involvement. (1)

Ethical dilemma: Conflict of two or more moral issues; a situation in which there are two or more conflicting, equally right answers. (7)

Ethnic group: A social grouping of people who share a common racial, geographic, religious, or historical culture. (11)

Ethnocentrism: The belief that one's own culture is superior to others. (11)

Eudaemonistic model of health: A model that includes the medical, role performance, and adaptive models, as well as movement toward self-fulfillment. (15)

Eustress: A moderate level of stress that acts as a positive stress response with protective and adaptive functions. (20)

Exhaustion phase: The phase of stress response in which symptoms of serious mental disorganization and physical collapse occur. (20)

Extrinsic values: Values that are not essential to the maintenance of life, such as love of music. (7)

Family: A self-identified group of two or more individuals whose association is characterized by special terms, who may or may not be related by blood lines or law, but who function in such a way that they consider themselves to be a family. (13)

Family communication: The transactional process of sharing information and creating meanings within a family system; the element that binds the family together. (13)

Family function: A measure of normality or health that occurs as a result of adaptation to stress. (13)

Feedback: The response given by the receiver to the sender about the message. (1)

Focus charting: A charting format using a focus (a sign or symptom, a nursing diagnosis, a behavior, a condition, a significant event, or an acute change in condition) and three steps: data, action, and response (DAR). (23)

Focused questions: Questions that limit the response to a certain informational area but require more than a yes-or-no answer. (23)

Formal operations period: Piaget's developmental stage in which abstract reality and logical thought processes emerge; independent decisions can be made. (18)

Functional communication: Communication in which the content and relational aspects of the message are clearly and directly sent and received; it is based on valid assumptions, trust, and a firm sense of self. (13)

Global aphasia: A form of aphasia in which the client has difficulty with both expressive language and the reception of messages. (17)

Group: A gathering of two or more individuals who share a common purpose and meet over a period of time in face-to-face interaction to achieve an identifiable goal. (12)

Group dynamics: All of the communication processes that take place within a group. (12)

Group process: The identifiable structural development of the group that is needed for a group to mature. (12)

Group think: Fear of expressing conflicting ideas and opinions because loyalty to the group and approval by other group members has become so important. (12)

Health: A broad concept that is used to describe an individual's state of well-being and level of functioning. (1)

Health teaching: A flexible, person-oriented process in which the helping person provides information and support to clients with a variety of health-related learning needs. (16)

High-risk nursing diagnosis: A state for which the client is at high risk and that is validated by the presence of risk factors (formerly referred to as "potential" diagnosis). (23)

Holistic construct: The unified whole of a person, with each functional aspect of self-concept fitting together, and each single element affecting all other parts. (3)

Homeostasis: A person's sense of personal security and balance. (20)

I–Thou relationship: A relationship in which each individual responds to the other from his or her own uniqueness and is valued for that uniqueness in a direct, mutually respected, reciprocal alliance. (1)

Individuation: Finding and acknowledging all parts of oneself; being true to one's nature. (1)

Informed consent: Assurance that the client fully understands what is happening or is about to happen in his or her health care and knowingly consents to care. (16)

Intercultural communication: Communication in which the sender of a message is a member of one culture and the receiver is from a different culture. (11)

Interpersonal: Between two or more people. (14)

Interpersonal competence: The ability to interpret the content of a message from the point of view of each of the participants and the ability to use language and nonverbal behaviors strategically to achieve the goals of the interaction. (9)

Interpersonal process record: A three-part record of the nurse–client interaction: (1) a written anecdotal record of the client's and the nurse's words as well as their nonverbal behavior; (2) a written analysis of the interaction, identifying communication skills and interventions; and (3) written suggestions for making more effective comments. (23)

Intrapersonal: Within a particular individual. (14)

Intrinsic values: Values that relate to the maintenance of life, such as eating to survive. (7)

Laissez-faire attitude: Allowing others to do as they please without intervening. (7)

Laissez-faire leadership: The style in which the leader provides little or no structure and essentially abdicates leadership responsibilities. (22)

Leadership: Interpersonal influence, exercised in situations and directed through the communication process, toward the attainment of a specified goal or goals. (12)

Leveling: Communication that is healthy and direct. (13)

Linear communication: An activity involving the transmission of messages by a source to a receiver for the purpose of influencing the receiver's behavior. (1)

Lived experience: The personal meaning of an experience as described by the person experiencing it. (3)

Maintenance functions: Group role functions that foster the emotional life of the group. (12)

Medical model of health: Health as the absence of signs and symptoms of disease or injury. (15)

Message: A verbal or nonverbal expression of thoughts or feelings intended to convey information to the receiver and requiring interpretation by that person. (1)

Message competency: The ability to use language and nonverbal behaviors strategically to achieve the goals of the interaction. (9)

Metacommunication: All of the factors that influence how a message is received. (9)

Metaphor: An anecdote in which one idea or object is substituted for another in a way that implies their similarity. (10)

Modeling: The transmission of values by presenting oneself in an attractive manner and living by a certain set of values, hoping that others will follow one's lead; teaching by performing a behavior that another observes. (7, 16)

Moral dilemma: *See* **Ethical dilemma.** (7)

Moral distress: A feeling that occurs when one knows what is "right" but is bound to do otherwise because of legal or institutional constraints. (7)

Moral uncertainty: Difficulty deciding which moral rules (values, beliefs, etc.) apply to a given situation. (7)

Moralizing: The transference of the values of the parents directly onto the child. (7)

Morphostasis: The tendency of a system to want to stay the same. (13)

Motivation: The forces that activate behavior and direct it toward one goal instead of another. (12)

Multiculturalism: A term used to describe a heterogeneous society in which diverse cultural worldviews can coexist with some general characteristics shared by all cultural groups and some perspectives that are unique to each group. (11)

Mutuality: Agreement on problems and the means for resolving them; a commitment by both parties to enhance well-being. (5)

Narrative charting: A chronological record of events happening to the client. (23)

Networking: A form of peer collaboration whereby individuals take advantage of making and using contacts. (22)

Neurolinguistic programming (NLP): A theory suggesting that people have a preferred representational mode: visual, kinesic, or auditory. (1)

Nursing: Involved interaction with persons in a caring mode. (1)

Nursing diagnosis: A two-part statement that labels the problems requiring nursing intervention and the etiology of the health care problem. (2)

Objective data: Data that are directly observable or verifiable through physical examination or tests. (2)

Open-ended question: A question that is open to interpretation and that cannot be answered by yes, no, or a one-word response. (10)

Operative values: Values used on a daily basis to make choices about actions, such as the value of honesty. (7)

Optacon: A reading device that converts printed letters into a vibration which can be felt by the deaf/blind person. (17)

Orientation phase: Period in the nurse–client relationship when the nurse and client first meet and set the tone for the rest of their relationship, assessing the client's situation and setting goals. (4)

Overt: That which is readily observable in one's behavior and verbal expression. (14)

Paradigm: A worldview reflecting the knowledge developed about a phenomenon of interest within a scientific discipline. (1)

Paralanguage: The oral delivery of a verbal message expressed through tone of voice and inflection, sighing, or crying. (9)

Paraphrasing: Transforming of the client's words into the nurse's words, keeping the meaning intact. (10)

Parataxic mode: A mode of experiencing whereby a person is able to describe the relationship between the past and the present. (1)

Participatory leadership: The style in which the leader maintains final control but actively solicits and uses the input of group members. (22)

Passive response: A response designed to protect the self against feeling the full emotional pressure of the perceived threat by refusing to engage actively in resolution of the conflict; a response that denies one's own rights in order to avoid conflict. (14)

Passive-aggressive behavior: Giving the appearance of cooperation and verbal acquiescence but with no real self-exposure or intent to change. (14)

Perception: A personal identity construct by which a person transforms external sensory data into personalized images of reality. (3)

Person: A unitary concept that includes physiological, psychological, spiritual, and social elements. (1)

Person-centered communication: Communication that is focused on the client; a medium that involves building an individualized relationship structure which allows clients to share their innermost personal experiences and the meanings they have for them with safety and trust. (4)

Persona: The social mask a person shows the world. (1)

Personal identity: All of the psychological beliefs and attitudes people have about themselves: perceptual, cognitive, emotional, and spiritual. (3)

Personal space: An invisible and changing boundary around an individual that provides a sense of comfort and protection to a person and that is defined by past experiences and culture. (5)

Physical motivators: Internal and external circumstances stimulating a person to learn as a way of avoiding physical discomfort. (15)

Position: An external context that formalizes roles and makes them understandable to others in the community or group; relates to the status one holds in the community. (6)

Possible diagnosis: A suspected problem for which additional data are needed. (23)

Preinteraction phase: A period in the nurse–client relationship when the nurse explores his or her professional goals, creates a supportive environment, and plans with other staff members the most appropriate ways to achieve the goals of the relationship. (4)

Preoperational period: Piaget's developmental stage in which learning by the toddler is developed through concrete experiences and devices and the child is markedly egocentric. (18)

Primary group: Spontaneous group formation characterized by an informal structure and social process; it can be automatic, like a family, or based on a common interest; it has no defined time limit. (12)

Primary prevention: Educational/preventive activities taken to preclude illness or prevent its natural course from occurring. (15)

Problem-oriented record (POR): A chart containing four basic sections: a database, a list of the client's identified problems, a treatment plan, and progress notes. (23)

Profession: A calling requiring specialized knowledge and often long and intensive academic preparation. (6)

Professional: One characterized by or conforming to the technical or ethical standards of a profession. (6)

Prototaxic mode: A mode of experiencing whereby one can focus only on the present and may not be able to recall past events or contemplate the future. (1)

Proxemics: The study of an individual's use of space. (5)

Psychomotor learning: Learning a skill by taking knowledge and applying it with "hands on." (15)

Quality circles: Small temporary work groups focused on developing problem-solving and decision-making strategies to enhance the work of the organization. (22)

Receiver: The recipient of a message, the person who translates the message into word symbols that make sense to the receiver. (1)

Reflection: A communication strategy linking the client's apparent emotion with the content of the client's message; it is used to clarify what the client is feeling and to affirm that the client's feelings are acceptable. (10)

Reframing: A strategy in which the nurse helps the client look at a situation in a new way. (10)

Reinforcement: The consequences of performing identified behaviors; positive reinforcement increases the probability of a response, and negative reinforcement decreases the probability of a response. (16)

Resistance phase: The second phase of the General Adaptation Syndrome (GAS) stress response, in which hormonal and chemical changes attempt to stabilize the physical response to the stress agent. Such metabolic changes can influence the development or advance the progression of stress-related chronic diseases. (20)

Role: A set of expected standards of behavior established by the society or community group to which a person belongs; role represents the social aspects of self-concept. (6)

Role ambiguity: A situation in which roles are not clearly defined. (6)

Role conflict: An incompatibility between one or more role expectations. (6)

Role mastery: The ability to meet the role expectations set by society. (6)

Role overload: The unrealistic attempt to meet the demands of too many roles simultaneously. (6)

Role performance model of health: Health as assessed by functioning and work performance behaviors. (15)

Role pressures: The external or internal circumstances, which are capable of change, that interfere with role performance. (6)

Role stress: A subjective experience that is associated with lack of role clarity, role overload, role conflict, or temporary role pressures. (6)

Secondary groups: Groups that are formally established to achieve certain agreed-upon goals; they have a prescribed structure and a designated leader, and they last for a specified length of time. (12)

Secondary prevention: Actions that are taken to promote early diagnosis of symptoms and to institute treatment after the onset of disease. (15)

Self-actualization: The level of development in which a person balances interdependence with individual self-awareness. (1)

Self-awareness: The means by which a person gains knowledge and understanding of all aspects of self-concept. (3)

Self-concept: An abstract structural construct that is used to describe the different images which make up the self in each person's mind. (3)

Self-differentiation: The capacity to stay involved in one's family or group without losing one's identity. (13)

Self-esteem: The value and significance people place on their self-concepts; an emotional process of self-judgment; an orientation to the self, ranging on a continuum from feelings of self-efficacy and respect to feelings that one is fatally flawed as a person. (3)

Sender: The source or initiator of a message. (1)

Sensorimotor period: Piaget's developmental stage in which the infant explores its own body as a source of information about the world. (18)

Shamans: Highly respected spiritual medicine men and women of the Native American culture. (11)

Shaping: Changing a person's behavior through a behavioral learning process. (16)

SOAP format: A four-step method of documentation that lists all of the client's subjective (S) comments, all of the current objective (O) information noted by the nurse, the nurse's analysis or assessment (A), and future interventions or plans (P) for care. (23)

SOAPIE format: An expanded SOAP format that adds interventions (I) and evaluation (E) of the outcome. (23)

Social cognitive competency: The ability to interpret message content within interactions from the point of view of each participant. (9)

Social incentives: The approval and disapproval of others who potentially have the power to reward or punish. (15)

Social support: All of the social and environmental factors that contribute to a person's sense of well-being. (20)

Standing committees: Permanent, ongoing task groups within an organization. (22)

Stereotyping: Attributing characteristics or behavior, generalized opinions, attitudes, and beliefs to a group of people as if all persons in the group possessed them. (5)

Stress: A physiological and psychological response to the presence of a stressor. (20)

Stress response: A nonspecific physiological response to the pressures that affect an individual during the course of daily living. (20)

Stressor: Any demand, situation, internal stimulus, or circumstance that threatens a person's personal security and balance. (20)

Subculture: An ethnic, regional, or economic group of people who are joined together by distinguishing characteristics that differentiate the group from the predominant culture or society. (11)

Subjective data: The client's perception of the data and what the client says about the data. (2)

Summarization: Reworking a lengthy interaction or discussion into a few succinct sentences. (10)

Symmetrical exchanges: Interactions in which each person has equal power and the exchanges mirror each other. (13)

Syndrome diagnosis: A cluster of actual or high-risk diagnoses that are predicted to be present because of a certain event or situation. (23)

Syntaxic mode: A mode of experiencing whereby a person can connect the past, the present, and the future. (1)

Task force. *See* **Ad hoc committee.** (22)

Task functions: Group role functions that facilitate goal achievement. (12)

Tellatouch: A portable machine into which the nurse can type a message that emerges in braille. (17)

Termination: The deliberate separation of two or more persons from an intimate and meaningful relationship. (8)

Termination phase: The period in the nurse–client relationship when the nurse and client examine and evaluate their relationship and its goals and results; the time when they deal with the emotional content (if any) involved in saying good-bye. (4)

Tertiary prevention: Rehabilitation strategies designed to minimize the handicapping effects of a disease. (15)

Theory: An organized, conceptual representation or explanation of a phenomenon. (1)

Therapeutic communication: A goal-directed, focused dialogue between nurse and client that is fitted to the needs of the client. (10)

Transference: Behaviors in which the client projects irrational attitudes and feelings from the past onto people in the present 1

Triangle: A three-person emotional system in which there is tension between two members and a third person steps in to stabilize the relationship. (13)

Trust: Reliance on the consistency, sameness, and continuity of experiences that are provided by an organized combination of familiar and predictable things and people. (5)

Validation: A form of feedback involving verbal and nonverbal confirmation that both participants have the same basic understanding of the message. (1)

Values: A set of personal beliefs and attitudes about truth, beauty, and the worth of any thought, object, or behavior. (7)

Values acquisition: The conscious assumption of a new value. (7)

Values clarification: A process that encourages one to clarify one's own values by sorting them through, analyzing them, and setting priorities. (7)

Values indicators: Attitudes, beliefs, feelings, worries, or convictions; they are not values because they have not been clearly established. (7)

Violence: Physical force used by one person against another. (21)

Wellness diagnosis: A statement reflecting a transition to a higher level of wellness. (23)

Working phase: The period in the nurse–client relationship when the focus is on communication strategies, interventions for problem resolution, and enhancement of self-concept. (4)

YAVIS syndrome: The tendency of physicians and other health care providers to want to treat the *y*oung, *a*ttractive, *v*erbal, *i*ntelligent, and *s*uccessful client. (19)

Index

Note: Page numbers in *italics* indicate illustrations; those followed by t refer to tabular material.